Roadfood

CLARKSON POTTER/PUBISHERS ✳ New York

Roadfood

The Coast-to-Coast Guide to 800 of the Best Barbecue Joints, Lobster Shacks, Ice Cream Parlors, Highway Diners, and Much, Much More

Jane and Michael Stern

Copyright © 2011 by Jane Stern and Michael Stern

Published in the United States by Clarkson Potter/Publishers, an imprint of the
Crown Publishing Group, a division of Random House, Inc., New York.
www.crownpublishing.com
www.clarksonpotter.com

CLARKSON POTTER is a trademark and POTTER with colophon is a
registered trademark of Random House, Inc.

This work was originally published in the United States by Random House, Inc., New York,
in 1978. Subsequent revised editions were published in the United States by Random House,
Inc., New York in 1980, Alfred A. Knopf, a division of Random House, Inc., New York,
in 1986, Harper Perennial, a division of HarperCollins Publishers, New York, in 1992,
and Broadway Books, a division of Random House, Inc., in 2002, 2005, and 2008.

Library of Congress Cataloging-in-Publication Data
Stern, Jane.
  Roadfood: the coast-to-coast guide to 800 of the best barbecue joints, lobster shacks, ice
cream parlors, highway diners, and much, much more/Jane Stern and Michael Stern.
      p.   cm.
  Includes index.
  1. Restaurants—United States—Guidebooks.   2. United States—Guidebooks.
3. Automobile travel—United States—Guidebooks.   I. Stern, Michael, 1946–
II. Title.   III. Title: Road Food.
  TX907.2.S84 2011
  647.9573—dc22   2010050608

ISBN 978-0-307-59124-1
eISBN 978-0-307-59125-8

Printed in the United States of America

Book design by Caroline Cunningham
Maps designed by Jeffrey L. Ward
Cover design by Dan Rembert
Cover photography: (large sign) Car Culture/Collection Mix: Subjects/Getty Images; (roof)
Brand X Pictures/Getty Images; (fried chicken) © Radius Images/Corbis; (Kowalski's hot dog
sign, Hamtramck, Michigan) © DetroitDerek Photography

10 9 8 7 6 5 4 3 2 1

First Clarkson Potter/Publishers Edition

To Steve Rushmore and to Stephen Rushmore, Roadfood pioneers

Acknowledgments

To freewheel around this country and eat side by side with citizens of every stripe at café counters, picnic tables, pig pickin's, and chicken booyahs is heaven on earth. As much as we relish the taste of a superior donut or a green chile cheeseburger, what we savor most is the experience of finding the great dishes and meeting the people to whom they matter. There is no way to adequately thank the thousands of cooks, staff, fellow diners, and good-eats tipsters who continue to make our journey such an excellent adventure. Without the enthusiasm of Roadfood restaurateurs as well as of the loyal fans of those restaurants, we would be lost.

We are so grateful for the community of passionate eaters, debaters, raconteurs, photographers, and culinary pioneers who comprise Roadfood .com. Their generous road-trip reports and no-holds-barred participation in forum discussions are, for us, a daily inspiration. There would be no Road-food.com had not Stephen Rushmore, Jr., conceived it eleven years ago. Our debt to Stephen is incalculable. We also thank Roadfood team members Bruce Bilmes and Sue Boyle, Chris Ayers and Amy Breisch, Tony Balda-menti, Marc Bruno, and, of course, Big Steve Rushmore—all of whom have helped turn a website into a family and cyberspace into an unfolding joy.

For many years, *Gourmet* magazine was our publishing home, and we still are inexpressibly indebted to Ruth Reichl, Gail Zweigenthal, Alice Goch-man, James Rodewald, Bill Sertl, John "Doc" Willoughby, and Larry Karol for all the support they provided while we were there. When *Gourmet* died, we were welcomed with open arms by the good people at *Saveur* magazine—in particular, James Osland, Dana Bowen, and Betsy Andrews—where once again we feel we belong and have the opportunity to do what we love to do.

We are proud to say we have been part of NPR's *The Splendid Table* almost since its beginning. Our weekly chats with Lynne Rossetto Kasper, aided and abetted by Jen Russell and conducted so ably by Sally Swift, are high on our list of reasons life is good.

We owe a huge debt of gratitude to our literary agent, Doe Coover, for being such a staunch advocate and ally in good times and bad, and we particularly want to thank Charlie Conrad at Random House for keeping the lights on and the hearth warm.

Contents

Welcome to the biggest *Roadfood* yet. We have added two hundred new restaurants since the last edition and updated reviews of old favorites in the hope that this book leads you to many unforgettable meals and inspires you to find new ones. We urge you to share your own restaurant discoveries with us and with fellow eaters who are equally passionate about unique dining experiences and food with real character.

There are so many people today who travel around the country with an itinerary of pulled pork, po-boys, green chile cheeseburgers, and buttermilk pie that it is almost incomprehensible to think that some thirty years ago when we conceived the idea of *Roadfood*, publishers thought we were crazy. They said there could not be a guidebook to American food because America didn't have any interesting food to find. Back then, the belief among gourmets (the term "foodie" hadn't yet been coined) was that ours was a nation with such an impoverished palate that anyone interested in eating well needed to go to another continent. Fifty years ago when John Kennedy became president, no one was shocked that he hired a French chef to cook at the White House.

After the original edition of *Roadfood* was published, we still spent a lot of time convincing people that to eat their way across this land or simply to "eat local" could be a glorious dining adventure. Even food-savvy readers were unaccustomed to thinking of our country's regional food as delicious and well worth seeking out; indeed, most people were not even aware that it existed. But over time, as hungry travelers have sought alternatives to junk food and ventured into small towns and city neighborhoods to find underappreciated gastronomic treasures, America has outgrown its culinary inferiority complex. Today, few people doubt what we have spent our career pointing out—that this country is an appetizing crazy quilt of amazing things to eat. Indeed, the subject we named Roadfood has enjoyed an incredible media vogue in the last several years. Just turn to cable TV and you can't miss one wacky host or another taking a thrill-seeking camera to all the sleeves-up eats we have been championing since we first wrote the book.

Although countless media chefs and eaters have become celebrities by waving the flag for real American food, truly great Roadfood is not celebrity-driven. It is less like a unique virtuoso symphony and more like folk music. It was not created by experts and does not reflect one genius's talent and ego; it was (and continues to be) created by the people; it is of the people and for the people; it is a true taste of our diverse national identity. Like the population itself, American food is freewheeling, iconoclastic, kitschy, and alternately humble and audacious, pious and devil-may-care, tradition-minded and traditions-be-damned. That's what makes Roadfood an endlessly rewarding quest.

So, please: Eat and be merry . . . and join us at the website Roadfood .com, where passionate eaters come together to share the joys of appetite-adventuring. Users are welcome to post reviews and to participate in discussion forums that include trip reports, meet 'n' greet get-togethers, and opinions about anything food-related. If you have a particular restaurant you want to review or recommend, or if you have a comment on one that we have recommended, please visit Roadfood.com and let the world know, or get in touch with us directly at Jane&Michael@roadfood.com.

Until then, we hope to see you at a roadside picnic table, at a diner counter, or in the hickory haze of a wonderful barbecue parlor somewhere down the road!

—Jane and Michael Stern

✳ If you are planning a special trip to any restaurant in this book, we urge you to call ahead to make certain it is open and is serving what you want to eat. Hours of operation change over the course of the year and proprietors sometimes go fishing. Our notation of BLD, meaning breakfast, lunch, and dinner, can mean different times in different places. For instance, many heartland restaurants do serve dinner, but dinner hour can end as early as seven o'clock. Also, some specialties are seasonal. (When calling, be aware that telephone area codes are changing all the time.)

✳ The vast majority of Roadfood restaurants require no reservations and are come-as-you-are. A few pricier ones do require a reservation. We've made note of which ones get insanely crowded, and what you can do about it. But again, if in doubt, please call ahead.

✳ We have given an approximate cost guide using dollar signs, but be aware that this can vary dramatically. Many Roadfood restaurants that offer $5 sandwiches for lunch also can serve $40 dinners. Also, wine, beer, cocktails, and multiple desserts can seriously jack up prices.
   ✳ $ = one full meal is under $12
   ✳ $$ = one full meal is between $12 and $30
   ✳ $$$ = one full meal is over $30

✳ Just because a restaurant from a previous edition of *Roadfood* does not appear here does not mean it's out of business or that we don't like it anymore. Either circumstance might be true, but it also is possible that we excised it simply to make room for one of the two hundred new places we believe deserve your attention.

✳ We welcome tips for inclusion in future editions, comments, and even complaints. Please e-mail us at Jane&Michael@roadfood.com or tell us what you think at our website: www.roadfood.com.

New England

Connecticut ✳ Maine ✳ Massachusetts

New Hampshire ✳ Rhode Island ✳ Vermont

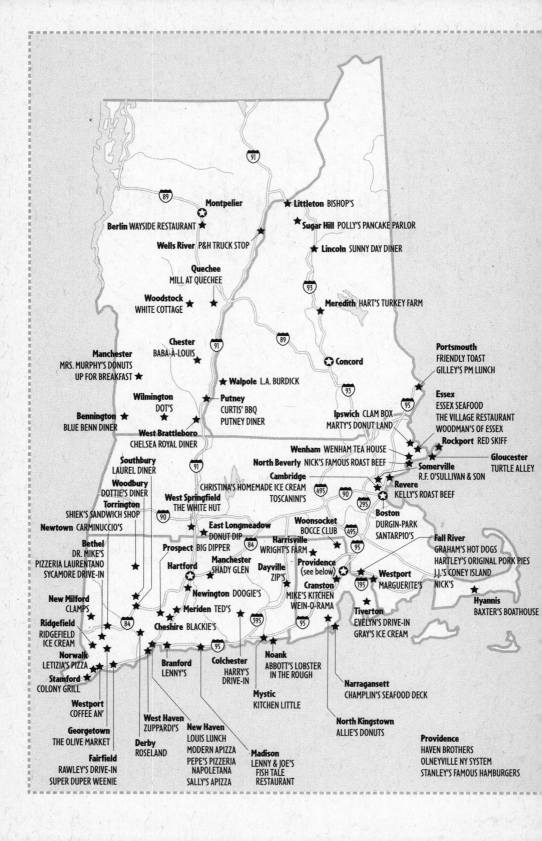

Montpelier

Littleton BISHOP'S

Berlin WAYSIDE RESTAURANT

Sugar Hill POLLY'S PANCAKE PARLOR

Wells River P&H TRUCK STOP

Lincoln SUNNY DAY DINER

Quechee
MILL AT QUECHEE

Woodstock
WHITE COTTAGE

Meredith HART'S TURKEY FARM

Chester BABA-À-LOUIS

Concord

Portsmouth
FRIENDLY TOAST
GILLEY'S PM LUNCH

Manchester
MRS. MURPHY'S DONUTS
UP FOR BREAKFAST

Walpole L.A. BURDICK

Essex
ESSEX SEAFOOD
THE VILLAGE RESTAURANT
WOODMAN'S OF ESSEX

Wilmington
DOT'S

Putney
CURTIS' BBQ
PUTNEY DINER

Ipswich CLAM BOX
MARTY'S DONUT LAND

Rockport RED SKIFF

Bennington
BLUE BENN DINER

West Brattleboro
CHELSEA ROYAL DINER

Wenham WENHAM TEA HOUSE

North Beverly NICK'S FAMOUS ROAST BEEF

Gloucester
TURTLE ALLEY

Cambridge
CHRISTINA'S HOMEMADE ICE CREAM
TOSCANINI'S

Somerville
R.F. O'SULLIVAN & SON

Southbury
LAUREL DINER

Revere
KELLY'S ROAST BEEF

Woodbury
DOTTIE'S DINER

West Springfield
THE WHITE HUT

Boston
DURGIN-PARK
SANTARPIO'S

Torrington
SHIEK'S SANDWICH SHOP

East Longmeadow
DONUT DIP

Woonsocket
BOCCE CLUB

Newtown CARMINUCCIO'S

Harrisville
WRIGHT'S FARM

Prospect BIG DIPPER

Fall River
GRAHAM'S HOT DOGS
HARTLEY'S ORIGINAL PORK PIES
J.J.'S CONEY ISLAND
NICK'S

Bethel
DR. MIKE'S
PIZZERIA LAURENTANO
SYCAMORE DRIVE-IN

Hartford

Manchester
SHADY GLEN

Dayville
ZIP'S

Providence
(see below)

Westport
MARGUERITE'S

Cranston
MIKE'S KITCHEN
WEIN-O-RAMA

Hyannis
BAXTER'S BOATHOUSE

New Milford
CLAMPS

Newington DOOGIE'S

Tiverton
EVELYN'S DRIVE-IN
GRAY'S ICE CREAM

Ridgefield
RIDGEFIELD
ICE CREAM

Meriden TED'S

Cheshire BLACKIE'S

Norwalk
LETIZIA'S PIZZA

Noank
ABBOTT'S LOBSTER
IN THE ROUGH

Stamford
COLONY GRILL

Branford
LENNY'S

Colchester
HARRY'S
DRIVE-IN

Narragansett
CHAMPLIN'S SEAFOOD DECK

Westport
COFFEE AN'

Mystic
KITCHEN LITTLE

Georgetown
THE OLIVE MARKET

West Haven
ZUPPARDI'S

North Kingstown
ALLIE'S DONUTS

Derby
ROSELAND

Fairfield
RAWLEY'S DRIVE-IN
SUPER DUPER WEENIE

New Haven
LOUIS LUNCH
MODERN APIZZA
PEPE'S PIZZERIA
NAPOLETANA
SALLY'S APIZZA

Madison
LENNY & JOE'S
FISH TALE
RESTAURANT

Providence
HAVEN BROTHERS
OLNEYVILLE NY SYSTEM
STANLEY'S FAMOUS HAMBURGERS

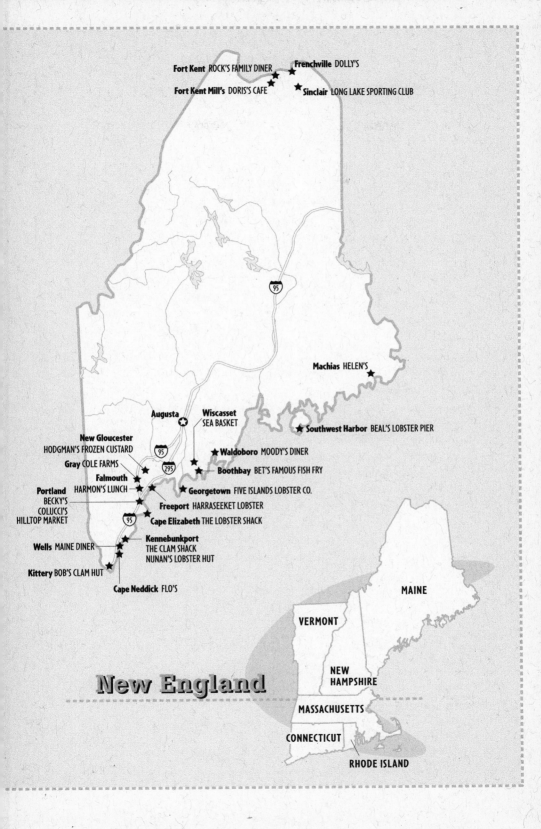

Fort Kent ROCK'S FAMILY DINER
Frenchville DOLLY'S
Fort Kent Mill's DORIS'S CAFE
Sinclair LONG LAKE SPORTING CLUB

95

Machias HELEN'S

Augusta
Wiscasset SEA BASKET
Southwest Harbor BEAL'S LOBSTER PIER

New Gloucester HODGMAN'S FROZEN CUSTARD
Waldoboro MOODY'S DINER
95
Gray COLE FARMS
Boothbay BET'S FAMOUS FISH FRY
295
Falmouth HARMON'S LUNCH
Georgetown FIVE ISLANDS LOBSTER CO.
Portland BECKY'S COLUCCI'S HILLTOP MARKET
Freeport HARRASEEKET LOBSTER
Cape Elizabeth THE LOBSTER SHACK
95
Wells MAINE DINER
Kennebunkport THE CLAM SHACK NUNAN'S LOBSTER HUT
Kittery BOB'S CLAM HUT
Cape Neddick FLO'S

MAINE
VERMONT
NEW HAMPSHIRE
MASSACHUSETTS
CONNECTICUT
RHODE ISLAND

New England

Connecticut

Abbott's Lobster in the Rough

117 Pearl St.   860-536-7719
Noank, CT.   LD May-Labor Day, then weekends through
                                  mid-October | $$

"In the rough" was never so agreeable. On an al fresco dining area perfumed by sea breezes and protected from marauding seagulls, one dines on lobster steamed to such perfect plumpness that the meat seems to erupt when the shell is broken. If cracking the carapace of a whole one seems too labor-intensive, the alternative is a hot lobster roll, which is hunks of lobster bathed in butter and sandwiched inside a warm bun. Cold lobster salad rolls are also available, as are hot and cold crab rolls.

While you can get excellent lobsters all up and down Yankee shores, one item you'll find only in this southernmost area is clear-broth clam chowder, of which Abbott's makes the best. Not nearly as creamy-dreamy as New England chowder and lacking the cacophony of vegetables in Manhattan chowder, as well as the pink tomato blush of Rhode Island shore dinner hall chowder, the clear-broth stuff is focused and intense. It is the essence of the ocean, and although it is dotted with bits of clam and little nuggets of potato, it is the liquid itself that commands attention. Unadulterated as it is, this is a dish strictly for seafood lovers. If you need something creamy, Abbott's lobster bisque is dramatically so.

Big Dipper

91 Waterbury Rd. 203-758-3200
Prospect, CT (limited winter hours) | $

Inspired by the traditional Good Humor bar but infinitely more delicious, Big Dipper's toasted almond ice cream delivers the luxury of marzipan and the euphoria of Independence Day. It is but one of a multitude of flavors that includes plain vanilla, silky chocolate, silly cotton candy, and a shockingly sophisticated cinnamon-coffee Café Vienna. Because it is not cloyingly rich, Big Dipper ice cream begs to be eaten in large quantities, or in such indulgences as a triple-dip fudge sundae. The line stretches far out the door on a pleasant night, and the staff is famously fun to deal with.

One thing we especially like about this place is that you are not limited to scoops as a measurement of your serving. You can buy exactly as much or as little ice cream as you want. Each customer is charged by weight (of the ice cream).

Blackie's

2200 Waterbury Rd. 203-699-1819
Cheshire, CT LD (closed Fri) | $

Hot dogs are so entirely the specialty of the house at Blackie's that regular customers walk in the door and simply call out a number, indicating how many they want. The dogs are pink Hummel-brand plumpies that are boiled in oil to the point that their outside surface bursts apart from the heat. One variation to consider is to add the suffix "well" to the integer you name. This means well-done, which adds extra crunch to the hot dog's skin.

The dog is served plain, and it is up to each eater to spoon out mustard and relish from condiment trays that are set out along the counter. The mustard is excellent, and we recommend a modest bed of it applied to the top of each wiener, all the better for the relish to cling to. The relish is transcendent: thick, luxurious, dark green, and pepper-hot enough that the nerve endings on your lips will want to hum. Blackie's—and its devoted clientele—are happy enough with this formula for frankfurter perfection that the kitchen doesn't even bother to offer sauerkraut or chili. Service is nearly instantaneous, so if your preference is *hot* hot dogs, it is entirely practical to order them one by one until you can't eat any more.

Blackie's (since 1928) has oodles of old-fashioned charm, although you ought not come if you feel like kicking up your heels. A sign on the wall warns "No Dancing." We especially like it in good weather when the long counter offers semi–al fresco seating.

Carminuccio's

76 South Main St. (Route 25)   203-364-1133
Newtown, CT   LD | $

At the small array of bare-topped indoor tables or on the patio to the side of this inconspicuous yellow house by the side of the road, customers eat pizzas on a level with New Haven's best.

The underside of the crust is a mouthwatering fright, tawny dough smudged and blackened and speckled with crumbs. Patted out extra-thin, Carminuccio's crust has such a sturdy crunch that you can hold a hot slice by the circumference and the center will not wilt. Even with meat and vegetables on top it stays sturdy from the outer edge almost to the point, and no matter what ingredients you get, topping slippage is rare.

New Haven–made sausage, strewn edge-to-edge in countless little pinches, is cooked and well drained of fat before a sausage pie is assembled and baked, thus ensuring the cheese stays cheesy and the crust dry. Vegetables are precooked in a convection oven, a process that not only saps crust-threatening moisture but dramatically intensifies the flavor of such toppings as spinach, onions, and tomatoes. Garlic especially benefits from the process, each whole clove caramelized to its soft essence. Before learning how it is done, we would have sworn the brilliant flavor of the kitchen's supple red pepper strips came from marinade and/or seasoning. But they are unadulterated, nothing but red peppers roasted to a sunny concentrate as vibrant as *pumate*. Combine the peppers with roasted garlic and sausage and you have a magisterial combo, one of the earth's essential pizza-eating experiences.

Clamp's Hamburger Stand

Route 202   no phone
New Milford, CT   LD April–Sept | $

Despite its lack of a sign, street address, and telephone number, Clamp's is easy to find. Head north on Route 202 out of New Milford and when you see a crowd of cars on the right, you have arrived. Open from late April to early September from 11 A.M. to 2 P.M. and from 5 P.M. to 8 P.M., this little al fresco food stand has been a Litchfield County summertime ritual since 1939. (Those hours are exact. We arrived one day at 2:05 and got nothing to eat!)

Tables are arrayed on grassy groves on either side of the shack where you order, pay for, and pick up food. While the menu lists many drive-in dishes, from chicken tenders to chili dogs, hamburgers and cheeseburgers are the basis of Clamp's reputation. Made fresh daily and cooked the way you request, they are medium-size patties that leak enough juice to give the bun its own beefy appeal. Their edges slightly crisp, the fibers of the meat infused with a smoky taste that sings of summer afternoons, they are picnic food par excellence. All condiments are available; we highly recommend fried onions, which are cooked until caramel-sweet. Deep-fried onions and French fries are okay, but it's the burger that's memorable.

Coffee An'

343 Main St.   203-227-3808
Westport, CT   BL | $

A good donut is like a flower in bloom or a splendid sunset—the magic has something to do with the knowledge that its allure is fleeting. By tomorrow, even the best donuts might barely be edible. That's especially true of Coffee An's devilish devil's food sinkers, which, when fresh, are as rich as expensive chocolate cake—crisp-skinned and with a roundhouse chocolate punch. Definitely some of the best chocolate donuts anywhere. The next day, you don't want to know about them; you don't even want to take them home for later. That's okay; this is a delightful place to dine—at window stools or around the low counter where locals come for their pastry fix in the morning and for sandwiches at lunch. We've never had anything but donuts, and can highly recommend the plain cake variety and the cinnamon-coated ones, each of which has a memorably crunchy surface.

Colony Grill

172 Myrtle Ave.   203-359-2184
Stamford, CT   LD | $$

Pizza is the only food on the menu of this old neighborhood tavern, and it is available in one size, about a foot-and-a-half in diameter with crust as thin as a saltine. Aside from the wild crunch of its crust, Colony pizza is known for locally made sweet sausage and for the optional topping called "hot oil": peppery olive oil that imbues the pie with luscious zest unlike any other. Pizzas are served on age-dented metal trays along with paper plates so flimsy they are useless, except for when a waitress can't find any other paper and uses the back of one as an emergency order pad. Each slice is crisp and yet so sumptuously oily that your fingers are guaranteed to glisten, even if you forgo the wonderful hot oil. Postprandial wreckage on the table is a giddy bedlam of severely battered trays piled with countless balled-up and knotted paper napkins. Napkins are the only essential utensil for eating a Colony Grill pizza.

Doogie's

2525 Berlin Tpk.   860-666-6200
Newington, CT   LD | $

Doogie's used to boast that it was "home of the two-foot hot dog," but re-
cession economics have reduced the size of the jumbo dog to sixteen inches.
Firm-fleshed and with a chewy skin that gets slightly charred on the grill, it
has a vigorously spicy flavor that not only holds up under any and all extra-
cost toppings, but does well when spread with Doogie's superb homemade
hot relish or ordinary mustard. For those of meek appetite, the same good
frank is available in a mere ten-inch configuration, too.

Doogie's hamburgers, cooked on the same charcoal grill where the hot
dogs are made, have a delicious smoky flavor. The top-of-the-line hamburger
is described on the menu as "the ultimate"; and while not as awesome as the
elongated hot dog, it is quite a sight: two five-ounce patties with bacon,
cheese, grilled onions, and sautéed mushrooms. Its formal name on the menu
is the Murder Burger.

Beyond hot dogs and hamburgers, Doogie's makes a heck of a good
Philly cheese steak as well as all sorts of other sandwiches, New England–
style clam chowder, a hot lobster roll, and that junkiest of junk foods, so
beloved hereabouts—fried dough. Doogie's fried dough, a plate-size disk of
deep-fried dough, is available veiled in cinnamon sugar or under a blanket of
red tomato sauce. Either way, it is a mouthful!

Dottie's Diner

740 S. Main St. (Route 6)   203-263-2516
Woodbury, CT   BLD | $$

Dottie's is one of the few places we know where you can still get an old-
fashioned chicken pie: savory crust loaded with nothing but warm, moist
chicken meat served under a mantle of gravy. Dottie also makes a more
familiar chicken pot pie that includes gravy, peas, and carrots. On the side,
mashed potatoes are the genuine article; they and cranberry sauce are supplemented on the plate with a sprig of al dente broccoli and a few thin, buttery slices of cooked squash.

As for the donuts—which we have considered America's best since
Dottie's was known as Phillips Diner and run by the Phillips family—they
are, if possible, better than ever. Cinnamon donuts are creamy inside with
a wickedly crunchy exterior (unless the humidity is really high that day);
chocolate donuts come loaded with vast amounts of the glossy dark glaze
that so perfectly complements the cake within. Vanilla-frosted donuts have

been added to the repertoire, as have cinnamon donuts with a chocolate coat.

Since her tenure began some four years ago, Dottie has spiffed things up with retro aqua upholstery in the booths and a new counter; and she's even gotten a liquor license and has begun serving dinners. The friendly community feeling so essential to the soul of a diner is thriving.

Dr. Mike's

158 Greenwood Ave.   203-792-4388
Bethel, CT   (weekends only in winter) | $

Forget psychotherapy and medication! The best antidepressant we know is a visit to the good Doctor Mike of Bethel. The cones and cardboard cups dished out year-round by this little shop are a miracle cure. As hopeless ice cream addicts, we must tell you that there is nothing quite like Dr. Mike's, and there are occasions when its ultra-richness is actually too, too much. The longtime standard-bearer, "rich chocolate," is only sweet enough to coax forth maximum cocoa flavor, its chalky chocolate and smooth butterfat body hypnotically fused. "Chocolate lace and cream" is another Dr. Mike's invention, made with wisps of refined, chocolate-covered hard candy. The shards of candy are suspended in a pure white emulsion of sweetened cream: another dreamy experience, but in this case our warning is to get it in a cup. The crunch of the candy conflicts with the crunch of a cone.

We've named our two favorite flavors. Don't hesitate, though, if you find your personal favorite among the approximately eight varieties available any particular day. Each one is made the old-fashioned way, using cream from dairy buckets, in five-gallon batches; and we have fond memories of Dr. Mike's coffee, coconut, cinnamon, Heath Bar crunch, even prune, dazzling vanilla, and some real tongue-stunners made with fresh fruits in the summer.

Nota bene: Fudge sauce for sundaes is magnificent. Whipped cream is thick and fresh.

Harry's Drive-In

104 Broadway   860-537-2410
Colchester, CT   LD (summer only) | $

A completely al fresco eat-place with wood-slat picnic tables arrayed under groves of flowering trees, Harry's has been a favorite stop for more than eighty years for people on their way to and from the beach. One of the best things about coming here is waiting for a meal to be assembled. There is no curb service. Exit your vehicle and stand in line; place an order and pay; then slide sideways to the pick-up window. The view is breathtaking: two dozen hamburgers lined up on a glistening hot grill, sizzling and sputtering and oozing juice. They are formed from spheres of meat that get slapped onto the grill and lightly squished so they flatten a bit; but the gnarled patties remain enormously luscious inside their rugged crust. With a mantle of melted cheese and a few strips of bacon, garnished with slices of summer tomato, lettuce, pickle, and mustard, sandwiched inside a lovely bakery bun and held together with a long toothpick, this might be the best drive-in hamburger anywhere. Hot dogs are grill-cooked, too, and are especially excellent when bedded in a split-top bun atop a spill of Harry's chili sauce.

Kitchen Little

135 Greenmanville Ave.   860-536-2122
Mystic, CT   BL | $

"Kitchen Little" isn't just a cute name. This diner on the road to historic Mystic Seaport really is minuscule. You must expect to wait almost any day, especially on weekends. If the weather is pleasant, the delay can be delightful. There are a couple of wood-slat benches out front under a tall pole topped with a U.S. flag, and the steel-blue water lapping up against the grassy shore just beyond the café is hypnotic.

"AM Eggstasy" is the house motto and the omelets are stupendous, as is the Mystic Melt, which is eggs scrambled with crabmeat and cream cheese served with raisin toast on the side. There are benedicts, heart-healthy egg-white omelets, and sizzled-crisp corned beef hash. If you don't come for breakfast, there is a whole menu of fried clams (strips or whole-bellies), a fine hot buttered lobster roll, and a half-pound hamburger, plus excellent clam chowder. It is southern New England–style chowder—steel-gray and briny—a great winter warm-up meal.

Laurel Diner

544 Main St. S.   203-264-8218
Southbury, CT   BL | $

Table seats are available, but we recommend a stool at the counter facing the Laurel Diner's pint-size grill. Here you have a spellbinding vision of time-space management as two short-order chefs fry, scramble, and flip eggs, fold omelets, butter toast, pour pancakes, and squish down patties of the diner's legendary corned beef hash.

The hash is a coarse-cut mélange of spicy beef shreds and nuggets of potato cooked on the griddle until a web of crust begins to envelop the tender insides. If you ask, the grill man will cook the hash until it is brittle-crisp nearly all the way through, which is a great idea if textural excitement supersedes succulence in your hierarchy of culinary pleasures, but we personally enjoy it the regular way: forkfuls of corned beef that are brick-red and moist, their pickly zest balanced perfectly by the soft pieces of potato.

You have two choices of potato: chunky home fries, which are excellent, and hash browns, which are better. While the chefs regularly scrape debris into the grill's front gutter, their touch is light enough that the flavors of bacon, ham, sausage, and hash linger, ready to be sucked into heaps of shredded potatoes piled on the hot surface. A broad cake of three or four servings is flattened and remains untouched long enough for the underside to turn gold, then the still-soft top is crowned with a scoop of butter. As the butter melts, the potatoes are flipped and worried so that by the time they are plated, they have become mostly crunchy, but with enough tender white tips to sop up at least two sunnyside yolks.

Lenny & Joe's Fish Tale Restaurant
1301 Boston Post Rd. (Route 1)   203-245-7289
Madison, CT   LD | $$

Lenny & Joe's opened as a roadside fried-clam stand in 1979. It has since become two restaurants with vast seafood menus that range from muscular hot dogs to whole lobster dinners (summertime) to superior fried seafood. Whole-bellied fried clams are big and succulent with golden crusts. We love the fried shrimp and scallops, even simple fried fish. All fried items are available in an ample regular-size configuration as well as a "super" plate with double the amount of fish. This is one restaurant where the undecided customer who craves the crunch of fresh-fried seafood will be happy ordering a variety platter with some of everything. It is a gargantuan meal, including crinkle-cut French fries and a little cup of sweet coleslaw. The only other necessary item would be an order of fried onions; Lenny and Joe's are wicked-good!

Lobster fanatics know Lenny & Joe's as a reliable source for a *hot* lobster roll, meaning chunks and shreds of lobster meat drenched in butter and heaped into a butter-toasted long roll. This is pure bliss, with none of the whole-lobster hassle of shell-cracking and meat-extraction. In season, the kitchen also offers a softshell crab roll that is divine.

Also at 86 Boston Post Rd. (Route 1), Westbrook, CT (860-669-0767).

Lenny's

205 S. Montowese St.   203-488-1500
Branford, CT   LD | $$

A longtime fixture of the Indian Neck section of Branford's coast, this excellent restaurant is a neighborhood place with a menu that ranges from hamburgers and hot dogs to full shore dinners. The latter includes chowder (either creamy New England–style or clear-broth shoreline-style), a couple of cherrystone clams on the shell, a lobster, a heap of steamers, sweet corn, and a thick slice of watermelon for dessert.

Good as both kinds of chowder are, one should never begin a meal at Lenny's without "zuppa d'clams": steamed-open cherrystones in a bowl of briny, lemon-laced broth, a half-loaf of bread on the side for dunking. Delicious! Many of Lenny's best meals are fried: whole-belly clams, succulent oysters, scallops, fish and chips, and huge butterflied shrimp. Crunch-crusted and clean-flavored, this is exemplary fried seafood, and definitive proof that a crisp, clean crust can be the very best halo for seafood's natural sweetness.

Throughout the summer, strawberry shortcake is available for dessert. It is the true Yankee version, made from a sideways-split, unsweet biscuit layered with sliced berries in a thin sugar syrup, and a mountain of whipped cream.

Letizia's

666 Main Ave. (Town Line Shopping Center) 203-847-6022
Norwalk, CT   LD | $$

While the strip-mall setting isn't much, Letizia's name is part of Northeast pizza history, one of the first in the region to serve it—as a weekend-only item—when Joe Letizia opened his Italian restaurant down on Norwalk's Wall Street in 1937. Well after his death in 1962, Uncle Joe's was still known as a source of fine red-sauce meals at rock-bottom prices. The family sold the old place in 1985 (it is now in others' hands), but today's Letizia's, opened by grandson Dan in 1992, still offers baked ziti and manicotti, spaghetti with marinara, and hot-parm grinders on made-here rolls. Those things are fine; however, with pizza this good, they're immaterial.

As is true of New Haven's greats, crust matters immensely. Baked on a screen, then further toughened on the oven's brick floor, it is medium-thin Neapolitan-style, chewy more than brittle, with a full, earthy taste. Traditional mozzarella and sauce—the same food service brands the family has used since the beginning—meld into a creamy Italian-American slurry with veins of tomato tang. Add disks of pepperoni, weeping oil into the mix, and you've got a mighty bite that is outrageously juicy. It is best consumed the New York City way, by pulling one triangular slice from the circle and folding it in half along the radius—the crust is pliable enough to bend, not break—creating a trough that holds everything like an open-top calzone.

Louis' Lunch

| 261 Crown St. | 203-562-5507 |
| New Haven, CT | L \| $ |

A small brick building with school-desk seats and an ancient wooden counter with years' worth of initials carved into it, Louis' Lunch cooks hamburgers in metal broilers that yield pillowy moist patties with a crusty edge. The burgers are served on toast because when Louis Lassen began serving them in his little lunch wagon over a hundred years ago, there was no such thing as a hamburger bun. In fact, it is possible that there was no such thing as a hamburger. Some culinary historians believe that this is where the hamburger was invented. Others attribute it to the Tartars or to the Earl of Salisbury or to sailors from Hamburg, Germany; but Louis' Lunch devotees contend that it was born of Louis Lassen's thrifty nature. The hamburger was his way of doing something useful with the leftover trimmings from the steak sandwiches he sold at his lunch wagon.

Whichever origin is true, Louis' Lunch is an essential stop on America's burger trail. The hamburgers are unlike any others, available with a schmear of Cheez Whiz, if desired; and the place itself, now run by a fifth generation of the Lassen family, is a taste of culinary history.

Modern Apizza

| 874 State St. | 203-776-5306 |
| New Haven, CT | LD \| $$ |

While it is less famous than Pepe's and Sally's, Modern Apizza (pronounce that second word the Neapolitan way: "AH-beets"), a 1930s-era pizzeria on State Street in New Haven, is one of the earth's best pizza parlors. Many savvy pizzaphiles consider it *the* best. "Our brick oven reaches temperatures in excess of 700 degrees," Modern's menu warns. "Some pizzas may blacken around the edges, and even lose their perfect shape due to contact with the brick floor of the oven." Okay with us! While a few places around the edge may be charred, the whole pizza has a swoonfully appetizing smoky taste; and you see why when you devour slices off the paper on which the pizza rests atop its round pan. The paper appears strewn with charred little bits of semolina from the oven floor, most of which cling to the underside of the crust, creating a slightly burnt, hot-bread flavor that no wussy metal-floored pizza oven could produce.

Modern's specialty toppings include broccoli, sliced tomato, artichoke, and clams casino. It is known for the Italian Bomb, which is a joy to eat despite the fact that it totally overwhelms its crust: sausage, pepperoni, bacon, peppers, onions, mushrooms, and garlic. There is also a Vegetarian Bomb topped with spinach, broccoli, olives, peppers, mushrooms, onion, and garlic. As for the New Haven favorite, white clam pizza (hold the mozzarella, please), Modern uses canned clams, not fresh, meaning there is less soulful marine juice to infuse the pizza; nevertheless, it is delicious—ocean-sweet and powerfully garlicky, and built on a crust that puffs up dry and chewy around the edges but stays wafer-thin all across the middle.

The Olive Market

19 Main St.	203-544-8134
Georgetown, CT	BLD | $$

Although the main specialty of The Olive Market—Uruguayan food—doesn't exactly fit the definition of Roadfood as an expression of local culture, and although its inventory includes hoity-toity olive oils, imported cheeses, and boutique pasta, we love it enough to recommend it to anyone passing through, whether for excellent morning coffee or for eats from a menu that ranges from French toast and pancakes to exotic grilled sandwiches and ultra-thin-crust pizzas. Especially notable is a sandwich known as a *chivito*. That's a protein-eater's delight of sliced steak with thin layers of ham and provolone cheese plus a fried egg, all on a beautiful hunk of bread crowned with a single olive.

On weekend nights The Olive Market goes from casual to awesome. That is when chef Fernando Pereyra shows off the cooking of his native Uruguay by offering, among other things, a stupendous "Gaucho dinner" for two or four people: an immense platter crowded with skewers of filet mignon, individual pork ribs, spicy chicken wings, teriyaki chicken skewers, and unbelievably luscious little lamb chops. In the center of this feast are ramekins of peanut dipping sauce, garlicky chimichurri sauce, and, of course, olives.

Pepe's Pizzeria Napoletana

157 Wooster St.   203-865-5762

New Haven, CT   LD | $$

Dating back to 1925, Pepe's Pizzeria Napoletana is a brash neighborhood joint on New Haven's pizza parlor row that makes what we have long considered to be the best pizza on earth. Any toppings are fine (pepperoni especially so), and the crust is sensational—brittle at its edges, ruggedly chewy where it puffs up, scattered on its crisp underside with burned grains of semolina from the oven's brick floor. The emblematic pizza is white clam, which Frank Pepe created mid-century after discussing the idea with a vendor selling littlenecks in a Wooster Street alley near the pizza parlor. It is an uncomplicated pie strewn with freshly opened littleneck clams and their nectar, a scattering of grated sharp Romano, a salvo of coarsely minced garlic, and a drizzle of oil. No mozzarella, no tomato sauce: pure elegance.

In 2006, Pepe's Pizzeria opened a second store in Fairfield, Connecticut, and has since opened others in Manchester and at Mohegan Sun, as well as in Yonkers, New York, with more on the way. Despite our skepticism of such proliferation, the meals we've had at the new places have been every bit as good as the original. And usually the wait for a table—which can be daunting in New Haven—is somewhat shorter.

Wherever you have it, the Pepe's dining experience is no-frills. Pizzas arrive on metal trays and silverware is flimsy and useless. When two people order the same soft drink, the waiter suggests a quart, which is brought to the table along with tumblers full of ice for customers to pour themselves.

Pizzeria Lauretano

291 Greenwood Ave.   203-792-1500

Bethel, CT   LD | $$

There are many excellent things on the menu of this gracious pizza parlor in the town that gave birth to P. T. Barnum: a just-right walnut-cranberry-gorgonzola salad dressed with lemony dressing, panini sandwiches at lunch, and pine-nut-dotted meatballs; but as the name suggests, pizzas are its glory. And glorious pizzas these are, in their own way every bit as soulful as those from Connecticut's funkier famous places. Imported flour and a wood-fired oven that proprietor Michael Lauretano brought from Naples create a crust with exquisite chewy-brittle balance. It puffs up along the edge, so there may be a few spots that taste (quite deliciously) of carbon; the whole thing is insinuated with fire because just before the pizza is ready to be pulled off the oven's floor, the pizzaiolo slides his peel underneath and holds it directly over the smoldering woodpile for a few moments, giving it a smoky fragrance. We love the plain garlic pizza—really just a gilded flatbread; heaven for crust-lovers—as well as the mighty garlic and broccoli rabe white pizza; there are tradition-minded margheritas and puttanescas as well as occasional specials that include a ramp pizza in the spring and a fall harvest locavore's delight of multiple vegetables known as the Garden Pizza.

If you're lucky, when you dine here the kitchen will be passing out little lagniappes to each table to accompany salad or to munch while you wait for the pie to cook: thin strips of oven-hot crust, oh-so-ready to be dipped in seasoned olive oil.

Rawley's Drive-In

1886 Post Rd.   203-259-9023
Fairfield, CT   LD | $

Rawley's defined a way of cooking hot dogs that has become gospel for many of the important frank emporia in southwestern Connecticut. Here, a dog gets deep-fried. When plump and darkened, it is pulled from the hot vegetable oil and rolled around on the griddle with a spatula—a finishing touch that strains off excess oil and gives the exterior a delectable crackle. The dog is then bedded in a high-quality roll that has been spread open, brushed with butter, and toasted on the griddle until its interior surfaces are crisp, in contrast to the outside which remains as soft and pliant as an oven mitt. The kitchen does the dressing, the most popular configuration being mustard and relish topped with sauerkraut and garnished with a fistful of chewy bacon shreds. To our taste, it is a perfect combination, although "heavy bacon"— twice as much—is a popular option.

The restaurant is pint-size: four booths plus a six-stool counter on what used to be a front porch, where an open picture window provides a scenic view into the lively short-order kitchen. As plebeian as can be, it is known for attracting celebrities who live or summer in the area. Meg Ryan and David Letterman have been spotted eating these fine hot dogs, and Martha Stewart used to be a regular.

Ridgefield Ice Cream Shop

680 Danbury Rd.   203-438-3094
Ridgefield, CT $

A former Carvel stand, the Ridgefield Ice Cream Shop makes quintessential soft-serve ice cream by using machines from Carvel's early days, when the formula was not pumped full of air. The resulting lick—our favorite ice cream anywhere—is not sinfully rich or weird-flavored or in any way surprising. It is smooth, dense, and pure; and while it is available with all sorts of toppings, coating, nuts, and fruits, we like ours just the way it comes from the gleaming stainless-steel machine: a swirly mound of it piled up on an elegant wafer cone. For those who live nearby, there are also extraordinary ice cream cakes made from the same frozen manna and layered with icing and crumbled cookies.

Although it has a sunny, summertime feel, Ridgefield Ice Cream is open year-round, rain or shine. In good weather, customers have their cones while leaning on their cars in the lot, or at one of the picnic tables out front.

Roseland Apizza

350 Hawthorne Ave.   203-735-0494
Derby, CT   D Tues-Sun | $$

Roseland Apizza started as a bakery in 1934. Today it is a popular neighborhood restaurant that is a shining example of Connecticut's great Italian-American cuisine. Here you can eat exemplary ravioli, lasagna, and nightly specials featuring shellfish and pasta, as well as brick-oven pies of the highest order. The crust is New Haven–style: thin but not quite brittle, with enough brawn to support all but the weightiest combinations of ingredients and to allay the pizza-eater's primal fears: slice collapse and topping slippage.

The luxe of some pies is surreal. High rollers can get a lavish shrimp casino pie topped with bacon, mozzarella, fresh garlic, and too many snappy jumbo shrimp to count. We recently enjoyed one heaped with a mountain of cool arugula salad—a yin-yang adventure of hot-and-cool, bread-and-veg, sweet-cheese-and-bitter-greens. We love the Connecticut classic white clam pizza made without tomato sauce or mozzarella, just a crowd of clams strewn across a crust glazed with olive oil and scattered with bits of basil, parsley, and oregano, thin-sliced garlic, a twist of cracked black pepper, and a scattering of grated Parmigiano-Reggiano. The nectar of the clams insinuates itself into the surface of the crust, giving every crunch exhilarating marine zest.

Note: Prices at Roseland are high, and some items, such as the shrimp oreganate pizza we recently had, seem outrageous. That one was over $40. However, take into account the fact that everything served here is huge; virtually nobody leaves without boxes and bags of leftovers. That pizza satisfied two healthy appetites at dinner and provided a hearty lunch for two the next day.

Sally's Apizza

237 Wooster St.   203-624-5271

New Haven, CT   D | $$

Sally's has soul. The place glows with old-neighborhood feel: wood-paneled walls, booths with well-worn Formica-topped tables, ubiquitous images of Frank Sinatra (a fan of Sal's cooking) all over the walls. And the pizza packs a wallop. It is generously topped, well oiled, and built upon a thin crust that is smudged and gritty underneath. Of special note are summertime's fresh tomato pie and broccoli rabe pie, heaped with bitter greens when they are available at the Long Wharf produce market. Although it is not formally listed on the menu, Sally's multi-meat "Italian bomb" (sausage, pepperoni, bacon, plus lots of onions) is also significant.

Old friends of Sally's are treated like royalty. Newcomers and unknowns might feel like they have to wait forever, first for a table, then for their pizza, and they will likely endure a staff who are at best nonchalant; but no one comes to Wooster Street for polished service or swank ambience. It's great, thin-crust pizza that counts, and on that score, Sally's delivers the goods.

Shady Glen

840 East Middle Tpk.   860-649-4245

Manchester, CT   BLD | $

Shady Glen makes dramatic cheeseburgers. On a high-temperature electric grill, each circular patty of beef is cooked on one side, flipped, then blanketed with several square slices of cheese. The cheese is arranged so that only one-quarter to one-third of each slice rests atop the hamburger. The remainder extends beyond the circumference of the meat and melts down onto the surface of the grill. At the exact moment the grilling cheese begins to transform from molten to crisp, the cook uses a spatula to disengage it from the grill and curl it above the meat like some wondrous burgerflower—still slightly pliable, but rising up in certain symmetry. The petals of cheese, which may be topped with condiments and are crowned by a bun, are crunchy at their tip but chewy where they blend into the soft parts that adhere to the hamburger.

The restaurant originally was opened in 1948 by John and Bernice Reig in order to put something on the menu of their dairy bar other than home-made ice cream. The ice cream is fantastic, including such seasonal flavors as mince pie, cranberry, and pumpkin in the fall, and the outstanding February specialty, bing cherry and chocolate chip. Our personal flavor faves include Grape-Nuts and Almond Joy.

Shiek's Sandwich Shop

235 E. Elm St.   860-489-5576

Torrington, CT   BL | $

This little joint is a treasure, most especially for its hot roast beef sandwich: cut-to-order slices heated on the grill, then sandwiched in a grinder roll with provolone, romaine lettuce, roasted green peppers, grilled onions, and mayonnaise and/or mustard. Hot dogs are great, too: big plump ones available with all the usual condiments, plus a hot relish that is nearly as addictive as that served at Blackie's in Cheshire (p. 6). The broad menu also offers salads, top-notch diner breakfasts, and serious Yankee chili. Shiek's is strictly a breakfast-and-lunch operation, closing mid-afternoon six days a week; and at mealtimes, the counter and scattering of tables bustle with regulars who chitchat table to table, table to counter, in front of and behind the counter, and all across the cozy dining area.

The ringmaster of the whole affair is Gary Arnold, who manages to carry on at least a couple of conversations at the same time he works the grill, builds sandwiches, and packs lunches to go for the take-out trade. One day we were seated at the counter with a mother and her adult son who explained that whenever the boy returns home to Torrington, this is where they go, not only to eat but to feel very much a part of the community that is theirs.

Super Duper Weenie

306 Black Rock Tpk.   203-334-DOGS

Fairfield, CT   LD | $

We've been on the Super Duper Weenie bandwagon since it was a food truck. It's now a restaurant (and three food trucks for catering) and it has been featured on every TV show and in every publication that pays attention to hot dogs. In fact, several years ago when *Reader's Digest* asked us to name our single favorite drive-in eatery anywhere in America, this is the place to which we gave the nod. If you love hot dogs, it's a Holy Grail. (And if you don't love hot dogs, its soups and sandwiches are first-rate, too.)

The dogs are firm-fleshed Grote & Weigels made especially for SDW, which splits and grills them until their outsides turn a little crusty. They are sandwiched in lovely fresh-baked rolls and adorned with fabulous condiments that include superior sweet onion sauce and hot relish. Chef Gary makes choosing easy (and fast) with suggested basic configurations that include the New Englander (with sauerkraut, bacon, mustard, sweet relish, and raw onion), the New Yorker (sauerkraut, onion sauce, mustard, and hot relish), and the Chicagoan (lettuce, tomato, mustard, celery salt, relish, and a pickle spear). Whatever you get, you must get French fries: beautiful golden twigs served fresh from the fry basket and made extra-delicious by a perfect sprinkle of salt and pepper.

Sycamore Drive-In

280 Greenwood Ave.   203-748-2716
Bethel, CT   BLD | $

Hamburgers at the Sycamore Drive-In are golf ball–size spheres of meat that get slapped onto the grill then spatula-flattened so intensely that the edges are nearly paper-thin and develop a lacy crunch. You can have one plain, doubled, sizzled with onions, topped with bacon and/or tomatoes; and if you still have questions, the menu offers "The Final Answer to the Hamburger." That's a Dagwood burger: two patties with cheese and every garnish known to mankind. (Don't tell anyone, but a waitress, whose name we shan't reveal, advised that if you order a double tomato cheeseburger with the works you will get, in effect, a Dagwood burger . . . but pay 40¢ less!)

The Sycamore is rightly famous for root beer, made on premises and served in frosty glass mugs. It varies from sweet to dry, depending on where in the barrel the serving is drawn, but whatever its nature on any day, it always makes an ideal basis for a root beer float.

The Sycamore is a genuine drive-in with carhop service (blink your lights) and window trays for in-car dining. Indoors, there are booths and a long counter. In the summer, on Saturday evenings, "Cruise Nights" attract vintage car collectors in their finest restored and custom vehicles. It's a true blast from the past!

Ted's

1046 Broad St.   203-237-6660
Meriden, CT   L | $

Central Connecticut is home to about a half-dozen restaurants that all make steamed cheeseburgers, a regional specialty so geographically focused that even people in eastern and western Connecticut have never heard of it. A steamer, as served at Ted's (since 1959), is cooked not on a grill or grate, but in a steam cabinet, the meat held inside a square tin as it browns. Adjacent to the beef in the cabinet are tins into which are placed blocks of Vermont Cheddar. The cheese turns molten and is ladled atop the burger in a hard roll (preferably with lettuce, tomato, pickle, and mustard).

If you love crusty hamburgers that crunch before your teeth sink into the pillowy meat, beware: this one is soft, inside and out, and the cheese atop it is the consistency of custard. For many otherwise broad-minded burger fans, it's just too weird. But those who become addicted to steamed cheeseburgers know nothing else that delivers their squishy satisfaction. Interestingly, the dish was created in the 1920s, when eating steamed food was a health fad.

Zip's Dining Car

Routes 101 & 12	860-774-6335
Dayville, CT	BLD | $

Zip's Dining Car is a vision of gleaming silver chrome and neon from the halcyon days of streamliner diners. The word "EAT" towers high above, and when you exit the car in the parking lot, you will smell sizzling onions, frying bacon, mashed potatoes and gravy. Inside, to the beat of music from vintage pop tunes on Formica-mounted individual jukeboxes, conversation flows easily among the distaff waitstaff (famous for their comely charms) and customers in chrome-banded booths and at the counter.

Looking for a formal gourmet banquet? Drive on! But if it's a square meal you want, you've found it. Hotcakes and sausage in the morning (breakfast all day), big open-face sandwiches smothered with gravy for lunch, meat-loaf and mashed potatoes, milk shakes and hot fudge sundaes and handsome hunks of pie and coffee, always coffee. Take a few sips and your cup will be refilled. Don't sip and it is likely the waitress will be crestfallen next time she comes around, pot in hand, and finds you need no more.

Zuppardi's Apizza

179 Union Ave.	203-934-1949
West Haven, CT	LD | $$

Sitting with Roadfood.com co-founder Stephen Rushmore over a whole baby clam pizza one afternoon at Zuppardi's, we joked that perhaps we ought not to include this place in *Roadfood,* nor post it on the website. Do we really want to share such a treasure with others, risking its becoming so crowded that we can't get in?

Not that Zuppardi's is a secret. It has been around since 1934 and on weekend nights you will likely have to wait for a table, even if the second dining room is opened up. But given its location off the New Haven radar, it never is insanely crowded like the big guns on Wooster Street, and it remains what it always has been—a neighborhood pizzeria. The pizza it serves is among the best.

Crust: Neapolitan-style. Thin and crisp with a puffy circumference that tilts more toward crunch than chew, it lacks a raunchy underside (the brick ovens' floors are regularly vacuumed), but it resonates with yeasty savor. Available toppings include sausage that is made on premises in 200-pound batches and strewn across the pizza in rugged clumps, fresh tomato, broccoli rabe, escarole and beans, hot peppers and roasted peppers. Clam pizza is listed twice on the menu, as whole baby clams and fresh clams, the latter twice as expensive as the former. That is because the fresh ones really are fresh, opened when you order your pizza (you will wait) and spread about the pie in superabundance. One of the Zuppardi family told us that for years vendors have tried to get them to switch over to flash-frozen, cryogenic, or otherwise pickled clams, guaranteeing the embalmed ones are indistinguishable from fresh. "Frankly, I think even the canned ones are better," she scoffed.

But freshly shucked ones are best, and the star ingredient in a magnificent pizza. They are tender littlenecks, glistening with briny-sweet oceanic liquor, complemented by a surfeit of chopped garlic and herbs. "Some customers ask for mutz [mozzarella cheeese]," the pizzaiolo shared with a disapproving frown, "but that just weighs it down." Mutzless, Zuppardi's fresh white clam pie, however perspicuous, is dizzying.

Beal's Lobster Pier

182 Clark Point Rd. 207-244-7178

Southwest Harbor, ME LD (summer only) | $$

Beal's is on a working lobster pier. Picnic tables overlook the harbor; from them, you can see the mountains of Acadia National Park in the distance and listen to the water rippling against the hulls of berthed fishing boats. At sunset, it is magic.

Inside, select a lobster from the tank; while waiting for it to boil, eat your way through a bucket of steamer clams or dip into a cup of chowder. Lobsters come pre-cracked for easy meat-extraction, but it's still some work. If a handsome whole one is too challenging a proposition, you can also get a lobster roll—tightly packed, with plenty of fresh, cool meat atop a cushion of shredded lettuce. Burgers and a few other non-lobster meals also are available. Desserts vary; we have enjoyed blueberry cake and ice cream.

Becky's

390 Commercial St. 207-773-7070

Portland, ME BLD | $

Becky's has dramatically expanded since we first wrote about the little waterside diner many years ago, but it remains friendly, sociable, inexpensive, and delicious. If you are a newcomer and walk in the door any time after

5 A.M., by which time the joint is jumping, you might think you have suddenly been swallowed up in some sort of predawn party of ravenous coffee hounds. Becky loves her varied clientele. "No matter who you are 'out there,' when you walk into Becky's Diner, you are one of us," she says. "Side by side at my counter sit fishermen and captains of industry, college professors and paranoid schizophrenics. They talk to each other and they talk to those who work here. We are all family."

The breakfast menu includes homemade muffins, French toast made from locally baked Italian bread, and "loaded" hash brown potatoes, which are mixed with peppers and onions and blanketed with melted cheese. There is a full array of usual breakfast sandwiches, and one sandwich that isn't usual at all: peanut butter and bacon. "I guess it's a breakfast sandwich," Becky said with a chuckle. We love the "Titanic omelet," loaded with all three breakfast meats, cheese, onions, and peppers, and accompanied, preferably, with Portland's favorite morning breadstuff, Italian toast. Home fries come plain, with onions, with green peppers, with cheese, or with all of the above. If you are in the mood for fruit, we highly recommend Becky's fruit salad, for which everything is fresh, and is fresh-cut to order.

Bet's Famous Fish Fry

Route 27	207-208-7477
Boothbay, ME	L Tues-Sat, D Tues-Fri (seasonal) | $

A tip of the hat to Holly Moore of hollyeats.com for directing us to this delightful food truck just off Boothbay's town square. As its name says, fried fish is the dish to have—the only dish on the menu—either paired with chips (French fries) or in a gigantic sandwich or a very, very large half sandwich. The fish is haddock, some of which is caught by Bet herself, the rest of which is secured from nearby boats. It is creamy-fresh, cased in a fragile red-gold crust, and attains extra savor when dolloped with dill sauce. Get your beverage from the soda machine or bring your own.

Bet's a character, always gabbing with customers, her truck painted with a sign advertising "Free Beer Tomorrow."

Bob's Clam Hut

315 US Route 1	207-439-4233
Kittery, ME	LD | $$

Bob's motto is "Eat Clams." Fried clams, clam cakes, clam chowder, and clam burgers are all wonderful, but they are just the headliners on a long menu of excellent Downeast seafood.

Seafood rolls are showpieces, and not just those piled with fried whole-belly clams or clam strips. You can have them loaded with scallops, shrimp, and oysters (all fried) or with crab, shrimp salad, or lobster. The high-ticket lobster roll is a beaut, served in a nice warm bun that is buttered and grilled until toasty golden brown on both sides; the lobster meat inside is faintly chilled, but not so much that any of the taste has been iced. In fact, this lobster blossoms with bracing ocean flavor when you sink your teeth into the good-size pieces. On the side of most seafood dishes comes Bob's excellent tartar sauce, a perfect balance of richness and zest.

There is no table service. Either outdoors or at the indoor counter, read the posted menu, then place your order and pay in advance. You get a number, then dawdle around the pick-up window (different from the order window) until the number is called. Dine either from the dashboard of your car, indoors at utilitarian tables and counter, or at one of Bob's blue-checked picnic tables.

Clam Shack

Route 9   207-967-2560
Kennebunkport, ME   LD (summer only) | $$

The Clam Shack anchors one end of the bridge that connects Kennebunk to Kennebunkport. Fried clams, sold by the pint, are some of the best anywhere—crisp-crusted and heavy with juice. Lobster rolls are strato-spheric. Big hunks of fresh-picked meat are arrayed across the bottom of a round bakery roll. It is your choice to have them bathed in warm butter or dolloped with cool mayonnaise before the roll's top is planted. It is not a huge sandwich, dimensionally speaking, but its flavor is immeasurable: a Maine summer pleasure to make any lobster-lover weak-kneed.

Whole lobsters are boiled and sold from an adjoining store that is also a seafood market and bait and tackle shop. Upon receiving a cooked lobster, and maybe a half-pound of steamer clams, it is the customer's job to find a place to eat. There are benches on a deck in back and seats facing the side-walk in front, where fish crates serve as makeshift tables. (Town zoning for-bids proper seating here.) Potatoes? Rolls? Corn? Dessert? You are on your own. The store does sell bottles of beer and wine.

Cole Farms

Route 100
Gray, ME

207-657-4714
BLD | $

Opened as a farmland diner in 1952, Cole Farms still can be relied on to serve such parochial arcana as boiled corned-beef dinner and mince pie in the autumn, corn chowder every Wednesday, and a choice of sweet beverages that includes both milk shakes (no ice cream, just milk and flavoring) and frappes (what the rest of the world knows as a milk shake, made with ice cream). It is not, however, preserved in amber. Remodeled and expanded at least a dozen times, the building is now huge and features a gift shop as well as a banquet room. Lunch choices include wraps and modern salads with fat-free raspberry vinaigrette dressing alongside such longtime kitchen specialties as clam cakes and chicken pot pie. Even morning muffins aren't quite as dour as they used to be. "We've tweaked them over the years," says proprietor Brad Pollard. "People want their muffins sweeter. You have to keep up." Such changes notwithstanding, a Cole Farms muffin is demure, nothing like a cloying cake-batter pastry.

A good measure of Cole Farms' personality is American chop suey, a *déjeuner maudit* listed on the menu side by side with "Campbell Soups." Like Cole Farms' shockingly red hot dog, it is an archaic New England meal once popular in institutions and on the supper tables of frugal housewives: ground beef mixed with elbow macaroni and vaguely Italian tomato sauce. It is bland as can be—closet comfort for those of us who sometimes wax nostalgic for school lunch.

The enduring regional value we like best at Cole Farms is the importance of pudding. The lineup is the same every day: tapioca, bread, Indian, and Grapenut. Indian pudding, the rugged cornmeal samp sweetened with molasses, is served hot under a scoop of melting Cole Farms vanilla ice cream. Grapenut pudding comes as a cool block of custard topped by a ribbon of sweetened cereal that has an amber crust reminiscent of a swanky crème brûlée. Swanky, it is not; Yankee, it is.

Colucci's Hilltop Market

135 Congress St.
Portland, ME

207-774-2279
L | $

Portland, Maine, loves Italians. Although Italians are similar to hoagies, heroes, grinders, blimps, zeps, wedges, and submarines elsewhere, the Downeast version has a character all its own. Its uniqueness is not owed to the meats and cheeses, which are commonplace, but to the toppings and the bread. Thick-cut tomatoes, crunchy strips of pepper, briny olives, and a surfeit of spiced oil give the upper layer a brilliant sparkle. And the bread below, completely unlike the muscular, chewy lengths typical of mid-Atlantic sub sandwiches, is soft and light, something like a gigantic version of the split-top buns in which Yankee wieners typically are served. The layers of salami or ham and cheese form a barrier between the bread and the oily vegetables above, but once that barrier is breached (generally at first bite), the bread quickly absorbs what's on top and loses its ability to hold anything. The experience is similar to eating a hot buttered lobster roll: midway through, the absorbent bun has transformed from a foundation into just one element among the stuff it originally contained.

The best Italian we found was at Colucci's Hilltop Market. As proprietor Dick Colucci expertly assembled one for us behind the counter of his corner store, he told us that his place has been a source of Italians since the end of World War II. It is also a source for blueberry muffins set out each morning on the counter in muffin tins, for succulent cheeseburgers made from just-ground beef, and for such démodé hot lunches as mac 'n' cheese, beef chili, and chop suey. There is no place to eat in this family-run market; any meal you get is take-out.

Dolly's

17 US Route 1   207-728-7050
Frenchville, ME   BLD | $

Next to Dolly's cash register and adjacent to the coffee maker is a griddle about four feet square sided by a pitcher filled with *ploye* batter. A ploye is an Acadian buckwheat pancake that gets cooked very briefly and never flipped. It comes off the hot iron with an underside that is slightly crisp and a top that is tender enough to beg for melting butter and maybe a dollop of molasses or maple syrup.

Unless you say otherwise at Dolly's, supper will come with ployes rather than rolls; and these ployes are memorable. They are butter-yellow with a faint green tinge created by the buckwheat (which is botanically an herb rather than a grain) and they arrive three by three straight off the griddle, too hot to handle. They are a glorious companion for Dolly's Acadian chicken stew. More a curative soup than a casserole, the kindly bowl of schmaltz-rich, golden broth is crowded with large pieces of meat, nuggets of potato, and little free-form dumplings, plus a measured scattering of herbs. It's great to gather with fork and spoon, but we found ourselves using ployes like edible mitts to pluck out especially inviting pieces of chicken, then downing meat and cake together in greedy mouthfuls.

Old-time Acadians ask for *creton* with their ployes. Creton is a crazy-fatty-good pork spread not unlike French rillettes. Dolly's version is bright and flowery, a refreshing burst of unexpected spices, including cinnamon, that harmonizes just right with a warm buckwheat crepe.

Doris's Cafe

345 Market St.   207-834-6262
Fort Kent Mills, ME   BL | $

The Roadfood connoisseur will grin with joy upon entering Doris's Cafe, which shares a building with the Fort Kent Mills post office. On one wall hang patrons' coffee cups, which they grab upon entering (starting at 5 A.M.), then pour their own coffee while Linda Daigle (the late Doris's sister) makes sure the frying potatoes look good and the eggs are ready to crack.

With a couple of exceptions, the menu is unsurprising town-café fare, including stout toast made from baked-here bread and well-made desserts such as pecan pie, chocolate cream pie, Boston cream cake, and "JJ apple pie," which is an obscure name for a sensational creation made from big spicy apple chunks with a savory crust festooned with a ribbon of caramel. Hot meals come with homemade rolls; and just about anything should be sided by French fries. This is potato country, and Linda makes the most of it, producing irregularly cut, soft-centered fries from the deep fryer next to the griddle.

Fries are the foundation for the local specialty known as *poutine*. Atop a heap of just-cooked potatoes goes a blanket of dark gravy and a big fist-ful of mozzarella cheese that melts from the heat of the spuds. Known in many local restaurants as "mix" or "fry mix," *poutine* delivers a round-house punch that makes it a nice dish to split among two (or four). The other unique treat is *ployes,* which are crepe-like buckwheat pancakes cooked only on one side, resulting in a top that has a million holes and is able to absorb massive amounts of butter and syrup or gravy from the hot turkey plate or boiled dinner (here, made with ham).

Five Islands Lobster Co.

1447 Five Islands Rd.   207-371-2990
Georgetown, ME   LD (summer only) | $$

How to dine at Five Islands can be a little confusing—nothing like a restaurant with waiters or even an eat-in-the-rough seafood shack. The first thing to do is go into the red clapboard building where a sign above the open door says "Lobsters." In here, confer with one of the ladies about the size you want—they'll happily hoist ones out of the seawater tank for inspection—and let them know whether you want clams, corn, or potatoes thrown into the net and boiled alongside. You can buy a soft drink (or bring your own wine or beer), although we had to convince one old salt to sell us a bottle of Moxie, which she promised was too bitter for travelers unaccustomed to the Yankee beverage that was originally marketed as a nerve tonic. Slices of blueberry cake and brownies are sold on the honor system. Leave a dollar for each one you take.

After arranging for dinner in the red building, head outside and find a picnic table or, if too hungry to wait foodless for the twenty to twenty-five minutes it takes for everything to boil, go next door to the Love Nest Grill (so named because fishermen and their paramours used to tryst there) and pick up an order of fried clams that are Ipswich-good, their briny marine essence encased in microthin crust. The Love Nest menu also features lobster rolls, fish and chips, crab cakes, even hamburgers and hot dogs.

When we told Chris Butler, who, with his wife, Jenny, bought Five Islands only a few years ago, that his lobsters were the best we ever have eaten, he explained that the water around here is the deepest and coldest on the coast, meaning lobsters yield meat that is firm and radiant with clean marine flavor. Ours fairly burst out of the shell when we took a nutcracker to it, and the juices that dripped on corn and potatoes added saltwater radiance to the whole meal.

Tranquility reigns when you look out at the islands in the distance, even when all the picnic tables are crowded with happy eaters chattering with the joy of their sleeves-up meal. As we devoured our shore dinners, savoring the beautiful scene every bit as much as the food, a fishing boat glided into the harbor and tied up at the wharf a few yards from our table. We ate Maine blueberry cake while watching two lobstermen offload crates full of lobsters just trapped in the deep.

Flo's

Route 1

Cape Neddick, ME

No phone

L (closed Wed) | $

Flo's blubbery little pink weenies are not gourmet sausages; and the place itself feels like a crowded garage. Nonetheless, there are many roadside hot dog fans (ourselves included) who would put this wacky little place on any all-American top-ten hot dog list.

Hot dogs are the one and only thing on the menu, so when you enter the low-slung, six-seat diner and peer through the pass-through window into the kitchen, proprietor and chef Gail Stacey (the late Flo's daughter-in-law) will ask just one question: "How many?" They are small, so two is a mere snack. Normal-size men can eat a half-dozen easily, allotting no more than two good bites per dog. Like the wieners, buns are steamed to order; and these gentle buns, fresh out of the heat box, have a fine, silky texture that is itself a vital component of the singular culinary experience of dining at Flo's. Hot sauce, which is technically optional but culinarily essential, is Flo's secret weapon. Nothing like the beefy chili on a chili dog, it is meatless, a devilishly dark sweet/hot relish of stewed onions, glistening with spice and customarily finished with a sprinkle of celery salt. A "special" at Flo's is a hot dog with this sauce and a thin line of mayonnaise, a magic combination that makes the modest dog unspeakably luxurious. If instead of mayo you get mustard, the kick of the sauce/mustard interaction gives every bite a wicked-good bark.

Note: Flo's has no phone! It is open only for lunch, from 11 A.M. daily except for Wednesday, when it is closed.

Harmon's Lunch

144 Gray Rd. 207-797-9857
Falmouth, ME L | $

Doneness is not an issue at Harmon's. All hamburgers are cooked medium—nice and moist but not oozing juice or pink inside. They are lunch counter patties par excellence, sizzled on a seasoned old griddle and sandwiched inside soft Portland-bakery buns that are buttered and heated just enough that they become ultratender mitts perfect for hamburger-holding. Among the options you do have when you order a hamburger is a slice of cheese melted on top and, better yet, grilled onions. The onions are fried until melting soft, and they add sweet, smoky luxury to the little package. Also available are mustard and a vivid red relish. Lettuce and tomato? Forget about them. "They are not available on a Harmon's hamburger!" proprietor Peter Wermell informed us. "Never were, never will be."

The only side dish is French fries, and they're super: thick cut and delivered too hot to handle. However, when this little shop gets crowded, as it so often does, ordering French fries can delay delivery of the meal. You see, while fifteen hamburgers will fit on the grill at one time, the fry kettle has room for only four orders of potatoes. Therefore people who come only for burgers sometimes have their order put to the head of the line while potato-eaters wait. On a busy summer Saturday, it's not uncommon to wait a half-hour for a meal.

Harraseeket Lobster

Town Landing   207-865-3535
Freeport, Maine   LD May-Oct | $$

They tell us that it does rain in Freeport, but every visit we have made to town seeking lunch at Harraseeket Lobster, the sun was shining brightly and gulls were swooping overhead through the blue, blue sky. Picnic tables overlook the Freeport town harbor; meals are perfumed by the salt smell of the ocean and serenaded by the sound of an American flag flapping overhead. Here is one of the nicest places west of Bath to plow into a shoreline meal with a glorious view.

The specialty is boiled-to-order lobsters (also available live, to go), but don't ignore the seafood baskets. Whole-belly clams are giants, hefty gnarled spheres of golden crust enveloping mouthfuls of ocean nectar. On the side, you want onion rings: puffy circles of brittle sweet batter around a hoop of onion that still has crunch. Clam cakes are good, too, their puffy dough holding dozens of nuggets of marine goodness. Chowder is swell, as is the cool lobster roll, served splayed open in a broad cardboard dish and packed with briny-sweet chunks of meat. Have it with onion rings or an order of fried onion middles (sweet, slick nuggets that are to fried rings what holes are to donuts), and conclude with a fudgy, hand-fashioned whoopie pie.

Helen's

28 E. Main St.   207-255-8423
Machias, ME   BLD | $

Helen's is deservedly famous for blueberry pie: a dense slurry of cooked and fresh tiny wild Maine blueberries—one-fifth the size of the big ones you buy by the pint at the supermarket—is piled onto a flaky crust and heaped with whipped cream. If all you know are the store-bought ones, the flavor of these berries is astonishing: intensely fruity, sweet but not sugary, bright as the sun. You can get Helen's blueberry pie year-round, but the best time to have it is late summer, when fresh-picked lowbush blues are abundant.

The same fine blueberries find their way into morning muffins; and pies made from raspberries, strawberries, and boysenberries should not be ignored, nor should brownies, cakes, and turnovers. But Helen's is not merely a pastry shop. It is a dandy small-town restaurant that serves lunch of elegant fried clams or fried haddock, broiled halibut, hot turkey and mashed potatoes, a whole boiled lobster dinner, or a flawless bowl of fresh-picked lobster meat sopped with butter.

Hodgman's Frozen Custard

1108 Lewiston Rd.
New Gloucester, ME

207-926-3553
Mother's Day to Labor Day
(closed Mon & Tues) | $

A fair-weather destination north of Portland, Hodgman's is the sort of place that calls out to anyone with a sweet tooth and a love for mid-twentieth-century Americana. It is a roadside custard shop where they make their own in only the basic flavors—vanilla and chocolate—plus one special each day. There are no mix-ins, swirls, chunks, chips, cookie dough, or candies polluting this dairy-pure manna. It's just custard. But oh, what good custard it is: thick and creamy, totally unlike bland brands pumped full of air.

We like vanilla best, just plain. Nothing is more perfectly satisfying on a warm summer day, whether perched on a cone or served in a cup. Of course, you can doll it up if you wish. Hodgman's menu lists sundaes, frappes and floats, banana boats and thunderstorms, hot fudge royals, tin roofs, and tin lizzies. Whole custard pies are also available.

There is no indoor dining area, but facilities include a large covered picnic area to the side of the stand, where you can sit and lick in the shade.

Lobster Shack

225 Two Lights Rd.
Cape Elizabeth, ME

207-799-1677
LD (closed winter) | $$

Here is the most dramatic possible setting for lobster-eating—the water's edge, framed by a pair of lighthouses at the entrance to Casco Bay. A restaurant has perched here since the 1920s, and while you might find better fried clams and lobster rolls along the coast, you will find no more inspired place to eat them than at one of the picnic tables marshaled on a flat patch of sandy land between the take-out counter and huge rocks where the ocean splashes in. When the sea is rough and the wind is gusting, a foghorn sounds nearby and a fine mist of salty air blows across your meal, causing hot lobster meat to exude puffs of aromatic steam as you crack claws, vent the tail, and unhinge the back.

Beyond whole lobsters, the menu includes some pretty fair fried clams and onion rings, a lovely lobster roll dolloped with a dab of mayonnaise, lobster stew, and clam cakes. For dessert there are Yankee puddings and pies and the chocolate-crème sandwich known as a whoopie pie (but here spelled whoopy pie).

There is indoor seating, too, but as far as we're concerned there is no point in coming to the Lobster Shack unless you plan to eat outdoors.

Long Lake Sporting Club

48 Sinclair Rd.   207-543-7584
Sinclair, ME   D | $$

You wouldn't call the Long Lake Sporting Club blue-chip (swank restaurants do not exist in northern Aroostook County), but neither is it blue-collar. Set in a peaceful waterside location on Long Lake and accessible by auto, boat, or seaplane (or snowmobile in season), it is a north woods supper club to which locals and visiting outdoorsmen repair for cocktails and big-deal meals of prime rib, lobster, or fried chicken.

The chicken is especially good, pressure-fried so it develops a hard, toasty crust that shores in amazing amounts of juice and cooked-tender meat. Alongside the chicken comes a ramekin of translucent red barbecue sauce with powerhouse spices that give the mild-flavored chicken a welcome jolt. Chicken or whatever main course you choose comes as part of a ritual meal that includes a finely chopped cabbage and carrot salad bathed in a curious spicy tomato dressing not unlike that used on barbecue slaw in the mid-South. Well-salted French fries are thick, with a tough coat enclosing supremely creamy insides. All meals include a plate of *ploies,* the thin buckwheat pancakes that are popular in this part of Maine in lieu of dinner rolls. The *ploies* arrive wrapped in a thick white napkin accompanied by bubble packs of butter and margarine and a pitcher of corn syrup. Two plates are provided so you can pour a pool of syrup onto the second plate, peel a ploye from the stack on the other plate, butter it, roll it into a tight tube, then dab it in the syrup for between-meat bites.

Maine Diner

2265 Post Rd.   207-646-4441
Wells, ME   BLD | $

For us, no trip up Route 1 is complete without a visit to the Maine Diner, whether it's for lobster benedict or a plate of homemade baked beans at dawn, the world's most delicious seafood chowder and meat loaf at noon, or lobster pie at supper time. Truly special daily specials include New England boiled dinner every Thursday and red flannel hash (made from leftover boiled dinner) . . . while supplies last. We are especially fond of the fried clams, which are vigorously oceanic, just a wee bit oily, so fragile the crust seems to melt away as your teeth sink into them. Serious clam devotees can get a "clam-o-rama" lunch, which includes clam chowder, fried whole-belly clams, fried clam strips, and a clam cake!

Seafood rolls are outstanding—split buns piled with clams, haddock, scallops, or shrimp. And the lobster rolls are not to be missed. Yes, we said rolls, plural: The Maine Diner offers two kinds—a lobster salad roll, of cool meat and mayo, or a hot lobster roll of warm meat with plenty of melted butter to drizzle on it. Either one is terrific; for us, the hot lobster roll is heaven on earth.

The menu is vast, including such all-American items as buffalo wings and barbecued pork sandwich, plus a superb chicken pot pie. In our book, the single mustn't-miss dish is lobster pie, a casserole containing plump sections of lobster—soft claw and chewy tail meat—drenched in butter, topped with a mixture of cracker crumbs and tomalley. It is a strange, punk-colored dish, monstrous green and brown and pink, shockingly rich.

Moody's Diner

Route 1   207-832-7785
Waldoboro, ME   BLD | $

Moody's no longer is open around the clock, but it remains one of the top spots along the coast route for predawn breakfast. When the doors open at 4:30, morning muffins have been out of the oven long enough that you can pull one apart without searing fingertips; through the cloud of steam that erupts, a constellation of blueberries glistens in each fluffy half. "It's a good thing you came on Thursday," advises waitress Cheryl Durkee when we occupy a booth. "I think the girl who comes in today makes the best cinnamon rolls. They're the tallest." Cheryl also warns that the 1.36-ounce jug of maple syrup that costs $1.50 is enough for only two pancakes, so anyone who gets a stack of three should consider purchase of a second jug.

Thrift is a pillar of traditional New England cooking and a big part of Moody's echt Maine character. This is not the place you come to splurge on a full-bore shore dinner or a $12 lobster roll; in fact the restaurant's 208-page cookbook, *What's Cooking at Moody's Diner*, doesn't contain a single recipe for lobster. But it does offer "mock lobster bake" made with haddock fillets. Haddock, which costs less than just about any other edible fish, has been served with egg sauce every Friday for as long as any of the Moody family can remember. (At last count, over two dozen Moodys worked in the restaurant and at the motel and cabins just up the hill.)

The menu is a primer of Northeast diner fare: meat loaf and mashed potatoes, hot turkey sandwiches, a panoply of chowders, stews, and soups, red flannel hash, baked beans with brown bread, and a fabulous selection of pies, including a legendary walnut pie that is actually a gloss on southern-style pecan pie but, as Alvah Moody proudly notes, "not sickening sweet."

Nunan's Lobster Hut

9 Mills Rd.   207-967-4362
Kennebunkport, ME   D (summer only) | $$

No frills at Nunan's will distract you from the perfection of the lobster (except maybe the view, when the panels on the sides of the dining room are raised and reveal a pleasant vista of Cape Porpoise marshlands). Each lobster is steamed in a couple inches of salty water for exactly twenty minutes, emerging with silky tender claw meat, its knuckles and tail succulent and chewy. It comes to the table on a pizza pan with a bag of potato chips. Coffee is served in mugs. Water comes in paper cups. Bring your own wine or beer.

The Nunan family have been lobstering for three generations, so by now they have the process of enjoying their catch down to its essence. After you've polished off the lobster, there are homemade brownies or a slice of pie, the recipes for which have been perfected over the last thirty years. Blueberry and apple are memorable, their subtly sweetened fruits encased in sugar-dusted crusts.

Should you desire to wash your hands before, during, or after eating, sinks are available in the open dining room, ready for immediate action. They are serious, proletarian sinks, like you'd want to have next to your workbench in the basement. For drying hands, Nunan's supplies rolls of paper towels. It's all wonderful lobster-eating ambience, including a touch of romance in the form of a utility candle stuck in a thick cork on every table.

Rock's Family Diner

378 W. Main St.   207-834-2888
Fort Kent, ME   BLD | $

Rock's is ambiguously located smack between two scenic markers, one declaring this spot to be the beginning of Route 1—2,209 miles from Key West—the other saying it is the end of Route 1—2,390 miles from Key West. We've never measured, nor do we have an opinion about whether Route 1 starts or ends in Fort Kent; but we have eaten several meals at this diner in the northeasternmost corner of the United States and recommend it with no ambiguity at all.

Walk in, study the wall menu, place your order, and pay. Then find a seat at a table or booth or one of the communal counters. In a short while, out comes a member of the staff with your cheeseburger, chili dog, sandwich, or hot-lunch plate. The burgers are thin patties, squished hard on the grill but fatty enough to be plenty juicy. On the side, fried potatoes are the order of the day, available seven ways: jo-jo's, curly fries, plain fries, fries topped with gravy, hamburger, or Italian sauce, or as a mix (the local version of *poutine*): potatoes heaped with mozzarella cheese and dark brown gravy.

A case up front and the counter are arrayed with all kinds of kitschy, made-here desserts, including turtle cheesecake, Rice Krispies concoctions, and a wide array of oversized cookies.

In August, when Fort Kent holds its annual Muskie Derby and Ploye Festival, Rock's hosts a contest to see who can eat the most *ployes* (buckwheat crepes). When we attended in 2009, they served a traditional Acadian meal that included some of the best pot roast anywhere, plus stacks of *ployes* to mop up its gravy.

Sea Basket

303 Bath Rd.   207-882-6581
Wiscasset, ME   LD | $

Sea Basket is a neat and tidy functional roadside café with eat-in-the-rough service: place an order and wait for your number to be called. We are huge fans of its lobster stew, which is loaded with hunks of knuckle and claw meat and is creamy but not heavy, gilded with a glistening butter slick on top. Fish chowder and clam chowder are similarly excellent; and the baskets of fried shrimp, clams, and haddock—made using a process the management calls "convection deep frying"—are all fresh and crisp. To our taste, Sea Basket scallops are especially delicious—sweet, tender, and veiled in a crust that virtually melts when bitten. We also sampled a lobster roll, which was filled with good pieces of meat bound in just enough mayonnaise, but was made, oddly enough, with a sturdy bun similar to what you'd use for a hero sandwich.

The proper dessert for almost any Maine Roadfood meal is a whoopie pie, of which the Sea Basket has a whole selection: classic thick, soft chocolate cakes surrounding white sugar filling, as well as raspberry crème whoopie pies made with white cookies, peanut butter cream whoopie pies, and thin-mint whoopie pies ("Tastes Just Like One!" a sign boasts).

Note: Sea Basket closes in January and February, and it is always closed on Tuesdays.

Baxter's Fish & Chips

177 Pleasant St.   508-775-7040
Hyannis, MA   LD April-Columbus Day | $$

Baxter's is crowded and the prices are higher than at shoreline shacks, but you cannot beat the setting, overlooking Hyannis Harbor where ferry boats set sail for Nantucket and Martha's Vineyard. While it is possible to have table service in Baxter's Boathouse Club, it's quicker and, in our estimation, much more fun to go to the fish and chips part of the operation, where the modus operandi is to eat in the rough: Study the posted menu, place an order, then carry your own tray to a varnished table indoors or a picnic table overlooking the water.

However you experience Baxter's, the thing to eat is summertime Yankee shore fare: crisp fried clams served with decent fries, or indecently tasty clam fritters, which are deep-fried doughballs dotted with morsels of clam and served with honey for dipping. The lobster rolls are good, as is the Yankee-style (creamy) chowder. Or you can eat fine scallops, shrimp, or oysters. Steaks are available for fish-frowners.

Christina's Homemade Ice Cream

1255 Cambridge St.   617-492-7021
Cambridge, MA $

Christina's has two strikes against it. First, seating is severely limited and because the place is so popular, it is not uncommon even in inclement weather for crowds to hover on the sidewalk licking cones and spooning into cups. Second, it is virtually impossible to park anywhere nearby. Roadfood.com member Bruce Bilmes offered his solution to the latter problem, which was either to take mass transit or to "move to within walking distance." If you love ice cream, housing near enough to walk for a cup of Christina's would be Millionaire's Row.

Take, for example, the flavor called burnt sugar, an alchemical combination of high-butterfat ice cream and sweet sugar that teeters on the edge of bitter-burnt. It is a flavor that stimulates the appetite at the same time it sates it, inevitably causing return trips in twenty-minute increments and, finally, futile alcoholic-like promises to eat moderately the next time. Burnt sugar is only one of dozens of interesting flavors at the pinnacle of greater Boston's pantheon of great ice cream shops. Other must-licks include blood peach (in season), saffron, Mexican chocolate, *khulfi,* and banana-cinnamon.

Clam Box

246 High St.   978-356-9707
Ipswich, MA   LD (summer only) | $$

It's hard to believe that we ever wondered where the best fried clams are made. One taste of those served at the Clam Box is irrefutable evidence that there are none better. The whole-belly clams are not overly gooey and not too large, offering a subtle ocean sweetness that is brilliantly amplified but not the least bit overwhelmed by the crusty sheath outside. A whole clam plate is a magnificent meal that includes not only the native beauties sheathed in their fragile red-gold envelope, but also elegant onion rings, French fries, and bright, palate-refreshing coleslaw. Even the tartar sauce is a cut above. The lobster roll is loaded with meat; Jane declares the clam chowder to be among New England's best; and our friends Bruce Bilmes and Sue Boyle wrote, "Clam Box's fried clam strips are perhaps the only strips we've ever eaten that don't seem like a compromise. They are as good as the bellies, in their own way."

The place itself is a gas, shaped like a clam box, the trapezoidal container in which fried-clams-to-go are customarily served. It is a genuine roadside attraction that dates back to the 1930s and would be of interest for its looks alone. There is indoor seating, but across the parking lot are choice seats whenever the weather is nice: sunny picnic tables for al fresco dining. Throughout most of the summer, expect a wait in line at mealtimes. The Clam Box is famous, deservedly so.

Donut Dip

648 N. Main St.   413-736-2224
East Longmeadow, MA   BL | $

"What foods these morsels be!" is the motto on the box in which your dozen is presented at the counter of a modest store that happens to be one of New England's premier donut shops. The box also boasts of forty-nine different varieties, including elegant French crullers and long crullers, devil's-food-dark chocolate, toasted coconut, buttermilk, and jelly-filled, plus fritters and fruit bars. The flagship donut is apple cider, which Roadfood.com's Chris Ayers and Amy Breisch described as "the finest we've ever eaten, their crunchy, cracked exteriors bursting with cinnamon-y apple flavor."

Second location: 1305 Riverdale St., West Springfield, MA.

Durgin-Park

340 Faneuil Hall Marketplace   617-227-2038
Boston, MA   LD | $$

Durgin-Park attracts hoards of tourists. It is noisy and can seem impolite. It is a pillar of Yankee gastronomy that twice a day clatters out expertly made plates of regional food, many of which are getting hard to find elsewhere. Seated at the long, red-checked communal table, you holler your order to a waitress who soon slaps down some corn bread. You then move on to such old favorites as lobster stew, Boston scrod, fishcakes and spaghetti, roast turkey with sage dressing, pot roast, or pork loin. The house specialty is prime rib, a gargantuan cut that overhangs its plate. Side that with a mountain of mashed potatoes and a scoop of fresh applesauce, and please, please, an order of superb Boston baked beans—firm, silky, not too sweet—and you've got a meal to nourish a nation.

The dessert list is tradition itself, featuring hot mince pie in the autumn, apple pandowdy, deep-dish apple pie, strawberry shortcake on a biscuit, and the world's best Indian pudding, which is a steaming gruel of cornmeal and molasses that true Yankees love and for which others may or may not acquire the taste.

Essex Seafood

143R Eastern Ave.   978-768-7233

Essex, MA   LD | $$

The sweetest, tenderest soft-shelled clams—perfect for frying—are harvested from the mudflats on Essex Bay; and here at Essex Seafood, they are expertly cooked and informally presented. This place boasts a significant lobster pound, where people come to buy them live to take home and boil, or boiled and ready to eat. Adjacent to the market and the holding tanks is a quiet dining room with a window to the kitchen. Here diners select from a menu of various-sized lobster dinners as well as boats, plates, sandwiches, and side orders of fried clams, scallops, and shrimp, plus excellent clam chowder and corn on the cob. The lobsters are swell, and the fried seafood plates are beautiful to behold: a layer of French fried potatoes, topped with a layer of onion rings, topped with a heap of your seafood of choice.

Eat inside, at booths in the wood-paneled dining room that is decorated with nautical bric-a-brac, or choose a green-painted picnic table outdoors in back—a breezy retreat from Route 133 near the Essex-Gloucester town line.

Graham's Hot Dogs

931 Bedford St.   508-678-9574

Fall River, MA   L | $

Franks 'n' beans are a time-honored combo almost everywhere, but there are few places where they come together as nicely as in Fall River, Massachusetts. Hot dog shops (of which the city has multitudes) offer them in a bun, the beans serving as a condiment either below or on top of the wiener. Graham's beans are especially good: brown-sugar sweet, soft and goopy, laced with limp leaves of onion. The same good beans are available bunned with *chourico* sausage, or with kielbasa, or with a hamburger. Or for all of $1.15, you can buy beans-only in a bun.

Should you be interested in outfitting your hot dog with things other than beans, Graham's has a panoply: ground *chourico,* bacon, potato chips, Coney Island–style chili sauce, sauerkraut, onions sopped with hamburger juices (that one is known as a "whimpy"), and the moist grated Cheddar that is a local favorite.

Dating back to 1962, Graham's lacks the patina of culinary history that makes so many of the region's more ancient hot dog joints especially charming. Its school-desk seats along the wall are fairly modern and the facade is boring brickface. But the bean dogs and hot cheese sandwiches are exemplary.

Hartley's Original Pork Pies

1729 S. Main St.   508-676-8605

Fall River, MA   BL | $

Rant on: One often hears the argument that American cuisine is homogenized and that regional specialties are disappearing. Such miserable claims—usually made by fussbudgets who rarely venture beyond places that have been anointed by the culinary elite—have a grain of truth. Some once-common good eats have gotten rare; fine local eateries do disappear. But anyone who actually leaves the elitist cocoon and bothers to explore with an open mind and willing appetite will find endless treasures of regional Roadfood all around the country.

We now shall climb off our soapbox and tell you about Hartley's Original Pork Pies, a one-hundred-plus-year-old bakery in Fall River, Massachusetts, that continues to make and sell the meat pies that once were so popular among the Quebecoise and British Isles immigrants who came to this region to work in the mills. The savory pies (*tourtieres*) are made as family-size nine-inchers and as individual units the size of a large cupcake. In addition to traditional ground pork with gravy, variations include chicken pie, chorizo pie, and even Buffalo chicken pie with hot sauce and blue cheese. Salmon pies are available on Friday and Saturday. The fillings are hearty and unmistakably artisan; the crust is sensational—melting-rich and flaky the way only a crust made with lard can be. In addition to meat pies, Hartley's makes stuffed quahogs and chorizo pizza. Local enough for you?

There are no dining facilities. Although infused with gravy, the pies are fairly tidy and manageable as dashboard eats, using a plastic fork and several napkins.

J.J.'s Coney Island

565 S. Main St.   508-679-7944

Fall River, MA   BLD | $

Most hot dog joints, especially in southeastern New England, are places you likely wouldn't take your dear old grandmother. They are, let us be kind, rough around the edges. Not so J.J.'s. "We don't allow swearing," proprietor Albano Medeiros once told a reporter. "We want families to come here. . . . We wanted to offer a classier place." The large street-corner restaurant is accoutered with comfortable booths and tables—and even an espresso machine—for leisurely dining and sipping. There are no counter seats. And the menu extends beyond tube steak variations to include *chourico* pie, stuffed quahogs, chow mein, nachos, and bacon-and-egg breakfast.

Chris Ayers and Amy Breisch, who zeroed in on this place, said that the first time they went they assumed they should get some gaggers (localese for Coney Island hot dogs), which are the featured attraction on the menu. But while waiting in line at the counter (service is tote-your-own), they noticed that a person in front of them got a chourico roll . . . and it was a beauty. Sure enough, this is no roll from Cheap-Eats Central. It is a lovely twisted pastry enveloping a great load of rugged, spicy sausage. J.J.'s also is a prime source of the Fall River hot cheese sandwich, for which a hearty scoop of warm hashed Cheddar is retrieved from a steam table tureen (where, miraculously, it does not melt or clump) and put onto a burger bun. Harmonized by a measure of the fine-grind, meaty sauce used on Coney Island hot dogs and a sprinkle of raw onion, the sharp cheese sings a clear dairy melody.

Kelly's Roast Beef

410 Revere Beach Blvd.   781-284-9129
Revere, MA   LD | $

There are a couple of other Kelly's branches, but they do not compare to the charm of the Kelly's at Revere Beach, especially on a warm spring weekend when gulls screech overhead and occasionally panhandle from the sky over diners who don't closely guard their meals. The salty air of the ocean wafts in to add ineffable savor to the roast beef sandwiches; and the sun shines down, making the roast beef's special sauce glisten. While there is no indoor dining at Kelly's, the pavilions at the broad beach across the street are one of the nicest dining areas a Roadfood devotee could hope for.

The beef sandwich is a North Shore paradigm. There are many toppings available but the primary trio, and a fine combo, are cheese, sauce, and mayo. If the beef tends to be a little bit dry—and in our experience, sometimes it is—the sauce and mayo are superb compensation; and the cheese, of course, adds extra fatty luxury to beef that is fundamentally very lean. We're also fans of the tender sesame seed bun.

Beyond the signature beef, Kelly's menu is mostly beach cuisine: fried clams, lobster rolls, scallops, shrimp, and, of course, French fries and onion rings.

Marguerite's

778 Main Rd. (in Village Commons)   508-636-3040
Westport, MA   BLD Mon-Sat; BL Sun | $

Walking into Marguerite's at noon on a rainswept winter day, the aroma in the dining room was the nicest kind of welcome: sweet clam chowder, buttery bisque ballasted with hunks of lobster, and hot crust on chicken pot pie. A town lunch room with no more than a dozen tables and a short counter, this is where folks come for honest shoreline food and the good company of waitresses who seldom stroll the dining room without a coffee pot in hand for instant refills. We love the fried bay scallops, veiled in the thinnest possible crust, and the sweet-mussel billi-bi redolent of rosemary; but the dish that makes us loyal for life is stuffed quahogs: big clamshells piled with stuffing made from chopped clams and linguica sausage. Known as stuffies, these savories are found on many menus in southern New England; we've found none as good as Marguerite's.

Marty's Donut Land

8 Central St.   978-356-4580
Ipswich, MA   B | $

Except for the fact that you can't have a smoke with your coffee any more, Marty's seems never to change. Its big, hefty donuts are classics from long before recent donut fads, its "honey dew" a simple sinker with a substantial sweet cake texture that is perfect for dunking. On the lighter side are those that are "honey dipped"—airy raised rounds that want to evaporate on your tongue. Chocolate-frosted donuts are weighty and crunch-skinned; and there are jelly-filled and powdered and coconut-spangled, too. Many regular customers come for big goopy coffee rolls.

A simple storefront, Marty's has a counter where take-out dozens are sold and where customers sit and converse as life comes in and out. And there are counter seats in the front window that afford a view of passing traffic on Route 133. Years ago, after a really satisfying Marty's breakfast, we asked the cashier if she had a business card she could give us with the address, phone number, etc., of the establishment for our records. "This is Marty's, hon'," she informed us. "We don't do business cards."

Nick's

534 S. Main St.   508-677-3890
Fall River, MA   LD | $

Long known as Dirty Nick's, this little storefront may be the oldest weenie joint in Fall River, dating back to 1920, when Nicholas Pappas came to town with a hot-dog-sauce formula he learned in Philadelphia. Similar to the New York System weenies of adjacent Rhode Island (see page 61), a hot dog at Nick's is small and pink with a gentle flavor that begs to be doctored up. The standard "works" configuration is a squiggle of mustard, a thin line of the spicy, dark meat sauce, and a scattering of chopped raw onions, all loaded into a fleecy bun. No single ingredient is glorious (although an argument could be made for the sauce); nor is the whole package one of those swoonfully delicious things that induces love at first bite. No, the pleasure of these little things is more progressive, leading from taste-buds bafflement to intrigue to pleasure and ultimately, to addiction. One is only the beginning. Two is a nice snack. Four would be a meal, except for the fact that if you buy five at Nick's ($1.26 each), you get the sixth one free. Nick's weenies are the foundation also for a Fall River delight known as the "bean dog": It is a tube steak topped with a scattering of sweet baked beans.

Smoky *chourico* is huge in this region thanks to the Portuguese roots of so many citizens; another local creation is the *chourico* and fry plate, which is sliced disks of sausage along with a few French fries in a bun surrounded by lots more French fries. Nick's makes its fries as they are needed. When you order them, someone steps to the back, grabs a potato, puts it in the French-fry cutter, then takes the little white spud logs and throws them into a vintage Autofry machine that automatically dispenses the cooked potatoes after their allotted cooking time.

One more local specialty not to miss: the melted cheese sandwich. "Melted cheese?" you ask. "How boring is that?" Not at all. While Fall River's melted cheese sandwiches are by no means epicurean tours de force, they are irresistible. Other examples around town use Cheddar so finely shredded that it seems to have been through a ricer; Nick's makes its version using tiles of sharp Cheddar that melt but don't quite drip. With some of that magic hot sauce on top, sandwiched in a supersoft bun, it's a wonderful little sandwich.

What better place to eat these nostalgic treats than in one of the one-hundred-year-old school desks lined up along Nick's wall?

Nick's Famous Roast Beef

139 Dodge St.   978-922-9075
North Beverly, MA   LD | $

Roast beef is huge north of Boston. You can hardly drive a mile without passing a restaurant that advertises beef sandwiches. Some are chains, many are mediocre. Nick's, where the motto is "We're the Only One," is in the top tier of excellence.

Like most local roast beef houses, it is a self-service joint where you place your order and wait for a number to be called, then carry your own tray to a table somewhere in the small strip-mall storefront eatery. Choices include a large beef sandwich, a junior beef sandwich, and a super beef sandwich on an onion roll. (There are also many other kinds of sandwiches available.) Super beef is the one we recommend. It is a well-stacked pile of moist, tender, full-flavored pink beef inside a giant rectangular roll that is egg-yellow and studded with squiggles of onion. Many condiments and add-ins are available, including horseradish, cheese, mayo, and mustard, but the people's choice is barbecue sauce, which has a spicy sweetness that makes it beef's good companion. And speaking of companions, you definitely want onion rings! Nick's onion rings are beautiful—golden brown and wickedly crunchy—requiring only a hail of salt to attain perfection.

Decoration at Nick's consists of hundreds of snapshots taken of roast beef fans all over America and the world that show them standing in front of famous places holding up a "Nick's Beef" bumper sticker.

Red Skiff

15 Mt. Pleasant St.   978-546-7647
Rockport, MA   BL | $

Remodeled a couple of years ago by new owners, the Red Skiff remains a cozy town café that attracts enough tourists and locals that you can expect to wait for a table or counter seat any time after eight in the morning, especially on weekends. The most interesting item on the menu is anadama bread, which supposedly was invented in Rockport, when a fisherman grew so angry at his lazy wife Anna that he baked his own loaf of bread from wheat flour, cornmeal, and molasses . . . all the while muttering, "Anna, damn her." Whatever its origins, the Red Skiff makes a dark, sweet, and high-flavored anadama loaf that tastes just great when toasted and buttered. (Whole loaves are available to take home.) The unique bread is used to make interesting French toast, available plain or topped with strawberries, but in truth, we like simple toasted anadama bread better. The egg dip, frying, and strawberry topping tend to detract from the solid Yankee character of the bread itself. Other good breakfasts include elegant, plate-wide pancakes (buttermilk, blueberry, or chocolate chip) and a warm pecan roll that is served adrip with caramel frosting.

R.F. O'Sullivan & Son

282 Beacon St.   617-492-7773
Somerville, MA   LD | $$

This popular, boisterous watering hole makes quintessential pub burgers, meaning extra-large mounds of beef with a crusty surface and juice-oozing insides. They are half-pound pillows of sirloin so thick that they take a good fifteen to twenty minutes on the grill, even when cooked rare. A plain hamburger is pretty sloppy, and they get sloppier when you choose one of several dozen ways the kitchen has of tricking them out. Naturally, there are cheeseburgers and bacon cheeseburgers, but opportunities to go wild abound. How about a black and blue burger rolled in black pepper and draped with blue cheese? Or an Empire State burger covered with Italian sausage and mozzarella cheese and festooned with peppers and onions? Thick steak fries and sweet onion rings are superb on the side, and Sam Adams on tap is priced right.

Santarpio's

111 Chelsea St.   617-567-9871
East Boston, MA   LD | $$

Arriving on battered metal trays carried by a take-no-prisoners staff of guys and gals (who are as efficient as they are brusque), Santarpio's thin-crusted pies are proof of the Northeast's pizza glory. The outer rim is a balance of crunch and chew, featuring an occasional blistered-black spot from the oven; and while the inside tends to soften and become unwieldy under a lot of toppings, leading to the heartbreak of cheese slippage, even the flexible part of the crust has a taste that makes you want to keep on eating, then order more. Curiously, the most powerhouse toppings (garlic, onions, anchovies) do not seem to pack a really wicked flavor wallop on Santarpio's pizzas; these are tomato and cheese pies with plenty of soul, but with a mild, creamy disposition. In our experience, one pie, ranging from simple cheese or cheese and garlic (the latter with a halo of oregano on top) to a deluxe combo of sausage, mushrooms, etc., is just about enough to satisfy one normal appetite.

But if your appetite is extra-healthy, you need to know about Santarpio's barbecue. For if this establishment's reputation rides on pizza, it is barbecue that will lure us back again and again. Nothing like pit-cooked 'cue, this version is lengths of homemade Italian sausage and skewered hunks of lamb, or what Italians know as *spiedini*. The sausage is a taut tube with the flavor of the charcoal fire insinuating its high-spiced insides. The lamb has a vivid flavor—for lamb-lovers only—and it ranges from a pleasant chew to a serious chaw. Many folks get barbecue as a pre-pizza hors d'oeuvre, presented on a plate with hot cherry peppers and some crusty Italian bread. Plates of sausage and lamb, with peppers and bread, are the *only* thing other than pizza on Santarpio's menu.

The barbecue adds immeasurably to Santarpio's atmosphere. Literally. The grill is just inside the front door, and its wonderful aroma harmonizes with the smell of tomato sauce, cheese, and crust from the pizza ovens in back to make the air in this unkempt bar irresistibly appetizing.

Toscanini's

899 Main St.   617-491-5877
Cambridge, MA $

First, let us say that the vanilla ice cream made by Gus Rancatore at Toscanini's is some of the best there is: pure, uncomplicated, satisfying. And the regional favorite, Grape-Nuts, is as good as it gets, the familiar breakfast cereal blended into sweet cream so it becomes flavorful streaks of grain. We love such flavors as Cocoa Pudding and Cake Batter as well as such extreme exotica as Black Pepper Bourbon. But the true call to glory is Burnt Caramel. If you are one who enjoys the preciousness of the crust on a flawlessly blow-torched crème brûlée, you, too, will understand how a controlled sugar burn creates an ice cream that transcends sweetness and makes taste buds buzz.

Turtle Alley

91A Washington St.   978-281-4000
Gloucester, MA   L | $

Mayans knew long ago what modern cooks only recently have discovered, that flavoring chocolate with pepper has mouthwatering sex appeal like nothing else. Our favorite way to appreciate the culinary collusion is candy made by chocolatier Hallie Baker at Turtle Alley. She creates terrific-tasting terrapins in white, dark, and milk chocolate; the stunner is an almond chipotle turtle in which the pepper's smoky bite surges through the caramel filling and around the nuts like edible adrenaline, all its excitement robed in a silky sweet chocolate coat that assures on-fire taste buds that all is well.

Hallie's school of terrapins is vast, each single one handmade and as unique as a snowflake. You can get them with pecans, almonds, peanuts, and macadamias, as well as cashews, which she believes are the ideal nut, at least cosmetically, because cashews most resemble turtle flippers. Beyond turtles, the shelves are crowded with brittles, clusters and butter crunches, chocolate-robed candied fruits, nonpareils, and simple hunks of uncomplicated chocolate. The confectionery is a joy to visit, for Hallie's pleasure at running it is contagious—she is the proverbial kid in a candy store, but in this case grown up and running it. Turtles and chocolate samplers are available by mail order.

The Village Restaurant

55 Main St.   978-768-6400

Essex, MA   LD | $$

Dark, wood-paneled, comfortable, and staunchly middle-class, The Village has been a town fixture for over half a century. One veteran staff member recalled to us that when it opened as a five-booth café, the owner used to leave the door open so that before the staff arrived in the morning, regulars could let themselves in and cook their own breakfasts on the grill!

Menus from those early days are posted in the vestibule, and they are a joy to read, not only for the prices (a dollar for a full dinner), but because they list so many of the very basic items that are still on the Village menu, and that still make this such a true regional eating experience. "We serve Essex clams" boasts a menu from 1956. The Village still serves Essex clams, fried to golden perfection. For dessert, you can have a dish of baked Grape-Nuts custard or strawberry shortcake on an old-fashioned biscuit. Nowadays, the menu has something for everyone; and we must confess that there have been occasions, after long days of eating fried clams up and down Cape Ann, when we have come to The Village because we needed a sirloin steak or even, on one occasion, vegetarian pasta! But still, it's local seafood that stars on these tables, simply fried or broiled, or in more deluxe configurations such as haddock Rockefeller. Lobsters are available boiled, fried, or as a lobster pie that is baked in a casserole dish with luscious seasoned breadcrumbs.

Among desserts, we recommend the Indian pudding, a true Yankee dish. It is grainy with a powerful molasses kick, and it is served piping-hot with a scoop of vanilla ice cream melting on top. A bit fancier, but true to local character, is blueberry bread pudding, made of cornmeal and molasses bread and set afloat in a pool of sweet rum sauce.

Wenham Tea House

4 Monument St.   978-468-1398

Wenham, MA   B Tues-Sun, L Tues-Sat, Tea Thurs-Sat | $

A real ladies' lunch room going back to 1912, Wenham Tea House benefits the Wenham Improvement Society by selling books, antiques, china, and handwork, as well as baked goods and very tasty, very polite meals. Of course, there are several main-course salads, including a terrific Caesar salad and a chicken Waldorf cut into tiny bite-size pieces. Crab cakes, available as an appetizer or main course, are demure little disks with a nice sweet flavor and the soft texture of good white bread. There are club sandwiches, a Cheddar crab melt on eight-grain bread, chicken pot pie, and even modern paninis on focaccia. Count on a quiche of the day as well as a soup; we love the creamy smooth lobster bisque. Meals are accompanied by warm, fresh-baked muffins.

Delicate foods are what you expect in such a setting (lace-curtained windows, decorative plates on the wall), but do not underestimate the satisfaction of such full meals as Yankee pot roast or turkey with trimmings that include moist sage dressing, mashed potatoes, whipped butternut squash, and cranberry-orange sauce, followed by hot milk sponge cake for dessert.

Custom decrees that all able ladies (and the occasional gentleman visitor) help themselves to coffee and tea at the sideboard, where a sign advises, "No cell phones, please." Service is swift and efficient, provided by a staff of waitresses in crisp uniforms with white aprons that remind us of the golden days of Schrafft's.

The White Hut

280 Memorial Ave.   413-736-9390
West Springfield, MA   BLD | $

You want a fast meal? Really, really fast? Stop in The White Hut around lunchtime, and you can be in and out—and very well fed—in under five minutes. There are no more than a few counter seats, plus a couple of tables for eating while standing up, but it's not creature comforts that have drawn crowds to this little fortress near the Big E fairgrounds since 1939. It is cheeseburgers. The White Hut offers a modest-size patty topped with standard American cheese. What puts it into the pantheon is the tangle of grilled onions that every regular customer knows to order as a garnish. In fact, if you forget to order onions, the waitress will ask if you want them anyway. And if you say *hamburger,* she'll shoot back, "You mean cheeseburger?" Meat, cheese, onions: It's the only way.

Hot dogs are exemplary, too. Sizzled on the grill alongside the hamburgers, they are medium-size tube steaks that blossom under a mantle of mustard, relish, and raw onions (applied by the waitress, as you specify); and they are served in a bun that is soft on the inside, but buttered and toasted to a luxurious golden brown on the outside.

Woodman's of Essex

121 Main St.   978-768-6057
Essex, MA   LD | $$

Overlooking a scenic marsh in the heart of the clam belt, where towns have bivalvular names like Ipswich and Little Neck, Woodman's epitomizes a whole style of informal Yankee gastronomy known as "eat in the rough." That means you stand at a counter, yell your order through the commotion, then wait for your number to be called. The food is served on cardboard plates with plastic forks. Carry it yourself to a table (if you can find a table that isn't occupied).

A chart we made several years ago comparing and contrasting the top clam shacks along the North Shore evaluated Woodman's clams as follows: Crust crunch = crusty. Chew = resilient. Belly goo = overflowing. Flavor = clamorama! Quantity = substantial. Whole platter presentation = merry jumble. In our experience, Woodman's clams tend to be somewhat larger and gooier than those served in other local places, sometimes a bit too large. But there is no faulting the frying, which results in big mouthfuls that are shattering crisp. Also on the must-eat fried-food roster are onion rings and French fries, and big, spherical clam fritters. Nor is clam chowder to be ignored.

Woodman's gets bonus points for being the one North Shore clam shack that is open year-round.

Bishop's

183 Cottage St.   603-444-6039
Littleton, NH   April-Columbus Day | $

Bishop's ice cream flavors range from the baroque—Bishop's Bash is chocolate chips, nuts, and brownie chunks in dark chocolate—to basic. Vanilla is pure and creamy-white; chocolate is like iced chocolate milk more than some ungodly-rich chocolate mousse cake; the coffee is reminiscent of HoJo's—smooth and creamy more than ultracaffeinated. Here, too, you can savor the old Yankee favorite, Grape-Nuts ice cream, in which the little specks of cereal soften into grainy streaks of flavor in pudding-smooth ice cream.

There is something unusually civilized about coming to Bishop's for ice cream. You'd think that such a happy-time product would stimulate yelps of exuberance and that the interior of the shop would ring with rapture. On the contrary, there is a reverential hush about it, even when Bishop's is jammed and every little table is occupied with ice cream eaters and a hundred are waiting to get inside. Perhaps it's due to the stately old house in which the business is located or the polite way of doing business—wooden cone holders are provided for parking the cone while you pay; or maybe the civilized demeanor is owed to the charm of the ice cream servers, who are extraordinarily solicitous as you choose between a S'more sundae and a maple sundae, and who want to know, if you order a sundae with buttercrunch and coffee ice cream, which flavor you prefer on top.

The Friendly Toast
121 Congress St.   603-430-2154
Portsmouth, NH   BLD | $

Here is deluxe breakfast in kitschy-hip surroundings that include chrome-banded tables and vintage fashion mannequins. While there is no ignoring the menu's intriguing oddities—Almond Joy pancakes, pumpkin pancakes dotted with Raisinets, Caribbean waffles with bananas and pecans—neither should a first-timer ignore the namesake standout, toast. Whole wheat, ana-dama, cayenne-Cheddar, and cinnamon-raisin loaves all are made daily, cut thick, toasted, and generously buttered. There is a variety of egg scrambles available with chorizo sausage and Tabasco-spiked, brown-sugared sweet potato fries or spicy mashed potatoes. Home fries, laced with caramelized onion, are especially memorable. To drink: cocoas of all kinds, coffee drinks, and Mojito milk shakes.

Gilley's PM Lunch
175 Fleet St.   603-431-6343
Portsmouth, NH   LD | $

Gilley's is an old-fashioned night-owl lunch wagon made by the Worcester Dining Car Company, now semi-permanently anchored on Fleet Street in Portsmouth. It was named for Ralph "Gilley" Gilbert, an employee who slung hash here for over fifty years. If it is the wee hours of the morning and all the normal restaurants are closed and even the bars are shut, you can count on this joint to be serving up hamburgers with chocolate milk on the side to a rogue's gallery of city folk who range from derelicts to debutantes.

Many dine standing on the sidewalk, but there is limited indoor seating at a narrow counter opposite the order area and galley kitchen. Gathered here under some of the most unflattering lighting on earth are insomniacs, die-hard partiers, and late-shift workers with no other place to eat, feasting on such quick-kitchen fare as chili dogs, French fries gobbed with cheese, and fried egg sandwiches with ultrastrong coffee on the side. The best dish in the house, or at least the one that seems most appropriate in this reprobate restaurant, is the hamburger; actually the cheeseburger . . . no, make that a double cheeseburger. House lingo is as follows: works = mustard, relish, onion. Loaded = works + ketchup. Pickles and mayonnaise are available, but must be specified by name.

Hart's Turkey Farm

233 Daniel Webster Hwy. (Route 3)   603-279-6212
Meredith, NH   LD | $$

If you love Thanksgiving dinner, you need to know about Hart's Turkey Farm, where it is Thanksgiving every day of the year except Christmas, when the place is closed. Hart's is not a cozy café, that's for sure—the restaurant is gigantic with a theme-park feel—but there is no faulting the moist, full-flavored meat on the turkey dinners—white, dark, or mixed—in sizes that range from a small plate (3.5 ounces of turkey) to the jumbo plate, which is over a pound of meat. With the turkey you get stuffing, potatoes, gravy, and cranberry sauce; and a diner with a mighty appetite can pay $6.99 extra to augment the basic meal with beverage, soup, salad, and dessert.

If sliced turkey is not your style, alternatives include turkey tempura, turkey Parmesan, turkey nuggets, turkey livers, turkey croquettes, turkey pie, turkey marsala, and turkey Divan. Not to mention big slabs of prime rib and a full repertoire of pastas and seafood. For those entertaining at home, Hart's offers roasted and ready-to-carve birds up to thirty-six pounds.

L.A. Burdick

47 Main St.   603-756-2882
Walpole, NH   BLD | $$

L.A. Burdick, which also has a shop in Cambridge, Massachusetts, is a chocolatier specializing in high-quality bonbons. Among the stars are truffles with flavors that range from mint and honey-caramel to scotch whiskey (single-malt, of course), full-size tortes, chocolate fondue, marzipan, nougat, and pâte de fruits. The signature chocolate is a mouse—a small rodent-shaped delicacy (complete with ribbon tail) filled with dark ganache, milk chocolate, and mocha, or with dark chocolate and cinnamon. Chocolate-enrobed thin-sliced candied ginger packs a sweet-spicy kick with a just a hint of saltiness that amplifies its confectionery intensity. Thin-sliced candied pears are another of our personal heartthrobs.

All these sweets are available in beautiful boxes to take home (or to buy via mail-order—check out www.burdickchocolate.com), but there is more to this wonderful place than chocolate. It is also a café where you can come for coffee and amazing pastries (Viennese gugelhupf, anyone?) any time after 7 A.M., as well as for lunch and supper. The full-scale meals are swank indeed, featuring such upscale offerings as salad of arugula with truffled fennel and Parmesan and pepper-crusted yellowtail. The prices for these items are relatively high on the Roadfood scale, maybe $15 for lunch, twice that for supper. But for all its certified excellence, the eatery has the comfy, casual air of a town café, which is what it is.

Polly's Pancake Parlor

672 Route 117   603-823-5575

Sugar Hill, NH   BLD (closed in winter) | $$

A few years ago when a documentary film crew from Germany wanted us to take them to a restaurant that was echt New England, we knew exactly where to go: Polly's Pancake Parlor. They were worldly folks and knew about maple syrup, but its celebration at Polly's was, for them, a wondrous experience. If you like pancakes and maple syrup and lovely log-cabin restaurants in the heart of the White Mountain sugarbush, you, too, may find a visit to Polly's wondrous. We sure do.

Of course, pancakes are the specialty of the house; they are made from stone-ground flours or cornmeal, either plain or upgraded with shreds of coconut, walnuts, or blueberries. One order consists of half a dozen three-inchers, and it is possible to get a sampler of several different kinds. They come with the clearest and most elegant fancy-grade maple syrup, as well as maple sugar and mouthwatering maple spread (that last one the consistency of soft cream cheese, but pure maple). You can also get maple muffins, sandwiches made with maple white bread, a gelatinized dessert called maple Bavarian cream, ice cream with maple hurricane sauce (syrup and apples stewed together), and all sorts of maple candies to take home.

Polly's is surrounded by maple trees that get hung with taps and buckets in the spring, but the most wonderful time to visit is autumn, as the trees turn color. The dining room has a glass-walled porch that overlooks fields where horses graze, and its inside walls are decorated with antiques and tools that have been in the family since the late eighteenth century.

Sunny Day Diner

Route 3   603-745-4833

Lincoln, NH   BL (closed Tues) | $

It's a sunny day indeed that starts with breakfast at the counter or in a booth at the Sunny Day Diner. A gleaming mid-twentieth-century streamliner that used to be known as Stoney's when it was parked in Dover, it was moved to Lincoln in the late 1980's; and it became the place it is today about fifteen years ago.

If we describe it as a diner with an elevated culinary consciousness, please do not expect a menu of striving dishes or service that's in any way pretentious. This is a heart-and-soul hash house, its goodness amplified by the fact that nearly everything is made from scratch. Corned beef hash is rich and luxurious, as are biscuits and gravy. You can have French toast made with banana bread and served, of course, with real maple syrup. On the side of eggs and omelets, the toast choice includes white, raisin, oatmeal, rye, and wheat—all made right here. Bakery items are a specialty, and it would be wrong not to have at least one muffin or sticky bun with any breakfast you get.

We've yet to have lunch at the Sunny Day, but its Reuben sandwich is legendary.

Allie's Donuts

| 3661 Quaker Lane (Route 2) | 401-295-8036 |
| North Kingstown, RI | B \| $ |

Allie's is Rhode Island's premier donut stop, so popular that it has two doors, funneling people to separate counters to place their orders. The waiting area is fairly small, but the open kitchen behind it is an immense workspace where powerful mixers whir and deep-fryers bubble. There is no indoor seating. A couple of picnic tables are available outdoors, but most people get their dozens to go or to eat in the front seat of their car.

The variety of donuts made each morning is vast, including honey-dipped, glazed crullers, raised jelly sticks, plain cake donuts, coconut-glazed solid chocolates, and a rainbow of jimmie-topped extravaganzas. None are fancy-pants pastries; these are big, sweet, pretty things to eat, the cake variety boasting a crisp skin and creamy insides.

Bocce Club

| 226 St. Louis Ave. | 401-767-2000 |
| Woonsocket, RI | D \| $$ |

It was at the Bocce Club in the 1920s where the Rhode Island tradition of gigantic, family-style chicken dinners began when the Pavoni family decided to serve meals to friends who came to their house to play bocce. Over the decades, the ad hoc eatery grew and became a legend, known for rosemary-roasted chicken bathed in butter and olive oil. The main course is preceded by an effulgent antipasto salad, accompanied by crusty bread, pasta in a red sauce, and a motley heap of French fried *and* oven-roasted potatoes. Pass the platters, and eat until you cannot move: that is the Bocce Club way.

While a majority of customers do come for chicken, the Bocce Club has an extensive menu that also includes Italian and Portuguese dishes as well as steaks. Our waitress looked crestfallen when we chose chicken for two. "Chicken is where we started," she explained. "But our chef is so good, there is so much more to try." That may be, but to come to the Bocce Club and not eat roast chicken would be like visiting Seattle and drinking Sanka.

Champlin's Seafood Deck

256 Great Island Rd.   401-783-3152
Narragansett, RI   LD | $$

Champlin's is a casual eatery at the entrance to Galilee Harbor. Food comes on disposable plates and customers carry their own meals from the kitchen window to bare-topped tables, many of which are perched on a deck over-looking the harbor's boats.

The menu is all about local seafood. You can pick your lobster in the adjoining retail store and the kitchen will charge $3 to cook it and supply melted butter; and if you come without your nutcracker, you can get one by leaving a $2 deposit with the staff. To accompany lobsters, there are buckets of steamers with broth and butter. You can get almost any fried seafood, including clams and really good flounder—a broad fillet of sweet, moist meat encased in unobtrusive crust. The flounder is available by the piece or as half of a fish and chips plate. While the French fries are fine, we recommend substituting onion rings, which come enveloped in a hopsy batter, or boiled red potatoes, which are cream-textured with an earthy spud flavor.

While we like Champlin's plenty, we are puzzled by the kitchen's apparent aversion to garlic. There seems to be none in the snail salad, that Rhode Island specialty that is customarily radiant with a garlic halo, nor in the linguine with white clam sauce, which, while quite respectable, was ultimately bland.

Evelyn's Drive-In

2335 Main Rd.   401-624-3100
Tiverton, RI   BLD (summer only) | $$

Evelyn's is a fair-weather drive-in with the nicest possible outdoor dining area: a row of covered picnic tables perched over Sakonnet Bay with a view of pleasure boats and the Newport shores. The outdoor dining is strictly self-service—carry your own food from the order window. We actually saw one couple spread a tablecloth and open their own wine to accompany lobster plates.

Regular customers tend to eat inside at tables and a short counter, where the view is of each other and where the tight quarters are filled with conversation and the hum of air conditioning (rather than the lap of water and the screech of seagulls). We noted that many of the locals order non-seafood meals from the broad menu: meat loaf, burgers, chicken pie, and one local oddity we couldn't resist ourselves, a chow mein sandwich. It is a plate of frizzled-crisp chow mein noodles (made in Fall River), soy-sauce gravy, and vegetables (beef optional) with a hamburger bun floating in it. Weird!

Evelyn's is at its best being a seafood shack, where the blackboard menu lists market prices for fried clams, scallops, and lobster. Scallops and clams are available in small and large size plates, the large being immense. In our experience, the clams are extraordinarily uniform in shape—the classic diamond-ring formation, with a chewy hoop and a gooey belly. The lobster roll, available with a choice of butter or mayonnaise served on the side, is only pretty good—more shredded meat than chunked. Chowder and clamcakes makes a nice single-digit-priced meal—those market prices for seafood can take the better part of $20 for a single lunch. You want to have a little cash to splurge on the Rhode Island favorite for dessert: Grape-Nuts pudding.

Gray's Ice Cream

16 East Rd. at Four Corners   401-624-4500
Tiverton, RI $

On a summer day in Tiverton, Gray's parking lot is packed with people who come from miles around to indulge in the time-honored ritual of standing in line at the order window and getting cups and cones of ice cream that range from normal flavors to that Yankee oddity, Grape-Nuts. Gray's also is proof of our contention that Rhode Island is one of the most coffee-conscious places in the nation (where else is coffee milk so popular?). Coffee ice cream here is robust and just-right sweet. The other great Gray's flavor is ginger, made with bits of fresh root that give the creamy scoops a sparkling spicy bite.

Haven Brothers

Fulton and Dorrance Sts. at Kennedy Plaza   401-861-7777
Providence, RI   D (late night) | $

From the time the Haven Brothers truck pulls up to Kennedy Plaza alongside City Hall at 5 P.M. to its 3 A.M. closing, it hosts a colorful party of Providence characters who carry on continuous conversation with the staff, with other customers, or—if no one will listen—with the voices inside their own heads. To say that the clientele at this late-night lunch wagon is diverse is an understatement. Among the regulars are city big shots, cops, drunks who need to sober up when the bars close, and wackos who range from wildly entertaining early in the evening to wild and scary after midnight. Dining facilities include two stools at a short counter inside and the steps of City Hall. Most customers eat standing up on the sidewalk.

The sandwich menu includes lobster rolls and steak and cheese on toast, but most orders are for hot dogs or hamburgers. The dogs are plump and pink, served in soft steamed buns, available with chili and all the usual condiments. The hamburgers are modest-size patties, available from plain to deluxe (lettuce, tomato, mayo, etc.), but devotees of junk food will have what used to be known as the Murder Burger, which is a double topped with every condiment in the house plus bacon, cheese, and chili. Side a Murder Burger with cheese-glopped French fries and you have a seriously satisfying sidewalk feast.

The most popular beverage at Haven Brothers is coffee milk—like chocolate milk, but flavored with coffee instead. Or you can have a frappe made with ice cream, milk, and flavoring (what the rest of the world knows as a milk shake).

Mike's Kitchen

At Tabor-Franchi VFW Post 239   401-946-5320
170 Randall St.   LD | $$
Cranston, RI

If you happen to drive past Mike's Kitchen, you won't notice it's a restaurant. Located in a VFW hall with no sign outside other than the Post number, Mike's doesn't need to advertise. To those who seek out great Italian food at low prices, it is an appetite-stirring magnet. At mealtimes, its tables are always crowded. (Tuesday, Saturday, and Sunday nights, it is generally closed to the public; that's when the Vets meet and when private functions are held.)

The menu, posted on the wall, is extremely appetizing: a catalog of dishes that are mostly Italian, a little Portuguese, and very Rhode Island. You can begin a meal with a stuffie (a stuffed quahog clam) or the unique Ocean State appetizer known as snail salad, then move on to perfectly broiled swordfish or scallops; or it is possible to indulge in such delectable old-world favorites as sautéed broccoli rabe (or a rabe and provolone sandwich), gnocchi Sorrentino, sole Florentine, and chicken with cannellini beans. On the side of anything, you want polenta—a cream-soft block of steamy cooked cornmeal available with fennel-spiked sausage, meatballs, or a blanket of thick marinara sauce.

Many of the Italian dishes are familiar: veal cutlets in a variety of sauces, Parmesans galore, scampis, and even spaghetti and meatballs and linguine with nothing but oil and garlic. Seafood pastas are especially wonderful, offered with a choice of red or white sauce; the top of the line is seafood Diablo—lobster, scallops, and shrimp spread out across a bed of noodles.

To drink with your meal, wine and cocktails are available from a bar at one side of the dining room. You will pay for these separately, as the bar is run by the veterans who own the building.

Olneyville N.Y. System

20 Plainfield St.   401-621-9500
Providence, RI   LD | $

Rhode Island's distinctive New York System hot dog, known also as a hot wiener, is a small, pink, natural-casing, pork-beef-veal frankfurter that gets grilled, then nestled in an untoasted bun, topped with yellow mustard, chopped raw onions, and dark sauce of ground beef plus a sprinkling of celery salt. It's the sauce that makes the dog unique—spicy but not hot, the meat as fine as sand, the flavor vaguely sweet, reminiscent of the kaleidoscopic flavors that give Greek-ancestored Cincinnati Five-Way chili its soul.

Olneyville was opened in the 1930s by the Stevens family, Greek immigrants who came to Rhode Island by way of Brooklyn, New York. It is still a Stevens-family operation, and countermen continue to use the old-time wiener-up-the-arm technique of preparing the hot dogs, lining up six to eight bunned ones from wrist to elbow and spreading sauce, onions, and mustard on all of them in the blink of an eye. A sign posted outside announces the everyday special: "Buy ONE wiener for the price of TWO and receive the second FREE!"

One curious item on the short menu is beef stew, which is not beef stew at all. It is an order of salted French fries spritzed with vinegar and ribboned with ketchup. The beverage of choice is the Rhode Island favorite, coffee milk—like chocolate milk, but coffee-flavored.

Two other locations: 1012 Reservoir Ave., Cranston, RI, and 1744 Mineral Spring Rd., North Providence, RI.

Stanley's Famous Hamburgers

371 Richmond St.   401-270-9292
Providence, RI   LD Thurs–Sat until 2 A.M. | $

A swell blog called Small Bites ("spices and stories from local eateries in the smallest state") alerted us to the Stanleyburger, a crisp-edged patty customarily served with pickle chips and fried onions. While bigger than slider-size, Stanleyburgers are small enough that we highly recommend a double or two, preferably with cheese, maybe also with bacon and tomato. French fries are crisp and flavorful, available plain, topped with cheese or chili, or Quebec-style, here meaning smothered with mozzarella shreds and dark gravy, a version of *poutine*. Stanley's offers milk shakes, but to make it a unique Rhode Island dining experience, you probably want coffee milk (strawberry and chocolate milk also are available); and for dessert, the local favorite: Grape-Nuts pudding.

Note: A second Stanley's (actually, the original) is located at 535 Dexter St. in the minuscule Blackstone Valley town of Central Falls; 401-726-9689.

Wein-O-Rama

1009 Oaklawn Ave.   401-943-4990
Cranston, RI   BLD | $

"The best hot weiners anywhere!" crows the menu at Wein-O-Rama; and in a state crazy for little pink weenies topped with chili, that's a bold assertion. Unlike many wiener restaurants (most of which spell the word *ei* rather than *ie*), this one has a full three-meal-a-day menu, but when the waitress caught us actually reading it, she interrupted our study and demanded to know, "You are not going to try our weiners!?" Of course, we did; and as the boast suggests, they are beauties.

Curiously, the words "New York Style" or "New York System" appear nowhere at Wein-O-Rama, but the dogs served here are exactly what is known by those terms at most other Ocean State frankfurter depots: a fingerling frank nestled in a soft bun and dressed with fine-grind, Greek-accented meat sauce, bright yellow mustard, crisp bits of raw onion, and an aggressive shower of celery salt. The combo is divine. Not that you necessarily will find God or the Meaning of Life if you eat one, but the sum of the hot dog's parts is nothing short of revelation. To drink: Rhode Island's favorite nonalcoholic libation, coffee milk. And the rice pudding is excellent.

Wright's Farm

84 Inman Rd.	401-769-2856
Harrisville, RI	D | $$

In the early 1950s, after hosting chicken-dinner picnics for local clubs, the owner of Wright's Chicken Farm opened a restaurant. Today it is the biggest of the Blackstone Valley's chicken dinner halls—one of the biggest restaurants anywhere, with seats for up to 1,500 eaters at a time in multiple dining rooms. On a Friday or Saturday night, you'll park a quarter mile away and you might wait an hour for your party's name to be called on the speaker system. While biding time, you can shop for toys, fudge, and kitschy bric-a-brac in the 4,000-square-foot gift shop, try your luck at a window dedicated to selling lottery tickets, or play keno in one of the four bars. Tables are set up for groups of ten and twenty or more. Once seated, you will be waited on and served instantly. When you are done, you pay the waitress with cash. No credit cards are accepted (but there is an ATM machine in the lobby). Everything about the experience is so huge it is hallucinatory.

Once you are at a table, the meal comes quickly because everybody gets the same thing: hot rolls, cool salad, macaroni shells with red sauce, and fabulous thick-cut French fries all orbiting around bowls full of dripping-good roasted chicken enveloped in gossamer skin with booming flavor. What's so especially good about the chicken is that in addition to its fall-apart-tender mouthfuls, there are significant surface areas where the skin has pulled away during roasting and the bare exterior of the meat itself has turned firm, becoming chewy, moisture-beaded bark with flavor even more intense than the soft, juice-dripping parts within. Meals are all-you-can-eat. If ever a bowl is emptied, it gets replaced with a full one.

Chicken-frowners do have an alternative: steak. It is ordered by less than 1 percent of Wright's customers.

Baba-À-Louis

92 Route 11W   802-875-4666

Chester, VT   BL | $

While scarcely a restaurant—no hot meals are served in the morning, and only quiche, sandwiches, and a salad bar at lunch—Baba-À-Louis is one of Vermont's most noteworthy breakfast stops. Since they opened a small storefront bakery in Chester in 1976 (moved to the current location in '97), John McLure and Ruth Zezza have won a reputation for masterful yeast breads. If you are serious about bread, you can stop in any day after 7 A.M., find a seat at one of the tables opposite the bakery shelves, and enjoy a cup of coffee while you tear off pieces from a warm baguette, anadama loaf, or sourdough rye. Morning-specific pastries are breathtaking, especially Mr. McLure's sticky buns. Ribboned with a walnutty brown-sugar glaze, these buttery cylinders are so fragile and fine that they verge on croissant-hood.

Lunch is served cafeteria-style. There is pizza on the weekends; and Tuesday through Saturday, you can have a panini, open-face, or regular sandwich, quiche, or soup or salad.

The place itself is beautiful: a sun-bathed baking cathedral with a full view of the open kitchen where doughs are kneaded and hot breads pulled from ovens.

Note: The bakery is closed during April and most of November, but open again at Thanksgiving.

Blue Benn Diner

318 North St.   802-442-5140

Bennington, VT   BLD | $

In the morning, it is hypnotic to watch coffee-pot-armed waitresses maneuver the cramped confines behind the counter and along the short line of wooden booths of this creaky but ultra-energetic monitor-roof diner that got planted on this site along Route 7 in 1949. What a joy it is to slide a fork down into a steamy slice of corn bread French toast or a stack of crunchberry pancakes with turkey hash on the side. The true-blue hash house menu offers hearty soups and gravy-topped biscuits as well as more creative fare that includes grilled salmon Caesar salad, soya sausage, and Syrian roll-ups. Every available surface is festooned with handwritten signs advertising literally hundreds of specials, including many choices to please vegetarians . . . like a terrific no-meat enchilada.

Chelsea Royal Diner

487 Marlboro Rd. (Route 9)   802-254-8399

West Brattleboro, VT   BLD | $

Nestled at the foot of the Green Mountains, the Chelsea Royal (Worcester Dining Car #736) is like a culinary yacht: polished wooden booths and gracefully curving wood ceiling, tiny-check tile floor, everything old but oh, so shipshape. (A more modern dining area has been added.) "What can we eat that's real Vermont?" we ask our waitress, who wears a "Good Food Fast" T-shirt.

"Blue Plate Special!" she shoots back. Lucky us, it is chicken pot pie—comfort food supreme. We get macaroni and (Vermont) cheese and Yankee baked beans on the side and top it off with maple walnut pie and a bowl of that Yankee stalwart, Indian pudding, a luxurious hot cornmeal and molasses samp that arrives under a crown of melting-fast vanilla ice cream.

Open every day of the year, and serving breakfast all day long, the Chelsea Royal is a place to come for French toast with real maple syrup ($1.25 extra) in the morning and meat loaf at supper . . . or such unexpected exotica as a Cajun skillet breakfast or teriyaki chicken salad lunch. A full fountain offers real milk shakes, sundaes, floats, and splits as well as homemade root beer and black cherry soda. The kitchen makes Mexican food Tuesday through Saturday (including margaritas and Mexican beers), and prime rib with excellent mashed potatoes on weekend nights. April through October, an ice cream stand offers soft-serve and hard-pack as well as burgers and foot-long hot dogs.

Curtis' BBQ

7 Putney Landing Rd. (exit 4 off I-91)   802-387-5474
Putney, VT   LD April-Oct, Wed-Sun | $$

Pitmaster Curtis Tuff's self-proclaimed "Ninth Wonder of the World" serves fine ribs and chicken in high roadside style. By that we mean that this place is more a picnic than a restaurant. Place your order at the window of one of the blue-painted school buses planted in the meadow. When you have paid and the food is ready, you will be pointed to a stack of cardboard cartons that are useful in toting the plates to a table, either in the sun or covered. Dine al fresco, then toss your trash in a can and be on your way.

Of the two things Mr. Tuff smoke-cooks, we go for ribs. They are available as slabs, half-slabs, medium and small orders. A half-slab is a hearty meal. The ribs are cooked so the meat pulls off in big, succulent strips that burst with piggy flavor and the perfume of smoke. To dress these dandy bones, Mr. Tuff offers two sauces: mild and spicy, both of which are finger-licking good. On the side you want a nice baked potato, a cup of terrific beans, and/or ears of sweet corn.

Note that Curtis' BBQ closes in October and reopens in April. It is open for lunch and supper in the summer from Wednesday through Sunday, and fewer days of the week in the late spring and early fall. There is a second location in Chester.

Dot's

3 West Main St.   802-464-7284
Wilmington, VT   BLD | $

Dot's is the Wilmington, Vermont, town café—so much a part of everyday life that regular customers enter before dawn to brew and pour their own coffee. It is housed in an 1832 building that was a post office and a retail store, then a restaurant early in the twentieth century. Its past is visible on the wall in the form of nostalgic photos of waitresses in starched white uniforms, circa 1938, but history tends to fade into the background when you face a craggy-crusted bacon cheeseburger or a handsome hot turkey sandwich with lumpy mashed potatoes. Whatever its past, Dot's is today a highlight of Roadfood in New England.

There's no place better to stop for a really hearty breakfast. We love the kitchen's French toast made from cracked wheat bread, the berry-berry pancakes poured of a batter positively loaded with blackberries, strawberries, raspberries, and blueberries, and the McDot's breakfast sandwiches, which are based on the yellow arches' but are really, really good.

Year after year Dot's takes the People's Choice first prize in the New England chili cook-off; and while Southwest chiliheads wouldn't even recognize it as their beloved bowl of red, this Yankee chili is terrific. It is listed on the menu as Jailhouse Chili, but it's most respectable. Beefy, thick with beans, spicy but not ferocious, it comes as a cup or bowl under a thick mantle of melted Vermont cheese.

The Mill at Quechee

1760 Quechee Main St.	802-295-2711
Quechee, VT	LD | $$

Quechee is a magical New England village, known best for the nearby Quechee Gorge, "Vermont's Grand Canyon," and for the Mill at Quechee restaurant. Originally opened in 1985 as The Glassblower's Café, it is part of the Simon Pearce glassblowing factory, which is still downstairs. An airy dining room is perched high above the rushing waterfall that powers the glassworks' furnaces and has large windowed walls that look out over Quechee's covered bridge. The setting is New England at its most picturesque.

Pearce is Irish and his kitchen offers elegant renditions of such homeland comfort food as soda bread scones and Ballymaloe brown bread, beef and Guinness stew, and an unspeakably delicious shepherd's pie made from local grass-fed beef and topped with a savory cheese-enriched crust. Many dishes are a creative ode to favorite Yankee groceries, such as horseradish-crusted blue cod, a BLT salad made with local tomatoes, a Maine lobster club sandwich, Vermont cheese soup, and house-smoked trout. And there is a mesclun salad topped with crisp-fried spicy calamari.

Available libations include choices from an astonishing 900-label wine list, locally brewed beers and ales, and hot mulled cider. Desserts we've liked include Quechee's own Blue Moon sorbet and a blackberry cobbler topped with local ice cream and raspberry sauce.

Mrs. Murphy's Donuts

374 Depot St. (Route 30)   802-362-1874
Manchester, VT   BL | $

A counter stool at Mrs. Murphy's is a box seat in donut heaven. You can get deluxe ones—Boston creams, jelly-filled, iced, and jimmie-sprinkled—but we'll take plain sinkers every time. They are the polar opposite of the frivolous fat puffs sold by Krispy Kreme in other parts of the country (but *not* in Vermont). These hefty boys have a wicked crunchy skin and cake insides that love to sop a while in coffee; at Mrs. Murphy's, you'll see a virtual dough-si-donut line of dunkers sitting at the counter bobbing theirs in and out of mugs.

The storefront café is a locals' favorite; it occurred to us one breakfast hour that most customers didn't tell Cheryl the waitress what they wanted; she brought them the usual. One banker-looking guy in striped suit and brogues left his sedan idling outside, stepped to the take-out counter, grabbed a bag, and flapped it open for Cheryl to load with six sour cream donuts. As she rang him up, he nodded thanks to her and she nodded thanks to him, then he left and drove away; not a word was spoken between them.

P&H Truck Stop

Exit 17 off I-91   802-429-2141
Wells River, VT   BLD | $

P&H is a real 24/7 truck stop, not for the fastidious epicure. You need to pass through the aroma of diesel fuel outside to get to the smells of fresh-baked bread and of pot roast blanketed with gravy in the dining room. Soups and chowders are especially inviting: Tomato-macaroni soup is thick with vegetables, ground beef, and soft noodles; corn chowder is loaded with potatoes and corn kernels and flavored with bacon. We love the falling-apart pot roast and any kind of sandwich made using thick-sliced P&H bread, but the mashed potatoes (*purée de pommes de terre* on the bilingual menu, written for French-Canadian truckers) taste like they were made from powder, and the meat loaf is strictly for die-hard diner fans.

The homemade dessert selection is huge, including fruit pies, berry pies, custard pies, meringue pies, Reese's pie (a peanut-cream), a few types of pudding, and a maple-cream pie thick as toffee and topped with nuts.

Putney Diner

82 Main St.   802-387-5433
Putney, VT   BLD | $

The Putney Diner is a delightful little town eatery just minutes away from I-91 at Exit 4. Although it doesn't look like a classic diner, this place has the spirit . . . and the menu. In the morning, plates of plain or buckwheat pancakes come with only-in-Vermont maple syrup. Eggs can be had with kielbasa or corned beef hash. And broad-topped muffins are split and toasted on the grill. At lunch, you can count on square meals of mac 'n' cheese, franks 'n' beans, roast turkey 'n' stuffing, or the arcane Yankee favorite, American chop suey.

No meal, including breakfast, should end without a slice of Putney Diner pie. There are fine fruit pies throughout the summer and a glorious maple walnut pie year-round.

Up For Breakfast

710 Main St.   802-362-4204
Manchester, VT   BL | $$

It can be difficult to order pancakes at Up For Breakfast because the menu also beckons with red flannel hash, griddle-cooked muffins, Benedicts, frittatas, and French toast. But oh, those pancakes! Three kinds are available, with or without blueberries in the batter. Buttermilk pancakes are sunny-hued and fluffy, easy to eat; those made from buckwheat batter are dark and serious; the sourdough 'cakes are breathtaking. The first thing you notice about the sourdoughs is the sound they make when you press the edge of a fork to one of them. You hear a faint crunch as the tine breaks through a lacy crust. Inside the chewy web that encloses them, they are thin but substantial, with the vigorous disposition of an old sourdough starter that has had years to develop its tang. Pair this with a generous infusion of sweet-tart blueberries and some of that woodsy syrup—served warm, praise be—and maybe an order of Up For Breakfast's wild turkey hash, and you'll understand why Vermont can claim the title of America's Breakfast Destination.

You really do go *up* for breakfast—to a cozy, second-story restaurant with window views of Main Street. There is pleasant art on the walls; and if you sit toward the back, you can enjoy watching goings-on in the semi-open kitchen. Seats can be scarce, but if you are looking for something extra-special in the morning, Up For Breakfast is a gold mine worth the wait.

Wayside Restaurant

1873 US Route 302   802-223-6611
Berlin, VT   BLD | $

For some ninety years now, the Wayside Restaurant has been an oasis of such true-Vermont fare as salt pork and milk gravy, fresh native perch, old-fashioned boiled dinner, and red flannel hash. Most of these things are still available, although not every day. Perch can be had only during ice-fishing season, when it is lightly breaded and fried to a crisp; salt pork covered with creamy white gravy has become a Thursday tradition; boiled dinner and shepherd's pie are cold-weather specials; fiddlehead ferns are offered only a few weeks in the spring.

Whatever the season, you will eat well and very inexpensively any time you come to this cheerful town lunch room. You begin to sense that fact when you smell warm rolls being toted to the tables. They have a yeasty perfume that promises great things to come. What joy it is to tear off a shred from a roll and submerge it into a bowl of Wayside beef barley soup—a hearty brew so thick with meat and pearly grain that a spoon literally stands up in it. Wednesday is traditionally chicken pie and meat loaf day. What a feast the chicken pie is: piled into a big crockery boat with dressing and a crusty biscuit, with a great heap of gravy-dripping mashed potatoes on the side. The meat loaf is exemplary, too: a two-inch-thick slab with a sticky red glaze along the rim and rivulets of stout brown gravy dripping down its sides.

In addition to such classic north country sweets as tapioca pudding, Grape-Nuts custard, mince pie, and homemade gingersnaps, the dessert repertoire includes apple pie made with densely packed hand-cut apples in a fork-crimped crust and maple cream pie. Low and flat with barely whipped cream dolloped on top, the filling of the maple pie is too delicious for words. Its radiant band of amber cream is complex, powerful, and elegant the way only pure maple can be, and it resonates on your taste buds after a Wayside meal like a Yankee cordial.

White Cottage

462 Woodstock Rd.   802-457-3455
Woodstock, VT   LD (summer only) | $

It was the summer of 1957 when the White Cottage opened on Route 4 at the edge of the pretty Vermont town of Woodstock; and the menu is still a vivid expression of mid-century drive-in tastes. Residents and summer visitors come to these breezy tables for excellent made-to-order hamburgers, hot dogs and foot-longs served Yankee-style in grilled rolls, and fried clams, available whole-bellied or as strips. The French fries are good and the fresh, crisp coleslaw is terrific.

On the side of these classic vacation meals, you can drink a soda, a lemonade, a milk shake, or a frappe. Ever curious about the obscure taxonomy of New England soda fountain beverages, we asked the person behind the order window to explain the difference between a milk shake and a frappe. Here, a frappe is made with hard ice cream, a milk shake with soft ice cream.

Mid-Atlantic

Delaware ✳ District of Columbia ✳ Maryland ✳

New Jersey ✳ New York ✳ Pennsylvania

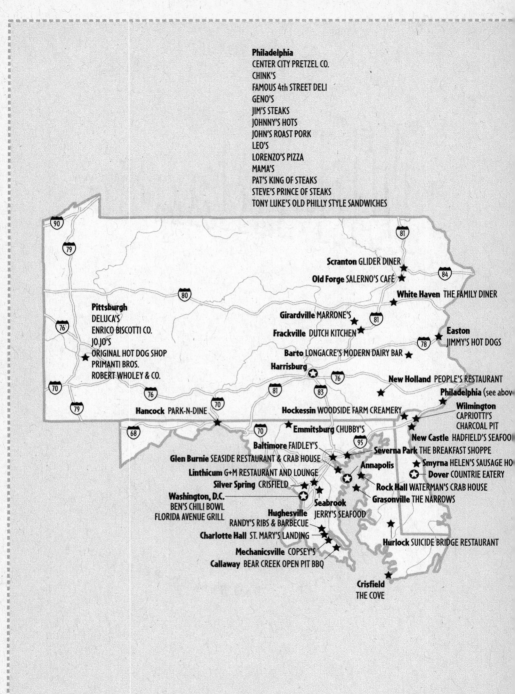

Philadelphia
CENTER CITY PRETZEL CO.
CHINK'S
FAMOUS 4th STREET DELI
GENO'S
JIM'S STEAKS
JOHNNY'S HOTS
JOHN'S ROAST PORK
LEO'S
LORENZO'S PIZZA
MAMA'S
PAT'S KING OF STEAKS
STEVE'S PRINCE OF STEAKS
TONY LUKE'S OLD PHILLY STYLE SANDWICHES

Scranton GLIDER DINER
Old Forge SALERNO'S CAFÉ
White Haven THE FAMILY DINER

Pittsburgh
DELUCA'S
ENRICO BISCOTTI CO.
JO JO'S
ORIGINAL HOT DOG SHOP
PRIMANTI BROS.
ROBERT WHOLEY & CO.

Girardville MARRONE'S
Frackville DUTCH KITCHEN
Easton JIMMY'S HOT DOGS
Barto LONGACRE'S MODERN DAIRY BAR
Harrisburg
New Holland PEOPLE'S RESTAURANT
Philadelphia (see above)
Hancock PARK-N-DINE
Hockessin WOODSIDE FARM CREAMERY
Wilmington
CAPRIOTTI'S
CHARCOAL PIT
New Castle HADFIELD'S SEAFOOD
Emmitsburg CHUBBY'S
Baltimore FAIDLEY'S
Severna Park THE BREAKFAST SHOPPE
Glen Burnie SEASIDE RESTAURANT & CRAB HOUSE
Smyrna HELEN'S SAUSAGE HOUSE
Linthicum G+M RESTAURANT AND LOUNGE
Annapolis
Dover COUNTRIE EATERY
Silver Spring CRISFIELD
Rock Hall WATERMAN'S CRAB HOUSE
Washington, D.C.
BEN'S CHILI BOWL
FLORIDA AVENUE GRILL
Grasonville THE NARROWS
Seabrook
Hughesville
JERRY'S SEAFOOD
RANDY'S RIBS & BARBECUE
Charlotte Hall ST. MARY'S LANDING
Hurlock SUICIDE BRIDGE RESTAURANT
Mechanicsville COPSEY'S
Callaway BEAR CREEK OPEN PIT BBQ
Crisfield
THE COVE

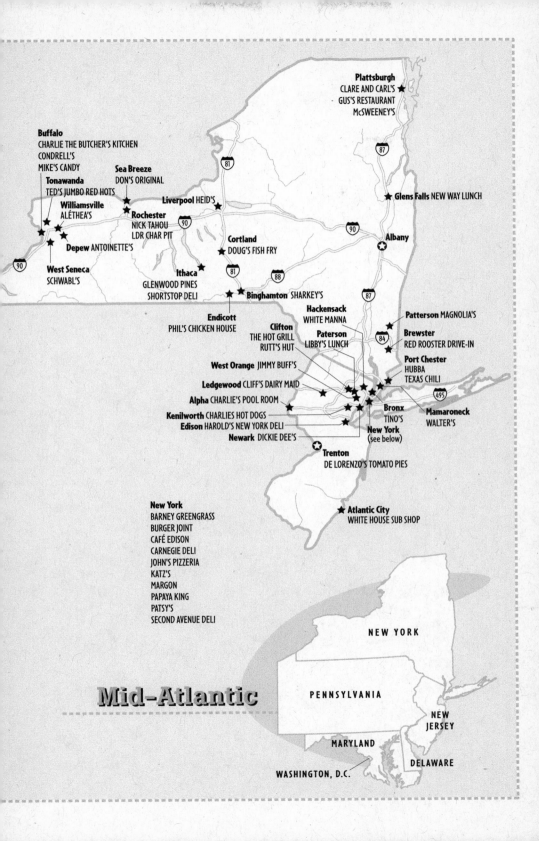

Plattsburgh
CLARE AND CARL'S ★
GUS'S RESTAURANT
McSWEENEY'S

Buffalo
CHARLIE THE BUTCHER'S KITCHEN
CONDRELL'S
MIKE'S CANDY

Sea Breeze
DON'S ORIGINAL

★ **Glens Falls** NEW WAY LUNCH

Tonawanda
TED'S JUMBO RED HOTS

Liverpool HEID'S

Williamsville
ALÉTHEA'S

Rochester
NICK TAHOU
LDR CHAR PIT

Albany

Depew ANTOINETTE'S

Cortland
DOUG'S FISH FRY

West Seneca
SCHWABL'S

Ithaca
GLENWOOD PINES
SHORTSTOP DELI

Binghamton SHARKEY'S

Endicott
PHIL'S CHICKEN HOUSE

Hackensack
WHITE MANNA

Patterson MAGNOLIA'S

Clifton
THE HOT GRILL
RUTT'S HUT

Paterson
LIBBY'S LUNCH

Brewster
RED ROOSTER DRIVE-IN

West Orange JIMMY BUFF'S

Port Chester
HUBBA
TEXAS CHILI

Ledgewood CLIFF'S DAIRY MAID

Alpha CHARLIE'S POOL ROOM

Bronx
TINO'S

Mamaroneck
WALTER'S

Kenilworth CHARLIES HOT DOGS

Edison HAROLD'S NEW YORK DELI

New York
(see below)

Newark DICKIE DEE'S

Trenton
DE LORENZO'S TOMATO PIES

New York
BARNEY GREENGRASS
BURGER JOINT
CAFÉ EDISON
CARNEGIE DELI
JOHN'S PIZZERIA
KATZ'S
MARGON
PAPAYA KING
PATSY'S
SECOND AVENUE DELI

★ **Atlantic City**
WHITE HOUSE SUB SHOP

NEW YORK

PENNSYLVANIA

NEW
JERSEY

Mid-Atlantic

MARYLAND

DELAWARE

WASHINGTON, D.C.

Capriotti's

510 N. Union St.   302-571-8929

Wilmington, DE   LD | $

Delaware a hotbed of great turkey sandwiches? We had no idea, and never would have known had not Roadfood comrades Bruce Bilmes and Sue Boyle alerted us to the large Bobbie at Capriotti's. If you are a fan of turkey—real, moist, full-flavored turkey from a roasted bird (as opposed to the blubbery loaf turkey common in sandwich shops)—the Bobbie is nothing short of spectacular. Loaded into a big, soft sub roll are juicy lengths of meat that have been hand-pulled off the bird, resulting in a textural kaleidoscope that cut slices cannot provide. Along with the turkey are sweet-tart cranberry sauce and just enough well-spiced stuffing to make a grand Thanksgiving sandwich.

Of course you can have a turkey sub without the cranberries and stuffing, as well as all sorts of other subs as well. Bruce and Sue noted that the Capriotti's on Union Street in Delaware is the original location, opened in 1976, and that the formula for success has led to branches elsewhere in Delaware as well as in Arizona, Florida, Pennsylvania, Utah, New Jersey, and Las Vegas, Nevada. As a matter of principle, we don't list chain restaurants in Roadfood, but once you've had a Bobbie in Wilmington, you will understand why this place demands inclusion.

Charcoal Pit

2600 Concord Pike (Route 202)   302-478-2165
Wilmington, DE   LD | $

Charcoal Pit's hamburger is a quarter-pound patty with a smoky taste served on a big, spongy bun either plain or in the deluxe configuration, which adds lettuce, tomato, and pickle. For those who crave extra meat, there is also a double-size eight-ounce hamburger, but in our opinion, that defeats the mid-twentieth-century charm of the meal. (The Charcoal Pit opened for business in 1956.) Fries on the side are savory, normal-size twigs with a nice tough skin and soft potato flavor. And the milk shakes come in silver beakers that hold at least two full glasses. (The shakes are so thick that a long-handled spoon is provided to help you get it from the beaker into your glass.) Crab cakes, while no competition for the Chesapeake Bay's best, are pretty nice: hardball-shaped spheres with crusty outsides and a fair measure of crab filling the interior. They're made here every Monday, Wednesday, and Friday.

We like this old-fashioned place with its comfy maroon booths and wall decor that includes vintage menus. Waitresses go about their job with aplomb and an attitude that make customers feel part of a cheap-eats ritual that has gone on forever.

There are other Charcoal Pits at 5200 Pike Creek, in the Fox Run Shopping Center on Route 40, and in Prices Corner at Kirkwood Highway and Greenbank Road.

Countrie Eatery

950 N. State St.   302-674-8310
Dover, DE   BLD | $

Breakfast, served all day, is swell at the Countrie Eatery: buttermilk pancakes or shillings (silver dollar 'cakes) filled with bananas or blueberries, or hefty biscuits topped with sausage gravy. The gravy, like the creamed chipped beef, is also available on regular toast or an English muffin. There are two noteworthy styles of French toast, one made with cinnamon bread, the other with seed-dotted sunflower bread. The latter is served as three long, thick pieces that are soft, moist, and nearly as eggy as pudding, dusted with powdered sugar. We got ours with a side order of scrapple—two thick slices from the loaf, fried until crunchy on the outside but moist and porky within.

At lunch you can have a sirloin burger, a hot sandwich made with turkey, pork, or beef and *real* mashed potatoes, or a terrific crab melt loaded with hunks of pearly-sweet Chesapeake Bay crabmeat. Every day the Countrie Eatery offers one all-you-can-eat special. Monday = chicken 'n' dumplings, Tuesday = stuffed peppers, Wednesday = lasagna, Thursday = beef stew, Friday = fried chicken, Saturday = chicken livers.

Ambience is country-craftsy Colonial with primitive art and old-time farm implements on the wall.

Hadfield's Seafood

192 N. Dupont Hwy. (Route 13)	302-322-0900
New Castle, DE	LD | $

You will have no trouble spotting Hadfield's as you travel north on Route 13. It is the shop with a crab hovering over the front door (a statue of a crab, that is). While many people buy crabs and other raw seafood to take home and cook, Hadfield's makes a specialty of selling whole meals to go. (No seats or table service here.) Whole crabs are the seasonal specialty; fried fish is always good—scallops, flounder, oysters, whiting, and shrimp. You also can get broiled crab cakes, stuffed flounder, a pair of shells filled with creamy crab imperial, and hot chicken wings by the ten-count, up to one hundred for $35.99, including blue cheese and celery. Dinners include coleslaw, French fries, a roll and butter, and tartar sauce; and it is also possible to get just about anything the kitchen makes by the pound or dozen.

Note: Hadfield's has a second location: 16 Wilmington Westchester Pike, Chadds Ford, PA; 610-459-3997.

Helen's Sausage House

4866 N. Dupont Hwy.	302-653-4200
Smyrna, DE	BL | $

If you are hungry and rushing north toward the Delaware Valley Bridge any time between four in the morning and lunch (or on Sunday starting at 7 A.M.), call Helen's and place a sandwich order. That's the way the truckers do it, and in this case, the truckers are onto a very good thing. Helen's Sausage House is a roadside eatery with huge sandwiches at small prices.

The sausages Helen's serves are thick and crusty giants with plenty of Italian zest. They spurt juice when you bite into them, and a normal sandwich is two in a roll (although wimpy appetites can get a single). With fried green peppers and onions, it is a majestic arrangement—a little messy to eat with one hand while driving, but nevertheless one of the great sausage sandwiches anywhere.

Helen's offers all manner of breakfast sandwiches on bread or rolls, made with eggs, bacon, scrapple, and fried ham; as well as lunchtime sandwiches of steak, cheese steak, burgers, hot beef, and hot ham. Other than the sausage, the must-eat (and must-see!) meal is Helen's pork chop sandwich. When the menu says *jumbo* pork chop, you better believe it. This slab of meat is approximately three times larger than the puny pieces of white bread that are stuck on either side of it. It isn't all that thick a chop, but it is tender, moist, and mouthwateringly spiced.

While most of Helen's clientele stop by for sandwiches wrapped to go, it is possible to dine here. Place your order at the counter and carry it to one of a few tables on ground level opposite the instant-order counter, or proceed up a couple of steps into a dining room decorated entirely with pictures of Elvis. Roadfood extraordinaire!

Woodside Farm Creamery

1310 Little Baltimore Rd.	302-239-9847
Hockessin, DE	(closed in winter)	$

Woodside Farm is home of the Hog Trough Sundae. That's five flavors of ice cream—two scoops of each—topped with three different toppings, a fresh banana, whipped cream, and a cherry. For less edacious sorts, there are normal-size cups, cones, and sundaes, too, all made from superior ice cream made the old-fashioned way, by taking high-butterfat milk and turning it into sweet cream. The sweet cream is mixed with fruit, flavors, and nuts, and frozen in small batches to be sold at the farm's stand. Jim Mitchell, whose family settled here in 1796, likes to tell visitors, "Two weeks ago, our ice cream was grass." Mr. Mitchell credits the goodness of his ice cream to the fact that the milk's source is his herd of Jersey cows (superior to Guernseys), which he keeps happy by grazing them on fields of sweet grass.

Flavors range from chocolate and coffee to pumpkin pecan and butter brickle toffee. It is wonderfully normal ice cream, by which we mean it is not sickeningly butterfatty or cloying with too many mix-ins. The ingenuous true-farm flavor is especially welcome in varieties made with fresh fruit: peach, strawberry, black raspberry, and black cherry. Turtle ice cream is choco-caramel-cream ecstasy. African vanilla is vanilla squared.

District of Columbia

Ben's Chili Bowl

1213 U St. NW   202-667-0909

Washington, DC   LD | $

It is possible to get only chili at Ben's Chili Bowl, the landmark lunch counter on U Street in the nation's capital; but even the president of the United
States (a Ben's customer) knows that the best way to enjoy the mahogany-
brown ground-meat stew is atop a half-smoke. That's the city's unique tube
steak—a plump, gently smoked beef-and-pork sausage link that gets sizzled
on a hot griddle until its skin turns snapping-crisp. Served in a bun with mustard and onions, it's swell without chili; but when smothered, it may well be
the ultimate chili dog. Ben's half-smokes are presented in a red plastic basket
and hopefully accompanied by the kitchen's fine French fries, then topped
off with an oh-so-mellow slice of sweet potato layer cake.

Big as its reputation is, Ben's remains a relaxed and easygoing diner, part
of the neighborhood since 1958, surviving urban unrest and economic ups
and downs. In 2001, its founders, Ben and Virginia Ali, were inducted into
the Washington, D.C., Hall of Fame. Today the restaurant is run by their
sons.

Florida Avenue Grill

1100 Florida Ave. NW   202-265-1586
Washington, DC   BLD | $

America is overpopulated with sub-par or merely adequate biscuits, which is why discovery of excellent ones is cause for joy. In the cool predawn hours at the counter or in a booth at the Florida Avenue Grill, they are served two by two, warm enough so you can only gingerly grab top and bottom of one to pull it into halves, all the better for the fleecy interior to absorb a cascade of spicy, sausage-crowded, cream-thick gravy. A smothered pair is adequate breakfast for modest appetites or an awesome side dish with fried pork chops and sweet stewed apples.

For lunch and supper, the menu is a soul-food primer of such dishes as pigs' feet and chitterlings, but unless you are a feet aficionado already, we suggest you begin with more familiar things to eat. Spare ribs, for example, glazed with breathless hot sauce, are rugged and satisfying. For a tender meal, how about meat loaf, served with a side of mashed potatoes and a heap of collard greens? True to southern custom, there are lots of vegetables to accompany the entrees: candied sweet potatoes, rich macaroni and cheese, lavish potato salad, rice, beans, peas, and always sweet corn bread for mopping up a plate.

Long a favorite destination for Washington's power brokers as well as blue-collar folk, and just a quick cab ride from Capitol Hill, the Grill's walls are plastered with 8x10 photos of office holders and sports stars who all are fans of the long-lasting soul-food diner. If you value honest eats, this humble restaurant with its sprung-spring booths, pink counter, and red plastic stools is choice. It is cheap, fast, and the motherly waitresses make even pale-faced strangers feel right at home.

Bear Creek Open Pit BBQ

21030 Point Lookout Rd.   301-994-1030
Callaway, MD   LD | $

One of several smokehouses in southernmost Maryland, Bear Creek is unique for its huge open pit. You'll see it on the left as you walk in the door. Here, pitmaster Curtis Shreve cooks pork and beef so tender that if you look at it hard, it falls apart. We are especially fond of the pork, either hand-pulled into shreds or sliced. It has a smoky flavor and a piggy richness that defies description. It is good enough to need no sauce whatsoever, all the better to savor the flavor of the meat. (Mr. Shreve's sauce, we should say, is excellent: sweet, gently spicy, and mildly addictive.)

Beyond superb barbecue and the St. Mary's County specialty stuffed ham, you can expect Bear Creek to have interesting game on the menu. Curtis Shreve is a hunter, and while he cannot serve what he kills (health department regulations forbid it), he does have a fondness for such meats as venison, alligator, frog legs, and rabbit stew.

Mr. Shreve originally hails from the Louisiana/Texas area; so his cooking reflects Southwest roots, too. The kids' menu contains corn dogs reminiscent of those at the Texas State Fair; and chili is the sleeper on the menu. It's a meat-and-bean stew with assertive but not incendiary spices, served under a mantle of grated cheese. Here also is that miraculous Texas twist on chili known as Fritos pie: a bed of crisp corn chips topped with chili and spangled with cheese. Shreve remembered, "When I was a kid years ago, they used to take a scoop of chili and put it right in the bag of Fritos and you ate it just like that. Now the bags are made of plastic that does not withstand the heat. So we serve our Fritos pie in a dish."

The Breakfast Shoppe

552-1 Ritchie Hwy.   410-544-8599
Severna Park, MD   BL | $

The Breakfast Shoppe is an inconspicuous one-room storefront café in a strip mall just south of Baltimore. Start with orange juice just-squeezed behind the counter; then move on to buckwheat pancakes with molasses syrup, any of a number of eggs Benedict variations, omelets and egg scrambles, or a mega-meal known as the Backpacker. That's eggs, sausage, ham, bacon, potatoes, peppers, onions, spinach, broccoli, tomatoes, and jack cheese, all loaded into a hot iron skillet that is set upon a trivet on the table.

Pancakes are terrific, available as tall stacks (5), normal stacks (3), short stacks (2), and singly. In addition to buckwheat, there are banana nut cakes and pancakes topped with strawberry marinade. Creamed chipped beef, a fairly scarce mid-Atlantic delight, is a house specialty, served on thick-cut challah bread with fried potatoes on the side.

The staff of swift waitresses makes life here friendly. Ours was always ready to refill coffee cups and to offer her own personal huzzahs about the items she likes best on the menu. When we told her how much we were enjoying our meal, she responded, "I know; it's so good. This is where I eat on my days off!"

Chubby's Southern Style Barbeque

16430 Old Frederick Rd.   301-447-3322
Emmitsburg, MD   LD | $$

A plain place in the beautiful countryside south of Gettysburg, Chubby's has become a destination dining spot for lovers of barbecued pork. Smokemeister Tom Caulfield marinates and dry-rubs ribs, cooking them low and slow until drippingly tender, serving them with a choice of sauces that include South Carolina mustard–style, North Carolina vinegar-pepper, and the most familiar tomato sweet/tangy. Caulfield's pulled pork is soft and smoky, and baked beans are liberally laced with shreds of it. Even the barbecued brisket is excellent, albeit more Texan than southern.

The menu is broad and also includes non-barbecued daily specials. About five years ago Washington Redskins lineman Randy Thomas made pig-out history by consuming six pounds of Chubby's food in less than an hour. His menu included a pound of brisket, two-and-a-half pounds of ribs, a pound of shrimp scampi, a pound of chili, three-quarters of a pound of crab dip, cheese-garlic toast, cheesecake, and pumpkin parfait. His beverage of choice was iced tea, of which he ingested a gallon.

The Cove

718 Broadway   410-968-9632
Crisfield, MD   LD | $$

Crisfield's water tower is emblazoned with the image of a crab; and while there are many seafood restaurants in town where the Chesapeake Bay crustacean stars, our favorite is The Cove. A modest place just off the main drag, it is well worth knowing about if you like crab cakes. The Cove's are especially creamy, perhaps not as lumpy-luxurious as those of crab houses farther north, but rich and fresh and satisfying. They are available as full-size cakes or as mini cakes on a bun, a.k.a crab cake sliders. The right way to have the full-size cake is broiled; and we think that works just as well on the slider version, but it is possible to have the cake fried. The result is a crunchy crust with moist meat inside, the good ocean flavor of the crab somewhat muted by its hot oil bath.

Several cakes are available for dessert, including the local specialty (and official state dessert of Maryland), Smith Island cake. Resembling a Hungarian *dobos torte,* it is ten microthin layers of yellow cake interleaved with ribbons of fudgy chocolate frosting. While the cake itself is not dramatically excellent, its extravagant layering is a sugar-rush indulgence. Several mainland bakeries in Salisbury and Ocean City make Smith Island cake, but The Cove is proud of the fact that the slices it serves are the real deal, cut from cakes brought by ferry from a baker on nearby Smith Island.

Crisfield

8012 Georgia Ave.   301-589-1306
Silver Spring, MD   LD | $$$

Crisfield is expensive, but no-frills. The room you enter is like a bar, with a long counter running along both sides and stools where people sit to eat and drink. The adjoining dining room has walls covered with white tile and cinder blocks, with all the charm of a locker room. Service is brusque and efficient and a full dinner can run over $20; even "light fare" meals are close to $15 and sandwiches are just under $10.

We'll happily pay these prices because some of the food served here is top-drawer. Crisfield is a fish house with regional specialties you simply don't find many places anymore. For example, seafood Norfolk style (i.e. swimming in butter) and huge fillets of flounder, broiled or fried or heaped with mountains of fresh lump crabmeat, as well as oysters and softshell crabs in season.

We have found the "Crisfield special" (lump crabmeat mixed with a bit of mayo and baked until golden brown) to be erratic: one time, fresh and sweet, another kinda tired; but the crab-stuffed flounder has never been a disappointment. It is a gigantic, milky-white fillet covered with a full-flavored crown of crab. We also liked the "Combination Norfolk"—hunks of crab, whole shrimp, and pieces of lobster all crowded into a skillet up to their waistlines in melted butter. It's a simple preparation, but unbeatable.

Faidley's

203 N. Paca St.   410-727-4898
Baltimore, MD   LD | $$

You may think you have had a great crab cake, but until you have eaten one at Faidley's you have not. Forget all the spongy, bready, fishy blobs that pass as crab cakes in most other places; here is the paradigm: a baseball-size sphere of jumbo lump crabmeat held together with minimal crushed-saltine filler and a whisper of mayo and mustard that is just enough to be a foil for the marine sweetness of the meat. While Faidley's offers "regular" crab cakes, made from shredded claw meat, and backfin crab cakes, made from slightly larger strips of body meat, the one you want is the "all lump crab cake." It is significantly more expensive than the others, but the silky weight of the big nuggets, which are the choicest meat picked from the hind leg area of the blue crab, is what makes these cakes one of the nation's most memorable local specialties.

Operated by the same family that started it in 1886—and which still forms each jumbo lump cake by hand—Faidley's is fortuitously located on one side of the boisterous, centuries-old food emporium known as the Lexington Market, where grazing opportunities range from Asian stir-fries to Polock Johnny's seven-inch sausage, and where Berger's Bakery offers a prodigious array of old-fashioned frosted cakes and fudge-frosted shortcake cookies. Amenities are minimal. Stand up to order, then stand up to eat at the chest-high tables provided. You can down raw oysters at the oyster bar, and in addition to crab cakes, the menu includes both Maryland crab soup (red) and cream of crab soup, as well as the unique Baltimore fish cake known as a coddie, composed of cod, mashed potato, and onion. Whereas jumbo lump crab cakes are the top of the line on the menu at $12.95 each, a coddie costs $2.50.

G&M Restaurant & Lounge

804 Hammonds Ferry Rd.   410-636-1777
Linthicum Heights, MD   LD | $$$

G&M is practically the only restaurant where we would recommend ordering stuffed shrimp. Given the icky breadiness of most versions, we were not inclined to do so until our waitress passionately recommended them, guaranteeing that the stuffing of these shrimp was all crab. We took the plunge and got a trio (for $25.50; G&M is not cheap). Each of three enormous shrimp was heaped with its own virtual crab cake—a pile of pearly white lumps separated by one-dimensional lines of spicy filler that do for crab what salt does for sirloin.

G&M's crab cakes, which come two to an order, sport the biggest possible lumps. You can count the pieces of meat in each one, those from the interior glistening, resilient, and all white, those forked off the outside offering a browned facet with faint crunch. The crab in this place is so regal that it is a perfect fit for crab imperial, the butter-rich casserole that here is infused with a vivid shot of Greek spice.

As noted above, G&M is at the high end of the Roadfood cost scale. A nice dinner for two with a few drinks easily can hit triple-digit prices. But if you are looking for a grand Baltimore meal in a dining room with such amenities as non-disposable flatware and tables with white tablecloths, it's hard to beat. Beyond legendary crabmeat, the menu is extensive, including such local seafood specialties as broiled rockfish and fried oysters, as well as such yet-to-be-sampled temptations as Chesapeake chicken (stuffed with crabmeat) and Baltimore's own take on German sauerbraten—sour beef and potato dumplings.

Jerry's Seafood

9364 Lanham-Severn Rd.   301-577-0333
Lanham, MD   L Mon-Fri, D Tues-Sat | $$$

Surefire tipster Joe Heflin described Jerry's Seafood to us as the "best overall Maryland seafood restaurant without a view." He warned that the ambience is nondescript—Jerry's is located in a strip mall—and we should expect long lines any evening, especially weekends.

No problem. We'll gladly wait for this extraordinary D.C.-area seafood treasure. Nor do we need to be soaking up ambience when we have one of Jerry's Crab Bombs on a plate in front of us. This is a fairly gigantic (ten-ounce) and expensive ($34) crab cake that is nothing more than fresh jumbo lump meat, Old Bay seasoning, and just enough mayonnaise to make it cling together, baked until a painfully fragile crust develops all around the edges but the inside is still dripping sweet. Even better for those with a yen for spice thrills is the Firecracker Crab Bomb, to which mustard and pepper are added. Jerry's also makes a six-ounce Baby Bomb ($26) and ordinary-size crab cakes.

Mr. Heflin's other recommendation was crab soup, which is a virtuoso balance of creaminess, crabbiness, and sharp spice. You can also eat vel-vety crab imperial perked up with peppers, crab dip, and crab bisque made with sherry. Those who are anti-crab can revel in fried shrimp, scallops, and oysters, all with a nice fragile crust, as well as good side dishes that include what the menu promises are from Jerry's mom's recipes: stewed tomatoes and coleslaw.

Jerry's has opened two other locations, at 169 West St. in Annapolis (410-268-7733) and 15211 Major Lansdale Blvd. in Bowie (301-805-2284).

The Narrows

3023 Kent Narrows Way S.   410-827-8113
Grasonville, MD   LD | $$$

Here is an extraordinarily handsome Eastern Shore restaurant in a breath-taking setting overlooking the Kent Narrows at the eastern end of the Chesapeake Bay Bridge. The menu is broad, including $30+ steak dinners, sandwiches and salads for lunch, hamburgers, cioppino, and barbecued quail accompanied by Smithfield ham in a balsamic glaze.

Great stuff, what little of it we have sampled, but we likely wouldn't include this place in *Roadfood* if it weren't for two great local specialties, crab cakes and oysters. The crab cakes are the purest ever: jumbo lump crab piled into a mound and just barely kissed by a bit of spice in the ridiculously minimal filler. As your fork touches the cake, chances are good it will tumble into big lumps, their outside surfaces faintly brown and barely crisp, the in-terior nothing but moist, warm, sweet ocean goodness.

Oysters, breaded in cornmeal and fried, are known hereabouts as White Gold, and what's so magnificent about them is that although they have been cooked, the meat of the oysters retains all of its fluid sensuousness—as much as a raw one, but even more intense because of its warmth and the fragile cornmeal crust with which the oyster melds. You can get a great big plate of them or have them as the ne plus ultra topping of a very nice Caesar salad.

Park-N-Dine

189 E. Main St.   301-678-5242
Hancock, MD   BLD | $

If you are driving—or riding your bicycle—through the narrowest part of western Maryland in Hancock and find yourself hankering for meat and potatoes, pull up to Park-N-Dine. Located alongside I-70 and at the end of the bike trail from Indian Springs along the C&O Canal, this venerable establishment is a blast from the past (1946) where uniformed waitresses are pros and where the kitchen still practices the craft of from-scratch cooking.

High kudos to the old-fashioned roast turkey dinner with mashed potatoes, stuffing, and gravy, followed, of course, by wedges of apple pie or actual from-scratch pudding (banana, tapioca, chocolate). Sandwiches and hamburgers are available, and breakfast is fine and dandy, but the charm of Park-N-Dine for us is its seven-day-a-week roster of Sunday dinner, i.e., pork chops, meat loaf, and plates of steaming-pink corned beef and cabbage. Portions are vast and prices are low.

Randy's Ribs & Barbecue

Route 5 (Leonardtown Rd.)   301-274-3525
Hughesville, MD   LD | $

Randy's opened in 1981 as a weekend-only roadside stand; and while its catering business has become large, the eatery remains charming. The sweet perfume of slow-smoking pork fills the air seven days a week throughout the year; and if you are one who considers barbecue foremost among the food groups, you will love what you find.

Sandwiches and platters are available: minced or sliced pork, ribs and ham, whole chickens, and slabs of ribs. "Slaw on that?" the order-taker will ask if you get a sandwich. "Yes!" we say, and then unwrap the foil around a big bun loaded with chunks of moist, full-flavored pork bathed in Randy's excellent spicy sauce, with which sweet slaw sings happy harmony. Ribs are large and chewy, their luscious meat infused with smoke; and on the side, we relished collard greens, macaroni and cheese, and baked beans.

Randy also offers a mighty fine half-smoke, which is a local variant of a hot dog: a plump sausage bisected lengthwise and smoke-cooked until its skin is taut and dark red, its insides dense and succulent. All the usual hot-dog condiments are available, but we recommend topping it with only one thing: Randy's sauce. That good sauce is available by the pint and gallon: an excellent investment in one's future culinary happiness.

Seaside Restaurant & Crab House

224 Crain Hwy. N. 410-760-2200
Glen Burnie, MD LD | $$

Beautiful crabs, especially big, come to the table stuck with a peppery, salty spice mix and too hot to handle. Grab your knife to pry away the outer shell, pick up the mallet to start pounding, and soon you will be rewarded with fat nuggets of the sweetest meat any crab ever delivered. Toss your shells into paper bags on the floor and hoist an ice-cold beer to quench the thirst that spicy crabs inevitably provoke: This is a true finger-licking feast, a royal mess, and incomparably fun.

Beyond blue crabs, the Seaside Restaurant has a menu of other local specialties, well worth sampling, especially if crabmeat-extraction is too daunting a task (it *is* hard work!). There are broiled shrimp, scallops, and flounder, and zesty crab cakes, plus fine crab soups, both Maryland-style (red, with vegetables) and creamy.

A busy place, especially on weekends. Expect to wait at mealtime.

St. Mary's Landing

29935 Three Notch Rd. 301-884-3287
Charlotte Hall, MD BLD | $$

St. Mary's County stuffed ham is a seasonal dish, generally served between Thanksgiving and Easter, but you can get it year-round at St. Mary's Landing. It's wonderful stuff: a corned ham packed with heaps of kale, cabbage, onions, and spice, served for breakfast on a plate with delicious potato cakes or for supper as a main course.

Lucky for us, they were out of stuffed ham one December night when we came for supper. That meant we discovered the kitchen's marvelously crabby crab cakes, a plate of big, snapping-firm spiced boiled shrimp, and barbecued ribs that had a delicate crunch to their outermost edges and meat that slid right off the bone.

This is a fascinating restaurant, a serious tavern as well as an eatery, with a wall-mounted TV monitor that displays keno numbers and a countdown to the next game. One morning when we arrived at 7 A.M., we were the first customers to take seats in the restaurant, but bar stools in the adjoining tap room were already occupied by ladies and gentlemen having shots and beers to start their day. Contrary to general principles of detecting good Road-food, St. Mary's County stuffed ham is almost always found in places where drinking and gambling are featured attractions.

Suicide Bridge Restaurant

6304 Suicide Bridge Rd.	410-943-4689
Hurlock, MD	LD	$$$

On two occasions, men shot and killed themselves on the bridge over Cabin Creek, then fell into the water. Another guy drove off the bridge. A subsequent jumper's body was fished from the creek and laid out on the wooden bridge, where his blood soaked into the boards, which stayed stained for five years. All this we learned from the take-out menu at this rather eerily named restaurant that is—bridge notwithstanding—extremely charming. Located on an Eastern Shore inlet from which paddlewheel boats glide into the Choptank River for dinner cruises, its broad windows offer views of the boats, the water, and the notorious bridge.

While the menu has a small section for "land lovers" listing steaks, ribs, and chicken, the reason we recommend eating here is seafood—primarily broiled rockfish, fried oysters, cream of crab soup with a shot of sherry, and first-rate crab cakes. There are backfin cakes, available either fried or broiled, their fine and wispy meat humming with a devilish pepper glow; and there are the fancier (and more expensive) Kool's Deluxe Crab Cakes made with jumbo lump crabmeat and available only broiled. Kool's deluxe cakes also have some sharp seasoning and their snowy hunks of meat are speckled with green herbs; nevertheless, the overwhelming goodness of those big pieces of crab puts all other seasoning into the background.

Suicide Bridge also makes a specialty of crab balls—peppery little orbs of crabmeat that get deep-fried to become a delightfully crunchy pop-in-the-mouth bar snack or hors d'oeuvre.

Waterman's Crab House

21055 Sharp St.	410-639-2261
Rock Hall, MD	LD	$$

A big, breezy eatery with an al fresco deck overlooking Rock Hall Harbor and shuttle service for those who arrive by boat at one of the nearby marinas, Waterman's is a good-time place. Live blues, rock, and 1950s oldies bands perform on weekends; and at dusk merrymakers gather at the forty-foot-long bar to savor cocktails, beer, and a spectacular sunset.

Tuesday and Thursday nights, customers come for an all-you-can-eat

Chesapeake Bay crab feast, and that is probably the one meal a first-timer ought to have; but Waterman's menu is broad and inviting. Other seafood temptations include crab soup served with a shot of sherry, alongside crusty-creamy crab cakes (fried or broiled), stuffed flounder, spiced steamed shrimp, softshell crabs, and a gorgeous broiled rockfish available with or without a side of crab imperial. Even fish-frowners will find plenty here: baby back ribs, ten-ounce hamburgers, and one-pound "Admiral's cut" prime rib.

Charlie's Pool Room

1122 E. Blvd.   908-454-1364
Alpha, NJ   L | $

"If you haven't had one, you ain't livin,'" wrote Roadfood.com insider aleswench about a Charlie's Pool Room hot dog topped with Grandma Fencz's sauce. A Kunzler-brand pork and beef dog fried in a deep skillet by John Fencz in a tiny kitchen in an old wood-frame house that used to be a barber shop and a jail, and now has a single table to eat at, the dog has an appealing surface crunch because it is cooked slowly in the hot oil. It gets snugged into a soft steamed bun, then sent into the culinary stratosphere when topped with an application of the thick, sweet-and-sour onion-tomato sauce prepared exactly according to specs set down by grandma Fencz. The sauce is not incendiary, but it has bite, and although it comes atop a bargain weenie, it has aristocratic complexity that reveals the skills of an accomplished cook. Grandma Fencz originally served her sauced hot dogs in 1925 so the boys playing pool at her place would have something to eat.

The one essential improvement on this high-class pool room dog is to order a "mealie," which adds onions and an artistic array of hot pepper slices to the top of the sauce. A meal of five mealies (they're not too big; customers in the ongoing eating contest are approaching two dozen) is known here as a blue-plate special.

Charlies Hot Dogs

18 S. Michigan Ave.   908-241-2627
Kenilworth, NJ   LD | $

While you can order what the menu calls a "push cart dog"—an ordinary street weenie on a blah roll with mundane condiments, Charlies' raison d'être is its Italian hot dog: one or preferably a pair of deep-fried, crisp-skinned, bursting-with-flavor franks stuffed into a half-circle of what's known hereabouts as pizza bread. It's a sizeable hearth-baked round loaf that vaguely resembles a pita pocket with muscle. The bread is chewy, soulful, and absorbent, that last quality essential for engulfing all the traditional garnishes that an Italian hot dog demands. These include a good measure of glistening fried peppers and onions and a heap of crisp-fried potato disks. The same ingredients can be used to accompany a sausage sandwich, also packed into pizza bread; and while we do like the sausage, it's the hot dog that has earned Charlies' landmark status in the Roadfood pantheon.

Service is do-it-yourself, and while there are a few tables for dining here, a majority of business is take-out.

Cliff's Dairy Maid

1475 Route 46   973-584-9721
Ledgewood, NJ   LD | $

Cliff's is a great place to know about if you and your sweet tooth are traveling along Route 80 through New Jersey. The 1975 drive-in is most famous for its ice cream, but is also a worthy source for foot-long hot dogs and chili dogs (especially good when topped with a tangle of fried-limp onions), hamburgers, and buckets of French fries.

Cliff's ice cream menu lists a few dozen "original homemade flavors," which range from utterly familiar chocolate and strawberry to bubble gum, cotton candy, and banana walnut chocolate chunk, plus another few dozen "fantasy flavors": tiramisu, holy cannoli, Bavarian cream raspberry truffle, etc. In addition to these hard-pack ice creams, Cliff's boasts several soft-serves, which are dense and rich. There is always a flavor of the month—and it can be swirled together with one of the regulars. We very much enjoyed a twist of chocolate and the March flavor, mint.

No indoor seating at this drive-in, but there is an array of picnic tables in back for dining al fresco.

De Lorenzo's Tomato Pies

530 Hudson St.   609-695-9534
Trenton, NJ   D | $$

De Lorenzo's is an extremely humble neighborhood joint that makes extraordinary pizzas, known hereabouts by their old Napoli name, tomato pie. And that is what they are: thin-crusted disks, edged with a little bit of oven char, topped with hand-crushed tomatoes, a judicious web of cheese, and—preferably—clumps of fennel-laced sweet Italian sausage.

Bruce Bilmes and Sue Boyle of Roadfood.com wrote, "It's mesmerizing watching Sam, or his father, Gary, prepare pies with both the casual assurance and precision of those who have practiced their craft for years and years. These are the most balanced pizzas around—no ingredient shouts down the others. They are not pies built on gross amounts of cheese or inferior toppings, and you'll find that a large pizza might not be enough for two hungry eaters."

When we describe it as humble, we mean really humble. There is nothing on the menu other than pizza and soda. Bruce and Sue warned: "Don't drink too much of that soda, though, because there's no bathroom, as all DeLo's regulars know. Any normal mealtime, there'll probably be a line of people waiting to get in. They take no reservations, except for Friday lunch (for which reservations are required, and it's the only day they're open for lunch). There are no menus." Decor on the wood-paneled walls is pizza-parlor classic: countless pictures of fans, ranging from nobodies to Frank Sinatra and Luciano Pavarotti.

A second De Lorenzo's is at 2350 US Route 33, Robbinsville, NJ; 609-341-8480. It has salads on the menu and a bathroom.

Dickie Dee's

380 Bloomfield Ave.   973-483-9396
Newark, NJ   LD | $

No ordinary weenie, Dickie Dee's specialty is an Italian-style (a.k.a. Newark-style) hot dog, meaning it is deep-fried and stuffed deep inside half a loaf of Italian bread along with fried peppers and onions and big chunks of crisp-edge, soft-center fried potatoes. All the ingredients are cooked in the same vat of oil next to the order counter; and they are plucked from the oil and inserted directly into the bread (no draining!), making for a wondrously oily double-handful of food.

Be prepared for serious attitude from behind the counter of this brash lunch room. When it's crowded—it usually is—the line moves fast, and woe to he who hesitates when placing an order. As the sandwich is made, the cook will demand to know what you want on it in the way of condiments; and this is another time you don't want to be slow responding. (We suggest that a spritz of ketchup is a nice complement for the potatoes that go atop all the other ingredients in the sandwich.)

Carry your tray to a table and ease into a permanently attached molded plastic chair. Lay out plenty of paper napkins for the inevitable spillage, and dig into a great hot dog meal that is a true North Ward original.

Harold's New York Deli

3050 Woodbridge Ave.   732-661-9100
Edison, NJ   BLD | $$$

Just because Harold's is comical doesn't mean it isn't seriously great. It may just be the best New York deli anywhere, even if it is in Edison, New Jersey. For intense chicken soup with matzoh balls, for spice-edged pastrami that is melting-rich, for creamy blintzes and even creamier egg creams, for the best ruggelah anywhere and a pickle bar to make the famous Guss' of New York blush, Harold's is the gold standard. The menu is vast, ranging from kosher hot dogs to triple-decker sandwiches, cold fish plates to hot suppers—all of it exemplary.

What's funny about the big, boisterous eatery is the size of its portions. While most New York delis offer sandwiches stacked extra-high and soup with very large matzoh balls, Harold's ups the ante to surreal proportions. A single matzoh ball is bigger than a softball; and yet, rest the edge of a spoon at its top and gravity is all that's needed to send the spoon sliding smoothly down into the ball's fluffy center. It is impossible not to gasp when you enter and see shelves of whole, wedding-size cakes, each two feet tall. When a towering "large sandwich" gets carried past your table to a party of four (who will divvy it up and each take home enough meat for more sandwiches the next day), no superlatives seem adequate to express the awe it inspires. Ridiculous, insane: the biggest food anywhere! While such protean portions of protein might seem wasteful (as well as expensive), remember that most dishes are split and that nearly everyone walks out with leftovers. On a recent visit, a single brisket sandwich provided a very filling lunch for one. Its remains became the basis of an excellent beef hash lunch for two the next day; and leftovers of the leftover hash became a pair of hearty breakfasts on day three.

The Hot Grill

669 Lexington Ave.   973-772-6000
Clifton, NJ   BLD | $

Texas weiners (spelled *ei*, not *ie*) are a big deal in this part of New Jersey, the word "Texas" being vintage hash-house code for chili. One of the best places to sample this Garden State specialty is The Hot Grill of Clifton.

Step up to the order counter, where empty trays await, and order a pair. *Nobody* gets just one Texas weiner! The counterman will holler out to the back kitchen, "Two, all the way!" And within ninety seconds, a pair of handsome little hot dogs will appear on the tray in front of you. Each is a deep-fried pup with rugged skin nestled in a too-short bun topped with mustard, onion, and spicy/sweet beef-chili sauce. Exemplary eats! On the side you definitely want gravy fries, or fries topped with gravy plus cheese and/or sauce. The preferred beverage with a Texas weiner is root beer.

It's fun to dine in The Hot Grill's vast modern dining room where, instead of music, you listen to the calls of the countermen back to the kitchen; and instead of sports, the overhead TV is tuned to "The Hot Grill Channel," which is a continuous program of hosannas to the hot dog.

Jimmy Buff's

60 Washington St.   973-325-9897
West Orange, NJ   LD | $

James Racioppi, proprietor of Jimmy Buff's, believes it was his grandparents, James and Mary Racioppi, who created the Newark hot dog. Mr. Racioppi says, "He played cards there every week. My grandmother served sandwiches to him and his associates. After a while, people started coming just to eat." As for the name of the store, James explains: "My grandfather Jimmy was an excellent card player. He was known for his talent to bluff, but with their Italian accents, they used to call him Jimmy Buff."

A Newark hot dog is built in a round of fresh, tawny-crusted Italian bread that is nothing at all like an ordinary, sponge-soft hot dog bun. It is sturdy, chewy, and delicious in its own right. It *needs* to be tough to hold all the ingredients that get piled into it. The bread is cut in half, forming two half-circles. Each gets squeezed open to become a pocket like a huge, spongy pita. Into the pocket go a pair of all-beef hot dogs that have been fried in hot fat until crunch-crusted, a heap of onions and peppers that have been sautéed until limp, and a handful of crisp-fried potato disks. The ingredients are forked directly from the frying cauldron into the sandwich, which is why the bread needs oomph—to absorb drippin's from the garlicky dogs and sweet vegetables. Options include ketchup and/or mustard and/or marinara sauce, and fire-hot onion relish.

There are three other Jimmy Buff's locations: in Castle Ridge Plaza in East Hanover, in Scotch Plains, and in the Prudential Center in Newark.

Libby's Lunch

98 McBride Ave.   973-278-8718
Paterson, NJ   LD | $

Texas weiners were invented in New Jersey prior to 1920 by John Patrellis, who worked at his father's hot dog stand at the Manhattan Hotel in Paterson. According to hot dog historian Robert C. Gamer of Wyckoff, Mr. Patrellis devised the formulation of a deep-fried frankfurter in a too-short bun topped with mustard, onions, and spicy meat sauce, traditionally accompanied by French fries and a mug of root beer. In 1920 the hot dog stand was renamed the Original Hot Texas Weiner because Mr. Patrellis believed the sauce to be like Texas chili. In fact, it is more Greek than Texan; but the Lone Star moniker stuck, and today Paterson is rich with Texas weiner shops.

Libby's Lunch, since 1936, is the best of the best. Here is a dog house with no pretense but with impeccable pedigree, countermen dish out dogs all the way, meaning topped with mustard, chopped onions, and sauce. Good as the spicy chili sauce is (you can buy it by the pint), it is the hot dog itself that makes this a memorable eating experience. Its insides are tender and succulent, while the exterior is blistered and chewy because of its hot-oil bath. Extra-large dogs (and cheese dogs) are available, but we believe the original size works best. A pair of these tube steaks with a side of crisp French fries blanketed with gravy is a grand plate of food: true New Jersey, and uniquely American.

Rutt's Hut

417 River Rd.   973-779-8615
Clifton, NJ   BLD | $

Raunchy wieners have made Rutt's Hut a cheap-eats legend among Garden State frank fanatics. The dogs are known as "rippers" because their skin tears and crinkles as they cook in hot oil and their exterior turns rugged and chewy. Weenie wimps can ask for an "in and outer," which gets plucked from the fat more quickly and remains thoroughly pink and plump; while those who crave maximum succulence can get one well-done, which is so porcine that it reminds us of fried pig skin.

The one stellar condiment for a ripper is Rutt's spicy-sweet relish, a dense yellow concoction made from onions and finely chopped carrots and cabbage. Hamburgers and hot-from-the-kettle French fries are nice, too; and we are fond of Rutt's chili: a chunky mid-Atlantic brew of clods of ground beef with an occasional bean in it, suspended in a vividly spicy tomato emulsion. With crumbled crackers on top, it's a formidable meal.

Rutt's serves hot-lunch meals as well as real drinks in an adjoining tap room with its own separate entrance. Here, amid wood-panel decor, one can quaff many beers with platters of such blue-plate fare as chicken croquettes, stuffed cabbage, Jersey pork chops, and that Garden State favorite, Taylor Ham on a bun. Prices are low, and the food we have tasted is mighty satisfying. But if you are coming to Rutt's only once, eat hot dogs at a counter. It's a Roadfood experience to remember: Dine in a wide-open mess hall with high counters at the windows that provide a view of the parking lot. Stand and eat off paper plates, and for entertainment, enjoy the calls of the countermen as they sing out, "Twins, all the way," meaning a pair of rippers with mustard and relish.

White House Sub Shop

2301 Arctic Ave. 609-345-1564
Atlantic City, NJ L | $

What makes a White House sub so good is more than superb bread and quality cold cuts. Its virtue is imparted by the artistry of its builders—the profusion of cold cuts without a hint of glut, the symmetry of the ingredients, the spring of the lettuce applied in all the right places, the perfect splash of oil. And there's the astounding size. One whole sub is more than two feet long, requiring a brace of paper plates to hold it. Ingredients range from fancy white tuna fish to meatballs and sauce; and the Philly cheesesteak (arguably a sub corollary) is excellent. The go-to variation is known as the White House Special—Genoa salami, ham, capicola, and provolone cheese all rolled and tightly packed inside the loaf, lubricated with olive oil, decorated with lettuce and bits of sweet pepper.

The White House is a landmark for sandwich connoisseurs; and like the cheesesteak shops of Philadelphia, it likes to boast of a stellar clientele. Pictures of celebrity customers line the walls, inscribed with praise for the excellence of the cuisine. News clippings tell of the time the astronauts came to scarf down subs, and of Frank Sinatra once having a bunch of them shipped from New Jersey across the world to a movie location. For all its stardust, the White House remains a humble Naugahyde-and-neon eatery with a row of booths along the wall and a counter up front. The lighting is harsh, the napkins are paper, and the service is lightning fast: It would be a sin to sell subs any other way. Expect a long wait at noon.

White Manna

358 River St.   201-342-0914
Hackensack, NJ   BLD | $

With good reason, New Jersey is famous for its vibrant hot dog culture; but here is one great hamburger joint that (rightfully) earns high marks from cheap-eats devotees. White Manna's burgers are paradigmatic sliders: little balls of freshly ground chuck that get slapped down onto a greasy griddle, preferably along with a handful of thin-sliced onions, mashed with a spatula, flipped, topped with cheese if requested, then crowned with the top of a tender potato roll. The roll is soft enough to sop up massive amounts of protein nectar that oozes from the beef as well as the sweet perfume from the steamed onions; and its yeasty blandness is just what the forceful ingredients need to hit their peak. Heaps of thin-sliced pickle chips come alongside. Four or six of these makes a nice meal. Alternatively, it is possible to order a few doubles, which start with a ball of meat twice the size of a regular one, but to our taste, that strategy tests the perfect balance of a true slider.

The place is a minuscule diner with hardly more than a dozen seats and minimal counter space. We've never been to White Manna when it isn't very crowded, meaning that although the hamburgers are definitive fast food, you might wait a while to get some.

Aléthea's

8301 Main St.   716-633-8620

Williamsville, NY   LD | $

Aléthea's is a top-rank source for such Buffalo-area specialties as sponge candy (chocolate-coated spun sugar) and Charlie Chaplins (marshmallow, coconut, cashews, and chocolate). Here, too, you will find the most delicious chocolate-covered ginger imaginable, made with smooth, crystalline ginger from Australia. All these can be purchased in the impeccably clean showroom in front of the large area in which everything is made or via mail order (www.aletheas.com).

The Roadfooder passing through who wants to sit down and have something more than bonbons needs to know about Aléthea's adjoining ice cream parlor, where truffled hot fudge, dark amber caramel sauce, freshly made marshmallow topping, and crunchy-crisp, well-salted nuts crown luxurious ice cream. Have a classic Mexicano (chocolate sauce and Spanish peanuts) or a Delphi Maiden of chocolate chip and coffee ice cream topped with marshmallow, chocolate sauce, and toasted almonds. Or just a regular sundae topped with devilishly chocolaty hot fudge. If you are a rice pudding aficionado and there happens to be a batch available (not always the case), you must eat Aléthea's, which has no peer: creamy, substantial, and radiant with cooked-sugar flavor reminiscent of crème brûlée.

Antoinette's

5981 Transit Rd.   716-684-2376
Depew, NY   L | $

There are two Antoinettes in the greater Buffalo area: the original, on Transit Road, and a second, at 1203 Union Road in West Seneca. Either one demands attention from the devotee of ice cream and/or masterfully made chocolates. Simply walking into the store will make you smile: The air is fragrant with cocoa perfume. Watching a sundae constructed is enchanting gastronomic foreplay. Starting at the top, nuts are fresh and crunchy. Whipped cream is, in fact, whipped cream and nothing else, not even sugar, piped onto the ice cream from a pastry tube in thick, luxurious swirls. Fudge sauce? Caramel sauce? Better yet, fudge and caramel and pecans on cream-pure vanilla ice cream to make a turtle sundae? It doesn't get better than this.

The candy selection is magnificent, including Buffalo's own sponge candy and Charlie Chaplin logs as well as a wide assortment of barks, clusters, molasses pops, truffles, cordials, chocolate pretzels, and chocolatized popcorn.

Barney Greengrass

541 Amsterdam Ave.   212-724-4707
New York, NY   BL (closed Mon) | $$

The food that put Barney Greengrass on the map is smoked fish. In the glass case of this restaurant and take-out store, you will find lean, silky sturgeon, salty cured salmon (known as lox), not-so-salty cured salmon (novie), snow-white whitefish, and luscious sable. In the dining room adjacent to the take-out counter, the fish are available on platters, with bagels and/or bialys, cream cheese, onions, tomatoes, and olives. These are the makings of a grand New York breakfast, and there isn't a restaurant in town that does it with the aplomb of bare-tabled Barney Greengrass.

Good as the smoked fish platters are, the single best dish in the house is the one known as eggs-and-novie. If you come in the morning, especially on a weekend, you will smell plates of it being carried from the kitchen to customers as soon as you enter. It is eggs scrambled with plush morsels of Nova Scotia salmon and onions nearly caramelized by frying. The combination tastes opulent; the textural range from the eggs' soft curds to the firm nuggets of fish they enfold to the slippery web of onions is a tongue's delight. The aroma of this omelet, as well as smells of freshly toasted bagels and of cold cuts, salamis, and garlic pickles from the take-out side of the restaurant, makes walking into Barney Greengrass one of the most appetizing experiences New York City has to offer.

Burger Joint

119 W. 56th St.	212-708-7414
New York, NY	LD | $

Roadfood on Manhattan's 56th Street? Just off the lobby of the luxurious Le Parker Meridien Hotel? The location does not fit any reasonable definition of Roadfood, but the place itself does; and the meal it serves is beyond reproach. What you will eat in this secretive alcove with less than a dozen worn tables and booths is a mighty fine hamburger. Despite the five-star address, it is by no means a gourmet hamburger; and at $7 (pricey compared to normal places in the U.S., but one of the cheapest meals anywhere in midtown Manhattan), you don't expect one. What you get is a medium-thick patty cooked to order on a charcoal grill, its fat quotient high enough that, if medium rare or less, it will ooze juice into its bun even before you bite into it. This may well be the ultimate lunch counter hamburger. Add cheese (for 50¢) and you get a melting blanket of two mixed Cheddars; ask for the works and you get lettuce, tomato, onion, mustard, ketchup, and mayo. French fries, served in a paper bag, are thin and crisp, a good burger companion if not among the great spuds of New York.

The above paragraph tells you the entire menu, except for a grilled cheese sandwich and a brownie for dessert. The beverage list includes Sam Adams by the single serving or pitcher, soft drinks, and, after 3 P.M. on Friday, milk shakes. Despite the hidden location of its entrance, the Burger Joint is easy to find once you enter the hotel lobby. Just inhale and follow the scent of sizzling beef. It it's lunch time, you'll know it by the inevitable line of customers waiting for a precious booth. Although tucked away behind curtains, this crazy little eatery has earned way too many fans for its very limited accommodations.

Café Edison

228 W. 47th St.	212-840-5000
New York, NY	BLD | $$

Known to regulars as "The Polish Tea Room," Café Edison offers a delicious taste of old New York unaffected by the corporate makeover of Times Square. Prices are moderate, the food is good, and the experience is unforgettable. In particular, we recommend ordering borscht, matzoh ball soup, braised brisket, kasha varnishkes, and homemade gefilte fish. Experts consider the cheese blintzes among the city's best; and we think the matzoh brei is superb.

Way back in the 1920s, this used to be a ritzy spot. Today, while it's no flophouse, the Edison Hotel is far from ultra luxurious. The café, which used to be the hotel's grand ballroom, still shows evidence of the glamour that once was, including bas-relief salmon-colored walls and elegant chandeliers. But now the walls are taped with signs advertising daily specials and the staff of weary waiters and waitresses will give any crabby deli help a run for their money in an angst-on-a-tray contest.

Carnegie Deli

854 7th Ave.   212-757-2245
New York, NY   BLD | $$

Expensive, rude, loud, uncomfortable, and overrun with tourists, the Carnegie Deli is a true taste of New York City. Its pastrami and corned beef are among the best anywhere; the kaleidoscopic menu of sandwiches, coffee shop hot lunch, and Jewish comfort food is definitive. Merely walking in from 7th Avenue is a gastronomic blast as the aroma of cured deli meats and sour pickles assaults your nose. A host points you to the back, and as you walk toward the tables, you pass a counter full of meats and smoked-fish salads behind which sandwiches are made. Salamis hang like a curtain over the counter, adding their garlicky perfume to the air. At the back of the restaurant, or in the adjoining dining room, you will be directed to a place at a table where you sit elbow-to-elbow with strangers.

Although purists gripe that the cured meats no longer are available hand-sliced, we have no complaints about the Carnegie's machine-sliced pastrami. It is mellow and not too zesty, utterly tender and infused with fatty savor. The sandwich is ridiculously large—so tall that the top piece of rye bread appears merely to be an afterthought applied to the tower of meat. In fact, it is difficult to eat the ordinary way, by picking it up in your hands and taking a bite. Many customers go at it piece-by-shred, directly from the plate. To accompany the monumental sandwiches, the Carnegie supplies perfect puckery accouterments—half-sour and sour dill pickles arrayed in silver bowls along the tables. Beyond sandwiches, culinary highlights include blintzes and potato pancakes, gefilte fish and pickled herring, borscht and kreplach soup.

Charlie the Butcher's Kitchen

1065 Wehrle Dr.	716-633-8330
Buffalo, NY	LD | $

According to Charlie Roesch, proprietor of Charlie the Butcher's Kitchen, it was beer that inspired the invention of beef on weck. He believes that back in the 1880s a now-forgotten local tavern owner decided to offer a sandwich that would induce a powerful thirst in his patrons. He had plenty of coarse salt on hand for the pretzels he served, so he painted a mixture of the salt and caraway seeds (*kummelweck* in German) atop some hard rolls, cooked a roast and sliced it thin, and piled the meat inside the rolls. As a condiment, he served hot horseradish. Slaking the thirst these sandwiches induced, beer sales soared. And Buffalo's passion for beef on weck was born.

Charlie the Butcher's father was a butcher, as was his grandfather (their slogan: "You know it's fresh if it comes from Roesch"). To honor the family trade, he wears a white hard hat on his head and a butcher's smock over his shirt and necktie as he carves beef on the butcher block in his open kitchen at the center of the restaurant. The beef on weck sandwiches are protein ecstasy, the rolls delicate but tough enough to sop up gravy and still stay strong.

Charlie's menu, we should note, extends well beyond beef on weck, and everything else we've sampled is first-rate: Buffalo-made hot dogs and sausages grilled over coals, chicken spiedie (a boneless breast that is marinated and grilled), melting-tender, full-flavored roast turkey, and such daily-special sandwiches as meat loaf, double-smoked ham, and prime rib. The beverage list includes the local favorite, loganberry juice, as well as Charlie's personal favorite, birch beer.

Clare and Carl's

4731 Lake Shore Dr.	518-561-1163
Plattsburgh, NY	LD (summer only) | $

A newspaper story posted on the wall at Clare and Carl's says that the region's unique weenie, the Michigan, owes its name to a Michigander named Eula Otis who came to work for Clare Warn in the early days of the drive-in (it opened in 1943) and went around to area restaurants saying, "I'm from Michigan. Would you like to try one of our chili dogs?" The state's name clung to the hot dog topped with Warn's sauce, which she had invented because New York–style hot dogs with mustard and sauerkraut weren't selling well. The Michigan became a passion unique to New York's North Country between the Adirondacks and Lake Champlain, served at summertime stands, in grocery stores, and even in the cafeteria at the Champlain Valley Physicians Hospital Medical Center.

Clare and Carl's presents its Michigans in a cream-soft bun that is similar to the traditional Northeast split-top, but is thicker at the bottom and closed at both ends, forming a trough to shore in the sloppy topping. The chili is thick with minced meat, kaleidoscopically spiced, not at all sweet, and just barely hot. It is intriguing and addictive.

There is another Clare and Carl's in town, but the original is a wonderful vision of long-gone roadside Americana, its clapboard walls so old that they appear to have settled deep into the earth. Carhops attend customers in a broad parking lot, and there is a U-shaped counter with padded stools inside. A menu posted above the open kitchen lists Michigans first; signs outside advertise the house specialty as Texas red hots.

Condrell's

2805 Delaware Ave.   716-877-4485
Buffalo, NY   LD | $

We're not sure if the formal name of this place is Condrell's or King Condrell's; both are used on menus, on signs, and when employees speak of it. No matter, because what's important here is the sundaes—some of the best on the planet. Atop locally made Perry's ice cream you can have basso profundo hot fudge, warm French chocolate sauce that is lighter than fudge and more pudding-like, or more traditional chocolate sauce that is thin and innocent. Marshmallow topping is smooth as cream, caramel is extra-buttery, whipped cream is utterly fresh, and nuts are crisp and salted just enough to be a perfect foil for everything sweet. Portions are big.

Do not neglect Condrell's candies. There are exemplary sponge candies and Charlie Chaplins (Buffalo faves), as well as more universally known delights including molasses paddles and molasses chips enrobed in dark or light chocolate, truffles of every kind, cashew or pecan turtles, chocolate-covered chunks of candied orange, pineapple, and ginger, dozens of varieties of cream centers, nut barks, chocolate-covered pretzels, and malted milk balls. To shop at Condrell's is to be a kid in a candy store. No metaphor exists to express the bliss of a Condrell's sundae.

Don's Original

4900 Culver Rd.   585-323-1177
Sea Breeze, NY   LD (summer only) | $

Say "New York hot dog" and most people will conjure up a street-corner
dirty-water dog or a kosher frank from an urban deli or Nathan's of Coney
Island. But culinarily, as in every other aspect of its culture, New York has
two personalities: downstate and everything else; and hot dogs on the far
side of the Southern Tier are a food group unto themselves, known as hots.
There are two primary subcategories: white hots and red hots. The white
hot, as served by Don's Original at the Lake Ontario summer playground
known as Sea Breeze, is an all-pork tube steak (which locals know to call a
porker) that wants to spurt juice when teeth sink into it. Split and grilled to
sputtering succulence, a white hot is right dressed with mustard and diced
onions. Don's red hot, known as a Texas hot, is firmer and looks more like a
traditional weenie and is customarily dressed with finely ground chili.

Even frankfurter-frowners will want to know about this happy Rochester landmark, which has been serving amusement park patrons since 1945.
The hamburgers and cheeseburgers are al fresco classics, cooked to order
and brought to their best selves by an application of bright red hot sauce.
Big, fat onion rings are made here, as is custard, available inside or at the
walk-up window.

Doug's Fish Fry

3638 West Rd.   607-753-9184
Cortland, NY   LD | $$

Located near Skaneateles Lake, which is so pure that local towns drink its
water unfiltered, Doug's is fish and chips–lovers' heaven. Your choice is either a sandwich, a fish dinner, or a fish onion dinner. The titles are mislead-
ing because the sandwich is in fact two or three large hunks of fried fish piled
in and around a modest bun that in no way is large enough to hold even half
its proposed ingredients. Like a tenderloin from the southern Midwest, the
presentation pushes the envelope of what, exactly, a sandwich is. A fish dinner adds beautiful chunky French fries to the pseudo-sandwich. A fish onion
dinner means onion rings.

The fish is Atlantic cod, bought fresh in Boston five times a week. It
is moist, sweet, and meek-flavored, encased in a sandy crust with just the
right amount of crunch. It comes with pickly tartar sauce that is surprisingly
unsweet. Sweetness comes in the form of Doug's superb coleslaw, which
is finely chopped and fetchingly spicy. And then there is sweet dessert: ex-

cellent soft-serve custard, dense and alabaster-pure. Throughout summer the custard is a foundation for warm fruit sundaes. The available compote, made right here from the fruit of the season, begins with strawberries and blueberries early in the summer, then moves to peaches and finally to apples in the fall. Glorious!

Service is eat-in-the-rough style: Place your order at the stand-up counter (from which you have an appetizing view of fish and fries coming out of the hot oil), pay for the meal, and wait for your name to be called. Fetch your own utensils from a table in the center of the dining room that holds plastic forks and knives, ketchup and mustard, and malt vinegar for spritzing on fries.

Glenwood Pines

1213 Taughannock Blvd.   607-273-3709
Ithaca, NY   LD | $

The primary attraction of this friendly roadhouse overlooking Cayuga Lake is a Pinesburger. That's a six-ounce beef oval topped with a couple of slices of cheese wedged into a length of Ithaca Bakery French bread with lettuce, tomato slices, onion slices, and your choice of Thousand Island dressing or mayonnaise. Connoisseurs told us that we had to have it with the Thousand Island, and it would be hard to argue against that. The sweetness of the dressing is a grand complement for the smoky meat and all its dressings. On the side, good companions include ultra-crunchy fried onion rings and creamy coleslaw.

We said the Pinesburger was the primary reason to visit. The secondary one is the fish fry. A huge, thick length of haddock is breaded and fried crisp and served with either tartar sauce or cocktail sauce. It is sweet, moist, flavorful fish, and a giant meal.

Ambience at the 1946-vintage Glenwood Pines is old-time tavern. When you walk in, you see a few pinball machines and a bowling game on the right, a pool table ahead of you, and beyond that, the bar where some folks sit and imbibe beers with (or without) their Pinesburgers as a TV delivers sports broadcasts from the upper right corner. To the left are tables and a small separate dining room; also a small case of trophies—for baseball, bowling, and volleyball—earned by teams that Glenwood Pines has sponsored.

Gus's Restaurant

3 Cumberland Head Rd.   518-561-3711
Plattsburgh, NY   BLD | $

In the same phylum as the Coney Islands of the heartland and the New York Systems of Rhode Island, the Michigans of New York's North Country are primarily summertime food. They are little porkers that come nestled in a soft bun and topped with a fine-grained, mildly spicy meat sauce.

Gus's serves Michigans year-round. It started as a dog stand in 1951, but it has grown to a three-meal-a-day restaurant with a full menu that boasts, "The restaurant features just about everything [even Lake Champlain perch], including their famous 'Michigan red hot,' which they invite you to try while dining." Each Michigan you order arrives in a cardboard boat. While condiments technically are optional, it is rare for anyone to order a Michigan topped only with sauce. Bright yellow mustard and chopped raw onions will be part of the picture unless you specifically ask for them to be omitted.

Heid's of Liverpool

305 Oswego St.   315-451-0786
Liverpool, NY   LD | $

Heid's has been around since before the hot dog was formally invented, but for as long as any living human can remember, hot dogs have been its claim to fame. For a while there were branches of the original, but today only one remains: a fast-food dog house with some tables inside and picnic tables outdoors under a tent.

The menu is wiener-centric. German franks, Texas hots (red wieners), or Hofmann-brand white hots made of beef, pork, and veal in Syracuse are quickly grilled, a process you can watch after placing your order. These are handsome sausages with a delicate casing and dense insides. In the old days the one and only available condiment was mustard. But since John and Randall Parker started running Heid's back in 1995, the topping choices have expanded to include chili, onions, sweet onion relish, and ketchup.

As always, the beverage list is a short one, including milk shakes, sodas, beer, and chocolate milk.

Hubba

24 N. Main St.　　　　　　　914-939-7271
Port Chester, NY　　　　　　BLD | $

In southeastern New York, central New Jersey, and western Connecticut, the word *Texas,* when used to modify the words *hot, hot dog,* or *weiner* (yes, *ei*), means chili. A Texas hot is a chili dog. The long-standing chili dog king of Port Chester is Hubba, formerly known as Pat's Hubba Hubba and, before that, Texas Quick Lunch. While there is a full menu written in permanent marker on white paper plates tacked to the wall, nine out of ten meals served are the same: two, four, or maybe even six split and grilled weiners blanketed with no-bean, ground-beef chili and garnished with crisp chopped onions. It is a wanton combo—hot, greasy, and messy—but with a personality so intense that when the yen for one strikes, not even prime filet mignon will cut the mustard. Those who need more sustenance than a brace of chili dogs get chili cheese fries on the side. To drink: Hubba water, which is tap water tinted pink by a dash of Hawaiian Punch.

Hubba's chili dogs are famous as the kill-or-cure conclusion to a night of heavy drinking. The restaurant stays open until just before dawn on weekends. No wider than an apartment hallway, with only about a dozen counter seats, it is known also for its eye-boggling decor: Every available piece of wall and ceiling is papered with dollar bills.

John's Pizzeria

278 Bleecker St.　　　　　　212-243-1680
New York, NY　　　　　　　LD | $$

John's looks extremely well lived-in and well eaten-in, its walls and the wooden backs of its rickety booths covered with a thicket of graffiti that represents the countless enthusiastic visitors who have dined here since 1934, when John's moved to Bleecker from its original location (opened in the '20s) on Sullivan Street. At the back of the front dining room, where two Italianate murals decorate the walls above the scarred wood, photographs of famous fans of John's are displayed. They include former mayor Giuliani and former Chairman of the Board Frank Sinatra.

Pizzas come large (eight slices) or small (six slices). There are no surprises on the ingredient list, except that the sausage is especially delicious, the mushrooms are fresh, and the mozzarella has a creamy goodness that makes magic with the brightly herbed red sauce. What makes John's pizza taste important is its crust. Cooked in a coal-fired wood oven, it has a dough that turns almost brittle at its outer edges in places where it blisters and blackens from the heat; and yet just fractions of an inch inside that circumference, it has a wondrous chew. The best part of it is the underside. Flip over a slice—you can do this, for the toppings cling well and each slice has enough structural integrity to stay together as it's handled—and gaze upon the bottom. It is charred from its stay on the floor of the old oven. Nearly black and on the verge of ashy, the crunchy bottom surface of this pizza is an addictive eating sensation unlike any other. For serious bread and pizza–lovers, this crust verges on a spiritual experience.

Katz's

205 E. Houston St.	212-254-2246
New York, NY	BLD | $$

The bad news: Katz's is slated to get demolished to make way for a big, modern building. The good news: It has not happened yet (as of the beginning of 2011), and this relic of bygone New York remains the wonderful culinary landmark it has been for well over a century. It is a cavernous eating hall with lined-up tables, the air filled with the noise of shouted orders and clattering carving knives and the aroma of the odoriferous garlicky salamis hanging along the wall. Pictures of happy celebrity customers ranging from comics Jerry Lewis and Henny Youngman to police commissioner Raymond Kelly are everywhere.

Ordinary table service by waiters is available, and quite easy. But the better way to do it is to personally engage with a counterman. Here's how: make eye contact with one of the white-aproned carvers who is busy slicing meats—by hand, of course—and making sandwiches behind the glass. Once you've gotten his attention, be quick and tell him what you want: pastrami on rye or on a club roll, or corned beef or brisket. They portion out meat and assemble sandwiches with the certainty and expertise of Dutch diamond cutters.

King of Katz's sandwiches is pastrami—not the hugest in the city, but very possibly the best: three-quarters of a pound expertly severed into pieces so chunky that the word *slice* seems too lightweight to describe them. Each brick-red, glistening moist hunk is rimmed black, redolent of garlic, smoke, and pickling spices, as savory as food can be. You can pay a dollar extra to have it cut extra-lean, but that would be sad.

Beyond superb cured meat: Katz's hot dogs just may be the city's best all-beefers; omelets are made deli-style, meaning open-face and unfolded; there are tender-souled matzoh ball soup and chicken noodle soup as well as potato latkes and blintzes; and to drink you can have a classic New York egg cream, chocolate or vanilla.

LDR Char Pit

4753 Lake Ave.   585-865-0112

Rochester, NY   LD | $

When you first see an LDR steak sandwich, you likely will be suspicious. The single broad cut of meat in its bun looks like it's got to be a challenging chew, especially considering the bargain price of $6.25 and the fact that the LDR Char Pit is a booth-and-counter diner, as far from a prime steak house as a restaurant can be. But when you take a bite, the faulty preconception vanishes. This slim steak, which is maybe a quarter of an inch thick and, mind you, cooked to order, is tenderness incarnate, oh-so-easy to chew and such a joy to savor, as buttery-beef flavored as a KC strip: a miracle sandwich.

It arrives completely unadorned. Condiments, including a meaty hot sauce, are available at a help-yourself counter; but we highly recommend you forgo them. The beauty of this steak sandwich is its simplicity: meat and bread. Anything else is only a complication.

LDR's menu also lists red hots and white hots—traditional upstate New York frankfurters—as well as grilled chicken and ham steaks, none of which we've tried. The steak is too compelling. When you are finished, walk a half-block toward Lake Ontario and you will find an Abbott's custard shop. Creamy, dense, dairy-pure, it is wonderful dessert. Our favorite flavor is chocolate almond.

Magnolia's

21 Front St.   845-878-9759

Patterson, NY   BL | $

Before K. C. Scott opened up the original Magnolia's in Carmel in April, 1999, it took a long while to come up with the right name. Then one day, standing in her kitchen, she found herself looking at one of the antique signs she had collected . . . for Magnolia Dairy Products. "I like Magnolia because it has a slow, southern feel," she explains, noting that her goal in starting this seductive little restaurant was to create a place that provided quality food at a reasonable price in a setting that was as relaxed as a friend's kitchen.

"We have an aversion to anything premade," K.C. says, noting that all the breads, the salad dressings, the pastries, and even the chocolates are made right here in the minuscule kitchen. They smoke barbecue brisket and pork butts for hours, then bathe the meats in a house sauce that will snap taste buds to attention. At breakfast, the repertoire includes omelets, French toast, pancakes, an egg-potato-cheese-salsa burrito, and waffles (weekends only).

Sandwiches are swell, especially the Local Hero portobello mushroom and pepper sandwich on focaccia bread and the Ludington cheese and tomato sandwich on hearth bread. We are fond of two always-available wraps: the Catalina, which is an assortment of vegetables, including delicious roasted peppers, in an herb wrap, and the Cortland, which is grilled chicken and Havarti cheese and pieces of locally grown Cortland apple.

Margon

136 W. 46th St.   212-354-5013
New York, NY   BLD | $

Margon is a personality-plus hole-in-the-wall around the corner from otherwise Disneyfied Times Square. Plush, it is not. A ramp leads downward to a long, narrow space with four stools jammed up against an impossibly uncomfortable counter near the front; tables are lined up on the right of an aisle that leads to the back.

On the left of the aisle is a buffet counter where arriving customers stand and place orders. Here is how it works: Walk to the back with your eyes looking left. This allows a full view of what's to eat, including pork chops smothered in gravy, glistening roast chicken, rice and beans, sweet plantains, and octopus salad. Place your order and have a seat. When it's ready, one of the counter help will call you to pick it up, or on occasion, they will bring it to your table.

The octopus salad can be a meal or a lip-smacking appetizer: tender leaves of meat glistening in a garlic marinade. While daily lunch specials include such exotica as tripe and pig's feet (Monday and Thursday) and *chicharron de pollo* (Tuesday), everyday entrees include stews and chops and roast chicken that are beautiful to see and a delight to eat. The Cuban sandwich is first-rate, a crisp-toasted length of bread enveloping roast pork, salami, ham, melted cheese, a surfeit of pickle slices, mustard, and mayo. Actually, any sandwich made on the good Cuban bread, then pressed and heated, is excellent. We love the plain roast pork that is anything but plain-tasting.

McSweeney's

535 N. Margaret St.   518-562-9309
Plattsburgh, NY   LD | $

It was only recently that we learned about Michigans, thanks to Roadfooders David Scheinberg, who used to spend summers in the Adirondacks, as well as to Adam Graham and to Cynthia Potts, all of whom alerted us to a style of chili dog unique to New York State's northland. Michigans go back to the early 1940s and have remained very popular in and around Platts-burgh, but virtually unknown elsewhere. Each place that makes Michigans has its own formula, but the basic idea is a piggy-pink wiener in a split-top bun, topped with a dark orange chili sauce in which the meat is sandy smith-ereens. The heft of the sauce contrasts with the fluffy bun and fatty frank, and while each separate ingredient is inarguably ignominious, the combo has charisma—especially when topped with a streak of yellow mustard and a scattering of crisp, chopped raw onions.

McSweeney's, which bills itself as "Plattsburgh's Red Hot Car Hop Stop," is a relative newcomer to the area, opening in 1991 and now boasting three locations. We visited the one on Route 9 North (Margaret Street), which features old-time carhop service and an inside counter as well as comfortable sit-down tables indoors. Its sauce is especially beefy, flecked with pepper that kindles a nice glow on the tongue. The package is substantial enough that Michigans come with a fork. Looking around the dining room and at people eating off trays hung on car windows, it appeared to us that most custom-ers forgo the utensil. A few people we observed had perfected a technique of hoisting the entire cardboard boat to chin level with one hand, then using the other hand to ease the Michigan from boat to mouth, bite by bite.

McSweeney's sells Michigan sauce by the pint ($11.50) and offers a Michigan without the hot dog: mustard, onions and plenty of sauce in the unique hollowed-out bun. This configuration is known, strangely enough, as a sauceburger, and as much as we like the sauce, we much prefer it in concert with a weenie.

Mike's Candy

2110 Clinton St. 716-826-6515
Buffalo, NY $

Of Buffalo's several claims to culinary fame (wings, beef on weck, char-cooked hot dogs), one of the lesser-known stars is sponge candy. Made of sugar that is cooked and spun and leavened to a state of desiccated near-weightlessness, then broken into diaphanous, double-bite-size hunks and sheathed in dark chocolate (or milk chocolate, if you prefer), it is similar to candy known in some parts of the Midwest as seafoam or fairy food.

We well remember our first bite at Mike's, a Buffalo chocolate shop where everything is made from scratch in a small back-room kitchen, and where sponge candy perfection is an obsession. We stood at the counter and sampled a piece, remarking that the molasses interior seemed actually lighter than air, as if it would float upward without the ballast of its thick chocolate coat. As soon as it was bitten and slightly moist, it evaporated into pure flavor with no corporeal residue at all. Susan Walter, daughter of founders Mike and Anastasia Melithoniotes, listened to us, but not to our words. "It sounds a little crisp today," she said, noticing the faint crunch it made when our teeth first met the sponge underneath its chocolate sheath. "It's breaking hard." The subtlety of her evaluation was lost on us, for it seemed absolutely perfect. Susan also clued us in to the uniquely Buffalonian favorite, the Charlie Chaplin, which is a log of freshly made marshmallow laced with coconut and rolled with cashews and chocolate. Neither she nor any other confectioner in town had a convincing explanation for how the Charlie Chaplin got its name and why it is an obsession in Buffalo and only in Buffalo.

(Sponge candy is almost always available in-store at Mike's, as well as for mail order throughout the year except in the hottest months of summer, when heat and humidity preclude shipping.)

New Way Lunch

54 South St.   518-792-9803
Glens Falls, NY   BL | $

New Way Lunch has a sign outside boasting that it has been world famous since 1919, and although it now occupies a new, modern building, its way with hot dogs is timeless. They are slim, non-kosher franks that are griddle cooked and slipped into soft, warm buns. The fundamental dressing formula is a trio of mustard, diced onions, and a finely textured beef sauce that has a peppery tang. It is a small package, costing just over a dollar. We observed that big guys ordered them by fours or sixes. Take-out customers come in for dozens.

There's a small menu of other items, too: char-cooked burgers, a Philly cheesesteak, fried fish and chicken, and a Greek salad. For a quick lunch not far from the New York Thruway, New Way is an easy detour.

Nick Tahou Hots

320 W. Main St.   716-436-0184
Rochester, NY   LD | $

Don't confuse a Rochester Garbage Plate with junk food that is tossed willy-nilly into a paper bag or bucket. At Nick Tahou Hots, where it was invented, a Garbage Plate is a carefully assembled meal. You cannot eat it on the front seat of a car. It demands a table and utensils, not to mention a big appetite and courage.

Construction of a Garbage Plate begins with your choice of two items from among home fries, French fries, macaroni salad, and baked beans. The duo is marshaled half-and-half on a carton-weight cardboard plate. Atop the foundation of starches is positioned a brace of hot dogs, hamburgers or cheeseburgers, Italian sausage or steak, or fried eggs. Piled onto the protein layer are meaty hot sauce and onions, and bread comes alongside to push, mop, and scoop. When we came to Nick Tahou's as part of the 2009 Roadfood.com eating tour of western New York, Bruce Bilmes and Sue Boyle declared the grilled cheese Garbage Plate the "sleeper winner." Instead of meat, this plate (the cheapest in the house) is built around a pair of grilled cheese sandwiches. Bruce and Sue wrote, "The flavors and textures just seem to be made for each other, and the toasted bread soaks up the juices (read grease) beautifully. A brilliant choice that we highly recommend!"

The Garbage Plate was created by Nick Tahou during the great Depression, when it was known as hots and potots—*hots* being the upstate New York term for hot dogs. The maximum-food/minimum-cost meal was renamed by happy customers and has been embraced by Rochesterians as a hometown specialty as dear as wings in Buffalo. Currently more than two dozen local restaurants serve its equivalent. *Equivalent* because Nick's son Alex trademarked the name Garbage Plate in 1992. No other chef can call this hash house symphony by that name; and so short-order kitchens all over Rochester resound with calls for Dumpster Plates, Trash Plates, Messy Plates, Sloppy Plates, and Rubbish Plates.

Call it what you will, there is nothing like having a Garbage Plate at the original Nick Tahou's, which is more than a restaurant to its most loyal clientele. It is home, it is family, it is a spirit of ragtag generosity with which Alex Tahou feeds needy kids at Christmas and takes care of neighbors and friends as well as newcomers all year-round.

Papaya King

179 E. 86th St. 212-369-0648
New York, NY LD | $

Incredibly, Papaya King began as a health-oriented juice store! That was 1932, when original proprietor Gus Poulos hired waitresses to do the hula on the sidewalk and lure people inside to taste "nature's own revitalizer." You still can have papaya juice, which is frothy and sweet if not necessarily salubrious, but it's for the hot dogs that this popular street-corner eatery has earned its stripes. A sign in the window boasts that they are "tastier than filet mignon." They do pack a booming garlic taste inside natural casing that pops when you bite it. They are modest-sized, so that two to four makes a meal, and they come in toasted buns. Available toppings include chili, sauerkraut, even coleslaw; the essentials are New York-style stewed onions and good ol' mustard.

Dine at an eating shelf that affords a nice view of the passing scene along Third Avenue and 86th Street.

Patsy's

2287 First Ave.   212-534-9783
New York, NY   LD | $

New Yorkers think nothing of picking up a slice of pizza for eating on the go. Patsy's is the Italian landmark in the midst of Spanish Harlem where street slices first were served back in the 1930s. To this day, customers stand around on the sidewalk outside or lean on an open-air counter facing First Avenue, wolfing down slices of pizza, which is the only thing on the walk-up menu. These are some of the most elegant slices you'll find anywhere in the city: wafer-thin charcoaled crust, minimal tomato, and just enough cheese to make it rich.

Whole pies are served at tables and booths inside. While all sorts of toppings are available, we like the most basic tomato-cheese combo: easy to hoist slice by slice, built on that marvelous fragile crust with charred spots all along the edge that have the smoky flavor that only a coal oven delivers. Two versions of plain cheese pizza are available: fresh mozzarella, with thin pools of creamy sliced cheese spread out within the microthin layer of tomato sauce, and regular mozzarella, on which saltier, slightly oilier shredded cheese is spread evenly all across the surface.

Phil's Chicken House

1208 Main Rd.   607-748-7574
Endicott, NY   LD | $

Phil's Chicken House was opened over forty years ago by Phil Card, who learned his skills at Endicott's Chicken Inn. His folksy wood-paneled restaurant is decorated to the hilt with country-crafty knickknacks (souvenir plates, angel statuettes, lighthouse miniatures) and it attracts customers that range from local families to well-armed state police SWAT teams (who practice marksmanship nearby).

As you might suspect by the name of this restaurant, its featured attraction is chicken—slow cooked and relentlessly basted on a rotisserie until the skin is glazed gold and the meat drips juice. The breast meat is velvet soft; thighs and drumsticks pack a roundhouse flavor punch; wings, which carry maximum marinade, reverberate with exclamatory gusto. The marinade is the classic Cornell chicken formula, devised by professor Dr. Robert Baker back in the late 1940s—a tomato-free vinaigrette, enriched with eggs and shot through with poultry spice, now used as a marinade and/or basting sauce by cooks throughout the region.

While nine out of ten customers come to Phil's for a half or a quarter barbecued chicken, square meals of all kinds are available, including pot roast, meat loaf, grilled ham, and steak. There's a lunch buffet every day and a breakfast buffet on weekends.

Red Rooster Drive-In

1566 Route 22   845-279-8046
Brewster, NY   LD | $

Although a roadside archeologist would definitely categorize the Rooster as a drive-in, there is no car service and there are no carhops. Still, there is a vast parking lot and plenty of people eat in their cars (or at one of three improbably small two-person tables in the cramped interior), and the service, cuisine, and ambience are *Happy Days* incarnate.

The hamburgers are not too big, not odd in any way, just pleasant handfuls fashioned by proprietor Jack Sypek or Andy the grill chef and sizzled on a smoky charcoal grill. We are particularly fond of cheeseburgers gilded by an order of onions that have been grilled until limp and slippery. They are served on tender buns—deluxe, please, with lettuce and tomato!—and accompanied by French fries, milk shakes, ice cream floats, or egg creams in a variety of flavors beyond the traditional chocolate.

In nice weather, customers can choose to eat at one of several picnic tables spread across the lawn in back. Adjacent to this open-air dining room is a modest miniature golf course where kids and carefree adults while away pleasant evenings in the Red Rooster's afterglow.

Schwabl's

789 Center Rd.   716-674-9821
West Seneca, NY   LD | $$

Now operated by former waitress Cheryl Staychok and her husband, Gene, Buffalo's best-known beef house didn't miss a beat when the Schwabl family left the business. Here is the benchmark version of that glorious Buffalo specialty, beef on weck. The beef itself is superb: thin slices (preferably rare) severed from a center-cut round roast just before the sandwich is assembled. The pillow of protein is piled high inside a *kummelweck* roll heavily crusted with coarse salt and caraway seeds, the roll's top momentarily dipped in natural gravy before it sandwiches the meat. The only thing this package could possibly want is a dab of horseradish, which is supplied on each table.

Of the several side dishes, mashed potatoes are very good (and topped with excellent gravy), but tangy-sweet German potato salad is our pick. That is all you need to know about Schwabl's, except for the nice hot ham sandwich on white bread in a pool of tomato-clove gravy. The ham is an interesting alternative to the beef, although it has none of the famous local sandwich's clout.

Schwabl's is a casual, well-aged eatery, attended by businesspeople at noon and families at suppertime. While liquor is served, the best beverage to pair with beef on weck is birch beer, which is available here on draft: a local brew with the faint twang of spearmint.

Second Avenue Deli

162 E. 33rd St.   212-689-9000
New York, NY   BLD | $$

The Second Avenue Deli has moved closer to Third Avenue, on 33rd Street, but it remains one of the ever-scarcer true Jewish delicatessens. You can smell its culinary character the moment you walk in and inhale the swirling perfume of sour pickles, aged salami, hot chicken broth, steamy corned beef, and pastrami. Where else can you begin a meal with *gribenes,* which are the unbelievably luxurious leftovers from rendering chicken fat? The Second Avenue Deli makes them in big batches, so they aren't as refined or as delicate as you might find on the kitchen counter at grandma's house, but they are nonetheless irresistible: squiggles and nibbles of skin along with limp caramelized shreds of onion that have been fried in the full-flavored oil. Dangerous to munch before a meal because they are so addictive and so corpulent, *gribenes* are the world's best complement to chopped liver, which here is smooth-flavored but ragged enough for textural excitement, rich the way only organ meat can be, and yet fresh and sparkling the way liver so seldom is.

Smoked fish platters are silky luxury; soups—especially the legendary mushroom barley—are some of the city's best; and deli sandwiches are delightful. While the sandwiches are not gargantuan, they are piled high enough that they are barely pickupable. Pastrami is especially excellent, more smoky than spicy; and unless you pay $2 extra for lean meat, it comes just-right fatty. Our only complaint is the rye bread, which as in so many otherwise first-rate delis nowadays, is second-class, pale, and flabby. We discussed this with the woman at the cash register and she shrugged knowingly, saying that the good old-time, double-baked bread, with its glossy crust and chewy body, has become too difficult to obtain.

Meals are topped off with a complimentary shot glass of chocolate phosphate ("Bosco and seltzer," explains the waitress). Second Avenue's kitchen actually is kosher, meaning you can't get cheese on a sandwich; and instead of butter to spread on bread, you may have to settle for chicken fat.

Sharkey's

56 Glenwood Ave.   716-729-9201
Binghamton, NY   LD | $$

Larry Sharak's father started making spiedies at a cookfire in the window at the family's tavern over fifty years ago. Skewered, marinated hunks of lamb were cooked on a charcoal grill and served with broad slices of bread. The custom was to grab the bread in one hand and use it as an edible mitt to slide a few hunks off the metal rod, thus creating an instant sandwich. Spiedies are still served and eaten this way at the bar and tables of Sharkey's. Lamb has grown too expensive, however, so today's spiedies are made from either pork or chicken. When you bite into a piece, it blossoms with the flavorful juice of a two-day marinade that tastes of garlic and vinegar, peppers and oregano, and, according to Larry Sharak, for whom the recipe is a family heirloom, "a lot of pinches of many spices."

Beyond the spiedie, Sharkey's serves Eastern European fare made by experts: *holupkis* (stuffed cabbage rolls) are the work of Larry's sister-in-law, Marie. Around Easter and Christmastime, the menu features homemade kielbasa sausages. And you can always count on buttery pierogi filled with seasoned mashed potatoes.

Sharkey's is a local institution to which families have come for generations. Old-timers know to enter through the back door rather than the front. Here, you walk into a dark dining room outfitted with ancient wooden booths and long family-style tables formed from pushed-together dinettes. Between courses, the young folks get up to play a few lines on the old Tic Tac Strike game, a pre-electronic diversion that seems at home in this historic tavern.

Shortstop Deli

204 W. Seneca St.   607-273-1030
Ithaca, NY   Always open | $

Any hearty eater who attended Cornell University in Ithaca, New York, in the last four decades years knows about Hot Truck, the mobile food wagon that invented French bread pizzas in the early 1960s. As served from the campus truck starting every night at 11 P.M. during the school year, these fusions of pizza and submarine sandwich are piled with ingredients, then baked open-face until the bread is shatteringly crisp, the cheese bubbles, and the meats sizzle.

The Hot Truck's hours are extremely limited, which is why we love the Shortstop Deli, to which proprietor Albert Smith and his son Michael have brought Hot Truck cuisine. More a big convenience store than a sit-down eatery, the Shortstop features shelves of snack foods, countless varieties of coffee, and a counter where you write your own order for Hot Truck. There are no tables and chairs, just some concrete benches outside the front window where it is possible to bring your wrapped sandwich and your cup of soda and dine al fresco.

The pizza subs are made on loaves of Ithaca Bakery French bread, and they range from the basic PMP (Poor Man's Pizza), which is nothing but bread, sauce, and cheese, to the extravaganza known as a Suicide (garlic, sauce, mushrooms, sausage, pepperoni, and mozzarella). These sandwiches have inspired a language all their own. For example, a Triple Sui, Hot and Heavy, G and G is a full Suicide with three extra home-made meatballs, a sprinkle of red pepper, extra garlic, mayonnaise, and lettuce. (G and G = grease and garden, i.e., mayo & lettuce.) An Indy includes link sausage, pepperoni, onion, sauce, and cheese, hot and heavy. A Flaming Turkey Bone (which contains no turkey and no bones and is not served on fire) includes chicken breast, tomato sauce, cheese, onions, extra hot and heavy, plus "spontaneous combustion" (double-X hot sauce).

Ted's Jumbo Red Hots

2312 Sheridan Dr.   716-834-6287
Tonawanda, NY   LD | $

Ted's began as a horse-drawn hot dog cart in Buffalo in the 1920s. It became a permanently anchored hot dog stand under the Peace Bridge in 1927, and opened as a bigger store on Sheridan Drive in 1948. There are now eight Ted's in western New York, and one in Tempe, Arizona; but the one to which we always want to return is Ted's of Tonawanda. It has modernized since 1948 and is as clean and sanitary as any fast-food franchise, but the hot dogs are like no others. Sahlen's-brand franks, available regular length or foot-long, are cooked on a grate over charcoal that infuses each one with pungent smoke flavor and makes the skin get crackling-crisp. As they cook, the chef pokes them with a fork, slaps them, squeezes them, and otherwise abuses them, thus puncturing the skin and allowing them to suck in maximum smoky taste.

In consultation with a person behind the counter known as "the dresser," you decide how you want to garnish your tube steak. The stellar condiment is Ted's hot sauce, a peppery concoction laced with bits of relish. You also want onion rings, sold as tangled webs of crisp fried batter and limp onion. To accompany a foot-long and a basket of o-rings, the beverage of choice in these parts is loganberry juice, which is a kind of *grand cru* Kool-Aid.

Texas Chili

8 S. Main St.	914-937-0840
Port Chester, NY	BLD | $

Although Texas Chili is neat, clean, and well lit, it delivers all the funky soul you expect in a chili-dog joint. Opened in 2009 by two partners who had worked down the street at the legendary greasy spoon Hubba (p. 110), it has a three-meal-a-day menu on which nearly everything, from omelets at dawn to wieners at 4 A.M. on Saturday night, features chili. It is a beanless ground-beef brew glistening with oil, so peppery that it is not listed on the menu as a stand-alone (although serious chiliheads do get it solo), that makes a brilliant complement for the little tube steaks that are split and grilled until their edges get crusty. Atop the chili on the hot dog, chopped onions are the standard garnish: crisp, cool and refreshing, a marvelous counterbalance for the chili dog, doing what onions so seldom do—uphold the invigorating banner of an actual vegetable. It is traditional for hot dogs in this area to be served in little, no-account white-bread buns; Texas Chili grills its buns in butter (or maybe buttery-flavored grease), adding a note of unctuous luxe to a package that is unctuous in so many other ways.

While a full array of soda pop is available to drink, the connoisseur's choice is what's known here as Texas water: plain water turned pink by a slight infusion of Hawaiian Punch.

Tino's

2410 Arthur Ave.	718-733-9879
Bronx, NY	L | $

The Bronx originally was part of Westchester County, so it makes sense that when you go to Tino's for a chicken parm hero, you'll hear some fellow eaters refer to it by its Westchester moniker, a wedge. Whatever you call it, this mighty log of lunch is authoritative. First, there's the bread. Many sandwiches of chicken Parmigiana (and eggplant Parmigiana) are built upon a toasted loaf. Not that there's anything wrong with that, but all too often toasting is simply a way of disguising a stale or inferior length of bread. Tino's doesn't toast, but if you want that crunch, get yours on a crisp-crusted Italian roll that is impeccably fresh and Arthur-Avenue soulful. Soft club rolls also are available. Then there's the chicken itself, a cutlet that's lightly breaded and glazed with fantastic sauce that tastes like it's really made from tomatoes, all of this crowned with creamy-fresh mozzarella. We nominate Tino's handsome hunk as King of Hot Italian Sandwiches.

Walter's

937 Palmer Ave.   No phone
Mamaroneck, NY   L | $

Even if you have another weenie you love more, you cannot deny that Walter's belongs on any list of America's top dogs. Each begins as a beef-pork-veal frank made exclusively for Walter's, as they have been since 1919. The frank is bisected lengthwise and cooked on a grill coated with a secret-formula sauce. It's a buttery sauce with an ineffable spice that insinuates flavor into the cut surface of the weenie and gives it a faint crunch that is a joy to bite, especially inside a soft bun that has been toasted on an adjacent grill. Some customers ask for their hot dog well-done and therefore more crisp than usual (not a bad idea) and others get a double dog (in our opinion, an imbalance of dog and bun), but whichever way you like it, please have it with mustard. It is Walter's own mustard, grainy and dotted with pickle bits. To drink? Walter's makes a fine malted milk shake.

The place is a vernacular-architecture hoot, designed to evoke a pagoda, complete with lanterns and a sign that spells out WALTER'S in letters that look vaguely like Chinese brushstrokes from a distance but turn out to be images of hot dogs strung together. On a pleasant day, you can dine in a grove of picnic tables suited to devouring multiple hot dogs and drinking excellent malts (or egg creams); but in inclement weather, you are on your own. Walter's has no inside seats.

Pennsylvania

Center City Pretzel Co.

816-18 Washington Ave.   215-463-5664
Philadelphia, PA $

Bad-tasting water = good-tasting food. There is no other good explanation for the excellence of Philadelphia soft pretzels.

We reached that conclusion when the Roadfood.com team went to Philadelphia on a cheesesteak-eating expedition several years ago. Between sandwiches, we cleansed our palates at Rita's Water Ice stand with cups of finely shaved ice saturated with bright red cherry syrup that was dotted with little bits of fruit. It was especially delicious (was that because of the water from which it was made?), so good that we all ate fast enough to suffer serious brain-freeze.

The other break in our cheesesteak hunt was at Center City Pretzel Company, where we picked up a half-dozen freshly made soft pretzels. By this point in the day, we had all eaten enough cheesesteaks that appetite was becoming a distant memory. But the aroma, then the taste, of these big soft pretzels proved irresistible. There is a brackish tang to the flavor of the pretzel, especially to its tan skin, that puts it a cut above pretzels from any other city. If it's morning when you get one—or, preferably, a bag of several—it likely will still be oven-warm, the absolute freshness bold-facing its dense, chewy nature. Some pretzel-lovers like to have a little mustard as a condiment. As far as we're concerned, these big softies need nothing to attain street-food perfection.

Chink's

6030 Torresdale Ave.   215-535-9405
Philadelphia, PA   LD | $

Chink's is a old-fashioned neighborhood cheesesteak shop staffed by young women who delight in what they do, which includes building banana splits supreme and blending chocolate milk shakes thick enough that trying to suck one up a straw will cause serious hollows in your cheeks.

The open kitchen—little more than a griddle—is up front at a picture window that allows pedestrians to stop and watch the cooks hack up frying meat, scoot around sizzling onions, layer on slices of cheese, then hoist the jumble into a long, chewy, toasty-edged roll. The result: a well-balanced, buttery confluence of meat and dairy and weeping sweet onion that welcomes a spill of sharp yellow peppers and pickle chips. It arrives not on a plate but on a square of butcher paper.

Chink's interior is vintage Americana: old wooden booths and a short five-stool counter. A sign up front reads, "Please do not lean on the counter. This is our work space. Thank you."

DeLuca's

2015 Penn Ave.   412-566-2195
Pittsburgh, PA   BL | $

If you need a really satisfying breakfast in Pittsburgh, we recommend a visit to DeLuca's. Located in the Strip District (an eater's paradise by any measure), this fine storefront café serves mighty morning meals. There are frittatas, pumpkin pancakes, extra-large egg sandwiches, and a showstopper called mixed grill: sausage or ham sizzled with a huge heap of peppers, onions, tomatoes, mushrooms, and zucchini, crowned with a couple of eggs (the eggs are optional) and sided by hunky home-fried potatoes and a couple of slabs of toast. Among the available varieties of toast are an aromatic cinnamon-raisin, rye, wheat, and white.

"Ordinary" omelets are jumbo, too, stuffed with hunks of fresh vegetables and/or your breakfast meat of choice. For many visitors, DeLuca's is an opportunity to indulge in one of the really outrageous breakfast items, such as the chocolate chip hotcake sundae, which is a stack of pancakes chockablock with melted and melting chocolate chips, topped with ice cream and strawberries. We are especially fond of blueberry French toast made with that sweet-smelling raisin bread.

DeLuca's is open for lunch as well as breakfast, with a nice menu of hamburgers, cold-cut hoagies, and such square meals as meat loaf or pork chops with potatoes. Milk shakes are served in silver beakers . . . and topped with a dab of whipped cream.

Expect to wait for a seat at peak mealtime hours, especially on weekends, when Pittsburghers throng to the Strip on a kind of eaters' holiday. For us, the choice place in DeLuca's is at the counter with a good view of the short-order chefs flipping eggs and hotcakes at lightning speed.

Dutch Kitchen

433 S. Lehigh Ave.   570-874-3265

Frackville, PA   BLD | $

The Dutch Kitchen is really convenient. At Exit 124B off I-81, it always seems to be just where we need it to be when hunger strikes south of the I-80 junction. It is a big, friendly place, a former dining car (still intact inside) to which has been added a whole dining room that is decorated to the max with country crafts, speckleware, homily plaques for kitchen walls, and souvenirs of Pennsylvania.

As for the food, it is wonderful. Look at the salad bar, which goes beyond the ordinary to include an effulgent array of vegetables that reflect co-owner Jennifer Levkulic's Pennsylvania Dutch ancestry. Here are pickled beets, seriously dark apple butter, chow-chow, and beans to augment your meal of real daily-roasted turkey, hearty bread filling, *genuine* mashed potatoes (with an occasional reassuring lump in the smooth, swirly spuds), and gravy.

The Dutch Kitchen is a traditional diner, and it is possible to stop here for bacon and eggs in the morning or a nice hamburger or sandwich at lunch, but we always are drawn to such hearty traditional dishes as smoked pork chops, turkey croquettes, and a stupendously good pot pie with homemade noodles, chicken and turkey, potatoes and vegetables. One of our favorite daily specials is a stew of ham, cabbage, and potato sided by a block of brown-top corn bread nearly as sweet as cake. For dessert, we like shoofly pie—a ribbon of molasses filling topped with a crumbly top—or shoofly cake, which is a different iteration of similar ingredients to become a dark spice cake that is a supreme coffee companion and is much easier to eat while driving.

Enrico Biscotti

2022 Penn Ave.   412-281-2602
Pittsburgh, PA   BLD | $

One of the fringe benefits of coffee's ascendance in recent years is the discovery of biscotti, the firm, twice-baked Italian cookie that dunks so well. Alas, like coffee itself, there are a lot of lame versions around. We didn't even think we liked them . . . until we visited Enrico Biscotti Company in Pittsburgh's historic Strip District. Here baker Larry Lagattuta makes them by hand using the finest ingredients, turning out such flavors as anise-almond, apricot-hazelnut, and pineapple-vanilla with white chocolate. They are firm enough that you'd never call them soft, but they do offer a tooth-pleasing resistance completely different from the desiccated, cellophane-wrapped variety.

Attached to the bakery is a European-style café where you can eat individual-size brick-oven pizza, *torta rustica* (quiche), soup, or a "big fat salad." Here, too, is the espresso machine, as well as a handful of tables both inside and outdoors in a sort of makeshift patio along the sidewalk. We know of no nicer place to start the day with strong coffee and biscotti, or to have a leisurely lunch of expertly made true Italian food. Bring your own wine.

The Family Diner

302 Main St.   717-443-8797
White Haven, PA   BLD | $

Interstate 80 through Pennsylvania is a challenging route for people who like to eat. There are truck stops and restaurants at nearly every exit, but most are mediocre. That is why we like The Family Diner, just a few minutes' detour from the highway. There is something for everyone in this friendly place, from blue-plate liver 'n' onions or meat loaf and mashed potatoes to one spectacular super-duper burger with the works to which the menu attributes a "college degree."

As in so many diners, breakfast is deeply satisfying, served here from dawn until the middle of the afternoon. The pancakes, while not what you'd call elegant, are colossal, so wide that they nearly eclipse the plate on which they're served. To add even more avoirdupois to this seriously high-caloric feast, you can get them blanketed with gooey, supersweet hot apple or blueberry topping. A real Pennsylvania favorite, creamed chipped beef, comes sided by hearty home fries or bite-size potato cakes. Eggs are available any way (including soft-boiled and poached) with a choice of bacon, ham, sausage, pork roll, or scrapple. Scrapple, as any true Pennsylvanian can tell you, is a local passion—thin slices from a loaf of ground pork and cornmeal that are sizzled in a pan until crisp.

Famous 4th Street Deli

700 S. 4th St.   215-922-3274
Philadelphia, PA   LD | $$

Since it opened in 1923, the Famous 4th Street Deli has had its ups and downs, but today it is a consummate kosher-style eatery: glass cases up front full of smoked fish, wrinkly salamis hanging from the ceiling, colossal sandwiches of cured meat, and such classic Jewish fare as matzoh ball soup, noodle kugel, and stuffed cabbage drenched in sweet-and-sour gravy.

Sinatra and Sammy Davis Jr. croon on the sound system in the background. A plate arrives with crisp coleslaw and a half-sour pickle. Dr. Brown's soda comes in a can along with an immense tumbler full of ice. And finally—ta-da!—the sandwich arrives. You can have it regular-size, which is large, or zaftig, meaning comically so. We love the pastrami, which is only modestly spiced even at its blackened edges. It is rich enough to feel like wanton indulgence, but not obscenely fatty.

Famous 4th cookies, which we described in the original *Goodfood* guidebook as "rich and toasty, big round beauties filled with large chips and nutmeats, an ideal balance between crispness and chew," are as good as ever, available in three basic forms: chocolate chip, walnut chocolate chip, and oatmeal raisin.

While not cloyingly so, the decor truly is nostalgic: an ancient black-and-white tiny-tile floor, vintage mirrored cabinets at the back of the dining area, and walls crowded with press accolades and pictures of the still-famous and long-forgotten personages who have eaten here.

Geno's

1219 S. 9th St.   215-389-0659
Philadelphia, PA   LD | $

Whichever of Philadelphia's cheesesteak shops we happen to consider our favorite at any particular time, we have always appreciated Geno's classicism. This is the cheesesteak as it originally was served (by Pat's, virtually across the street). It seems that here the meat is cut a little thicker than at other places (although it's still thin enough to be cooked through almost instantly when it hits the griddle), the rolls are sturdy, and the cheese choice includes provolone, American, or Whiz. Open into the wee hours of the morning, Geno's is a magnet for night owls who eat standing under carnival-colored neon, leaning forward at the waist so shreds of beef that fall from the sandwich hit the sidewalk rather than their shoes.

Be sure to order your steak properly: First give your choice of cheese, then say the word "with" or "without," indicating your decision on whether or not you want onions. In other words, "Whiz without" means a cheesesteak made with Cheez Whiz but no onions. Red sauce is another option, but for most aficionados, sauce is not an essential cheesesteak ingredient. On the other hand, you must have fries—or cheese fries—on the side.

Glider Diner

890 Providence Rd.   570-343-8036
Scranton, PA   Always open | $

Named because it originally was built from the packing crates that held a glider airplane, the wood-sided Glider Diner was replaced by a shiny silver Mountain View dining car in 1952. A large annex known as the Fireside Lounge was added in the early 1960s, but for blue-plate traditionalists, the old silver streamliner is the place to be. Here breakfast is served round the clock, and lunch and supper specialties include Gliderburgers and milk shakes and comforting hot sandwiches of roast beef, meat loaf, Virginia ham, and turkey.

Roadfood stalwarts Bruce Bilmes and Sue Boyle clued us in to the real specialty of the house, listed on the menu as *porketta* and available either in a toasted hard roll or as the centerpiece of a hot platter, surrounded by slices of white bread, accompanied by mashed potatoes and blanketed with gravy. Porketta is well-seasoned roast pork, sliced thin and dripping moisture: delish!

For dessert, there are fruit and cream pies, but we never can resist the specialty old diner cooks know as "cat's eye"—tapioca pudding.

Jimmy's Hot Dogs

2555 Nazareth Rd.   610-258-7545
Easton, PA   LD | $

We're not cheapskates, but we must confess that there is something irresistibly alluring about a decent meal that costs considerably less than coffee at Starbuck's. Maybe *decent* isn't the exact right term to describe what's served at Jimmy's Hot Dogs, for these skinless dogs are sinful little steamers—piggy and juicy and priced under one dollar each. This means you can have two hot dogs, dressed, of course, the Jimmy's way, with mustard, onions, and pickle spears, along with a bag of potato chips and a Coke or chocolate milk for under three dollars. If you've got a big appetite, you might want three or four hot dogs; but even if you and a friend indulged in four apiece, you could still walk out with change from a ten-dollar bill.

Want something other than a hot dog and chips? Too bad, because that is the extent of Jimmy's menu. There is no extra charge to kibitz with members of the Apostopoulos family, who have run the joint, without changing a thing, for decades . . . and who have perfected the art of freezing and overnight-shipping their beloved weenies to ex-Eastonites desperate for a taste of home.

Note: There are no seats. Business is take-out only.

Jim's Steaks

400 South St.   215-928-1911
Philadelphia, PA   LD | $

Opened in 1939, Jim's is Philadelphia's second-oldest cheesesteak shop (after Pat's), and it's definitely the sharpest looking with its deco black-and-white tile decor.

It's a very popular place, which is a good thing, because your wait in line will provide ample time for deciding how you like your steak garnished— "wit" or "witout" (onions)—and whether you want the standard Cheez Whiz or optional American or provolone. The wait in line also takes you past the back of the store, where an automatic slicer produces heaps of rosy-colored beef ready to be fried.

The steaks are made by hacking up the meat on the grill (with onions, preferably!) so it becomes a kind of onion-flavored steak hash. If you get sliced cheese, it is layered in the roll before the meat and melts underneath it. Whiz is ladled atop the meat. Pizza sauce and peppers are optional condiments. The bread is excellent, the fried onions are appropriately slippery, and the optional hot peppers are breathtaking. Have a Dr. Brown's soda on the side, and you've got a cheap-eats meal to remember.

Johnny's Hots

1234 Delaware Ave.   215-423-2280
Philadelphia, PA   BL | $

The name of this restaurant refers to a tube steak that is similar to a half-smoke or a Georgia hot: finely ground pork and plenty of spice packed into a taut casing. While it is not brutally hot, your tongue will glow; and if you like that glow, get your hot with hots, the latter being long hot peppers with an exclamatory punch. Johnny's is known for top-ranked cheesesteaks and breakfast sandwiches that include eggs along with the hot sausage, but the one item that most deserves attention if you are a devotee of recherché local taste is what wiseacres know as Philly surf 'n' turf: a hot dog and fish cake sandwich. Yup, snugged into a single sturdy roll is a split hot dog (or hot sausage, if you prefer) with a fish cake smooshed right on top of it. We got ours with that ever-rarer local condiment, pepper hash. The hash is wonderful. The fish cake and wiener combo may be more of an acquired taste.

Located on the Fishtown waterfront, Johnny's has no indoor dining room or tables and chairs. Place your order and pay for it at one window, pick it up at a window a couple of yards to the right, then marshal the meal on one of the metal counters provided at chest level against the shop's stone block wall and on the pillars in front. When finished—ten, fifteen minutes at most—gather the crumbs in the papers in which the food was wrapped, dispose your refuse in a garbage can, and drive away.

John's Roast Pork

14 E. Snyder Ave.   215-463-1951
Philadelphia, PA   BL Mon-Fri | $

John's roast pork sandwich is one of Philadelphia's culinary treasures, made from "Pop Pop's original recipe," cooked and boned on premises. The slices of pale, sweet meat are forked from a drippy trough and piled into a superb Carangi Bakery seeded roll, then preferably supplemented by clumps of spinach sautéed in olive oil with plenty of garlic. While the tonic shot of spinach is a welcome addition, we recommend forgoing optional cheese toppings, which only detract from the essential piggy pleasure of the pork itself.

John's cheesesteak, which is ordered from a separate station at the walk-up counter, also is one of the city's best. John Bucci, whose family started the place, explains why he thinks the steaks are so good: "When you order one, there is nothing on the grill. We start clean," he says. "Onions are not precooked; every steak is made for the person who orders it. I am a cheese fanatic. We put five slices on every sandwich, eight if you order extra." There is so much meat in a John's sandwich that the server tears out some of the roll's soft insides to make room for it. The onions are sweet, the beef juicy, the cheese abundant, the roll fresh: Is there a better formula for cheesesteak perfection?

John's is a working person's eatery, open only Monday through Friday for breakfast and for lunch. (The shipyard personnel who were its original clientele in 1930 all went home for dinner.) Heavy industry no longer dominates the neighborhood, which has become a Monopoly board of big box stores, strip malls, and discount warehouses that dwarf the modest sandwich shop and its patio picnic tables. There is no indoor dining, but heat lamps and shutters are set up for cold weather.

Jo Jo's

110 24th St.
Pittsburgh, PA

412-261-0280
Midnight to noon | $

A word of warning about Jo Jo's hours: Although its motto is "Breakfast Served All Day, Every Day," what that means here in Pittsburgh's produce market is that it is open from midnight until noon. The schedule is made to jibe with that of truck drivers who haul produce up from the South, arriving in the wee hours. They unload their reefers, then come for the Jo Jo Special, an impossibly overstuffed three-egg omelet containing peppers, onions, mushrooms, provolone and American cheese, bacon and/or sausage and/or ham, plus a spatula-load of superb hot fried potatoes. Unless you have the appetite of Gargantua, consider this plateload a meal for two. French fries are popular, too, ordered on the side of a meat loaf sandwich in lieu of home fries, and frequently served underneath a blanket of dark brown gravy.

Jo Jo's is located at the far end of Pittsburgh's colorful Strip District (where the all-night produce market thrives), and it gets mighty colorful at the counter and long tables of this former gas-station café about 2 A.M. As the music clubs close and truckers arrive to conduct business at the produce terminal a few blocks away, the late and early shifts come together to eat huge breakfast omelets cooked in individual skillets and served with pre-buttered slabs of Italian toast.

While the majority of Jo Jo's customers are sober, responsible folks who simply happen to be out late at night, chances are good you will meet a handful of, shall we say, eccentric types who drink too much. One superfan of the big omelet very carefully and precisely explained that he comes to the restaurant every morning about four for the purpose of drinking a Jo Jo omelet after eating beer all night.

Leo's

1403 Chester Pike
Folcroft, PA

610-586-1199
LD | $

A full-size Leo's cheesesteak is comically huge, more than enough for two normal appetites. A good half-yard of excellent Amoroso Bakery bread is split open and loaded with pounds of sliced-thin beef that has been sizzled and trowel-cut on the griddle, interlaced with caramelized onions, and saturated with melted cheese. Steaks are available without cheese, as hoagies (meaning lettuce and tomato added), as well as in the configuration known as a pizza steak, with sauce; but there is no improving on the classic configuration of meat and cheese and onions, plus a scattering of peppers and pickles to add a bit of sparkle.

Leo's offers no indoor seating. It's just a counter where you place your order and can watch the grill man cook it. Picnic tables are provided outside.

Longacre's Modern Dairy Bar

1445 Route 100
Barto, PA

610-845-7551
BLD (closed Sun) | $

The rolling land of eastern Pennsylvania, dotted as it is with black-and-white bossies roaming farm fields, is a perfect appetizer for one of Longacre's excellent milk shakes or malts, or an old-fashioned ice cream soda in a tall tulip glass. If you need an ice cream dish that is more substantial, choose a sundae made from your choice of over a dozen flavors of ice cream and nearly two dozen toppings including the usual fudge and marshmallow and butterscotch as well as such old-time fountain oddities as wet maple walnut and crushed cherries. The supreme such concoction is known as the Longacre Special (a.k.a. Garbage Sundae) and features ten scoops of ice cream, ten toppings, whipped cream, and a cherry, all served in a thirty-two-ounce goblet.

It is also possible to come to Longacre's for a handy-sized hamburger or hot dog, accompanied, of course, by a cherry Coke, vanilla coke, or Hadacol (that's a Coke and root beer combo).

We like the fact that Longacre's little eating area—a short counter and a handful of booths and tables (plus picnic tables outside)—opens at 7:30 A.M., a time when most ordinary customers come for coffee and an egg sandwich. But the waitress assured us that it is not uncommon for the doors to open at dawn for customers who order up a cookie dough sundae or a CMP (chocolate marshmallow peanut sundae) for breakfast. Humankind's fundamental need for excellent ice cream is a craving that cannot be controlled by the hands of a clock.

Lorenzo's Pizza

900 Christian St.
Philadelphia, PA

215-922-2540
LD | $

Located on a corner near the Italian Market, Lorenzo's is a real neighborhood place with little of the tourist traffic that finds the more famous market eateries. Its cheesesteaks are superb, made from frozen sheets of meat, which is not really a bad thing. After all, we are not talking about prime beef here.

Anyway, the frozen sheets get thrown onto the grill along with a pile of raw onions. As the meat and onions sizzle together, the chef hacks away at them with a spatula, winding up with a hodgepodge of meat and soft-cooked onions. The aromatic combo is shaped into an oval about the length of the Italian bread for which it's destined, and the oval is generously dolloped with molten Cheez Whiz. The cheese is insinuated into the hash, then the lengthwise-sliced bread is used to shovel up the whole mess and finally enclose it. We like this sandwich plenty; our Roadfood.com colleague Stephen Rushmore declared it the cheesiest steak in the city.

Mama's

426 Belmont Ave.	610-664-4757
Bala Cynwyd, PA	LD | $

Although the cheesesteak was invented in the hubbub of Philadelphia's Italian Market, the best one we've ever eaten is far from the urban core in the suburb of Bala Cynwyd. In fact, the cheesesteak made at Mama's just may be too good. Although the place is a modest pizza parlor and sandwich shop, one local we know contends that Mama's cooking is too masterly and that its refined cheesesteak defies the proletarian nature of a street-food sandwich most commonly made from stringy beef and Cheez Whiz. Okay, then, let's call this the über-cheesesteak.

Chef Paul Castellucci's beef is thin-sliced, lean, and scarlet, hitting the hot griddle in clumps that get hacked up with a trowel as they brown. He then applies a great mound of what looks like shredded mozzarella but is in fact a proprietary mix that, incredibly, does not stick to the hot iron surface. The beef and cheese are worked over so thoroughly that the cheese nearly disappears into the finished product, but its luxury saturates every bite. The onions are not cooked on the grill amongst the shreds of beef, which is the customary way steak chefs do it. Instead, Castellucci sautés them separately to the exact point where they tip from sharp to sweet and crisp to limp. They are added after the loose log of meat and cheese is hoisted from the griddle into the jaws of a length of muscular Italian bread. Long hot peppers, roasted in Mama's pizza oven, add brilliant red and jade-green hues as well as hot sparkle to the earthy combo.

Marrone's Cafe

31 W. Main St.   570-276-6407

Girardville, PA   LD | $

Pennsylvania has a pizza culture unlike any other place. There's Philadelphia, of course, with many excellent examples of classic Neapolitan-American thin-crust pie; and there is Old Forge, outside of Scranton, where the pizzas are thick-crusted and rectangular, available with toppings that range from bacon and eggs in the morning to Monterey Jack cheese and meatballs to Polish pizza with kielbasa and onion topping.

Marrone's of Girardville, down in Schuylkill County, serves its own unique variation of Old Forge pizza. Presented on a thin sheet of paper in a metal pan, it is rectangular with a lightweight crust that is about a half-inch thick and crisp around the edges but chewy-bready toward the middle. Most regular pizza toppings are available in addition to the gobs of cheese that are standard; and on the side comes a plastic cup full of bright-red, crushed-pepper hot sauce. A plastic spoon is provided to spread the sauce atop the pizza; and it is a brilliant addition. The pizza is mild-mannered; the sauce packs a punch. What a nice duet!

Marrone's is a seventy-plus-year-old brick-front tavern where many people come only to drink in the bar next to the dining room. The ideal beverage for its distinctive pizza is a pitcher of locally brewed Yuengling beer, known here in coal country as Pottsville Punch.

Original Hot Dog Shop

3901 Forbes Ave.   412-621-7388 or 687-8327 for delivery

Pittsburgh, PA   LD (late night) | $

The Original Hot Dog Shop has quite a large menu, including pizza, hoagies, fish sandwiches, and hamburgers; but if the name of the place doesn't clue you in to what's good, the view behind the counter will. There on a broad grill are row upon row of lovely hot dogs—pale pink ones barely warm and darker ones cooked through and ready to be bunned, as well as a formation of deep red all-beef kosher dogs. Regular or all-beef, these are fine franks with a seriously meaty flavor, available plain or gooped with cheese or in a "Super" configuration with cheese and bacon, and with a full array of condiments that include ketchup, mustard, relish, onion, pickle, chili, mayo, and kraut.

On the side of whatever hot dog suits your taste, you must get French fries. Big O fries are legendary: crisp and dark gold with a clean flavor and a wicked crunch that makes them such a good companion for just about any sandwich. Even a small order is a substantial dish. Although cheese for dipping is available, as are gravy, hot sauce, and ranch dressing, these exquisite potatoes want only a sprinkle of salt.

Aside from great fast food and post-midnight hours, one reason Pittsburghers are so fond of the Original Hot Dog Shop is that it can trace its heritage back to the Original Famous Sandwich Shop, where the foot-long hot dog was introduced in 1928. Syd Simon, who opened the Original Hot Dog Shop in 1960, worked for fifteen years at the old Famous.

Pat's King of Steaks

1237 E. Passyunk Ave.   215-468-1546
Philadelphia, PA   Always open | $

Street-food historians believe that Pat Olivieri invented the cheesesteak in Philadelphia in 1930. His family continues to operate the restaurant he began, and while aficionados of the cheesesteak enjoy debating the merits of the city's many cheesesteak restaurants (some operated by renegades from Pat's own family), there is no denying the absolute authenticity of Pat's sandwich, which is oily, salty, and meaty, i.e., everything nutrition prigs dislike. Thin flaps of less-than-prime beef are sizzled on a grill alongside onions and hefted into a roll (with or without some of those onions), then a trowel of melted Cheez Whiz is dripped on top. Peppers, mushrooms, pizza sauce, and extra cheese are all extra-cost options; and if you wish to dude it up further, there are big glass jars with hot sauce and peppers near the take-out windows.

The combination of plebeian ingredients transcends its lowly status and becomes something that is certainly not aristocratic, but carries a distinction all its own. Side your sandwich with a cup full of cheese fries (French fries blanketed with more of that melted Whiz), and eat standing up on the sidewalk under harsh lights. Observe the splattered hot sauce and dropped and crushed French fries underfoot. Listen to the rumble of trucks going past on their way to or from the Italian Market. Smell the mingling of cheap aftershave lotion and fancy fragrances on customers in line—both aromas overwhelmed, as the line approaches the take-out window, by the powerhouse aroma of steak and onions sizzling on a hot grill.

People's Restaurant

140 W. Main St.
New Holland, PA

717-354-2276
BLD Sun–Fri | $$

People's Restaurant is a civilized café on Main Street in a town where locals and tourists come for home-style food. Accommodations include tables with upholstered chairs and a counter toward the middle of the restaurant where townsfolk gather and exchange sections of the newspaper as they discuss current events.

Suppers include such local entrees as fresh-roasted pork with sauerkraut, smoked country ham steak, and lengths of light-bodied Lancaster sausage; and there are such all-American meals as tuna-noodle casserole and fried chicken. Alongside main courses, you choose from an inviting list of freshly prepared vegetables: whipped potatoes, Cheddar-macaroni salad, three-bean salad, pepper cabbage, etc. And dessert is a reminder of just how seriously Lancaster County takes its sweets. There are pies aplenty, including apricot crumb, coconut cream, French apple, strawberry Boston cream, shoofly (wet-bottom, of course), grasshopper, and peanut butter silk. Plus, there are always cakes, custards, and pudding.

Sunday is a great day to dine at People's if you don't mind crowds and a wait, for locals and visitors fill the place with the joy of family weekend dining. We also love coming when only a few regulars occupy the counter seats, very early in the morning, when we feast on either old-fashioned oatmeal or "baked oatmeal," which is like a coarse-textured bread pudding made from cooked oats and brown sugar. Another excellent breakfast, and a true mid-Atlantic specialty, is creamed chipped beef. This is the real stuff—spicy shreds of brined beef in a rich cream sauce, ladled over a plate of crusty fried potato disks. Of course, you can also get a dish of expertly crisped scrapple; and eggs are guaranteed to be from local hens.

Primanti Brothers

46 18th St.
Pittsburgh, PA

412-263-2142
Always open | $

If you like big sandwiches, you need to eat around Pittsburgh. In this brawny city, where the Big Mac was invented in 1968 by a local McDonald's franchisee, "the more the merrier" is the basic rule of sandwich-making. The city's longtime champion of huge sandwiches is Primanti Brothers, a raucous open-all-night beer-and-sandwich joint that throbs with the play-by-play broadcast of whatever local team is in action. Opened in 1933, the original Primanti's down in the Strip District is a city shrine where walls are painted with caricatures of native sons who range from Andy Warhol to Mr. Rogers and from Tom Mix to Roberto Clemente. (There are three other Primanti Brothers around town; none are open round the clock.)

The astonishing sandwiches were originally designed for truckers who hauled produce to the nearby wholesale market. While their trucks were being unloaded, they dashed over to Primanti Brothers with a big appetite but little time to eat a dagwood, slaw, and potatoes separately. The solution was to load hot French fries directly into the sandwich atop the customer's meat of choice, then top the fries with Pittsburgh-style (no mayo) coleslaw and a few slices of tomato. The sandwiches are assembled at the grill behind the bar at the speed of light, so when the sandwich is delivered, the fries and grilled meats are still steaming hot, the slaw and tomato cool.

Weird as this combination sounds, the regulars at Primanti's tables assert that such combinations as double-egg and pastrami (both sizzled on the grill) or hot sausage and cheese simply do not taste right without a layer of crisp-fried potatoes and another of slaw. The barely hoistable meal is presented wrapped in butcher paper so that when appetite flags, the paper's edges can be gathered like a drop cloth to pick up the spillage.

Robert Wholey & Co.

1501 Penn Ave.   412-391-3737
Pittsburgh, PA   LD | $

Located in Pittsburgh's appetite-inducing Strip District, Robert Wholey & Co. seems more like a culinary amusement park than a mere store. It has a toy train running around and singing mechanical pigs to amuse children and an extensive kitchenware department to amuse recipe-obsessed adults.

Once strictly a wholesale fish market, Wholey now carries a vast inventory of foodstuffs that range from baked ham by the haunch (or sliced super-thin, a.k.a chipped, the way Pittsburghers like it) to sides of tuna that are cut into steaks to order. For those of us who demand immediate gratification, there are a few makeshift tables for sit-down meals at the end of a cooked-food line, and more tables upstairs in the Pittsburgh Room. While you can order crab cakes, shrimp, even chicken, the meal most people come to eat is a fish sandwich on a tender, butter-rich bun. Whiting and cod both are available, the king of sandwiches being the Wholey Whaler: a pound of whiting sizzled crisp in the bubbling fry kettles toward the front. If that's not enough to sate you, simply ask the staff to fry (or broil) as much fish as you want to eat and they will charge you by the pound.

Salerno's Café

139 Moosic Rd.   570-457-2117

Old Forge, PA   LD | $$

Salerno's is a tavern where many people come only to drink. We recommend a visit for Old Forge pizza, a style of pie unique to this area around Scranton. Most of the Old Forge pies are squared off rather than round, airy-crusted, and topped with sweet marinara sauce and a mild blend of Italian and American cheese. It's an easy-to-eat pizza, simple and friendly.

At lunch you can only get red pizza, which is a twelve-slice pie big enough for two healthy appetites. At dinner, Salerno's better-known creation is a white pizza—a double-cruster made with a blend of several cheeses between the crusts.

There is a broad menu beyond pizza in this neighborhood tavern: sausage and peppers, chicken Parmesan sub sandwiches, *pasta e fagiole*. Many customers take their food at the bar, where they can knock back draft beers and watch the wall-mounted TV.

Steve's Prince of Steaks

7200 Bustleton Ave.   215-338-0985

Philadelphia, PA   LD | $

"The perfect balance of flavors and textures" is how Roadfood.com's Bruce Bilmes and Sue Boyle described the cheesesteak at Steve's Prince of Steaks in northeast Philadelphia. Unlike steak places that chop their meat into hash on the grill, Steve's slices it into flaps and sizzles the pieces in the traditional Italian Market way. The meat is not prime cut, that's for sure, but its flavor is a welcome, oily tsunami of beefy protein. Combine that with a load of Cheez Whiz and a heap of fried-soft sweet onions all piled into a chewy tube of fresh bread and you've got picture of cheesesteak perfection. It is presented on two sheets of wax paper, which helps to gather debris to be picked and plucked and popped in the mouth.

Here are the choices you'll need to make when you dine at Steve's: plain steak, cheesesteak, pizza steak (with sauce), or steak hoagie (with lettuce and tomato); normal weight or double meat. If you choose cheese: American, Whiz, provolone, or mozzarella. Extras? They include pizza sauce, mushrooms, and house-roasted hot red and green peppers. Dill pickles, relish, cherry peppers, yellow peppers, and hot sauce are available as garnishes. The French fry selection features cheese fries and pizza fries. Soft drinks include birch beer; or you can have a lovely chocolate soda, which is nothing but chocolate syrup mixed with seltzer water.

The dining experience is street food par excellence. Read the menus posted on the wall, place your order at two different windows (one for sandwiches, the other for fries and drinks, each paid for separately), then dine at the easy-wipe silver counter that runs along the wall.

Steve's has two other locations: at 2711 Comly Rd. in Philadelphia (215-677-8020) and 1617 East Lincoln Hwy. in Langhorne (215-943-4640).

Tony Luke's Old Philly Style Sandwiches

39 E. Oregon Ave.   215-551-5725
Philadelphia, PA   BLD | $

Tony Luke's is an old-time city haunt that provides convincing evidence of the Delaware Valley's sandwich hegemony. Mighty cheesesteaks, chicken parm and veal cutlets, hot sausage, cool hoagies, sandwiches of nothing but greens (spinach and/or broccoli rabe): all are exemplary. Best of all is roast pork. Is it moist? Yes, drippingly. Tender? Ridiculously so. Pure and piggy, lean but luxurious, glowing with garlic, the thin-sliced pork is piled in shreds and chunks inside a fine long hero roll and it would be delicious as is. But with broccoli rabe added, the combo becomes one of the earth's great sandwiches. The limp greens add a bitter twist that gives whole new meaning to the sweetness of the pork. Cheese and hot peppers are other available condiments; and while the former adds another layer of luxe and the latter a pleasing punch, we think the pork and broccoli rabe alone are simply impeccable.

Although Tony Luke's has spawned a small empire, eating at the original location is a pure Philly blast. It's a small place, the dining facilities little more than a covered patio with seating for maybe a few dozen people, the safe parking lot surrounded by razor wire (although many take-out customers just stop in the street). Walls are decorated in the traditional South Philly style, i.e., with autographed 8x10–inch pictures of celebrities. In this case, many of the glitterati are club boxers who apparently enjoy meals here between bouts. Service is brash and fast. When you place your order and pay for it, they take your name; and when the sandwich is ready, they call you to the counter, front and center.

Mid-South

Kentucky * North Carolina * Tennessee *

Virginia * West Virginia

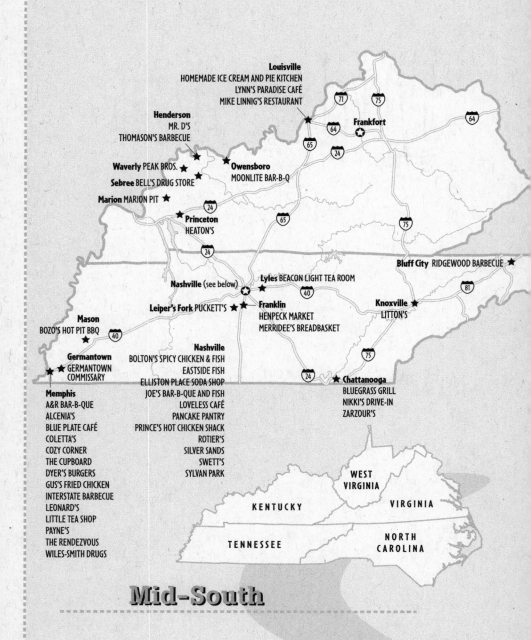

Louisville
HOMEMADE ICE CREAM AND PIE KITCHEN
LYNN'S PARADISE CAFÉ
MIKE LINNIG'S RESTAURANT

Frankfort

Henderson
MR. D'S
THOMASON'S BARBECUE

Waverly PEAK BROS.
Owensboro
Sebree BELL'S DRUG STORE
MOONLITE BAR-B-Q

Marion MARION PIT

Princeton
HEATON'S

Bluff City RIDGEWOOD BARBECUE

Nashville (see below)
Lyles BEACON LIGHT TEA ROOM

Leiper's Fork PUCKETT'S
Franklin
HENPECK MARKET
MERRIDEE'S BREADBASKET

Knoxville
LITTON'S

Mason
BOZO'S HOT PIT BBQ

Germantown
GERMANTOWN
COMMISSARY

Nashville
BOLTON'S SPICY CHICKEN & FISH
EASTSIDE FISH
ELLISTON PLACE SODA SHOP
JOE'S BAR-B-QUE AND FISH
LOVELESS CAFÉ
PANCAKE PANTRY
PRINCE'S HOT CHICKEN SHACK
ROTIER'S
SILVER SANDS
SWETT'S
SYLVAN PARK

Chattanooga
BLUEGRASS GRILL
NIKKI'S DRIVE-IN
ZARZOUR'S

Memphis
A&R BAR-B-QUE
ALCENIA'S
BLUE PLATE CAFÉ
COLETTA'S
COZY CORNER
THE CUPBOARD
DYER'S BURGERS
GUS'S FRIED CHICKEN
INTERSTATE BARBECUE
LEONARD'S
LITTLE TEA SHOP
PAYNE'S
THE RENDEZVOUS
WILES-SMITH DRUGS

WEST
VIRGINIA

KENTUCKY

VIRGINIA

TENNESSEE

NORTH
CAROLINA

Mid-South

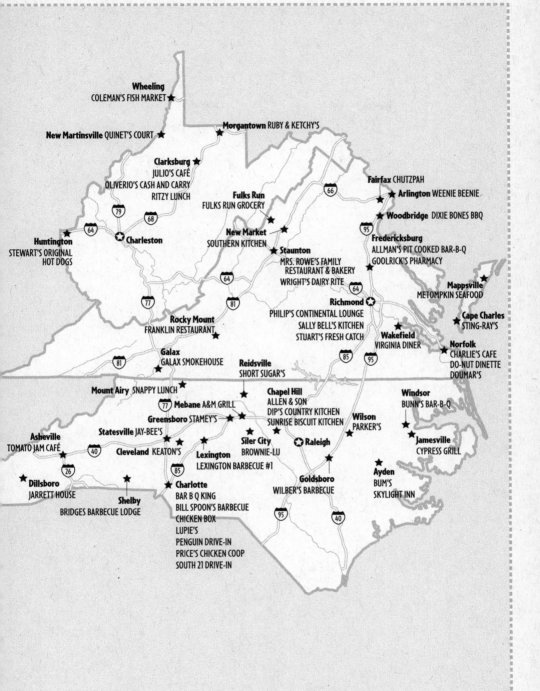

Wheeling
COLEMAN'S FISH MARKET ★

Morgantown RUBY & KETCHY'S

New Martinsville QUINET'S COURT ★

Clarksburg ★
JULIO'S CAFÉ
OLIVERIO'S CASH AND CARRY
RITZY LUNCH

Fairfax CHUTZPAH

★ **Arlington** WEENIE BEENIE

Fulks Run
FULKS RUN GROCERY

★ **Woodbridge** DIXIE BONES BBQ

New Market
SOUTHERN KITCHEN

Huntington
STEWART'S ORIGINAL
HOT DOGS

☆ **Charleston**

Staunton
MRS. ROWE'S FAMILY
RESTAURANT & BAKERY
WRIGHT'S DAIRY RITE

Fredericksburg
ALLMAN'S PIT COOKED BAR-B-Q
GOOLRICK'S PHARMACY

Mappsville
METOMPKIN SEAFOOD

Richmond ☆
PHILIP'S CONTINENTAL LOUNGE
SALLY BELL'S KITCHEN
STUART'S FRESH CATCH

Cape Charles
STING-RAY'S

Rocky Mount
FRANKLIN RESTAURANT

Wakefield
VIRGINIA DINER

Norfolk
CHARLIE'S CAFE
DO-NUT DINETTE
DOUMAR'S

Galax
GALAX SMOKEHOUSE

Reidsville
SHORT SUGAR'S

Mount Airy SNAPPY LUNCH

Mebane A&M GRILL

Chapel Hill
ALLEN & SON
DIP'S COUNTRY KITCHEN
SUNRISE BISCUIT KITCHEN

Windsor
BUNN'S BAR-B-Q

Greensboro STAMEY'S

Wilson
PARKER'S

Statesville JAY-BEE'S

Siler City
BROWNIE-LU

☆ **Raleigh**

Jamesville
CYPRESS GRILL

Asheville
TOMATO JAM CAFÉ

Cleveland KEATON'S

Lexington
LEXINGTON BARBECUE #1

Dillsboro
JARRETT HOUSE

Charlotte
BAR B Q KING
BILL SPOON'S BARBECUE
CHICKEN BOX
LUPIE'S
PENGUIN DRIVE-IN
PRICE'S CHICKEN COOP
SOUTH 21 DRIVE-IN

Goldsboro
WILBER'S BARBECUE

Ayden
BUM'S
SKYLIGHT INN

Shelby
BRIDGES BARBECUE LODGE

Bell's Drug Store

7107 Route 56   270-835-7544
Sebree, KY   L | $

As we drove into the small town of Sebree on a backroads eating tour in the company of Kentucky-food authority Louis Hatchett, Louis suddenly called out, "Orangeade!" We pulled into a parking place across from the sturdy old brick-facade building that is Bell's Drug Store. It is a working pharmacy with shelves of patent medicines and knickknacks for sale and a short soda fountain counter up front. Here is where milk shakes are whirled, sundaes and floats constructed, and cherry Cokes mixed to order.

We placed our orangeade orders and then a moment later, the soda jerk turned to us with a tragic look on his face. "We have run out of oranges," he lamented. But there was still a good supply of lemons, so we ordered lemonade and lemon ice and watched him go to work squeezing juice to make them. We ordered one lemonade made with an extra lemon (50¢ surcharge): what a mighty sweet/tart wallop! And the lemon ice was something different: nothing but fresh lemon juice poured over crushed ice and seasoned with a dash of salt. When the mixologist handed it to us, he pointed to a large sugar dispenser that had been filled with salt (and conspicuously so labeled!). "There's more salt if you'd like," he said. To our taste, it was just right as presented, the sprinkle of salinity enriching the pure citrus power.

Heaton's

619 Marion Rd.   270-345-2052
Princeton, KY   L | $

We admit to getting a slightly perverse, anti-snob pleasure from dining at a table opposite shelves of motor oil and other automotive necessities. Located in a service station, Heaton's resembles a thousand other quick-stop, quick-eat mini-marts around rural America. But the barbecue it serves is superb. It is real Kentucky 'cue, in this case pulled pork, served in a sandwich, large or small, as a plate with two side dishes, by the pound, and by the whole shoulder. It is hickory smoked, rugged-textured, and comes with a fascinating sauce that is slightly sweet with a bright citrus flavor.

Homemade Ice Cream and Pie Kitchen

2525 Bardstown Rd.   502-459-8184
Louisville, KY $

We arrived at the Louisville airport in the company of three sophisticated palates from New York; and before heading into Kentucky on a barbecue-eating expedition, we took them to one of America's great places to sate a sweet tooth. Our friends were flabbergasted by the variety of pies and cakes available, many of which are virtually unknown outside the South: chocolatey red velvet cake encased in thick white cream cheese frosting, chess pie that is purity itself, hummingbird cake that was actually not named because it would please a nectar-crazed avian. In addition to regular chess, which is little more than cream, sugar, and eggs, there are lemon chess and chocolate chess. And of course there are literally dozens of more universally known pies and cakes, including Key lime, lemon meringue, banana cream, apple, apple crunch, and Dutch apple with caramel.

Many of the handsome layer cakes come swirled with sweet-smelling buttercream frosting. A few of our favorite varieties include banana-pecan cake, coconut cake, mandarin orange cake with pineapple-filled whipped cream, and jam-spice cake with caramel frosting.

Because we visit Louisville for only short periods, coming to this little shop is inevitably frustrating. There is no way two people, or even five people, can sample a significant fraction of the lovely desserts available any one day. Nearly everything is sold by the slice as well as the whole cake, and dining tables are scattered about inside and on a front patio for drop-ins who require instant gratification.

Note: There are a handful of other Homemade Ice Cream and Pie Kitchens around Louisville.

Lynn's Paradise Café

984 Barret Ave.   502-583-3447
Louisville, KY   BLD | $

Lynn's Paradise Café is the most whimsical restaurant we know. The decor is wild and kitschy, featuring winners of the cafe's annual Ugly Lamp Contest; and the gift shop up front sells a panoply of useful appliances as well as silly souvenirs. For all its sense of fun, this is a place that serves some seriously good food. We love breakfast the most, from lovely local eggs with grits and biscuits on the side to bourbon-ball French toast and banana-split pancakes. There is also a good ol' plate of Kentucky country ham with eggs and warm Granny Smith apples. This is true country comfort food!

Not that we want to slight lunch and dinner. Mom's Meatloaf is a square-meal knockout made with marinara sauce, sided by real mashed potatoes and al dente lima beans. Louisville's own hot brown sandwich is built on sourdough bread, its turkey, bacon, and tomato slices fully gooped up under a mantle of sizzling broiled cheese. Hamburgers are lovely, available with good French fries or one of several side dishes such as creamy polenta, braised rosemary cabbage, crusty blocks of mac 'n' cheese, and grilled asparagus. Last visit, we relished a dinner of hot turkey, dressing, and cheese grits.

The beverage selection includes a "gigantic mimosa," and a "world famous Bloody Mary," made from Lynn's own mix and garnished with a skewer of peppers and olives.

Marion Pit

728 S. Main St.   270-965-3318
Marion, KY   LD | $

Marion Pit is open every day of the year except Christmas, Thanksgiving, New Year's Day, and Easter Day. Proprietor Jack Easley said that he usually cooks an especially large number of pork shoulders on Saturday because so many local churches purchase meat by the pound for Sunday suppers. At thirty-plus years in business, his is the oldest smokehouse around, and certainly the most unpretentious—a tiny hut on the outskirts of town with a few picnic tables for dining al fresco or inside a screened patio.

Place your order at a window in the small building to which hickory-cooked shoulders are brought from an adjoining cookhouse and readied for eating. Mr. Easley told us that he cooks his meat for seventeen hours, using no seasonings and no sauce whatever. The long roast at low temperatures results in pork that is unspeakably tender, so soft that it cannot be sliced because it would fall apart. You can buy it by the pound to go, by the sandwich, or by the plate (billed here as a "big pile of bar-b-q"). It is some of the best Q anywhere, served with a delicious sauce, the recipe for which is known only to Mr. Easley, his wife, and his son.

Mike Linnig's Restaurant

9308 Cane Run Rd.   502-937-9888
Louisville, KY   LD (closed Mon) | $$

Mike Linnig's opened some eighty years ago as a fruit and vegetable stand on the Linnig family farm. It is now a big restaurant with great picnic-style accommodations outside and cavernous dining rooms indoors. The menu includes just about every kind of seafood that can be fried, including sea scallops, crawfish, and salmon, but its highlights are such Indiana fish camp specialties as catfish, whitefish, and frog legs, all served in immense portions. We are especially fond of the spicy fish nuggets and the freshly breaded shrimp. The fish, the frog legs, the scallops, and the oysters have a seriously nice crunch to their crust, but are not otherwise memorable.

Onion rings are a specialty. They are big chunky things, extremely brittle and mostly crust with just a hint of onion flavor emanating from the slick ribbon within. By the way, the tartar sauce and cocktail sauce, while served in the sort of individual cups typical of institutional meals, are Mike Linnig's own recipe, and both are outstanding.

Among the beverage choices beyond bottled beer are iced tea (sweet or not), lemonade (which tastes a lot like the tea), and genuine Kool-Aid, listed on the menu as fruit punch.

Moonlite Bar-B-Q

2840 W. Parrish Ave.   270-684-8143
Owensboro, KY   LD | $$

There's not a lot of waitress contact at Moonlite Bar-B-Q, where everyone able to walk avails themselves of a spectacular buffet. But we have to say that the interaction we have had is a pleasure. On one delightful occasion, we arrived a good half-hour before the people we were joining. We were very hungry. We explained the situation and our waitress suggested we go fill some plates at the buffet and eat a while. "I'll have your plates cleaned and places set again, so when they arrive you can act like you haven't et yet."

Good plan, for a mere single trip to the Moonlite buffet doesn't provide nearly enough plate space to enjoy everything that needs to be tasted. The array of foods occupies one large room with salads and desserts on one side, vegetables and meats on the other. There is barbecued chicken, ribs, pulled pork, spectacularly succulent beef brisket, and even a pan of non-barbecued sliced country ham that is firm and salty as well as a tray of ready-made ham biscuits. And there is western Kentucky's favorite barbecue meat, mutton. Cooked until pot-roast tender, it is set out on the buffet two ways: chopped and pulled. Chopped mutton is pulverized to nothing but flavor: tangy lamb and wood smoke in a bold duet. The pulled version is a textural amusement park—rugged and chunky with a lot of hard outside crust among soft, juicy chunks of interior meat. Apply your own sauce at the table from the pitchers the waitress brings. One is a dark orange emulsion with gentle vinegar-tomato zest; the other is known as "mutton dip," an unctuous gravy that is used to baste the mutton as it cooks. For those who need heat, Moonlite also supplies bottles of Very Hot Sauce, which is brilliantly peppered and will set your lips and tongue aglow.

Beyond meats, we need to mention the impressive deployment of vegetables, including cheesy broccoli casserole, macaroni and cheese, creamed corn niblets, ham and beans, and butter-drizzled mashed potatoes, plus the western Kentucky soup/stew of mutton and vegetables known as burgoo (pronounced BUR-goo) and crusty corn muffins. One visit, we even sampled a silly but intriguing banana salad made with Miracle Whip and chopped nuts. And there are a couple of tables of terrific Kentucky pies.

Mr. D's

1435 S. Green St.　　　　　　270-826-2505
Henderson, KY　　　　　　　LD | $

A fiberglass chicken about as tall as a grizzly bear stands outside of Mr. D's, beckoning customers to drive in. While Mr. D's is a full-menu drive-in with a repertoire of hamburgers, hot dogs, and sandwiches, chicken rules. It is fried chicken made from a recipe popularized decades ago by a legendary chicken man named Colonel Jim, and like the stupendously good chicken on which the Bon Ton Mini Mart built its reputation, it has a wickedly crunchy crust that is spicy enough to make your eyes water.

Because Mr. D's is a quick-service drive-in with car service only, the chicken you order will be delivered to your window in five minutes or less, meaning that the kitchen cooks it ahead of time rather than to order. This is good if you are really, really hungry, but not so good if you are a crisp-skin connoisseur, because the crust loses its crunch. Make no mistake: this is four-star fried chicken and puts just about any non-Kentucky fried chicken to shame. But the next time we order some, we are going to do as Henderson tipster Louis Hatchett advises: request that the kitchen cook it to order. If that twenty-minute wait means crust that cracks when bitten, we'll happily endure it.

Peak Bros.

5363 US Hwy. 60   270-389-0267
Waverly, KY   LD | $

Peak Bros., which had become a legend among western Kentucky barbecue parlors since it opened in 1948, burned down in 2006. It has been rebuilt and is as good as ever. Originally guided here by Duncan Hines biographer and Kentucky tipster Louis Hatchett IV, who referred to Waverly as "the western edge of barbecued muttonland," we began our Peak Bros. love affair with chipped mutton sandwiches. Chipping, a local term for intensive chopping, turns the meat into a hash sopped with the potent natural gravy that is known as dip.

Debbie Britt, whose father and uncle started the restaurant, assured us that chipped is good, but sliced is even better. At her urging, we got some slices and they were really good, although our preference is chipped. Peak Bros.' ham, edged with pepper, was a sweet harmony of pork and smoke, luxuriously tender; the sliced mutton was moist and mellow with none of the rank bite typical of mature lamb elsewhere.

The most punishing interview we have ever conducted was in Peak Bros.' old kitchen, with Tony Willett, who has cooked meat here since the early 1970s. The pit door was open and he was busy throwing spice on pork ribs, peeling skin off hams, and turning briskets and hunks of lamb on the grate. Hellish heat and blinding puffs of smoke emanating from the pit didn't bother him at all, but our eyes teared, our glasses fogged, and our lungs resisted taking in the cloudy air. The fumes of burning wood and cooking meats were penetrating. "When I go home, my wife makes me stay outside until I take off my clothes," Willett confided. "When I walk into a store, you can hear people say, 'Here comes Peak Brothers.' "

Thomason's Barbecue

701 Atkinson St.   270-826-0654
Henderson, KY   LD | $

Kentucky tipster Louis Hatchett IV brought us to Thomason's for barbecue beans, which are magnificent—rich and smoky, laced with shreds of meat and so vividly spiced that they taste like Kentucky Christmas—but the barbecue itself is worth a trip, too.

Thomason's barbecues everything: pork, mutton, beef, spare ribs, baby back ribs, chicken, ham, and turkey. You can get your choice of meat on a plate, which includes pickle, onion, bread, and beans, on a tray, which includes only pickle, onion, and bread, or in a sandwich. Like all other sandwiches in this area, Thomason's can scarcely be picked up by hand because juice from the meat saturates the lower piece of bread, causing it to disintegrate. The pork is velvet-soft, moist, and seductively smoky; mutton is sopped with gravy and gentle-flavored.

A simple, free-standing eatery with an order counter and a scattering of tables, Thomason's does a big carry-out business, selling its specialties by the pound and gallon. On a shelf below the order counter are for-sale bottles of dip, which is a sauce with natural, au jus character.

A&M Grill

402 E. Center St.   919-563-3721
Mebane, NC   BLD | $

The A&M Grill looks as plain as can be, but the aroma of the barbecue pit that surrounds the eatery is a sure sign it is something special. Tables inside are covered with checked blue cloths and outfitted with rolls of paper towels for the messy business of barbecue eating. In fact the menu is a broad one, including southern fried flounder, steaks, even an item titled "grilled chicken fettuccini," available with alfredo or marinara sauce. We chose barbecue and were delighted with what we ate. It's pork, of course, available chopped or sliced and served as a dinner, a tray, or a sandwich. We ordered pork trays about 8 A.M., and shortly after the waitress took the order, we heard the appetizing sound of cleavers hacking away in the kitchen, chopping meat that was soon to be ours.

The meat's texture is one of extremes, ranging from velvet soft to nearly crunchy, some parts crisp and others oozing juice—all of it infused with the fine flavor of smoke. The pork comes sauced with a thin emulsion that has a sharp tomato-vinegar tang. On the side are crunchy hush puppies and coleslaw chopped so fine it looks almost like mashed vegetables.

Allen & Son

6203 Millhouse Rd.   919-942-7576

Chapel Hill, NC   LD | $

Cinder-block walls, plastic tablecloths, and pork slow-smoked over hickory coals: here is a definitive North Carolina barbecue parlor. Sandwiches are available, but we recommend getting Allen's meat on a plate, which includes a pile of sparkling coleslaw and about a half-dozen crisp-skinned hush puppies. The hush pups are arranged like a sculptor's work, *on top* of the pork. It is a field of spheres atop a heap of meat: a lovely, aromatic, and absolutely mouthwatering sight. Meat is served sauceless, but you can dress it up with Allen & Son's butter-rich, vinegar-based hot sauce loaded with spice and cracked pepper.

If you get the combination plate known to some locals as "stew and que" (highly recommended), the pile of good smoked meat is supplemented by a bowl of Brunswick stew, another traditional companion to smoked pork in these parts. Unlike the meatier Brunswick stews of southern Virginia, this luscious stuff is mostly vegetables with a few shreds of meat, all cosseted in a tomato-rich sauce. It is a hearty, rib-sticking food that makes a wonderful contrast to the exquisite pork.

Bar B Q King

2900 Wilkinson Blvd.   704-399-8344

Charlotte, NC   LD | $

Bar B Q King is an American drive-in par excellence, complete with vintage Servus Fone ordering system whereby you study the menu, then press a button to speak with the kitchen and place your order. Meals are brought to the car on blue plastic trays, and while the Servus Fone apparatus has its own counter on which to set the trays, it was a bit too low for our vehicle, so we dined off the dashboard.

Our first visit, we made the mistake of asking for a "pork sandwich." What we got was a perch sandwich. We ate it anyway, and it was marvelous—moist, sweet white meat so satisfying it reminded us of the best pork, but encased in a golden crust. In fact, the perch was so good, we subsequently ordered trout, shrimp, and oysters—all fried in that only-in-the-South soulful way that's guaranteed to convert even a diehard fish-frowner.

What we learned from our experience—other than to recommend BBQK as a fried-fish restaurant—is that if you want smoked pork hereabouts, you don't say "pork"; you say "barbecue." Pork is the only pit meat there is. It is available sliced or minced (the latter really is pulverized, the former "hacked"), and it, too, is a winner—tender, succulent, veiled in a subtle sauce that does not overwhelm the meat's fundamental fineness.

Bill Spoon's Barbecue

5524 South Blvd.   704-525-8865
Charlotte, NC   L | $

A sign on the front of Bill Spoon's announces WE COOK THE WHOLE PIG. IT MAKES THE DIFFERENCE. That's no lie. As swell as shoulders and butts may be when they are slow-smoke-cooked, they cannot match the rousing diversity of hacked-up whole hog, from creamy to crunchy, which you can have here on a partitioned plate with a couple of side dishes or packed into a bun and crowned with bright, pickly mustard slaw. Spoon's Brunswick stew is so dense with meat and vegetables that you can clean the bowl using only a fork; and tubular hush puppies with a vivid onion punch provide cornmeal counterpoint to the spice of barbecue or barbecue-laced beans. If there is a pork-frowner at your table, Spoon's chicken, cooked moist and ultratender, encased in succulent skin, is a fine alternative.

To drink: sweet tea, refilled approximately every ninety seconds by a roving member of the waitstaff. For dessert: banana pudding. It all adds up to an archetypal barbecue meal, just what you'd hope for in a place that's built a grand reputation pit-cooking pig since 1963. Founder Bill Spoon learned the barbecue trade from John Skinner, who learned his craft at North Carolina's first sit-down barbecue restaurant, opened by Bob Melton in Rocky Mount in 1924.

Note: Since Bill Spoon's passing, the gauntlet has been taken up by Steve Spoon. During a visit in 2010, we noted that some members of the staff were wearing "Steve Spoon Barbecue" apparel—perhaps signaling a name change. As for quality, that remained foursquare four-star.

Bridges Barbecue Lodge

2000 E. Dixon Blvd.   704-482-8567
Shelby, NC   LD (closed Mon and Tues) | $

Bridges has no written menu, just the slip of paper used by the waitress to take orders: sandwich, tray, or plate. A tray is barbecue and barbecue slaw; a plate also holds French fries, lettuce, tomato, and pickle. Both are accompanied by hush puppies, and whether you select sandwich, tray, or plate, you must decide if you want your meat (pork shoulder) minced, chopped, or sliced. It is a major decision, for they are almost like three different foods.

Bridges is one of the few places that offers minced barbecue, an old-time configuration from traditional pig-pickin's. It is pulverized into moist hash with some little shreds of darkened, chewy crust among the distressed pork. The mound is held together by a good portion of uniquely North Carolinian sauce with a strong vinegar punch. Chopped is the more typical way modern North Carolinians like it—chunky and easily chewable, and with only a smidgen of sauce. Sliced barbecue comes as big, soft flaps. With the pork comes a Styrofoam cup of warm sauce for dipping.

The hush puppies are elongated crescents with a wickedly brittle, sandy-textured crust. The slaw is strange, too, if you are expecting anything like coleslaw typical of other regions. This is *barbecue* slaw, meaning finely chopped cabbage bound together with—what else?—barbecue sauce! It's got a brilliant flavor and a pearly-red color that handsomely complements your pork of choice. The small tray, by the way, is only about three by five inches and an inch-and-a-half deep, but it is astounding how much meat and slaw get packed into it.

Bridges' dining room is plain and soothing, with the kind of meditative atmosphere unique to the finest pork parlors of the mid-South. Square wooden chandeliers cast soft light over green-upholstered booths and a short counter up front where single diners chat quietly among themselves as they sip buttermilk or iced tea and fork into barbecue. During our first meal here, five police officers with gleaming automatics in their patent leather holsters occupied a table toward the back. Even they spoke in hushed tones, as if it would be sacrilegious to be raucous in this decent eat-place.

Brownie-Lu

919 N. Second Ave.   919-663-3913
Siler City, NC   BLD | $

Brownie-Lu chicken is broasted, meaning that it is cooked in Broaster equipment, a unique combination of frying and pressure-cooking that goes back to the mid-1950s. The result is chicken that is so tender that it wants to slide off the bone of its own accord, encased in crunchy-brittle skin so thin you can practically see through it. The meat has a full but mellow flavor, like something an ideal grandma might make. It is served with nice rolls and such laudable side dishes as butter beans cooked with ham and genuine mashed potatoes. In fact, there are enough good vegetables on the menu that a health-food type could come here and have a totally meatless, delicious meal. A full breakfast is served—country ham is a must—and lunch and supper demand a slice from one of the kitchen's homemade cream pies.

Bum's

566 Third St.   252-746-6880
Ayden, NC   BL | $

Many people think of Bum's as a barbecue restaurant, and that in itself is a high compliment, considering its "competition" in Ayden is the Skylight Inn (p. 164), which any sane person must agree is one of the best barbecue restaurants on this planet. Some others think of it as a chicken restaurant. You'll wait a good twenty minutes for the bird to fry, but the reward for your patience is crisp-crusted chicken on a par with North Carolina's finest. We relish the barbecue and the chicken, but we love Bum's most for its vegetables and side dishes.

It's small torture to go through the cafeteria line and have to choose among corn sticks and corn bread, luxuriously porky boiled cabbage, pieces of crisp pork skin, butter beans, and collard greens. The last, those greens, are actually grown by proprietor Latham "Bum" Dennis in his home garden; and they are cooked to a point of supreme tenderness and savor at the restaurant. There are a few desserts from which to choose; banana pudding is the one not to be missed.

Bum's breakfast buffet features excellent biscuits (with or without gravy) and a choice of pig meats that includes homemade sausage, pork tenderloin, and fried ham.

Bunn's Bar-B-Q

127 N. King St.   252-794-2274
Windsor, NC   L | $

Bunn's building started life in the mid-1800s as a doctor's office. It became a filling station in 1900, and in 1938 barbecue was added to the menu of gasoline and motor oil. There's still an old Texaco pump outside, and the place is decorated with vintage signs, ads, and ephemera. The atmosphere is vaguely similar to what the Cracker Barrel chain aims to create; but in this case, it is real.

When you enter, you have a choice of sitting on a bench at a counter in a room to the left or at a table in a room to the right, in back. Wherever you sit, service is lightning-fast. That's because there is virtually no choice on the menu. What you eat is pork, with or without Brunswick stew, on a plate or in a sandwich, accompanied by supremely fresh coleslaw. The pork is chopped ultrafine, a mix of soft white meat from the inside of the roast laced with chewy brown bark from its surface. It comes ever-so-lightly sauced with what the locals like: vinegar and spice; but if you want it moister or hotter, other sauces are provided on the counter and tables. Plates are topped with a lovely square of thin, extremely luscious corn bread that has a serious chew and is the ideal medium for pushing Brunswick stew around on the plate.

Chicken Box

3726 N. Tryon St.   704-332-2636
Charlotte, NC   LD | $

When hungry for fried chicken in Charlotte, our first choice always has been Price's. But for excellent fried chicken as well as a full soul-food menu, there's an alternative: a very humble eatery named the Chicken Box. Located in a drab building that used to be a fast-food eatery, this place serves chicken with big flavor and crust that crackles. Wings, drumettes, drumsticks, thighs, and breasts are sold by the plate with French fries or your choice of fine vegetables (mac 'n' cheese and collard greens are especially noteworthy) or in party-size quantities to take home.

Amenities are minimal. Carry a tray with your food from the counter to a molded seat in the dining area. And it would be appreciated if you cleaned up the table when you are done.

Cypress Grill

1520 Stewart St.   252-792-4175
Jamesville, NC   D Jan-Apr | $$

For those of us who grew up thinking of herring as a pickled hors d'oeuvre, North Carolina river herring is a shock. For one thing, it looks like a fish. And for another, it really tastes like a fish—not the least bit like chicken or anything else. There is no better place to get to know it than at the Cypress Grill on the banks of the Roanoke River. Here is the last of the old-time herring shacks, quite literally a cypress wood shack, open only for the herring run, January through April. (In recent years, even in those months, herring depopulation has sometimes meant a no-herring menu early in the year.)

There is nothing on the Cypress Grill menu other than fish. Not even a gesture is offered for fish-frowners. Other than herring, you can have rock (striped bass), perch, flounder, shrimp, oysters, devil crab, clam strips, trout fillet, or catfish fillet. Tuesday, Thursday, and Saturday, roe is available. Side dishes include a choice of vegetables, which are fine but not particularly interesting: boiled potatoes, fried okra, slaw.

The herring are served with their heads lopped off, each one veiled in the thinnest possible sheath of cornmeal, its flesh scored with notches so that when it was tossed into the boiling oil, it cooked quickly deep down to the bone. The big issue among river herring–lovers is degree of doneness. Some ask for it sunnyside up, meaning minimal immersion in the fry kettle, resulting in a fish from which you can peel away the skin and lift moist pieces of meat off the bones. The opposite way to go is to ask for your herring cremated: fried until hard and crunchy and so well cooked that all the little bones have become indistinguishable from the flesh around them. The meat itself is transformed, its weight lightened so the natural oiliness is gone but the flavor has become even more intense. The crust and the interior are melded, and they break off in unbelievably savory bite-size pieces, finally leaving nothing but a herring backbone on the plate.

While some herring-crazed patrons fill up on four, five, six, or more of the plush fish, we must advise first-time visitors to the Cypress Grill to leave appetite for dessert. That's the one non-fish item on the menu worth singing about. Every morning, proprietors Leslie and Sally Gardner make pies. When we stopped to visit one day around 10 A.M., Mr. Gardner led us right over to the pie case—a wooden cupboard built by a neighbor to be so sturdy, he says, "you could dance on it." He insisted we feel the bottom of a pie pan, still nearly too hot to touch. We sat down then and there and forked up a piece of chocolate pie that was modest-sized but intensely fudgy.

Dip's Country Kitchen

408 W. Rosemary St.   919-942-5837
Chapel Hill, NC   BLD | $$

"Mama Dip" is Mildred Council, founder/owner/chef at Chapel Hill's beloved soul-food restaurant. Ms. Council, nicknamed "Dip" by her siblings because she was such a tall kid, wrote *Mama Dip's Kitchen* in 1999, and it is a valuable cookbook that includes many of the recipes used in her restaurant.

Three meals a day are served in the nouveau-rustic quarters to which Dip moved a few years ago. Lunch and dinner offer great southern classics—fried chicken, chitlins, Brunswick stew; at breakfast, you can't go wrong with eggs, pork chops and gravy, biscuits, and grits. Other hearty wake-up meals include salmon cakes, brawny country ham, and blueberry pancakes.

Later in the day, what we love most about Dip's meals, aside from the lumpy, crunchy, brightly salty crust of the fried chicken, is the vegetables. The daily list includes long-cooked greens, black-eyed peas, crunchy nuggets of fried okra, mashed potatoes and gravy, porky string beans, okra stew with tomatoes, corn-dotted coleslaw, always a sumptuous vegetable casserole, and cool sweet potato salad. For mopping and dipping, there are buttermilk biscuits, corn bread, and yeast rolls.

Jarrett House

100 Haywood Rd.　　　　　　　828-586-0265

Dillsboro, NC　　　　　　　　LD (closed in winter) | $$

Hoo-eee, talk about country cooking! How about a skillet-fried, center-cut slice of country ham with red-eye gravy and biscuits on the side? Or chicken and dumplings with fried apples, and locally grown beans and squash? Catfish and fried chicken are also on the lunch menu; battered and fried mountain trout is available at supper. And for dessert? A nice slice of vinegar pie ("like pecan pie without the pecans") or warm peach cobbler. Yes, this is the real thing, all right, served in the gracious dining room of a Smoky Mountain inn built in 1884.

Lunch is swell, served by the plate, but full enjoyment of this grand restaurant is found at dinnertime or on Sundays, when meals are served by the platter and bowl, family-style, and guests are welcome to keep eating until it's time to lean back and let out the belt a notch or two.

Jay-Bee's

320 Mocksville Highway　　　704-872-8033

Statesville, NC　　　　　　　LD | $

The brash personality of this drive-through (or dine-in) eat-place is irresistible. "This Ain't No Fast Food Joint!" a sign outside brags. "We Proudly Make All Our Menu Items to Order And It Takes a Little More Time." That would be about a three-minute wait until you are presented with a ready-to-eat Prairie Dog topped with barbecue sauce, chopped onions, and melted cheese or a Northerners' Fancy Dog under sauerkraut and mustard.

Although Jay-Bee's pride is hot dogs, hamburgers are impressive. Available in quarter-pound or half-pound configurations, they are hand-formed from beef ground daily and sizzled to appealing succulence, particularly good when dressed with a heap of sautéed onions.

The beverage menu ranges from sweet tea and milk shakes to Dr. Pepper and Mountain Dew; and if you dine inside, a refill of any soda is free. One-quart-size drinks—yes, thirty-two ounces—are available at the drive-through window.

Keaton's

17365 Cool Springs Rd.   704-278-1619

Cleveland, NC   LD Wed-Sat | $

A cinder-block bunker in North Carolina cattle land between the High Country's natural beauty and High Point's unnaturally low-priced furniture outlets, Keaton's serves some of the best fried chicken you ever will eat.

Step up to the counter and order an upper or a lower (the polite country terms for breast and wing or thigh and drumstick). Pick side dishes from a soulful repertoire of mac 'n' cheese, baked beans, hot-sauce slaw, or white-mayo slaw; choose iced tea (sweet, of course) or beer; then go to your assigned table or booth, to which a waitress brings the food.

In Keaton's kitchen, the chicken is peppered and salted, floured and fried, at which point it is simply excellent country-style pan-cooked chicken. Then comes the distinctive extra step: Just-fried pieces are immersed in a bubbling vat of secret-formula red sauce, a high-spiced, opaque potion similar to what graces High Country barbecued pork. This process takes only seconds, but the throbbing sauce permeates to the bone. You eat this chicken with your hands, pulling off crisp strips of sauce-glazed skin, worrying every joint to suck out all the flavor you can get.

Lexington Barbecue #1

10 Hwy. 29 & 70 S.   336-249-9814

Lexington, NC   LD | $

Welcome to Lexington, North Carolina, a small city with more than one barbecue restaurant per thousand citizens. Of the approximately twenty eateries that specialize in hickory-cooked pork, Lexington Barbecue, which opened in 1962, is king of the hill. "Monk's Place," as locals know it (in deference to founder Wayne "Honey" Monk), looks like a barn with six smelters attached to the back. From their tall chimneys issues the scent of burning hickory and oak wood and slow-cooking pork, one of the most appetite-arousing perfumes in the world. Honey Monk's is a straightforward eatery with booths and tables and carhop service in the parking lot. Much business is take-out.

There are no complicated techniques or deep secrets about Lexington barbecue. After about ten hours over smoldering smoke, pork shoulders are shredded into a hash of pieces that vary from melting soft (from the inside) to chewy (from the "bark," or exterior). The hacked meat is served on a bun with finely chopped, tangy coleslaw or as part of a platter, on which it occupies half a small yellow cardboard boat, with slaw in the other half. Like the meat, the slaw is judiciously flavored with a vinegar/sweet red barbecue sauce. As part of the platter with the meat and slaw, you get terrific, crunch-crusted hush puppies. For dessert, there's peach cobbler and, on rare occasions, berry cobbler, too.

Historical note: In 1983 the North Carolina General Assembly designated Lexington as the "Hickory-Cooked Barbecue Capital of Piedmont North Carolina." That same year the White House asked Mr. Monk to cook barbecue for President Reagan and other heads of state at the Williamsburg International Economic Summit.

Lupie's

2718 Monroe Rd.   704-374-1232

Charlotte, NC   LD | $

Lupie's is the sort of place locals love but outsiders seldom discover. It's been part of the Elizabeth neighborhood since 1987, and it has an unvarnished charm that is increasingly rare in a world of corporate restaurants with carefully plotted themes. If it has a theme of any kind, you might call it "Square Meals: Square Deals." Prices are in the mid-single-digit range. Sweet tea is served in Mason jars. Decor includes odes to Elvis as well as portraits of the waitstaff from years past. Lupie's isn't just a restaurant; it is a vital part of its community.

Much of the food is true South. The four-vegetable plate is a meat-and-three benchmark. We had one with painfully tender disks of yellow squash with sweet onions, green beans (non-canned, well cooked) saturated by tidal waves of pork flavor, large hunks of carrot sweetened with brown sugar, and super-cheesy mac 'n' cheese. On the side came a square of good corn bread. The menu lists three kinds of chili: Texas, vegetarian, and Cincinnati-style. We've enjoyed them all. Burgers, too, are beautiful: thick and craggy, all the better to hold massive quantities of melted Cheddar cheese. You get your choice of Kaiser or onion roll, potato chips or coleslaw.

For dessert, we've yet to go beyond banana pudding, which is creamy-good, thick with crumbled vanilla wafers. One portion will feed two or three.

Parker's

2514 US Hwy. 301   252-237-0972

Wilson, NC   LD | $

Parker's goes back to the 1940s, when Wilson was the place tobacco farmers sold their crop. A big barbecue meal was how they celebrated the harvest; buyers ate here and spread the word up and down Highway 301, which was the main north-south road prior to I-95. Still, the interstate is only seven miles away, making Parker's an extremely convenient stop for those traveling the four-lane.

It is a spacious eating facility with multiple dining rooms. Customers crowd the lined-up tables for family-style combo platters of chopped pork, fried chicken, Brunswick stew, boiled potatoes, corn sticks, and coleslaw. Cooked over hardwood and chopped into hash, the pork is a mix of lean inside meat and crunchy shreds, scarcely sauced at all. A hint of vinegar and peppers is all that's needed to bring out the wood-smoked sweetness of the pork. If you do want to doll it up, tables are set with plain vinegar and a hot sauce that has a vinegar base. As for Parker's chicken, we like it even better than the pork. Its seriously crunchy crust encloses juice-dripping meat, the dark pieces especially luscious.

From the moment it opens each day, Parker's always seems to bustle. As you enter, it's an adventure maneuvering your way to a table as waiters zoom past toting platters piled high with food.

Penguin Drive-In

1921 Commonwealth Ave.   704-375-6959
Charlotte, NC   LD | $

The Penguin used to have a reputation as a rough bar in a bad neighborhood. The neighborhood has improved and the Penguin isn't really all that rough, but it definitely is rough around the edges. Patrons come to whoop it up as much as to eat; and the staff—always efficient and usually quite polite—seem to be contestants in the World's Ghastliest Tattoo and Piercing Pageant. While it most definitely is not the place to bring your sweetheart for a marriage proposal or your dear old mother, it is a great destination for first-class hamburgers in a lively dive.

The broad menu includes decent North Carolina barbecue (bunned along with coleslaw), an ode-to-Elvis peanut butter and banana sandwich, fried bologna, pimiento cheese, and a panoply of hot dogs (including a very nice battered corn dog). But it's the hamburgers we most recommend. Named to honor North Carolina's passion for stock cars, the burgers come as a one-third-pound single (known as the Small Block), two one-third-pound patties (Large Block), and three on a bun for a pound of meat (the Full Blown Hemi). Any burger can be had all the way, meaning topped with lettuce, tomato, onions, mustard, and pickle, or southern style, the latter including chili, mustard, onions, and coleslaw. Cheese or pimiento cheese and bacon are optional. The best thing about these large-bore burgers is the meat itself, a thick patty that oozes juice and radiates ultrabeef flavor. Amazingly, although they are huge, the condiments copious, and the bun normal-sized, even the mighty Hemi is wieldy enough to pick up and eat without significant spillage.

Note: The Penguin changed hands late in 2010. Its future is uncertain.

Price's Chicken Coop

1614 Camden Rd.   704-333-9866
Charlotte, NC   LD (take-out only) | $

Once inside the door of this little South End storefront, two-thirds of which is dedicated to cooking and one-third to ordering (no dining facilities whatsoever), you pick your place in one of six or seven lines leading to a counter with three cash registers, each of which is flanked by white-uniformed, hairnetted servers. The cinder-block room thunders with kitchen clatter undershot by the syncopation of bubbling oil, and everything happens double-fast. Customers' orders are haiku-simple:

> *Quarter, white, and tea*
> *Plus an order of gizzards.*
> *Add a fried pie, too.*

Box of chicken in hand, you exit and find a place to eat: back at work, in your car, or on the pleasant grassy berm of the light-rail line across the street. Amenities are minimal, but the fried chicken is maximal. It's the best in North Carolina—maybe the best in the South and therefore the best anywhere. There is nothing dramatically unusual about it. It is cooked in peanut oil and while brothers Steve and Andrew Price keep their seasonings a secret, it is not the spice that makes it unforgettable. What's so great is the surfeit of crunchy skin imbued with the silky goodness of chicken fat. The skin is substantially chewy and you can hear its juices when you apply your teeth to it—just before it dissolves into pure chicken flavor on your tongue. Expectedly, the meat of the dark parts oozes savory juice. Not so predictably, even the big, meaty breasts are moist and big-flavored in a way that white meat almost never is. If fried chicken isn't rich enough for you, Price's also fries up dramatically delicious chicken livers. And if you need a pop-in-the-mouth snack a whole lot easier to eat than the juice-oozing parts, gizzards are always in good taste.

Short Sugar's

1328 S. Scales St.   336-342-7487

Reidsville, NC   BLD | $

Carhop service is still available at Short Sugar's, which opened as a hamburger joint in 1949. It now serves three meals a day, and the menu is vast, including breakfast, sandwiches, and a burger roster with a "teenage burger" (a double cheeseburger). Chili dogs are raunchy little things topped with chili so fine that it is more a paste than hash. Barbecue is the featured attraction, a point that is obvious if you walk in the door that leads to the take-out counter, for here you have a view of quarter hogs on the grate, soon to be chopped up and served on a plate (with fries, slaw, and hush puppies), on a tray (with just slaw and hush puppies), or as a sandwich. The meat is sweeter than most due to Short Sugar's fascinating sauce, which is mixed in and also available in squeeze bottles on the table if you want more. The slaw is brilliant, fresh as can be, and the hush puppies provide a welcome crunchy counterpoint for the tender pork. Our only disappointment was a ham biscuit. The biscuit was blah.

A big restaurant with a long counter, booths, and tables, Short Sugar's has the patina of a place that has been around for many decades. Most of the clientele are regulars, but the staff treats strangers as welcome guests.

Skylight Inn

1501 S. Lee St.   919-746-4113

Ayden, NC   LD | $

Hickory-smoked, whole-hog barbecue, unaffected by time or trends, has made the Skylight Inn a legend. Unlike pyrotechnical kick-ass Q's, Skylight's mating of smoke and pork is a subtle nuptial, elegantly abetted by the addition of a little vinegar and Texas Pete hot sauce, salt, and pepper—nothing more—as it is chopped with cleavers on a rock-hard maple cutting board. Beyond exquisite flavor, what is most striking about whole-hog barbecue is the texture. Along with soft shreds from the interior are chewy strips from the outside as well as shockingly crunchy nuggets of skin. The cooked skin conveys terabytes of lusciousness, its firmness adding edible drama that is lacking in barbecue made only from upscale hams or shoulders. Any sauce beyond the vinegar and Texas Pete is anathema. There are two and only two ways to have meat at the Skylight Inn: in a cardboard tray or on a bun. Other than a tile of primitive, unleavened corn bread and some coleslaw, there is nothing else on the menu.

Sandwiches are a twentieth-century addition to the Jones family repertoire, but their pairing of barbecue and corn bread goes back to 1830, when ancestor Skilton M. Dennis, who cooked whole hogs in pits dug in the ground, brought some of the meat to sell at a nearby Baptist convention. "As far as we know that was the first time barbecue was served to the public in North Carolina," says Samuel Jones, Dennis's seventh-generation descendant, who operates the Skylight Inn along with his father, Bruce. Sam is the grandson of Pete Jones, the longtime pitmaster, who started in the business with his uncle, Emmett Dennis, when he was six years old. Pete built the current Skylight Inn in 1947 and in 1988 he put a jumbo replica of the Capitol Dome atop the building after a journalist declared his place the Barbecue Capital of America.

Snappy Lunch

125 N. Main St.   910-786-4931
Mount Airy, NC   BL | $

As Yankees, we had never heard of a pork chop sandwich until we traveled south. Even in Dixie, it is not all that common, but you'll find it on menus in various configurations ranging from a bone-in chop with superfluous bread that serves merely as a mitt so you can eat the meat without utensils to the boneless beauty at Snappy Lunch. Surely this is the king of pork chop sandwiches. It is a broad slab of meat that is breaded and fried, similar to the tenderloins of the Midwest, but with more pork and in batter rather than breading. It is soft and luscious, as tender as a mother's love.

Few customers of Snappy Lunch get a plain pork chop sandwich. The ritual here in Mount Airy (Andy Griffith's hometown and the inspiration for TV's Mayberry) is to have it *all the way,* which means dressed with tomato, chopped onion, mustard, meaty/sweet chili, and fine-cut cabbage slaw speckled with green peppers and onions. The total package is unwieldy in the extreme. Served in booths or at the counter in a wax paper wrapper, this is a sandwich that requires two big hands to hoist and eat. There are no side dishes available other than a bag of potato chips, and the beverage of choice is tea—iced and presweetened, of course.

There are, however, other items on the menu, including a weird Depression-era legacy known as the breaded hamburger, for which ground beef is extended by mixing it with an equal portion of moistened bread. The result is a strange, plump hamburger that resembles a crab cake. Definitely an acquired taste!

South 21 Drive-In

3101 E. Independence Blvd.   704-377-4509
Charlotte, NC   LD | $

If you like classic American drive-ins and don't already know about Charlotte's South 21, allow us to introduce you to your new best friend.

When South 21 Drive-In boasts that its Super Boy burger is a meal in itself, that's only partially true. It's a lot of food, for sure: two good-size patties with the works in a sesame bun crowned with a quartered pickle spear and sided by a heap of French fries. While that may indeed be a meal, all aficionados of this vintage 1952 drive-in know that no meal is complete without an order of onion rings. They are individual hoops that arrive so greaseless that they first appear to have been baked, not fried. But after a few bites, the luxury of the fry kettle becomes deliciously apparent. With some salt added, these are four-star o-rings. The other thing necessary to complete the meal is either Cherry Lemon SunDrop (a tradition hereabouts) or one of South 21's excellent milk shakes, blended to order.

While we love this old-fashioned drive-in with its articulated window-side trays and Servus-Fone ordering equipment at every car slip, we do believe the hamburgers need doctoring up; they tend to be dry enough to beg for extra condiments. That's why many regulars prefer the heftier and juicier hamburger steak or the fried chicken.

Stamey's

2206 High Point Rd.   336-299-9888
Greensboro, NC   LD | $

Stamey's makes Lexington-style North Carolina barbecue, which means that the meat is pork shoulder pit-cooked over smoldering hickory wood until eminently tender, then chopped or sliced. "Chopped" is nearly pulverized. Slices are more like shreds of varying sizes, some soft, others crusty. The sauce is peppery with a vinegar tang, and thin enough to permeate the soft pork rather than blanket it. If you get a platter (as opposed to a sandwich), it will be accompanied by a powerfully zesty coleslaw and odd-shaped, deep-fried corn squiggles that are Stamey's version of hush puppies. This is a Piedmont meal that connoisseurs put in the top tier of a big state that is fanatical about barbecue and has at least six different regional variations from the coast to the western mountains. Be sure to leave room for dessert. Stamey's peach cobbler is nearly as famous as the barbecue. Served warm with ice cream, it's an epiphany.

There is a second Stamey's at 2812 Battleground Ave. (US 220 North); 336-288-9275.

Sunrise Biscuit Kitchen

| 1305 E. Franklin St. | 919-933-1324 |
| Chapel Hill, NC | BL \| $ |

If you have a cramped and uncomfortable car, you might find Sunrise Biscuit Kitchen problematical. It is drive-through only, offering no place to eat. But if you are a biscuit-lover, you will want to come here even if you're in a minimicromobile. Sunrise biscuits are big and buttermilky with an outside surface that is golden crisp. The kitchen pulls them into halves and loads in resounding slices of grilled country ham, succulent pork tenderloin, and luxurious pillows of expertly fried white-meat chicken. Coffee is available, but so is sweet tea, which is a good biscuit's soul mate.

Tomato Jam Café

| 379 Biltmore Ave. | 828-253-0570 |
| Asheville, NC | BL \| $ |

Biscuits earn Tomato Jam Café high standing on the Roadfood honor roll—cat head biscuits in particular, so named because they are closer to the size and shape of a big cat's knobby noggin than they are to a smooth and symmetrical hockey puck. Made using whole-grain flour, they are biscuits of color rather than the more familiar lily-white ones. Yet there is nothing cloddish about them and they are seriously flavorful. They are probably best enjoyed with nothing but butter and a schmear of the café's wonderfully fruity tomato jam, but they are sturdy enough to be a great mitt for a breakfast BLT that includes apple-smoked bacon and broiled tomato. You even can have a biscuit topped with vegan sausage gravy!

Vegetarian items are not an afterthought at TJC; and if you can forgo an order of creamy, buttery, stone-ground grits, it's possible to eat vegan. At lunch, in addition to hamburgers made from grass-fed cow meat, the menu lists a black bean burger and a pseudo-burger made of a marinated portobello cap. There are lots of different grilled cheese options as well as pimiento cheese, available hot or cold, with or without roasted tomato, and with the option of that good apple-smoked bacon.

Side dishes not to be missed include chunky cinnamon-spiced applesauce, griddle-crisped potato cakes, and slow-roasted tomatoes (heirloom tomatoes in the summer). Desserts that demand attention include banana pudding, red velvet cake, and cashew-studded brownies.

There's a nice attitude about this place. It is fun and funky with thrift-shop-retro decor and a cavalcade of characters, especially at breakfast, who make eavesdropping on other diners' discussions irresistible. The proprietors are so dedicated to using local groceries that they have put up a chalkboard listing suppliers, farms, and bakeries with which they deal. Their mission statement is to make food "a rich part of daily being"; and their philosophy avows, "We at Tomato Jam consider our customer's health and well being as important as our own."

Wilber's Barbecue

4172 US Hwy. 70 E.   919-778-5218
Goldsboro, NC   BLD | $

Pilots who take off from Seymour Johnson Air Force Base have flown the fame of Wilber's far and wide, and legends abound regarding the pounds of barbecue carried aboard strategic flights. Even if it weren't at the end of the runway, Wilber's reputation for serving first-class Lexington-style North Carolina barbecue could never have remained merely local. This place is world-class! Since 1962, when Wilber Shirley stoked the oak and hickory coals in old-fashioned pits, he has been known for whole-hog barbecue, chopped and judiciously seasoned with a peppery vinegar sauce. After eight hours over the coals, the meat is soft as a sigh, its natural sweetness haloed by the indescribably appetizing tang of hardwood smoke. It is served with potato salad, coleslaw, Brunswick stew (a pork hash with Veg-All-type vegetables), and squiggle-shaped, crunch-crusted hush puppies.

Beyond terrific barbecue, the original Wilber's has the added attraction of serving breakfast, in the form of a buffet with smoky sausages, thick-cut bacon, chewy cracklin's, biscuits and gravy, grits, and sweet muffins. By late morning, chopped barbecue reigns, and it is served until about nine at night . . . or until the day's supply runs out. When that happens, the management locks the door and hangs up a sign that advises, *Out of Barbecue!*

A&R Bar-B-Que

1802 Elvis Presley Blvd.   901-774-7444

Memphis, TN   LD | $

At the counter where you stand and place your order at A&R you can hear the blissful smokehouse lullaby coming from the kitchen: chop-chop-chop on the cutting board as hickory-cooked pork gets hacked into mottled shreds and pieces for plates and sandwiches. The sandwich is the classic Memphis configuration: pork mixed with tangy red sauce piled in a bun and crowned with a spill of coleslaw. It occurred to us as we plowed through a jumbo that the slaw in a Memphis barbecue sandwich is as important for its texture as for its pickly sweet taste. The cabbage provides such nice little bits of crunch among the velvety heap of pork.

Beyond pig sandwiches, the A&R menu is full. You can have ribs (wet or dry), catfish dinner, hot tamales, meatballs on a stick (!), and that only-in-Memphis treat, barbecue spaghetti. That's a mound of soft noodles dressed not with ordinary tomato sauce, but with—what else?—barbecue sauce, laced with shreds of pork. It's weird, but in this city, where restaurants also offer barbecue pizza and barbecue salad, it makes sense.

The ambience of A&R is unadulterated BBQ parlor: quiet enough so you can hear the chopping in the kitchen while you concentrate on enjoying the meal. It is a big place with a lot of elbow room. Raw brick walls and fluorescent lights set a no-nonsense mood; and however hot it is outside, you can count on the air conditioning system to be running so high that it's practically like going into hibernation. Or is the trance we experienced a result of hypnotically good food?

There are three other A&Rs in Memphis.

Alcenia's

317 N. Main St.   901-523-0200
Memphis, TN   BL | $

Everyone who eats at Alcenia's gets a hug from proprietor from B. J. Lester-Tamayo, either on the way in or out, or both. "I feel so guilty if I haven't hugged you, I'll chase you down the street when you leave," she says with a laugh. Her restaurant, named for her mother and granddaughter, is a modest lunch room decorated in a style that is an intriguing mix of 1960s psychedelic beaded curtains, primitive folk art, odes to African American culture, and white wedding-veil lace strung up across the ceiling over the large table.

B. J. learned to cook from her mother, who lives in Meridian, Mississippi, but comes to visit and makes tea cakes and egg custard pie and coaches B. J. on the phone when she is making chowchow or pear preserves. B. J.'s turnip greens are extraordinary, flavored not with pork but with what she calls turkey "tails." Even more wondrous is the cabbage, which, when we first saw it, we assumed was steamed with greens because dark leaves were laced among the white ones. B. J. explained that those are the cabbage's outer leaves. "The best part!" she declared. "Most people throw them away because they are tough. They need an hour extra steaming; that makes them soft and brown." Flavored with a hail of spice that includes jerk chicken seasoning and lots of pepper, this is cabbage with a tongue-searing punch. On the side comes a basket of hot-water corn bread: cushiony-moist griddle-cooked cakes that are the perfect foil for ecstatically seasoned vegetables.

Aside from Alcenia's exemplary southern vegetables, dining delights here include a delicious fried pork chop that is crisp-crusted and dripping with juice, crunch-crusted fried chicken, and bread pudding that the Memphis *Commercial Appeal* declared to be one of the ten best desserts in the city.

Beacon Light Tea Room

6276 Hwy. 100   931-670-3880
Bon Aqua, TN   D Tues–Fri; BLD Sat & Sun | $

Opened in 1936 by Lon Loveless, who went on to open the renowned Loveless Café in Nashville, the Beacon Light Tea Room is a lesser-known gem

of Tennessee country cooking. Loveless fans will have déjà vu upon opening the menu, for it is the same as the Loveless's used to be. Brittle-crusted
fried chicken and country ham with red-eye gravy are the only entrees
to know about, and among essential sides is the sumptuously rich mid-
century Home-Ec triumph, hash brown casserole. Potato shreds are mixed
with cheese, sour cream, and—you guessed it—a can of chicken soup, then
baked until bubbly with a crust on top.

Meals are sided by biscuits with homemade peach and blackberry preserves. They are set out on the table in spoon-it-yourself crocks. There are
whole, soft hunks of peaches in the amber one, and the blackberries have a
sultry flavor that is a brilliant counterpoint to super-salty country ham.

Although it was originally named for the revolving spotlight that directed planes flying mail between Memphis and Nashville, the term "Beacon Light" now has another meaning. For the proprietors of this upright
restaurant, the beacon is Jesus, and His image is everywhere in art on the
old wood-paneled walls. Each table, which is clad in a leatherette cloth, is
outfitted with a "Scripture Bread Box," a small plastic loaf hollowed out to
contain cards about the size of fortune-cookie fortunes, but in this case with
scriptural advice on each side.

Blue Plate Café

5469 Poplar Ave.   901-761-9696
Memphis, TN   BLD | $

In this cheery café that was once a private home built by Holiday Inn founder
Kemmons Wilson, breakfast is served any time and it is good enough to draw
some daunting crowds on the weekend. Omelets are good, French toast is
better, pancakes are best. (Waffles stink; Blue Plate has gone from thin, elegant ones to fat-ass Belgians.) We are particularly fond of the kitchen's
banana pancakes, whose fruity sweetness is magnificently complemented
by crunchy peanut syrup that is nut-sweet more than sugar-sweet. Flavorful knobby-top biscuits are served with cream gravy dotted with bits of
sausage.

Lunch is good ol' meat-and-threes, with such entrees as pot roast, baked
pork chops, chicken and dumplings, and fried shrimp (that last one is every
Friday). The vegetable roster is about twenty items long, including real
mashed potatoes, turnip greens, creamed corn, mac 'n' cheese, etc., etc. If
you want something simpler than meat-and-three, there are salads, soups,
and sandwiches, including a fried peanut butter and banana sandwich. Apparently that one is health food: It is served on whole wheat bread.

Bluegrass Grill

55 E. Main St.   423-752-4020
Chattanooga, TN   BL | $

We get lots of suggestions about where to eat. Some pan out, others aren't so impressive. Ever since John Reed tipped us off to Zarzour's (p. 190), we have learned to put full faith in any of his suggestions. That is how we came upon the Bluegrass Grill, to which Mr. Reed directed us for "heavenly muffins, granola, cinnamon rolls, biscuits and breads all made from scratch starting at 3:30 A.M. by Father Jonas." Fr. Jonas Worsham, along with his family, including his wife, Joan Marie, have created a beckoning breakfast destination that also is open for lunch.

Big, squared-off biscuits, given extra character by the inclusion of whole wheat flour, arrive hot enough to melt butter pats. Add gravy on top and get a bottomless cup of coffee, and you will have a mighty morning meal for under $6. French toast is made from a choice of four house-baked breads, including raisin and multigrain; superb home fries—red potatoes sautéed with onion and garlic—are offered as a side dish to omelets or as a bed for toppings that range from gyro meat to chorizo to beans and cheese. Muffins, cinnamon rolls, whipped-cream-topped brownies: all first-class!

We've yet to eat lunch at Bluegrass Grill. (Breakfast is served from 6:30 A.M. to closing at 2 P.M. weekdays or 1 P.M. Saturday.) The menu is soup, chili, sandwiches, and salads. If you have a party of fifteen or more and want dinner, the Worsham family also offers a weeknight "Greek feast" for which you consult about the menu. For that, of course, advance notice is required.

Bolton's Spicy Chicken & Fish

624 Main St.   615-254-8015
Nashville, TN   LD | $

Bolton's manager Dolly Graham once said, "Our chicken is hot, but it won't cause you to lose your composure." That depends. If you are squeamish about high-capsicum fare, Bolton's chicken might indeed be reason for a meltdown, especially if you ask for it hot. What's great about it, for those who do like inflammatory food, is that the heat is deep in the meat, right down to the bone itself. It is much more spicy than it is salty, making each bite a taste-bud adventure.

It is beautiful chicken with a thin, red-gold crust that flakes off in delicate strips. You can get breast, leg, or wings; and side dishes include vigorous turnip greens, sweet coleslaw, strangely soupy mac 'n' cheese, and that

Nashville soul-food favorite, spaghetti. In addition to chicken, Bolton's sells a whiting sandwich that is available garnished in the locally favored way, with mustard, onion, pickles, and enough hot sauce to make your tongue glow.

A tiny East Nashville shop with a carry-out window to its side and a dining room with a handful of tables (oilcloth-covered), Bolton's is an essential stop for anyone in search of a true taste of Music City.

Bozo's Hot Pit BBQ

342 Hwy. 70   901-294-3405
Mason, TN   LD Tues-Sat | $$

In the nine decades since it opened, Bozo's has earned a sterling reputation for barbecue. Slow-smoked shoulder is served white or dark, the former unspeakably tender shreds, the latter more chewy and crusty outside meat. (Many savvy eaters get a combination of the two.) You can have it the classic Memphis way, in a sandwich with slaw (although here the slaw has a more pronounced vinegar tang), or on a plate with beans and/or onion rings. Sandwiches are immense, loaded with more meat than any bun could possibly contain. Tables are armed with three sauces, mild, sweet, and hot. The hot is *very* hot.

Although barbecue is the must-eat meal, Bozo's menu also includes steaks, shrimp, and wicked pies, including pecan, coconut, and chocolate.

Named for founder Thomas Jefferson "Bozo" Williams, the restaurant was engaged in a trademark battle with Bozo the Clown back in the 1980s that went all the way to the U.S. Supreme Court. But Bozo's is still Bozo's, its well-worn Formica tables showing only about a half-century of use. (The original Bozo's was destroyed by fire in 1950.)

Coletta's

1063 S. Parkway   901-948-7652
Memphis, TN   LD | $

If you've eaten around Memphis enough to have encountered barbecue spaghetti, barbecue pizza will not be a complete shock. Memphians like everything barbecued. At Coletta's Italian Restaurant (the oldest restaurant of any kind in the River City), a medium-thick-crust pie with a glaze of melted mozzarella is topped not with Italian sauce and sausage or pepperoni, but with a bouquet of barbecued pulled pork in zesty cinnabar pit sauce. Weird as it may seem, it works pretty darn well. No, it is not one of the world's great pizzas; nor is it in the highest echelon of mid-South barbecue; but it is a specialty worth noting—and eating—for all who want to savor America's rules-be-damned cuisine.

Coletta's also serves barbecue salad, which is like any ordinary salad (iceberg lettuce, carrot shreds, tomatoes) but adorned with barbecue—the same moist mix of fine shreds and a few chewy nuggets as on the pizza. The meat on the salad is unsauced. Dressing is the customer's choice, and it makes all the difference in the salad's character. Italian vinaigrette nudges it in the direction of minimally sauced eastern North Carolina 'cue; Thousand Island or Russian is more like mountain smokehouse meals; ranch dressing brings it close to that strange Alabama variety of sauce that is based on mayonnaise.

Barbecue pizza and salad are just two items on a full-range menu of familiar Italian-American fare, including more universally known pizzas, house-made sausage, ravioli, and spaghetti and meatballs.

It should be noted that the original Coletta's on South Parkway, around the corner from Graceland, has a sad and foreboding look from the outside. Inside, however, you will find all the hospitality and warmth of a stereotypical mid-twentieth-century Italian-American eatery, including paper placemats that explain Italy's charm to diners and bunches of breadsticks to start the meal. There is plenty of cognitive dissonance in the fact that the old wood-paneled walls hold massive amounts of Elvisiana and the waitresses speak in syrupy southern drawls.

Cozy Corner

745 N. Parkway   901-527-9158
Memphis, TN   LD | $$

In America's premier barbecue city, the number one barbecue restaurant is the Cozy Corner, a family-run storefront that serves sauce-glazed spare ribs packing huge sweet-pork punch, baby backs with meat that slips from the bone in glistening ribbons, plus thick disks of barbecue bologna and that delightfully monomaniacal Memphis side dish, barbecue spaghetti. Cozy's unique house specialty is Cornish hen, a plump little bird that emerges from its long smoke bath with painfully fragile, burnished skin wrapping meat that throbs with spicy flavor right down to its bones.

Despite its fame, the Cozy Corner remains humble, its front room clouded with haze from the smoker behind the self-service counter. It was established back in 1977 by Raymond Robinson, who, until his death early in 2001, oversaw his small, sweet-smelling empire from behind the order counter, haloed by the glow of his smoke pit. Today his widow, Desiree, keeps up the high culinary standards and the friendly air that has always made this such a happy place to visit.

The Cupboard

1400 Union Ave.   901-276-8015
Memphis, TN   LD | $

The Cupboard is a hugely popular restaurant in what used to be a Shoney's, where a sign outside boasts "Freshest Veggies in Town." Proprietor Charles Cavallo is a fresh-food fanatic, a joy he credits to his uncle, who sold watermelons. "One day when I was twelve, he gave me a few he had left over. I sold them by the side of the road, and from that moment, I had the passion." He drove a produce delivery truck for ten years, and in 1993 bought The Cupboard (then a much smaller place) with the goal of making it a showcase for vegetables. Tomatoes direct from the field in Ripley, local squash, crowder peas, onions, cabbage, and sweet potatoes appear not only on the menu (which features a five-vegetable, no-meat meal), but also on the floor of the restaurant, in the vestibule and around the cash register, from which they are sold by the peck and bushel when they are in season.

One of the best cooked vegetables here is the simplest: a whole baked sweet potato, starchy sweet and soft as pudding. And The Cupboard's full-flavored turnip greens are made without pork or poultry, just boiled and seasoned. "My greens taste like greens," Charles says, stating the obvious. "Sometimes I have people who come in and say, 'You've changed the recipe. These are different.' Yes, they are different, I say: maybe younger, maybe winter greens, which have a softer taste, maybe they are from Georgia instead of Tennessee. Every bunch has a flavor of its own."

Non-vegetable notables at this high-spirited eatery include fantastic corn bread gem muffins and yeast rolls, warm fruit cobbler, and brilliant lemon icebox pie.

Dyer's Burgers

205 Beale St.   901-527-3937
Memphis, TN   LD | $

A modest-size round of raw ground beef is held on the cutting board under a spatula and the spatula is whacked a few times with a heavy hammer, flattening the meat into a semi-compressed patty at least four inches wide. Now the good part: The patty is submerged into a deep black skillet full of bubbling-hot grease, grease that the management boasts has not been changed since Dyer's opened in 1912! It's the grease that gives a Dyer's burger a consummately juicy interior while it develops a severe crust outside and a unique, shall we say, intriguing flavor.

Our waitress explained that the grease is carefully strained every night after closing hour (on weekends, around dawn—this is Beale Street, after all), and besides, the really old grease is always burning off, so the supply that supposedly never changes is, in fact, always changing. Whatever. The fact is that this is one heck of an interesting hamburger, if for no other reason than its ability to drive nutrition wardens wild. Burgers are assembled in many ways: as doubles or triples, or as double or triple "combos" (with layers of cheese). Good hand-cut French fries are available on the side.

If hamburgers are not your passion, allow us to suggest another Dyer's specialty: the Big Rag Baloney sandwich. That's a half-inch-thick slab of baloney that is fried to a crisp in the same skillet, and in the same vintage oil, as the burgers.

Eastside Fish

2617 Gallatin Pike   615-227-8388
Nashville, TN   LD | $

The Giant King, the signature dish at Eastside Fish, is immense. A pair of whiting fillets, each at least a half-pound, are dredged in seasoned cornmeal and crisp-fried, then sandwiched between four slices of soft supermarket white bread. The fish is cream-moist and delicate, its brittle crust mottled with splotches of four-alarm Louisiana hot sauce and enveloped in a harmony of crunchy raw onion, dill pickle chips, and smooth yellow mustard. Standard companions for the fish are white bread, hush puppies, coleslaw, and, strangely enough, meat-sauced spaghetti.

The small storefront tucked back from Gallatin Pike has a single tall table with a couple of stools for those who need a place to eat, but Eastside's business is virtually all take-out. Whiting is traditional; you also can get catfish, tilapia, or trout. There is no heat lamp to keep fish on hold, so from the time an order is placed, it takes a good 10–15 minutes to get it. The brown paper bags in which customers receive their fish out the order window are steaming hot and splotched with oil, the sandwich inside wrapped in wax paper and held together with toothpicks.

We also recommend Eastside's hot wings: jumbo drumettes fried so the skin turns luxuriously chewy. They are served sauceless, so they don't look hot, but they will clear your sinuses.

Elliston Place Soda Shop

2111 Elliston Pl.   615-327-1090
Nashville, TN   BL | $

It bills itself as a soda shop, and a fine one it is; but we like Elliston Place more for meat-and-three lunch. Choose sugar-cured ham, salt-cured country ham, southern-fried chicken (white or dark meat), a pork chop, or liver 'n' onions; then select three vegetables from a daily roster of at least a dozen. On Mondays and Thursdays the house special is turkey and dressing, a casserole of shredded roasted white and dark meat with steamy corn bread dressing: delicious! If you want to skip meat altogether (Elliston Place vegetables are so good, such a strategy makes sense), there is a four-vegetable plate, accompanied by hot bread, for under $5. The vegetable repertoire includes lovely whipped potatoes, turnip greens, baked squash, fried bite-size rounds of okra, black-eyed peas, baked squash, and congealed fruit salad (the Dixie name for Jell-O).

For breakfast, biscuits are crunchy brown on the outside with a soft interior that begs to wrap itself around a slice of salty country ham. Many locals ignore the excellent ham and choose fried bologna as their breakfast meat of choice. On the side comes a bowl of firm, steamy white grits—mild-mannered companion for full-flavored breakfast meat.

A city fixture since 1939, this is a restaurant with personality! Its tiny-tile floor is well weathered and its tables wobble. Above the counter, vintage soda fountain signs advertise banana splits, fruit sundaes, sodas, and fresh fruit ades. Each green-upholstered booth has its own jukebox with selections that are, suitably enough, country classics.

Germantown Commissary

2290 S. Germantown Rd.   901-754-5540
Germantown, TN   LD | $$

Here's well-made down-home food, served in decorator-rustic surroundings in an upscale neighborhood. The Germantown Commissary has barnboard walls chockablock with old tin signs, wind-up telephones, and vintage advertisements. Many of its tables wobble as much as those in a juke joint, and the air has the unmistakably seductive aroma of a working smoke pit.

It is best known for ribs, which truly are first-rate: crusted with sauce, scented by hickory, meaty as hell with enough chew to provide maximum flavor. You can order them by number of bones, from five to twelve (a full rack), or as part of a half-and-half plate with another barbecued meat. We suggest the latter, because it would be a crime to come to the Commissary and *not* have pulled pork. It is shoulder meat, pulled into slightly-more-than-bite-size strips and hunks, some edges crusty, some parts velvet-soft. You can also get the meat chopped, which is okay but deprives your tongue of the pleasure of worrying those long strips of meat you get when it's pulled.

For dessert, there are smokehouse classics: banana pudding with softened vanilla wafers in the custard and tongue-soothing lemon icebox pie.

Gus's Fried Chicken

310 S. Front St.   901-527-4877
Memphis, TN   LD | $

The sign outside Gus's says that it is world famous. The menu says its fried chicken is hot. Both claims are debatable: Gus's certainly is known among chicken connoisseurs, but it has yet to gain fame on the order of other Roadfood shrines such as, say, Arthur Bryant's or Pepe's Pizzeria. As for hot, it is not ferocious like hot fried chicken in Nashville. Having now said what it is not, let us say what Gus's *is*: one of the best fried chicken restaurants anywhere. Each piece, dark and white, is encased in a zesty envelope that vigorously crunches, then offers plenty of rewarding chew, all the while radiating the ecstatic flavor combo of chicken fat and pepper. These are chicken parts that will have you worrying every little edible piece from everywhere on every bone.

Other than catfish a couple of nights a week, chicken is Gus's only entree; any pieces are available in any combination; side dishes include baked beans, coleslaw, fried rice (!), fried okra, and spiced French fries. Even those who aren't fans of fried green tomatoes and fried dill pickles should consider ordering some of Gus's to start the meal. No novelty in this kitchen, the pickles maintain nice al dente firmness inside their crunchy coat, which, like the batter on the chicken, is an elegant balance of spice and lusciousness.

To call the restaurant casual underestimates its humility. On a crappy street the wrong side of Beale, it regularly posts a security guard on the sidewalk so that visitors will feel safe between car and front door. The interior, where mismatched chairs are arranged around a couple dozen tables topped with miscellaneous checked easy-wipe tablecloths, it seems like a chaotic madhouse as customers mill around near the door, waiting for their turn to sit. Once seated, you will deal with a staff who are nothing but courteous and efficient.

Henpeck Market

1268 Lewisburg Pike   615-794-7518

Franklin, TN   BLD | $

A gas station, a grocery store, a live bluegrass venue, and a café serving the finest possible versions of classic mid-South fare, the Henpeck Market is a Roadfood vision. Simply getting to it is a pleasure, for the rolling-pasture landscape around Franklin is achingly bucolic.

Service is cafeteria-style, which is a good thing because it allows you to study the beautiful desserts and to see other people's meals get plated. Casual though it may be, there is a refinement about the experience that makes this charming place something much more compelling than any other gas station/convenience mart that happens to serve hot meals. Yes, it is a country store and the menu items are mostly familiar, but the food is a cut above.

For us, the standout dish is a pimiento cheese sandwich. It's fine on white bread, better when grilled, best when smoky bacon is included. Other deliciocities include corn bread salad, biscuits and country ham, and fried grits squares. Desserts are a sight to behold, and there are so many that choosing only one or two is a real challenge. We like the seven-layer carrot cake, meringue-topped banana pudding, and cream cheese chocolate brownies.

The last Saturday of each month, the Henpeck Market features a live bluegrass jam that includes a supper of catfish, turnip greens, white beans, and slaw; and every Tuesday night, meals are served family-style.

Interstate Barbecue

2265 S. Third St.   901-775-2304

Memphis, TN   LD | $$

Interstate's Jim Neely is a master barbecue man, and in the city of Memphis, to be a true pitmaster is to be a god. His restaurant is a modest pork house serving four-star ribs, shoulder meat, sausages, and bologna with all the proper fixin's, including addictive barbecue spaghetti (soft noodles in breathtaking sauce). You eat at a table in a dining room where the "Wall of Fame" is decorated with critics' accolades and 8x10s from celebrity fans; or enter next door and get it to go, by the sandwich, plate, or whole slab of ribs.

Each big rib packs deep savor haloed by the perfume of wood smoke; chewing it generates massive infusions of flavor that literally exhaust taste buds after a while. Chopped pork shoulder is a magnificent medley of shreds, chunks, wisps, and ribbons of smoky meat, all crowned with Neely's spicy-sweet red sauce. A chopped pork sandwich is the most Memphian dish on the menu, made as per local custom with a layer of cool coleslaw atop the well-sauced meat.

Joe's Bar-B-Que & Fish

3716 Clarksville Pike   615-259-1505
Nashville, TN   LD | $

Joe's just might be the world's slowest fast-food restaurant. It looks quick: no indoor seating, just a drive-through line with a large menu to study and a microphone to speak into when the time comes to place your order. A few yards beyond the menu is the window where you pay and receive the food. We were third in line for lunch, and based on the timing, we almost believe that each car's order is started from scratch, bagged, and served before the next car's order is taken.

The thirty-minute wait was well worth it! This food is indeed made to order. Whiting is crisp and hot from the deep-fryer, served the Nashville way with mustard, dill pickle chips, raw onion, and plenty of hot sauce. The corn bread that enfolds pulled pork in Joe's wonderfully soulful pork-on-corn-bread sandwich comes off the grill so steamy that the unwieldy sandwich is almost too hot to handle. Rib tips are succulent and sauced with gusto.

Dining amenities? There is a small gazebo in back with a few tables where customers are welcome to bring their bagged meals. The only problem is that the quickest way to get there is to drive from the pick-up window out onto Clarksville Pike—against the flow of traffic—then quickly cut back into the drive-through line. Or it is possible to pull out and make a legal U-turn in one of the parking lots across the road. That's the slower way, and at Joe's, slow is good.

Leonard's

5465 Fox Plaza Dr.   901-360-1963
Memphis, TN   LD | $$

In 1922 Leonard Heuberger configured the barbecued pork sandwich that has become a regional icon: shreds of smoked shoulder meat topped with tomato-sweet, vinegar-tangy sauce, festooned with a heap of creamy, cool coleslaw. It is a mesmerizing confluence of sugar and spice, meat and bread and sauce.

Choices at Leonard's range beyond the famous sandwich. There are slabs of ribs, platters and plates, barbecued bologna, and even a roster of Italo-Dixie combo plates that include spaghetti with ribs and barbecue with ravioli.

Leonard's is worth visiting not only for its pork, but also for its sign, which is one of the great images in porklore: a neon pig, all decked out in top hat and tails, wielding a cane, captioned, "Mr. Brown Goes to Town." Years ago, a waitress explained its significance: "Mr. Brown was the term used for brown-meat barbecue. It is the outside of the shoulder that gets succulent and chewy from the sauce and the smoke in the pit. The inside part of the roast, which is moist but has very little barbecue flavor, is known as Miss White. People in Memphis used to ask for plates and sandwiches of 'Mr. Brown and Miss White.'"

Little Tea Shop

69 Monroe Ave.   901-525-6000
Memphis, TN   L | $

Memphis is our favorite place to eat pork, but there's none served at the Little Tea Shop down by old Cotton Row. Proprietor Suhair Lauck is Muslim, and yet despite her religion's prohibition against pigs, she serves some of the most soulful eats in the city. We were aghast when Sue told us that her greens were in fact completely meat-free. It had always seemed to us that the opulent "likker" in which they wallow in their serving bowl—a spruce-green broth retrieved from the pot in which they have boiled—gets its intoxicating character at least as much from the hambone as from the collard, turnip, or mustard leaves that the boiling process turns soft and mellow.

But tasting is believing, and let us tell you that a serving of pork-free turnip greens with pot likker at the Little Tea Shop is positively tonic. If a flavor can be verdant, here it is: the heady soul of a plant with leaves that marinate in sunlight. Turnip greens are the centerpiece of Sue's most popular lunch on the printed-daily menu. For $6.50, you get a bowl filled with sultry dark greens sodden in their likker, the once-tough leaves cooked so limp that you can easily separate a small clump of them with the side of a soupspoon and gather it up with plenty of the liquid. Atop the greens are slices of raw onion, leaching pungent bite into the leaves; and atop the onions are bright red slices of tomato, which are shockingly sweet compared to everything below. On the side are crisp-edged, cream-centered corn sticks well suited for crumbling into the bowl.

We love the do-it-yourself ordering process at the Little Tea Shop. Every customer gets a one-page printed menu of the day—there is a different menu for each day of the week—with a little box next to each item. Like voting with an old-fashioned ballot, you put a check mark in the box next to each dish you want to elect for your lunch. Other than greens and pot likker, some of the outstanding dishes are the Lacy Special (named for a cotton trader), in which corn sticks sandwich a chicken breast topped with gravy, and such vegetables as sliced candied yams, fried corn, baked squash, black-eyed peas, and scalloped tomatoes.

Litton's

2803 Essary Rd.   423-688-0429
Knoxville, TN   LD | $

With a catalogue of hamburgers that range from minimalist beef patties to a "Thunder Road" burger (named for the movie about moonshining in these parts) topped with zesty pimiento cheese, onions, and hot peppers, Litton's is burger-lovers' heaven. For each one, freshly ground meat is formed into a patty that is nearly one-half pound and is cooked to order, then sandwiched in a made-here bun, preferably with at least lettuce, tomato, and onion, and, at most, bacon, pickles, or chili. Hamburgers—and other sandwiches—are available with onion rings, French fries, or any number of classic southern sides.

At least as famous as the hamburgers are Litton's desserts: coconut cream pie, old-fashioned red velvet cake, creamy banana pudding, and Italian cream cake, a creamy, buttery concoction with old-fashioned simplicity that goes perfectly with a lingering cup of after-meal coffee.

Loveless Café

8400 Hwy. 100   615-646-9700
Nashville, TN   BLD | $$

Long before it became a national shrine of country cooking, the Loveless Café was a favorite haunt among Grand Ole Opry performers, whose pictures line the walls and whose tour buses frequently could be seen parked toward the back of the lot. In those days, to eat here was to feel like one of a small group of cognoscenti privy to down-home southern cuisine of the highest order.

The Loveless has received great press over the last two decades, not only from *Roadfood* but also from national magazines and the many TV food-show hosts who go around showing people Roadfood eateries. Now there are all kinds of Loveless souvenirs to buy, a thriving mail-order business for "hams & jams," and a sometimes-exasperating wait for a table.

Bleeding deacons averse to change complain that the biscuits aren't as good as they were when the late Carol Fay Ellison used to make them and that the crust on the fried chicken isn't as crisp and . . . yada yada yada. In our experience, the red-checked tablecloths still offer up a tableau of truly artisan (but not affected) vittles. Peach preserves are the color of a summer sunset, sweet and deeply fruity, just perfect in conjunction with a faintly sour biscuit. Blackberry preserves are more tart: wonderful on biscuits or toast or waffles, or on ice cream, or (we confess) spooned straight from the jar.

As much as the exalted preserves, ham is the pride of the Loveless kitchen. It is country ham, slow-cured and salty, fried on a griddle until its rim of fat turns translucent amber and the coral-pink meat gets speckled a sandy brown. It comes sandwiched in biscuits or on a plate with red-eye gravy, cream gravy, sorghum molasses, or honey, and bowls full of each of the preserves. What delirious fun it is to permutate all these good things: dip the biscuits, spread the sorghum, make little sandwiches with ham.

Saved from extinction several years back by new owner Tom Morales, the Loveless has added all sorts of new items to the traditional menu: barbe-cue and smoked pork, a green-tomato BLT, and a dessert menu that includes some of the best banana pudding in the South. It's different than it used to be, but it remains a Roadfood treasure.

Merridee's Breadbasket

110 4th Ave. S.   615-790-3755
Franklin, TN   BL | $

Merridee's is a casual kind of place where people come early in the day to buy breads and pastries to take home or to sit down for breakfast or lunch. Place an order at the counter and they'll call your name when it is ready, by which time, hopefully, you have found a table. The large menu includes hot breakfasts and a vast array of oven-fresh rolls (almond swirl, cinnamon twist, sticky bun, muffins, biscuits, scones, etc.) as well as lunch of sand-wiches, salads, and crescents ("No, not croissants!" says the menu), which are homemade bread doughs wrapped around turkey and honey mustard, spinach and feta cheese, or roast beef and Swiss.

While the choice of sandwiches is vast, pimiento cheese, a mid-South passion, is essential. It is not dramatically different from ordinary cheese spread, but that subtle difference is just the point. Pimiento cheese is all about nuance: the slight zip of chopped pimientos and sweet relish and their red and green sparkle in the gentle-flavored cheese. While hearty and satisfy-ing, it has a refined character that sings of ladies' lunch rooms, afternoon tea, and Dixie finesse.

For dessert: cake, pie, fudge brownies, and sugar tea cakes, available with espresso coffee drinks.

Nikki's Drive-In

899 Cherokee Blvd.   423-265-9015
Chattanooga, TN   LD | $

Although carhop service no longer is available, Nikki's remains a timeless mid-twentieth-century drive-in, complete with long counter, jukebox at every booth, and Coke served in glass bottles. Signs atop the brick building do not boast of hamburgers (although the burgers are very nice lunch-counter patties); they advertise dishes that have been house specialties for decades: jumbo Gulf Coast fried shrimp and southern fried chicken. The shrimp are relatively pricey (near $20) but stupendously meaty, fresh, and lush-crusted. We thank tipster John Reed for telling us we had to have bacon-wrapped, deep-fried chicken livers (oh, mama, are these ever rich!) as well as Nikki's justifiably famous big-hoop battered onion rings. We topped things off with very good pecan pie.

If the weather is nice, take time for a seat at one of the picnic tables on the patio. The view to the south is downtown Chattanooga, especially lovely at night when the lights twinkle.

Pancake Pantry

1796 21st Ave. S.   615-383-9333
Nashville, TN   BL | $$

We suffer from anxiety at the Pancake Pantry. First we worry about getting in. There is almost always a long line of hungry Nashvillians waiting for a precious seat in this singular restaurant that transcends generic pancake-house dining. Second, simply choosing from the menu induces paroxysms of indecision. If we order sweet potato pancakes that are so good drizzled with cinnamon cream, then it doesn't make sense also to eat onion-laced potato pancakes. And if we get stacks of pancakes, how much appetite can possibly remain to enjoy what are surely the best hash browns in the South? We don't know if they're cooked on the same griddle as the pancakes, or if it's just pancake scent in the air, but Pancake House potatoes are as buttercream-fluffy as the best flapjack. Fried to a golden crisp, they are counterpoise for the salty punch of a brick-red slab of griddled country ham.

A few other favorites from the broad and inviting menu: Smoky Mountain Buckwheat Cakes, which appear dark and somber but are featherlight, arriving in a stack of five with plenty of butter and a pitcher of very warm syrup to pour on top; Caribbean buttermilk pancakes; and thin and eggy Swedish pancakes wrapped around lingonberry preserves.

The Pancake Pantry is a big restaurant with plenty of space among the tables and a high-spirited ambience throughout the dining room. It is impossible to imagine being in a bad mood when eating here. After all, what's not to be happy about when you are eating excellent pancakes with plenty of butter and syrup and good coffee on the side?

Payne's

| 1762 Lamar Ave. | 901-272-1523 |
| Memphis, TN | LD \| $ |

As in most barbecue parlors of the mid-South, the counterman at Payne's will not ask if you want coleslaw when you order a pulled pork sandwich. It is automatic: Tender pork shoulder is hacked with a cleaver on a wooden block and piled into a bun with hot or mild sauce; and to balance the meat's smoky profundity, a big pile of pickly sweet slaw goes on top. This configuration, formally known as a pig sandwich, is a brilliant, wide-spectrum presentation that combines warm meat with cool slaw, spicy sauce with creamy dressing, piggy pork with crunchy cabbage.

Expect no frills in this very basic place, where accommodations are just a few scattered tables to which you carry your own food, which is presented ready-wrapped. The menu is posted on a movable-letter board above the order counter, where the short list includes beef barbecue, sausages, rib tips, and bologna, with sides of beans, slaw, and French fries. In our experience none of these is stellar, but the pig sandwich is.

Prince's Hot Chicken Shack

| 123 Ewing Dr. | 615-226-9442 |
| Nashville, TN | LD Tues-Sat \| $ |

Pay attention to the name: Prince's *Hot* Chicken Shack. You can take that to the bank. The fried chicken is available mild, medium, hot, and extra-hot. Even the mild packs a punch. We tried hot and it had us tearing up . . . with joy! What's great about this crisp-fried wonder is that it isn't merely hot. It is radiant with flavor; its chewy skin has soulful character; the meat is moist and luxurious. To say it is addictive is not hyperbole. We met several customers who told us they come to Prince's five times a week (it's closed Sunday and Monday), and any day they didn't get their extra-hot was a sad one. If we lived in Nashville, we could easily get hooked.

Chicken is all you need to know, except for the French fries, which are terrific, too. The chicken comes in halves and quarters. It is delivered in a paper bag near the window where you placed your order and paid. There are a handful of tables in the restaurant and many people simply step outside to dine on the walkway of the small strip mall where Prince's is located. Beverages are sold from vending machines inside.

Puckett's Grocery & Restaurant

4142 Old Hillsboro Rd.   615-794-1308
Leiper's Fork, TN   BL | $

Puckett's is a grocery store, a live music venue, and a restaurant (actually two restaurants; there's another in Franklin). A scattering of mismatched tables occupy the front of the store, to the side of which is an open kitchen where meals are cooked and assembled. The menu varies day to day, but when barbecue is available, that's the ticket: pulled pork that is moist and sweet, needing no sauce whatsoever but beautifully accompanied by a couple of onion-speckled corn cakes. Hamburgers are also excellent: thick, hand-pattied rounds sizzled to order and piled into buns with bouquets of garnishes and condiments. You can also get a fried bologna sandwich and the local favorite, pimiento cheese. And every day, there's a choice of meat-and-threes, so you can accompany your pork or roast chicken with the likes of broccoli rice casserole, green bean casserole, fried pickles, and a pair of moist, onion-dotted corn cakes hot off the grill. The dessert selection features chocolate and buttermilk chess pies and, on occasion, red velvet cake.

The Rendezvous

52 S. Second St.   901-523-2746
Memphis, TN   D | $$

Famous as they are as an icon of Memphis barbecue, Charles Vergos's ribs technically are not barbecued; they are charcoal broiled. Instead of being bathed in sauce, which is the more typical Memphis way, they are dry. Dry, but not drab. Indeed, these are some of the most flavorful ribs you will eat anywhere. Instead of sauce, the meaty bones arrive at the table encased in a crust of powerful spice. The spice accentuates the sweetness of the pork and also seems to contain and concentrate its succulence. Vergos's ribs are lean, tender, and flavorful beyond description.

With its semi-subterranean dining room where the decor is antique bric-a-brac and thousands of business cards left by decades of happy customers, The Rendezvous is more reminiscent of a beer hall in *The Student Prince* than a mid-South barbecue. To accompany the beer you must drink before (as well as during) any meal, there are plates of sausage and cheese that are a merry hors d'oeuvre. Sound like a lot of food? Eating large is part of the

Rendezvous experience; of all the restaurants in town, we nominate this one as the worst to visit on a diet.

Ridgewood Barbecue

900 Elizabethton Hwy.   423-538-7543
Bluff City, TN   LD | $$

Ridgewood Barbecue has defined excellence for decades. Hams are hickory-cooked in a pit adjacent to the restaurant, sliced into fairly thin pieces, then reheated on a grill when ordered. The meat is souped with a tangy, dark red, slightly smoky sauce (available by the pint and quart near the cash register) and served as a platter, under a heap of terrific dark gold French fries or in a sandwich that spills out all sides of the bun.

We love the platter presentation, because it allows one to fork up a French fry and a few flaps of sauced meat all at the same time, making for what we believe to be one of the world's perfect mouthfuls. Prior to the arrival of the platter, you will be served a bowl of coleslaw—cool, crisp, sweet—surrounded by saltine crackers. We also recommend ordering a crock of beans. They are soft, laced with meat, and have a fetching smoky flavor.

A word of warning: If you arrive at a normal mealtime, expect to wait. Despite its fairly remote location, this place attracts barbecue-lovers from far away, some of whom come to take vast party platters home; but there are almost never enough seats. We like to arrive at about 4 P.M., when chances are good we will get one of the really choice booths adjacent to the open kitchen in the old dining room. From here, the view is magnificent. You see the cooks heating meat on the grill, making sandwiches and platters, and immersing potatoes into the bubbling-hot deep-fryers. Once a meal is plated and ready to be sent to the table, it is set on a holding counter just inches from your booth, separated only by a short glass partition. If you arrive hungry and are waiting for your food to be delivered, this sight—and its accompanying aromas—is tantalizing beyond description.

Rotier's

2412 Elliston Pl.   615-327-9892
Nashville, TN   LD | $

A longtime favorite of Vanderbilt students, Rotier's is a blast from the past, its burger one-of-a-kind. A thick, irregularly shaped patty of ground beef is grilled to glistening perfection and stacked with lettuce, tomato, pickle, and hopefully a layer of bright orange cheese and a good squirt of mustard between two handsome tiles of toasty French bread. The package is tall enough that it arrives stuck together with a toothpick.

Although everyone in town knows Rotier's as the hamburger place, it also happens to be one of Nashville's premier hot-lunch restaurants, where you can choose from a menu of such entrees as pork barbecue, country-fried steak, fried chicken, and meat loaf. On the side pick two vegetables from a list of southern classics: black-eyed peas, turnip greens, fried okra, baked squash casserole, crowder peas, white beans, etc., etc. Or it is possible to get a plate of nothing but vegetables—an excellent strategy if for some reason you are going meatless. With the vegetables come good rolls or warm corn bread; and if you don't want to drink beer, the menu lists milk shakes, chocolate milk, sweet milk, and buttermilk. And, of course, sweet tea.

Silver Sands

937 Locklayer St.   615-742-1652
Nashville, TN   BL | $

Great breakfasts and meat-and-three lunches are portioned out from a short cafeteria line that gives Silver Sands customers a view of what's to eat as well as the opportunity to discuss options with one of the team of servers behind the counter: What's good with smothered pork steak? (Answer: stewed apples and fried potatoes with onions.) Don't be surprised if the helpful gals dipping plates refer to you as honey, darlin', sweetheart, and baby.

We recommend the country ham, but when the kitchen runs out of it, a good fallback meat is fried bologna, which is served under a mantle of sweet, soft fried onions. Grits are thick, full-flavored, and especially wonderful when ladled with plenty of butter. Huge chicken wings are dished out with a mantle of brown gravy; and among the worthy vegetables at lunch are greens, green beans, and macaroni and cheese (in the South, mac 'n' cheese is a vegetable).

Silver Sands is a low-slung cinder-block building tucked into a corner in an otherwise residential neighborhood just west of the Farmers Market in North Nashville. There are about a dozen tables—much business is carry-out—and despite circulating overhead fans, the air in the cream-colored dining room is thick with the homey aromas of good cooking.

Swett's

2725 Clifton Ave.   615-329-4418
Nashville, TN   LD | $

Swett's is a visible success story: Opened in 1954 as a small soul-food meat-and-three café, it became a large, modern cafeteria, burned down, and was built again. Portraits of the founding Swetts adorn the walls, and their legacy is well reflected by a kitchen that continues to serve hearty soul-food meals at reasonable prices.

Like so many cafeteria lines, this one starts with dessert: pies ranging from low-profile chess to lofty meringues, plus a couple of hot fruit cobblers. Beyond the sweets are the meats: masterful fried chicken, spice-encrusted baked chicken, sausages, country steak, and beef tips. Now comes the real fun: vegetables. Swett's repertoire is a southern symphony of steamed or fried okra, fried corn, squash casserole, candied yams, mashed potatoes, mac 'n' cheese, stewed cabbage, candied apples, baked beans, turnip greens, rice and gravy, etc. Most customers get one meat and two or three vegetables. Some fill their tray with nothing but four or five vegetable dishes . . . accompanied, of course, by corn bread, either baked as a loaf and sliced or in the more typical local formation, as a cake fried on a griddle.

Draw your own iced tea (sweet or unsweet) at the end of the cafeteria line.

Sylvan Park

4502 Murphy Rd.   615-292-9275
Nashville, TN   LD | $

With all the ambience of a prison cell, Sylvan Park remains one of the most charming meat-and-threes in Tennessee. Serenaded by the loud hum of an ice cooler, you sit at one of the dozen tables scattered through the small cinder-block dining room and order off a short menu that includes such entrees as country ham, fried steak, and salmon croquettes, as well as a long list of vegetables and side dishes. The standard meal is one meat and three vegetables, but we often forgo the meat and get a four-vegetable plate.

For dipping and mopping the juices and for serving as uncomplicated punctuation among the assertive flavors of the vegetables, Sylvan Park offers tender little biscuits with great absorbent qualities as well as tangy corn bread muffins with a rough texture that crumbles nicely over a serving of creamy white beans.

Sylvan Park is known also for its pies: chocolate, chess, butterscotch, egg custard, sweet potato. Cut to order in the kitchen, a slice might arrive half-fallen-apart on the plate. That's because these pies are very, very delicate, with fragile meringue on top of the creamy ones. A highly recommended alternative to pie, when available, is banana pudding. Its flavor is immense, and it is made the classic southern way, with softened vanilla wafers and streaks of meringue throughout the custard.

Wiles-Smith Drugs

1635 Union Ave.	901-278-6416
Memphis, TN	BL | $

Just up the road from the Sun Records studio, where Elvis made his first recording, is a drugstore that opened when The King was nine years old. Wiles-Smith has been remodeled, so it doesn't look ancient, but its culinary values are tradition itself. You can sit at the boomerang-pattern Formica counter and enjoy a nice breakfast or lunch sandwich or meal-size beef stew for under $5. Ice cream concoctions are classic, including perfectly blended sodas, cherry and chocolate sundaes, and milk shakes that come in tall silver beakers so you can refill your glass approximately one-and-a-half times. When Memphis sizzles in the summer, this is the place to come for an icy fruit freeze.

Zarzour's

1627 Rossville Rd.	423-266-0424
Chattanooga, TN	L Mon-Fri | $

When you get lost trying to find Zarzour's, don't bother looking in the phone book to call and ask driving directions. There is no evidence of it in the Yellow Pages; its number is in the residential listings, under the name of the manager's mother-in-law. And if you do finally locate the no-man's-land café, you will not be able to eat unless you arrive during the fifteen hours a week that it's open for business: Monday through Friday from 11 A.M. to 2 P.M.

When you walk in, chef Shannon Fuller will call out, "Are you having a cheeseburger or dining off the menu today?" The burgers are hand-pattied, thick and juicy and satisfying. The menu is a 5x7–inch piece of paper with three entrees handwritten every day above a printed list of vegetables. The murky turnip greens are especially delicious: pork-sweet, as tender as long-steamed cabbage, and heavy with tonic pot likker. Certain menu items are immemorial, including roast beef every Friday. We adore the antediluvian dish baked spaghetti, which is toothless pasta laced with crumbled beef, chewy shreds of cheese scraped from the edge of the casserole, and a web of hardened noodles from the top. No hot meal is more popular than the every-Wednesday salmon croquettes (known to some fans as "redneck crab cakes"). "I make twenty-five or thirty plates of them," Shannon says, showing how she forms each one from a mix of salmon, egg, onion, flour, and milk, then pan-fries it so the luxurious pink mash inside is encircled by a good crunch.

Shannon's mother-in-law, Shirley (granddaughter of the founder), makes dessert. Her glories include lemon icebox pie, banana pudding, and the amazing millionaire pie. That's pineapple chunks, walnut pieces, green grapes, and mandarin orange slices suspended in a mix of frozen Cool Whip and sweetened condensed milk.

Allman's Pit Cooked Bar-B-Q

1299 Jeff Davis Hwy.   540-373-9881

Fredericksburg, VA   LD | $

For over fifty years, Allman's has been building a reputation on smoke-cooked pork shoulder, sliced or minced. Sliced is more like pulled—irregular shreds and nuggets that are soft and lean with a subtle flavor that can be amplified quite nicely by an application of sweet, thin sauce. You can have it on a plate or in a bun, or as the main ingredient in pork stew by the cup or bowl. Good fries and crisp coleslaw come alongside and milk shakes are made to order.

The pork is good, but to a large degree the allure of Allman's is the place itself: a brick storefront with a counter and stools and a scattering of bare tables in a room that feels untouched by time. (Thanks to Hetty Lipscomb for tipping us off to this place.)

Charlie's Cafe

1800 Granby St.   757-625-0824

Norfolk, VA   BL | $

When we asked locals for Roadfood suggestions in Hampton Roads, many recommended Charlie's Cafe, describing it as a great greasy spoon. The old wood-frame house does have a well-worn feel and cheap-eats accommodations: bare tables, counter with stools, unbreakable heavy-duty china. And the menu is hash house cuisine par excellence. But if Charlie's is a greasy spoon in ambience, it is a cut above in food and service. Even the walls are interesting: a gallery for strange and intriguing paintings that's a far cry from standard-issue diner decor.

There is a full lunch menu with burgers of all kinds, sandwiches, salad, and homemade soup, as well as daily specials that always include a full turkey dinner every Thursday; but it's breakfast that is the big draw (very big on weekends; prepare to wait for a table). Omelets are notable. Ingredients are not unique—choices range from fajita chicken or chili filling to vegetarian specials—but the eggs from which they're made are grand. We sat at the counter and watched a potato omelet made (at the suggestion of regional food savant Patrick Evans-Hylton, it was a potato omelet topped with habinaro [*sic*] salsa) and didn't see the cook do anything special; yet the fluffy cloud of eggs that arrived before us was sheer elegance. In concert with a filling of crisp-fried potatoes and melted jack cheese, as well as a hot-pepper "habinaro salsa" topping, it was one splendid breakfast. Potential accompaniments include biscuits, corn bread, Texas toast, and butter-gobbed grits. Coffee is bottomless and tea is sweet. Other morning choices include country ham, pork chops, and pancakes with chocolate chips, strawberries, pineapple, or creamed chipped beef.

Chutzpah

12214 Fairfax Towne Center   703-385-8883
Fairfax, VA   BLD | $$

While Chutzpah is not by any means a regional restaurant, it had come highly recommended to us by members of Roadfood.com, and so one afternoon on the outskirts of D.C., desperately in need of comfort food, we sought it out. Located at the far end of a nondescript Fairfax shopping center, it is a modest-size storefront with an immodest personality. Billing itself as a *real* New York deli, Chutzpah features gigantic sandwiches, smoked fish platters, bagel plates, hot or cold borscht, and a full repertoire of Dr. Brown's sodas.

Meals begin with bowls of sour and half-sour pickles and creamy coleslaw. We spooned into matzoh ball chicken noodle soup, which was as homey as can be, then feasted on wiener schnitzel, a big, thick slab of juicy meat in an envelope of crunchy, dark brown crust. It is served with lemon wedges and a large side dish of serious meaty gravy. We thought the gravy superfluous, but the latke (potato pancake) on the side was excellent. Of course we also had to have a sandwich, but which to choose? Pastrami (annotated on the menu with the advice, "Please don't embarrass yourself and ask for mayonnaise"), hot brisket, or chopped liver? We went for a Reuben, which is an extremely unwieldy heap of steamy corned beef, sauerkraut, melted Swiss cheese, and Russian dressing between two crisp-grilled slabs of rye bread. It comes with thick-cut steak fries and it is delicious!

For dessert, we walked out with a nice black-and-white cookie, forgoing the seven-layer cake, carrot cake, and genuine New York cheesecake.

Dixie Bones BBQ

13440 Occoquan Rd.   703-492-2205
Woodbridge, VA   LD | $$

Roadfood adventurer Laura Key tipped us off to Dixie Bones for its macaroni salad, iced tea (available sweet or unsweet), and hickory-smoked pork. As far as we've tasted, the pork is the best barbecue in the greater D.C. area and an essential Roadfood stop along I-95. Cooked at least a dozen hours over smoking hickory logs, the meat is velvet-soft and gentle-flavored, served in sandwiches heaped on a platter with such side dishes as Laura's favorite creamy-lush macaroni salad, French fries, baked beans, limp greens, and a terrific item known as a muddy spuds. That last item is chopped-up baked potato dressed with barbecue sauce.

Dixie Bones offers three heat levels of Carolina-style sauce (tomato-sweet/vinegar-tangy), the hottest of which is not incendiary. In addition to boneless pork, there are ribs sold by the rack and half-rack, pork sausage, beef brisket, pulled chicken breast, and fried catfish fillets.

Pies are made here, and we found the apple pie endearingly soulful, i.e., well sweetened and cooked long enough that the pieces of apple inside were as tender as the pork that preceded dessert. Thursday is lemon chess pie day. Friday and Sunday feature coconut cream. Saturday's pie is sweet potato.

Do-Nut Dinette

1917 Colley Ave.   757-625-0061
Norfolk, VA   BL | $

Diner-lovers alert! On an unlikely corner in the rather trendy Ghent neighborhood of Norfolk, Do-Nut Dinette is the real deal. Early one morning, we were thoroughly entertained by the back-and-forth palaver among stool-sitters and staff, the topics covered including tattoos gotten while drunk and why hash brown potatoes are good for you. As the name suggests, donuts are the specialty: raised and glazed, light enough that three or four or even a half-dozen doesn't seem like too many for a healthy appetite. They are vaguely like Krispy Kreme, but donuts of quality that are good even if they're not hot from the fryer.

However, you do want to get to Do-Nut Dinette early in the day when the donuts are fresh. Only one batch is made each morning, and it can be gone by noon. The rest of the menu is a repertoire of Mid-South diner classics including sizzled country ham and well-buttered grits. If grits are not your thing, do consider the hash browns. They are good and greasy, brightly seasoned—the sort of spud that seems just right in a dinette.

Note the limited hours of operation: Daily from 6 A.M. to 2 P.M. The Dinette has been known to also be open on weekends in the wee hours.

Doumar's

1919 Monticello Ave.   757-627-4163
Norfolk, VA   BLD | $

Doumar's has been at the corner of 20th Street and Monticello Avenue in Norfolk since 1934, but it was thirty years before that and in the city of St. Louis that the Doumar name first gained fame. At the World's Fair of 1904, Mr. Doumar introduced a novel way of serving and eating ice cream: the cone. The cone made it possible for fairgoers to walk and eat ice cream at the same time and without utensils—surely one of the great ideas in culinary history.

Today's Doumar's of Norfolk is marked by a sign with two big ice cream cones on either side, but it's known also for pork barbecue, double-meat hot dogs, burger-and-French-fry plates, and flat grilled cheese sandwiches. As for ice cream, if you choose not to get a traditional waffle cone (still made the old-fashioned way), you can order what is known here as a Reggie (a chocolate milk shake with crushed cone chips), a June Bride (chocolate ice cream topped with strawberry sauce), a Scope (hot fudge atop vanilla ice cream and orange and lime sherbet), or a Kingston Flat (strawberry shortcake with bananas). Milk shakes are superb, served in glasses made of . . . glass!

Best of all, Doumar's delivers its classic drive-in fare in the classic drive-in manner—on trays that hang on the window of your car.

Franklin Restaurant

20221 Virgil H. Goode Hwy.   540-483-5601
Rocky Mount, VA   BLD | $

Traveling from Roanoke toward Winston-Salem along the Virgil H. Goode Highway (Route 220) early one morning, we spotted a bunch of vehicles with local license plates pulled into the parking lot at the Franklin Restaurant in Rocky Mount. Upon opening the car door, we were suddenly intoxi-cated by the smell of sizzling country ham. This is the real stuff, salt-cured to a concentrated essence-of-pig flavor that no other meat can match. You can get a big serving as part of a meal with eggs et al. or have it more simply sandwiched in one of Franklin's tender, crumbly homemade biscuits, which have enough body to sop up a full charge of ham essence.

A return trip confirmed that while breakfast may be the most important meal of the day, it's not the only good one in this friendly diner. Supper of turkey with all the trimmings was glorious. It is nothing out of the ordinary: a meal where the much-abused encomium "home cooking" would seem to fully apply, except for the fact that salad is retrieved from a (very nice) salad bar. We only wish the wonderful warm peach cobbler that came for dessert had been served alongside the full-flavored ham steak that was our other main course. There aren't too many taste sensations more thrilling than the sweet-salty punch of these two.

Fulks Run Grocery

| 11441 Brocks Gap Rd. | 540-896-7487 |
| Fulks Run, VA | $$ |

Finding Fulks Run Grocery in the Shenandoah Valley just south of the West Virginia border is a pleasure. Although it is less than a half-hour's drive from I-81 along Route 259, it feels alluringly remote, surrounded by nothing but countryside. Built in 1949 by Garnett Turner and now run by his progeny, it is a grocery store, not a restaurant. But we cannot resist tipping friends off to any ham house we find, especially Turner's Ham House, which is located behind the store and is considered by those in the know to be the finest small-scale producer of sugar-cured country ham anywhere.

Many people who know Turner Hams never go to Fulks Run; it has been a thriving mail-order business for years. Of course, you can buy a nice ham right here to take home and prepare. The big beauties, wrapped in cheesecloth, are displayed helter-skelter in various shopping carts all around the store.

Galax Smokehouse

| 101 N. Main St. | 276-236-1000 |
| Galax, VA | LD | $$ |

A sign on the front of this friendly corner storefront announces "Genuine Pit Barbecue," and that is a promise you can believe. Ravishing ribs, available in slabs from four to twelve bones, come with hush puppies, corn on the cob, sauce-absorbent bread, and such other sides as barbecue beans, fried potatoes, and smoked mashed potatoes. Brunswick stew, generally served as a side dish but also available by the bowl, is a fork-thick gallimaufry of hunky vegetables.

If ribs are not your dish, the Smokehouse also offers pulled pork, brisket, and chicken (white or dark) as well as hugely handsome half-pound hamburgers and smoky all-beef hot dogs. Big smoked potatoes are available with just butter and sour cream or loaded with your choice of barbecued meat. Smokehouse banana pudding is some of the best anywhere: big-flavored, smooth, and soulful.

Goolrick's Pharmacy

901 Caroline St.   540-373-9878
Fredericksburg, VA   L | $

Goolrick's is a vintage pharmacy lunch counter where shakes are still assembled from ice cream, syrup, and milk, whirred by wand and served in the tall aluminum beaker in which they were mixed. Not only are the shakes great, so is the lemonade, which is freshly squeezed. And while nothing on the lunch menu will win huzzahs on the Food Network, we love a roster of nice, modest sandwiches such as BLT, chicken salad, grilled cheese, cream cheese and olive, and even peanut butter and jelly. If a shake or lemonade doesn't suit your fancy, how about a cherry Coke, vanilla Coke, or chocolate Coke—each made by squirting fountain syrup into the bottom of the glass before the Coke is drawn.

Accommodations are limited to counter stools and a handful of tables along the wall. In back, a compounding pharmacist can actually fill prescriptions the old-fashioned way, by customizing medicines to meet patients' special needs.

Metompkin Seafood

14209 Lankford Hwy.   757-824-0503
Mappsville, VA   Tues-Sat 9-6 (closed six weeks, Jan into Feb) | $

Cruising along Highway 13 between Temperanceville and Modest Town on Virginia's Eastern Shore, there is no ignoring Metompkin Seafood. Brightly painted yellow signboards set up by the roadside like a flurry of vintage Burma-Shave ads are emblazoned with red script calling out "soft crabs," "steamed shrimp," "fried fish," "oysters," and "home made crab cakes." The place is a shack with a wooden crab mascot hung on its clapboards overlooking picnic tables and hand-written menus posted on the wall. Inside is a seafood market and take-out counter along with a single round table and a couple of rocking chairs where customers who have placed their orders can sit and wait for them to cook.

When we stopped by one Saturday in February, Metompkin had only just opened after a winter hiatus and spirits among customers standing inside were high. "Finally!" one woman called out, ordering a couple of pounds of steamed shrimp, a fried scallop platter, and a crab cake sandwich. "I've been hungry since Christmas." A man in a camouflage hunting outfit said he'd driven forty-five minutes to Mappsville three times in the last week just to have plates of seaside (as opposed to bayside) oysters.

Fast food, this is not. When owner Ellen Hudgins takes your order at the counter, she writes it on a slip of paper and carries it to the back room, where the fish is fried, oysters opened, and shrimp steamed. While you wait, you can peruse raw seafood in the case, shop for seasonings and hush puppy mix on the wall shelves, and watch TV at the single table, which is outfitted with paper towels, hot sauce, a local real estate guide, and a Bible. After about fifteen minutes, Ellen announces, "I've got some orders here." Hungry hopefuls listen to see if their time has come. Platters come in Styrofoam clamshells, sandwiches are wrapped in foil; serve yourself canned beverages from the cooler, then dine at a picnic table or in your car.

Prices are unbeatable—a big oyster and shrimp platter costs $11.95; a bounteous fish sandwich is a ridiculously low $3.95. That fish—flounder the day we visited—comes cased in a vividly seasoned crust, expertly fried so the meat within is moist and sweet. The fried crab cake is not the deluxe jumbo-lump-style cake but it is unimpeachably crabby, and at $4.95 for a crab cake sandwich, it is a bargain meal.

Beyond fine seafood from the ocean and the bay, Metompkin is Roadfood par excellence: part of a community that loves and appreciates it, completely tuned in to local foodways, informal and friendly. Here is one very convincing piece of evidence that American regional food is alive and well and a joy to discover and to eat.

Mrs. Rowe's Family Restaurant and Bakery

74 Rowe Rd. (Exit 222 off I-81)   540-886-1833
Staunton, VA   BLD | $$

Mrs. Rowe's is not what it used to be, but that doesn't mean you won't enjoy its freshly baked biscuits and sticky buns, the crunchy fried chicken with mashed potatoes and/or mac 'n' cheese on the side, the pork chop and stewed apple plate, and the creamy, meringue-crowned banana pudding. Opened by the late Mildred Rowe decades ago as a small mom-and-pop café, the once-homey eatery has become a big roadside enterprise. Its fame and its location at the end of a highway exit ramp attract crowds on busy travel weekends (a million people per year!), and sometimes it can seem like an assembly-line eatery. But we've never found the staff less than courteous, and once the food starts coming we easily drop any prejudice engendered by Mrs. Rowe's conspicuous success and eat hearty.

Philip's Continental Lounge

5704 Grove Ave.   804-288-8687
Richmond, VA   LD | $

A haunt of students at the University of Richmond since 1939, Phil's is famous for outsize sandwiches ranging from grilled cheese to Reubens and Reuben variants. The turkey club is imposingly tall and the unfancy hamburgers are diner delights, especially when topped with cheese and accompanied by an order of brittle-crusted beer-batter onion rings or French fries. Crunchy pickle wedges come alongside.

Beyond sandwiches, Phil's offers a broad menu of hot suppers: fried chicken, fried shrimp, even steak. Among libations, adult and otherwise, are terrific milk shakes, tart limeade, and the house signature cocktail, vodka limeade.

Ambience is that of a mid-century college-town lounge with its decor of pennants and giant droopy inflated beer bottles hanging from the ceiling.

Sally Bell's Kitchen

708 W. Grace St.   804-644-2838
Richmond, VA $

Sally Bell's Kitchen was conceived in 1924 as a bakery, and that is what it is today—a charming little relic from the past with Sally Lunn muffins, pies, tarts, and that nearly lost icon of the Old South kitchen, beaten biscuits. The biscuits are crisp, tan rounds with silky tops that are an ideal companion for bisque or a fluffy little salad or Sally Bell's tomato aspic. Cupcakes are notable because they are iced all over, not just on top. We love the strawberry cupcakes, so pretty in pink.

There is no place to eat here, but you can get a boxed lunch that sells for well under $10. Inside a white cardboard box, inscribed with the trademark feminine silhouette, you will find a sandwich on a made-here roll or bread, a cup of macaroni or potato salad, a cupcake . . . and this marvelous thing called a cheese wafer. It is delicate and fragile—a couple of bites and it is gone—a taste of a more refined era long before supersizing. Among available sandwich ingredients are, of course, pimiento cheese as well as chicken salad, egg salad, Smithfield ham, and cream cheese with nuts.

While we travelers generally confine ourselves to cupcakes, little tarts (apple, peach, or pecan), muffins, and boxed lunches, people with a dinner table nearby come to Sally Bell's for full-size cakes. The devil's food and yellow batter cakes are picture-perfect.

Southern Kitchen

9576 S. Congress St.	540-740-3514
New Market, VA	BLD | $

A conveniently located town café just minutes from I-81, the Southern Kitchen has remained true to its name for decades. If you want something real to eat, something *real southern,* drive past the franchised junk-food restaurants clustered near the highway and have a seat in the dining room to the right or at the counter or in one of the old booths along the wall. Here you will find genuine country ham at breakfast and Virginia peanut soup at lunch (although a while back we convinced the waitress to warm some of the latter up for us at 7 A.M.). The soup is creamy but not too thick, nutty-flavored but not like liquid peanut butter, and laced with a fetching onion sweetness. A little of it goes a long way; it is an Old Dominion specialty whose svelte character is a perfect hors d'oeuvre before a supper of powerhouse country ham.

If a thick slice of that good ham is just too hammy for dinner, consider the kitchen's gorgeous fried chicken, encased in a succulent golden crust, or even fried oysters, which, considering the location hundreds of miles from seawater, are shockingly good. Among noteworthy side dishes are stewed tomatoes made the traditional southern way—extra sweet—so they are a perfect balance for the ham.

Pies are homemade and worth saving some appetite for—especially the coconut meringue.

Sting-Ray's

26507 Lankford Hwy.	757-331-1541
Cape Charles, VA	BLD | $$

It is rare to find good food in a gas station restaurant, which is why it's such fun to find a place such as Weikel's in Texas (p. 470) or Oklahoma Joe's in Kansas City (p. 413). Located on Virginia's Eastern Shore and known to locals as Chez Exxon, Sting-Ray's shares space with fuel pumps, a pottery shop, and a boat storage facility. Instead of the familiar gas station repertoire of breakfast sandwiches, corn dogs, and cellophane-wrapped honey buns, it is a source of superb local cuisine.

Oysters and shrimp are expertly fried (marinated shrimp are gorgeous). A not-to-be-missed kitchen specialty is sweet potato biscuits. Made from a recipe that is decades-old, they are particularly good sandwiching thin slices of country ham which, being Virginia ham, isn't all that brackish. Regional highlights also include ultra-luxurious crab imperial and flounder stuffed with crab imperial as well as a creamed crab dish that isn't really a stew but is too thick to pass as soup.

Deluxe though some dishes may be, service at Sting-Ray's is down-home. Place your order at the counter and pay. Find a seat (which can be difficult on weekends) and your food will be brought out by one of a staff of professional waitresses. One named Etta turned out to be a font of Sting-Ray's history as well as a top-notch advisor when it came to ordering, steering us toward sweet potato pie for dessert (sweet potatoes are a local crop). Its creamy goodness was accented by a dollop of bright-flavored damson plum preserves.

Stuart's Fresh Catch

2400 Mechanicsville Tpk.   804-643-3474
Richmond, VA   LD | $

Stuart's is a storefront seafood market with no place for customers to eat. Everything is sold fried (or grilled), either ready to eat by the tray, dinner, piece, or sandwich, or ready to take home and cook. We accompanied our sandwich of cream-fleshed fried lake trout, fried oysters, and fried shrimp with individual orders of exemplary collard greens, fried okra, macaroni and cheese and, best of all, spoonbread. A rarity in any other region and ever more difficult to find even in the South, this billowy corn pudding has a kind of gaiety that tastes as much of corn as any sweetener. It is earthy but elegant, and even though it does require a utensil (preferably a spoon), it makes an ideal companion for hunks of golden-crusted lake trout with its dense meat and crisp golden crust that is so right to pick up and eat with fingers.

Virginia Diner

408 Country Dr. N.   804-899-3463
Wakefield, VA   BLD | $

Wakefield's Virginia Diner is the epicenter of the peanut universe. Here you can buy pounds of Virginia peanuts, which are 100 percent better than any other peanuts: big, crunchy, dark, and rich. They come salted or un-salted, spiced with Old Bay seasoning or Cajun pepper, butter-toasted, in the shell or shelled, and as the foundation for a truly aristocratic peanut brittle.

Curiously, there are not a lot of peanuts served in the restaurant, al-though it used to be that Virginia ham had to be made from peanut-fed pigs (no more). This diner's ham is terrific, available baked or fried. Fried chicken, having nothing to do with peanuts, is also mighty good, sheathed in a brittle crust. With these fine southern entrees, you can choose turnip greens, candied yams, spoonbread, black-eyed peas, or stewed tomatoes.

For dessert, you definitely want peanut pie. It is a simple dish, similar to pecan pie but not so cloying.

Weenie Beenie

2680 Shirlington Rd.   703-671-6661
Arlington, VA   BLD | $

Weenie Beenie is the sole survivor of a small Washington-area chain of drive-ins specializing in half-smokes. No one knows for sure how the half-smoke got its name (perhaps because it's only half smoky or because many places, like Weenie Beenie, bisect them horizontally before they are grilled), but it is the one dish unique to the area. Here you can have one at lunch dressed with chili (known as a chili smoke), mustard, onions, and relish. At breakfast your half-smoke will be matched with a fried egg and a slice of bright orange cheese.

Regular hot dogs also are available, but they look pretty boring to us. You also can order barbecue pork or just a bowl of beefy chili. Picnic tables are arrayed along the side of the take-out-only restaurant for those who choose not to eat in their cars.

Wright's Dairy Rite

346 Greenville Ave.   540-886-0435
Staunton, VA   LD | $

Three years before Ray Kroc began franchising McDonald's, Wright's Dairy Rite of Staunton, Virginia, started serving Superburgers. Two beef patties with cheese and lettuce, topped with a special sauce and layered in a triple-decker bun, this architectonic hamburger is still served as it was in 1952—by carhops at the window of your vehicle, in a car slip at the side of the restaurant. Wright's added a dining room in 1989, so it is also possible to eat inside, where decor includes a handsome Wurlitzer jukebox and vintage Wright's menus from the 1950s and 1960s.

Handsome as the Superburger is, we suggest serious burger-lovers forgo it for a Monsterburger or a Carolina burger; they are bigger patties of beef that tend not to lose their juice, which can be a fault of the smaller patties. On the side, you want Wright's homemade onion rings. To drink with this festive heap of food, one needs a shake. At Wright's, milk shakes are the real thing, available in chocolate, strawberry, or vanilla, as well as with real bananas or strawberries (mmmm!), and with or without malted milk for additional richness. It is, after all, Wright's *Dairy* Rite, so don't hesitate to have a banana split, a float, or a flurry (candy and/or cookies blended into soft-serve ice cream).

Wright's menu goes well beyond burgers. There are regular and foot-long hot dogs, corn dogs, pork barbecue on a bun, sandwich baskets, submarines, chili with beans, even a veggie wrap with fat-free dressing. In addition to milk shakes and soda pop, the beverage list includes freshly brewed, pre-sweetened iced tea, served in twenty-ounce cups.

West Virginia

Coleman's Fish Market

2226 Market St.   304-232-8510
Wheeling, WV   LD | $

Coleman's fish sandwich is simplicity itself: two pieces of soft white bread holding a cluster of steaming hot fried fish fillets. If you want tartar sauce, you have to ask for it, and you pay 7¢ extra. The sandwich is delivered across a counter, wrapped in wax paper; it is your task to find a table somewhere on the broad floor of the renovated century-old Wheeling Centre Market House, unwrap it, and feast!

The crust on the North Atlantic pollock fillets is made of cracker meal, thin as parchment. When you break through it, your sense of smell is tickled by a clean ocean perfume, and as the pearl-white meat seeps its warm, luscious sweetness, you taste a brand-new food, like no other fish sandwich ever created.

After you've eaten several dozen over time, you might want to branch out and try some of the many other excellent foods Coleman makes, all delivered over the counter in a bag for toting to a table: Canadian white sandwich (a bit blander and "whiter" tasting than the regular fish), shrimp boats and baskets, fried clams, oysters, deviled crabs, and Cajun-spiced catfish. Coleman's really is a fish market, and if you wait in the "Special Line" (as opposed to the "Regular Sandwich Line"), you can ask the staff to cook up just about any raw fish in the case, and pay for it by weight. On the side of whatever fish you get, there are good French fries and Jo-Jo potatoes, and onion rings every day but Friday (when the deep-fryers are totally devoted to making only fish sandwiches).

Coleman's was started by John Coleman in 1914 in the old city market (which itself dates back to 1890). Joe Coleman, grandson of John, keeps things up-to-date with the latest advances in nutritionally virtuous cooking oils. And the iron pavilion in which the market is located was handsomely renovated about fifteen years ago. In the heart of a muscular city known for steel and coal more than for cooking, Coleman's is a thriving legend of American gastronomy.

Julio's Café

501 Baltimore Ave.　　　304-622-2592

Clarksburg, WV　　　　LD | $$

Across from the train station in the old Elk Point section of Clarksburg, Julio's is a first-rate Italian restaurant with a tin ceiling, carved wooden bar, and plush leather booths that are, incongruously, outfitted with Lava Lamps. While the food is excellent, and clearly prepared by a chef with culinary expertise, prices are reasonable and service is neighborhood-friendly.

A printed menu lists lots of inviting pastas, including four different versions of *pasta e fagiole*—with cream sauce, with marinara, with potatoes and kale, and *en brodo* that twinkles with fennel—and primavera made with uncooked vegetables in red sauce. But some of the best dishes are not in print; waitresses recite extremely appetizing lists of the day's appetizers, entrees, and desserts.

For hors d'oeuvres, we loved our "paisano salad," a cold antipasto plate topped with the kitchen's jade-green garlic basil dressing, and roasted peppers with gorgonzola served atop tiles of garlic toast. We devoured entrees of vivid red peppers stuffed with hot ground sausage atop a bed of al dente spaghetti, a supremely comforting bowl of *pasta e fagiole,* and a stylish plate of tuna pomodoro. The meal commenced with a basket of swell garlic toast with a smoky taste and concluded with an outrageously rich house-made éclair loaded with French cream and blanketed with good chocolate.

Oliverio's Cash and Carry

427 Clark St.　　　　　304-622-8612

Clarksburg, WV　　　　$

"This was once *the* spot in Clarksburg," Angela Oliverio told us several years ago as she slid a long length of pig gut onto the spout of her hand-cranked sausage-making machine. "We had everything here in Elk Point [the

Clarksburg neighborhood where her grocery is located]: prostitution, gambling, big business, street-corner business, thriving industry."

While not by any means a bustling metropolis, Elk Point is coming back and, most important, Oliverio's is as wonderful as ever. What a gem: a vintage, family-run grocery store where Angela sits in back and with the help of her brother John cranks out lengths of coarse-textured Italian pork sausage seasoned with paprika, fennel seed, and plenty of hot pepper. She also prepares bowls full of peppered green and black olives that she will sell you by the pint. On the front shelves of the store are a wide assortment of roasted peppers and vegetable relishes that Angela's other brother, Frank, makes in his workshop just down the street. Peppers are how Oliverio's has been best known, ever since mama Antoinette Oliverio began canning them in the back of this store in the early 1930s. Some of the choice varieties made by son Frank today include diced hot cherry peppers, a spicy *giardiniera* (garden mix), and peppers in hot red sauce.

We need to point out the rather obvious fact that Oliverio's is not a restaurant. It is a little grocery store; and unless Angela takes a liking to you and you happen to be lucky enough to arrive just when she's cooked up a batch of her sausage for tasting purposes, you cannot eat here.

Quinet's Court

215 Main St.   304-455-2110
New Martinsville, WV   BLD | $

"We use the area's finest hobby chefs' recipes often," boasts the printed menu of Quinet's Court, where the choice of items on multiple buffet tables is cornucopic. Although presented in big institutional pans on room-length steam tables, most of the dishes do indeed seem like home cooking at its finest—from cake-smooth corn bread to stuffed peppers to cream pies, cobblers, cookies, and pudding.

To accompany baby back ribs, kielbasa, chicken casserole, or ham loaf with pineapple glaze, customers avail themselves of a vegetable smorgasbord to make even a devoted vegetarian smile. Silk-tender butter beans, sweet hunks of carrot, scalloped potatoes, homemade noodles, five-cheese mac 'n' cheese, and baked beans can fill a plate with a variety of wonderful flavors that, even meatless, can be a more than filling meal.

The buffet rule is that you pay one price and help yourself to as much as you want. A sign at the beginning of the first table does warn, however, that a $1 surcharge will be added to the bill of anyone who wastes food. Our waitress was especially generous. As we walked in the door, early during lunch hour, we noted a couple of beautiful sticky buns in a pan left over from breakfast. When we asked her if we could have one, she brought it, no charge, and told us simply to consider it part of our lunch buffet.

Accommodations are appropriately vast: big tables in several spacious dining rooms. Decor includes an awesome picture of prizefighter Jack Dempsey (who ate here in the 1940s) and a thousand pictures of town history and local citizens. It is possible to dine non-buffet-style: Breakfast, lunch sandwiches, and a selection of hot meals are listed on the menu under the heading "Great Specials for Our Not-So-Hungry Friends."

Ritzy Lunch

456 W. Pike St.   304-622-3600
Clarksburg, WV   LD | $

"A hot dog without chili is not a hot dog!" proclaims John Selario, known in Clarksburg as Hot Dog John. Mr. Selario's parents opened Ritzy Lunch in 1933, and he shows us pictures of his father in front of the same storefront sometime in the 1940s with hot dogs listed on the window for 7¢ each, hamburgers a dime. "Ritzy Lunch has always been known for hot dogs," he tells us. "Clarksburg itself is an important hot dog town, not so much because of the weenies but because of the way we make our chili. There are so many immigrants and sons and daughters of immigrants—Greeks and Italians, mostly—that when we spice up our chili, we know how to do it right!"

Hot Dog John will get no argument from us. His dogs are lovely little pups, buried deep inside a steamed-soft bun and topped with a zesty ground-beef sauce that is judiciously peppered and earthy flavored. If you want to add a sweet note, ask for a layer of coleslaw to go atop the chili—a popular configuration throughout most of West Virginia.

Although hot dogs are the *spécialité de la maison,* you should also consider sampling an unusual kind of hamburger in one of Ritzy's old wooden booths. Listed on the menu as a Giovanni, it is a patty of meat topped with melted cheese and roasted peppers served between two slices of butter-and-garlic-infused toast. Excellent!

Ritzy Lunch is an immensely happy place, a sort of nonalcoholic tavern where old friends and town characters hang out on the ancient counter stools to kibitz back and forth with each other and the waitresses, and where, on any pleasant day, two or three wiseacres are likely to be found out on the sidewalk joshing with each other and making friends with newcomers.

Ruby & Ketchy's

2232 Cheat Rd.   304-594-2004

Morgantown, WV   BLD | $

Ruby & Ketchy's is a charming out-of-the-way diner in the Cheat Lake area east of Morgantown. It's open for three meals a day, and its knotty-pine booths and counter are favorite places for locals to come for good eats and conversation. Opened by Ruby Nicholson in 1958, who was soon joined by husband Ketchy, it's still run by descendants of the beloved couple; and many of the recipes, including the vegetable soup, chili, and every-Tuesday meat loaf, are Ruby's.

Hot meals range from crab cakes to sirloin steak, and such lunch specials as bean soup and corn bread (every Thursday) and salmon patties with mac 'n' cheese on Friday. We enjoyed our ham dinner, of which the menu boasts "served over 30 years." The ham was pan-sizzled and had a rewarding chew. Hot roast beef was also good: pot-roast tender and accompanied by a sphere of mashed potatoes covered with gravy. We're not sure what to say about the potatoes, which didn't taste all that real to us but were a fine gravy conduit.

Blackberry pie is the go-to dessert. It is dark purple and winey, with a rugged berry texture. The crust could have been flakier, but the filling was first-rate.

Stewart's Original Hot Dogs

2445 Fifth Ave.   304-529-3647

Huntington, WV   LD | $

With countless little stands and storefronts that specialize in spicy little weenies topped with chili and coleslaw, West Virginia considers itself the hot dog capital of the known universe. The best place to test that claim is Stewart's, a curb-service drive-in since 1932. The formula includes local Logan hot dogs and Heiner's buns and, most important, all the trimmings: onions, mustard, and—drum roll, please—Stewart's secret-recipe chili sauce. The sauce is thick and pasty, not too hot. West Virginia hot dog connoisseurs believe the picture is not complete unless it also includes coleslaw as part of the trimming constellation; Stewart's is creamy with a bit of pickle bite.

To drink, nearly everybody swills renowned Stewart's root beer, available in quantities that range from a four-ounce mug for kids to a thirty-two-ounce drink to a gallon jug. Or you can enjoy it as the basis of an ice cream float.

Note: There are four other Stewart's locations in the Huntington area: First St. and Adams Ave. in West Huntington; in the Huntington Mall; 1025 Oak St. in Kenova; and 205 Towne Center Dr. in Ashland.

Deep South

Alabama * Arkansas * Florida * Georgia *

Louisiana * Mississippi * South Carolina

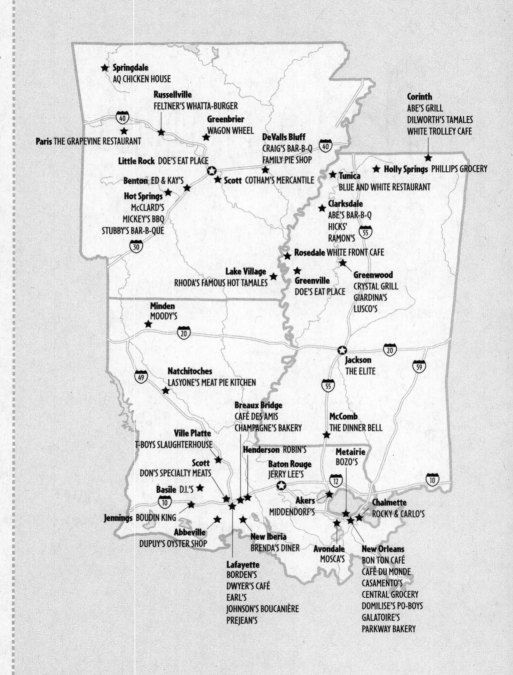

Springdale
AQ CHICKEN HOUSE

Russellville
FELTNER'S WHATTA-BURGER

Greenbrier
WAGON WHEEL

DeValls Bluff
CRAIG'S BAR-B-Q
FAMILY PIE SHOP

Corinth
ABE'S GRILL
DILWORTH'S TAMALES
WHITE TROLLEY CAFE

Paris THE GRAPEVINE RESTAURANT

Little Rock DOE'S EAT PLACE

Scott COTHAM'S MERCANTILE

Holly Springs PHILLIPS GROCERY

Benton ED & KAY'S

Tunica
BLUE AND WHITE RESTAURANT

Hot Springs
McCLARD'S
MICKEY'S BBQ
STUBBY'S BAR-B-QUE

Clarksdale
ABE'S BAR-B-Q
HICKS'
RAMON'S

Rosedale WHITE FRONT CAFE

Greenwood
CRYSTAL GRILL
GIARDINA'S
LUSCO'S

Lake Village
RHODA'S FAMOUS HOT TAMALES

Greenville
DOE'S EAT PLACE

Minden
MOODY'S

Jackson
THE ELITE

Natchitoches
LASYONE'S MEAT PIE KITCHEN

McComb
THE DINNER BELL

Breaux Bridge
CAFÉ DES AMIS
CHAMPAGNE'S BAKERY

Ville Platte
T-BOYS SLAUGHTERHOUSE

Henderson ROBIN'S

Metairie
BOZO'S

Scott
DON'S SPECIALTY MEATS

Baton Rouge
JERRY LEE'S

Basile D.I.'S

Akers
MIDDENDORF'S

Chalmette
ROCKY & CARLO'S

Jennings BOUDIN KING

Abbeville
DUPUY'S OYSTER SHOP

New Iberia
BRENDA'S DINER

Avondale
MOSCA'S

New Orleans
BON TON CAFÉ
CAFÉ DU MONDE
CASAMENTO'S
CENTRAL GROCERY
DOMILISE'S PO-BOYS
GALATOIRE'S
PARKWAY BAKERY

Lafayette
BORDEN'S
DWYER'S CAFÉ
EARL'S
JOHNSON'S BOUCANIÈRE
PREJEAN'S

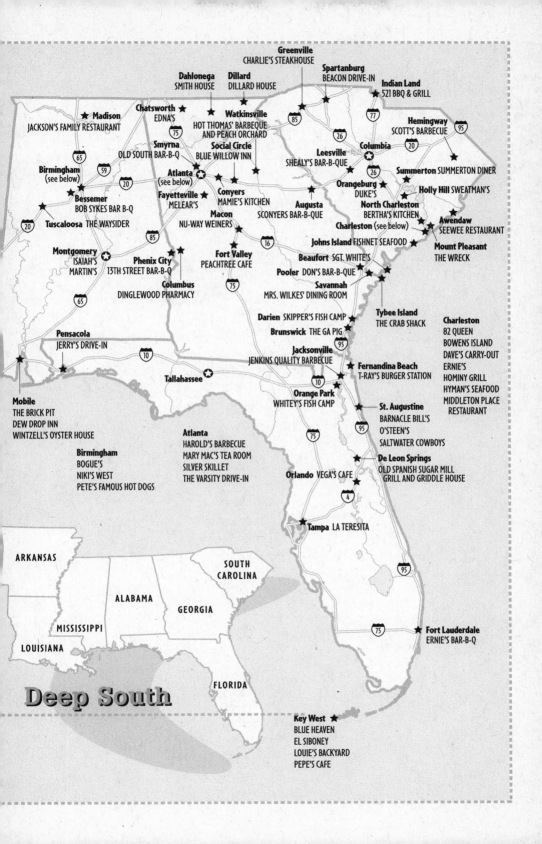

Greenville CHARLIE'S STEAKHOUSE

Spartanburg BEACON DRIVE-IN

Dahlonega SMITH HOUSE

Dillard DILLARD HOUSE

Indian Land 521 BBQ & GRILL

Madison JACKSON'S FAMILY RESTAURANT

Chatsworth EDNA'S

Watkinsville HOT THOMAS' BARBEQUE AND PEACH ORCHARD

Hemingway SCOTT'S BARBECUE

Smyrna OLD SOUTH BAR-B-Q

Social Circle BLUE WILLOW INN

Columbia

Leesville SHEALY'S BAR-B-QUE

Summerton SUMMERTON DINER

Birmingham (see below)

Atlanta (see below)

Orangeburg DUKE'S

Holly Hill SWEATMAN'S

Bessemer BOB SYKES BAR-B-Q

Fayetteville MELEAR'S

Conyers MAMIE'S KITCHEN

Augusta SCONYERS BAR-B-QUE

North Charleston BERTHA'S KITCHEN

Tuscaloosa THE WAYSIDER

Macon NU-WAY WEINERS

Charleston (see below)

Awendaw SEEWEE RESTAURANT

Johns Island FISHNET SEAFOOD

Mount Pleasant THE WRECK

Montgomery ISAIAH'S MARTIN'S

Phenix City 13TH STREET BAR-B-Q

Fort Valley PEACHTREE CAFE

Beaufort SGT. WHITE'S

Pooler DON'S BAR-B-QUE

Columbus DINGLEWOOD PHARMACY

Savannah MRS. WILKES' DINING ROOM

Tybee Island THE CRAB SHACK

Charleston
82 QUEEN
BOWENS ISLAND
DAVE'S CARRY-OUT
ERNIE'S
HOMINY GRILL
HYMAN'S SEAFOOD
MIDDLETON PLACE RESTAURANT

Pensacola JERRY'S DRIVE-IN

Darien SKIPPER'S FISH CAMP

Brunswick THE GA PIG

Tallahassee

Jacksonville JENKINS QUALITY BARBECUE

Fernandina Beach T-RAY'S BURGER STATION

Mobile
THE BRICK PIT
DEW DROP INN
WINTZELL'S OYSTER HOUSE

Orange Park WHITEY'S FISH CAMP

St. Augustine
BARNACLE BILL'S
O'STEEN'S
SALTWATER COWBOYS

Atlanta
HAROLD'S BARBECUE
MARY MAC'S TEA ROOM
SILVER SKILLET
THE VARSITY DRIVE-IN

Birmingham
BOGUE'S
NIKI'S WEST
PETE'S FAMOUS HOT DOGS

De Leon Springs OLD SPANISH SUGAR MILL GRILL AND GRIDDLE HOUSE

Orlando VEGA'S CAFE

Tampa LA TERESITA

ARKANSAS

SOUTH CAROLINA

ALABAMA

GEORGIA

MISSISSIPPI

LOUISIANA

Fort Lauderdale ERNIE'S BAR-B-Q

FLORIDA

Deep South

Key West
BLUE HEAVEN
EL SIBONEY
LOUIE'S BACKYARD
PEPE'S CAFE

Bob Sykes Bar B-Q

1724 9th Ave. N.   205-426-1400
Bessemer, AL   LD | $$

Bob Sykes opened in 1957 as a hamburger stand. Bob soon built a pit and started cooking barbecue. At one time there were fourteen Bob Sykes barbecues in northern Alabama, but in 1977 the Sykes family decided to concentrate on one location in Bessemer, southwest of Birmingham. Since then, this smokehouse, now run by a third generation of Sykeses that still uses the original recipes, has been a smoke signal of good eats.

Cooked over slow-smoldering hickory wood, the pork is finely chopped and succulent; ribs are beautiful burnished mahogany with great hefty ribbons of meat around each bone; chopped beef is particularly flavorful. Big Bob dinner plates include your barbecued meat of choice with baked beans, coleslaw, and French fries or potato salad, plus rolls. There is even a version of the barbecue salad so popular farther west: lettuce, tomatoes, carrots, cheese, and croutons topped with your choice of pork, chicken, turkey, or ham. For those with a lot of hungry mouths to feed, Sykes's menu lists extra-large orders to feed five or ten (the latter is based on two-and-a-half pounds of barbecue and comes with a gallon of tea). Carry-out meals and big feeds are sold at a drive-through window that the menu advises is ideal for "church functions . . . hunting trips . . . tired mothers . . . unexpected guest."

Pies are excellent, sold by the slice, whole pie, or mini-pie. You can get chocolate, pecan, and coconut, but the one that must be sampled is the meringue-topped lemon pie: sweet, creamy, and southern to its soul.

Bogue's

3028 Clairmont Ave.	205-254-9780
Birmingham, AL	BL | $

Souvenir matchbooks say, "It's vogue to eat at Bogue's," but if you are looking for an epicurean breakfast, for obsequious service, or for the trendy restaurant where fashionistas dine, Bogue's is all wrong. If, on the other hand, you want a cheap, rib-sticking breakfast featuring grilled country ham or pork chops, buttered grits, and biscuits so richly endowed with cooking grease that your fingers glisten after you split one in half, this is where you want to be. If for some reason you don't want biscuits, we highly recommend the sweet rolls. "Are they made here?" we ask our waitress.

"Every morning," she reassures us, speaking loud enough to be heard over the blast of Bogue's high-powered air-conditioning and, without being asked, bringing us Tabasco sauce for a plate of eggs.

No, the pea green walls and upholstered booths are not glamorous, but to connoisseurs of good ol' urban Roadfood and of the rock-ribbed waitresses who serve it, Bogue's is a gem in the rough.

The Brick Pit

5456 Old Shell Rd.	251-343-0001
Mobile, AL	LD | $$

The Brick Pit calls itself "The Best Damned Smoked Barbecue in the State of Alabama." We do not disagree. Pitmaster Bill Armbrecht operates a room-size cooker into which he piles hickory and pecan logs and smokes meats at the lowest possible temperature for the longest possible time. Pork shoulder sizzles for some thirty hours; ribs for twelve; chicken for six. During the process, the meats' natural fat becomes their basting juices, and by the time they are done, each piece of pork and chicken is virtually fatless, yet moister than moist.

We're especially smitten with the pulled pork—so much so that when we were asked by the erstwhile Gourmet Institute to have a few great regional foods shipped to New York for attendees to taste, Brick Pit shoulder headed the list . . . and earned universal accolades. It is presented as a pile of motley chunks and shreds—some as soft as warm butter, others with a crunchy crust. Ribs are blackened on the outside but extravagantly tender, with many areas so gentled by their tenure in the smoke pit that the lightest finger pressure causes pieces of meat to slide off the bone.

The low-slung dining room at The Brick Pit is painted white and completely covered in signatures, tributes, and other assorted happy graffiti. Orders are taken at a back window; once you've said what you want, you find a seat, and in no time a waitress brings the meal on a partitioned plate that holds the meat of choice separate from the beans and coleslaw that come with it.

Dew Drop Inn

1808 Old Shell Rd.   251-473-7872
Mobile, AL   LD | $

Frankfurter purists, skip this entry and move on. South Alabamians put ketchup on their hot dogs—a boner in most places, a criminal act in most of the Midwest. But talk to any wiener-lover who grew up in Mobile, and you will see eyes mist with nostalgia for the unique joy of their hometown hot dog as dished out by street vendors during Mardi Gras and as served at the Dew Drop Inn year-round. They are bright red steamed franks of medium size, and the presentation is a work of art, the wiener nestled in a toasted bun, topped with cool sauerkraut and a layer of warm, beefy chili with spicy-sweet zest. Standard condiments include mustard and pickles as well as ketchup. Aesthetes order them upside-down (the dog sits atop the condiments) and others like them "shaved" (without kraut).

A comfy, wood-paneled roadhouse that opened in 1924 and introduced hot dogs to southern Alabama, the Dew Drop Inn also offers a full menu of po-boys, gumbo, Gulf shrimp, and hot dinners accompanied by such good vegetables as turnip greens and rice and gravy. Coca-Cola is served the true-South way, in its shapely classic bottle alongside a glass full of ice. Banana pudding is the choice dessert. Service is speedy; checks are delivered with meals.

Isaiah's Restaurant

135 Mildred St.   334-265-9000
Montgomery, AL   L Tues-Fri & Sun | $

Roadfood warrior Cliff Strutz (a.k.a. Buffetbuster at Roadfood.com) pointed the way to this locally loved but elsewhere little-known restaurant and bed-and-breakfast near the capitol. The cuisine is easy-to-like soul food, the signature dish being a big slab of catfish (boneless) with a golden crisp coat and a shot of lemon-pepper seasoning. Other entrees on the menu, which is a piece of paper on which each customer marks what he wants, are chicken, ribs, and pork from the smoker. But it's the side dishes that star: collard greens, field peas, candied yams, lima beans, and that honorary southern vegetable, macaroni and cheese, of which Isaiah's makes some of the best. It is baked so that some noodles attain a good measure of chew while the whole package—thick enough to be doled out in a single piece the size of an ice cream scoop—remains creamy. Fried corn, another interesting choice, is a goopy kind of dish, the kernels suspended in bacon-fat gravy: maybe too rich.

The dessert choice is limited to either cheesecake or peach cobbler. The latter is what you want, served warm in a jumbo soda fountain tulip glass and preferably à la mode.

Jackson's Family Restaurant

234 Lime Quarry Rd.   256-772-0191
Madison, AL   BL Mon-Fri | $

Halfway between Huntsville and Decatur, the small town of Madison is home to a great small-town restaurant. What a pleasure it is to ease into a Naugahyde booth and open up a menu to find a piece of paper clipped inside that lists all the various elements from which you can choose your fundamental southern plate lunch of meat-and-three. That means one meat and three vegetables from a choice that might include, among the former, country-fried steak or barbecue, and among the latter, fried okra, vinegar slaw and mayo slaw, greens, beans, and hush puppies.

Catfish, fried whole, comes crusted with fine, crumbly cornmeal. You get two per order, the obligatory sides being hush puppies, coleslaw, and French fries. To drink: Coke or iced tea. And for dessert, you'll want a slice of pie that is baked locally for the café, preferably pecan or apple. Jackson's is also a terrific place for an early morning breakfast of country ham and biscuits.

(Please note that Jackson's closes the weeks before and after Independence Day and Christmas.)

Martin's

1796 Carter Hill Rd.   334-265-1767
Montgomery, AL   LD | $

Oh, such biscuits begin supper at Martin's! Warm, flaky-crusted with gossamer insides, they would be insulted by the use of butter. The only thing better than the biscuits is the corn bread, in the form of soft-textured muffins, also warm.

The dinner menu is good-size, including such main-course choices as whole fried catfish, stuffed deviled crabs, and fried chicken livers. At lunch, choice is limited to daily specials: catfish fillets, smoked sausage, country-fried steak, chicken and dumplings. At either meal, you can count on a roster of side dishes that honor the southern way with vegetables: velvet-soft cooked cabbage, pot-likker-sopped collard greens, pole beans, buttery mashed potatoes, plus, of course, Jell-O salad in rainbow hues. Of all the things to eat at Martin's, the standout is fried chicken. Its crisp gold crust has a nice jolt of spice, it is easy to handle (i.e., grease-free), and it is dripping moist inside. One serving includes a meaty white breast and a dark-meat thigh. With biscuits, mashed potatoes, and greens, it makes a memorable meal . . . followed, of course, by a piece of Martin's coconut meringue pie.

A wood-paneled, colonial-themed restaurant that moved to its current location in a strip mall about ten years ago, Martin's is busier at lunch than at supper; in fact at noon, you will likely wait, and watch, as early-arriving customers devour their plates of irresistible fried chicken with hedonistic gusto.

Niki's West

233 Finley Ave. W.   205-252-5751
Birmingham, AL   BLD | $

In the Deep South, vegetables are grown nearly year-round, and many of those vegetables are trucked to the produce center in Birmingham, where they are then shipped to destinations all over the East. Niki's West, surrounded by warehouses and loading docks, is where the produce-haulers come to eat. We counted more than three dozen vegetables along the steam table line—far too many to even contemplate sampling some of each; so prepare yourself to make some hard choices among the likes of yellow squash casserole, fried green tomatoes, black-eyed peas, and three different kinds of seasoned greens (turnip, collard, and spinach). Some items from the market are austere enough to please even the strictest dieter: unadorned sliced tomatoes, raw vegetable vinaigrette, and baby lima beans. But the more temptatious segment of Niki's produce repertoire is prepared according to voluptuous southern-café tradition. Broccoli is mixed with cheese and rice in a crazy-rich mélange; tomatoes are stewed with sugar and shreds of torn white bread until they become as sweet as cobbler; bright orange yams are infused with sugar; crunchy-fresh okra is sheathed in a deep-fried crust.

The decorative theme at Niki's is the Aegean Sea (fishnets, scenic art of fishing boats, etc.), and when it comes to choosing an entree, we recommend baked fish Creole, broiled mackerel, and grilled amberjack. For fish-frowners, there is always a selection of beef and pork as well as a baked Greek chicken that is terrific.

We used to not like dessert at Niki's, but recent visits have made us happily eat our words. Lemon meringue pie is lofty and light, lemon icebox pie is vibrant, and banana pudding, sweet and rich as caramel, is one of the South's best.

Pete's Famous Hot Dogs

1925 2nd Ave. N.   205-252-2905
Birmingham, AL   L | $

Pete's has been declared the narrowest restaurant in Birmingham and can feel as snug as an MRI machine. Dishing out cheap eats since 1915, it entered our book of must-eats thanks to a Roadfooder who goes by the handle "The Don." The Don described Pete's hot dogs as "the absolute best in the land, perfectly grilled every time, always on a fresh steamed bun." He said that Pete's hot dogs are "so good I have to hit myself in the head with a brick to stop eating them."

We can relate. Pete's hot dogs are modest-size crisp-grilled weenies almost always served "all the way"—with onions, sauerkraut, and tangy-sweet sauce, as well as a shot of mustard. Pete's "special" supplements the mix with dark, beefy chili. Cheese adds a whole other level of taste to the combo and is highly recommended. If you eat twelve of them in one sitting, the thirteenth is free.

Other than hot dogs and hamburgers, there is nothing on Pete's menu, not even French fries. If you need something on the side, bags of chips are available; and the beverages of choice are Coca-Cola and a curiously tangy grape-flavored bubbly bug juice known as Grapico. For dessert, choose from a selection of candy bars that includes Goo Goo Clusters. Expect to dine standing up.

13th Street Bar-B-Q

1310 7th Ave.   334-291-1833
Phenix City, AL   LD | $

We've eaten a few memorable pork chop sandwiches around the country, from Helen's Sausage House in Delaware to Don's Specialty Meats in Cajun country and, of course, the hallowed Snappy Lunch in Mount Airy, North Carolina. Here's a real beauty, in an extremely inconspicuous storefront smokehouse that bills itself as "Home of the Pork Chop Sandwich." You get a thick, boneless slab of tenderloin dressed with a measure of slaw and your choice of mild or (very) hot mustard sauce. It arrives in a tender poppy-seeded roll that serves not only as a good mitt for lifting the chop but also as a quiet, bready counterpoint for the succulent meat and spicy sauce.

The full barbecue menu also includes extremely meaty ribs crusted with vivid glaze as well as barbecue sandwiches and plates: chipped, chopped, or sliced.

There are four locations of the 13th Street Bar-B-Q in Alabama and Georgia, none of them located on 13th Street.

The Waysider

1512 Greensboro Ave.   205-345-8239
Tuscaloosa, AL   BL | $

For about half a century, The Waysider has been a treasured source of streak o' lean, once a familiar farmhouse dish that's now pretty hard to find. If you like your bacon well fatted and thick enough so that it has a crust that encases a thin ribbon of pig meat, you will love it. Four fried-crisp slabs, each a good quarter-inch thick, arrive on the plate—with gravy and biscuits, of course. The word *luscious* simply is not luscious enough to describe its overwhelming sumptuousness. It is bacon squared, bacon to the nth degree, with its chewy, lean veins of meat striating a strip of amber fat so tenuous that it melts on your tongue. For a slightly less piggy breakfast, consider country ham with red-eye gravy, served with dainty, fluff-centered, crisp-topped biscuits, grits, and honey. The triple-whammy flavor combo of salty ham, steamy biscuit, and sweet honey makes a taste experience that is, for us, as close to heaven as earthly food ever gets.

Waysider lunch is good Dixie café fare: fried chicken or steak with slews of such satisfying southern vegetables as fried okra, field peas, collard greens, squash soufflé, candied yams, and fried corn. Warm fruit cobbler and cream pies top things off with a super-sweet exclamation mark.

Wintzell's Oyster House

605 Dauphin St.   251-432-4605
Mobile, AL   LD | $$

Wintzell's used to be one of a kind. There now are six of them in Alabama and one in Hattiesburg, Mississippi. We've heard mixed reviews about the others, but have only good things to say about the original in downtown Mobile. Aside from impeccable, opened-as-you-watch raw oysters, you can sample such definitive Gulf Coast specialties as seafood gumbo and crisp-fried crab claws, oyster po-boys, and crusty-fried catfish, as well as an authoritative version of the unique Mobile specialty, West Indies salad. A simple dish, it's really nothing more than crabmeat marinated in oil and vinegar with grated onions. If the crab is good—and you can count on that here—it is a dish that is rich and ocean-sweet, so addictive that many customers forgo it as an appetizer (its usual role) and get a couple of large orders for their main course, accompanied by saltine crackers.

The restaurant itself is heaps of fun. Opened by Oliver Wintzell as a six-stool oyster bar in 1938, it has survived hurricanes and floods, rebuilt and expanded into a big place. There still is an oyster bar where you can sit and knock 'em back by the dozen; and it continues to keep score in the ongoing contest to see who can eat the most raw oysters in one hour. The walls are plastered with thousands of little signs offering bons mots and politically incorrect rules of life put there by the late Mr. Wintzell, starting in the 1950s. For example: "When a wife looks high and low for her husband at a party, she usually finds him high." *Bits of Wit and Wisdom (The Signs at Wintzell's Oyster House)* and *Oysters and Politics,* Mr. Wintzell's self-published books, are available for sale at the cash register.

AQ Chicken House

1207 N. Thompson St.   479-751-4633
Springdale, AR   LD | $

Fried chicken? There is none better. Charcoal-cooked chicken? AQ's is the best. Barbecued chicken? There are a few around the country we like better than AQ's, but these crusty pieces, sticky with dark red, spicy-sweet sauce, will never get kicked off our plate. The point is: If you like chicken, you need to come to Springdale (or AQ's second location on Highway 71B in Fayetteville) and test this fine stuff for yourself. Fried is juice-spurting tender, encased in a chewy-crisp envelope of well-seasoned crust. Charcoal-cooked is nearly as indulgent, its spicy skin imbued with the flavor of smoke and a vigorous lemon-pepper smack. If you can't make up your mind, the menu does offer a sampler platter of three pieces, each cooked a different way. An all-you-can-eat plan is available for $11.99 per person.

Meals at this big, family-friendly restaurant begin with glossy-topped cloverleaf rolls hot from the oven; and among essential side dishes are a slightly spicy sweet potato casserole, batter-dipped French fries (over-the-top, deliciously oily), seasoned green beans, smoky baked beans, and real mashed potatoes. Unless you have a note from your doctor, you must order fried peaches for dessert: slices of al dente peach are battered and fried and served hot under a pile of ice cream.

Cotham's Mercantile

5301 Hwy. 161 S.   501-961-9284
Scott, AR   L Mon-Wed, LD Thurs-Sat | $

In the Grand Prairie southeast of Little Rock, Cotham's Mercantile is perched on stilts above a slow-flowing river. Built in 1917, it has been a general store, a jail, and a military commissary. Contemporary Arkansans know it as a plate-lunch destination.

The old wood building is fronted by a broad porch. Enter a swinging door into a dining room packed literally to the ceiling with vintage house and farm bric-a-brac, from garden tools to primordial television sets. Remote the restaurant may be, but it is rare to see an empty chair. Bare wood tables are surrounded by customers who come for noonday meals built around catfish, chicken-fried steak, or chicken-fried chicken, and such daily specials as fried pork chops (Monday), chicken and dumplings (Tuesday), meat loaf (Wednesday), and southern-fried chicken (Thursday). Side dishes include corn fritters, hush puppies, collard greens, and fried green tomatoes.

A large number of customers make the pilgrimage for a hamburger. It's not just any hamburger, but a Hubcap Hamburger: an immense circle of cooked ground beef—close to a foot in diameter and a half-inch thick—that comes in a bun that nearly fits, dressed with a salad's worth of mustard, lettuce, tomato slices, pickles, and hoops of onion. Incredibly, it is possible to lift it with two hands from plate to mouth. The outlandish specialty has earned such renown that the store's pushpin map of the United States has no room left for any more pins to show where Hupcap-loving customers have come from; business cards from visitors around the globe are tacked up all around it.

Desserts include Arkansas fried pies and peach or blackberry cobbler.

Craig's Bar-B-Que

Hwy. 70 W.   870-998-2616
DeValls Bluff, AR   LD | $

Craig's pork is deeply smoked and brushed with a thick orange sauce that is big on spice and nearly sugarless, with a twist that tastes vaguely like citrus. To balance the devilish sauce, which is available ultra-hot if specially requested, sandwiches are constructed with a layer of sweet coleslaw inside the bun. That bright slaw sings a fine tune when it dresses one of Craig's Polish sausages, also lined with mustard and topped with hot sauce. Dinner plates include beans and slaw; the only other available side dish is a bag of chips. And the only proper thing to drink is iced tea—very sweet tea, of course.

During a visit to this tumbledown roadside shack in summer 2010, we chatted with a waitress who had returned after starting at Craig's twenty-plus years ago. "Nothing has changed," she said with a certain amount of pride, pointing to the ducks-in-flight wall panel pattern that gives the place a hunting-lodge ambience. Pinned to the walls are business cards and hand-penned ads who-knows-how-old: lost dogs, pre-owned shotguns, beauty salons, deer processing, and taxidermy. Diners' attire ranges from still-wet camouflage waders to pressed pinstripe suits and well-worn overalls. Although the dining room is bisected (a legacy of segregation days), quarters are close enough that conversations are wide open among seated eaters as well as take-out customers hovering around waiting for their food. We shared thoughts with Arkansawyers about political vice and bird-dog virtue.

Doe's Eat Place

1023 W. Markham St.   501-376-1195
Little Rock, AR   LD | $$$

Doe's is no longer the dilapidated eatery with worn linoleum floors that made it such a deliciously déclassé place to eat high-class steaks. After a kitchen fire early in 2010, it reopened in the spring with clean new floors and spiffed-up dining areas. But nothing important has changed. The steaks remain aristocrats. Porterhouses, T-bones, and rib-eyes are served by weight, family-style. That means that the cut of your choice comes hot from the kitchen already sliced, along with tongs for everyone to hoist their own from the serving plate. Are you stumped as to what porterhouse poundage your table needs? No problem. The menu advises, "If you are a new customer at Doe's and wish assistance ordering, our experienced staff will be glad to help you." In fact, the staff at Doe's is friendly and obliging, even those times when the place is packed, as it is on weekend nights.

Along with succulent, charred-edge slabs of beef come skillet-cooked French fries. And before the arrival of the meat you get a bowl of memorable marinated salad slick with garlicky, lemony olive-oil dressing. There are serious appetizers, too, and we highly recommend them for those of limitless appetite. Fried or broiled shrimp are available by the half-dozen, and Doe's hot tamales with chili are tip-top (but also very, very filling).

Note: There now are franchised Doe's throughout the South. This one and the one in Greenville, Mississippi (p. 272), are family-owned.

Ed & Kay's

15228 I-30   501-315-3663
Benton, AR   BLD | $

Best known for its showstopping pies, Ed & Kay's also happens to be a good stop for a hamburger with onion rings or a yeomanly plate lunch. There may be only one or two hot entrees any day—stuffed peppers, fried chicken, ham, pork chops—but the list of side dishes is awesome, including mac 'n' cheese, purple hull peas, creamed corn, and skillet-fried potatoes. Most people get an entree and two or three vegetables, but it is possible to neglect a main course altogether and have a wonderful meal of four different side dishes.

Meringue pies are amazing-looking, their tops a perfect volcano shape that is two or three times the height of the filling itself. Of course there are chocolate cream, coconut cream, and lemon meringue. Our personal favorite from this phylum is peanut butter cream. But neither should one ignore the non-meringue pies. Pecan is masterful; and the one known as PCP is the ultimate, its initials standing for pineapple, coconut, and pecan.

Family Pie Shop

Hwy. 70 W.   870-998-2279
DeValls Bluff, AR   Erratic hours; call ahead | $

Mary Thomas, who used to be a barbecue cook for Mr. Craig, at Craig's Bar-B-Que on the other side of Route 70 (p. 222), opened her little bakery in 1977; and while it is merely a cinder-block garage hidden from easy view, aficionados consider Mary's the finest pie stop in the state: high honor hereabouts, where pie consciousness is as elevated as in Iowa.

Mary's dining facilities are virtually nonexistent, other than a couple of stools and a random kitchen chair in a disheveled storage room next to the kitchen. Most people get whole pies or small ones for two to eat in the car or at home. Mary told us that when Bill Clinton lived in Little Rock, he stopped in all the time and ate pie at the counter with his friends and family. He didn't have a favorite. "He liked them all!" she confides. She also advised that former Governor Mike Huckabee used to love her pies, too. But then he went on a diet.

Mary's simple egg custard pie is nothing short of perfect, as are the luxurious "Karo nut," a.k.a. pecan, and the sweet potato pie. But filling almost doesn't matter; the crust lifts them all heavenward. Honey-brown, ready to flake with slight pressure from a plastic fork, it is as fine as a Viennese sugar cookie. The crust's savor is amplified in Mary's version of the Arkansas favorite, fried pie—apple, peach, or apricot filling inside a crescent of pastry dough that is deep-fried until brittle.

Feltner's Whatta-Burger

1410 N. Arkansas Ave.   479-968-1410
Russellville, AR   LD | $

There are Whatta-Burger shops throughout the Southwest, but none like this one, where the well-nigh-perfect "custom made hamburgers" are served with ravishing French fries and milk shakes in cardboard flagons that are more like buckets than cups.

In addition to big and good meals, Feltner's offers the kick of an only-in-America experience that is fast food at its finest. The instant you enter the low-slung brick building, an order taker virtually accosts you at the door to find out what you want. At the head of the line, you convey the precise details of your order, from a simple Whatta-burger (that's a quarter-pound patty on a five-inch bun) to a Whatta-burger with double meat and double cheese. At the end of the line, you pay and receive your meal on a tray in a white bag, beverage on the side. Find a booth in the big dining room, where the walls are lined with humorous and inspirational homilies: "We guarantee fast service no matter how long it takes"; "The hurrier I go, the behinder I get"; "Cherish yesterday, dream tomorrow, live today."

Feltner's is *the* town burger joint, a favorite for families, teens on dates, and Arkansas Tech students. We well recall our first visit, when we shared the dining room with a happy stampede of approximately three dozen fresh-faced six-footers attending basketball camp at the college, each of whom carried a tray with a brace of double-doubles (double meat, double cheese) and a heap of French fries.

The Grapevine Restaurant

105 E. Walnut St.   479-963-2413
Paris, AR   BLD | $

The Grapevine defies categorization. It is a worldly restaurant in a country town. Its repertoire ranges from catfish to coconut shrimp, veggie plates to surf 'n' turf, sweet tea to chocolate milk to wines from France and Arkansas. The staff is folksy and down-home, but able to walk you through the menu with the savvy of a learned gastronome. It's the finest food for miles around, and you will be hard-pressed to spend more than $10 for a meal.

You know you are in for something special when the bread basket arrives. Crisp-crusted tawny loaves with a slightly sweet edge are hand-cut into irregularly sized slices and served with a ramekin of honey butter. Hamburgers are one-third-pound beauties; the salad selection includes Greek, Cobb, and a "Santa Fe" concoction topped with unbelievably tender grilled chicken and served with creamy avocado dressing. Full dinners, including barbecued beef, chicken-fried steak, and house-smoked brisket, come with such sides as fried okra and four-star mac 'n' cheese.

Bread pudding is huge: physically and flavorfully. It is a dense block of bread that has become custard, served floating in a pool of sweet praline sauce.

McClard's

505 Albert Pike   501-623-9665
Hot Springs, AR   LD | $$

Pork is king in this smokehouse, the pulled pork ineffably tender and moist, its smoky sweetness especially radiant when spread with hot sauce. The signature dish is a rib and fry plate. The ribs are a meat-heavy slab with a sticky glaze of peppery red sauce. They are presented under a pile of gorgeous honeytone French fried potatoes and sided by fine, bright coleslaw to create what may be the most perfectly balanced barbecue meal anywhere.

A whole section of McClard's menu is devoted to tamale plates, ranging from plain tamales with beans to a full spread. A "spread" is McClard's term for a pair of tamales topped with sauce-sopped chopped smoked meat, beans, crisp Fritos chips, raw onions, and shredded orange cheese. Spreads remind us of the locally favored Fritos pie, but with the added zest of genuine pit barbecue.

The neon-lit 1942 stucco building that houses McClard's once offered toot-your-horn carhop service, but now hordes of happy eaters line up to fill the booths inside. The recipe for its sauce supposedly dates back to 1928, when a customer at the McClard family trailer court couldn't pay his bill and so offered his barbecue sauce recipe instead!

Mickey's BBQ

1622 Park Ave.   501-624-1247
Hot Springs, AR   BLD Tues-Sat | $

Hot Springs is a barbecue hot spot, its highlights not only ribs and pulled pork, but also great beans and pit-cooked potatoes. You'll find all of the above at Mickey's, a snug hut where the "Hickory Nut" dining room features napkin holders carved from tree limbs as well as wood paneling branded with scenes of animals that hunters like to see in front of the bead on a shotgun: deer, ducks, pheasants. The beef and pork are terrific; ham is exemplary; and Mickey's hot, complicated sauce infuses each of them with a delicious glow.

And what fine side dishes. The potato, slow-cooked over hickory smoke just like the meats, has a leathery skin and cream-soft center. You can have it gobbed with butter or, even better, stuffed with the barbecue meat of your choice (beef, pork, or ham), then heaped with just-right spicy-sweet barbecue sauce, coleslaw, and beans. That treatment is more of a meal than a side. Beans, by the way, are also top-drawer, larded with shreds and chunks and chewy debris off the good ham roast.

Rhoda's Famous Hot Tamales

714 Saint Mary St.   870-265-3108
Lake Village, AR   BL | $

The name of Rhoda Adams's café is no lie. The tamales well deserve the fame they have earned throughout the Mississippi Delta. She makes them with a combination of beef and chicken; the meats combined with steamy cornmeal are wrapped in husks that when unfolded, emanate an irresistibly appetizing aroma and are a joy to eat as a snack or meal any time of day.

Beyond tamales, the menu at James and Rhoda Adams's little eat-place by the side of the road is a roster of great, soulful regional specialties. For fried chicken or pigs' feet, pork barbecue or catfish dinner, you won't do better for miles around. Early one morning Rhoda made us breakfast of bacon and eggs with biscuits on the side. Even this simple meal tasted especially wonderful. Rhoda is one of those gifted cooks who makes everything she touches something special.

We've always considered Arkansas one of America's top-seven pie states (along with Iowa, Wisconsin, Minnesota, Virginia, Texas, and Maine). Rhoda's pies are proof. She makes small individual ones as well as full-size pies. We've yet to taste the coconut pie, but we can say that her sweet potato pie, lemon pie, and pecan pie are world-class.

Stubby's Bar-B-Que

3024 Central Ave.   501-624-1552
Hot Springs, AR   LD | $$

Chris Dunkel, whose family bought Stubby's from founder Richard "Stubby" Stubblefield, Sr., in 1977, is known now to regulars as "Stubb" because he carries on the traditions that have made this place a required barbecue destination since it opened in 1952. "There are three things that mark a good barbecue," Chris told us. "A woodpile, mismatched chairs, and high-quality meat."

Stubby's has all of those, and more important, the food is sensationally delicious. Ribs, pork, and ham each in its own way presents the magical duo of swine and smoke; even the brisket is Texas-tender and dripping juice. Chicken, which in our book of barbecue tends to be a secondary consideration, is not to be dissed in this place; its skin is nearly blackened by smoke exposure in the pit, its meat moist and ludicrously tender. No matter what your meat preference, two side dishes are essential. The pit-smoked potato is a pound-plus spud that emerges from a long, slow heat bath with insides that are fluffy and delicious even before massive amounts of butter and sour cream are applied. Stubby's pot-o-beans is laden with hunks of smoky ham and a thick blanket of sauce. That sauce, made in the back room daily, is tangy, peppery, and so beguilingly spiced that we find ourselves dipping plain old white bread in it after the beans are gone and the meat on our plate is a glowing memory.

Wagon Wheel

166 S. Broadview St.   501-679-5009
Greenbrier, AR   BLD | $

Having recently enjoyed a good conversation with Ari Weinzweig—creator of Zingerman's in Ann Arbor, Michigan, and a brilliant food historian—about chocolate gravy, which, he informed us, is not some modern affectation but in fact a time-honored Appalachian cook's recipe, we were eager to return to the Wagon Wheel and retaste their version of it. It is fascinating stuff, at first shocking, blasting normal standards for gravy into foggy puzzlement. But after a few forkfuls, the combination of smooth, not-too-sweet chocolate and tangy biscuit gets agreeable. If you don't want to take your taste buds where few taste buds have gone before, Wagon Wheel's more familiar sausage gravy is excellent: thick, meaty, and powerfully peppery.

The biscuits, by the way, are top-drawer: big, knobby critters that are so especially nice when paired with eggs and Petit Jean bacon; and whether you come for breakfast, lunch, or supper, you must have pie. In the pie-rich state of Arkansas, Wagon Wheel is a standout. In particular we like the classic coconut meringue; and for those who want to go baroque, there is banana split pie, containing banana, pineapple, and chopped pecans.

Barnacle Bill's

14 Castillo Dr.   904-824-3663

St. Augustine, FL   LD | $$

Barnacle Bill's is not an undiscovered Roadfood hole-in-the-wall. It is big
and popular and in fact there are two of it, the second location (dinner only)
at 451 A1A Boulevard in St. Augustine, phone: 904-471-2434. (But these
two are no relation to the several other Barnacle Bills found along the Atlantic coast.)

Shrimp brought in on boats to nearby Mayport are the main attraction: They are firm, juicy butterflies available simply fried in an envelope
of melting-crisp crust, in a coconut crust, or, best of all, in a crust enhanced
by the heat of locally grown datil peppers. The datils, which also give lively
snap to Bill's Minorcan clam chowder, are, curiously, unknown on the island of Minorca. The story is that they arrived in the eighteenth century in
the hands of Minorcans who, on their way to Florida, probably stopped
somewhere in the Caribbean and picked up datil seeds. The pungent pepper,
which seems to be a sport variety of the habanero, has become St. Augustine's signature flavor agent.

For first-timers and those who have a hard time making up their mind
what kind of shrimp they want, there are plates of a dozen, four of each
variety. The menu offers all sorts of other seafood and even a selection of
"landlubber fare"; but we agree with tipster Meg Butler, who first clued us

in to this restaurant: "I can't say much other than fried shrimp, fried shrimp, fried shrimp."

Blue Heaven

729 Thomas St.   305-296-8666

Key West, FL   BLD | $$

Off the beaten path in the Bahama Village area of the sunny never-never land known as the Conch Republic, Blue Heaven is a breakfast-lover's dream. Dining is al fresco on a broad outdoor patio under the shade of opulent banyan trees, where your companions include the café's flock of hens and roosters who hop and peck around tables and chairs. Their cock-a-doodle-dooing is a natural companion for hefty omelets, but our favorite dishes are the tropical-tasting banana pancakes and the seafood Benedict built upon ocean-fresh fish and topped with lime hollandaise. To drink? Who can resist a mimosa made with fresh-squeezed OJ? Lunch items include wonderful barbecued shrimp, fresh local fish, and jerk chicken.

An incredibly colorful place to eat, Blue Heaven has been the home of a boxing ring (Ernest Hemingway sparred here), a bordello (the tiny rooms upstairs are now part of an art gallery), a bookmaking parlor, and a cockfighting pit (heroic roosters are buried in a little graveyard behind the dining area), as well as the inspiration for Jimmy Buffett's song "Blue Heaven Rendezvous." It is delightfully disheveled, casual in the extreme, and one of Key West's most evocative dining experiences.

El Siboney

900 Catherine St.   305-296-4184

Key West, FL   LD | $$

When you consider El Siboney is just ninety miles from Cuba itself—closer to Havana than to Miami—you understand why its Cuban food tastes so right. This is the best place we know on Key West to taste grilled garlic chicken, a half-bird with a crisp skin and meat so tender that going at it with utensils feels abusive. Plantains on the side are slightly crusty and caramelized around their edges. And yuca, a side dish served with roast pork, beans, and rice, is a revelation not quite like any other vegetable. Soft and glistening white hunks, reminiscent of a well-baked potato but more luscious and substantial, are served in a bath of heavily garlicked oil and garlanded with onion slices.

The Cuban sandwich is a beaut, made on a length of fragile-texture toasted bread that is cut in half at a rakish angle and loaded with ham, roast pork, salami, and cheese with pickles, lettuce, and tomato. Conch chowder is thick with conch meat, and provides a great opportunity for dunking shreds of the buttered Cuban bread that comes with every meal. The grandest dish in the house is paella Valenciana for two (call ahead; it takes an hour to prepare), a vast fisherman's stew served with rice, black beans, and plenty of Cuban bread for mopping juices. Dessert choices include Key lime pie, flan, and rice pudding, accompanied of course by espresso or café con leche.

El Siboney is a clean, pleasant place with red-striped tables topped with easy-wipe plastic and silverware presented in tidy little paper bags. If you don't speak Spanish, the waitresses do their best to help you understand the menu. Ours explained that El Siboney was a Cuban Indian, and that the Indian-themed art on the walls is a tribute to him.

Ernie's Bar-b-que & Lounge

1843 S. Federal Hwy.   954-523-8636
Fort Lauderdale, FL   LD | $$

Conch chowder is served throughout Florida, but none is so fully satisfying as that served at Ernie's, where the menu declares "Conch is King." It is potent stuff, vividly peppered, thick with sweet bits of nicely clammy conch and chopped vegetables, with sherry available to add a whole other layer of intoxicant to the heady Caribbean classic. Ernie's version delivers maximum ocean flavor and is hearty enough to be a meal or, in a smaller portion, a sturdy companion to one of Ernie's fine barbecue sandwiches, constructed on thick-sliced Bimini bread and accompanied by a bowl of barbecue sauce for dipping. Even if you don't have a sandwich, get some of that bread to go with the chowder. It looks pretty much like white bread but is dense and nearly cakelike, with an alluring sweetness that partners nicely with the briny flavor of mollusk. Conch fritters and conch salad are also featured on Ernie's menu. As for the barbecue, you can do better elsewhere.

Jenkins Quality Barbecue

830 N. Pearl St.   904-353-6388
Jacksonville, FL   LD | $

Jenkins smokes beef, pork, and chickens in a pit fired by oak logs, then serves them with sauce made from a recipe that is a long-held family secret. The sauce is unusual stuff, peppery but not ferocious, mustard-orange, and as thick as Thanksgiving gravy—a righteous companion especially for Jenkins's superb roast chicken, but also swell on ribs or beef and delicious soaked up straight with the white bread that is used for sandwiches.

The sandwiches are sandwiches only in name. The spare rib sandwich is four slices of white bread surrounding four or five big spare ribs, the whole thing drenched with enough sauce that picking it up whole is impossible. Instead, one folds back the thick butcher paper in which it is presented and alternately gnaws a rib and peels off pieces of sauce-drenched bread. Very good! And multi-napkin messy. On the side, you want an order of corn nuggets, which look like hush puppies but are creamy-centered corn fritters. For dessert, there is fine red velvet cake.

The store on Pearl Street, in a fairly desolate part of downtown Jacksonville, is the main location. There are a few other Jenkins around the city. Dining facilities include a handful of upholstered booths and a couple of concrete picnic tables outside.

Jerry's Drive-In

2815 E. Cervantes St.   850-433-9910
Pensacola, FL   BLD | $

Jerry's opened for business in 1939, and frankly, it doesn't look like it's changed much since then. It is a Formica-counter café with a few tables and booths and help-yourself rolls of paper towels for customers to use as needed. The walls are decorated with college pennants and graffiti going back decades. Jerry's has character to spare . . . but it also has important hamburgers—good-size, juicy patties of beef beautifully dressed with lettuce, tomato, chopped onions, mustard, and mayo, served with sweet coleslaw and crisp French fries. Not gourmet burgers, not unusual burgers, just good, satisfying hamburgers in a classic lunch-counter setting.

Although many visitors to the "Redneck Riviera" know Jerry's as the hamburger place, regulars come for three square meals a day. The breakfast menu features all the usual configurations of eggs and luncheon meat (with grits and/or hash browns), plus an extraordinarily luxurious chicken liver omelet. At lunch, you can have such regional delights as smoked mullet, deviled crab, and broiled grouper, as well as big deep-fried oysters with hush puppies on the side.

La Teresita

3248 W. Columbus Dr.   813-879-4909
Tampa, FL   BLD (open all night Fri & Sat) | $

A Cuban sandwich is a beautiful thing: ham, roast pork, and cheese along with mustard, mayonnaise, and pickles encased in elegant bread that is toasted to a crisp. There is no better place to eat one than Tampa, especially at the neighborhood café called La Teresita.

Choice seats (and swift service) are at a sweeping serpentine counter where whole families line up on the rows of stools at dinnertime. Regulars come for breakfast of buttered Cuban bread and café con leche; lunch favorites include *carne asada, ropa vieja, vaca frita,* and the best black beans and rice in town. Throughout the day, you'll see groups of happy gents gathering in the street after dining at La Teresita. Here they fire up big made-in-Tampa cigars and look like kings who have just enjoyed a royal feast.

Louie's Backyard

700 Waddell Ave.   305-294-1061
Key West, FL   LD | $$$

Louie's is not cheap or in any way typical. It is one of a kind. But when we visit Key West and think about dinner, our thoughts immediately take us to a table at Louie's Backyard, where the best seats are located on a multilevel terrace overlooking the Atlantic. Here you dine while pleasure boats sail past and pelicans graze the waves.

The gracious pink classical-revival house could serve TV dinners and it would be irresistible on a moonlit night; but it happens to be one of the innovators of Key West cuisine, known for such tropical delights as Bahamian conch chowder with bird-pepper hot sauce, grilled local shrimp with salsa verde, and cracked conch with pepper jelly and ginger daikon slaw. The Louie's supper forever etched in our book of great culinary memories was our first: a pair of lovely grilled strip steaks glazed with hot chipotle chile sauce, sided by garlic mashed potatoes and red onion corn relish. To top things off, we had fancy coffee and feathery Key lime tarts. Soft island breezes made hurricane lamps flicker. Bulbs strung among branches in overhead trees formed a radiant canopy above the patio. The ocean glowed cobalt blue when distant, soundless lightning storms at sea ignited over the horizon.

Old Spanish Sugar Mill Grill and Griddle House

Inside De Leon Springs State Park   386-985-5644
601 Ponce de Leon Blvd.   BL | $
De Leon Springs, FL

Are you ready to cook? At the Old Spanish Sugar Mill in De Leon Springs State Park, you are your own pancake chef. Tables have griddles built into their center. The staff brings two pitchers from the kitchen—a milled-here, stone-ground, buckwheat-style batter as well as a more traditional butter-milk batter—plus whatever mix-ins you feel you need (bananas, blueberries, pecans, apple chunks, peanut butter, chocolate chips, and applesauce are all available for a slight extra cost), and you pour and flip your own. Sausage, bacon, and ham are also available . . . but cooked by professionals in the kitchen. Pancake toppings include molasses, honey, and syrup.

It's fun to punctuate the process of eating pancakes by cooking them at your own speed and in your own favorite size; you can keep pouring batter until you bust. At $4.50 per person (plus the park entrance fee and obliga-tory 18 percent tip), this is one of the bargain breakfasts of the South. The pancakes are served from morning until closing time, mid-afternoon; but if you're not in the mood to cook for yourself, the kitchen also will make a fine sandwich on house-made whole-grain bread (the BLT is extremely well endowed with bacon) or a salad.

The restaurant is located in an old mill building in the beautiful area where explorers once sought the Fountain of Youth. The park around it is an idyllic recreation area with boat rides and picnic tables and opportunities to hike and bird-watch. It is a popular destination and the restaurant is a small one, so almost any time of day you will likely wait for a table.

O'Steen's

205 Anastasia Blvd.   904-829-6974
St. Augustine, FL   LD | $$

With about a dozen tables and a six-stool counter, O'Steen's is a no-frills café: no credit cards, no tablecloths, no cocktails, wine, or beer. A sign on the wall reads, "If you have reservations, you are in the wrong place." It is so popular that there always is a wait, even at 11:30 A.M. and 5 P.M. There's good reason for the crowds. The north Florida coast is the center of America's shrimping industry, a fact immediately apparent when you bite through the crunchy veil that encloses the dense pink flesh of O'Steen's fried shrimp, which are as rich as nutmeat and ocean-sweet. O'Steen's sells them in orders of nine, twelve, eighteen, or twenty-four; they are medium-size and each butterflied to resemble the lines inside the circle of a peace symbol.

"Have you been here before?" the waitress asks as she sets down a plate of them. When we say no, she points to a plastic ramekin that holds the kitchen's special pink sauce for dipping. She then hoists a Grolsch beer bot-tle. "And this is the datil pepper sauce we make. Don't start with it alone. Mix it with the pink." O'Steen's hot sauce, turbocharged with datil peppers, is bright and fragrant and even when prudently blended with the milder pink stuff engenders a back-of-the-throat roar that rumbles forward with inexorable titillation.

Pepe's Cafe

806 Caroline St.   305-294-7192
Key West, FL   BLD | $$

Breakfast at Pepe's, from 6:30 every morning, is heaps of fun, always featuring a bread of the day in addition to a big menu of omelets, pancakes, homemade granola, and creamed chipped beef on toast. Later in the day, Apalachicola Bay oysters by the dozen make Pepe's a destination for insatiable oyster-lovers who consume them raw, baked, or roasted Mexican-style. Weekly traditions include a Sunday night barbecue that features beefsteaks, pork ribs, tenderloin, chicken, salmon, and mahimahi. And who can resist a lunch menu that offers both a blue-collar burger and a white-collar burger? (The former is six ounces, the latter four.)

Pepe's boasts that it is "the eldest eating house in the Florida Keys," and it sure does have the feel of a place that's seen it all. The old wood dining room is covered with knickknacks as miscellaneous as grandma's attic, including pictures of famous people and nobodies, nautical bibelots, and scenes of old Key West. Each varnished booth is outfitted with a shelf that holds about a dozen different hot sauces for oyster eating. Out back is a bar where locals congregate. (The bar opens at 7 A.M.!) And to the side on an open patio strewn with mismatched tables, illumination is provided by an array of fixtures that includes a crystal chandelier, green-shaded billiard lamps, and year-round Christmas lights strung among the trees.

Saltwater Cowboys

Dondanville Rd.   904-471-2332
St. Augustine, FL   D | $$

Named for founder Howard Dondanville, who was affectionately called Cowboy, and designed to look like a salt marsh fish camp from long ago, this way-too-popular restaurant serves excellent Minorcan clam chowder (a St. Augustine specialty) and a slew of southern seafood: freshly opened oysters and fancy-cooked ones, boiled crawfish with Cajun vibes, snapper, deviled crabs, softshells, and shrimp. A whole portion of the menu is headlined "Florida Cracker Corner" and devoted to frog legs, cooter (soft-shelled turtle), catfish, alligator tail, and even fried chicken with a vividly flavored breadcrumb crust. We suggest starting a meal with oysters Dondanville, served on the half-shell and glistening with a mantle of garlic, butter, wine, and finely chopped onions, then moving on to Cowboy's jambalaya, which is a profusion of shrimp, oysters, chicken, ham, and sausage on a pile of seasoned rice.

Fish camp fare–frowners can have open-pit barbecue, including ribs, chicken, and shrimp. What we saw on other people's plates looked good, but the opportunity to indulge in so much seafood precluded a sample.

When we wrote "too popular," we meant that chances are good you will wait for a table at any normal suppertime. It's a big place with four dining rooms, but reservations are not accepted. Waiting facilities are an open-air deck where cool frozen drinks (and sweet tea in mason jars) are served. The place has great ramshackle beauty, occupying a restored old home with its bentwood chairs and walls decorated with antique fishing gear, snake skins, and "cracker" memorabilia. Windows look out over marshland and dusk on the Intracoastal Waterway.

T-Ray's Burger Station

202 S. 8th St.	904-261-6310
Fernandina Beach, FL	BL | $

As the name suggests, burgers are what's to eat. They come in two sizes and dressed in many ways. We like the Big T Bacon Burger—extremely juicy and full-flavored. For beef-frowners there is a portobello mushroom burger. Beyond burgers, T-Ray's offers salads and fried chicken and delicious cheese grits, too. Locals know it as the place to get superb chicken and dumplings every Thursday as well as banana pudding for dessert every day. And they flock here in the morning for masterful hot-from-the-oven biscuits.

It's easy to miss. It looks like every other Exxon station, except for the cars circled around it every day at breakfast and lunch times. Dine at the counter or one of the mismatched tables. Ray's the guy who does the cooking. His father, Terrell, runs the gas station.

Vega's Cafe

1835 E. Colonial Dr.	407-898-5196
Orlando, FL	BL | $

The place that is now Vega's started as a gas station. Today it is the best informal Cuban restaurant in central Florida. For the price of a soulless Happy Meal, you can walk into this friendly little fast-food shop and not only satisfy your hunger, but also uplift your spirit with the joy of real food and a staff of people who care.

There are soups and sandwiches of all kinds, as well as chicken and beef platters, but the one must-eat dish is a Cuban sandwich. Thin slices of sweet ham, moist fresh pork, and Swiss cheese (nearly melting from the warmth of the other ingredients) are combined with dill pickles and mustard in a length of glorious Cuban bread (baked in Tampa and bought daily) that is toasted until fragile-crisp and buttered while still warm so the butter simply becomes part of the fleecy interior. This combination of ingredients is simply one of the great sandwiches anywhere. A whole one is a giant meal. A half, with a side of black beans and rice, is a perfect lunch . . . with caramelized flan and a cup of high-octane espresso for dessert.

(Special thanks to Jerry Weeks of Nashville for tipping us off to this fine restaurant that is all too easy to drive right past.)

Whitey's Fish Camp

2032 CR 220   904-269-4198
Orange Park, FL   LD | $$

When we hit the road some thirty years ago, our first trips through the heart of Florida were a bonanza. One Sunday we accidentally stumbled into the Zellwood Sweet Corn Festival, leaving town well fed and with butter-splotched shirtfronts; in Cross City we found a fast-food shop called Mr. Mullet, whose owner was determined to create a nationwide empire of drive-through Mullet restaurants boasting the motto "Any Time Is Time For Mullunch"; and we ate dinner at a strange outfit southwest of Jacksonville called Whitey's Fish Camp. Whitey's was a tackle shop, boat launch, mobile home park, and extremely informal restaurant fashioned out of a storage shed and bait locker. The kitchen served wild-caught catfish, which was so delicious it made us instant fans. Subsequent encounters with farm-raised catfish revealed that the flavor punch of genuine, bottom-feeding river cats is something special. Pond-raised are fine—mild and polite, receptive to all kinds of character-building treatments such as blackening and Cajun-spicing. But farmed fish are no comparison to the wild ones at Whitey's, where the menu and the place have expanded dramatically and where catfish still reigns.

Served AYCE (local fish-house shorthand for All You Can Eat), the cats vary from three inches to over a half-foot long. Unless you specify what size you want, each plate delivered to the table will hold one or two big ones and two or three little ones. The tiniest are so fragile that experienced diners eat even the tender rib bones, leaving nothing but vertebrae. Big ones, with a skeleton that demands respect, provide supremely easy access to meat. Simply poke the tines of a fork through the sandy cornmeal girdle just below the backbone, then pull downward. A nice mouthful slips cleanly off the ribs. Atop the patch of brittle crust on your fork is a nugget of dense meat as luxurious as prime beefsteak but with freshwater sparkle that evokes vacation campfires and balmy summer nights. We have never eaten anything so indisputably outdoorsy in a normal cloth-napkin restaurant. (In lieu of napkins, Whitey's supplies each table with a roll of paper towels.)

It wasn't only the robust character of the fish that impressed us when we first found Whitey's. Our idea of what a Roadfood eatery could be was dramatically expanded by this full-fledged fish camp that is a community as much as it is a restaurant: boat launches, bait-and-tackle shop, oyster bar and beer bar, campground and RV park complete with hair-styling salon. With its out-of-fashion video games for kids and two-dollar claw machine that grabs a live lobster rather than a stuffed toy, Whitey's is not quaint like some bucolic farm-town café or vintage diner. It is a taste of what locals like to call cracker culture, meaning it evokes the old, pre-air-conditioned Florida that had its own special brand of sporting lifestyle long before the great influxes of northerners. A blatant patch of cracker living such as Whitey's is a good reminder of the old saw that the farther north you go in this state, the deeper south you are.

Blue Willow Inn

294 N. Cherokee Rd.   770-464-2131
Social Circle, GA   LD | $$

"We have two rules," says the waitress when you are seated at a table and receive your sweet iced tea (known here as the champagne of the South). "Rule one is that no one goes home hungry. Rule two is that everybody has to have at least two desserts." Each guest is given a plate and invited to go to the serving tables as often as possible to help himself. Every day here is Sunday supper, southern-style. The beautiful, bounteous buffet is located in a room full of food that includes far more dishes than any single appetite can sample in a single meal. A few of the must-eats are fried chicken, fried green tomatoes, collard greens that are long-cooked to porky tenderness, chicken and dumplings, and, of course, biscuits. Using a recipe from Sema Wilkes's legendary boardinghouse in Savannah, the Blue Willow kitchen creates tan-crusted domes with fluffy insides and a compelling fresh-from-the-oven aroma. Their tops are faintly knobby because the dough is patted out rather than rolled.

For dessert, there are pies, cakes, cookies, and pudding, but the one we recommend (assuming you have an inkling of appetite by the end of the meal) is warm fruit cobbler. The Inn provides rocking chairs on its broad front porch for postprandial snoozing. It is a magnificent place, a grand Dixie mansion that is said to have inspired Margaret Mitchell to conceive of

Tara in *Gone with the Wind*. And although meal service is help-yourself, the serving staff couldn't be more gracious.

The Crab Shack

| 40 Estill Hammock Rd. | 912-786-9857 |
| Tybee Island, GA | LD \| $$ |

It may not be the most romantic come-on in the restaurant world, but what Roadfooder could resist The Crab Shack's catchphrase, "Where the Elite Eat in Their Bare Feet"? Need we say that this is not a formal dining room? Park among heaps of oyster shells and eat off paper plates at picnic tables to the sound of Jimmy Buffett tunes. Toss your shells and refuse into the big garbage bins provided. The deckside view of the broad tidal creek is lovely—a true waterside picnic—but even lovelier are the great heaps of sloppy, hands-on seafood that Savannahns come to gobble up with beer and/ or frozen margaritas.

The fundamentals include boiled shrimp (served the Lowcountry way with corn, potatoes, and sausage), steamers by the bucket, raw oysters on the half-shell, crawfish in season, and your choice from a list of four kinds of boiled crab: Alaskan, blue, golden, or, when available, stone crab (claws only, of course). In addition to these simple seafoods, The Crab Shack offers deviled crabs, crab stew, and shrimp and crab au gratin. Couples can always opt for a shellfish feast for two: mountains of whatever's in season accompanied by corn, potatoes, and sausage.

Dillard House

| 768 Franklin St. | 800-541-0671 |
| Dillard, GA | BLD \| $ |

Dillard House isn't really a boardinghouse, but it serves its meals boardinghouse-style. Everything is set out on the table on platters and in bowls. Friends, family, and strangers reach, pass, and grab for what they want. There is no fixed menu; the meal consists of everything the kitchen is offering at the time you sit down, the blackboard list changing hour by hour as new dishes are cooked and others eaten up. It is essential to come to Dillard House with a big appetite; it would be wrong to practice moderation. And be prepared to grab what you like. At a boardinghouse feed like this, nobody wants to waste time being polite.

Fried chicken always is on the table, and it's crunch-crusted gold. Country ham, prime rib, and barbecue chicken are the other entrees. But it's the vegetables we like best at a Dillard House feed. Not Spartan, health-food veggies, they are lavish, ultra-flavored, stars-and-bars Dixie vegetables such as acorn squash soufflé loaded with coconut and raisins, creamy vanilla-scented yams streaked with mini-marshmallows, and limp-leaf collard greens pungent with the smack of a salty hambone. Plus dinner rolls and biscuits and, of course, iced tea in mason jars. The dessert to eat is peach cobbler. Breakfast is awesome, too, with eggs a merely minor note in a repertoire that includes sausage, ham with red-eye gravy, bacon, and pork tenderloin, fried potatoes, grits, stewed apples, biscuits with sausage gravy, cinnamon rolls, and blueberry muffins.

The Dillard House dining room is huge and boisterous, just one part of a vast good-time complex in the scenic mountains that includes hotel and cottages, riding stables, hiking trails, and opportunities to whitewater raft, fish, and golf.

Dinglewood Pharmacy

1939 Wynnton Rd.	706-322-0616
Columbus, GA	L | $

The Northeast, where we live, has plenty of excellent hot dogs of all kinds, but nothing like a scrambled dog. When you sit at Dinglewood's counter (or at one of a few tables and booths) and receive your dog, you won't at first recognize it as a member of the wiener family. A shallow rectangular dish comes with the handle of a spoon sticking out from below a pile of oyster crackers, meat-and-bean chili, pickle slices, and chopped raw onions. Use the spoon to poke around a bit and you soon will discover the hot dog, a modest little red-skin weenie already cut into bite-size pieces, buried underneath everything else. The spoon, of course, is essential. This take on the scrambled dog, Dinglewood's contribution to American gastronomy, cannot be picked up. It doesn't even pretend to have a bun.

The movable-type menu above the counter lists a few other sandwiches, a chili dog, and a bun with nothing but chili in it, as well as milk shakes, sundaes, and fresh lemonade.

Don's Bar-B-Que

217 E. US Hwy. 80	912-748-8400
Pooler, GA	LD | $

"I'm most certainly a barbecue snob," wrote Meg Butler in her recommendation of Don's, which she described as a "tiny shack, great for lunch." If, indeed, one were a Deep South barbecue snob, Don's might prove disconcerting, as the meat served here is more North Carolina–style—pulled pork hacked to smithereens, dressed with a thin, tangy pepper sauce, and best eaten in a bun. On the side you want onion rings, and the thing to drink is sweet tea served as per local custom in gigantic portions.

Don's is a minuscule place with barely room for a dozen people inside. But there is plenty of room for al fresco dining at outdoor picnic tables.

Edna's

Hwy. 411 S.   706-695-4951
Chatsworth, GA   LD | $

Every day Edna's puts out a short list of entrees and a long list of vegetables from which you choose one main course and three side dishes. In many meat-and-three restaurants, it is the vegetables that matter, and some customers forget the meat altogether, getting a four-vegetable plate for lunch. At Edna's the all-vegetable strategy would be a big mistake. We don't know about the meat loaf or the country-fried steak, but we can tell you that the fried chicken is delicious, a fact that becomes apparent if you look around the restaurant and note that probably half the clientele choose it. Edna's logo is a chicken wearing a chef's toque with the proclamation, "Our chicken dinners are worth crowing about."

The side-dish list includes not only vegetables such as mashed potatoes, fried potatoes, green beans, pole beans, etc., but also mac 'n' cheese and Jell-O salads. And whatever you get, it comes with a corn bread muffin that crumbles very nicely over a heap of cooked greens. For dessert, there could be no better choice than Edna's peanut butter pie—a grand ode to the Georgia goober.

The GA Pig

2712 Hwy. 17 S.   912-264-6664
Brunswick, GA   LD | $

On the sign of The GA Pig you see a merry pig playing a fiddle and doing a jig. You, too, will dance for joy when you eat at this oh-so-convenient restaurant less than a mile from Interstate 95. GA Pig pork, slow-cooked over hickory wood, basted with a tongue-teasing red sauce, then hacked into juicy hunks and shreds to be served on a platter or stuffed into a toasted-bun sandwich, is soul-of-the-South classic. There are ribs, too—a joy to gnaw— and on the side, thick and meaty Brunswick stew.

A fun place to stop, The GA Pig is log-cabin rustic with picnic-table seating and a genuine pine grove set back from the road for al fresco dining. Eating here is a welcome break from the monotony of highway travel; or if you are really in a hurry, you can get anything to go and pig out as you drive along the highway. However you experience The GA Pig, we bet you will find a sweet place for it in your bank of culinary memories.

Harold's Barbecue

171 McDonough Blvd. SE   404-627-9268
Atlanta, GA   LD | $

Harold's is Atlanta's most respected beacon of velvet-soft sliced pork, ribs painted with intensely seasoned translucent red sauce, and the vegetable-and-smoked-meat gallimaufry known as Brunswick stew. The stew comes as a meal unto itself or as a companion to ribs or pulled pork; its vegetable sweetness is quietly accentuated by a distant vinegar tang. It can be improved only by crumbling a square of Harold's corn bread on top.

Outside, a cheerful pig in sunglasses occupies the sign by the side of the road—a beacon of comfort in an otherwise scary neighborhood near Atlanta's federal prison. Although it is a stark building with bars on every window, Harold's interior has a comforting patina of age and hickory smoke. The wood-paneled walls are hung with earnest religious homilies, including this one above the door to the rear dining room: "God has time to listen if you have time to pray."

Hot Thomas' Barbeque

3753 Hwy. 15   706-769-6550
Watkinsville, GA   LD Tues-Sat | $

Hot Thomas' used to be only a peach orchard. It's still in the middle of fruit-growing country, and inside the restaurant you can buy jams, chutney, and syrup made from peaches and bearing the Hot Thomas brand.

The main reason for coming to this sun-bleached white building in Watkinsville, ouside Athens, is to eat pork. Step up to the counter and order a plate, and while it is being assembled, nab yourself a Coke or a Mr. Pibb from the cooler.

Find a seat and fork into delicious hickory-cooked pork, hacked to smithereens with a good measure of "Mr. Brown" (crusty dark meat from the outside) laced among the supple, sweet pieces from the center of the shoulder. Traditional Georgia side dishes to accompany this lovely entree (really, the only one on the menu) include Brunswick stew (a kind of tomato-onion-and-some-other-vegetable mélange with a mild pork flavor), sweet coleslaw, and soft white bread suitable for dunking in the stew and mopping up hot sauce. The sauce is available mild, hot, and extra-hot, that last one being *extra* hot with a breathtaking pepper punch. Like the peach products, the sauce is available in bottles to take home.

Mamie's Kitchen

1295 N. Main St. NW   770-922-0131
Conyers, GA   BL | $

Jack Howard started in the biscuit business in 1962 when he opened an eat-shack in an industrial section of Atlanta. Named for a skillful cook in his employ, Mamie's Kitchen has since expanded to four locations east of the city. "In the early days, I used to go to the mountains and buy big cakes of butter from the farmers," Jack recalls. "I brought jars of preserves they made and put them on my tables. My slogan was, 'I am rolling in dough.' "

Any time you order a biscuit at Mamie's, it comes hot from the oven. Its knobby golden surface has a gentle crunch, and although the inside is fleecy, it is not fragile. While it is delicious plain or simply buttered, you can also get it topped with sausage gravy or sandwiching streak o' lean or fried chicken. Its greatest glory is to be pulled into two circular, gold-topped halves so it can sandwich a slice or two of deliriously flavorful country ham grilled until its rim of fat becomes translucent amber and the brick-red surface starts to turn crisp. The power of the ham—its complexity, its salty punch, its rugged, chewy texture—is perfectly complemented by the fluffy gentleness of the biscuit around it.

Mary Mac's Tea Room

224 Ponce de Leon Ave.   404-876-1800
Atlanta, GA   LD | $$

Originally opened in 1945, Mary Mac's is an old-fashioned urban lunch room in the heart of Atlanta that offers a broad menu of dishes that exemplify Dixie cooking. You can start a meal with pot likker—that's heaps of soft turnip greens wallowing in a bowl with their flavorful cooking liquid—sided by a corn bread muffin. Entrees include such classics as baked chicken with corn bread dressing, pork barbecue with Brunswick stew, and country-fried steak with gravy. Fried chicken is crust-crunching, moisture-spurting delicious, some of the best anywhere.

Side dishes are choice; many customers come to eat a four-vegetable plate with no meat at all. Standouts include a sweet potato soufflé that is spiced Christmas-sweet, macaroni and cheese in which the noodles are suspended in an eggy cheese soufflé, fried green tomatoes, hoppin' John, and crisp-fried okra.

An airy place with soothing pastel yellow walls, Mary Mac's offers old-style tea room service, which is great fun. When you sit down, you are given an order pad and menus. Once you've made your decisions, you write your own order and hand it to your waiter or waitress, who in the meanwhile has brought you an immense tankard of what the menu lists as the table wine of the South—sweet iced tea.

Melear's

GA Hwy. 85   770-461-7180
Fayetteville, GA   BLD | $

Melear has been a big name in Georgia barbecue since 1927, when John Melear opened a smokehouse in LaGrange. The Melear's south of Atlanta goes back over half a century and is open seven days a week, even for breakfast Monday through Sunday.

Pork is the meat to eat: chopped, mixed with a bit peppery vinegar sauce and served in a sandwich, on a tray, or as a dish with the irresistible name "bowl of pork." The sandwich is notable because it comes on grilled slices of bread (as opposed to barbecue's usual spongy-white companion slices), adding a nice crunch to the sandwich experience. The same pork, but more of it, is the anchor for a full-bore barbecue dinner that also includes potato chips, pickles, white bread, and smooth-textured, rib-sticking Brunswick stew. Extra-hot sauce is available, and it is good, but Melear's pork has a fine, subtle flavor that we believe is better complemented by the mild version.

To accompany Melear's classic "Q," the proper beverage is iced tea—dazzlingly presweetened, as is the custom in this part of the country, presented in tumblers that are a full foot tall and about half again as wide at the mouth. When you get to the bottom of this tub, it is refilled on the house, and it will continue to be refilled for as long as you are parked in a high-backed chair at one of Melear's aged wood tables eating barbecue.

Mrs. Wilkes' Dining Room

107 W. Jones St.   912-232-5997
Savannah, GA   L | $

West Jones Street is a boulevard of antique brick houses with curving steps and graceful cast-iron banisters. At eleven o'clock each morning a line begins to form at number 107. At 11:30, the doors open and the lunch crowd finds seats at tables shared by strangers. And so begins Mrs. Wilkes's daily feast, boardinghouse-style.

The tabletops are crowded with platters of fried chicken and corn-bread dressing, sweet potato soufflés, black-eyed peas, okra gumbo, corn muffins, and biscuits. As at any southern banquet worth its cracklin' corn bread, there are constellations of vegetable casseroles: great, gooey, buttery bowls full of squash au gratin and scalloped eggplant, cheese grits, corn pudding, pineapple-flavored yams topped with melted marshmallows, creamed corn enriched with bacon drippings, green rice (mixed with broccoli and celery), brown rice (with mushrooms and soy sauce), and the Lowcountry legend, Savannah red rice. The food comes fast; everybody eats fast in a spirit of joyful camaraderie. ·

When the late Mrs. Wilkes first started serving meals in this dining room in 1943, there were many similar places in cities throughout the region, where boarders as well as frugal local citizens gathered to enjoy the special pleasure of a meal shared with neighbors and strangers. Now the take-some-and-pass-the-bowl style of the old boardinghouse is a rarity. Mrs. Wilkes' is a prized opportunity to indulge in the delicious dining style of a culinary tradition that values sociability as much as a good macaroni salad.

Nu-Way Weiners

428 Cotton Ave.   478-743-1368
Macon, GA   BLD | $

There are other Nu-Way Weiner shops in central Georgia, but the one on Cotton Avenue in Macon is the original, established in 1916 by James Mallis and now run by his descendants. It is a shoebox-shaped restaurant with tables and a counter, instantaneous service, and addictive hot dogs. They are bright red little private-label links that are grilled and bedded in a steamed-soft bun. Nu-Way's glory is having it all the way, which means topped with mustard and onions and a fine-grained chili that is sweetened with porky-rich barbecue sauce. One other good topping is coleslaw, which is creamy sweet. Or you can order that peculiar Georgia configuration, a scrambled dog, which is a splayed-open bun topped with a hot dog and smothered with chili and beans.

Chocolate milk is the only reasonable alternative to soft drinks that are served extra-cold over Nu-Way's famous flaky ice.

Old South Bar-B-Q

Windy Hill Rd.   770-435-4215
Smyrna, GA   LD | $$

We first ran into barbecue salad in Memphis, but have since seen a claim for its invention in Alabama and found the exemplary one in Georgia, at Old

South Bar-B-Q, a family-run eatery that's been slow-smoking meats since 1968. No paradigm exists telling exactly what such a salad should be; there are more ways to make it than there are to spell the word "barbecue." Some are regular green salads topped with barbecue sauce and/or salad dressing; Jim Neely's Interstate Barbecue in Memphis adds bacon bits but no other meat; others pile dressed salad greens on top of sauced barbecue.

Old South calls its version a "chef's bar-b-q salad." It is a big plate of cold, crisp lettuce and grated orange cheese topped with pork (pulled, chopped, or sliced), beef brisket (chopped or sliced), or chicken, the whole meal-on-a-plate accompanied by your choice from a selection of eight salad dressings and four sauces (original, sweet, hot, or hot-sweet). Pour or dip: It's up to you. Our first-timer recommendation is pulled pork with hot or hot-sweet sauce and honey mustard dressing. Purely speaking, it's neither salad nor barbecue. But what it is is weirdly satisfying.

If you are more a traditionalist, be assured that the regular barbecue plates and sandwiches are first-rate, the latter available on either bun or garlic toast.

Peachtree Café

Lane Southern Orchards   800-277-3224
50 Lane Rd.   L | $
Fort Valley, GA

The Peachtree Café at Lane Southern Orchards, which farms over 5,000 acres of peach and pecan trees, has a nice menu of barbecue, sandwiches, and salads; but it's dessert that is compelling. That is especially true during summer peach season, when over two dozen different varieties ripen, week by week, on company trees. Peach muffins and peach ice cream are swell, as is butter pecan ice cream made from Lane Company nuts. Best of all is pecan pie, crowded with Lane Company nuts that are rich and sweet and fresh-from-the-shell crunchy. Top this with fresh peach ice cream, and your taste buds will be humming "Georgia on My Mind."

Sconyers Bar-B-Que

2250 Sconyers Way   706-790-5411
Augusta, GA   LD Thurs-Sat | $$

Sconyers is an immense barbecue complex with seating for hundreds in multiple dining rooms, plus drive-through service. Hams are cooked a full twenty-four hours over oak and hickory, resulting in meat that is ridiculously tender and sopping in its own smoke-perfumed juices. Curiously, it is a lot like Lexington-style barbecue, but with a sauce that has more of a pepper punch. It comes on a plate along with hash and rice, pickles and coleslaw, and plenty of nice soft white bread for mopping, or in a sandwich or à la carte by the pound.

For people afraid of their food, Sconyers has added something called T-loin, which is billed as 96 percent fat-free, low-sodium, and low-cholesterol "choice pork." We have yet to try it. Ribs, chopped beef, turkey, and chicken are also available off the pit. Sweet tea is, of course, the most popular thing to drink.

Silver Skillet

200 14th St.   404-874-1388
Atlanta, GA   BL | $

The Silver Skillet diner is a charismatic blast from the past, its glass windows tilting outward like mid-century tailfins. Booths are upholstered in green and orange Naugahyde, tables topped with boomerang-pattern Formica, and the clientele ranges from blue-collar boys in overalls to visiting celebrities with an entourage in tow.

Breakfast is fine: skillet-cooked ham afloat in a pool of dark red-eye gravy with biscuits on the side; plate-wide pancakes; fried pork chops with grits. At lunch, there is meat loaf or fried chicken and always a good list of southern-style vegetables from which you can make a bounteous four-vegetable plate.

And for dessert? Ah, dessert. The banana pudding is dandy, as is peach or blackberry cobbler, but the lemon icebox pie is stellar. Cool, creamy and neatly poised between sugar-sweet and lemon-zesty, it is a superlative exclamation point after any meal, but especially after a slab of country ham.

Skipper's Fish Camp

85 Screven St.   912-437-FISH
Darien, GA   LD | $$

Unlike most fish camp restaurants, Skipper's is refined and polite, its walls decorated with handsome nautical decor and a whole stuffed alligator. Service is solicitous; meals come on non-disposable plates. There is a boat launch next door, dating back to the time this place really was more like a fish camp; but now Skipper's is adjoined by a prestigious waterside condominium development where no worms are sold.

The handsomest meal we've seen here is crisp-fried flounder, a fish so big that it hangs over both ends of a good-size plate. The vast plateau of meat below its craggy orange-gold crust is moist and sweet, easy to lift in bite-size nuggets right off the skeleton. Fried shrimp, caught locally, are firm and fresh, accompanied by red-crusted hush puppies in which the cornmeal is infused with a beguiling swirl of sweetness and garlic. By comparison to the muscular shrimp, fried oysters are shockingly fragile, so tender that they virtually melt in the mouth. Excellent sides include brown-sugary sweet potato casserole and bitter greens. Thick, hearty Brunswick stew is available as a formidable hors d'oeuvre or entree companion.

The essential dessert is Georgia peach cobbler, a one-two punch of fruity sweetness and buttery crust. It is served hot, and of course you want a globe of vanilla ice cream melting on top.

Smith House

84 S. Chestatee St.	706-867-7000
Dahlonega, GA	LD | $$

Did you know that Dahlonega, Georgia, had a gold rush in 1828? The Smith House likes to say it was built atop an untapped vein, but today's treasure is in the form of puffy yeast rolls, cracklin' corn bread muffins, fried chicken, ham with dumplings, and true-South vegetables that range from candied yams to chestnut soufflé. Since 1922, when Henry and Bessie Smith turned the old house into an inn, service has been family-style: Pay one price and eat your fill. There is no menu to look at; there are no choices to make. Everything the kitchen has prepared that day is brought to the communal tables in large serving dishes. Local folks and visitors all behave as though they were at a family party, passing platters back and forth, chattering happily about the good ol' southern food they are eating.

Varsity Drive-In

61 North Ave.	404-881-1706
Atlanta, GA	BLD | $

Like a nation unto itself, the Varsity is a teeming, overpopulated place that even has its own language. If you order a heavyweight, a ring, and a string, you will receive a hot dog with mustard and extra chili, onion rings, and French fries. Although curb service is an option, full and true communion with the V requires that you get out of your car and stand in line at the inside counter. Here, as you go eye-to-eye with an order taker, he will bark out "What'll ya have?" with all the vigor of a Marine drill sergeant. The food will appear before you have a chance to reach for your wallet.

To drink, there's a full menu of reliable southern favorites: ice-cold buttermilk, gigantic cups full of Coke, PCs, and FOs. PC is Varsity lingo for chocolate milk ("plain chocolate") as opposed to a chocolate milk *shake* (with ice cream). FO means frosted orange, reminiscent of a Creamsicle-in-a-cup. With or without chili dogs, frosted oranges are one heck of a way to keep cool.

Lest you have any doubts, this is health food. Varsity founder Frank Gordy, who lived well into his seventies, once proclaimed, "A couple of chili dogs a day keep you young."

Bon Ton Café

401 Magazine St.   504-524-3386

New Orleans, LA   LD | $$$

Magazine Street was laid out in 1788; the building holding the Bon Ton Café is slightly newer, going back to the 1840s. The restaurant opened in 1953. Its menu is old-time Cajun, which means a rustic Louisiana cuisine that is *not* kicked up a notch, not overspiced or overhyped or blackened or infused, but simply delicious. This is the place to know the joy of crawfish étouffé, an unspeakably luscious meal especially in May, the peak of the season when crawdads are plumpest. You can have étouffé as a main course or as one part of a wonderfully monomaniacal meal of bisque, étouffé, Newburg, jambalaya, and an omelet, each of which is made with crawfish. Or you can start dinner with an appetizer of fried crawfish tails. They look like little fried shrimp, but taste like shrimp's affluent relatives.

Dinner begins with the delivery of a loaf of hot French bread, tightly wrapped in a white napkin. When the napkin is unfurled, the bread's aroma swirls around the table. Then comes soup—either peppery okra gumbo made with shrimp and crab or turtle soup into which the waitress pours a shot of sherry. Other than crawfish in any form, the great entree is redfish Bon Ton, which is a thick fillet sautéed until just faintly crisp, served under a heap of fresh crabmeat and three gigantic fried onion rings. For dessert, you want bread pudding, which is a dense, warm square of sweetness studded with raisins and drenched with whiskey sauce.

A big, square, brick-walled room with red-checked tablecloths, Bon Ton is soothingly old-fashioned. There is no music, just the sounds of knife, fork, and spoon and happy conversation, interspersed by the occasional ringing of the pay phone at the back near the bar. Service, by a staff of uniformed professionals, is gracious and Dixie-sweet. As we prepared to take a picture of our redfish, a waitress rushed over and insisted on taking the picture herself, so she could include the two of us along with the lovely meal.

Borden's

1103 Jefferson St.   337-235-9291
Lafayette, LA $

"What is a frappe?" we asked as we studied the drink section of the posted movable-letter menu above the counter at Borden's dairy bar.

"That's frapp-AY," replied the mixologist, a soda-fountain veteran to whom the differences among a shake, malt, freeze, flip, frappe, and soda are elementary. She explained that here in Lafayette, a frappe is four scoops of ice cream and your choice of flavor, all blended together. It is like a milk shake without the milk. "You eat it with a spoon," she advised.

Nice as that sounds, we went for a traditional chocolate malt. It was a pleasure to watch her assemble ingredients in the tall cup with aplomb, then tend the cup as the mixer strained to whir them all together. It was a lot of work rearranging it round and round, up and down and at a cant so that unblended clods of ice cream were hit by the blades. The ultimate result: a classic malt, served with spoon and straw, with nary a single hunk of unmixed ice cream.

Sundaes are masterfully made, too—but served, alas, like the shakes, in paper cups rather than traditional soda fountain glassware. Among the broad choice of toppings, we are partial to hot fudge, marshmallow cream, and syrupy "wet nuts."

Boudin King

906 W. Division St.   337-824-6593
Jennings, LA   BLD | $

Yes, the boudin at Boudin King is wonderful—densely packed, spicy, and deeply satisfying. Buy it mild or hot, by the link; it is a Cajun classic. But so is just about everything else on the menu of this unlikely source of greatness. We say "unlikely" because Boudin King appears to be a fast-food restaurant, even including a drive-through window. Meals are served on disposable plates. Prices are little more than McJunkfood.

And yet here is stupendously good gumbo, smoky-flavored and thick with sausage and big pieces of chicken. And speaking of chicken, we would rate the fried chicken served by Boudin King as some of the most delicious in southern Louisiana, a part of the world where frying chicken is a fine, fine art. Other specialties include crawfish in the spring and nice fried pies for dessert.

The late Ellis Cormier, who founded this place back in the 1970s, once told us, "Nowhere else in America, except perhaps where the Mexicans live, is food properly spiced." Monsieur Cormier was one of the leading lights in America's rediscovery of its regional food, and of Cajun food in particular. It was primarily thanks to his good cooking that in 1979 the Louisiana State Legislature proclaimed Jennings "The Boudin Capital of the Universe."

Bozo's

3117 21st St.
Metairie, LA

504-831-8666
LD | $$

Metairie's time-honored, family-run tavern is a plain-looking place that is a bonanza of south Louisiana seafood: redfish, trout, shrimp remoulade, hugely hearty gumbo, daily-delivered oysters either on the half-shell or fried up for a magnificent po-boy on fragile French bread, and insanely luxurious barbecued shrimp, plus wild-caught catfish with succulent sweet meat that puts blah farm-raised cats to shame.

Those allergic to seafood can have a plate of red beans and rice with smoked sausage. Meals begin with crisp-crusted, fluffy-center bread that comes toasted and buttered. Dessert? Bread pudding, of course—topped with pecan praline rum sauce.

Brenda's Diner

409 W. Pershing St.
New Iberia, LA

337-367-0868
BLD | $

Brenda's brought tears of joy to our eyes. "It doesn't get better than this," we agreed out loud halfway through a lunch of fried chicken, fried pork chops, red beans with sausage, rice and gravy, candied yams, and smothered cabbage. Each dish Brenda Placide had cooked was the best version of itself that we have had since, maybe forever. The pork chop was audibly juicy with a tender taste that had us gnawing to the bone. The chicken's fragile crust shored in juice-dripping meat. The red beans were New-Iberia *hot*; the smothered cabbage, speckled with nuggets of garlicky sausage, brought high honor to the vegetable kingdom.

We ate this soul-stirring food in a tidy little dining room where a CD of southern gospel music set a rapturous tone. There are seats for no more than twenty people. The neighborhood is run-down, but the diner is immaculate inside; the walls are a gallery of Brenda's gratitude: prints and posters celebrating African American culture, as well as photos marking the achievements of Brenda's kin (graduations, weddings, reunions).

We had to ask her how she cooks such magnificent food, but we weren't surprised when she had no satisfactory answer. "It's from my mamma's kitchen," she said. "I cannot tell you how to do it because she never taught me to measure anything. You add seasoning and spice until it's right." It occurred to us that even if we studied Brenda as she cooked, taking scrupulous notes about every grain of every ingredient she used, we couldn't in a lifetime make food like this. It would be like watching Isaac Stern play the violin, then copying his every move.

Café des Amis

140 E. Bridge St. 337-332-5273
Breaux Bridge, LA BLD | $$

A sign in the window of Café des Amis boasts that it is "the essence of French Louisiana." It's the real deal, all right, a French-accented mix of South and Soul, with a dash of Caribbean spice and Italian brio. But it's ridiculous to try to define it by its roots; better to describe what it is.

At breakfast, it is beignets, little crisp-edged twists of fried dough under an avalanche of powdered sugar; it is "Oreille de Couchon," a long strip of fried dough so named because it resembles a pig's ear, available plain or filled with boudin, also spread with powdered sugar. It is biscuits topped with crawfish étouffée, omelets filled with tasso ham, and cheese grits with andouille sausage.

The menu for lunch and supper is a veritable encyclopedia of local favorites, including turtle soup, andouille gumbo, barbecue shrimp, corn bread filled with crawfish tails, softshell crab, and crawfish pie. Desserts include bread pudding with rum sauce, which is more of a New Orleans thing than a Cajun one, and *gâteau sirop*, which is extremely local. Made from sugarcane—grown and processed all around here—it is a block of moist spice cake with the distinctive smoky sweetness of cane sugar.

A friendly old brick-wall storefront that has been renovated to serve as an art gallery and live-music venue (check out the Saturday morning zydeco breakfast) as well as a restaurant, Café des Amis is a gathering place for locals and an easy destination for passersby. If you are looking for a full, true, and joyous taste of Acadian Louisiana, make Breaux Bridge your destination.

Note: Breakfast is served only on Friday, Saturday, and Sunday.

Café du Monde
800 Decatur St.   504-525-4544
New Orleans, LA   Always open | $

Café du Monde is a New Orleans institution, serving café au lait and beignets to locals and tourists for more than a century and a half. It is always open, and the characters you'll meet here—any time of day, but especially at odd hours in the middle of the night—are among the Crescent City's most colorful. The best seating is outdoors, where the chances are you will be serenaded by street musicians of the French Quarter as you sit under the awning and watch life go by.

There is not much to the menu: chicory coffee, either black or au lait (with a lot of milk), white or chocolate milk, orange juice, and beignets. Beignets are wonderful: dense, hole-less donuts, served hot from the fry kettle and so heaped with powdered sugar that it is not possible to eat one without getting white powder all over your hands, face, and clothes.

After leisurely coffee-sipping and beignet-eating, you can buy New Orleans souvenirs inside the restaurant, then stroll across Decatur Street to the place where fortune tellers, tarot card readers, and palmists set up shop every evening and, for the right price, reveal your future.

Casamento's
4330 Magazine St.   504-895-9761
New Orleans, LA   LD (closed in the summer) | $$

Oyster loaves are served throughout New Orleans and Cajun country, and we've yet to find one that's bad. But for many loaf-lovers Casamento's is the ultimate. Oysters aren't the only item of note on the menu of this spanking-clean neighborhood oyster bar that closes for a long summer vacation, when oysters aren't in season. You can also have fried fish and shrimp and springtime soft-shell crabs; and there's even a plate of that arcane Creole Italian meal, daube, which is flaps of pot roast in gravy on spaghetti noodles.

Casamento's oyster loaf is nothing short of magnificent: a dozen crackle-crusted hotties piled between two big slabs of what New Orleans cooks know as pan bread, a.k.a. Texas toast. Each single oyster is a joy, its brittle skin shattering with light pressure, giving way to a wave of melting warm, briney oyster meat across the tongue. When we asked proprietor Joe Gerdes what made his oysters so especially good, he modestly replied that his method is "too simple to call a recipe." Of course he uses freshly shucked local oysters, and he does recommend frying in lard, but the real secret is ineffable. "Everything is fried by feel and sound," he said. "It requires a lot of personal attention and experience."

Central Grocery

923 Decatur St.   504-523-1620
New Orleans, LA   LD | $

The term "muffuletta" once referred only to a chewy round loaf of bread turned out by Italian bakeries in New Orleans. Grocery stores that sold the bread got the fine idea to slice it horizontally and pile it with salami, ham, and provolone, then top that with a wickedly spicy mélange of chopped green and black olives fragrant with anchovies and garlic. The place that claims to have done it first is the Central Grocery on Decatur Street.

While it has become a tourist attraction and muffulettas are now the only sandwich on the menu, the Central Grocery still feels like a neighborhood store, its yellowed walls decorated with travel posters, the air inside smelling of garlic and sausage and provolone cheese. There is no table service. Step up to the counter and give your order, then watch the sandwich assembled. Once the sandwich is ready, it is cut into quarters (enough for four normal appetites) and wrapped, at which point you can take it to a counter toward the back of the store to unwrap and eat it.

Champagne's Breaux Bridge Bakery

105 S. Poydras St.   337-332-1117
Breaux Bridge, LA $

This charming nineteenth-century one-room bakery in the crawfish capital of the world caused us to stomp on the brakes as we drove past early in the morning. The smell of just-baked bread was irresistible. Inside the door, a small card table was arrayed with loaves. They are the familiar-looking south-Louisiana torpedoes, like French baguettes but about half the weight. Some are wrapped in paper, the others in plastic bags. "You want soft, you get the plastic," advised the gent behind the counter. "For crisp, paper." Our paper-wrapped loaf had a refined crunch to its crust and ineffably feathery insides. It's delicious just to eat, but oh, how well this would scoop out to be become a seafood boat filled with fried oysters or shrimp!

Cooked meat pies were displayed along the bakery counter, and good as they looked, we hesitated about getting one because who wants a cold meat pie? "We have a microwave," said the woman behind the counter.

"Lots of people, they come in and they take two or three, hot, to eat," said the man who had been our bread counselor. The warmed one we took out to the car was nothing short of spectacular: rich, moist, and vividly spiced.

We also walked away with a bag full of sugar cookies and one big, flat cookie filled with coconut. Delicious!

D.I.'s

6561 Evangeline Hwy.   337-432-5141
Basile, LA   LD | $$

Big round beer trays heaped with crawfish emerge from the kitchen trailing hot spiced steam through the dining room as accordion notes with a triangle beat bounce from the bandstand like manic Brick Breaker balls. Set back from the two-lane in the middle of nothing but rice fields and crawfish ponds, far from any town or major highway, D.I.'s is a brimful measure of Acadian pleasure. If it hadn't been for Sulphur policeman and good friend Major Many McNeil, we never, ever would have come across it. When we told Many we were on the lookout for a true Cajun eating experience, he said D.I.'s was it.

Daniel Isaac ("D.I.") Fruge has been known to neighbors for his well-seasoned crawdads since the 1970s. He was a rice and soybean farmer who began harvesting the mudbugs, boiling and serving them on weekends to friends and neighbors: $5 for all you could eat. They were served in his barn the traditional way—strewn in heaps across bare tables—with beer to drink on the side.

D.I. and his wife, Sherry, now run a restaurant with a full menu that includes steaks, crabs, oysters, frog legs, flounder, and shrimp; but vividly spiced crawfish are the draw. The classic way to enjoy them is boiled and piled onto the beer tray—a messy meal that rewards vigorous tail-pulling and head-sucking with an unending procession of the vibrant sweetwater richness that only crawdads deliver. You can have them crisp-fried into bite-size morsels with a salty crunch; and there is crawfish pie, étouffée, and bisque.

No longer a makeshift annex to Monsieur Fruge's barn, D.I.'s is a spacious destination with multiple dining rooms and dance floor. The Cajun music starts at 7 P.M., with an open-mike jam session Wednesday.

Domilise's Po-Boys

5240 Annunciation St.   504-899-9126

New Orleans, LA   L | $

You won't likely drive past Domilise's bar/sandwich shop by accident, for it is located in an unscenic blue-collar neighborhood; and if you did accidentally drive by, you might not guess that it is a source of great New Orleans sandwiches. It looks like a small, no-frills neighborhood tavern, and in some ways, that is what it is. We guess it would be possible to walk in, sit at the bar, and knock back longnecks or boilermakers all day long. To do so, you'd have to have no sense of smell, for the air of this tavern is wildly perfumed with shrimp, oysters, and catfish hoisted from the fry basket and heaped onto fresh po-boy loaves.

You may have to take a number before you can place your order. At the height of lunch hour, Domilise's is packed, for its superior po-boys attract eaters from all over the city; table space is precious (strangers often share); and the house phone rings unanswered.

For the newcomer, delay is a good thing because it provides an opportunity to read the menu on the wall and to observe the sandwich makers construct different combos before you decide which is the right one for you. Hot smoked sausage with gravy is the one we recommend above all others. Get it "dressed," meaning topped with tomato, lettuce, and grainy Creole mustard. A large one is constructed on a length of bread so long that it must be cut in thirds. While the sandwich is being made, buy your drink at the bar and hope that by the time you are ready to eat, space at a table is available.

Don's Specialty Meats

730 I-10 (S. Frontage Rd.)   337-234-2528

Scott, LA   L (butcher shop is open daily

from 6 A.M. to 7 P.M.) | $

A big modern building located just off the interstate, Don's is a destination for boudin and cracklin's, hot lunch, po-boys, fried pork chops, fried chicken, and just about any kind of Cajun meat you need for cooking at home. There is a large indoor dining room as well as picnic tables outside. Service is do-it-yourself.

Weekends are an especially good time to eat at Don's. Saturday, the smoked pork chop draws fans from Lafayette Parish and beyond. Slices of white bread hold a giant, bone-in chop that oozes juice at first bite and is even more delectably messy if you have it dressed with barbecue sauce. Sunday, the place is thronged with locals who come for pork steak, stuffed brisket, and ribs.

Dupuy's Oyster Shop

108 S. Main St.　　　　　　337-893-2336
Abbeville, LA　　　　　　　LD (closed Tues) | $$

There's a broad menu at Dupuy's, including sirloin steak, fried catfish, pastas, and wonderful onion rings, plus a bountiful Sunday brunch; but as the full name of the place suggests, oysters are its raison d'être. The very best way to have them is raw on the half-shell by the dozen, served on a tray of ice with a full complement of condiments. Or, if you like things cooked, have them fried and stuffed into bread with mayonnaise and mustard. In addition, there is oyster stew and an intriguing grilled oyster salad.

The one other dish that is essential to eat at this friendly, always-crowded town café is Cajun seafood gumbo, a boldly spiced stew that you can retrieve from the bowl with only a fork.

Dwyer's Café

323 Jefferson St.　　　　　　337-235-9364
Lafayette, LA　　　　　　　BL | $

No one makes lunch sound as good as Mike Dwyer does. You will hear his pitch as you approach the cafeteria area of Dwyer's Café, where he enumerates the day's choices, one by one, with pride and exuberance to make appetites growl. It's a joy to hear him, but in fact, this food needs no hard sell. It is superlative plate lunch.

Parenthetically, Dwyer's hamburgers are excellent. But it's the hot lunches we love. Dwyer's is a meat-and-three affair, the daily meats including such expertly cooked stalwarts as smothered pork chops, lengths of pork sausage, roast beef with dark gravy, and chicken-fried steak with white gravy. One day in the winter, Mike was pitching crawfish fettucine, a fabulous cross-cultural Franco-Italian-Cajun noodle casserole loaded with high-flavored crawdads. Among the notable side dishes are dirty rice, eggplant casserole, red beans, and sausage jambalaya. On cold days, you can get gumbo or chili.

Dwyer's is also a notable breakfast opportunity. We love the tender sweet potato hotcakes with their faintly crisp edge (which Mike says he added to the menu for low-carb dieters!). When you order pancakes, the waitress will ask what kind of syrup you want: cane or maple. Sugarcane is a major crop around here, and the pancake syrup made from it is thick, dark, and resonantly sweet . . . but not at all white-sugar sweet.

Earl's

510 Verot School Rd.   337-237-5501
Lafayette, LA   L | $

West of New Orleans from Baton Rouge to St. Charles and from the swamps of Avery Island to the prairies of Evangeline Parish, hundreds of places sell boudin sausage. It is served on plates in some restaurants, but it is most commonly obtained from groceries and quick-stop stores where it is made. Among the best of them is Earl's, which sells it by the link from a hot box near the cash register. Customers buy it to take home or to eat in the car. There's no place to eat on premises.

Earl's boudin is ideal for off-the-dashboard dining, each link so dense that once the casing is breached with a sharp knife, you can fork out pieces in tidy clumps. Each bite is a country-style symphony of pork and rice, pepper and onion, needing only beer (or Barq's root beer) on the side to be a complete meal.

Earl's also serves a plate lunch, including fine fried chicken, po-boys, red beans and rice, and catfish on Friday—again, all on a take-out basis.

Galatoire's

209 Bourbon St.   504-525-2021
New Orleans, LA   LD | $$$

Galatoire's is far more formal than most Roadfood restaurants—no jeans allowed, jackets are required for men—and at a good $50 per person, it is more expensive. But if you've got the money and want the definitive Creole dining experience, it's a must. (Guys: House jackets are available if you come to New Orleans without yours.) With its mirrored walls, bright lights, and dark woodwork, white linen tablecloths and black-tie waiters, it is a crystalline image of a bourgeois dining room from the turn of the nineteenth century: solid, dependable, with a bounteous larder of the highest quality. The staff is polite but not obsequious, and they are able to clearly and appealingly describe every item on the multipage menu without making the description a grocery list or trying too hard to sell it. Nor will these pros offer the ridiculous "Good choice!" if you happen to select something of which they approve.

A surfeit of options makes the menu more than a little frustrating. Deciding is sweet agony. Do you like crabmeat? You can have it au gratin, ravigote, Sardou, Saint-Pierre, maison, or Yvonne. There's shrimp Clemenceau, Creole, Marguery, au vin, étouffée, deep-fried, and the kitchen's famous remoulade (which bears little resemblance to remoulades anywhere else). There are seven kinds of potato, nine different omelets and egg dishes, and a choice of soups that includes oyster-artichoke, Creole gumbo, and turtle.

We've sampled only a fraction of what Galatoire's offers. Not once have we been disappointed; more often, we are inspired to rave that the plate before us holds what surely is the paradigm of whatever it's supposed to be. Highest on our hit list are the shrimp remoulade, trout amandine, crab Sardou (with spinach, artichoke hearts, and hollandaise sauce), soft-shell crabs (the tenderest ever!), and the inconspicuous but conspicuously potent garlic green salad.

Meals begin with warm loaves of the fragile-skinned, fluffy bread found nowhere outside of southern Louisiana and, if you're a tippler, the classic New Orleans aperitif, a Sazerac. And they can end with a fiery climax: *café brulot* for two, flamed tableside.

Jerry Lee's

12181 Greenwell Springs Rd.   225-272-0739
Baton Rouge, LA   L | $

Like most of the great boudin makers in southern Louisiana, Jerry Lee's is a store rather than a restaurant. There are no dining facilities. It is common to see customers sitting in their trucks or cars and dining off the dashboard or, on a nice day, eating al fresco off the hood. A neon sign in Jerry Lee's window shows a boiling pot (presumably where the pork is cooked) with this legend underneath: "If it's not Jerry Lee's, it's not Boudin." While a lot of Cajun boudin is fire-hot, Jerry Lee's is only haloed by pepper . . . all the better to savor the flavor of the rice that is its dominant ingredient, along with the luxe of the ground pork that is its soul.

In a heated case near the cash register, you will find the boudin already extracted from its casing and piled into rolls along with cheese—the latter, in our opinion, completely overwhelming the refined flavor play of the former. The better choice is to forgo the fixins and get a couple of links, which cost about $1.75 each. Their casing is really tough, virtually impossible to cut with teeth alone, but once it is opened up with the plastic knife provided by the management, out wafts a balmy aroma that is unique to southernmost Louisiana. Grab a bag of Zapp's potato chips and a Barq's root beer and you have the makings of a local feast.

Johnson's Boucanière

111 Saint John St.   337-269-8878
Lafayette, LA   L | $

Boucanière means "smokehouse" in Cajun, and smoking pork and beef is
what the Johnson family has done since they opened up a grocery store in
Eunice in 1937. Today they live above their smokehouse in Lafayette, making it easy for them to come downstairs about 3:30 in the morning to get
the meats on the grate, where they cook low and slow for hours. The results
compose a lunch menu featuring sinfully tender pulled pork, beef brisket,
tasso ham, and sausage made from pork or turkey. There's even a barbecue
salad of your choice of pork, brisket, or chicken combined with lettuce, onions, tomatoes, and shredded cheese, dressed with Johnson's barbecue sauce.

Finally, but by no means the least of Johnson's accomplishments, is
boudin sausage, the savory Cajun treat that may be eaten with a fork but is
even more fun when squeezed directly from its natural casing. The fabulous
website boudinlink.com gave Johnson's Boucanière an A+ rating, declaring
the boudin to be perhaps the ideal blend of rice and meat with an overall
flavor that is complex but clean.

Much business is take-out, but a covered porch provides casual accommodations for those who come to eat a plate lunch.

Lasyone's Meat Pie Kitchen

622 Second St.   318-352-3353
Natchitoches, LA   BLD | $

When we surveyed visitors at the first annual Louisiana Roadfood Festival
of 2009 to find out what food they liked best from among the several dozen
local specialties sold by street vendors, the winner by a landslide was the
meat pie dished out by Lasyone's. Second place was Lasyone's crawfish pie.
Half-circle pastry pockets about the size of tacos with a rugged crimp around
their edges, Lasyone's deep-fried pies have a golden crust that is brittle and
crunchy near the crimp, pliant near the mounded center. Inside each flaky
sheaf is a good-size portion of deftly seasoned ground beef, moist enough to
make gravy irrelevant. Spicy but not fire-hot, complex and succulent, it is an
honest piece of food that satisfies in an old-fashioned way. Lasyone's serves
them for breakfast, accompanied by eggs and hash browns, but most customers come midday to get a pair of them for lunch, with soulful dirty rice
on the side, darkened with plenty of gizzards and topped with zesty gravy.

Middendorf's

30160 Hwy. 51 S.   985-386-6666
Akers, LA   LD Wed-Sun | $$

Middendorf's has been remodeled with a waterfront deck and air-condi-
tioned kitchen, but it remains the casual, noisy, and fun place it has been
for seventy-five years. There is nothing like its catfish, whether you get thick
or thin. Thick is a meaty cross-section of fish, similar to a steak wrapped in
breading. It is sweet-smelling and has resounding vim that is unlike any seawater fish. Thin catfish is more elegant. Sliced into a diaphanous strip that is
sharply seasoned, lightly breaded, and quickly fried, a thin cat fillet crunches
loudly when you sink your teeth into its brittle crust, which is sheer enough
to let the rich flavor of the fish resonate. With the catfish, thick or thin, there
are perfectly good and unsurprising companions: French fries, hush puppies,
and coleslaw salad.

Beyond catfish, just about any seafood on the menu is well worth eating. We have had some great gumbo here, made with shrimp and crabmeat,
which was surprisingly delicate compared to the more overpowering versions sold in the city's best gumbo houses. There are fabulous barbecued
shrimp and oysters, sautéed soft-shell crabs, po-boy sandwiches, and Italian
salads loaded with olives and spice.

Moody's

601 Martin Luther King Dr.   318-377-5873
Minden, LA   L | $

If you are traveling through Webster Parish along Interstate 20 east of
Shreveport, we highly recommend taking Exit 47 and driving five minutes
to the north. Here in Minden (where Hank Williams married his Billie Jean
in 1952) you will find Moody's, where heavy-duty partitioned plates carry
some of the highest-quality, lowest-priced meals in the South. Expertly made
fried chicken, pork chops, or meat loaf is accompanied by such soulful vegetables as turnip greens, cheese-enriched broccoli, and candied yams. Filling
out the plate are cylinders of hot-water corn bread—baked, then fried to
a crisp. Peach and blackberry cobblers compete for your dessert vote with
coconut pie and strawberry cream pie.

Mosca's

4137 US 90 W.   504-436-9942
Avondale, LA   D | $$

Despite catastrophic hurricanes and not-quite-cataclysmic changes in the American diet, Mosca's never seems to change. All the great things about this legendary destination still deserve legendary status, especially oysters Mosca—a festival of garlic, olive oil, Parmesan cheese, and breadcrumbs, all cosseting little nuggets of sweet oyster meat.

The parking lot remains a gravel wreck; the outside is dark and nefarious; in fact, on a recent trip to New Orleans, we were told that Mosca's for many years was the hangout of the region's chief Mafioso. If it's your first time, we guarantee you will think you are lost when you make the drive. And even when you find it, you will wonder: Can this two-room joint with the blaring jukebox and semi-secret kitchen dining area really be the most famous Italian roadhouse in America? Inside, conviviality reigns, and we saw only friendly sorts of folks eating; no one looked like a cast member of *The Godfather* or *The Sopranos*.

Aside from the setting and location, the primary thing you'll notice upon arriving at Mosca's is the smell. Garlic reigns. There are whole cloves of it in the painfully tender chicken à la Grande—wine-sautéed pieces that arrive in a pool of rosemary-perfumed gravy. Thank God for spaghetti bordelaise, which is little more than a heap of thin noodles bathed in oil and butter and garlic. It is an ideal medium for rolling up on a fork and pushing around in extra chicken gravy or the last of the oysters Mosca breadcrumbs to sop up their goodness.

Go with friends: the bigger the group, the more different dishes you can sample—and you do need also to taste Mosca's sausage, chicken cacciatore, and Louisiana shrimp. Everything is served family-style.

Parkway Bakery & Tavern

538 Hagan Ave.   504-482-3047
New Orleans, LA   LD (closed Tues) | $

After much arduous research, it is our opinion that the best roast beef po-boy in New Orleans (a city that takes its roast beef po-boys very seriously) is made by the Parkway Bakery & Tavern, overlooking Bayou St. John. The sandwich is presented tightly wrapped in a tube of butcher paper that already is mottled through with gravy splotches when you pick it up at the kitchen window. Unwrap it and behold a length of fresh, brawny bread loaded with beef so falling-apart tender that it seems not to have been sliced but rather hand-pulled, like barbecued pork, into myriad slivers, nuggets, and clumps. It is difficult to discern where meat ends and gravy begins because there is so much gravy saturating the meat and so many carving-board scraps, known as debris (say DAY-bree), in the gravy.

That meaty gravy makes the city's ultimate dining bargain. At $4.85 for a full-length sandwich, $3.65 for an eight-incher, Parkway's gravy po-boy is a minimalist sandwich of the good, chewy bread filled only with gravy. The bread is substantial enough to absorb massive amounts of the liquid and a booming beef scent, becoming the most appetizing savory loaf imaginable, its surface crowded with debris that is the concentrated essence of roast beef.

Parkway has a full repertoire of po-boy fillings, including oysters, crunchy fried shrimp (that, mysteriously, makes a fabulous partner with the roast beef in the surf 'n' turf po-boy), and a brunch version that includes sausage, bacon, eggs, and cheese and is served with a side of syrup!

A note about the restaurant name: The original Parkway on this site indeed was a bakery, so beloved that lines of customers would stretch out the door at times when it was known fresh bread would be coming out of the brick oven. The bakery closed in the early 1980s and today's Parkway does not make its own, but the name lives on.

Prejean's

3480 I-49 NE
Lafayette, LA

337-896-3247
LD | $$

Prejean's is big and noisy (the live music starts every night at 7 P.M., and be sure to wear your dancing shoes), and the food is classic Cajun. In some other part of the country, a restaurant this brash might seem too "commercial" to qualify for Roadfood—walls hung with Acadiana, a stuffed alligator in the center of the dining room, a gift shop with tacky souvenirs—but for all its razzle-dazzle, Prejean's is the real thing, a fact about which you can have no doubt when you dip a spoon into the chicken and sausage gumbo or the dark andouille gumbo laced with smoked duck.

The menu is big and exotic, featuring dozens of dishes you'll not find on menus outside Louisiana, from crisp-fried crawfish boudin balls and catfish Catahoula (stuffed with crawfish, shrimp, and crab) to eggplant "pirogues" (canoes) hollowed out, fried, and filled with crawfish and red snapper fillet, drizzled with buttery lobster sauce. It is possible to get a monomaniacal all-crawfish meal of crawfish bisque, fried crawfish, crawfish étouffée, crawfish pie, crawfish boulettes, and a salad dotted with crawfish. There are two significant desserts: red velvet cake and bread pudding with Jack Daniel's sour mash sauce.

Robin's

1409 Henderson Hwy. 337-228-7594
Henderson, LA LD | $$$

Lionel Robin cooks some of the most distinctive restaurant meals in swamp country. Year-round, but especially in crawfish season from early in the year through spring, this is the place to have it either simply boiled or in all the many ways Cajun chefs like to celebrate it. A crawfish dinner starts with bisque, which is smoky, complex, and rich. You then move on to a few boiled and fried ones, étouffeé over rice, boulettes, stuffed pepper, and a superior pie in which the little crustaceans share space with vegetables and plenty of garlic in a translucent-thin crust.

The one crawfish dish we might not recommend here is gumbo—not because it isn't good (it is), but because the shrimp and okra gumbo is even better. And chicken and sausage gumbo, while containing none of the seafood for which Robin's is renowned, is wonderful—brilliantly spiced, thick with sausage you will remember for a long time.

For dessert: How about some of Monsieur Robin's Tabasco ice cream?

Rocky and Carlo's

613 W. St. Bernard Hwy. 504-279-8323
Chalmette, LA LD | $

Way out in St. Bernard Parish, Rocky and Carlo's is a spacious eating hall featuring that essential trinity of south Louisiana cuisine—Italian-Cajun-Dixie fare. Walk along the cafeteria line and select from a broad hot-lunch menu that includes pork chops with greens, braciola, veal parm, stuffed peppers, muffalettas, fried shrimp or oysters, and gorgeous baked chicken. Rocky and Carlo's seafood gumbo, loaded with shrimp, crab, and crawfish and thickened with okra, just may be the best in or out of New Orleans. The blackboard menu also lists wop salad, the locals' politically incorrect term for garlicky iceberg lettuce with green olives, and many customers come for the excellent roast beef po-boys. Heaps of wispy, deep-fried onions adorn almost every table.

No matter what you eat at Rocky and Carlo's, the single dish that you likely will remember best is the inconspicuous menu listing "macaroni." There is none better. Very different from typical mac 'n' cheese made with elbow noodles, this mountain of baked pasta is built from substantial perciatelli tubes that come plastered with orange cheese—tender gobs from the heart, chewy strips from the top, and crisp webbed bark from the casserole's edge. Some people get it topped with sweet red marinara sauce or glistening mahogany brown gravy, each of which adds unique character.

T-Boy's Slaughterhouse

2228 Pine Point Rd. (Hwy. 104)   337-468-3333
Ville Platte, LA   L | $

The trip from the swamplands of the South to T-Boy's Slaughterhouse winds through Evangeline Parish prairies where cattle and horses graze and native zydeco music sets the cultural beat. Once you arrive, you are in for a true taste of country life. As its name suggests, this place is not a restaurant. It is a from-scratch butcher and convenience store selling sausages and meats from the smokehouse, including paunce (stuffed stomach) and tasso ham. For those just passing through, it is a premier source of the visceral Cajun sausage known as boudin. In spring crawfish season, especially during Lent, crawfish boudin is a Friday special. It is moist, sweet, and swampy with a slow-rolling pepper kick.

Boudin is sold hot by the long link, which proprietor T-Boy Berzas is happy to scissor into pieces two or three inches long, making it easy simply to squeeze the luxuriant filling from casing to mouth without the trouble of utensils. We strongly suggest accompanying boudin with some of T-Boy's fabulous hot cracklin's, which are assertively seasoned, pop-in-the-mouth chunks and squiggles of deep-fried pig skin, fat, and shreds of meat that shatter when you bite into them, then dissolve into an ethereal slurry of pork and pepper—the flavor of Cajun Louisiana in bite-size pieces.

T-Boy's has a second location in Eunice.

Abe's Bar-B-Q

616 State St.   662-624-9947
Clarksdale, MS   LD | $

Folklore designates the crossroads of Highways 61 and 49 in Clarksdale as the spot where Robert Johnson sold his soul to the devil in exchange for music mastery. In 1924, when Johnson was thirteen, Abraham Davis began selling sandwiches in Clarksdale. He opened Abe's Bar-B-Q at the crossroads in 1937, and today his grandson Pat Davis runs the place, which is known for pecan-smoked pork and hot tamales.

Abe's barbecue is Boston butt that is cooked over pecan wood, cooled overnight, then sliced and heated again on the griddle when it is ordered. While on the grill it gets hacked up. The result? Pork hash with lots of juicy buzz in its pale inside fibers and plenty of crusty parts where it has fried on the hot iron of the grill. You can have it on a platter or in a sandwich, the latter available in two sizes—normal and Big Abe, which is twice the pork loaded into a double-decker bun. Clarksdale is close enough to Memphis that it is served city-style, i.e., with the slaw inside the bun.

Abe's sauce is dark red, tangy, with the resonance of pepper and spice—a sublime companion for the meat. Pat Davis told us that it is made from the original recipe his grandfather developed, except for one ingredient, which he swears he doesn't use any more. We wondered aloud if that secret ingredient might be opium, considering its addictive qualities. Pat denied it with a sly smile.

Served three to an order, with or without chili on top, Abe's tamales are packed into cayenne-red husks, their yellow cornmeal moist with drippings from a mixture of beef and pork. The recipe is Abe Davis's, unchanged. "No doubt granddaddy got it from someone in town," Pat suggests, reminding us that Abe had come to the United States from Lebanon, where tamales aren't a big part of the culinary mix. Why Abe thought they would sell well in his barbecue place is a head-scratcher. "There were no Mexican restaurants here then," Pat says. "And as far as I know, not many Mexicans."

Abe's Grill

803 Hwy. 72 W.   662-286-6124
Corinth, MS   BL | $

A tip of the hat to Michael Medley, whom we met in Salt Lake City, where he slipped us a tempting list of eateries in northern Mississippi. Otherwise, we might never have traveled out Highway 72 to Abe's Grill. What to eat at Abe's? "Breakfast!" Michael said. And sure enough, if you are looking for hot biscuits made the true-South way with Martha White flour, for country ham and eggs, or even for a plate of pork brains, you must stop at this colorful roadside attraction that is plastered inside and out with vintage advertising signs, license plates, postcards, calendars, and photographs.

No praise is too high for Abe's biscuits, which are lightweight but substantially savory, and especially delicious if you arrive early and they are oven-fresh. Sawmill gravy is a well-known classic to top them, but curiously enough, chocolate gravy is a classic, too. (Ari Weinzweig of Zingerman's Deli [p. 339] did the research on this.) While it takes some getting used to, the chocolate gravy makes a seductive alternative to ordinary biscuit companions. Split and buttered or sandwiching sausage or bologna, the biscuits are good, too. Coffee is included with most breakfasts, but if you eat enough pig meat to rouse a powerful thirst, do consider Abe's iced tea, served in a one-quart frosted mason jar.

We have yet to have lunch at Abe's, but we do look forward to a hamburger, which Abe's makes from beef ground here daily, as well as to Abe's "original recipe" corn dog along with fresh-cut French fries.

Blue & White Restaurant

1355 US Hwy. 61 N.   662-363-1371

Tunica, MS   BLD | $

Tunica has gone from cotton fields to gamblers' paradise, but out on Highway 61, the old Blue & White Restaurant is operating pretty much the same as it's been since opening day in 1937. The gas pumps are gone, so it is now only a restaurant rather than a full-service travelers' stop; but if you are looking for good southern food at reasonable prices in an atmosphere that is more down-home than high-stakes, this is the place to go.

We were lucky enough to visit on the cusp of breakfast and lunch hour. "You have ten more minutes to order breakfast," our waitress warned. "Then the lunch buffet will open." Naturally, we did both. For breakfast we had a classic country ham plate, the vigorous, well-aged slab of pig accompanied by eggs, biscuits, chunky sausage cream gravy, coffee-flavored red-eye gravy, and a bowl of stout, buttery grits. What a great morning meal!

When the buffet opened up, we helped ourselves to chicken and dumplings, which was superb: powerfully chickeny, loaded with meat, and laced with free-form mouthfuls of tender flavor-infused dough. On the side, we spooned up black-eyed peas, creamed corn, escalloped potatoes, and some of the most amazing turnip greens we've ever eaten. These greens were oily, salty, luscious, and rich, almost more like the pork that was used to flavor them than the green vegetable they appear to be. On the side of this good meal came a sweet-dough yeast muffin and a crisp corn stick: both oven-hot and delicious.

We paid extra for an order of that weird specialty invented a few decades ago in the Delta, fried dill pickles. Blue & White's are ultra-thin slices with a veil of crust, nearly weightless, served with ranch dressing as a dip. Light as they are, the pickles have a resounding brine flavor that induces a mighty thirst. If you are a beer drinker, you will have instant cravings.

Crystal Grill

423 Carrollton Ave.   662-453-6530

Greenwood, MS   LD | $$

Years ago, the Crystal Grill was known for a neon sign that glowed "Never Sleep." Open from 4 A.M. until midnight, it hosted the locals for their pre-dawn coffee klatch as well as C&G Railroad men who'd stop their train on the tracks just across the street for a late-night supper. Breakfast no longer is served; at lunchtime, townsfolk flock here with the gusto of celebrants arriving at a church picnic. Multiple remodelings over the years have created a labyrinth of small dining rooms that can seat over 200 people in neighborly surroundings.

The menu is an eccentric spectrum of local treasures (peppery Delta tamales, Biloxi flounder, Belzoni catfish) and such saccharine Dixie oddities as pink velvet frozen salad (crushed pineapple, Cool Whip, cherry pie filling, and condensed milk) and "fruit salad" that is canned pear halves topped with grated yellow cheese. Proprietor John Ballas said that the recipe for his kitchen's aromatic yeast rolls came from a friend's mother who was a home-ec teacher at Greenwood High and that the spaghetti sauce is made from a recipe that his father obtained years ago by writing a letter to Heinz. Our favorite dishes on the menu are shrimp and crab Newburg, fried oysters, turnip greens, and sweet, sweet tea. And pie.

Oh, what pie! Annie Johnson's legendary mile-high slices are significantly taller than they are wide, the great meringue triangle on top about twice the height of the ribbon of cream it surmounts. It's quite an adventure to ease the edge of a fork onto the top of the fluffy white crown and allow nothing more than gravity to carry it through to the filling, where its downward progress slows but doesn't stop. Finally the fork hits bedrock—a completely wrong term for a lard-laced savory crust that shatters under an ounce of pressure. Not to slight coconut cream, which is fantastic, but chocolate cream is Crystal Grill's crowning glory. Not overwhelmingly fudgy or thick, it is more like Swiss milk chocolate, its creamy soul as prominent as its chocolate flavor. It reminds us of fine chocolate pudding, all the more delicious for being sandwiched between a cloud of delicate meringue and a stratum of meltingly flaky crust.

Dilworth's Tamales

702 Wick St.   662-665-0833
Corinth, MS   L | $

At $3 per dozen, Dilworth's tamales are a terrific bargain. You actually can eat a dozen, maybe even two dozen if you're hungry, for they are panatela-thin. Wrapped in parchment, they are a simple mixture of beef, cornmeal, and spice steamed in the wrapper long enough to become a single, pleasing chord. Dilworth's sells them hot or mild, the former bright but not incendiary, the latter sheer Miss-Mex comfort.

All business is drive-through, and while your dozen will come well wrapped inside a brown paper bag, we advise being armed with plenty of napkins when you open up the butcher paper that contains them.

These tamales have a long history in Corinth. Proprietor Lisa Edmond's father used to ride through the streets of town on a three-wheel bike with a large basket, hawking tamales from street to street. The house motto is "Dilworth's Are The Best Yet."

The Dinner Bell
229 5th Ave.   601-684-4883
McComb, MS   L | $$

The Dinner Bell's reputation for grand southern meals has unfurled since it opened in 1945. Now run by the Lopinto family, who took over in 1981, it is the place to go in Mississippi to experience revolving-table dining.

The whole tables don't revolve. They are round, and in the center of each is a lazy Susan that those seated at the circumference can set in motion. It is piled with a lavish array of food. Spin it and take what you want. When a serving tray starts getting empty, out comes a full one from the kitchen. Grab as much as you want and eat at your own speed.

It isn't only quantity and convenience that make Dinner Bell meals memorable. This is some mighty marvelous food: chicken and dumplings, catfish, ham, corn sticks, sweet potato casseroles, black-eyed peas, fried eggplant, and fried okra. The dishes we cannot resist are the flamboyant vegetable casseroles supercharged with cheese and cracker crumbs: our kind of health food. Spinach casserole enriched with cream cheese and margarine and cans of artichoke hearts is good for the soul . . . not to mention the fact that it is scrumptious. To drink with all this good food, there is only one proper libation: sweet tea.

Doe's Eat Place
502 Nelson St.   662-334-3315
Greenville, MS   D | $$$

Located on the wrong side of town in the back rooms of a dilapidated grocery store, Doe's does not look like a restaurant, much less a great restaurant. Its fans, ourselves included, love it just the way it is. Mississippians have eaten here since 1941, when segregation was a way of life. Back then, blacks entered through the front door for meals of fried fish and tamales; white patrons came in the back door and ate in the kitchen. Today, many dining tables still are located in the kitchen, spread helter-skelter among stoves and counters where the staff dresses salads and fried potatoes in big iron skillets. Plates, flatware, and tablecloths are all mismatched. It is noisy and inelegant, and service—while perfectly polite—is rough and tumble. Newcomers may be shocked by the ramshackle surroundings, but Doe's is easy to like once the food starts coming.

Start with tamales and a brilliantly garlicked salad made of iceberg lettuce dressed with olive oil and fresh-squeezed lemon juice. Shrimp are usually available, broiled or fried, and they are very, very good; but it's steak for which Doe's has earned its reputation. "Baby Doe" Signa, son of the founder, told us that it is merely "U.S. Choice" grade, which, frankly, we don't believe. To us, it tastes like the primest of the prime, as good as any steak we have eaten anywhere: booming with flavor, oozing juice, tender but in no way tenderized. The choices range from a ten-ounce filet mignon up to a four-pound sirloin. Our personal preference is the porterhouse, the bone of which bisects a couple of pounds of meat that is very different in character on either side of the bone. The tenderloin side is zesty and exciting; the other side seems laden with protein, as deeply satisfying as beef can be. With steak come some of the world's most delicious French fries—dandy to eat "neat," even better when dragged through the oily juices that flow out of steaks onto the plate.

Note: Please do not confuse this great eat place or its family-run sibling in Little Rock (p. 223) with franchised Doe's throughout the South.

The Elite

141 E. Capitol St. 601-352-5606
Jackson, MS   BLD | $

Despite its name, The Elite is a restaurant for people of every social class: white-collar downtowners at breakfast, white and blue collars at lunch, whole families and even starry-eyed couples on dates for supper. A Jackson fixture now for one hundred years, it belongs to a small, little-acknowledged genre of great southern restaurant: the polite, square-meals café with a Greek accent.

Most of what you'll eat is copybook southern-comfort fare: country-fried steaks and veal cutlets with gravy, Delta-style tamales, fried crab claws from the Gulf, Mobile Bay West Indies salad, crisp-fried shrimp, and a choice of vegetables, from simple sliced tomatoes to elaborate casseroles. The Elite also offers a selection of Mexican food, including an enchilada plate that Roadfood.com's Bruce Bilmes and Sue Boyle described as "simply as good as it gets: gooey, laced with raw chopped onions, topped with a mantle of orange cheese." Breakfast biscuits are delicate; yeasty dinner rolls are famously good. There is excellent house-made baklava for dessert, but do not ignore the intense lemon chess pie.

Giardina's

314 Howard St.   662-455-4227

Greenwood, MS   D | $$$

Opened in 1936, Giardina's started as a fish market but soon became a restaurant popular among cotton growers, known for its private curtained booths where bootleg booze could be drunk in secrecy. As King Cotton lost its economic hegemony late in the twentieth century, Giardina's fortunes waned along with those of Greenwood, the South's cotton capital. But then the Viking Range Corporation came to town in 1989 and the presence of the stove maker turned everything around. The Mississippi Heritage Trust has given awards to Viking for its rehabilitation of local properties, including the transformation of the historic Irving Hotel from a ratty embarrassment to a stylish boutique hotel called The Alluvian. What we like about The Alluvian, beyond its feather beds and 300-thread-count sheets, is the fact that it is the new home of Giardina's (pronounced with a hard G).

Giardina's is stylish, modern, and expensive. Service is polished. Tables are outfitted with thick white cloths and snazzy Viking cutlery. The wine collection—stored in state-of-the-art Viking wine cellars—is impressive. And yet for all that, the dining experience is down-home Delta. When you enter, Mary Rose Graham, a second-generation Giardina, will escort you to a private dining compartment just like in Prohibition days. The menu is upscale cotton country fare, including hefty steaks and elegant pompano, hot tamales, and a bevy of dishes that reflect the powerful influence of Italian immigrants on Greenwood's cuisine. These include garlicky salads and a marvelous appetizer called Camille's bread, which our waiter described as "like a muffuletta but without the meat"—a hot loaf stuffed with olives, sardines, and cheese.

Hicks'

305 S. State St.   662-624-9887

Clarksdale, MS   LD | $

"I am sixty-one years old, and I made my first tamales at age sixteen," Eugene Hicks told us a few years ago when we asked him why the ones he makes are so especially good. Rich and with a hard kick of pepper spices, each one is hand-wrapped; and they are available by threes, sixes, or twelves. A plate of three is served with chili and cheese, baked beans, and Italian-seasoned coleslaw.

Tamales are what put Hicks' on the map, but there is a whole menu of ribs, rib tips, and chopped pork shoulder cooked over flaming hickory logs and topped with house-made sauce. In addition, there are Hicks-made pork sausages, fried catfish, and a fourteen-inch "Big Daddy" sandwich that is made with a combination of sliced barbecued pork and smoked turkey.

The first day we stopped in, a sign by the drive-up window advertised hog maws at $3.69 for a pint container. While the car ahead of us loaded up what looked like a meal for twelve, we debated for a moment what, exactly, hog maws are. Jane was sure maws were some part of a pig's mouth (inferred from the expression, "shut your maw"); Michael believed they came from the far other end of the animal. When it came our turn, Jane asked the woman behind the window, "Is this maw you are serving a mouth or a rectum?" She looked at us wide-eyed and explained that they are parts of a pig's stomach. For us, they are an acquired taste we have yet to acquire.

Lusco's

722 Carrollton Ave.   662-453-5365
Greenwood, MS   D | $$$

To occupy one of Lusco's back-room private dining booths and to hear the plaint of blues musicians that floats from the sound system above the partitions that segregate the parties of diners is a weird and compelling taste of cotton country history. Planters around Greenwood came to know Charles "Papa" Lusco as a grocer in the 1920s. His wife, Marie "Mama" Lusco, sold plates of her spaghetti at the store, and Papa built secret dining rooms in back where customers could enjoy his homemade wine with their meals.

Mama and Papa were Italian by way of Lousiana, so the flavors of the kitchen they established are as much Creole as they are southern or Italian. Gumbo, crab, and shrimp are always on the menu, and oysters are a specialty in season—on the half-shell or baked with bacon. The menu is best known for its high-end items: Lusco's T-bone steaks are some of the finest anywhere—sumptuous cuts that are brought raw to the table for your approval, then broiled to pillowy succulence. Pompano has for many years been a house trademark (when available, usually the spring), broiled and served whole, bathed in a magical sauce made of butter, lemon, and secret spices.

Lusco's is also known for its New Orleans–style salad of iceberg lettuce dolled up with anchovies, capers, and olives and liberally sopped in a fragrant vinaigrette; but third-generation Lusco Karen Pinkston is a serious salad buff who has made it her business to concoct more modern alternatives. One evening's choices included Mediterranean salad, made with feta cheese; traditional Caesar salad; and a salad billed as Gourmet's Delight, made with arugula, radicchio, endive, red lettuce, and spinach. "Andy [Karen's husband] likes to tease me about that one," Karen said about the latter. "He tells me it's just weeds I've picked by the side of the highway. But the fact is that the Delta is different now than it used to be, and the new people have more educated palates. Even this place has to change with the times."

Phillips Grocery

541 E. Van Dorn Ave.   601-252-4671
Holly Springs, MS   L | $

Located in a two-story wood-frame house that was a saloon in the nineteenth century, Phillips became a grocery store in 1919 and has built its reputation on hamburgers since the 1940s. Some customers buy them to go, but there are seats here, too: a short counter with stools, a handful of old wooden school desks, and a few odd tables (including one really odd one made from the cross section of a huge tree trunk). Outside on the front porch, a couple of picnic tables provide a view of the railroad depot.

The menu, written on a blackboard, lists side dishes including fresh-from-the-freezer Tater Tots and morsels of deep-fried, bright green okra enveloped in a golden crust. Corn nuggets are something special—bite-size fritters with lots of kernels packed inside a sweet hush-puppy-like jacket. You can get spicy or regular French fries. And if a MoonPie off the grocery shelf isn't your dish for dessert, Phillips also offers fried pies for a dollar apiece. A fried pie is a folded-over half-circle of dough fried until reddish brown and chewy, enclosing a heavy dollop of sugary peach or apple filling.

Hamburgers are presented wrapped in yellow wax paper inside a bag for easy toting, and when you peel back the wrapping, particularly on a half-pound Super-Deluxe, you behold a vision of beauty-in-a-bun. It is a thick patty with a wickedly good crunch to its nearly blackened skin. Inside, the meat is smooth-textured and moist enough to ooze juice when you gently squeeze the soft bun wrapped around it. The flavor is fresh, beefy, and sumptuous: an American classic.

Ramon's

535 Oakhurst Ave.   662-624-9230
Clarksdale, MS   D | $$

We thank Roger and Jennifer Stolle, infallible tipsters for all things relating to food and culture in the Mississippi Delta, for taking us to Ramon's. It's not the sort of place anyone would find accidentally. But it is a Roadfood treasure. "I wouldn't tell everyone to eat here," Roger said, pointing at the water-damaged acoustical ceiling tiles and explaining that local lore blames a lax landlord for the decomposition that makes the place a bona fide dump. Still, Thomas and Barbara Ely, the couple who run Ramon's, valiantly create a pleasing milieu in the form of empty fifths of Jack Daniel's and three-liter jugs of Taylor chablis that have been made into decorative lamps, and they serve magnificent butterflied fried shrimp nearly as big as moon pies. "We were taking bets in the kitchen if you-all would be able to finish," the waitress admitted when Michael, dispossessed of all appetite, left two of his dozen shrimp uneaten on the plate.

Roger said his favorite thing to eat was a plate of chicken livers and spaghetti, a reminder of the significant Italian influence in Delta cooking. The livers are sensational: unspeakably rich and luxuriously crunchy. They are so filling that we barely forked into the heap of noodles that came alongside them.

White Front Cafe
902 Main St. 662-759-3842
Rosedale, MS L | $

Joe Pope is gone, but his youngest sister, Barbara, holds the reins of this little wood-frame house that has become a Delta landmark to which people travel a hundred miles from Memphis for tamales—the one and only thing on the menu. Many people buy them to take home, but there's special pleasure in eating here at one of four kitchenette tables in the front room. Order three or four; they are served tightly wrapped in their corn husks. You can eat them one of two ways: Pick up a tamale and squeeze out a mouthful of the succulent insides or peel away the husk and use a saltine cracker to scoop some up.

Mr. Pope once told us that he got his recipe from the daughter of John Hooks, who learned how to cook tamales from a Mexican from Texas who traveled through the Delta back in the 1930s. We believe they are some of the very best: all-beef (no pork), a well-nigh perfect blend of meat, cornmeal, and just enough peppery spice to excite but not overwhelm your tongue.

White Trolley Cafe
1215 Hwy. 72 E. 662-287-4593
Corinth, MS BL | $

The slugburger originally was configured in Corinth, Mississippi, during the First World War. The pint-size patty, sometimes called a doughburger, was formed by mixing ground beef with potato flakes and flour. At first it was called a Weeksburger because the man who invented it was a diner owner named John Weeks. Over the years, soybean grits have become the meat-extender of choice for the oddball blimpy, which gets deep-fried to a crisp and garnished with mustard, pickle chips, and onions. The name "slug-burger" came about during the Great Depression, when you could buy one for a nickel and the five-cent piece was known as a "slug." The belief that the recipe calls for ground-up garden snails is a culinary canard.

With its dozen counter stools, mostly male clientele, and in-your-face hash-house ambience, the White Trolley Cafe is an ideal place to confront a slug. White Trolley's is thicker than most with a crust that's tough or—if you ask for yours well done—brutally crunchy. The interior, however it's cooked, is soft but not too juicy. Native Corinthians seem to adore them; for those accustomed to a red-meat hamburger that oozes juice, the slug is a taste that demands some acquiring. The White Trolley also offers all-beef burgers, but if you don't say beef when you order, you get a slug.

Much business at the White Trolley is take-out; hence it makes sense that the popular dessert is a packaged Mrs. Sullivan's individual pie—pecan, coconut, or chocolate. Mrs. Sullivan's pies are another old-time inamorata, invented during the Depression in Jackson, Tennessee.

Beacon Drive-In

255 John B. White Sr. Blvd.   864-585-9387
Spartanburg, SC   LD | $

Drive-in service at the Beacon is swell, but any newcomer must avail himself of the serving line inside. Here you enter a fourth dimension of restaurant-going, unlike anywhere else. The moment you enter and approach the counter, an employee behind it will demand, "Call it out!" And you better give your order quickly or else stand back and allow other, swifter folks to say their piece. On a good weekend day, the Beacon serves five thousand people.

Once you give an order, it is shouted back to the huge open kitchen. Then you are asked in no uncertain terms to "move on down the line!" Grab a tray and by the time you have moved twenty paces forward, there your order will be—miraculously, exactly as you ordered it, with or without extra barbecue sauce, double bacon on the burger. A bit farther down the line, you get your tea, lemonade, or milk shake and pay the cashier, then find a seat. Total time from entering to digging in: maybe two minutes.

The menu is big, ranging from gizzard plates to banana sandwiches. We recommend Pork A-Plenty, which is chopped and sauced hickory-cooked hot barbecue on a bun that also contains cool coleslaw. The sandwich comes buried under a mountain of intertwined deep-fried onion rings and French fries. The only correct libation to accompany this tremendous meal is sweet tea, served in a tall tumbler over crushed ice so cold that gulpers run the risk of brain-freeze headache. The Beacon sells more tea than any other single restaurant in the USA.

Bertha's Kitchen

2332 Meeting Street Rd.   843-554-6519
North Charleston, SC   L | $

Bertha's Kitchen, an out-of-the-way soul-food eatery now in its fourth decade, is small enough that the cafeteria line isn't so much a line as it is a counter where you stand and tell one of the several kitchen staff if you want your pork rib niblets on rice, which parts of the fried chicken you prefer, and if you're having just lima beans or lima bean dinner. The beans alone are a soupy, khaki-colored side dish. Dinner pairs them with hunks of neck from which weighty nuggets of meat are easily detached by probing with a fork. With the neck or in place of it to accompany the beans, you also can choose pig tails, which are little more than cylinders of glistening, warm pork fat that melts as it hits your tongue. Who knew a menu item called lima beans could be so mighty a meal?

Beyond those great beans, the menu is a primer in Lowcountry soul food: red rice with sausage, fried chicken encased in fissured red-gold crust, pork chops with meat as wanton as gravy itself, turkey prileau (a doppelganger of pilau), hoppin' John, and macaroni and cheese fetched from the baking pan with shards of crunchy-chewy crust. As inexpensive and informal as Bertha's is, every meal is prepared exactly as you order it from a member of the kitchen staff: Do you want more pig tails or less in the limas? Will you have red rice, white rice, or hoppin' John—on the side or underneath? How much gravy will you have with your stewed gizzards? For all the precision ordering, meals come on disposable plates and it is difficult for one person to spend more than $10 for a tray-filling feast.

Bowens Island Restaurant

1870 Bowens Island Rd.   843-795-2757
Charleston, SC   D Tues-Sat | $$

Bowens Island oysters are hideous to see, all gnarled and splotched with pluff, which is the oysterman's term for the fine silt that is stuck on them when they are harvested and clings to them when they are roasted so that merely touching a cooked cluster will smudge your fingers. Experienced customers, who come for the $22 all-you-can-eat deal, bring their own oyster-eating gloves. Amateurs, who might eat only a cafeteria tray's worth, are given a clean-looking washcloth along with a dull knife for prying the shells open (an easy task on roasted oysters) and cutting the meat loose. However you do it, eating pluff is an inevitable part of the meal, and while it has what proprietor Robert Barber calls "a unique stinky smell," it is a good stink, an ocean aroma that adds mineral salubrity to the flavor. On the door of the hut where you go to place your order, a bumper sticker reads, "Pluff Mud: The Goo That Holds the Earth Together."

"Most people who aren't from around here think of oysters as cold on the half-shell, all wet and slimy," Barber told us. "They've never had them steamed, hot and juicy." The cooking process, which takes only a few moments, infuses the meat of the oyster with its own juices, concentrating the flavor and while it takes nothing away from the sensual mouthfeel of a raw one, the lick of fire adds balmy bliss.

Oysters are the reason to come to Bowens Island, but they are not the whole story. You can eat hearty Frogmore stew (a Lowcountry slumgullion of sausage, shrimp, corn, and potatoes); and the hush puppies served alongside other oyster alternatives—expertly fried shrimp and fish—are among the best anywhere, their dark red, spherical surface hard and crunchy, their insides creamy rich.

Ambience is fish-camp rough-and-tumble, the tables conveniently outfitted with holes in the center where you can throw shells after you have extricated the meat from the heaps of inner tidal bivalves that are shoveled onto the table hot from the roaster. (The verb *shovel* is not a metaphor; a garden shovel actually is used to serve the oysters.) The heavy *kerplunk* of emptied shells getting tossed into the garbage cans beneath the tables' holes is the backbeat of dining at Bowens Island; the melody is the slurp of sucking slippery nuggets of marine meat straight off the oyster knife, then drinking down warm, salty liquor from the shell.

Charlie's Steakhouse

18 E. Coffee St.   864-232-9541
Greenville, SC   D | $$

Dinner at Charlie's is built upon time-honored rituals that citizens of Greenville (and their parents and grandparents) have come to know and appreciate since this fine old steak house opened in 1921: apply-your-own dressing service for salad or slaw (the latter just a huge heap of cut cabbage), a bottle of Charlie's own steak sauce on every table, thick china plates rimmed with a pattern of magnolias, silver presented wrapped in thick linen napkins, and tables cushioned so well that highball glasses wobble as you slice into a steak.

The arrival of any steak is a glorious event, for it comes on a hot metal plate (resting on a wood pallet), sizzling and sputtering so loudly that all conversations stop in wonderment. It is nice meat, dense and juicy, although like so many modern steaks, it lacks the delirious beef taste of a good old prime cut. Still, who could resist a menu that boasts "All beef shipped direct from Waterloo & Des Moines, Iowa; St. Joe & Kansas City, Mo"? The roster includes a T-bone, a filet mignon, and a porterhouse for one, but many regulars who come in groups opt for a jumbo sirloin cut into portions for two, three, or four people.

Charlie's is a low-key sort of place—polite, but not overly impressed with itself and not ridiculously overpriced like the national prime-steak chains. Waitresses are friendly as can be, but also real pros, constantly positioning and repositioning the dressings, sour cream bowl, bread plate, and butter-pat dish on the table so everything is arrayed for maximum convenience.

Dave's Carry-Out

42 Morris St.	843-577-7943
Charleston, SC	LD | $

Not to disregard Tuesday's jumbo turkey wings and red rice or Thursday's melting-tender Cornish hen with hoppin' John, but it is Dave's everyday shrimp that must be eaten. These taut pink crescents are veiled in a film of elegant crunch reminiscent of the legendary frying done by the long-gone Edisto Motel. It is hypnotic to watch the cook bread them one by one, then toss them into a fry basket that gets dropped into hot oil above the pieces of fish and pork chop that sizzle down below. Yes, everything goes into the same hot soup, and everything comes out with its own flavor—pork, fish, chicken—complicated by a multi-flavored zest that is the hallmark of Low-country cooking.

Dave's is a tiny corner storefront with only two tables for eating on premises and a reputation for staying open long into the morning when everything else in town has closed. A few years ago it moved from its original oil-saturated disreputable location to the current corner storefront, which is freshly painted and shipshape. While purists bemoan the cultural elevation, the current Dave's is a restaurant where anyone will feel welcome, any time of night. As the name suggests, it is designed mostly for the take-out trade. Still, when it's crowded, as it inevitably is late at night, you can wait up to an hour for your food to be cooked and plated (in Styrofoam). Everything is cooked to order, order by order.

Duke's

789 Chestnut St.   803-534-9418

Orangeburg, SC   LD Thurs-Sat | $

When connoisseurs of southern food refer to Orangeburg-style barbecue, they mean Duke's. Here is a definitive eastern South Carolina barbecue parlor, including—please note—the very limited hours of operation, Thursday through Saturday. The limited schedule hearkens back to an old-fashioned pig pickin', which was a weekend celebration at which hogs were enjoyed from beard to tail, or *barbe à queue*.

There's nothing at all charming about Duke's decor, at least not in an HGTV sort of way. It is a stark place with a single purpose: to celebrate hickory-smoked pork. Hacked into chunks at a cutting board in back, it is pork with a complex flavor that is just faintly smoky. Each piece is a tender mouthful that is a joy to savor in the peace of this room, where the only music is the cadence of more pork being hacked into hunks back in the kitchen.

Obtain the pork from a serve-yourself buffet line that also includes rice, hash (a stewlike mixture made from pig innards), a choice of red sauce that is four-alarm hot or yellow mustard sauce that is sweet and tangy (unique to central South Carolina), and pickles. Dish out as much as you want in your partitioned plate, grab a plastic fork, and find a place at one of the long picnic tables in the cavernous eating hall. The drink of choice is presweetened iced tea; and each table is outfitted with a few loaves of Sunbeam bread, which is just the right thing for mopping a plate of juice and sauce.

82 Queen

82 Queen St.   843-723-7591

Charleston, SC   LD | $$$

Eighty-two Queen is not typical Roadfood. At a good $50 per person, maybe it isn't Roadfood at all. But if you want to eat some of the most inspired versions of coastal Carolina's regional specialties, many of which are hard to find at any restaurant, it is a destination to treasure. For instance, there are good versions of shrimp and creamy grits throughout the Lowcountry, but 82 Queen chef Brad Jones enhances the formula by making his with barbecued shrimp—muscular sweeties whose coat of fire is dramatic balance for the earthy grits below. Enriched with cheese, sprinkled with a bounty of crisp bacon pieces and chopped green onions, this is an unforgettably good meal. The same good grits serve as a pedestal for grilled mahimahi, adorned with pumate butter and crisp fried green tomatoes. If you need to wait at the bar for your table, the not-to-be missed munch plate is fried oysters, which are little lodes of marine meat encased in crisp, Tabasco-charged crust, served with crushed red pepper marmalade.

A whole section of the menu is devoted to "Lowcountry Specialties": crab cakes with hoppin' John, Frogmore stew (a hearty gallimaufry of shrimp, sausage, corn, okra, and potatoes), and good ol' buttermilk fried chicken served with skillet corn bread and a luxurious portion of macaroni and cheese. Sunday brunch features a spiced shrimp boil, crab Benedict, French toast casserole, and a BLT that promises a quarter-pound of apple-smoked bacon. Desserts are a joy unto themselves, including bourbon pecan pie, peach praline cobbler, raspberry-glazed Key lime pie, and outrageously indulgent Toll House pie.

Ernie's

64 Spring St.   843-723-8591
Charleston, SC   L | $

Charleston is filled with restaurants that are famous, most of them deserving the acclaim. It also has a number of superb eateries that aren't famous but are treasured by locals as sources of four-star soul food. Ernie's is one of the greats, well known enough to regulars that there is no sign outside.

One of the most satisfying low-cost meals anywhere is Ernie's lima bean dinner, a huge presentation that arrives on one plate (for rice) and in two bowls, one for beans, the other for an impossible amount of brick-red neck bone meat dripping with hammy flavor. Cost: $6. Ernie's offers both okra soup and okra soup *dinner,* the latter poured over rice and supplemented by great chunks of meat. This soup has a dense vegetable flavor that is at once hugely satisfying and salubrious. Even the white rice that accompanies Ernie's fine fried chicken isn't just plain white rice. It is laced with soft wisps of cooked onion; it glistens with chicken fat and bristles with grains of hot pepper.

A few other items that are favorites among regulars: turkey wings (gargantuan), turkey necks either as a dinner or simply with rice, gizzards, red rice with pork chops, hoppin' John, and huge, heavy hunks of stupendous bread pudding.

Fishnet Seafood

3832 Savannah Hwy.   843-571-2423

Johns Island, SC   LD | $

A fundamental rule for finding good things to eat while traveling is to look for restaurants located in former gas stations. We don't know why, but they're some of the best Roadfood stops. To wit: Fishnet Seafood. It isn't really a restaurant at all; it is a fish market with no tables, not even provisions for stand-up eating. But if you point to just about any fish in the house, the staff will bread it and fry it to order, and in this part of coastal South Carolina, cooks know how to fry things. Flounder is particularly wonderful, sheathed in a brittle gold crust, its sweet white meat dripping moisture. If you order it as a sandwich, you get one huge, falling-apart-tender fillet with two token slices of white bread: finger food, for sure!

Another fine dish is Jesus crab, which is the management's name for what other places refer to as devil crab. When we inquired about the name, a woman behind the counter explained that the dish was simply too good to be named for the prince of darkness. Indeed, Fishnet is a very religious place, its decor featuring not only the expected inventory of nautical nets and buoys, but also signs everywhere reminding guests of Jesus's goodness and His ultimate importance. We've seen a lot of barbecue where religion is a fundamental aspect of the dining experience, but not so many seafood places. This is one where the original fisher of men is the star of the menu.

521 B-B-Q & Grill

7580 Charlotte Hwy.   803-548-7675

Indian Land, SC   LD | $

An inconspicuous storefront in a commercial strip by the side of the two-lane, 521 B-B-Q & Grill is a conspicuously worthy barbecue destination. Not that there's anything wrong with the menu's extra-thick fried bologna sandwich, but it would be a crime to come here and not eat chopped pork and/or ribs. The former—Boston butt that is hand-rubbed and slow-smoked for fourteen hours—becomes rough-hewn hash that is served sauceless. Please, savor some unadorned forkfuls for full appreciation of the refined synergy of swine and smoke. But then, bring on the sauce. Two kinds are arrayed in squeeze bottles on every table (next to the roll of paper towels): a thin, pepper-powered vinegar dressing that adds a boldface exclamation mark to the flavor and a thicker, sweeter, and extremely tangy tomato sauce. Both are winners.

The ribs are just about the meatiest baby backs we've ever run across.

Huge amounts of juice-sopped meat slide off the bone at the slightest provocation. Like the pork butts, the ribs are slow-smoked so the woodsy flavor of the pit completely insinuates itself into every fiber of the meat. Then they are painted with some of that tangy sauce and grilled until the sauce begins to caramelize. The glaze hugs the pork, and those two tastes together define the joy of ribs.

We haven't yet mentioned what some people consider to be the very best thing on the menu, included on every plate or tray of barbecue: hush puppies. Irregularly shaped with dark, red-gold skin that offers both crunch and chew, their interiors are moist and sweet-corn sweet, laced with perfumy onion. Nor are the baked beans to be ignored. They fairly vibrate with barbecue zest.

And finally, we need to mention the staff: a corps of waitresses who are as much fun as they are efficient, eagerly replacing a couple of hush puppies that accidentally tumbled into the baked beans and lost a touch of their crispness and taking great joy when a customer is caught licking every bit of sauce off his fingers. In brief, if you like barbecue, put 521 on any short list of must-visits in the Carolinas.

Hominy Grill

207 Rutledge Ave. 843-937-0930
Charleston, SC BLD | $$

Our first meal at the Hominy Grill was breakfast, and it was spectacular. The sausage patties that came alongside our sunny-side-up eggs were rugged and crusty and brilliantly spiced—a joy to eat when pushed through some yolk or sandwiched inside a tall biscuit. Bacon was excellent, too—double-thick, crisp, and full-flavored, just begging to be cosseted in that biscuit or eaten in alternating mouthfuls with a forkful of smooth-textured grits. A great breakfast option, even if a bit biscuit-redundant, is house-made bread, either pumpkin-ginger or banana-nut, both of which are moist, full-flavored, and elegant.

We were equally impressed when we returned for lunch and plowed into thick shrimp gumbo and a serving of Brunswick stew sided by good corn bread. And who could resist a distinctly southern BLT made with crunchy disks of fried green tomato? Buttermilk pie was the perfect dessert, surpassed only by what we both agree is the best chocolate pudding anywhere. And did we mention caramel layer cake, the little known and hugely wonderful Charleston fave?

The Hominy Grill building was at one time a barber shop, and the striped poles that signify the tonsorial profession still flank the inside of the front door. It's a spacious room with an old stamped tin ceiling, wood-slat walls, and slow-spinning fans overhead. There also is an outdoor patio. You can expect to wait for a table, especially on weekends. It is no secret that this place serves some of the best Lowcountry food anywhere, and at very reasonable prices.

Hyman's Seafood

215 Meeting St.   843-723-6000
Charleston, SC   LD | $$

What we didn't eat one evening at Hyman Seafood: amberjack, cod, flounder, mahimahi, mako, monkfish, snapper, hokie, salmon, tilapia, trout, tuna, and black drum. Those were the fish of the day on the blackboard, and below them were grouper, stuffed wahoo, and fried lobster tails, which we didn't sample, either. Local oysters were coming in and available on the half-shell or fried, and we didn't even have appetite enough for them. The point is that Hyman has a big, big menu—mostly seafood, with a few token meats and pastas—and it's bound to be a little frustrating to pass up so many good things.

What we *did* have was swell: she-crab soup that is ridiculously thick, rich as cream sauce itself, and loaded with meat; a broad dish with thirty steamed spiced shrimp; and a house specialty, crispy flounder. This is one large, beautiful fish that has been scored in a diamond pattern and broiled so the fork-size sections of meat get a crusty edge and seem virtually to lift off the bone: one of the East Coast's top fish-eating experiences.

Hyman's is a tremendously popular place, frequented by tourists and locals alike. If you're looking for a romantic restaurant, cozy accommodations, or a funkier setting, Charleston and vicinity have plenty, but for large-party ambience and impeccable local seafood, Hyman's is a good choice.

Middleton Place Restaurant

4300 Ashley River Rd.   843-556-6020
Charleston, SC   LD | $$$

It costs a lot of money to have lunch at the Middleton Place restaurant: $16.95 prix fixe for the food plus $25 per person just to get on the grounds where the restaurant is located. It is part of a vast interpretive environment built on the plantation that once was the home of Henry Middleton, president of the First Continental Congress. If you have a taste for Colonial history, the cost of admission is money well spent, providing access to sweeping terraces, gardens, walks, and artificial lakes that proffer beauty from a bygone age. Attractions include "Eliza's House," a freedman's dwelling that shows what life was like for African Americans who stayed on the plantation after the Civil War, and the plantation stable yards where farriers, potters, carpenters, and coopers demonstrate their eighteenth-century skills. Mounted trail rides (right past sneaky-looking alligators) are available at the nearby Equestrian Center, and the mansion itself is full of priceless antique furniture.

The restaurant is very much part of the effort to honor the Lowcountry's cultural heritage. When it opened as a tea room run by the Junior League in 1928, its specialties were okra soup and sandwiches. In more recent times, crack southern cook Edna Lewis came on board to develop recipes that provide a sampler of beguiling southern specialties. We don't know any other place that serves Huguenot torte, a sticky-gooey apple dessert that is something like a cobbler, but more intense. Peanut soup, thickened with sweet potatoes, is smooth and smoky, the earthy duet becoming a single note rather than two. Even the more ordinary dishes tend to be extraordinarily good. Fried chicken is hugged by thin buttermilk batter that is radiant with spice, its skin succulence incarnate. Greens are curiously not cooked totally limp and yet are totally tender, pungent with tonic punch. Pulled pork barbecue—smoke-cooked on premises, of course—has simple authenticity that puts it right up there with South Carolina's best.

Meals are three-course affairs, served in a charming modern-rustic dining room with windows that overlook green grass and grazing sheep.

Scott's Barbecue

2734 Hemingway Hwy.   843-558-0134
Hemingway, SC   LD | $

Whole-hog pork, cooked all night over smoldering oak and hickory coals, is pulled into shreds and served on disposable plates along with hunks of pig skin and servings of peppery, just-barely-sweet sauce for dipping. Two kinds of skin are available—fried to a crisp and stripped off the hog, the latter as chewy as the former is crunchy. White bread comes alongside, and you can get boiled peanuts for munching. Chickens and steaks, also slow-smoked, are sometimes available.

Founded in 1972 by Ella and Rosie (short for Roosevelt) Scott, and now presided over by the Scotts' son, Rodney, this much-loved local place was anointed as "authentic" by the national press a few years ago. That, plus

Scott's proximity to Myrtle Beach, means you can expect big crowds, especially on weekends. Pilgrims notwithstanding, the meal on the plate and the place itself are the real deal.

SeeWee Restaurant

4808 US 17 N.   843-928-3609
Awendaw, SC   LD | $$

A former grocery north of Charleston along US 17, SeeWee is now a hugely popular restaurant that includes an outdoor patio for al fresco dining. It still looks a bit like a roadside store—shelves stocked with supplies, higgledy-piggledy decor of nautical bibelots. But Charlestonians now come for local seafood, down-home vegetables, and magnificent cakes.

Daily specials are chalked up on a board: country-fried steak, whole catfish, Jamaican jerk chicken, Buffalo shrimp or oysters (fried in a spicy Buffalo-wing style), fish stew by the cup or bowl. We are partial to the regular menu and its roster of fried seafood. You can get a platter or a sandwich with very good extra-large French fries and coleslaw on the side. Our shrimp were snapping firm and veiled in a fine, crisp crust.

One of the great only-in-the-South meals to get here is an all-vegetable plate. Choose four from a list of more than a dozen available, including such local faves as red rice, butter beans, fried squash, fried okra, and rice and gravy. We went for fried green tomatoes (deliciously al dente with a tangy smack), sweet potato casserole (super-spicy), macaroni and cheese (dense and thick with cheese), and collard greens (salty, oily, luxurious).

As you walk into the restaurant you will see a shelf of the day's layer cakes, and desserts are listed on a blackboard. When we saw chocolate cake with peanut butter icing, we knew we had to have a piece. So we ordered it as we ordered lunch. The cake came before the meal. "I cut this for you because I was worried there wouldn't be any left by the time you were ready," our waitress kindly explained as she set it down with our sweet teas. We are so grateful she was watching out for us, because this cake was superb . . . as was our caramel layer cake and goober pie.

No bill arrives after the meal. When you're done eating, the waitress will instruct you to go up to the cash register and tell the man your table number. He's got your check and will tally it up and get you squared away.

Breakfast is served Saturdays only.

Sgt. White's Restaurant

1908 Boundary St.   843-522-2029
Beaufort, SC   LD | $

Upon entering this little restaurant you are faced with the steam table from which the server puts together your plate. While it is possible to order off a menu—and the fried chicken and shrimp therefrom are exemplary—we cannot resist the array of barbecue and side dishes in the trays. You get either pulled pork, which is a medley of velvet-soft shreds from inside and crunchy strips from the outside of the roast bathed in the Sergeant's brilliant tangy-sweet sauce, or ribs, which are crusty and unspeakably luscious, also caked with the good sauce. Each side dish is a super-soulful rendition of a southern classic: smothered cabbage richer than ham itself, broccoli gobbed with cheese, brilliantly seasoned red rice, a vivid mix of collard and turnip greens, *real* mashed potatoes, candied yams, etc., etc. A normal meal is one meat and two sides, served with a block of corn bread on top. Even that corn bread is extraordinary: rugged-textured and sweet as cake.

Shealy's Bar-B-Que

340 E. Columbia Ave.   803-532-8135
Leesville, SC   LD (closed Wed & Sun) | $

We found out about Shealy's thanks to tipster Paul McCravy, who wrote that "the vegetables surpass any I've had at the three family reunions I attend each year in Pickens County." Greens and beans, boiled, fried, and mashed, served plain and in elaborate casseroles—the array of vegetables is awesome. And they are merely the side dishes to some magnificent meals of fried chicken with cream gravy, including pulley bones for those who are feeling lucky.

For us, the main attraction is pork barbecue, which is presented at the buffet with all the glory of a traditional South Carolina barbecue feast, meaning you will find just about every part of the pig from the rooter to the tooter. That includes meat, ribs, hash, skin, gravy, and a rather bizarre creamy/spicy mush apparently quite popular in these parts known as liver nips. Of special interest on the tender shreds of smoked pork is Shealy's sauce (available by the bottle), an alluring mustard-tinged sweet-and-sour condiment unique to the South Carolina Midlands.

Summerton Diner

33 Church St.　　　　　　　803-485-6835
Summerton, SC　　　-　　　BLD (closed Thurs) | $

Since Lois Hughes opened it for business in 1967, this little café on the out-skirts of town has been a favorite of locals and a beacon for travelers along I-95. After Lois's daughter Lynelle Blackwell took over in 1987, she en-larged and remodeled it, but today the diner has the feel of an ageless eatery: well-worn Formica counter, blond wood-paneled walls, each table set with bottles of hot vinegar peppers for brightening up orders of collard greens.

There's a full menu, and such items as fried chicken or steak and quail are always available, but at lunchtime the thing to order is the special. For well under $10, you get an entree, three vegetables, dessert, and tea. Plus corn bread and biscuits. We love baked chicken supreme, which is crusty and fall-apart tender; the waitress asks if you want white or dark meat. Like all entrees, it comes on a partitioned plate along with two of the vegetables you choose. (The third vegetable, for which the plate has no room, comes in its own bowl.) As you might expect in a true-South café such as this, the side dishes are superb: earthy fresh rutabagas, spicy stewed apples, porky sweet greens that still have an al dente oomph to their leaves, mashed pota-toes blanketed in gorgeous beef-shred gravy, hefty blocks of macaroni and cheese with crusty edges and creamy insides, rice infused with soulful gravy. Et cetera!

The serving of pudding is small but classic: balmy custard in which sliced bananas and softened vanilla wafers are suspended, all under a Kewpie-doll spiral of whipped cream.

Note that the Summerton Diner is closed Thursdays. It is open for three meals a day the rest of the week.

Sweatman's

1313 Gemini Dr. (Route 453)　　803-492-7543
Holly Hill, SC　　　　　　　　LD Fri & Sat | $

Please note Sweatman's hours of operation. Inconvenient, yes? But utterly true to the tradition of a country pig-pickin', the point of which is to kick back and feast after a hard week's work. Decades ago, it used to be that the menfolk of the Sweatman family did all the cooking and hosted these big feeds only for relatives and friends, but in 1977 Bub Sweatman turned the informal ritual into something like a restaurant. We say *something like a restaurant* because it is a place without waiters, menu, or choice of food. The menu is whole hog. Serve yourself, and dine in the former living quarters of the family home, where tables are covered with oilcloth and windows dressed with calico curtains.

The buffet is spectacular. Among the choice of things to eat are chunks of shoulder meat—both creamy white from the inside and crusty-brown from closer to the fire—ribs for gnawing, rib meat only (minus the bone), pig skin stripped and fried into mottled brindle strips with a wicked crunch, and pungent hash made from the jowls, liver, and other ignominious portions of the hog. The hash is ladled over rice. The chunks of barbecued pork are as succulent as food can be, presented plain and glistening with their own copious juices. This meat needs nothing in the way of condiments, but if you do want to gild it there are two sauces available, one made with hot peppers and the other a typical South Carolinian sauce built around mustard.

Sweatman's has few frills, but it is no rough-and-tumble smoke pit. A barbecue meal in this smoky shrine is a serene and meditative experience, and one that will linger in your memory as sweet as pork itself.

The Wreck

106 Haddrell St.   843-884-0052
Mount Pleasant, SC   D | $$

The docks at Shem Creek in Mount Pleasant, just north of the city, are lined with seafood restaurants, all quite pleasant-looking and with similar shoreline menus; but if you meander farther along the water, out Live Oak Road to Haddrell Point, you will find a Roadfood jewel in the rough. And we do mean *find,* for the restaurant known as The Wreck (formally named The Wreck of the Richard and Charlene for a boat hit by Hurricane Hugo) has no sign outside—it's tucked between the Wando Seafood Company and Magwood & Sons Seafood—and we also mean *in the rough,* for it is located in a former bait locker, and decor is mostly piles of cardboard beer cartons. Seats are plastic lawn chairs at tables clothed with fish-wrapping paper (but romantically lit by candles at night). If the weather is cool, you are warmed by a couple of fireplaces that get lit in the concrete-floored dining room. The view of docked shrimp trawlers couldn't be more appetizing. And the food is impeccable.

Place your order by using a marking pen to circle what you want on the paper menu. Meals begin with a bowl of soft boiled peanuts. She-crab soup is served in the traditional manner with a shot of sherry to pour on top just before spooning in. Then come crunchy fried shrimp, scallops, oysters, or broiled fish accompanied by zesty slaw and tubular hush puppies. Depending on your appetite, you can get a meal either "Richard-sized" (copious) or "Charlene-sized" (normal portion). Everything is presented on cardboard plates with plastic utensils; beer comes in the bottle. Dessert is a choice of Key lime bread pudding or banana pudding.

If you are a fish-frowner, The Wreck does offer London broil. However, the menu warns, "This is a seafood house claiming no expertise in the preparation of red meat. So, when you order red meat it is yours . . . No returns!!!!!"

Midwest

Illinois * Indiana * Iowa * Michigan *

Minnesota * Missouri * Ohio * Wisconsin

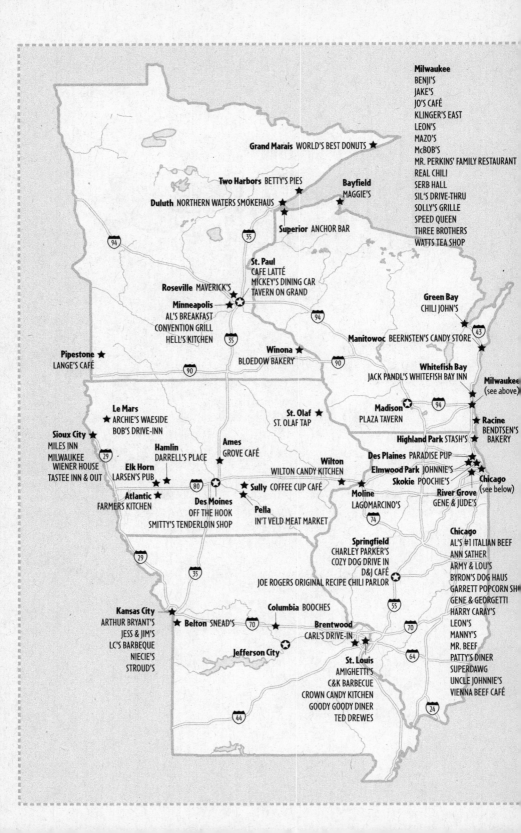

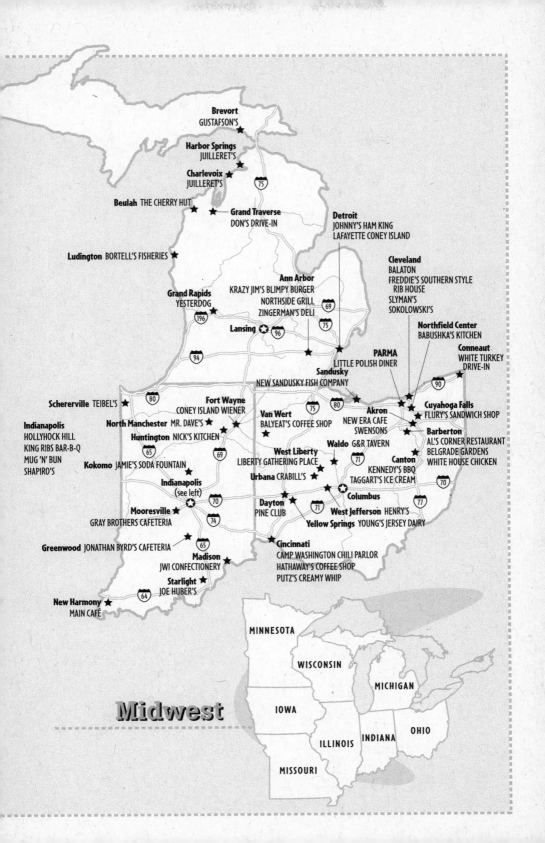

Brevort
GUSTAFSON'S

Harbor Springs
JUILLERET'S

Charlevoix
JUILLERET'S

Beulah THE CHERRY HUT

Grand Traverse
DON'S DRIVE-IN

Detroit
JOHNNY'S HAM KING
LAFAYETTE CONEY ISLAND

Ludington BORTELL'S FISHERIES

Cleveland
BALATON
FREDDIE'S SOUTHERN STYLE
RIB HOUSE
SLYMAN'S
SOKOLOWSKI'S

Ann Arbor
KRAZY JIM'S BLIMPY BURGER
NORTHSIDE GRILL
ZINGERMAN'S DELI

Grand Rapids
YESTERDOG

Lansing

Northfield Center
BABUSHKA'S KITCHEN

PARMA
LITTLE POLISH DINER

Conneaut
WHITE TURKEY
DRIVE-IN

Sandusky
NEW SANDUSKY FISH COMPANY

Schererville TEIBEL'S

Fort Wayne
CONEY ISLAND WIENER

Van Wert
BALYEAT'S COFFEE SHOP

Akron
NEW ERA CAFE
SWENSONS

Cuyahoga Falls
FLURY'S SANDWICH SHOP

Indianapolis
HOLLYHOCK HILL
KING RIBS BAR-B-Q
MUG 'N' BUN
SHAPIRO'S

North Manchester MR. DAVE'S

Huntington NICK'S KITCHEN

Waldo

Barberton
AL'S CORNER RESTAURANT
BELGRADE GARDENS
WHITE HOUSE CHICKEN

West Liberty
LIBERTY GATHERING PLACE

G&R TAVERN

Canton
KENNEDY'S BBQ
TAGGART'S ICE CREAM

Kokomo JAMIE'S SODA FOUNTAIN

Urbana CRABILL'S

Indianapolis
(see left)

Mooresville
GRAY BROTHERS CAFETERIA

Dayton
PINE CLUB

Columbus

West Jefferson HENRY'S

Yellow Springs YOUNG'S JERSEY DAIRY

Greenwood JONATHAN BYRD'S CAFETERIA

Madison
JWI CONFECTIONERY

Cincinnati
CAMP WASHINGTON CHILI PARLOR
HATHAWAY'S COFFEE SHOP
PUTZ'S CREAMY WHIP

Starlight
JOE HUBER'S

New Harmony
MAIN CAFÉ

MINNESOTA

WISCONSIN

MICHIGAN

IOWA

Midwest

ILLINOIS   INDIANA   OHIO

MISSOURI

Al's #1 Italian Beef

1079 W. Taylor St.   312-226-4017
Chicago, IL   LD | $

Al's, which claims to have invented the Chicago Italian beef sandwich, started as a small shop in old Little Italy with no seats for dining, just waist-high counters along the wall. It has since franchised out to other locations in the area, but the original is still the greatest, not only for the beef, but also for the fact that Mario's Italian ice shop is directly across the street when it comes time for dessert.

The beef is thin-sliced, gravy-sopped, and garlic-charged. It gets piled into a chewy length of Italian bread. You can ask for big beef (about twice as much) or have your sandwich double-dipped, which means totally immersed in a pan of natural gravy so the bread is soaked through. "Beef with hot" is a request for the relish known as *giardiniera,* an eye-opening garden mélange of finely chopped marinated vegetables, capers, and spice that is roast beef's perfect complement. "With sweet" is what you say if you prefer the popular alternative to giardiniera: big, tender flaps of roasted green bell pepper with a charcoal taste.

"Combo!" or "Half and half!" is a call for a sandwich that contains not only beef but also a plump, four-inch length of Italian sausage, retrieved from the appetizing haze that hovers over the hot metal grate just behind the order counter. Taut-skinned, succulent, and well spiced, the sausage is itself a major lure for many customers who sidestep beef altogether and order double-sausage sandwiches, hot or sweet.

Ann Sather

909 W. Belmont   773-348-2378

Chicago, IL   BL Mon & Tues, BLD Wed-Sun | $

Two words of advice: cinnamon rolls. You get two fluffy big ones per order, each blanketed in sweet glaze. Among Ann Sather's other breakfast icons are Swedish pancakes, which are folded-over crepes with a lace edge. They are available with a cup of lingonberry sauce, with a side of eggs, or with a couple of meatballs. Potato pancakes are superb, as is the French toast with peach compote. The item that rivets our attention is the waffle, two waffles to be exact, Swedish waffles, the menu says. We're not exactly sure what makes them Swedish, but we do know that they are not big fat Belgians. They are thin, crisp, and aromatic waffles, baked in an iron that gives them a fetching scalloped shape and served two to an order.

Although most Chicagoans think of it (rightly) as a breakfast destination, there are few places that offer such wonderful comfort-food supper. Chicken croquettes with candied sweet potatoes, anyone? There is roast tom turkey with all the fixins, broiled Lake Superior whitefish, shepherd's pie, and roast loin of pork with caraway seed sauerkraut. And, of course, there are Swedish meatballs.

Army & Lou's

422 E. 75th St.   773-483-3100

Chicago, IL   BLD | $$

A friendly storefront open since 1945, Army & Lou's is the place to go for soul food—breakfast, lunch, or dinner, and, Friday evenings, jazz performed by South Side artists. We were the only white people in the place the day we went for lunch, and the wall decor is exclusively pictures of African Americans. It is said that the city's first black mayor, Harold Washington, ate here all the time.

While the menu features a wide array of soul food, including chitterlings (served with spaghetti!) and ham hock with mixed greens, there are plenty of items that appear to be just what you'd expect in any neighborhood café, black or white. We say "appear" because the smothered pork chops we ordered were soulful to the nth degree, and the fried chicken would never, ever be mistaken for KFC's flabby bird parts.

All entrees come with a choice from a long list of appetizing side dishes, including candied sweet potatoes and corn bread dressing with giblet gravy. Dessert is a choice of fruit cobbler (ooey-gooey peach the day we were here), sweet potato pie, or bread pudding with lemon sauce.

Byron's Dog Haus

1017 W. Irving Park Rd.   773-281-7474
Chicago, IL   LD | $

As plump Polish sausages sizzle on the grill, the Dog Haus counterman dips a ladle into the fryolator to get some hot fat to pour over the grilling tube steaks. The grease helps give them a blackened, crisp skin; it also gives them a look of glistening, sinfully swollen avoirdupois. These are some of the most cumbrous Polish sausages in a city where Polish sausages, along with their all-beef brothers, hot dogs, are matters of serious culinary consideration. If you are a Polish-sausage fanatic, it isn't likely you will be blasé about the big, charred tubes they serve up at Byron's Dog Haus; you will love them or hate them.

The hot dogs are more civil; we recommend them to all who appreciate a substantial, all-beef frank. They are Vienna brand, steeped to plump succulence, with a faint crackle as you sink your teeth into them. Our only complaint is about the buns. They are a bore—small, plain (no poppy seeds), forked straight from their plastic-wrapped container (not well warmed).

On the other hand, Dog Haus condiments are fine: eleven different toppings that include strips of green pepper, cucumber disks, piccalilli, squeeze-on yellow mustard, onions, sport peppers (hot!), and whole tomatoes that happen to have been cut into slices. Yes, there resting atop your hot dog and all its other condiments is one tomato, not quite still round because it has been cut into slices; but because the slices don't go all the way through, it stays in one piece . . . until you try to eat the dog, at which time everything falls into a splendid mess. The tomato is customarily gilded with a sprinkle of celery salt.

Alongside this good specimen of frankfurter pulchritude, you want French fries. They are skinny and crisp—a suitable spuddy companion to the highly seasoned sausages that are this restaurant's specialty. Unless you really love French fries, one order is plenty for two.

Charlie Parker's

700 North St.   217-241-2104

Springfield, IL   BL | $

Don't rely on your GPS if you come hunting for Charlie Parker's, an out-of-the-way trackside Quonset hut that has a sense of scale as out of whack as its lat/long coordinates. One single pancake is the size of a large pizza. No one ever has been able to eat a Four Giant Stack (but if you do, they're free). Even a single one is enough for two to four people. But what's most amazing is that it's really good, made from a fresh, farmy batter and griddle-cooked so that it develops a faintly crunchy skin that forks love to crack through.

Charlie's is also a good place to eat a horseshoe, that outrageously huge Springfield specialty that is basically a pile of everything on a plate. Breakfast 'shoes are especially awe-inspiring: big oval mountains built upon a foundation of white bread. Atop the bread are eggs, breakfast meats, hash browns, cream gravy, and/or hot cheese sauce.

Cozy Dog Drive In

2935 S. Sixth St.   217-525-1992

Springfield, IL   LD | $

Invented during World War II by Ed Waldmire when he was in the Air Force stationed in Texas, the corn-clad, deep-fried Cozy Dog was originally called Crusty Cur and was a big hit with flyboys at the Amarillo PX. After the war, Waldmire's wife convinced him that his wiener needed a more appealing name, and in 1946, they opened Cozy Dog (so christened because no one eats a single, lonely one). You don't have to be a street-food connoisseur to savvy the difference between a Cozy Dog and an ordinary corn dog. The Cozy's batter jacket has a vivid crunch and earthy corn flavor; the dog within is plump with juice. Family baskets include four Cozy Dogs and a large order of (freshly cut) French fries.

D&J Café

915 W. Laurel St.   217-753-1708

Springfield, IL   BLD | $

The horseshoe is one of the most regionally restricted of all local specialties, found nowhere beyond Springfield, Illinois, where it was first devised at the Leland Hotel back in 1928. It is one of America's most outlandish meals, in a class with the Rochester Garbage Plate (p. 115) and super nachos. Food lore says it was named because it resembled a horse's shoe (a slice of ham) on an anvil (a hot metal plate) with farrier's nails (French fries) scattered around, but modern 'shoes are way more than that, always including lots of cheese sauce and sometimes gravy, too. The original ham and cheese configuration has been joined by burgers, sausage, Buffalo-sauced chicken, even vegetarian combos as possible options. Best of all is the breakfast 'shoe, which may or may not contain ham (or bacon or sausage patties), and which will more likely be heaped with hash browns than French fries. And of course, it will contain two to four eggs. Cheese sauce may be supplemented by or replaced by cream gravy.

At the humble D&J Café, everything on the breakfast 'shoe is completely blanketed by hash browns that have a crisp outside coat and enough thickness that below the crunch is plenty of plush spuditude—essential for mopping eggs if you like runny yolks. What's notable about this particular 'shoe, other than the spuds, is its balance—a magnificent harmony of gravy, cheese, meat, and potatoes.

Garrett Popcorn Shop

625 N. Michigan Ave.   312-943-4200
Chicago, IL $

Most candy-coated popcorn is frivolous junk food. CaramelCrisp—Garrett's name for caramel corn—is serious and soulful. It really doesn't taste candied at all. The popcorn is an earthy note within a caramel sheath that is deeply buttery and has dark flavor that teeters at the edge of tasting burnt. Like singed crust atop a well-made crème brûlée, the corn's coat smacks of fire as much as sugar.

Another thing that makes it good is that it is served hot and fresh. Once mixed with caramel, it is spilled into an L-shaped trough against the front wall where a woman worries it with two large scoops, ensuring the caramel corn doesn't clump into pieces larger than three or four popped kernels. As it achieves the perfect consistency, it is shoveled forward into the other end of the trough, where it is scooped into wax-paper bags that are weighed out for customers.

Almost equally excellent is Garrett's cheese corn, which is impossible to eat without your fingers turning bright orange from the cheese that coats and infuses the hot popped kernels. The vivid cheese immeasurably enhances the starchy corn flavor of the puffy kernels, making a savory snack that is almost unimprovable.

But it can get better. Instead of ordering either CaramelCrisp or cheese corn, you can ask one of the women working the counter for a "mix," also known as a "Chicago mix." She fills a bag half full with caramel corn, then tops it off with cheese corn and shakes the bag. The combo is a giant taste sensation that seems to cover the whole spectrum of what a tongue can appreciate: salty, sweet, buttery, earthy, crisp, and chewy. Frankly, even a mini-mix, which is a mere eight ounces, exhausts our ability to eat anything else for hours. It is, for us, a perfect food.

Gene & Georgetti

500 N. Franklin St.   312-527-3718
Chicago, IL   LD | $$$

Gene & Georgetti's sirloin, filet mignon, and T-bone are all, in our opinion, benchmarks by which other steaks should be measured. Perfectly cooked as ordered (medium rare, please), with a glistening charred crust and velvet pink-to-red insides dense with full-flavored juice, these are the hunks of meat we dream about any time we are on the way to Chicago.

It is all too tempting to precede a steak with "garbage salad," a piled-high plate that is a mishmash antipasto of cured meats, cheeses, olives, peppers, one big shrimp, and lettuce all in a garlicky marinade. *Too tempting* we say because a whole garbage salad is a big meal. Even a half is mighty filling if you've got steak and potatoes on the way.

On the side of G&G's steaks, the top starch is cottage fries, big round disks with crisp edges and soft centers. There is a large menu beyond beef: lamb chops are excellent; shrimp de Jonghe (or lobster de Jonghe) is surely the most buttery version of the dish anywhere in the city. We also love G&G's chicken Vesuvio, a mountainous plate of winey, garlicky roasted chicken wallowing in pan juices along with chunks of potato.

Impeccable meals are delivered by a staff of professional waiters who are all business. No fawning service here, no annoying "Is everything okay?" will interrupt your dinner conversation. Gene & Georgetti is no nonsense, all quality.

Gene & Jude's

2720 N. River Rd.   708-452-7634
River Grove, IL   LD | $

Gene & Jude's has no tables or chairs. As is Chicago custom, it offers a counter to which you may bring your meal, unwrap it, and eat standing up. When finished, use the wax paper in which the food was served to gather up any scraps and heave them into one of the large garbage cans in the corners of the room. The arrangement is comfortable and eminently practical for eating extremely messy food; however, many customers choose to dine in their cars in the parking lot.

You get a hot dog or a double dog. The natural-casing, all-beef Vienna brand links are slim and snappy; they are inserted into soft buns and dressed with mustard, onions, piccalilli, or sport peppers as you request. Tipster Glen Stepanovic told us that some hot dog historians consider this the "original" Chicago-style dog, before the more baroque garnishes of pickle spear, tomato slice, and celery salt.

A fine, fine hot dog . . . but wait, there's more! Whatever toppings are included, each dog gets heaped with a large fistful of French fries . . . some of the best French fries in Chicago. Fresh? Check it out: As you wait for your hot dog to be prepared, you can watch the counter folks peel and cut whole potatoes, then fry them, drain them, and pile them onto waiting dogs. They spend a good long time in the bubbling oil, emerging a dark brown with some pieces crunchy through-and-through, others thick and potato-creamy inside.

Harry Caray's

33 W. Kinzie St.   312-828-0966
Chicago, IL   LD | $$$

We tend not to frequent sports bars because the food is usually less important than what's on TV. Harry Caray's is one huge exception. It is the sports bar to end all sports bars—especially heavenly for Chicago team fans—and it is loaded with memorabilia not only from the Cubs, but from the life of legendary announcer Harry Caray.

Beyond his antics in the broadcast booth, Caray was known as a man who loved to eat. And the place he opened is testimony to that passion, too. This is one truly great Chicago restaurant. For example, there is not a better prime steak in Chicago. We like the sirloin best, grilled in a coat of cracked peppercorns. Other highlights of the menu include such familiar Italian specialties as lasagna, veal parmigiana, and a risotto of the day.

Among the "Italian" dishes is one that we've found only in Chicago, and it is magnificent: chicken Vesuvio. Chicken Vesuvio is several bone-in pieces of chicken, sautéed and then baked to utmost succulence, encased in a dark, red-gold crust of lush skin that slides from the meat as the meat slides off its bone. Is it tender? Forget about it! The dark meat in particular sets new standards for chicken tenderness. Piled among the chicken are wedges of potato, long-sautéed in a bath of white wine, garlic, olive oil, and spice until they are soft as mashed inside but have developed crunchy edges. Even if you don't get chicken Vesuvio, "Vesuvio" potatoes are available as a side dish to go with any steak or chop. The only problem about ordering them is that you likely won't also be ordering Harry Caray's garlic mashed potatoes, which are superb.

The setting is vintage: an 1895 Dutch Renaissance–style limestone building now on the National Register of Historic Places, its interior a luxuriously muscular space of mahogany woodwork and broad tables covered by thick white napery. Although a sumptuous place to which many customers come in pinstriped business suits, there is a democratic feel about this dining room that makes any decently dressed customer feel right at home. Harry Caray was a people's hero, and that's the way he liked it.

Joe Rogers Original Recipe Chili Parlor

820 S. 9th St.   217-522-3722
Springfield, IL   L | $

Springfield chili, as made at Joe Rogers, is wild stuff, definitely not for the fastidious epicure. Cooked ground beef, which resembles loosemeats, comes virtually swimming in grease—known slightly more politely as hot oil—and is almost always accompanied by beans. It is possible to ask for the oil to be skimmed off when you order a bowl, but that would negate the purpose of the little oyster crackers that come alongside. They are a nice sponge for the oil, sopping up its chili pepper zest. The chili comes in six different degrees of hotness, from mild to Firebrand, the latter known as the J.R. Special. If you eat a bowl of Firebrand, your name will be inscribed on the Joe Rogers honor roll posted on the restaurant wall so that your survivors can come and salute your daredevil spirit.

Note that Joe Rogers spells chili the normal way, with one *l*. That is unusual in Springfield, Illinois, because in 1993, when the state legislature formally declared the downstate capital to be the "Chilli Capital of the Civilized Universe," it purposely used the rare double-L spelling of the word, ordained by force of Senate resolution.

Johnnie's

7500 W. North Ave.   708-452-6000
Elmwood Park, IL   LD | $

We do not eat Italian beef often enough to anoint one place the very best. Chicago (and Chicago alone) has so many good ones, and as a native, Michael gets too deliriously sentimental at the very sight (and smell) of shaved-thin, garlic-sopped beef loaded into a brawny length of bread and crowned with pickly-hot giardiniera to make any sort of reasoned judgment.

But let us say that the last time we were at Johnnie's and had a combo sandwich (that's beef plus sausage), we found it hard to believe that Chicago's great signature sandwich can get any better than this. The beef is soft and fairly softly seasoned—just garlicky enough to halo its protein magnitude—and the sausage is dense, taut, and chewy. This glorious duo plus Johnnie's vibrant giardiniera compose a taste-buds epiphany. To accompany Italian beef or to savor its afterglow, Johnnie's makes delicious Italian ice that is a tantalizing balance of sweet and tart.

Lagomarcino's

1422 5th Avenue   309-764-1814

Moline, IL   LD | $

Started as a Moline, Illinois, candy store in 1908, Lagomarcino's is still renowned for hand-dipped chocolates, as well as fancy fruit baskets. You won't find better sponge candy anywhere. (Sponge candy is crunchy chunks of spun sugar enrobed in dark chocolate, also known as "fairy food," "sea-foam," and "violet crumbles.") And the chocolate-dipped fruit repertoire includes orange, apricot, pineapple, pear, and kiwi.

What we like best is the hot fudge sundae, its fudge made from a recipe acquired in 1918 from a traveling salesman for the princely sum of twenty-five dollars. It is a bittersweet, not-too-thick elixir that just may be the best hot fudge in this solar system or any other. When you order a sundae, the great, dark stuff is served in a manner befitting its distinction: in a small pitcher alongside the tulip glass full of ice cream and whipped cream, so you can pour or spoon it on to taste. This serving technique provides a fascinating demonstration of how one's soda fountain habits reflect one's personality. Do you pour on all the fudge at one time, willy-nilly, risking that some will spill over the sides of the serving glass? Do you pour it on spoonful by spoonful, carefully ensuring that every bite will have just the proper balance of ice cream and fudge? Or do you eat all the ice cream, with maybe just a dash of fudge poured on, so you can then conclude your snack by downing all the hot fudge that remains in one dizzy chocoholic binge?

Leon's

1640 E. 79th St.   773-731-1454

Chicago, IL   LD | $

Chicago's original Leon's (since 1941) delivers spare ribs that are big and brawny, dripping juice as soon as your teeth cut down below the crust. Leon's also serves exemplary rib tips, a lower-cost option that is harder to eat, demanding more tooth work, but is perhaps even more rewarding. The tips deliver meat that is tenderloin-tender, dizzyingly swirled with the potent flavors of hickory and oak smoke. Another specialty is the Chicago hot link, a vividly spiced, coarse-cut sausage, vaguely Italian in character, that is served, like the pork, smothered in good sauce.

For the Roadfooder traveling through town, eating all this good food is a royal pain. Meals are take-out only, presented in cardboard boats, the entree covered with a mess of French fries sopped with sauce, plus a couple of slices of clean, spongy white bread. It adds up to some of the messiest barbecue meals anywhere. On a pleasant afternoon, it might be great to dine standing up off the trunk of one's car, but local gulls are wise, and as soon as any food is out in the open, they start flocking and squawking and making threatening dives toward your meal. While we have never actually been attacked, these birds make outdoor dining feel downright dangerous. So you eat in your car, winding up with sauce on your fingers, the steering wheel, the seats, the gear shift, *everywhere.*

Customers and staff are separated by bulletproof glass. As in a bank, you slide your money through a slot, and when your meal is packed, they send it out via a lazy Susan that ensures you can't shoot them, or, we suppose, vice versa. But our experience is that Leon's looks scarier than it is. We wouldn't likely visit at midnight, but every lunch we've had here has been a totally pleasant experience, the staff helpful and clientele friendly. It's only the birds in the parking lot that feel threatening.

Leon's other locations in Chicago are 8249 S. Cottage Grove, 1158 W. 59th, and 4550 S. Archer.

Manny's

1141 S. Jefferson St.	312-939-2855
Chicago, IL	BL | $$

We usually return to our favorite Chicago cafeteria-style deli with the vow *not* to eat corned beef sandwiches. There are so many other good-looking things to eat: kasha and bowtie noodles, chop suey, short ribs of beef, oxtail stew, and pierogies, not to mention matzoh ball soup, blintzes, and potato latkes. But most often, the beauty of the warm corned beef, thin-sliced before one's eyes and piled between slices of glossy-crusted rye bread in a pile of rosy-red cured-meat moistness, wins out and that's what we eat, sided by potato latkes.

Gino Gambarota, Manny's corned beef man for the last twelve years, will cut the meat the way you like it—lean, fatty, or regular—but he will not cut it thick. "The art of cutting corned beef is to cut it as thin as possible, and against the grain," Gino says. His slices are shaved so thin they verge on disintegration, but they stay intact and miraculously succulent.

Manny's charm goes far beyond its great deli sandwiches and inviting hot meals. At the edge of Chicago's Loop, not far from where the everything-goes bazaar known as Maxwell Street once thrived, it remains a magnet for Chicagoans of every stripe. Dining room tables are occupied by politicians and businesspeople, wise guys and university professors, and cured-meat lovers from distant suburbs. When a newspaper photographer joined us at a recent meal, a nearby Chicago cop just couldn't resist coming over to investigate the reason the camera was out. When he saw the lensman focusing on a corned beef sandwich, he beamed with understanding and gave us the high sign.

Mr. Beef

666 N. Orleans   312-337-8500
Chicago, IL   LD | $

Mr. Beef is a premier source for the Second City's premier street food, Italian beef. Great heaps of ultra-thin-sliced, garlic-infused beef are piled into a length of muscular Italian bread that gets soft as beef juices soak into it, but retains the oomph to stay in one piece even if you order your sandwich "dipped," which means double-soaked in gravy. An important choice you'll need to make is whether or not you want your sandwich topped with roasted red peppers or the peppery vegetable mélange known as *giardiniera*, which is crunchy, spicy, and a brilliant contrast to the full-flavored beef.

Sausages here are excellent as well—cooked on a grate until taut and bursting with juice. You can get a sausage sandwich in similar configurations as beef, and it is also possible to have a combo, which is a length of sausage and a pile of beef loaded into the bread.

Accommodations are minimal. There is an adjoining dining room with actual tables at which to sit as well as a counter up front with stools, but the Italian beef connoisseur's choice is to stand at the chest-high counter that rims the perimeter of the main room. Here, the wax paper that wraps the sandwich can be unwrapped to catch all the spillage and keep it at handy plucking distance while you dine.

Paradise Pup

1724 S. River Rd.   847-699-8590
Des Plaines, IL   L | $

The name is Paradise Pup and the hot dogs are indeed excellent—Chicagoland classics that are available topped with a wheelbarrow's worth of condiments. And the Italian beef sandwiches are top-tier. But the Pup's primary claim to fame is its cheeseburger. A hefty patty charcoal-grilled to crusty succulence, all the more delicious when ordered with a sheaf of bacon on top or perhaps raw or grilled onions, it comes on a seeded kaiser roll. You get your choice of cheese—American, mozzarella, or the connoisseur's choice, Merkts, which is a tangy Cheddar from Wisconsin that matches perfectly with the beef.

Seasoned French fries are excellent, too, whether you order them plain or loaded, which means heaped with cheese, bacon, and sour cream. To drink: a cream-rich milk shake.

Dining accommodations are virtually nonexistent—a handful of counter seats and outdoor tables with umbrellas—and the small eat-shack is almost always crowded. Expect to wait.

Patty's Diner

3358 Main St.   847-675-4274
Skokie, IL   BL | $

We originally went to Patty's strictly for the old potatoes, a brilliant concept of gathering together shreds and hunks of griddle-cooked potato and deep-frying them until wickedly crisp. But old potatoes are only one item on a big and enticing breakfast menu that includes handsome slices of ham cut to order off the bone, corned beef hash (plus ham hash), egg sandwiches on made-in-house rolls, immense omelets, and biscuits buried under peppery sausage gravy. Along with coffee, customers are given a dish of sweet little fritters to enjoy while waiting for breakfast to be made.

A Roadfood treasure, Patty's embodies diner soul. It's a plain-looking storefront with a handful of tables and a long counter that provides a terrific view of the short-order chefs at work.

Poochie's

3832 Dempster St.   847-673-0100
Skokie, IL   LD | $

Poochie's red hots are the best. Standard hot dogs are all-beef Vienna franks, boiled to perfect plumpness and served in tender, seeded Rosen's-brand buns. Char dogs, cooked over coals, are crusty, blackened versions thereof. Polish sausages are plumper, porkier variants slit in a spiral pattern to attain maximum crunchy surface area. If one in a bun of any of these tube steaks is insufficient for your appetite, you can get either a jumbo dog or a double. Our personal favorite meal is a jumbo char dog with Cheddar fries (superb fries!) on the side.

Poochie's is proud of its char-cooked hamburgers, and we like them very much, especially piled high with those sweet grilled onions. But if you are passing through Chicago and stop at Poochie's with time for only one street-food indulgence, make it a red hot with the works and a side of fries. It is an only-in-Chicago meal, and a jewel in the crown of America's Roadfood.

Stashs

1825 Second St.   847-432-6550
Highland Park, IL   LD | $

If you are north of the city and in need of a great Chicago hot dog, find Stashs in Highland Park's Port Clinton Square. You can have your all-beef frank steamed, but we prefer ours charred, meaning its surface gets crusty all around the edges while the inside still drips juice. It is pocketed in a fresh Rosen's-brand poppy-seed bun and topped with a choice of nine different condiments, from mustard and relish to sport peppers and celery salt. If you get it "dragged through the garden," the hot dog itself will be completely eclipsed by long pickle spears, tomato slices, onions, etc. This is a beautiful wiener, and delicious. There are jumbo dogs and Polishes, too, as well as double dogs in a single bun; but it's our opinion that a single one of Stashs normal dogs, garnished with a plentiful supply of condiments, is one perfect food.

Beyond hot dogs, Stashs has a vast menu that includes a pasta bar from which the management will create whatever sort of dish you want from ten kinds of noodle, six different sauces, and all sorts of vegetable and cheese toppings. In addition, there are hamburgers, beef sandwiches, gyros, wraps, pockets, and quesadillas. We've never tried any of these things, but we do have one other important recommendation to make: French fries. With a Stashs dog, they are essential. These are four-star potatoes with a creamy center and crunchy edge. Cheddar cheese is available as a topping, but in this case, all we want is a sprinkle of salt.

Superdawg

6363 N. Milwaukee Ave.   773-763-0660

Chicago, IL   LD | $

Everything at Superdawg really is super, starting with taut-skinned, all-beef tube steaks in steamed-soft buns. They're available with the complete Chicago panoply of condiments and share the menu with crisp-edged Superfries, Superonion chips, Superburgers, Supershakes, and Whoopskidogs (the house name for a Polish sausage).

You'll have no trouble spotting Superdawg as you approach along Milwaukee Avenue: A pair of ten-foot statues of a male and female wiener (Flaurie and Maurie) wearing leopard-skin togas stand high atop the roof, winking electronically. Opened in 1948, this Roadfood landmark still features the once-modern "Suddenserver" automated order system and serves its dogs in cardboard boxes that announce, "Your Superdawg lounges inside contentedly cushioned in Superfries, comfortably attired in mustard, relish, onion, pickle, and hot pepper."

There is a second Superdawg at 333 S. Milwaukee Ave. in Wheeling. Phone: 847-459-1900. (The Midway Airport Superdawg has closed.)

Uncle Johnny's

500 W. 32nd St.   312-225-6111

Chicago, IL   L | $

Uncle Johnny's breaded steak, a sandwich unique to Chicago's South Side, is a wonderful thing: pounded-thin sheets of beef that are lightly breaded and pan-fried to super-succulence, then rolled into a bundle and stuffed in a loaf of Italian bread with a coat of red gravy (tomato sauce) and melting mozzarella, plus roasted peppers and/or spicy giardiniera. The steak is more tender than Kobe beef and the in-your-face Italian flavors of the sandwich are a grand indulgence.

Once a working butcher shop and now a neighborhood grocery with a short list of great sandwiches (the Italian beef is swell), Johnny's has only a couple of random seats indoors and, when weather permits, a picnic table on the sidewalk. Beware if you plan to eat a breaded steak sandwich in your car. It is a sloppy thing that demands undivided attention from its eater, as well as a large stack of napkins on the side.

Vienna Beef Café

2501 N. Damen Ave.   773-278-7800
Chicago, IL   L | $

Chicago's hot dogs, a.k.a red hots, are famous for the splendor of their condiments, but it's the wiener itself that matters most: a dense, garlicky, all-
beef tube steak. Nearly all of the city's top purveyors get theirs from the
Vienna Beef Company, which happens to run its own factory store café. You
won't find a more perfect version of the Chicago classic: a wiener steamed
to bursting plumpness, the tenderest possible fresh poppy-seed roll, crisp
pickle spears, tomatoes, brilliantly spicy-sweet piccalilli. Even the bright yellow mustard tastes like it was made that morning.

But that's not all. Vienna Beef also happens to make superior corned
beef, Polish sausages, pastrami, hard and soft salami, and Italian beef, all of
which are on the café lunch menu. The flagship item is a 3XL corned beef
sandwich, which is nine ounces of spicy beef piled between slices of very
good rye bread.

Coney Island Wiener

131 W. Main St.   219-424-2997

Fort Wayne, IN   LD | $

Coney Island wiener shops abound throughout the Midwest, "Coney Island" being the old term for hot dog, which folks in the heartland used to associate with New York. Fort Wayne's Coney Island, a Main Street storefront formally known as The Famous Coney Island Wiener Stand, was established in 1914 and has built its reputation on the classic Greek-American frankfurter: a modest-size bright pink weenie nestled in a soft bun and topped with Coney sauce, which is a fine-grind chili with a rainbow of seasonings and fetching sweetness. Although all condiments are technically optional, everyone orders their hot dogs with Coney sauce, as well as a line of mustard and a good sprinkle of chopped raw onion. The only other things on the menu are baked beans, chili (more a soup than a stew), and hamburgers.

Seating is at counter stools, many of which offer a nice view not only of the doings behind the counter and between staff and customers, but also through the big window out onto Main Street.

Tipster Brett Poirier, who encouraged us to seek out these fine weenies, pointed out that Fort Wayne makes a great way station for anyone traveling America's original coast-to-coast thoroughfare, the Lincoln Highway.

Gray Brothers Cafeteria

555 S. Indiana St.   317-831-3345

Mooresville, IN   BLD | $

Gray Brothers is gigantic, and quite deluxe as far as cafeterias go: leaded glass windows in the doors, plenty of tasteful decor. Almost any time you walk in, it will be crowded, but that's no problem because the cafeteria line moves really fast; and besides, your wait takes you along the "preview line," which allows you to study the dozens of food items from which you will soon be choosing. The trays are big, but if you're at all like us, you'll find yours fully occupied well before you get to the rolls and beverages at the end of the line.

It's hard to know what to recommend because we've never had anything at Gray's we didn't like. Among the most memorable dishes are chicken and noodles, meat loaf (with mashed potatoes, natch), chicken livers, and fried chicken with an ultra-flavorful crust that pulls off the bird like strips of pork cracklin's. The way things work in Gray's line is that you tell the servers what entree you want; they put it onto a nice flower-patterned partitioned plate, then slide the plate down to the vegetable area, where it is weighted with whatever sides you desire.

Who can resist the corn bread stuffing? Or mac 'n' cheese? We also love the heartland salads, especially creamy pea and carrot-raisin-marshmallow. Desserts are dazzling, with whole pies arrayed on shelves below the individual slices (many pies get bought and taken home). Fruit pies abound, of course, and there are swell butterscotch, banana cream, and pumpkin flavors, but the Indiana favorite, and a specialty of Gray's, is sugar-cream pie . . . as simple and pure and good as the name suggests.

Hollyhock Hill

8110 N. College Ave.   317-251-2294

Indianapolis, IN   D | $$

In 1928, on a quiet street at the northernmost outskirts of Indianapolis, a restaurant named The Country Cottage started serving family-style chicken dinners. The city has grown around it and the name was changed to honor the hollyhock bushes on the lawn, but the specialty of the house is still fried chicken dinners. The ritual banquet begins with pleasant enough but unmemorable pickled beets and cottage cheese and salad with sweet-and-sour vinaigrette, then upshifts to unforgettably good chicken. Fish, shrimp, and steak are options, but this chicken is skillet-fried and wonderful, served with pan gravy. To go with it there are bowls of mashed potatoes, green beans, and corn niblets, as well as hot breads with apple butter. All these trustworthy selections are replenished for as long as anyone at the table wants to keep eating them, but it's only the chicken that makes you want to eat 'til you bust.

Dessert is ingenuous and fun: Make your own sundae. Sauces of butterscotch, crème de menthe, and chocolate are provided to dollop as desired on your ice cream. The normal ice cream flavor is vanilla, but true Hoosiers opt for the state favorite, peppermint.

Jamie's Soda Fountain

3320 S. Lafountain St. 765-459-5888
Kokomo, IN $

Jamie's is an old-fashioned Main Street soda fountain where there are enough syrups on hand to offer a near-infinite variety of drawn-to-order drinks. Chocolate Coke? How about a diet chocolate Coke? Or a cherry ginger ale or a vanilla root beer or a diet vanilla/strawberry phosphate? Of course there are green rivers and black cows and black-and-white sodas and pink lemonades. Plus shakes, malts, sundaes, and floats. The swankiest shakes are made with hot fudge and/or black raspberry flavoring.

Beyond confectionery beverages and dessert, Jamie's food menu is a catalog of lunch-counter fare. The fried ham sandwich is excellent. Hoosier tenderloins are available breaded and fried or grilled. There are hamburgers, cheeseburgers, bacon cheeseburgers, and burger baskets (including fries). If you wish to exercise knife and fork, you can have chicken and noodles or gravy-blanketed hot beef Manhattan. For breakfast, which is served all day, the choices range from bacon and eggs and wraps and sandwiches to biscuits and gravy.

Good French fries are available on the side, as are hot potato chips and deep-fried macaroni and cheese.

Joe Huber's

2421 Engle Rd. 812-923-5255
Starlight, IN LD | $$

For a long time, cynicism kept us from enjoying supper at Joe Huber's. People had been telling us about this restaurant since the early days of Roadfood, but it wasn't "pure" enough for us. It is part of a tourist-oriented taste of rural life that includes a farmer's market, gift shop, wagon rides for kids, a zoo of farm animals, concerts, and car shows. Finally, encouraged by a glowing review and appetizing photos posted at Roadfood.com by "Cecif," we went. And we were won over.

No, Joe Huber's is not a charming little town café. But we defy you to sink your teeth into the crust of the fried chicken or gather a silky dumpling from its chicken broth or fork up some of those real mashed potatoes and not concur with Joe Huber's many fans that it is a worthy Roadfood destination. And the fried biscuits? Inspired! Cecif described them as "similar to beignets . . . but a bit less greasy and very fluffy and light." With or without the apple butter that comes alongside, they are impossible to stop eating. And that's a problem, because as soon as your biscuit basket looks empty, you will be served more.

There are other items on the menu, including pork chops, steak, and catfish; and groups of people can have the chicken served family-style along with slices of honey ham and a constellation of slaw, potatoes, gravy, green beans, corn, and, of course, biscuits. Desserts include fruit cobbler, pie, and a $12.99 extravaganza listed as a Three Acre Sunday, about which the menu suggests, "Share it with everyone at your table!"

Jonathan Byrd's Cafeteria

100 Byrd Way   317-881-8888
Greenwood, IN   LD | $

Jonathan Byrd's boasts that it is America's biggest cafeteria, a claim with which we would not argue. The serving line is eighty-eight feet long with a minimum of twenty entrees at any one time (serving continuously from 10:45 to 8:45 daily) as well as countless vegetable side dishes, Jell-Os, salads, desserts, bread, and rolls. In need of comfort food when we stopped by, we dined on turkey pot pie and a bowl of chicken and noodles, the latter an especially salubrious bowl of thick, soft pasta and shreds of chicken in just enough broth to keep it all moist.

Among the memorable side dishes were macaroni and cheese with a good portion of crusty, chewy top-cheese mixed in with the creamy noodles from below, a buttermilk drop biscuit that was a textural joy, and bread pudding laced with slices of cooked-soft apple and plenty of sweet caramel sauce.

The late Jonathan Byrd, founder and proprietor, was a man on a mission from God. "I was impressed by how many significant biblical events involved people eating together," he wrote for a story in *Guideposts* (reprints of which are available in the vestibule). As a matter of principle, no liquor is served in the cafeteria, not even in its banquet rooms, and the Jonathan Byrd function rooms regularly play host to gospel concerts.

JWI Confectionery

207 W. Main St.   812-265-6171
Madison, IN   L | $

A beautiful restoration, complete with nostalgic photos of long-gone high-school days on the wall, makes a visit to this old soda parlor an irresistible taste of history as well as a worthwhile detour for Roadfood of the sweetest kind. The building that houses JWI Confectionery was built when Andrew Jackson was president . . . in 1835! Madison, Indiana, is an Ohio River town with a great historical feel to it, and this Main Street storefront shop, which old-timers know as Betty Mundt's Candies, dates back to 1917. JWI still makes candies from heirloom recipes in vintage molds, and the ice cream is manufactured in a machine at the back of the store.

Lunch is served from about 11 A.M. until early evening, and the meals we've seen look dandy—meat loaf, roast beef, cold-cut sandwiches, soups, quiche, etc.—but to be honest, we've only seen them. When we come to JWI, we want pie, cake, candies, cookies, and ice cream. The ice cream is especially excellent, ranging from cones and single scoops in a dish to sundaes topped with real whipped cream. Of course we could not resist the top-of-the-line pig's dinner known as The '37 Flood—a ten-scoop, multi-topping extravaganza that JWI says will feed four to six people.

King Ribs Bar-B-Q

4130 N. Keystone Ave.   317-543-0841
Indianapolis, IN   LD | $

King Ribs is a former automobile garage with no dining facilities. All business is drive-through, walk-up, or home delivery. It is the sort of barbecue you smell before you see. The scent of more than a dozen drums lined up, smoldering wood inside them and pork sizzling atop the wood, perfumes the neighborhood for blocks. The house motto is "Fit for a King," and of all the regal meals to eat here, ribs top the list. They are tender enough so that the meat pulls from the bone in heavy strips, barely glazed with sauce, but chewy enough that the pork flavor resonates forever. It is a pure, sweet flavor, just faintly tingling with smoke. The house sandwich is known as pork on a bun, and that is what it is: an outlandishly messy load of hacked-up pork dripping with sauce and surrounded by a bun too messy to be hoisted by hand.

Side dishes include macaroni and cheese that is thick as pudding and intensely cheesy, with noodles so soft they are almost indistinguishable from the cheese. Also: baked beans, fine-cut slaw, and white bread for mopping. For dessert, there is a choice of sweeties: chess pies or sweet potato pie.

Main Cafe

520 Main St.   812-682-3370
New Harmony, IN   BL | $

The southern Indiana countryside for miles around New Harmony is farmland: no business or industry, no malls, no convenience stores, no chain
restaurants. Just rolling green landscape and two-lane roads. A former uto-
pian community created by folks who sought heaven by living simply, New
Harmony remains a bucolic small town with a Main Street café. Despite
lively table-to-table conversations (everybody who eats here knows everybody else), we found it to be a meditative sort of place, ideal for getting centered, as well as nicely fed, before or during a day of travel along the Ohio
River Valley.

In truth, the breakfast menu is not all that interesting, the baking powder biscuits are slightly overweight, and dairy products are virtually unheard
of (buttery spread for biscuits, powdered creamer for coffee). But we relished
the very piggy, crisp-fried tenderloin that came alongside our plate of eggs.
On a return trip, we delighted in the ploughman's lunch of ham, beans, and
corn bread. And the pies—coconut cream and chocolate cream—are blue-
ribbon beauties.

Mr. Dave's

102 E. Main St.   219-982-4769
North Manchester, Indiana   LD (closes mid-afternoon in winter) | $

Indiana is the easternmost outpost of tenderloin love. The tenderloin, formally known as a breaded pork tenderloin sandwich, sometimes abbrevi-
ated BPT, is a slice of pork pounded flat and wide, breaded and fried, and
sandwiched in a bun, preferably with pickle slices and mustard. There are
few restaurants as proud of this heartland treasure as Mr. Dave's, where
the tenderloins are neither too thin nor ridiculously wide (as so many are).
Four-ounce boneless pork medallions are cut and pounded out so there is
still good heft to the meat; they are breaded in cornmeal and fried, coming
out crunchy, luscious, tender, and piggy-sweet—just right inside a bun with
lettuce, tomato, and mustard.

Although tenderloins have been its glory since "Mr. Dave" Clapp
opened up in 1962 (the business is now run by his son Kevin), there is a full
short-order menu to make all but a strictly kosher Roadfood traveler happy.
You can get your pork tenderloin grilled rather than fried, and there is pulled
pork barbecue as well. Cheeseburgers, broasted chicken, and corn dogs fill
out the menu.

Mr. Dave's used to do a brisk mail-order business selling breaded, frozen, and ready-to-fry tenderloins to homesick Hoosiers in tenderloin-free parts of the world, but a dozen years ago Indiana's elected officials decided to protect us against such evil by ruling that pork cannot be shipped without federal inspection.

Mug N' Bun

5211 W. 10th St. 317-244-5669
Indianapolis, IN LD | $

The *mug* is root beer; the *bun* is a Hoosier tenderloin; together they are a paradigmatic Midwest drive-in meal. This timeless joint not far from the Indianapolis Motor Speedway gives customers a choice of eating off the dashboard or at outdoor picnic tables umbrella'd by radiant heaters for cold weather. In-car diners blink their lights for service and food is presented by carhops on window trays. People seated at tables summon the kitchen by using a buzzer that adjoins the posted menu.

We were tipped off to Mug N' Bun by writer Dale Lawrence, who described its root beer as "legitimately creamy, yes, but also smoky, carrying hints of vanilla fudge and molasses, as rich and smooth as a dessert wine." In other words, not like your average soda pop! It is served in thick frosty mugs and in sizes that include small, large, giant, quart, half-gallon, and gallon. As for the tenderloin, it too is big, if not the juiciest in town. We were more fond of the double cheeseburger that filled out its bun with meat to spare. Also, the onion rings are something special: battered thick, crisp, and sweet.

Nick's Kitchen

506 N. Jefferson St. 260-356-6618
Huntington, IN BLD | $

It was 1904 when Nick Frienstein started frying breaded pork cutlets to sell in sandwiches from a street cart in Huntington; four years later he opened a small café called Nick's Kitchen. His method of preparing the fried pork cutlets was finessed one winter shortly after Nick moved to the café and his brother Jake suffered such severe frostbite that he lost the fingers off his hands. Jake, whose job it was to bread the slices of pork, found that his stumps made good tools for pounding the meat to make it tender. Since then, a tenderloin (no need to say pork tenderloin) has been defined as a sandwich of pork that has been either beaten tender (with a wooden hammer) or run through a mechanical tenderizer (or both).

Now run by Jean Anne Bailey, whose father owned the town café starting in 1969, Nick's Kitchen lists its tenderloin on the menu with a challenge that's more than a little ironic, considering its culinary history: "Bet You Need Both Hands." Two hands are barely adequate for hoisting the colossal sandwich, which is built around a wavy disk of audibly crunchy pork that extends a good two to three inches beyond the circumference of a five-inch bun, virtually eclipsing its plate. Soaked in buttermilk that gives a tangy twist to the meat's sweetness and tightly cased in a coat of rugged cracker crumbs (not the more typical fine-grind cracker meal), the lode of pork inside the crust fairly drips with moisture. Jean Anne tells us she buys the meat already cut and cubed. She pounds it, marinates it, breads it, and fries it.

Nick's Kitchen isn't only a tenderloin stop. It's a wonderful three-meal-a-day town café with big breakfasts and a noontime blackboard of daily specials. We loved our plate of ham, beans, and corn bread, and we were bowled over by Jean Anne's pies. "My father served frozen ones," she says. "I knew I wanted something better." Made using a hand-me-down dough recipe that incorporates a bit of corn syrup, her fruit pies have a flaky crust that evaporates on the tongue, melding with brilliant-flavored rhubarb or black raspberries. Butterscotch pie—which she learned to cook from her grandmother—is more buttery than sweet, nothing at all like cloying pies made from pudding filling. Sugar-cream pie, an Indiana signature dessert, is like cream candy in a savory crust.

Shapiro's

808 S. Meridian St.   317-631-4041
Indianapolis, IN   BLD | $

Shapiro's serves deli meals cafeteria-style. In addition to a full repertoire of traditional kosher-style fare from gefilte fish to matzoh ball soup, its menu includes such midwestern specialties as buttered perch plates (Friday) and Hoosier sugar-cream pie. The corned beef sandwich is one of the best anywhere, the meat cut lean but not too much so; each slice is rimmed with a thin halo of smudgy spice and is so moist that it glistens. The slices are mounded between slabs of Shapiro's own rye bread, which has a shiny, hard, sour crust. Slather on the mustard, crunch into a dill pickle to set your taste buds tingling, and this sandwich will take you straight to deli heaven.

Get some latkes (potato pancakes), too. They are double-thick, moist, and starchy: great companions to a hot lunch of short ribs or stuffed peppers. Shapiro's supplements ordinary latkes with cinnamon-scented ones—wonderful when heaped with sour cream. And soup: bean, lentil, split pea, and chowder are daily specials; you can always order chicken soup or red beet borscht.

Teibel's

1775 Route 41   219-865-2000
Schererville, IN   LD | $$

Teibel's is one of a handful of restaurants that continue to serve the favorite big-eats Sunday-supper sort of meal so beloved in northern Indiana: buttered lake perch. When it opened in 1930, it was a mom-and-pop café, and today it is a giant-size dining establishment (run by the same family), but the culinary values that made it famous still prevail.

The feast starts with a relish tray—scallions, olives, celery, and carrots—followed by a salad (superfluous), then a plate piled high with tender fillets of perch glistening with butter. It is a big portion, and this fish is full-flavored; by the time our plate was empty, we were more than satisfied. Our extreme satisfaction was due also to the fact that we had to have an order of Teibel's fried chicken, too. Perhaps even more famous than the perch, this chicken is made from a recipe that Grandma Teibel brought from Austria many years ago. It is chicken with a crumbly red-gold crust and juicy insides, in a whole other league from the stuff that comes in a bucket from fast-food franchises. Some other interesting items from Teibel's menu: frog legs (another local passion) and walleye pike. For fish- and frog-frowners, there is a turkey dinner.

After a family-style feed like this, what could be nicer than a hot apple dumpling? Teibel's flake-crusted, cinnamon-scented dumpling is served à la mode with caramel sauce on top.

Archie's Waeside

224 4th Ave. NE   712-546-7011

Le Mars, IA   D | $$$

A steak-eaters' destination since Archie Jackson started it in 1949, Archie's is now run by grandson Bob Rand, who is a fanatic for excellence and produces some of the best steaks anywhere in America. They arrive a little crusty on the outside, overwhelmingly juicy, and bursting with the full, resonating flavor of corn-fed, dry-aged beef. Even the filet mignon, usually a tender cut that is less flavorful, sings with the authority of blue-ribbon protein. Bone-in rib eye is deliriously succulent. And an off-the-menu item called the Benny Weiker (named for a good customer of years ago who was a famous cattle buyer in the Sioux City stockyards) is simply the most handsome piece of meat we have ever seen presented on a plate: an eighteen-ounce, center-cut, twenty-one-day dry-aged filet mignon.

And by the way, the things that come before and during the beef are pretty special at Archie's. Along with salad you get a relish tray and a plate of cured-here corned beef: super-lean, high-flavored, beautiful to look at. The waitress suggested we do like regular customers do and shred the spicy beef on our salads. Available companions for meat include a well-browned patty of hash brown potatoes and a trio of substantial corn fritters.

Archie's is a big, happy restaurant with capacious booths and hordes of happy customers who come from miles around to enjoy the beefy pride of Siouxland.

Bob's Drive-Inn

Highway 75 S.	712-546-5445
Le Mars, IA	L | $

You will not find "loosemeats" on the menu that hangs above the order window at Bob's Drive-Inn. That is because it is listed by one of its several aliases, a "tavern." The dish is so big hereabouts that Bob's menu doesn't even offer a hamburger. If you want beef, you get loosemeats. Bob's are definitive. Browned, strained of fat, then pressure-cooked with sauce and spice, then drained again, this meat is moist, full-flavored, and deeply satisfying. Each sandwich is made on a good-quality roll that proprietor Myles Kass secures from Le Mars's own Vander Meer Bakery, and most are served with cheese, mustard, and pickle.

If for some reason you don't want loosemeats, or if you, like us, need to sample every good hot dog that exists, get a couple of franks at this fine place. They are natural-casing Wimmer's-brand beauties made in Nebraska. In the best-of-both-worlds department, have a Bob Dog, which is one of these snappy franks topped with loosemeats.

Root beer is house-made, and fruit shakes are made from real summer fruit.

Coffee Cup Cafe

616 4th St.	641-594-3765
Sully, IA	BLD | $

If you are southeast of Des Moines looking for the sort of town café where locals come to eat and shmooze, here's the place. Breakfast is lovely— plate-wide golden pancakes and big rounds of sausage; there are eggs and potatoes, of course, and modest-size but big-taste cinnamon buns with a translucent sugar glaze, served warm with butter on the side. The meal we like best is lunch. The menu lists hot beef sandwiches and tenderloin steaks, and there is one square-meal special every day—last visit, it was baked ham with mashed potatoes and apple salad. Any time of day you can order Dutch lettuce, a locally preferred salad of crisp, cold iceberg leaves bathed in a warm sweet-and-sour creamy mustard dressing with pieces of bacon and slices of hard-cooked egg.

No matter what meal you eat, or what time of day you eat it, you must have pie at the Coffee Cup Cafe. Iowa is major pie country, and it is in just such inconspicuous small-town cafés that some of the very best are eaten. Looking for a good cream pie? Have a wedge of Coffee Cup banana cream. It quivers precariously as the waitress sets it down on the table, the custard jiggling like not-quite-set Jell-O, the foamy white meringue on top wafting like just-spun cotton candy. Below these ribbons of white and yellow is a thin, tawny crust that doesn't *break* when met with a fork; it *flakes*. The whole experience of cutting a mouthful, raising it to one's mouth, and savoring it is what we imagine it would be like to eat pastries on the moon or some planet where gravity is only a fraction of earth's; for the word "light" barely does justice to the refinement of this piece of pie.

Darrell's Place

4010 1st St.   712-563-3922
Hamlin, IA   LD | $

Darrell's Place looks more like a large utility shed than a restaurant, but aficionados of the tenderloin know that it is a culinary gem. Winner of the 2004 Iowa Pork Producers Association award for the best tenderloin in the state, Darrell's serves tenderloins that are thick and juicy, enveloped in a crisp, fine-textured crust that is more crunch than breading. The ribbon of meat is a good half-inch thick, making for an ultra-opulent eating experience. And while it is a very large sandwich, the crisp-edged patty extends only a bit beyond the bun, not outrageously far, meaning you can easily pick it up, even with one hand.

Hamlin is a tiny town with a population of less than three hundred. It's a charming place in the heart of farm country and seems light-years away from civilization. And yet it is just fourteen miles north of I-80, a supremely convenient detour for interstate travelers in the west of the state. While visiting, you might consider visiting Nathaniel Hamlin Park, home of the world's largest collection of nails.

The Farmer's Kitchen

319 Walnut St.   712-243-2898
Atlantic, IA   BLD | $

When a fellow with the screen name "blizzardstormus" started posting in the forums at Roadfood.com about a half-dozen years ago, our appetites perked up. He gave his location as Atlantic, Iowa, a small town not too far from I-80 in the western part of the state where long ago we bought one of our most treasured locally published, spiral-bound cookbooks—the Atlantic community's collection of recipes for the likes of breaded pork loin, corn bread muffins, and sour cream raisin pie. All of these, and much, much more, we soon discovered, are on the menu of Mr. Blizzardstormus's café in the heart of town—The Farmer's Kitchen.

That name is no lie. Farmers eat here and much of the food is farm-kitchen good. Bread and pies are made daily; beef, bacon, eggs, and produce are local; just about everything—including the excellent gravy that smothers hot beef and meat loaf—is made from scratch. If you are not in the mood for such Iowa-specific fare as a breaded pork tenderloin sandwich or a casserole-like skillet dinner, consider the hamburger. The Farmer's Kitchen offers more than a dozen variations, including a Wisconsin butter burger, a one-pounder, and the notorious Cy-Hawk burger, which is a half-pound of beef, smoked Cheddar, bacon, grilled onions, lettuce, tomato, and mayonnaise dolled up with roasted garlic and chipotle chilies.

There always are several pies for dessert, including the chocolate peanut butter that was declared No. 1 in the American Pie Council's National Pie Championships and French apple (guaranteed: a whole apple in every slice), but the one to eat is baker Charlene Johnson's mighty sour cream raisin, crowned with a vast meringue cloud.

Grove Cafe
124 Main St.   515-232-9784
Ames, IA   BL | $

When you say "pancake" at the Grove Cafe, you might want to separate the word. In this place, a pancake is a pan cake—a good-size layer of cake that has been cooked in a pan, or in this case, on the grill. Nearly an inch thick in its center, it is wide as its plate—a round of steamy cooked batter that has an appealing orange hue. It comes with a couple of pats of butter and a pitcher of syrup (all of which this cake can absorb with ease). With some peppery Iowa sausage patties, one of these cakes is a full-size meal. Two of them, listed on the menu as a "short stack," is a breakfast for only the tallest of appetites.

Grove Cafe also offers omelets with hash browns and happy little slices of French toast for breakfast, as well as hamburgers, hot beef, and meat loaf at lunch. But to many of its longtime fans, including hordes of Iowa State alumni who have consumed tens of thousands of calories in these bare-tabled booths and on the low stools at the counter, pancakes are all that matter. To its most devoted fans, Grove Cafe is a pancake parlor.

Located in the old business district, it has a weathered character with faded cream-colored walls decorated with photos and mementoes from the riding exploits of the proprietor. Among them is a blue ribbon he won at the state fair showing Appaloosa horses. A large sign painted on the wall above the grill jokes, "Just Like Home: You Don't Always Get What You Want."

In't Veld Meat Market

820 Main St.   641-628-3440
Pella, IA   L | $

Most customers come to In't Veld to shop for meat rather than to eat; and even those of us who are just passing through will find such good travel companions as summer sausage, dried beef, and wax-wrapped cheeses. For those in search of regional specialties, the meat to eat is ring bologna, also known as Pella bologna because this town is the only place it is made. It is a tube of sausage about as thick as a pepperoni stick, curled into a horseshoe shape, cured, smoked, cooked, and ready to eat. It is delicious sliced cold with a hunk of cheese and a piece of bread; it's even better when you can warm it up and cut it into thick disks like kielbasa. Smoky, vigorously spiced, and firm-textured, this bologna is an only-in-Iowa treat.

For travelers, what is especially good about In't Veld Market is that you can sit down right here and have a hot bologna sandwich: five thick slices on a fresh bakery bun . . . pass the mustard, please! In fact, a whole menu of meat-market sandwiches is available for eating here (or taking out) until mid-afternoon each day. In addition to the famous bologna, you can have house-dried beef on a bun, homemade bratwurst with sauerkraut on a hoagie roll, ham and Swiss, or a ground-here beefburger. Side orders are limited to potato salad, macaroni salad, beans, slaw, and Jell-O; and for dessert, we suggest a walk across the square to Jaarsma Bakery, a Dutch-accented shop with beguiling pastries, sweet cakes, and cookies as well as locally loved Dutch letters.

Larsen's Pub

4206 Main St.   712-764-8026
Elk Horn, IA   LD | $

Winner of the 2007 Iowa Pork Producers Association award for the state's best tenderloin, Larsen's Pub makes one that is approximately a half-pound of meat, pounded tender so that it extends beyond its bun in all directions, but still so thick that the big vein of pork within the golden crust spurts juice when you sink your teeth into it. Squirted with mustard and bunned with lettuce, tomato, and pickle chips, this fine sandwich is a good explanation for why the tenderloin has earned such stalwart devotees.

Larsen's is an extremely inconspicuous storefront tavern in a Danishancestored town known also for its authentic Danish windmill, the Danish Inn (*frikadeller* meatballs, *medisterpolse* sausage, and *smørrebrød* sandwiches), and its annual end-of-May Tivoli Fest, featuring folk dancers, a costumed parade, and Danish-themed food vendors.

Miles Inn

2622 Leech Ave.   712-276-9825
Sioux City, IA   LD | $

If you look through the Sioux City Yellow Pages for the Miles Inn, you won't find it under R, for Restaurants. It is listed under T, for Taverns. This makes sense in two ways. First, and most obvious, is that it is, in fact, a tavern—a place people come to for long, leisurely afternoons or evenings sipping beer, watching the overhead TV, and kibitzing with each other. Built in 1925 by bricklayer John Miles, it is a sturdy edifice that sells suds by the case as well as by the draught. The only hot food you can get in this place is a sandwich, which the sign on the wall calls a Charlie Boy. That's reason number two that its listing under Taverns makes sense, because the sandwich sold here as a Charlie Boy is known by many Sioux Cityans as a tavern.

In northwest Iowa, taverns are more popular than hamburgers. Dozens of restaurants serve them, and each has its own twist on the basic formula, which is ground beef that is gently spiced and cooked loose so it remains pebbly when put upon a bun. A scoop of meat is generally garnished with pickle chips and mustard, most often with cheese; and the sandwich is almost never served on a plate.

Miles Inn's Charlie Boys, named after Charlie Miles, who was founder John Miles's son, are served in wax paper. They are rich and well fatted, with a concentrated beef flavor that even a sirloin steak cannot match. (Raise your hand if you agree with us that the one meal that most fully satisfies the deepest hunger for beef is a great burger, even more than a great steak.) Two or three Charlie Boys makes a hearty lunch, and the right libation is beer from the tap.

Milwaukee Wiener House

309 Pearl St.   712-277-3449
Sioux City, IA   BLD | $

Milwaukee Wiener House specializes in Coneys, formally known as Coney Island hot dogs, which are diminutive franks blanketed with chili. You see them marshaled on the grill by the window as you walk in. The formation is impeccable: row upon row, side by side, each identical in shape, not one out of place. All condiments are available, but connoisseurs know there is only one way to go: mustard, chili, and chopped raw onions. Each dog comes nestled in a warm bun so soft and fresh that it shows finger-mark impressions from the gentlest grasp. The hot dogs themselves are snappy, natural-casing tube steaks well complemented by the zest of the house-made fine-grind beef chili. Three or four such steamy babies makes a nice meal.

The Milwaukee Wiener House is a big rectangular dining room with rows of booths to which you tote your own meal after ordering at the counter. It opens at six in the morning, and has done so for more than eighty years. Old advertising posted on the wall boasts that it has served 4 million hot dogs, but about five years ago proprietor Gus Demetoulis told us that statistic was true when he and his partner, Thomas Eliades, took over the restaurant in 1960. He estimated the current tally at well over 10 million.

Off the Hook

| 1100 East 14th St. | 515-265-1662 |
| Des Moines, IA | LD \| $ |

A pleasant, bare-tabled café and fresh fish market, Off the Hook specializes in meals based around fish, but not your typical middle-of-the-road, no-flavor fishes that people on diets tend to eat. Here you eat fish with character, like catfish with juice-heavy meat fairly dripping flavor, or buffalo fish that is as funky as the darkest dark-meat chicken, or carp encased in earthy cornmeal batter.

The fish-frowner among us Sterns declared the fried chicken to be some of the best she has eaten outside the Deep South—crisp-crusted and thoroughly tender. We both agreed that the vegetables that come alongside meals are soul-food classics. They include collard greens, an insanely opulent dish of fried cabbage, red beans and rice, fried green tomatoes, mac 'n' cheese, southern fried potatoes (sliced and cooked with onions), and creamy-cool coleslaw.

For dessert: smooth, silky sweet potato pie.

Smitty's Tenderloin Shop

| 1401 S.W. Army Post Rd. | 515-287-4742 |
| Des Moines, IA | LD \| $ |

"Home of the REAL Whopper" says a cartoon on Smitty's wall; and if you know the taste of Iowa, you know that in this case "Whopper" does not refer to a hamburger. It means a tenderloin: pork tenderloin, pounded thin and plate-wide, breaded and fried crisp and sandwiched in a bun. Smitty's

Tenderloin Shop has been a pork connoisseur's destination since 1952, and its loyal clientele put it in the pantheon of sandwich shops.

Like all top tenderloin tenderers, Smitty's is a humble setting. It has a scattering of tables and a friendly counter where locals sit and shoot the breeze at lunch hour. Although the menu includes a handful of other lunch-counter meals—hamburgers, double hamburgers, Coney Island hot dogs, a lovely corn dog, a bowl of chili—King Tenderloin is the dish to eat. Available in small or large sizes (small is large; large is nearly a foot across), Smitty's tenderloin is served on an ordinary burger bun. The bun is virtually irrelevant except as a method for keeping ketchup, mustard, onions, and pickles adjacent to the center section of the ten-inch-diameter cutlet, and as a kind of mitt to hoist the vast tenderloin from plate to mouth. It is a marvelous disk of food, its inside a soft and flavorful ribbon of pork succulence, its crust brittle and luscious.

St. Olaf Tap

106 S. Main St.   563-783-7723

St. Olaf, IA   LD | $

One full pound of pork tenderloin is pounded out until it becomes a tender, ragged-edged circle larger than a dinner plate but still thick enough to become a juicy white ribbon of meat when it is breaded and fried crisp. The colossal hunk of food is presented between two halves of a normal-size hamburger bun that is so relatively small it reminds us of a Tater Tot. Or you can ask for it between halves of two buns, or three or four. Even a quartet is dwarfed by the meat within.

Without question, St. Olaf Tap serves the biggest of all tenderloins in the southern Midwest's tenderloin belt. It is also one of the most delicious: a savory balancing act of crunchy crust and succulent white pork, beautifully abetted by jumbo onion rings and/or corn fritters. Half-size and quarter-size versions also are available, but if you are more than one person (or if you have an insatiable appetite), we highly recommend getting the super jumbo; it's an only-in-Iowa dining experience.

Tastee Inn & Out

2610 Gordon Dr.   712-255-0857

Sioux City, IA   LD | $

Tastee Inn & Out is strictly take-out. Meals are procured at either a walk-up or drive-through window, and they are eaten either in the car or at a picnic table in the parking lot. Run by the Calligan family for over a half-century now, this ingenuous eatery specializes in what it calls a Tastee sandwich, known elsewhere in northwest Iowa as a tavern or a loosemeats: seasoned, barely sauced ground beef shoveled into a bun with a slice of bright orange cheese, pickle chips, and onion. It is sloppy and unjustifiable but strangely addictive; its only possible companion is an order of onion chips, which are bite-size, crisp-fried petals of sweet onion, customarily served with a creamy dip similar to ranch dressing, known farther west as fry sauce.

Wilton Candy Kitchen

310 Cedar St.   563-732-2278
Wilton, IA   L | $

We've never sampled Hadacol, the high-proof patent medicine that Colonel Tom Parker used to hawk before he became Elvis Presley's manager. But we do endorse the teetotaler's version of it made at the Wilton Candy Kitchen. Fiz-biz historians trace a fountain on this spot to the mid-1880s; today's Candy Kitchen dates back to 1910, when a young immigrant named Gus Nopoulos came to town and rented the place to make candy and sell soda and ice cream. Now run by grandson George Napoulos and family, the Candy Kitchen is a trip back to a world of long-forgotten concoctions such as a pink lady (strawberry, cherry, and vanilla flavoring), an oddball (strawberry and vanilla), and a dipsy doodle (six different flavors). Cokes and cherry Cokes are not poured from a glass or bottle; they are mixed to order, using water carbonated on premises and Coke syrup. Mr. Nopoulos told us that Coke syrup, once a fountain staple in every American town, is getting hard to find. "We've got to go all the way to Cedar Rapids for it now," he lamented. That syrup is half the formula for the Nopoulos family version of the hadacol (cola plus root beer), the name of which George explained to us thusly: "They 'hada call' it something."

Bortell's Fisheries

5528 S. Lakeshore Dr.
Ludington, MI

231-843-3337
L (summer only) | $

You catch it, they'll cook it. BYO seafood to this old fish market and smoke-house across from Summit Park where the menu includes walleye, catfish, trout, and whitefish from nearby waters. Bortell's also imports ocean perch and Alaskan salmon; so even if you don't have your own catch, you will have a wide variety of flavorful smoked fish from which to choose. It is sold by the piece or pound.

On the road between Pentwater and Ludington, it's easy to drive right past the sign that says "Hot Fried Fish to Go," but if the car windows are open, you will likely smell sweet wood smoke in the air. Step up to the counter, place your order, and pay. There is no dining room and business is strictly take-out. Once you get your fish, find a picnic table and eat outside in the shade under the grove of ancient beech trees.

The Cherry Hut

211 N. Michigan Ave.
Beulah, MI

231-882-4431
LD Memorial Day-mid-Oct | $

Comfort-food lunch is grand at this 1920s roadside eatery: sandwiches, tur-key dinner, lovely cinnamon rolls, and turkey salad brightened up with cherries. But it is pie baked from locally grown cherries that is the destination dish. A single serving is one-quarter of a full-size pie; spilling out its sides are bright red cherries whose sweetness is balanced by a beguiling tart undertone. The crust is melt-in-the-mouth savory. Topped by a scoop of creamy vanilla ice cream, it's a perfect all-American dessert.

Dining facilities include outdoor picnic tables as well as indoor tables, and part of The Cherry Hut experience is buying things to take home. The restaurant shop sells not only whole fresh pies (five hundred per day) but also jellies, jams, and a wide array of Cherry Jerry, the Happy Pie Faced Boy, souvenirs.

Don's Drive-In

2030 N. US Hwy. 31 N.   231-938-1860
Grand Traverse, MI   LD | $

Don's is a real drive-in that opened the year Elvis joined the Army (1958). Selections on its jukebox evoke days of American mid-century car culture at its prime, and the ambience is rock-and-roll: Hubcaps and album covers decorate the walls and you can dine inside or in your car, where meals are served on window trays. The menu is basically burgers and fries, featuring the old-fashioned "basket" presentation, meaning a sandwich sided by French fries and coleslaw.

The tough decision to make at Don's is whether to get a hamburger or a brace of Coney Island hot dogs. The burger is thick and juicy; a Coney, topped with chili sauce, is a Midwest paradigm. Whatever you get to eat, there should be no question about the beverage. Make it a milk shake. Don's blends its shakes to order, either large or small, both of which are big enough to fill at least a couple of glasses, and both of which are thick enough to require powerful suction with a straw. Chocolate and vanilla shakes are good all the time; in the summer, strawberry shakes are made with fresh fruit.

Gustafson's

4321 US 2   906-292-5424
Brevort, MI   L | $$

The full name of this alluring roadside attraction is Gustafson's Smoked Fish and Beef Jerky. It is a gas station and party store that has delicious food that is oh-so-ready-to-eat, but it does not offer full-service meals.

Even with your eyes closed, you'll find it as you cruise along the shore road (we don't recommend driving this way) because a sugar maple haze from a quartet of smoldering smokers outside clouds the air with the unbelievably appetizing smell of whitefish, trout, menominee, chub, and salmon turning gorgeous shades of gold. Inside, coolers are arrayed with the firm-fleshed beauties, which you can buy by the piece, wrapped in butcher's paper. Utensils and plates are unnecessary; it's a pleasure to use one's fingers to pick flavorful chunks of fish straight from the paper in which they're wrapped.

Beef jerky is also a specialty of the Gustafson family, which marinates strips of top round for a day and a half, then slow-smokes it over maple for six hours. Jerky is made with a traditional smoky-sweet taste, Cajun-spiced, or barbecue flavored. Vacuum-packed jerky is available through the mail, by the pound.

Michigan's Upper Peninsula lends itself to waterside picnics. A few chaws of jerky, a moist hunk or two of freshly smoked freshwater fish, a fifty-cent stack of saltine crackers, a bag of fried cheese curds, and a beer, plus the scenic beauty of Lake Michigan: What's better than that?

Johnny's Ham King

2601 W. Fort St. 313-961-2202
Detroit, MI BL | $

If Motor City muscle doesn't cut the mustard any more and Motown is mostly memory, we suggest another sobriquet of which Detroiters still can be proud: Ham Haven. Thanks to a truck driver named Joe, who tipped us off to what he called "out of this world" ham, we discovered that this is a city where little diners make a big deal of ham at low prices. Mike's Famous Ham Place in Corktown, the Ham Shoppe on St. Antoine, and Johnny's Ham King are the Big Three, where the pinkest part of the pig is sliced to order and sizzled on the griddle, served on the side of eggs for breakfast or sandwiched, still warm, in soft onion rolls for lunch.

Gearjammer Joe, who especially recommended Johnny's four-egg omelet with ham and buttery, extra-crisp potatoes, noted that a swivel stool at the long counter was the place to sit. Here is where you get to watch Pete, a short-order cook with a quarter-century of experience, wield his spatula like a samurai sword and entertain customers with impassioned political soliloquies. At lunch, in addition to the Ham King Sandwich, ham and bean soup is a must.

Juilleret's

1418 Bridge St.　　　　　　231-547-9212
Charlevoix, MI　　　　　　BLD | $$

The menu at Juilleret's is town-café fare, but the quality of all that's served is a cut above (as are the prices). We love just walking in the door and gazing upon the case of just-baked loaves of cinnamon, cinnamon-raisin, white, banana-walnut, and whole wheat bread. Plus maple rolls, nutty rolls, and cinnamon-raisin rolls.

Juilleret's pancakes belong on our short list of the nation's best. They are large, so large that one is a nice-size meal, but amazingly they are not gross or doughy. In fact, each cake is a rather elegant piece of food, like a fine pastry but with all the good buttery character of a griddle-cooked flapjack. They are made plain or infused with raspberries or blueberries and available with house-made syrup, powdered sugar, honey, or peanut butter, or (if you pay extra), maple syrup from a nearby farm.

At lunch, mashed potatoes for the side of hot sandwiches are the real deal, topped with homemade gravy. Local whitefish is broiled to a fine, fragile, crisp-edged succulence, sandwiched in Juilleret's bread and served with excellent pickly-sweet tartar sauce. Hamburgers are served on made-here buns; even the tuna salad, made fresh the Midwestern way with Miracle Whip, is a cut above.

Desserts? Couldn't be better. Juilleret's coconut cream pie is one of the best anywhere, its dense, coconut-chocked custard so intensely flavorful that you want to call it savory, its meringue topping light as a puff of steam.

Juilleret's

130 State St.　　　　　　231-526-2821
Harbor Springs, MI　　　　LD | $$

The oldest restaurant in Michigan and still run by the family that started it in 1895, Juilleret's is a soda fountain and sweet shop that also happens to be the great Great Lakes source for planked whitefish. The old-time way of cooking starts with a heap of milky-white fillets spread out on a seasoned hardwood plank. They are broiled in rivers of butter until their edges turn crisp and brown. They are strewn with slices of lemon and tomato and surrounded by a wall of piped-on mashed potatoes that shores in all the juices. What a feast! Planked whitefish is available only for dinner, after five in the afternoon, for any number of people from two to ten.

At the fountain, soda jerks are proficient at using house ice cream to make sodas, sundaes, banana splits, tin roofs, cream puffs, coolers, rainbows, and a couple of exclusive items, the Velvet and the Thundercloud. The Thundercloud is vanilla ice cream, bittersweet chocolate sauce, and chopped nuts all layered in a slender tulip glass and topped with a blob of marshmallow fluff. A Velvet is the same ingredients, minus the nuts, blended smooth.

Many customers come to Juilleret's only for hamburgers or ice cream, and some come just to hang out. It is a big, tin-roofed town lunch room, favored by generations of vacationing Michiganders, and its ambience is noisy, extremely casual, and fun. It is a place to table-hop, carry on across-the-room conversations, and flirt with the new kids in town.

Krazy Jim's Blimpy Burger
551 S. Division St.   734-663-4590
Ann Arbor, MI   L | S

While you are waiting in line at the Blimpy—and you will wait in line—please do your homework: figure out how to order your hamburger. When you get to the counter (the line moves fast), you will be asked if you want something fried. This refers to side-dish vegetables, including broccoli stalks, steak fries, and big, irregular onion rings in self-detaching crust. Next, tell the burger cook how many patties you want. At ten-to-a-pound, two is minimal. Triples, quads, and quints are the norm. Now, name your roll: kaiser, regular, or onion? Want cheese? Say Cheddar, Swiss, provolone, American, bleu, or feta. Fifth question: Any extras on top? These include fried eggs, bacon, salami, grilled onions, banana peppers, and mushrooms. Finally, when everything else is settled, give the assembler a list of condiments you want applied, naming the wet ones first. By this time, you are at the cash register at the end of the line. The fried things have arrived in overflowing cardboard boats and your burger, precisely built to your specifications, is wrapped in wax paper and ready for you to tote to a table.

To our knowledge, no one has been evicted or banned for inappropriate ordering such as asking for a hamburger with everything—you must be specific—or naming cheese prior to naming bun, but the staff is notorious for not hiding their exasperation at dumbstruck customers who gum up the works. In this place, there are no computer terminals, not even order pads. Everything is verbal, and it can seem like chaos. But everyone gets exactly what they ordered exactly when they reach the end of the line.

According to generally accepted rules of griddle frying, Krazy Jim's hamburgers are cooked all wrong. Each sphere of freshly ground chuck, about the size of an ice cream scoop, is squished flat on the hot iron, slapped and flipped, sometimes hit so vigorously that it disintegrates like Iowa loosemeats (but is reintegrated with a deft spatula), finally leaned on hard before getting dressed and bunned. Call it burger cruelty, but these hamburgers are fatty enough to take it and still come off the griddle oozing juice. No doubt, a single plain one on a bun would be boring. But no one gets a single, and the only reason to get one plain is if you've given up condiments for Lent. A proper Blimpy is baroque.

Lafayette Coney Island

118 W. Lafayette Blvd.   313-964-8198
Detroit, MI   LD | $

Although the term "Coney Island" comes from the Brooklyn beach resort where the hot dog supposedly was invented in 1867, you will find virtually no Coney Island hot dogs in the New York area or anywhere east of the Delaware River. And the Coneys you do find nearly everywhere else in the nation bear only scant resemblance to the hot dogs of New York. While Coneys vary, their common denominator is chili topping, which never was part of the boardwalk formula. About 99 percent of them also are served with mustard and chopped raw onions.

Nowhere is the passion for Coneys more intense than in Detroit, where an adjoining pair of rival storefront doggeries known as American Coney Island and Lafayette Coney Island serve franks that might look pretty much alike to the casual observer but are cause for adamant partisanship. We recently received a photo of the two places, taken by Cliff Strutz, who wrote, "I had one of my all-time favorite Roadfood moments while I was in Detroit last weekend. After finishing a couple of Coneys, I was standing in the middle of the street taking photos of Lafayette and American Coney Islands. A car pulled up with two guys dressed in Red Wings clothing, obviously going to the game. Well, one headed for the door at Lafayette and one for American, both ribbing each other for their poor taste in hot dogs. I find it very amusing that one just didn't say 'whatever,' and eat with his friend. But Coney loyalty is apparently more important." The photograph shows the two guys each going to his favorite place.

Make no mistake, Lafayette's Coneys (or American's—we're as neutral as Switzerland on this issue) are not aristocratic; they are plebeian. But the harmony of spicy hot dog, soft white bun, smooth chili, bright yellow mustard, and crisp onions (and maybe shredded cheese, too) is culinary magic. When the craving for one (or more likely, four) of them strikes, no prime steak could scratch the itch. It is possible to order one with "heavy chili," but we believe that throws the precious balance off. Better to have your extra chili blanketing French fries or cheese fries.

Northside Grill

1015 Broadway St.   734-995-0965

Ann Arbor, MI   BL | $

The Northside Grill is not a pancake house. The popular pine-paneled café has a full menu for breakfast and for lunch, but other than drinking lots of its really good coffee, we've not been able to get much beyond the superb pancakes. Best of the bunch may be the apple–oat bran 'cakes with their rugged, apple-chunk texture and cinnamon twist. A similar configuration is available with blueberries. Plain buttermilk pancakes are too dairy-delicious to be called plain. And potato pancakes are crisp and crunchy on the outside but creamy within and sparkling with herbs and spices, topped with slivers of grilled red onion, and accompanied by ramekins of sour cream and apple-sauce.

We loved our Big Easy omelet made with andouille sausage and a full measure of Cajun spice, and did manage to sample a piece of masterful apple pie, but there are so many subjects for further study, including cinnamon swirl French toast and breakfast burritos, not to mention a good-looking lunch repertoire of burgers, chili, Mexican plates, and salads.

Yesterdog

1505 Wealthy St. SE   616-336-0746

Grand Rapids, MI   LD | $

Courteous service? No way. Comfortable, modern accommodations? Not here. Neat and tidy meals? Not a chance! Excellent snappy-skinned boiled hot dogs loaded into steamed soft buns and smothered with sloppy chili sauce, cheese, onions, mustard, pickles, sauerkraut, and just about any other condiment you can name? This is the place. Chili is pretty much de rigueur; you can pick your toppings one by one or simply ask for an ultra, which is some of everything.

Yesterdog has been around for decades, and today it is a self-consciously old-timey sort of place with vintage advertising signs all about (sharing wall space with pictures of happy customers wearing Yesterdog T-shirts) and a pre-electric cash register for ringing up sales. It is almost always crowded, so much so that there is frequently a mob of people out on the sidewalk waiting to get in, and it doesn't empty out until long after midnight. Tips are given to the staff by tossing coins into the bell flare of a tuba.

Zingerman's Deli

422 Detroit St.
Ann Arbor, MI

734-663-3354
BLD | $$

It started small, but Zingerman's has become a culinary colossus that includes a mail-order business, creamery, bake house, coffee shop, and estimable full-service roadhouse (at 2501 Jackson Avenue). While not every such conspicuous success proves the adage that they must be doing something right, the fact is that Zingerman's doesn't merely do something right; it does everything fantastically well.

Sandwiches are our favorite things, made with such top-notch ingredients as Nueske's bacon, Amish free-range chicken, Niman Ranch pastrami, Michigan-grown vegetables, Italian salami, Arkansas ham, and smoked salmon from Maine. They are assembled on the best bread in the Midwest— world-class baguettes, the best old-fashioned double-baked Jewish rye in the nation, sourdoughs, chile-Cheddar, pecan-raisin, or challah. And let's not even get into such peripheral (*not*) items as excellent pickles, olive tapenade, smoked fish salads, and multiple cheese spreads, including a pimiento cheese that competes with anything in the South.

Obtaining lunch can be confusing. You enter the surprisingly small deli, which is primarily a retail operation selling meats, breads, cheeses, et al., and browse a menu posted all over the wall. While you are figuring out what you want, a server will approach to take your order and your name. You are then given a check that you take to a register and pay. Find a seat (lots of nice ones outdoors for fair-weather dining), to which your food will soon be brought. The staff is extremely friendly and patient, and they are full of helpful recommendations if you can't decide between, say, halloumi and Muenster cheese.

Zingerman's is more expensive than an average sandwich shop. A BLT is $9.50 or $10.99 depending on size; grilled cheese is $6.50–$7.99. But what you get is far superior to, and considerably bigger than, an average sandwich. Roadfood omnivores will find it frustrating because a single visit, no matter how much you order, will provide only a glimmer of all the good things there are to eat . . . and to see and to smell.

Al's Breakfast

413 14th Ave., SE   612-331-9991

Minneapolis, MN   BL | $

Al's is open year-round, but the coziest time to eat in this pint-size diner near the University of Minnesota is from October through April, when the windows cloud with breakfast-scented steam from the well-seasoned griddle where pancakes, eggs, hash browns, and corned beef hash sizzle. It is impossible to convey the joie de vivre at Al's, where a patron once rhapsodized to us, "Al's is an organism. It is not some soulless concept restaurant that a corporate idea man at a drawing board designed. Good things happen here; people's lives change. If you want a car, or an apartment, or a sweetheart, come in and sit at the counter. Come in, have coffee, and chat a while. Pretty soon, I promise, you will get what you need. Al's has a life of its own, above and beyond any of us. I truly believe it is a crossroads of the universe."

The buttermilk pancakes are broad, thin, and slightly sticky inside, with a good, sour smack. Rivulets of butter and sweet syrup complete their flavor perfectly; or you can get them made with blueberries or giant blackberries in the batter. The other basic batter variation is whole wheat, which has a wholesome, earthy flavor; and either batter can be studded with corn kernels or walnuts as the pancakes cook. For garnishing these distinguished flapjacks beyond ordinary syrup, you can choose extra-cost maple syrup, sour cream, or bowls of berries. Other than pancakes, Al's offers lovely poached eggs, corned beef hash, omelets, and crunchy hash browns.

Betty's Pies

1633 Hwy. 61   218-834-3367
Two Harbors, MN   BLD (limited winter hours) | $

Betty's makes gorgeous fruit pies with lightweight crusts, really creamy cream pies that are thick and pure and satisfying, and a sensational chocolate creation that is dark chocolate cream, cinnamon meringue, whipped cream, and chocolate whipped cream on a flaky crust. While the rustic café sports a big menu that includes walleye sandwiches, hamburgers of all kinds, wraps, salads, and Upper Peninsula pasties, it is the pies that make it a worthy destination. Pies and a relatively new item known as a pie shake. Yes, it is what it sounds like. One entire piece of pie of whatever flavor you choose is blended with ice cream and milk! Our waitress dissuaded us from getting one made with fruit pie, as it would have too grainy a texture, so we chose banana cream, which made us think of pie à la mode in a tall glass. Pieces of banana and bits of crust inevitably clogged the straw, making it a drink that must be gulped or spooned.

Betty's is famous and gets crowded in the summer when travelers come to enjoy the beauty of Lake Superior's North Shore. Although rebuilt and remodeled since its opening in 1956, and now under new management with Betty retired, it remains a charming place with blue-and-white kitchenette decor and waitresses who are outspoken in the best diner tradition.

Note: Betty's has limited hours in winter months, so be sure to call ahead.

Bloedow Bakery

451 E. Broadway   507-452-3682
Winona, MN   B | $

Southwest Minnesota food lore tells the story of the little home-grown bakery (in business for some eighty years) that ran Krispy Kreme out of town. It was back in aught-three that the national chain moved in, setting up its products throughout town in groceries and convenience stores. But the interloper donuts did not impress Minnesotans, who knew better. In less than two years, KK had vanished from the shelves and Bloedow reigned supreme.

It's a sweet story for those of us who prize eateries with genuine character over those cookie-cuttered in the corporate boardroom, and the fact is that the glazed and cake donuts, sweet rolls, maple-frosted long johns, and cookies at Bloedow's (rhymes with *Playdoughs*) deserve their renown. We found out about the place thanks to Roadfood.com tipster Vanessa Haluska, who directed us to a Bloedow specialty, the peanut butter roll. It's a big, circular pastry made with sweet dough and swirled with peanut butter where you might expect cinnamon. For P.B. lovers it is a very large taste of heaven, and so we salute Vanessa, who described this charming place as "the best small town bakery that I have ever visited!"

Cafe Latté

850 Grand Ave. 651-224-5687
St. Paul, MN LD | $$

Get your food cafeteria-style. If you like Caesar salad, this place is a dream, because you can get the classic version as well as a Caesar supplemented by artichoke hearts, Greek olives, or sliced tomatoes. Each individual salad is made to order, so you can specify if you want a little more of this or that. Breads from the prodigious bakery in the back of the store are arrayed along the line and regal cakes are on display at the beginning.

We'll be drooling on our computer keyboard if we try to describe too many of the cakes, so let's just say that the turtle cake, an intense mountain of chocolate, caramel, and pecans, is monumentally good. Other available layered chocolate wonders are chocolate-chocolate, orange blossom, German chocolate, and chocolate banana.

Whether you are in the mood for cake or a salad, a sandwich and soup, or just scones and espresso, this is a fine, inexpensive place to enjoy yourself. We are always a wee bit frustrated for the simple reason that there is no appetite huge enough to sample all the things that look good, particularly from the bakery.

Convention Grill

3912 Sunnyside Rd. 952-920-6881
Edina, MN LD | $

Here is a great American hamburger: a bun-filling patty sizzled to crusty perfection on an extremely well oiled grill. It oozes juice and radiates beefy savor, and is especially good topped with a mantle of melted cheese and/or California style (with lettuce, tomato, and mayonnaise). Other available toppings include bacon and mushrooms; or you can have a Plaza Burger, which comes with sour cream, chives, and chopped onions and is sandwiched in a dark bun.

For burgers alone, we'll happily make the pilgrimage to this 1934-vintage diner in Edina, but we can guarantee our California cheeseburgers will be accompanied by French fries. Beautiful fries, cooked until bronze-hued, each portion a mix of cream-centered, full-size sticks and darkened crunchy little twigs and burnt ends of potato debris from when the spuds are hand-cut in the kitchen.

On the side you want a malt. So thick they must be spooned from their silver beaker because pouring is impossible, Convention Grill malts are available in a rainbow of flavors: chocolate, wild blueberry, butterscotch, strawberry, coffee, banana, vanilla, caramel, honey, hot fudge, butterfinger, mint, and Reese's Peanut Butter Cup. For 50¢ extra, you can have fresh banana added. The only problem with ordering a malt is that it makes it less likely you will have stamina for a hot fudge sundae. It comes in a broad tulip glass with gobs of fudge underneath the ice cream and whipped cream on top, and on the side is a good-size cup of extra hot fudge to pour on as you eat your way through.

All this excellent Roadfood is dished out by a staff of white-uniformed waitresses who are utterly efficient and, in our experience, omnipresent. It was Lynne Rosetto Kasper, host of the radio program *The Splendid Table,* who said we needed to go here; and while Lynne is best known as an expert on Italian food, this suggestion alone earns her an exalted chair in the Burger Lovers' Hall of Fame.

Hell's Kitchen

80 S. 9th St.   612-332-4700
Minneapolis, MN   BLD | $$

Our first visits to Hell's Kitchen were for breakfast—some of the best breakfasts anywhere. Every table is supplied with chef Mitch Omer's magnificent preserves and marmalade and extra-luxurious chunky peanut butter, which are themselves a compelling reason to eat at this downtown hot spot. Among the stars of the morning menu are huevos rancheros of the gods—a huge plate of food that includes spicy beans, eggs, cheeses, sour cream, and fresh salsa on a crisp flour tortilla. Rosti potatoes come alongside, too, and they are available as a dish unto themselves. Chef Omer's rostis are less like the Swiss spuds that are their namesake than they are glorified hash browns, the shreds of potato mixed with bacon, onions, chives, and scallions and grilled in sweet cream butter. A few other breakfast specialties: lemon ricotta hotcakes, extra-spicy maple-glazed bison sausage, and a quarter-pound caramel pecan roll featuring extra-crunchy pieces of nut and a refined glaze that is a sweet tooth's dream.

The most unusual and perhaps the most delicious dish on the breakfast menu is Mahnomin Porridge, a recipe that the promethean Mr. Omer came up with from reading trappers' accounts of native Cree Indian meals that featured wild rice. His version includes hazelnuts and cranberries and is topped with maple syrup and cream. What an amazing hot cereal!

The lunch menu is every bit as inviting. How about a walleye BLT made with cornmeal-dusted fillets and lemon tartar sauce instead of the homemade mayo the kitchen uses on its regular BLT? Who cannot love the ham and pear crisp sandwich on sourdough bread, draped with a mantle of Swiss and fontina cheeses? We instantly became addicted to the house Bread Bucket, which is all the chewy, freshly made baguette you can eat served along with sweet cream butter, Omer's preserves, and peanut butter.

Rather than rave on, let us simply say that if you are in Minneapolis and want to wow your taste buds, go to Hell's Kitchen. It is inspired and inspiring.

Lange's Café

110 8th Ave. SE
Pipestone, MN

507-825-4488
always open | $

The moment we walked into Lange's Café, we looked at the case of caramel rolls and knew we had hit pay dirt. And sure enough, as we ate our way through as much of the menu as possible, we swooned with pleasure over and over again. Beef is the entree not to miss. Listed as roast beef if it comes on a plate with mashed potatoes, green beans, and gravy, and as hot beef if it is served in a sandwich with mashed potatoes on top and gravy all over, it is pot roast—tender and deep-flavored. Mashed potatoes are the real thing; dinner rolls that come alongside are freshly baked.

The caramel rolls that so many people eat for breakfast must be sampled any time they are available. They are immense blocks of sweet, yeasty dough—about 3 inches square—and they are bathed in a buttery warm caramel syrup that has a burnt smack to its sweetness.

Now, we have saved the best for last: sour cream raisin pie. It's a specialty of bakers in Minnesota, Wisconsin, and Iowa, and over the years we have made it our business to sample every SCR pie we come across. Lange's is built upon a custard that is dense, packed with raisins, creamy, and sweet with the sour-cream edge that makes its sweetness all the more potent. Its meringue is air-light; the crust flakes when poked by a fork. It was our supremely lucky day, for we walked into Lange's about 10 A.M. and the pie had been out of the oven only a short while. Our pieces were faintly warm, like baby food, and as we ate, we declared this the best sour cream raisin pie ever made . . . 10 on a 1–10 scale . . . the crème de la crème . . . the Mother Lode.

Not too long after we included this great place in a previous edition of *Roadfood*, we got a note from Peg Lange saying, "We have breathed *new life* and commitment into our business: new sign, new canopy, new landscaping, new atrium glass, new display cabinet, and new uniforms." We're thrilled at the renaissance, but even more thrilled to report that the food hasn't changed at all. This is still southwestern Minnesota's premier Roadfood café.

Maverick's

1746 N. Lexington Ave.   651-488-1788
Roseville, MN   LD | $

Maverick's specialty is roast beef sandwiches: soft, pink, velvety slices cut to order and piled into a soft white bun while the meat is still hot and moist. Rick Nelson of the *Minneapolis Star-Tribune* told us that the restaurant concept was inspired by the proprietor's desire to improve on Arby's. If that was his goal, he has more than succeeded, for this is a super roast beef sandwich—simple, pure, and satisfying.

It is served cafeteria-style, along with a short menu of other beefy things, including brisket (offered on a dark pumpernickel bun) and barbecued beef, plus pulled pork, ham, chicken, and fish fillets. When we stopped by, open-face roast beef sandwiches were the day's special: the same good beef piled on a plate with the roll on the side and a couple of mounds of mashed potatoes. While the beef in this one was the same good beef as in the simple sandwich, we much preferred Maverick's crisp French fries to the ersatz mashed potatoes.

Ambience at this inconspicuous strip-mall eatery is that of a workman's café. Once you get your food, you stop by a condiment bar where the choices range from horseradish and horseradish cream to hot peppers, ketchup, mustard, and pickles. Then you find a place at one of the four-tops along the side of the room or at the long banquet table that runs down the middle. We walked out happy and satisfied.

Mickey's Dining Car

36 W. 7th St.   651-222-5633
St. Paul, MN   BLD | $

The best thing about Mickey's Dining Car is Mickey's Dining Car itself—a yellow-and-red enamel streamliner built by the Jerry O'Mahony company in 1937. Although it has been well used over decades of twenty-four-hour service, it is still in magnificent shape. Complementing the Deco dazzle of the diner (which is listed on the National Register of Historic Places) is a juke-box featuring Elvis and Del Shannon, and a staff of waiters and waitresses who have honed the art of service with a snarl. It's not mean service, and it's not bad service; in fact, it is efficient and polite . . . unless you are one of the frequent gawkers (we plead guilty) who come in to look around at the hand-some joint and its colorful regular denizens. We who are too preoccupied to place our order can swiftly and with no hesitation find ourselves at the mercy of the hash-slingers, one of whom once told us, in no uncertain terms, "A museum, it's not. You gonna eat or kick tires?"

We're not going to tell you that the cuisine at Mickey's Dining Car rates four stars. There are some things they serve that we wouldn't recommend at all. The pies, for example, are more easily identifiable by their color (red, yellow, blue) than by their designated ingredient (could it be fruit?).

On the other hand, breakfast is foursquare. Eggs are whipped up in a flash, blueberry buttermilk pancakes are pretty fine, and the hash brown potatoes are available O'Brien-style, meaning mixed with diced ham, onion, and green peppers. We like the French toast made from the diner's extra-thick white bread, and the morning special of pork chops or steak and eggs. While these chops bear little resemblance to the thick, tender ones you'll get for supper in a high-priced restaurant, they have a flavorful hash-house charm all their own. The milk shakes are real, blended to order. And how many other joints do you know that still offer mulligan stew?

Northern Waters Smokehaus

394 Lake Ave. S., Suite 106   218-724-7307
Duluth, MN   L | $

Before he came to Duluth, Eric Goerdt was a fisherman in Sitka, Alaska, where he perfected his techniques for smoking fish as well as meats. When you listen to him talk about the firm luxury of a hunk of salmon that has been hand-trimmed, marinated, and smoked over maple wood, you are hear-ing a man on a mission to make delicious smoked food. Mission accom-plished! His little smokery in the DeWitt-Seitz Marketplace in Canal Park is a culinary gem for passersby as well as lovers of smoked fish and meats who are willing to mail-order their favorites.

It is a tiny retail store with a few tables for sitting down and eating such fine sandwiches as bison shoulder braised in Schlitz and barbecue sauce on a bun, wild Alaskan sockeye gravlax with pickled ginger, vegetables, and wasabi mayonnaise on a baguette, and an insanely opulent gloss on the tra-ditional Reuben, this one made of hot bison pastrami, caramelized onions, pepperoncini, mayonnaise, and provolone on a crusty hard roll. We also treasure this place as a source of provisions. It is a secure feeling to hit the road with a stack of saltines and hunks of perfumy Lake Superior whitefish and smoked salmon for noshing between meals.

Tavern on Grand

656 Grand Ave.   651-228-9030
St. Paul, MN   LD | $$

Walleye sandwiches are a big deal in Minnesota, the best of them, no doubt, made at North Country campfires by walleye fishermen. For those who don't catch and cook their own, the place to go is Tavern on Grand in St. Paul.

Billing itself as "Minnesota's State Restaurant Serving Minnesota's State Fish," this friendly place will start you off with an appetizer of sautéed walleye cakes or a walleye basket of deep-fried bites. The sandwich is a fillet—grilled or fried—served on a length of French bread with tartar sauce that does a marvelous job of haloing the sweet meat of the lake fish. You can get a walleye plate for lunch (with steamed vegetables and red potatoes, known as a "shore lunch") or a walleye supper of one or two fillets with the works. There is even a Lakeshore Special that is a single fillet accompanied by a half-pound sirloin steak. On the side of almost anything, turkey wild rice soup is essential. To accompany your meal, there are beers galore, domestic and imported, on tap and by the bottle.

Tavern on Grand feels like the right place to enjoy a true Minnesota meal. It is designed to resemble a log cabin lodge in the woods, and no matter where you sit in the bar, you have a good view of one of the many TVs positioned for everyone to watch whatever game is currently broadcast. You'll know it by the big neon fish in the front window.

World's Best Donuts

10 E. Wisconsin St.   218-387-1345
Grand Marais, MN   BL mid-May to mid-Oct | $

"The only donut that has ever rivaled my late grandmother's donuts," wrote tipster Paul Swindlehurst, attributing the excellence of World's Best Donuts to its frying medium: lard. "Best when warm," Mr. Swindlehurst advised. Heeding his advice, we arrived shortly after the shop opened at 4:30 one spring morning. Amen and hallelujah! Still warm from the fryer, these circular sylphs are donut royalty. We were awestruck by the plain cake donut, a hand-cut beauty that is substantial but in no way leaden, sweet enough and yet with deep, savory satisfaction. Chocolate-frosted and cinnamon-sugar cake donuts are simple and unimprovable, and the locally loved skizzles (a.k.a. elephant ears), which are crisp-surfaced and featherweight, provide a great way to maximize the joy of lard-cooking.

Regulars keep their cups on the Mug Shelf so they can pour their own and sip while waiting in line to place an order. Travelers who become a registered donut eater (sign up for free) are entitled to a free donut when they return the next year.

Amighetti's

5141 Wilson
St. Louis, MO

314-776-2855
LD | $

Amighetti's is a serve-yourself sandwich shop that has become a beloved culinary institution on "The Hill," St. Louis's old Italian neighborhood. Eating here is casual and fun, especially on a pleasant summer day. Place your order at the window and wait for your name to be called. Find yourself a seat on the sunny patio, and feast on a legendary Italian sandwich. Right next door to the restaurant, Amighetti's bakes its own bread—a thick-crusted loaf with sturdy insides ready to be loaded with slices of ham, roast beef, Genoa salami, and cheese, garnished with shreds of lettuce and a special house dressing that is tangy-sweet. All kinds of sandwiches are available, including a garlicky Italian hero, roast beef, and a three-cheese veggie sandwich—all recommended primarily because of the bread on which they're served.

Each sandwich is wrapped in butcher paper secured by a tape inscribed with Amighetti's motto: *Often Imitated, Never Duplicated.*

Arthur Bryant's

1727 Brooklyn Ave.   816-231-1123
Kansas City, MO   LD | $$

Arthur Bryant used to shock reporters by calling his esteemed barbecue restaurant a "Grease House." Although the master of Kansas City barbecue
passed away in 1982, his business heirs, bless them, have never tried too hard
to shed that moniker. The "House of Good Eats" (another of Mr. Bryant's
appellations) remains a cafeteria-style lunch room with all the decorative
charm of a bus station. (There are branches at the Kansas City Speedway,
Ameristar Casino, and airport.)

Because Arthur Bryant and his brother Charlie hailed from Texas, it
makes sense that the smoked brisket—a Texas passion—is the best meat
in the house. It drips flavor. Have it in a sandwich or if you come as a
large party, order a couple of pounds of beef and a loaf of bread and make
your own at the table. Pork ribs are wonderful, too, glazed with blackened,
burnt edges and loads of meat below their spicy crust. Skin-on French fries
are bronze beauties and the goopy barbecue beans are some of Kansas
City's best.

What makes Arthur Bryant's unique is the sauce. It is beautiful—a gritty,
red-orange blend of spice and sorcery that is not at all sweet like most barbecue sauces. It packs a hot paprika wallop and tastes like a strange soul-food
curry, a nice complement to any meat. Once you've tasted it, you'll understand why this old Grease House is a foodie legend.

Booches

110 S. 9th   573-874-9519
Columbia, MO   LD | $

A billiard parlor/tavern where the beverages of choice are beer (in a bottle)
and iced tea (in a pitcher), or maybe Coke in a paper cup, Booches is a
magic name to hamburger aficionados. The hamburgers—known among
old-timers as "belly bombers"—are thick, juicy, and maddeningly aromatic,
served unceremoniously on a piece of wax paper. It is difficult to say what
exactly makes these hamburgers so especially delicious. They are normal-
size, available with or without cheese, and the condiments are standard-
issue onions, pickles, mustard, or ketchup; yet their smoky/meaty flavor
is extraordinary from first bite to last. In 1999, Booches won kudos from
the *Digital Missourian* as an especially earth-friendly eatery, not only because each hamburger is cooked to order (thus, no meat is wasted), but
because "no one can leave a Booches burger half-eaten."

Some of the food's charm is no doubt due to the offhand way in which it is served in colorful surroundings. Booches is the oldest pool hall in Columbia, and it is likely your burger—or good chili dog—will be eaten to the wooden clack of pool shooters as well as the noise of whatever sports event is blaring on the television. Decor is a combination of sports memorabilia, kudos from famous artists who have enjoyed the beer and burgers, and some delightful politically incorrect humor, including one sign that advises, "Parents . . . Keep your ankle-biting little crumb-gobblers on a leash or I will put them in the cellar to play with the rats."

C&K Barbecue

4390 Jennings Station Rd.	314-385-8100
St. Louis, MO	D | $

St. Louis has always been a great barbecue town; C&K represents the best of this tradition. It is a small, out-of-the-way former service station with no seating (all take-out) and late-night hours well suited to those of us who get a craving for ribs after midnight.

Ribs, rib tips, chopped meat, even chicken, all bathed in proprietor Darryle Brantley's exclamatory sauce, are served in Styro boxes with sweet potato salad and soft white bread that makes a good sponge for drippy extra sauce. These are extremely messy meals, so even though each order is packed with napkins, we recommend getting extras.

In addition to all the expected smokehouse specialties, C&K offers a few rarer items such as snoots (pig snouts baked until crisp and bathed in sauce) and ears (yes, pig ears, cooked until butter-soft and served between two slices of white bread, with or without sauce). These items are for the advanced barbecue connoisseur. We recommend the first-time visitor start with a slab of ribs!

Carl's Drive-In

9033 Manchester Rd.	314-961-9652
Brentwood, MO	LD (closed Sun & Mon) | $

A tiny sixteen-stool diner on old Route 66, Carl's is the place to belly up for elegant-oily hamburgers and foot-long hot dogs that stretch far beyond the bun and come smothered with chili. The burgers are mashed flat on the grill so that their edges turn into a crisp filigree of beef, and they are thin enough that a double or a triple makes good sense, as does the addition of cheese. Ketchup is supplied in small paper cups.

Burgers are the main attraction, but Carl's is also a source for three-way chili and tamales topped with chili or sauce. Shoestring French fries are a great companion for any meal, and the beverage of choice is house-brewed root beer drawn straight from the barrel, served in a frosted mug. (Root beer floats are not to be missed.)

Expect to wait for a seat at lunchtime. But not too long. The turnover is quick, and it is an amazing thing to watch the staff juggle cooking for sit-down customers, take-out customers, and customers whose orders come in via the house pay phone.

Crown Candy Kitchen

1401 St. Louis Ave.   314-621-9650
St. Louis, MO   LD | $

The Crown Candy Kitchen is an old-time sweet shop that makes its own chocolate candy and serves all kinds of malts, shakes, sodas, and sundaes. We are especially fond of the chocolate banana malted and the hot fudge malted, not to mention the excellent house policy of giving five malts free to anyone who can consume them in thirty minutes (except during the lunch-hour rush).

Other than superb ice cream treats, Crown has a nice lunch-counter repertoire of sandwiches, tamales, chili, and chili mac. Items of special interest from the kitchen are what the menu calls a Heart Stopping BLT, guaranteed to be made with Miracle Whip, and house-made chicken salad, available only on Tuesdays and Thursdays.

Goody Goody Diner

5900 Natural Bridge Ave.   314-383-3333
St. Louis, MO   BL | $

Breakfast is served all day (until closing mid-afternoon) Wednesday and Friday at Connelly's Goody Goody Diner, and other days only until 11 A.M. The menu is vast, ranging from omelets, breakfast sandwiches, pancakes, waffles, and French toast to boneless catfish fillets with eggs and one amazing dish known as the Wilbur. "We're bringing a popular St. Louis diner breakfast to Connelly's," the menu notes in its description of the Wilbur. Known in other local diners and chili parlors as a slinger, the Wilbur is an omelet filled with chili, fried potatoes, peppers, onions, and tomatoes. It is a soulful meal, profoundly satisfying . . . although not necessarily what we crave to eat early in the morning!

The chili that gives the Wilbur its avoirdupois can be ordered as a side dish. It is stout and salty, made with chunks of beef, and it is the fundamental element in a once-popular but now rare midwestern diner dish, chili mac. Goody Goody's chili mac is prepared with blunt hash-house style: well-cooked spaghetti noodles are topped with chili and crowned by a mass of shredded Cheddar cheese.

"We've changed many items on our menu over the years," the Goody Goody credo goes. "But the way we prepare our hamburgers will never change. They're not fancy—they're just *good*!" We agree. Regulars and doubles, patty melts and cheeseburgers, slawburgers and barbecue slawburgers are all outstanding, available with sides that include onion rings, French fries, cheese fries, and, of course, chili. Each burger is mashed down hard enough on the grill that it becomes a thin, rugged patty with a lacy-crisp circumference, its rugged nature nicely gentled by the soft yellow bun in which it is served.

Jess & Jim's

517 E. 135th St.　　　　　816-941-9499
Kansas City, MO　　　　　LD | $$$

Jess & Jim's, a Kansas City landmark that opened in 1938, is all about beef. This is apparent even from a distance when you spot the huge statue of a bull atop the roof of the restaurant. Steaks arrive from the kitchen exuberantly sputtering, crusty from an iron griddle. The top-of-the-line KC Playboy Strip is two inches thick, and unlike the super-tender bacon-wrapped filets, it demands some chewing. Not that it is tough, but neither is it a cut of meat for milquetoasts. Dense and intense, this is steak-lover's steak, which is not to say that the T-bones, porterhouse, and strips are anything less than excellent.

On the side of regal meat, excellent potatoes are essential. There are cottage fries, French fries, and immense bakers available, of course, with sour cream, bacon, and shredded cheese as condiments. The sleeper on the menu here is fried chicken. It's a reminder that as much as it is a beef lode, Kansas City is a serious fried chicken town.

Note: On weekends especially, this place gets very crowded. Call-ahead seating is available . . . and much advised.

LC's Barbeque

5800 Blue Pkwy.　　　　　816-923-4484
Kansas City, MO　　　　　LD | $$

It is a good thing that LC's sandwiches come in little trays, because they are so messy that no flat plate could contain them. An abundance of sauce-sopped meat comes piled onto a puny slice of white bread and topped with another slice. The bread underneath has disintegrated before it arrives at your table, so this sandwich cannot be lifted by hand. You either use plastic utensils or pick at it by hand. (All tables are outfitted with rolls of paper towels.)

Beef, ham, turkey, pork, sausage, and ribs are all expertly pit-cooked, and among the "specialty meats" on the menu is burnt ends. These are crisp, chewy, extra-luscious nuggets cut from the outside edges of smoked brisket. Many pieces are laced with an obscenely delicious amount of fat; there are chewy pieces and crunchy pieces; and while some of the ends might be dry all by themselves, LC's excellent sauce makes them sing.

Amenities are minimal. All dinnerware is disposable. A television set is always on in one corner of the room and a few dusty game-animal trophies adorn the walls. Place your order and pay for it at the counter, where you have a great view (and sniff) of the pit, and it will be delivered to your table posthaste.

Niecie's

5932 Prospect Ave.   816-444-6006
Kansas City, MO   BLD | $

Niecie's is a long-running soul-food café opened by Denise Griffin Ward in 1985. Since then it has become a sort of community center, and every morning except Sunday you can expect to see a table with a dozen or more Baptist and Holiness Church pastors gathered for breakfast and conversation. As we sat down in a booth one day, a couple nearby were praying over their fried pork chops before digging in.

We really like breakfast of chicken and waffles; in this case it is three jumbo wings, beautifully fried with lots of gnarled, crisp skin, along with a waffle and a big plastic jug of Hungry Jack syrup. Other breakfast choices include biscuits and gravy (we're not all that fond of the biscuits), pancakes, country ham, and eggs with grits on the side.

Among the daily lunch specials are salmon croquettes on Monday, a legendary smothered chicken Tuesday, short ribs Friday, and fried catfish Saturday. An every-day specialty of the house we highly recommend is Niecie's grilled wings. They're seasoned and cooked with onions and are powerfully flavorful. If you order them, expect a twenty- to thirty-minute wait.

The most exotic item on the menu, at least for those of us who don't have easy access to southern Midwest soul-food specialties, is the pig ear sandwich. "You get two ears!" beamed waitress Ms. Myra C., whose badge identified her as having nineteen years of service at Niecie's. Yes, indeed; it is two whole ears in a bun. We got ours with the works: lettuce, tomato, onion, and ultra-hot horseradish. We've got to admit that ears are a little scary, not so much because they're the worst part of the pig—there are plenty of parts that are far worse on the *ick!* scale. The problem is that they look exactly like what they are: large, pointy porker ears. Their taste is not objectionable—it's something like the fatty parts of bacon or streak o' lean—but the gelatinous texture is, to say the least, a little weird.

Snead's

1001 E. 171st St.   816-331-7979
Belton, MO   LD (closed Mon & Tues) | $$

Snead's is one of the greats, if not the greatest, among Kansas City barbecue restaurants. Its menu lists so many good things that it is impossible to sample all of them in one visit. At the top of list: beef and/or ham brownies, which are the crusty, smoky chunks stripped from the ends and tips of the meat. Order a sandwich or a plateful. They aren't as soft as the ordinary barbecue, but they fairly explode with the flavor of meat and smoke.

Snead's meats are cooked in large kettles in a brick pit fueled by hickory wood. The result is barbecue with supreme tenderness and powerful smoke flavor. Sliced pork does not pack the potency of brownies, but it is hugely satisfying and one of the softest foods on earth. Beef brisket is shockingly fatless; and even though it isn't dry, sauce is a natural companion. Snead's offers two variations: a slightly sweet mild sauce and a vigorously peppery orange brew that is reminiscent of Arthur Bryant's, not at all sweet. Then there are log sandwiches, named for their shape: tubular mixtures of finely ground barbecued beef, pork, and ham, all minced together and wedged into a long bun. The result is a salty, powerful mélange reminiscent of a Maid-Rite. On the side: hand-cut, freshly made French fries, barbecue beans, and finely chopped coleslaw that is perfectly suited to brightening a fatigued tongue.

A low, rustic dining room decorated with quilts, farmy pictures, and a small collection of vintage wooden coat hangers, Snead's is way out in the country where urban sprawl hasn't yet arrived. One customer with whom we chatted recalled coming here as a child when the place opened in the mid-1950s on the corner of Bill Snead's farm.

Stroud's

5410 NE Oak Ridge Dr.   816-454-9600
Kansas City, MO   D Mon–Thurs, LD Fri & Sun,
                               Sat open from 2 P.M. | $$

Stroud's location on Oak Ridge Drive lacks the tumbledown charm of the original restaurant Mrs. Stroud opened in the 1930s on the location of the family fireworks stand, but in some ways the modern restaurant is even better: an expansive frontier farmhouse with dining tables overlooking green grass on the rolling countryside. What better spot on earth could there be to enjoy the ultimate fried chicken dinner?

The chicken is slow-sizzled in an iron skillet, emerging with a coat of gold that is noisy to crunch and not the least bit bready; there is just enough of it to shore in all the juices. Once you break through, those juices flow down chin and fingers and forearm. You become an unsightly mess, but you don't care because the juices are ambrosia. Chicken is the lodestone; around it are a constellation of side dishes straight from heaven's table. Pour some peppery cream gravy onto the thick white cloud of mashed potatoes, tear off a piece of warm, buttery cinnamon roll, spoon into lovely chicken soup with homemade noodles. All exemplary. Even the green beans, which passed al dente long ago, pack a surprising porky sparkle.

Meals are served family-style. Stroud's is hugely popular and most of the time you will have to wait for a table, then wait while your chicken is fried. You will be glad you did.

Second location: 4200 Shawnee Mission Pkwy., Fairway, Kansas; 913-262-8500.

Ted Drewes

6726 Chippewa   314-481-2652
St. Louis, MO   (closed in winter) | $

For anyone in search of America's most delicious ice cream (and who is not?), here's a name to put on the short list of candidates for greatness: Ted Drewes. Technically, Drewes's product is not ice cream. It is frozen custard, meaning it is egg-rich and ultra-creamy. There's nothing more purely dairy-delish than the vanilla, but you can mix it with your choice from a list of dozens of different flavoring agents from chocolate and strawberry to fudge, cherries, cookies, nuts, and candy bars.

The best-known dish in the house is called a Concrete, which is a milk shake so thick that the server hands it out the order window upside down, demonstrating that not a drop will drip out! Beyond Concretes, there are sundaes, cones, floats, and sodas.

Ted Drewes has two locations (the second is at 4224 S. Grand; 314-352-7376), both of them mobbed all summer long with happy customers spooning into huge cups full of the creamy-smooth delight. In autumn, the custard operation closes and Ted goes into the Christmas tree business.

If you are far away and seriously crave this superb super–ice cream (as is the case for many St. Louis expatriates), Ted Drewes is equipped with dry ice to mail-order its custard anywhere you need it.

Al's Corner Restaurant

545 W. Tuscarawas Ave.   L Mon–Fri | $
Barberton, OH

This immaculate storefront luncheonette, open only for weekday lunch, is a treasure trove of blue-plate Hungarian meals at blue-collar prices. Service is cafeteria-style. Step to the right when you enter and there Beth Gray will show you what's to eat, put it on a plate, and then on a tray. Dine either at a table or at the long U-shaped counter in the center of the room.

Lunch specials, at well under $10 each, include the likes of chicken paprikash with dumplings, pierogies, cabbage and dumplings, and Al's sausages. The sausages are made down the street at Al's Quality Market, and they are stupendously delicious: taut, muscular, and oozing savory juices. Jane, whose father was a Hungarian epicure and taught her well, declared the paprikash to be one of the best she ever ate: creamy with a real paprika punch, the chicken falling-off-its-bone tender. The only problem we had was deciding which starch to eat more of: the dumplings are buttery and satisfying; the mashed potatoes are . . . buttery and satisfying, too!

Note: Al's has no phone, but the number of Al's Quality Market, at 563 W. Tuscarawas Ave., is 330-753-7216. Carry-out orders may be placed at this number.

Babushka's Kitchen

9199 Olde Eight Rd.   330-468-0402

Northfield Center, OH   LD | $$

For those just passing through, a visit to Babushka's can be hugely frustrating. This Polish restaurant between Akron and Cleveland has so many good things on the menu that even a party of four who each order something different will miss out on great specialties.

Do you start with legendary *czernina* soup, a sweet-and-sour brew made with duck, prunes, and dumplings and served in a charming little ramekin with a bird on its lid? Or chicken soup with *kluski* noodles? Or stuffed cabbage soup? Or tomato dumpling soup? Of course, you must have pierogies, but these are so huge that two make a meal. Do you have them filled with potato and Cheddar? Roasted sauerkraut? Sweet dry cottage cheese? On the side of dinner, how can one choose a single item from the likes of sauerkraut and dumplings, cabbage and noodles, classic cucumber salad, and real mashed potatoes with roast pork gravy?

Among Babushka's special dinners, we do highly recommend one called the Warsaw, which is a heap of sinfully tender roast pork mixed with grilled onions, sauerkraut, and gravy sandwiched between two potato pancakes with a big crown of sour cream. Smoked kielbasa—made here, of course—is firm and juicy, so well accompanied by kraut and dumplings. (Unsmoked fresh kielbasa also is available.) And if you like stuffed cabbage, you must get Babushka's. These *golabki,* enveloped in a rich sweet-and-sour tomato gravy, set the standard.

On a rural road not too far from a main artery lined by soulless fast-food outlets, Babushka's feels like another world. It is a simple place with homespun charm. Service is informal: Read the menu on the wall, place your order at the counter, and find a seat to which the kitchen staff brings the meal when it is ready. For those in search of food with a real connection to local culture, it's a gem. The house slogan is "Revive your memories and reunite your family."

Balaton

13133 Shaker Square   216-921-9691

Cleveland, OH   LD (closed Mon) | $$

Great Hungarian food is one of Cleveland's culinary treasures, and there is no better place to enjoy that fact than at a table in the Balaton. Located in a storefront that was once a men's clothing store, the magnificent little restaurant first opened on Buckeye Road in 1964. The current location, since

1997, is a lovely space that has the feel of a long-standing European café without airs, the family that operates it very much on hand and making sure everything runs smoothly.

Meals are abundant (half-orders of most items are available), but it is quality, not quantity, that makes the Balaton superior. Wiener schnitzels are crunch-crusted and moist inside; paprikash (chicken or veal) is brightly spiced and luxurious; goulash is comfort food supreme. We were especially smitten with Hungarian *lecso,* a gorgeous length of smoked sausage served atop a stew of yellow peppers, tomatoes, and onions. And the potato pancakes? Fantastic! They arrive hot and crisp, the freshly shredded spuds shot through with a subtle pepper kick. Chunky applesauce comes on the side.

Desserts include a classic multilayer *dobos* tort, flaky strudel, and *palas-cinke,* which are slim crepes rolled around apricot or poppy-seed filling.

Balyeat's Coffee Shop

131 E. Main St.   419-238-1580
Van Wert, OH   BLD (closed Mon) | $

Fried chicken stars on Balyeat's menu, but good though it may be, it is just the headliner on a menu that is an honor roll of mid-American square meals. Here is a place to sit down for a plate of roast pork or roast beef, cooked that morning, served hot and large, with piles of mashed potatoes and gravy. Sauerkraut and sausage is on the menu every day but Friday, and you can usually count on a choice from among barbecued ribs, meat loaf, and liver and onions. If mashed potatoes don't ring your chimes, how about the fine alternative, escalloped potatoes?

Ahh, dessert! Pie is king in this part of the world, and Balyeat's pies are pastries to behold. There are cream pies, fruit pies, custard pies, and pecan pie; our personal favorite is the one known as "old-fashioned pie" (O.F. pie). It is like custard, but tawnier, and with a sort of layered effect that happens as its cream rises to the top. It is pure, simple, and utterly satisfying: culinary synecdoche for Balyeat's Coffee Shop.

Belgrade Gardens

401 E. State St.   330-745-0113
Barberton, OH   D | $$

Barberton chicken, served at a handful of restaurants in the Akron suburb, is cooked in lard. Dark meat, even white meat, is drippingly juicy; its red-gold crust crunches just before it dissolves into pure savory flavor that further enhances the luxury of the moist bird it had enveloped. Belgrade Gardens, which opened in 1933 and is now a huge, happy function hall, is the original source of Barberton chicken, and while the menu is vast—including steaks, chops, seafood, sandwiches, and some really good chicken paprikash—first-time visitors need to get the full chicken dinner. You can get white or dark meat or a combination or a plate of nothing but legs, thighs, backs, wings, or tenders. Each is available small, medium, and large.

In restaurants throughout the area, chicken is the focal point of a ritual feast that also includes a bowl of spicy tomato-rice hot sauce that is positively addictive. At a table near ours, a woman was telling her friends that she used to come to Belgrade Gardens every week. "My mother would always take home hot sauce to try to duplicate the recipe," she said. "She came close, but Father never allowed that she had done it." In addition to the sauce, you get a timbale of sweet coleslaw, and a fistful of French fries plus a basket of white and dark bread.

Camp Washington Chili Parlor

3005 Colerain Ave.   513-541-0061
Cincinnati, OH   BLD | $

Camp Washington sets the standard for Cincinnati's unique style of chili—an edible layered hillock of limp spaghetti noodles topped by vividly spiced ground beef, then kidney beans, raw onions, and, finally, a fluffy crown of shredded Cheddar cheese. Oyster crackers are used as a garnish and one traditional side dish is a Coney Island hot dog topped with chili, cheese, and onions.

The other notable Queen City specialty on Camp Washington's menu is the double-decker sandwich, the basic principle of which is similar to five-way chili: layered ingredients as impressive for looks as for multileveled tastes. Possible double-decker ingredients range from eggs and breakfast meats to roast beef, ham, and cheese. Theoretically, it requires no utensils. While half of a well-made one can indeed be picked up in two hands, it cannot be eaten like a normal sandwich, i.e., all strata going into the mouth at one time. It must be nibbled at, top to bottom, or bottom to top, in such a way that some bites are more the top layer and others more the bottom.

While proprietor John Johnson has expanded and modernized the open-all-night restaurant since taking over from his uncle and a partner in 1977, he has—bless his soul—maintained the welcoming, democratic spirit of a great American urban diner.

Crabill's

727 Miami St.   513-653-5133

Urbana, OH   L | $

Thick, heavy hamburgers are great. But they're just one sort of greatness. Another is the minuscule slider. Once an accursed branch of hash-house gastronomy, the griddle-fried micropatty has become strangely fashionable, as in the Kobe beef sliders we've encountered as hors d'oeuvres in striving restaurants. You'll even come across non-beef so-called sliders made of crab cakes and tuna tartare. Let us assure you that the sliders you will eat at Crabill's are not trendy or upscale, and they are, as tradition demands, made of ordinary hamburger beef (and optional ordinary cheese) on spongy little buns. They're addictive and delicious. Eating one (that's about two bites' worth) is a unique experience: Cooked in deep oil on the grill, it has an outside surface with formidable crunch, and it is so skinny that there is virtually no interior! Six or eight make a decent meal, but if you have a competitive spirit, you might want to try to beat the record currently held by Hank Carpenter of thirty-three singles in one sitting.

Flury's Sandwich Shop

1300 Sackett Ave.   330-929-1315

Cuyahoga Falls, OH   BL | $

This tiny diner seats scarcely over a dozen people and there is nothing revolutionary on the menu, but if you are in greater Akron and looking for a hospitable slice of Americana, we highly recommend it. There is always a pancake of the day—we enjoyed cornmeal and banana-nut—and lunch opportunities include meat loaf sandwiches and mac 'n' cheese, preceded by proprietor Kim Dunchuck's homemade soup. For dessert, choose from among Kim's homemade cookies and shortcake laced with blueberries or blackberries.

Freddie's Southern Style Rib House

1431 Saint Clair Ave. NE   216-575-1750

Cleveland, OH   LD | $

Oh, yes, the ribs are very good at Freddie's—meaty bones with plenty of chew that delivers big pig flavor, dramatically enhanced by Freddie's sweet-hot-spicy-tangy sauce. And the wings are eye-opening. But it is for the Polish Boy we recommend a visit. A sandwich unique to the soul-food restaurants of Cleveland, the Polish Boy depends on excellent barbecue sauce to bring its dramatically disparate elements all together. Its central ingredient is a length of kielbasa that Freddie's cooks until its skin turns crisp while the inside stays pink and juicy. The sausage is enclosed in a big, spongy white bun along with a fistful of French fries, the unwieldy package generously blanketed with sauce. Incredibly, most regular customers do not use utensils to eat this sandwich. They actually pick the thing up in their hands as French fries fall and sauce seeps from inside the bun.

Freddie's is dark and tavernous, a rather disheveled place that might not win any awards for restaurant design or decor but nonetheless is a beacon for sandwich connoisseurs from around the country.

G&R Tavern

103 N. Marion St. (off US Route 23) 740-726-9685
Waldo, OH   BLD | $

Since 1962, the G&R Tavern has built its reputation on bologna sandwiches that put pale, thin-sliced supermarket bologna to shame. In this family-friendly sports bar, the bologna is dark and smoky, firm as a knoblewurst salami, and sliced as thick as a good-size hamburger patty. It is fried until its exterior turns crisp, then loaded into a sandwich with sweet pickles and onion (a great condiment combo) or your choice of mustard, mayonnaise, or tomato. Fitting side dishes include a variety of deep-fried vegetables and curly fries.

If for some reason you are a fried-food-frowner, G&R also offers a bologna salad sandwich, and because this bologna is so much better than the spongy packaged stuff, the salad reminds us of something made with good ham, but smoother.

Hathaway's Coffee Shop

441 Vine St.   513-621-1332
(in the Carew Tower Arcade)   BL | $
Cincinnati, OH

Here's a good Cincinnati breakfast for you: Hathaway's French toast, bright with cinnamon flavor and dusted with powdered sugar and splotched with melting butter. On the side, the locally loved pork-and-pin-oats loaf known as *goetta,* sliced thin and fried crisp. To drink: a bottomless cup of coffee, never allowed below half-full by the watchful waitstaff.

Located on the first level of Carew Tower, Hathaway's is one of an endangered species: the downtown coffee shop. Seating is at one of three U-shaped counters or at a steel-banded dinette table against the wall. In addition to plate lunch, sandwiches, and well-respected hamburgers, there's a full soda fountain menu of sundaes and banana splits, plus traditional malts and yogurt shakes. These latter include a banana whisk, a pink cloud (made with strawberries), and a crème sickle (orange juice and milk). The yogurt shakes evoke an era when yogurt was an alternative to normal food. The menu touts them as "Healthful Pick Me Uppers," for when one needs that sweet supercharge in the middle of the shopping day.

Henry's

6275 Route 40   614-879-9321
West Jefferson, OH   LD | $

No traveler in a hurry wants to be on Highway 40, the side road parallel to I-70, but anyone with an appetite for home cooking needs to make the detour. Here, set back from the south side of the road, is what looks to be a defunct gas station. The pumps are long gone, but the on-premises restaurant is alive and well—a slice of Roadfood heaven.

The meals are country-style fare: baked ham, hot roast pork sandwiches with mashed potatoes and gravy, creamed chipped beef on corn bread. But it's not the savories that put this unlikely knotty-pine-paneled roadside café on the map. It is pie. Here are some of the best pies in Ohio, in the Midwest, anywhere. Every day, baker Shelley Kelly has a list of six or eight she has made: peach, banana, chocolate, peanut butter, cherry, coconut, etc. The butterscotch pie is thick and dense, full-flavored the way only real (not from a mix) butterscotch can be, and it comes topped with a creamy meringue. Custard pie is modestly thin, a sunny yellow wedge dusted with nutmeg. It is balmy, lightweight, melt-in-the-mouth tender. The flavor of the rhubarb pie is as brilliant as the bright summer sun, intensely fruity, sweet but not cloying, and balanced by a crust that flakes into luscious shards.

Kennedy's B.B.Q.

1420 7th St. NW   330-454-0193
Canton, OH   L | $

Relish the relish! Whichever barbecued meat you get in your sandwich at Kennedy's, you must get it topped with cabbage relish. Vaguely similar to the sort of slaw that goes into a pig sandwich in the South, but more pickly than sweet, it is bright and refreshing, an especially good partner for pork. And oh, what lovely pork this is: butter-tender with occasional chewy shreds, it is piled so high and huge in a bun that well over half the sandwich must be eaten with a fork or fingers. That much tumbles out if you try to lift it by hand.

Other pit-cooked meat choices are ham (fabulous), beef (yet to be tried), and turkey (not impressive). The rest of the menu is chili and bean soup. Plus corn bread and Amish pies. That's the extent of it. The connoisseur's choice, other than a sandwich, is a bowl of bean soup loaded with chunks of pit ham and crowned with crumbled corn bread.

A Canton landmark since 1922, when it opened as Spiker's, the pint-size eatery was bought and renamed in 1960 by Jack Kennedy, who ran it for forty-nine years. After Mr. Kennedy died in 2009, it was taken over by Ernie Schott, proprietor of Canton's superb Taggart's Ice Cream Parlor. Mr. Schott extended the lunch hour to 5 P.M. but otherwise made no changes in the time-honored formula.

Liberty Gathering Place

111 N. Detroit St.   937-465-3081
West Liberty, OH   BLD | $

"We have girls who come in at four in the morning to make the coleslaw and macaroni salad," a Gathering Place waitress boasted when we asked if the side dishes were good. "Good" turned out to be not a good enough word to describe them, for the little bowl of macaroni salad set before us was inspired: blue-ribbon, church-supper, Independence-Day-picnic fabulous! It was creamy with a pickle zip, dotted with hunks of hard-cooked egg and a few crunchy shreds of carrot, the noodles themselves cooked just beyond al dente but not too soft.

Noodle rapture proved to be a paradigm for the dining experience at what appears to be a typical Main Street café but is in fact an extraordinary one. During a week we spent in Dayton having suppers at the Pine Club, the Gathering Place became our destination lunch stop for moist ham loaf and deep-flavored smoked pork chops sided by mashed potatoes and breadcrumb-enriched escalloped corn. We were astounded by the fried tenderloin sandwich—totally unlike the brittle-crisp, foot-wide 'loins typical of Midwest cafés. Here, the tenderloin is a thick pork steak with only hint of crust—a slab of meat that is folded over inside the bun so you get a double layer of pork as juicy as a pair of chops. For dessert, we had cool coconut and peach crunch pie, the latter served hot and veined with melted butter.

Little Polish Diner

5772 Ridge Rd.   440-842-8212
Parma, OH   LD | $

The name of the Little Polish Diner is not a cute affectation. It is really little: six counter stools and five tables in a space about the size of a walk-in closet. And it is really Polish, too. Its motto: "Our food is just like mom used to make." How we wish we had a mom who made such fine pierogi (big buttery filled dumplings), *golumbki* (stuffed cabbage), and marvelous pork-and-kraut *bigos* (hunter's stew).

We happened to stop in on a Wednesday, when the special lunch was a Warsaw Combination Plate consisting of a crisp breaded boneless pork chop, a stuffed cabbage glistening with sweet-tart sauce, a serving of *bigos,* and mashed potatoes. The soup of the day was chicken noodle, which was homey to the nth degree, filled with shreds of savory dark meat and spoonfuls of vegetables. We also got what the menu calls a Polish Boy—a length of kielbasa with sauerkraut in a roll; the sausage was bursting with juice and flavor. We want to return on a Saturday, when the special is chicken paprikash with potato dumplings and cucumber salad.

New Era Cafe

10 Massillon Rd.   330-784-0087
Akron, OH   LD | $

Since 1938, the New Era Cafe has been a gathering place for Canton Serbs and others who like Serbian food. The well-weathered old facility was replaced in 2005 by a somewhat sterile, spanking-new building; but even if architectural charm is lacking, the staff remains avatars of old-world charm and, more important, the kitchen continues to serve classic Middle European fare of the highest order.

"Where do you get your strudel?" we asked a young waitress when it came time to order dessert. She looked at us like we were crazy and pointed to the New Era kitchen. "We get it from there," she answered. "My grandmother makes it." It might be the best strudel in a city with many fine pastry chefs, its multiple layers of skin ineffably flaky, the warm apple compote at its heart sweet like ripe fruit, not like sugar.

Paprikash is the house specialty. Unlike the more common Hungarian versions that are creamy rich, this paprikash is more a thin broth, insinuating its pepper flavor into the velvety little dumplings that surround pieces of chicken on the plate. Roast duck with stuffing and mashed potatoes is worthy of a holiday feast. *Cevapi,* skinless Serbian sausages with a good chaw and a pepper bite, come either five or ten to an order and are wonderful sided by the kitchen's genuine mashed potatoes and rich brown gravy as well as a scattering of crisp chopped onion. Meals come with bakery-fresh bread, and the beverage list includes frighteningly dark Turkish coffee.

New Sandusky Fish Company

235 East Shoreline Dr.	419-621-8263
Sandusky, OH	LD | $

Virtuoso Roadfooders Bruce Bilmes and Sue Boyle turned us on to this little take-out-only shack that offers sandwiches and whole dinners at single-digit prices. Located on Lake Erie's southern shore, it boasts fresh yellow perch and walleye fried to golden-crusted tenderness and piled into buns with abandon, as well as catfish and bass fillets. Frog legs are available at dinner along with fries, onion rings, hush puppies, etc.

Many customers are anglers who bring their catch here to have it cleaned (in a building out back) and have a sandwich while they wait. While all business is take-out, we travelers who prefer outside-the-car dining will find nice bench seats in a gazebo across the street.

The Pine Club

1926 Brown St.	937-228-7463
Dayton, OH	D | $$$

The Pine Club is paradise for meat eaters. You have your choice of filet mignon, porterhouse, or sirloin, each cut and aged on premises and cooked on a grill so the outside gets a good dark crunch but the inside is still swollen with juice. Perhaps even more wonderful than steak is chopped steak, made from a mix of prime beef and dry-aged lamb, its succulence as luxurious as steak tartare, but with the added pleasures of all that released gravy and a crusty skin.

Regulars know to begin a meal with scallops—sweet, firm nuggets with a pale light crust and smoldery sea taste. All meals are served with a basket of dinner rolls, and steaks come with a handful of onion rings and choice of potatoes that includes Lyonnaise: a crunchy, plate-wide pancake of shredded 'taters woven with veins of sautéed onion. As for salad, although a mesclun mix was added to the menu a while ago, the traditional Pine Club salad is iceberg lettuce—cold, crisp chunks served "red and bleu," which is French dressing loaded with enormous clods of dry blue cheese.

Dessert? There is none. If you're in dire need of something sweet and don't necessarily want a high-proof libation such as a grasshopper or a

Golden Cadillac, you can step outside and go next door to the Ben & Jerry's store.

The Pine Club is a true Midwest supper club, open only in the evening, until midnight on weekdays, 1 A.M. on Friday and Saturday. No reservations, no credit cards, no nonsense.

Putz's Creamy Whip

Putz Place & West Fork Rd.   513-681-8668
Exit 17 off I-74   LD (closed in winter) | $
Cincinnati, OH

Putz's is a drive-up stand with a menu of hot dogs, foot-longs, burgers, and barbecue, but everybody comes for the custard. It is smooth and rich, an ivory-hued soft-serve product that is great swirled into a sugar cone or waffle cone or heaped into a cup and enjoyed for its pure, creamy goodness. Or you can have it whipped up for an extra-thick milk shake or malt or mixed into a soda.

The best way to enjoy it, in our opinion, is in a sundae or banana split, the latter made in a long plastic boat that holds three mounds of ice cream plus all the toppings. Sundaes are medium-size plastic cups filled with custard and topped with whatever you like. Best of all sundaes is the turtle, for which the bottom of the cup is filled with caramel, the caramel is topped with custard, then the custard topped with chocolate syrup. The chocolate syrup is mounded with whipped cream, chopped nuts, and a cherry.

Putz's is just off the highway in a little grove all its own (on a street that was rechristened to honor the longtime favorite destination–dessert place). There are pleasant picnic tables alongside that are an ideal place to spoon into creamy-whip perfection.

Slyman's Restaurant

3106 St. Clair Ave.   216-621-3760
Cleveland, OH   BL (closed Sat & Sun) | $$

A vintage Near East Side deli where the corned beef slicing machine never stops, Slyman's is open only for breakfast and lunch, the morning menu including a dandy corned beef, egg, and cheese breakfast sandwich. At lunch, there's a full menu but corned beef stars—on rye, of course. The sandwich is very big, the meat sliced thin. It is extremely tender and somewhat lean, lacking the lasciviousness of fatty hunks of corned beef. That is exactly why Slyman's Rueben is so popular. The addition of cheese and sauerkraut, plus a crisp crust of griddled rye, adds the reckless luxury that lean beef does not deliver.

Culturally, this is an interesting place. The menu includes a long list of slang unique to Slyman's sandwich-makers. Mummy = mustard + mayonnaise. Special K = hold the sauerkraut. Cake = mayonnaise + horseradish. Grill Brick = grilled bread only. Waitresses are all business, and the guys behind the counter are full of joie de vivre. The menu is classic Jewish deli, but brochures at the cash register invite customers to know Allah better and the menu includes praise to Jesus in the form of a reference to John 3:16.

Sokolowski's University Inn

1201 University Rd.   216-771-9236
Cleveland, OH   L (D Fri & Sat) | $$

What hungry person could not be happy walking along the cafeteria line of this 1923-vintage tavern in Cleveland's Tremont district and gazing upon beautiful pans full of pierogi, kielbasa, sauerkraut, breaded lake fish, and stuffed cabbage? The hearty Polish food is of high quality and dished out with good cheer in abundance. Pierogies are the most famous dish in the house, and they are awesome: big, tender pockets filled with cheese and smothered in the onions with which they were sizzled in butter until the onions turned caramel-soft and sweet. The kielbasa is as buff as a sausage can be, nearly too muscular for the flimsy cafeteria knife and fork provided, and it delivers megatons of smoky, piggy, spicy flavor. We especially like the balance of Sokolowski's *halushka,* which is a mix of salubrious sautéed cabbage and little squiggles of dumpling. On Friday nights, the menu features beer-battered cod and Lake Erie perch, plus live piano music. Sokolowski's is open for supper only on Friday and Saturday nights, when the menu expands to include grilled rainbow trout, prime rib, and chicken paprikash.

To drink, you can pluck a bottle of beer from one of the coolers, which feature all kinds, domestic and exotic, and there is Vernors ginger ale on tap. For dessert, we love the egg custard pudding dotted with fat grains of rice.

A hale, rollicking place. Our first visit was a few weeks before Christmas, when the sound system throbbed with familiar carols and holiday songs, all with a polka beat. In addition to the usual welcome signs in Polish and countless pictures of the celebrities who have come to enjoy this landmark restaurant, effigies of Santa and his elves were everywhere.

Swensons

18 S. Hawkins Ave.   330-864-8416
Akron, OH   LD | $

Pull into a space and flash your lights. Out sprints a curb boy to take your order. King of the menu is the Galley Boy, a double cheeseburger dressed with two sauces, one mayonnaisey with bits of onion added, the other zesty barbecue. Optional condiments include ketchup, relish, sweet pickles, horse-radish, Worcestershire, Tabasco, cocktail, honey mustard, tartar, and Cajun spice. Garnish choices are tomato, lettuce, olives, grilled onions, hot peppers, bacon, Coney sauce, and coleslaw. It's a drippy, fully satisfying drive-in burger.

Beyond hamburgers, the menu lists a quarter-pound all-beef bologna sandwich, salads, soups, fried chicken, and shrimp. Among the beverages are milk shakes and malts, something called a California (reminded us of Kool-Aid), and half-and-half (tea and lemonade). French fries, which we didn't try, are listed as "Only Idaho's," the dubious apostrophe apparently having migrated from the restaurant name, Swensons, which doesn't contain one on the outdoor sign or menu.

Swensons has no indoor seats. Meals to be eaten here are presented on sturdy trays that clip onto the inside of car windows in such a way that it's possible to dine in comfort even when it's raining.

Taggarts Ice Cream

1401 Fulton Rd. NW   330-452-6844
Canton, OH   LD | $

Taggarts hot fudge is not too thick nor intensely sweet. It is the consistency of chocolate syrup, deeply fudgy-flavored, served just warm enough to dramatically pair with cool ice cream. Although Taggarts is an ingenuous midwestern ice cream parlor that goes back to the early twentieth century, there is something sophisticated about this hot fudge. Elegant. Suave. It just might be the best hot fudge on the planet.

You'll get whipped cream on a Taggarts hot fudge sundae and that is crowned with a bright red maraschino cherry, but the real cherry atop these soda fountain marvels are spills of pecan halves. They are roasted to a crisp, which brings out their buttery richness, and they are salted with enough brio to provide an ideal savory halo for fudge and ice cream. The only possible improvement on the package is to make it a turtle sundae, which adds caramel sauce, or a banana split.

Great as the sundaes are, the signature concoction of Taggarts's fountain

is something else, known as a Bittner. Invented in the 1930s when a customer dared the staff to make a milk shake so thick that a spoon would stand
upright in it, the Bittner is three-quarters of a pound of vanilla ice cream
blended with chocolate syrup and heaped with those good roasted pecans.

Beyond sundaes, shakes, malts, floats, sodas, coolers, and ice cream pies,
Taggarts offers a full menu of sandwiches, burgers, hot dogs, soups, and
salads. We've tried the wonderfully old-fashioned olive-nut cream cheese
on toast, as well as a grilled cheese sandwich with bacon, and both were
great. But it's hard to pay attention to the main course when dessert is so
compelling.

White House Chicken

180 Wooster Rd. N.   330-745-0449
Barberton, OH   LD | $$

White House chicken is for skin-lovers. Each piece is enveloped in a chewy,
spicy, super-savory coat so thick that the meat inside—white as well as
dark—yields no juice until the envelope is breached. While we would hesitate to call any chicken too juicy, the soft, moist meat simply cannot compete
with the assertive crust around it. In fact, nice as the meat is, we find that
a full plate of this fine chicken with the works, which in Barberton means
French fries, spicy rice, coleslaw, and bread, has so much of that good, red-
gold skin on it that we might leave meat behind just to make sure we get all
the really good stuff.

Aside from a judicious shot of seasoning, what makes White House
chicken skin such a marvel is that the frying medium is lard, insinuating
every bite with wanton luxe. Like all the Barberton chicken houses, White
House cuts its bird the old-fashioned way: into wing, drumette, breast, leg,
thigh, and back, an economical technique left over from Depression days
when cooks tried to maximize the number of pieces they could get from
one bird. When you sink your teeth into a piece, you may find meat where
you don't expect it or not enough meat where you want it (in the back), but
who cares, when the additional pieces mean more of that can't-stop-eating
skin.

The original location is a big white corner building with a neighborhood-
tavern feel. The last time we ate here, a kindly old lady walking out the door
smiled at us, poked a finger in our direction, and said, "You found it!" We
have yet to visit any of the other Akron-area locations of the White House,
which apparently is looking to franchise nationally.

White Turkey Drive-In

388 E. Main Rd.   440-593-2209
Conneaut, OH   LD Mother's Day–Labor Day | $

"If you find yourself along Lake Erie in the northeast corner of Ohio, pull into the White Turkey, a seriously vintage drive-in." So wrote a Roadfood tipster in a note with no return address and no ID. So we don't really know who to thank for this suggestion, but we sure would like to! This Richardson's Root Beer stand is a quintessential Roadfood stop along old US 20, offering seats at high stools where you can feel a lake breeze and watch the cars cruise past while you dine on true mid-American, mid-century drive-in fare. Its namesake turkey sandwich is the real thing. No compressed loaf here! You can get a plain one or a Large Marge, which also includes cheese and bacon. Beyond turkey, there are Big Ed one-third-pound burgers, hot dogs, and chili cheese dogs.

While only one flavor of ice cream is available—vanilla—the variety of soda fountain drinks and desserts is mesmerizing. Of course there are cones, shakes, and malts; there are sundaes topped with your choice of pineapple, cherry, chocolate, hot fudge, butterscotch caramel fudge, strawberry, grasshopper, or mint. You can get a black cow (here, a blend of root beer and ice cream). And the root beer floats are divine, available in sizes from kiddie (80¢) to Super Shuper, created with a quart of root beer and a quantity of ice cream to match.

Young's Jersey Dairy

6880 Springfield-Xenia Rd.   937-325-0629
Yellow Springs, OH   BLD | $

There's something for everyone at Young's Jersey Dairy: a goat-petting zoo, a farm-themed gift shop, a miniature golf course (Udders and Putters), picnic grounds where you can have catered meals, summertime wagon rides around the farm, a serious restaurant (just up the road) that serves local produce, identified by which farm it came from, and a June-to-October art exhibit of statuary cows painted by local artists. A few years back, a gourmet coffee shop was added, offering espresso drinks, gelato, and wireless Internet access. All great stuff, but for us, Young's will always be the place to get a milk shake.

Using ice cream and milk from their own farm, Young's blends regular shakes and extra-thick shakes (spoon required), as well as bullshakes that are extra-large, extra-thick, and come with one additional scoop of ice cream floating on top. There are exotic flavors galore, but give us a vanilla or chocolate shake every time, preferably with plenty of malt powder added. There's none better. The dairy store counter is also a fine source of sundaes, banana splits, and bowls of ice cream from a choice of more than two dozen flavors. And you can have a nice little meal here, too: breakfast of sausage gravy and biscuits or pancakes, or lunch-counter hamburgers and sandwiches.

Anchor Bar

413 Tower Ave.   715-394-9747
Superior, WI   LD | $

The Anchor Bar is a spare-looking tavern in an industrial non-neighborhood near the Duluth shipyards. The inside is nearly pitch-dark. Customers at the bar and big round tables include rugged-looking seamen having rugged-sounding conversations. The aroma of grilling beef is irresistible. The Anchor Bar is a destination hamburger-lovers need to know.

Each burger is a thick, hand-formed patty made of meat fat enough to weep juice into the bun even before you apply finger pressure to lift it. It is not high-end prime beef, but its stout, blue-collar satisfaction is undeniable. And its proletarian price is unbelievable. A single burger, served in over a dozen guises including topped with cheeses, hot sauces, even cashews, costs three dollars. A heap of hot-from-the-kettle golden fries—big, square, spuddy logs laced with lots of crisp squiggles and burnt bits—adds exactly one dollar to the price. An amazing, under-five-dollar meal!

Big eaters, take note. The Anchorburger is a sandwich of two one-third-pound patties. The Gallyburger is three of them, with a layer of cheese on top of each. "That's what we call meat loaf on a bun," the waitress joked when she set down a Gallyburger. It is served with a plastic fork and knife, but with care, it is edible by hand with nominal spillage.

Beerntsen's Candy Store

108 N. 8th St.   920-684-9616

Manitowoc, WI   LD | $

In the back of Beerntsen's, past the confectionery shelves and through an elaborately carved archway, handsome wooden booths are occupied by customers who come for such ice cream fancies as a Sweetheart (caramel, vanilla ice cream, marshmallow, crushed nuts) or a Sunset (strawberry and vanilla ice cream, pineapple, marshmallow, crushed nuts). Up front are more than a hundred different kinds of hand-dipped candy including a chocolate cosmetology set (brush, mirror, hair dryer), smoochies (like Hershey's kisses, but bigger), raspberry and vanilla seafoam dainties, and—pièce de résistance—a bonbon known as fairy food, which is a two-inch square of brittle spun-sugar molasses shrouded in deep, dark chocolate. We are very happy we live nowhere near Manitowoc, Wisconsin, and that fairy food is too delicate to be shipped; otherwise, we'd be addicts.

Bendtsen's Bakery

3200 Washington Ave.   262-633-0365

Racine, WI   L | $

Bendtsen's calls its kringle "the world's finest Danish pastry," a claim with which we would not disagree. If you don't know what kringle is, think of an ordinary Danish, like you have with morning coffee. Now, imagine its crust buttery and feather-light, almost like a croissant, and fill it with a ribbon of pecan paste and chopped nuts, or a layer of almond macaroon paste, or a tunnel of cherry and cheese. Picture it as big as a Christmas wreath, a ring that is about a foot and a half across and iced with sugar glaze or flavored frosting. Finally, have it warm with butter melting on top, accompanied by a leisurely pot of coffee. There you have one of the great breakfast (or teatime) treats in America, a dish that has become the signature of Racine, Wisconsin.

Bendtsen's has pictures on the wall that show the time they made the world's largest kringle, but size isn't what makes their pastry so wonderful. Each kringle made here, whether simply filled with apricot jam or fancy-filled with a mash of cranberries and walnuts, is a beautiful sight—a broad oval rather than a perfect circle, quite flat, and ready to slice into small pieces (of which you'll want three or four).

There is no place to eat at Bendtsen's, although samples of kringle are often available on the counter for tasting.

Benji's

4156 N. Oakland Ave.   414-332-7777
Shorewood, WI   BLD | $$

Benji's is an old-fashioned deli in a modern shopping area. It is an authentic taste of Milwaukee, by which we mean it offers a reassuring menu of old-country ethnic dishes (chicken-in-the-pot, cabbage rolls, fried matzoh) along with plenty of midwestern Americana, such as a Friday night fish fry, a deluxe hamburger plate with French fries, a French dip sandwich on a poppy-seed roll, and that mysteriously named heartland meal-in-a-skillet, hoppel poppel, for which no ethnic group we know has taken credit. Hoppel poppel is a griddled breakfast mélange of chewy salami chunks, scrambled eggs, tender potato, and (optional) onions. Benji's offers it also in a "super" version that adds peppers, mushrooms, and melted cheese to the formula. Either way, it's delicious.

The other specialties of the house are deli food: piled-high corned beef sandwiches on rugged-crusted sour rye bread, lox-and-bagel platters, sweet-and-sour cabbage borscht, buttery warm blintzes (available filled with cheese, cherries, or blueberries), and crisp potato pancakes served with applesauce. For dessert, we recommend noodle kugel (a cheesecake-rich block of cooked egg noodles and sweetened cheese), served hot with sour cream. And for a beverage to drink with your meal, Benji's offers true melting-pot variety: domestic or imported beer, kosher wine, Dr. Brown's in cans, Sprecher's soda in bottles, and chocolate phosphates (seltzer water and chocolate syrup).

Chili John's

519 S. Military Ave.   920-494-4624
Green Bay, WI   LD | $

In 1916, "Chili John" Isaac devised a recipe for ground beef cooked with a rainbow of spice. His recipe featured an eye-opening measure of peppery oil, but the way he served it at his little eat-place, in concert with spaghetti noodles, beans, and cheese, the heat became part of a well-balanced plate of food. It is served with spoon-size oyster crackers, which some say were invented at Chili John's request. The story is that sometime in the 1920s, he realized that the old-fashioned store cracker, at least an inch in diameter, was too unwieldy to garnish his chili, so he convinced cracker manufacturers to downsize. Historians have found evidence of little crackers prior to 1916, but not as a chili companion.

Although some locals still call the multilayered configuration Texas-style chili (an appellation Texas chili–heads no doubt would abhor), variations of the formula are now known throughout the state as Green Bay–style chili, and the legendary chili parlor Chili John created has become a culinary guiding light.

Jack Pandl's Whitefish Bay Inn

1319 Henry Clay St.   414-964-3800
Whitefish Bay, WI   LD | $$

Jack Pandl's (since 1915) serves German-flavored Dairyland cuisine in a friendly, wood-paneled dining room with a wall of windows that look out over elegant Lake Drive. Waitresses wear dirndl skirts and there is lots of old-world memorabilia for decor (including one of the planet's biggest collections of beer steins), but the menu is at least as midwestern as it is Middle European. At lunch, when the steel-banded tables are set with functional paper place mats, you can eat a julienne salad, or a Reuben sandwich made with Wisconsin cheese, or pork chops, or a Denver omelet. In addition to broiled whitefish ("always purchased fresh," the menu guarantees), there is that lean but luscious local specialty, walleyed pike, filleted and broiled to perfection. This being Milwaukee, Friday is fish fry night, of course. Pandl's perch is lovely—whole fish filleted so their two halves hold together, encased in a golden crust and accompanied by first-class potato pancakes.

We love *schaum torte* for dessert. That's a crisp meringue dolloped with freshly made custard. On the other hand, we never can resist the German pancake. It's not really a dessert item, and many people have it as their main course, but somehow it makes a grand conclusion to a meal. This gorgeous edible event, a Jack Pandl's specialty, is a big puffy cloud of batter similar in texture to Yorkshire pudding, but slightly sweeter. It arrives at the table piping hot and shaped like a big bowl, its circumference crisp and brown, risen high in the oven, its center moist and eggy. Dust it with a bit of powdered sugar and give it a spritz of lemon, creating a sophisticated syrup, then dig in immediately. It is a big plate of food, a joy to share with friends.

Jake's

1634 W. North Ave.   414-562-1272
Milwaukee, WI   L | $

It took us a long time to realize that Milwaukee was a major corned beef city, but if we had any doubts, Jake's erased them. Here is a vintage urban deli where the hand-sliced corned beef is steamy-moist, unspeakably tender, and vividly flavored.

Proprietor Michael Kassof suggested that one reason for his beef's deliciousness might be that a dozen or more briskets are boiled together, their pot becoming a slurry of spice and beef flavor that re-insinuates itself into the fibers of the meat. Just as the counterman prepares to slice a whole brisket for sandwiches, it is sprinkled with paprika, adding a little extra jolt to the taste. The beef is sliced medium-thick, then piled into slick-crusted, Milwaukee-made Miller Bakery seeded rye: not an outrageously huge sandwich like you might get in Chicago or New York, but in no way skimpy, either. We see the meat-to-bread ratio as perfect.

There are a few other items on Jake's menu: pastrami, turkey pastrami, hard salami, hot dogs, and soups-like-mama-should-have-made; and you can have the corned beef as part of a Reuben with sauerkraut and cheese. But for us, and for generations of Milwaukeeans, Jake's is synonymous with corned beef on rye.

With its pale yellow walls, its tables topped with worn linoleum, its ancient wood booths equipped with out-of-order buzzers once used to summon service, Jakes exudes faded charm. It has been around since 1935, when the neighborhood was mostly Jewish. Original proprietor Reuben Cohen sold it to Jake, who sold it to Michael Kassof's dad in 1967, and now Michael runs the place—the last Jewish business in a neighborhood that is mostly African American. Superlative corned beef is a cross-cultural infatuation.

Jo's Café

3519 W. Silver Spring Dr.   414-461-0210
Milwaukee, WI   BL | $

Hoffel poffel isn't widely known anywhere in the United States that we are aware of, although we have seen versions of it (also called hoppel poppel) in Iowa. It is one gigantic breakfast plate of a few eggs scrambled with chunks of potato, some onions, and, at Jo's, lots of nuggets of spicy salami and, optionally, some cheese on top. The only reason we would recommend not getting it for breakfast at Jo's is that the *other* kind of potatoes—the thin-cut hash browns—are delicious. Cooked in a flat patty until brittle-crisp, they too are available under a mantle of melted cheese. Actually, either sort of potato dish will leave precious little room for Jo's terrific pecan rolls and cinnamon rolls; nor should a first-time visitor miss out on one of the large omelets cooked on Jo's griddle.

We generally think of Jo's for breakfast, but lunch is good, too. Blue-plate cuisine is the order of the day, including such daily specials as meat loaf, beef stew, pork chops, and country-fried steak with real (of course!) mashed potatoes, homemade gravy, and a yeasty fresh-baked dinner roll. Every day you can order barbecued pork ribs or chicken.

Klinger's East

920 E. Locust St.   414-263-2424

Milwaukee, WI   D | $$

When we went to Milwaukee on a mission to eat at its best fish fries, our buddies Jessica Zierten and Brad Warsh, both lifelong Milwaukeeans, insisted that any significant expedition needed to include a visit to their favorite tavern in the Riverwest neighborhood, Klinger's East. We're glad they recommended it, because this shadowy bar is not one that we would necessarily feel obliged to enter. It doesn't look like a great place to eat. Despite the fact that half of it is a pool hall with bleak decor, it is a comfy place to eat, even for out-of-towners like us. Customers include wholesome-looking families you'd never see dining in such an establishment in other parts of the country. But in Milwaukee, taverns aren't just for drinkers; they are community centers.

The fish fry is brilliant. Of course cod is on the menu, sheathed in a crunchy coat of beer batter. You can also get smelt, which Brad informed us is properly pronounced "shmelt" hereabouts. It is a fish-lover's fish with vivid oily character—a heap of crunch-coated two-inch sprats well accompanied by a short stack of silver-dollar-size potato pancakes.

Leon's

3131 S. 27th St.   414-383-1784

Milwaukee, WI $

There is no place to eat at this neon-rimmed, Eisenhower-era hangout other than in your car or standing in the parking lot along with other happy pilgrims who have come for the ultimate frozen dessert. Leon's menu is all custard: cones, cups, sodas, sundaes, malts, pints, and quarts. (Hot dogs are available, but they are irrelevant.)

Milwaukee is fanatical about custard, which is heavy, smooth, and pure—denser than the richest super-premium ice cream and nothing like wan frozen yogurt. As made by Leon's, it is egg-rich, sweet but not cloying, and uncomplicated. No mix-ins, no silly names for flavors, no cookie dough or brownie chunks. Choose vanilla, chocolate, strawberry, or butter pecan. Have it in a cone or cup. Or have a sundae topped with the sauce of your choice and some of the most delicious toasted nuts on the planet: pecan halves that have a wicked crunch, a salty punch, and an earthy flavor that only helps accentuate the heavenly clarity of the superior custard itself.

Maggie's

257 Manypenny Ave.   715-779-5641
Bayfield, WI   LD | $$

There is something especially good about savoring whitefish at Maggie's
in the old lakeshore village of Bayfield in northernmost Wisconsin, where
the twenty-two Apostle Islands punctuate a horizon of enamel-blue sky and
steel-gray waves. It is almost always on the menu at the screaming-pink town
café where tourists line up to eat during the summer and where North Shore
locals come for refuge and companionship when temperatures head into the
way-below-zero range. A few days each year Maggie's does not serve whitefish because the kitchen cannot get it fresh from the boats that work within
thirty miles of town. Caught-that-morning is the rule, and during October
and November, when Wisconsin prohibits angling for whitefish, Maggie's
reaches out all of forty miles to fishermen who ply Michigan waters, which
do not close for the season. "If we can get their morning catch later in the
day, we will serve it," says Jeff Shannon, who runs the place. "If they're late,
or if they don't have a truck on the road, I invite you to have a hamburger."
(Maggie's Wisconsin Burger is a Dairyland tour de force, topped with aged
Cheddar, Colby, Amish blue, and Swiss cheeses.)

Whitefish fillets, which also are available broiled without the plank and
sautéed in butter, are supremely easy to eat. The fishermen deliver them
with a dozen pin bones still attached to the top of each piece, but Maggie's
kitchen staff removes the bones one by one with needle-nose pliers. On most
Friday evenings, you can get a special of headless but otherwise whole whitefish with all its bones, skin, and fins. It is sautéed in a pan full of butter, and
even if you've never faced a whole fish like this, getting all the meat is a snap.
The waitstaff will show you how to peel back the skin, then start at the top
and easily separate moist forkfuls from off the bone. The flavor of whole
whitefish is not significantly different from those that are filleted and broiled
or sautéed, but the presentation adds fish-camp fun to the dining experience.

You'll not likely find whitefish livers on the menu of a restaurant anywhere other than around the shore of Lake Superior. Because it takes a lot
of fish to gather a small amount of livers—they're about the size of a quarter
and a dinner of them might include fifteen or twenty—mongers who sell to
local restaurants and markets traditionally have thrown them away. But old-
time fishermen have long considered them a delicacy, and in recent years as
Bayfield has gone from quiet fishing village to popular tourist destination,
livers have begun to appear on the menus of a handful of plain and fancy
restaurants in the area. Like the flesh of the whitefish, the livers' most distinguishing characteristic is their pure, inland water taste, more mellow than

chicken livers or any mammal organ meat we know. Maggie's rolls them in spiced flour and sautés them with peppers, onions, and mushrooms until their outsides have a bit of crunch and the inside of each turns melting soft.

Mazo's

3146 S. 27th St.   414-671-2118
Milwaukee, WI   BLD Tues–Sat | $

One of Milwaukee's lesser-known culinary attractions is excellent hamburgers. Many connoisseurs believe Mazo's serves the best. It is a tiny place, now run by Nick Mazo, whose grandparents started it in 1934, and if you come at lunchtime, prepare to wait a while once you find a precious seat in the dining room. These burgers are *not* fast food, but they are worth the wait. They are not outlandish in any way. They are normal-size patties of good ground beef in lovely toasted buns, but what sends them into orbit is the fact that they are grilled in butter—the Milwaukee way!—resulting in a confluence of the two most wickedly good fats: meat and dairy. Available toppings include fried onions, sautéed mushrooms, and of course a layer of cheese. Other choices for dressing up the burger are bacon, lettuce, and tomato as well as Thousand Island dressing. On the side, have coleslaw, French fries, or baked beans.

Bonus: Mazo's is directly across the street from the excellent Leon's custard stand (p. 379).

McBob's

4919 W. North Ave.   414-871-5050
Milwaukee, WI   BLD | $$

Roadfood.com users Jessica Zierten and Brad Warsh said we needed to come to McBob's several years ago when we were in their home city of Milwaukee looking for fish fries. Every Friday, McBob's offers three choices: perch, walleye, or grouper; or you can have a combo of perch and walleye, or a super combo of all three. With the fish come American fries or potato pancakes, coleslaw, and bread. "This is the real deal!" Brad proclaimed. "All fresh, all real." Each fish fillet is encased in a highly seasoned, fragile crust. The walleye is light and ephemeral; the grouper is mild with a sweet oily flavor. The perch is snowy white. If you get the meal with potato pancakes— you must!—the pancakes are fanned out on the plate as a kind of edible trivet for the fish. They are laced with bits of onion and have a potato flavor that perfectly complements the crisp fish.

If you happen to be a fish-fry-frowner, McBob's is not to be ignored.

Every day of the week it is a source of A-1 corned beef. Big chunks of steamy-hot meat from a super-tender spiced brisket are piled into a sand-wich of plain rye or in toasted rye with sauerkraut, horseradish mustard, and Swiss cheese (a Reuben). The meat is extraordinarily lean and yet veritably dripping with flavor. The ideal condiment is horseradish mustard. The next morning, McBob's turns the corned beef into some of the best hash we've ever eaten.

Mr. Perkins' Family Restaurant

2001 W. Atkinson Ave.   414-447-6660
Milwaukee, WI   BLD | $

Mr. Perkins' is a city lunchroom with a mostly African American clientele, but all visitors are made to feel welcome at this counter and in these booths. With a large menu (and a reliable rotation of daily specials, i.e., neckbones every Wednesday), this neighborhood Milwaukee café is a destination soul-food eatery.

While certain dishes may be an acquired taste—chitterlings, for example—many specialties are comfort food for anyone. Baked chicken with dressing is tender and vividly spiced; meat loaf is firm and satisfying; those pork neckbones on Wednesday are some trouble to eat (they're little), but the meat virtually falls from the bone as you savor it. We must also mention the fried perch, which is a plate of about three large boneless fillets encased in a sandy cornmeal crust. The meat of the fish is amazingly juicy, with fla-vor as lusty as beefsteak.

One of the most delightful aspects of lunch and supper at Mr. Perkins' (which also serves breakfast) is choosing side dishes. Macaroni and cheese has a perfect balance of tender noodle and crusty edges; fried okra is veg-etable-sweet; fried green tomatoes are tangy and brittle-crisp; there are pot-likker-sopped turnip greens, and turnip bottoms made into an intriguing squash-like mash with butter and sugar. Corn bread is Tennessee-style, i.e., a griddle-cooked cake that is buttery, tender, golden-colored, and an ideal tool for mopping gravy and vegetable drippings from a plate. Desserts include pineapple coconut cake, individual-size fried peach pies, sweet potato pie, or a plate of sweet yams. And to drink, the beverages of choice are lemonade and iced tea, both served southern-style, i.e., sooo-eeeet!

Plaza Tavern

319 N. Henry St.   608-255-6592
Madison, WI   LD | $

We found out about the Plaza Tavern at Minneapolis's Convention Grill, which boasts that its hamburger is modeled after the one served in Madison. We were intrigued by the one we had in Minnesota, so next time we were driving west of Lake Michigan, we stopped at the source to check it out.

Not merely intriguing, a Plazaburger is downright delicious, addictively so. What makes it different from a regular hamburger (which is also available) is the secret-sauce condiment that drenches the patty to a degree that it seems to seep right into it. It is thinner than ketchup and its texture reminded us of some eastern North Carolina barbecue sauces, although it doesn't have the vinegar tang. It's spicy but not even three-alarm hot, and in addition to infusing the meat with its flavor, it gets deeply imprinted into the tawny bun on which the burger is served. Connoisseurs have it on their French fries, too. You can buy a cupful for 60¢.

The Tavern menu is an otherwise unremarkable array of sandwiches, plus, of course, cheese curds. Beers are sold by the pint and pitcher. Ambience is pure Midwest saloon: long bar, tight booths, and wall murals showing scenic Wisconsin.

Real Chili

419 E. Wells St.   414-271-4042
Milwaukee, WI   BLD | $

Real Chili serves bowls of chili—mild, medium, or hot—with spaghetti or beans, or spaghetti *and* beans, the latter arrangement known as the Marquette Special (to honor the many Marquette University students who are frequent chili eaters). Atop this heap of food, you can have your choice of sour cream, cheese, or onions; and on the side, you'll get some oyster crackers to crumble on top or to eat as a palate-cleanser between bites of chili.

This déclassé joint is the kind of beanery you once could find in big cities throughout the heartland. With the exception of Cincinnati, the Midwest has lost most of its chili parlors, and although this style of chili gets no respect from southwestern purists, it is a culinary adventure you don't want to miss. Sit at a counter or at one of two communal tables with backless stools; uniformed waitresses dole out second helpings at half price, and the preferred beverages are beer or cherry Coke.

There is a second location at 1625 W. Wells St.; 414-342-6955.

Serb Hall

5101 W. Oklahoma Ave.
Milwaukee, WI

414-545-6030
D (Fri only) | $$

Serb Hall is the largest fish fry in the United States. The chandelier-crowned eating stadium seats 950 people at hundreds of four-tops and dozens of big-party tables as a loudspeaker voice reverberates above the din with announcements of birthdays and anniversaries and clusters of diners cheer from a hundred yards away. By 6 P.M., the South Side banquet hall is filled; the line of people waiting outside stretches for city blocks.

Fish fries are the only meal regularly served, fifty-two Fridays per year, Good Friday being the big blowout when over two tons of fish are served along with a ton and a half of French fries and seventy-three gallons of tartar sauce. Most people come here to eat Icelandic cod—thin-crusted blocks of soft white meat served in a plastic basket with French fries, tart coleslaw, and rye bread on the side. Beer-battered cod is frequently available, its hopsy coat shoring in an abundance of cream-rich fish juices.

When we inquired about Serb Hall serving hours, our very busy waitress took time to carefully explain that the "In" door closes precisely at 8 P.M., but customers already seated are allowed to finish eating and drinking.

Sil's Drive-Thru

1801 E. North Ave.
Milwaukee, WI

414-225-9365
BLD | $

Sil's mini-donuts come to you piping hot from the fryer in a paper bag. Dusted with either powdered sugar or cinnamon sugar, each is two-bite size, and even when it's cooled to room temp, the donut is a masterpiece of balance, small enough to match plenty of not-quite-crisp skin with creamy insides. Sil's makes good coffee and espresso drinks as companions.

A modernistic hut that once was a bus shelter, Sil's is open until 2:30 A.M., by which point the six-per-serving donuts are less interesting to most customers than the $1.50 snack known as "wieners for the wasted."

Solly's Grille

4629 N. Port Washington Rd.
Milwaukee, WI

414-332-8808
BLD Tues–Sat | $

Hamburgers are a passion in Milwaukee, where butter is the staff of life. Ergo, the butter burger. At Solly's, it is a fairly thin patty of beef, cooked through, served on a bun saturated with melted butter. Not margarine, not flavored oil: pure, dairy-rich, delicious butter. You can get a Super Burger (two patties, and a good idea—a single is overwhelmed by its bun) or a Super Special, which adds lettuce, tomato, and mayo to the mix (also a good idea), as well as cheeseburgers and burgers topped with onions, mushrooms, and Monterey Jack cheese. The biggest of all is the Cheesehead—a half-pound of sirloin with Swiss and American cheese, stewed onions, raw onion, and mushrooms. It is impossible to eat with one's hands, but it's fun to try!

There are other sandwiches on Solly's menu, none of which we've tried, also omelets and fish fries, excellent crinkle-cut French fries, and made-here pie. If you've got a sweet tooth, apply it to a milk shake, which is Dairy State–rich and made in flavors that include chocolate, hot fudge, strawberry, pineapple, vanilla, and the superb fresh banana malt. Another confectionery alternative is a black cow made with Sprecher's root beer. And, this being a city where ice cream is even more beloved than butter burgers, there is a full array of sundaes, too.

Seating is at two horseshoe-shaped counters with stools, and the staff of uniformed waitresses go about their business with well-seasoned hash-house aplomb.

Speed Queen

1130 W. Walnut St.   414-265-2900
Milwaukee, WI   LD | $

Speed Queen's neighborhood is iffy, but the barbecue is definitive. Pork, beef, and turkey are slow-cooked and glazed with sauce, either mild—robust and slightly sweet—or hot, which is an explosive, dark orange emulsion reminiscent of Arthur Bryant's in Kansas City. For many customers, the mild is a little too mild and the hot is too lip-burning; so it is not uncommon to hear orders for "half and half." (Sauce is sold in bottles to take home: *highly recommended*!)

There are two kinds of pork available: shoulder or outside meat. Shoulder is thick slices that are almost chunks, tender as velvet. Outside meat is a motley pile of nearly blackened shreds and nuggets, some of which are tender, some of which are crusty, and some of which quite literally melt on the tongue. It is smokier-tasting than inside meat, like essence of barbecue. A favorite way to eat at Speed Queen is to order a half-and-half plate (ribs and outside, rib tips and shoulder, etc.) that consists of meat, sauce, a couple of slices of spongy white bread (necessary for sopping sauce), plus a cup of coleslaw. Beans and potato salad cost extra. You can also get a sandwich; but beware: These "sandwiches" are, in fact, lots of meat and sauce piled onto white bread in such a way that it is inconceivable to hold it in your hands.

Everything is delivered at the order window in a Styrofoam container, and while most business is take-out, Speed Queen offers a row of functional booths for dining in. Decor is minimal, consisting of two identical photo murals of the Wisconsin Dells on opposite walls. While there is a jukebox, it seems seldom to be plugged in or playing. Room tone is a hush punctuated by lip-smacks, sighs of pleasure, and the quietest kind of reverential conversation—the pensive hush induced by good barbecue.

Three Brothers

| 2414 S. Saint Clair St. | 414-481-7530 |
| Milwaukee, WI | D | $$ |

Branko Radiecevich's Serbian restaurant, which his father named for Branko and his two brothers, is a Milwaukee landmark that attracts eaters from all walks of life and all ethnic groups. Accommodations are polite but humble. Start with lemon-and-wine-marinated rice-stuffed grape leaves served with black olives and firm sticks of nut-sweet *kashkaval* (a goat's-milk cheese) or a "Serbian salad" of tomatoes, green peppers, and onions veiled with a web of finely grated *bryndza,* a soft goat's-milk cheese.

One autumn a while back when we came for supper, Branko reminded us that it was leek season and brought out a savory pastry pie layered with caramelized peppered leeks. He was even more enthusiastic about roast lamb, a Three Brothers signature dish that is basted for four hours in its own juices with tomato, pepper, onion, and garlic, and served *just barely* on the bone. Poke it with fork tines, and bite-size hunks of meat separate from the haunch and fall into the juice on the plate. The menu describes it as a must for the lamb-lover, but we suspect that even non-lamb-lovers might find its refined taste irresistible.

The building in which Three Brothers serves these fine meals is a corner tavern that was built in 1897 and for decades was owned and operated by the Schlitz Brewing Company. The Schlitz insignia—a globe—still crowns the peak of the roof. There are no longer seats at the old bar, which runs the length of the front room and is now a service area, but the wood-floored saloon retains the warmth of a community gathering place.

Watts Tea Shop

| 761 N. Jefferson St. | 414-290-5720 |
| Milwaukee, WI | BL & T Mon-Sat | $ |

When we wrote the cookbook *Square Meals* in 1984, we described the ritual of ladies' lunch as culinary history. We were wrong. At the Watts Tea Shop, on the second floor of George Watts & Son fine china shop, ladies' lunch is alive and well . . . along with afternoon tea and lovely breakfasts of ginger toast and hot chocolate.

Such a pleasant place! At the front door downstairs, you are greeted by a member of the staff and directed to the elevator. Past display cases of Limoges and Wedgwood, you find yourself on the second floor in a broad lunchroom with a window view of Jefferson Street below. The tables are well-worn bare wood; the floral carpet is a muted blue. Coffee is served in Royal Worcester Hanbury-pattern cups, and napkins are white linen. Of course, waitresses wear tidy uniforms.

Sandwiches are served on tender-crumb homemade whole wheat bread. While we adore the mixed green and black olive salad sandwich, and the BLT is exemplary, and a quiche of the day is always available, what dazzles us about the menu is its many ways with chicken. You can have chicken salad, minced chicken, all-white chicken, sliced chicken, or chicken salad Polynesian, that last one mixed with coconut shreds, pecans, and a citrus vinaigrette.

To drink, there is tea and lemonade and the wonderful house specials known as a Waterford spritzer (lemonade, lime, and sparkling water) and a cold Russian (coffee, chocolate, and whipped cream). Dessert is splendid: filled sunshine cake, made from a decades-old recipe for triple-layer sponge cake with custard filling and seven-minute frosting.

Southwest

Arizona * Colorado * Kansas * Nevada *

New Mexico * Oklahoma * Texas * Utah

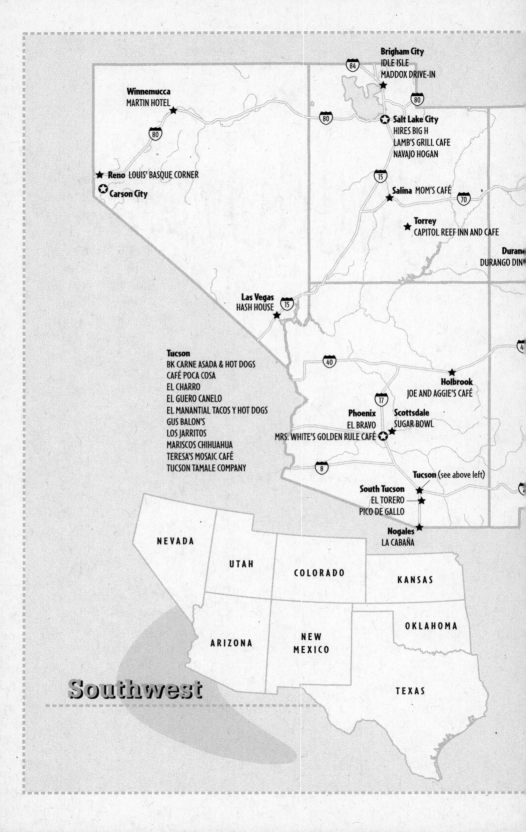

Brigham City
IDLE ISLE
MADDOX DRIVE-IN

Winnemucca
MARTIN HOTEL

Salt Lake City
HIRES BIG H
LAMB'S GRILL CAFE
NAVAJO HOGAN

Reno LOUIS' BASQUE CORNER

Carson City

Salina MOM'S CAFÉ

Torrey
CAPITOL REEF INN AND CAFE

Duran
DURANGO DIN

Las Vegas
HASH HOUSE

Tucson
BK CARNE ASADA & HOT DOGS
CAFÉ POCA COSA
EL CHARRO
EL GUERO CANELO
EL MANANTIAL TACOS Y HOT DOGS
GUS BALON'S
LOS JARRITOS
MARISCOS CHIHUAHUA
TERESA'S MOSAIC CAFÉ
TUCSON TAMALE COMPANY

Holbrook
JOE AND AGGIE'S CAFÉ

Phoenix
EL BRAVO
MRS. WHITE'S GOLDEN RULE CAFÉ

Scottsdale
SUGAR BOWL

Tucson (see above left)

South Tucson
EL TORERO
PICO DE GALLO

Nogales
LA CABAÑA

NEVADA

UTAH

COLORADO

KANSAS

ARIZONA

NEW
MEXICO

OKLAHOMA

TEXAS

Southwest

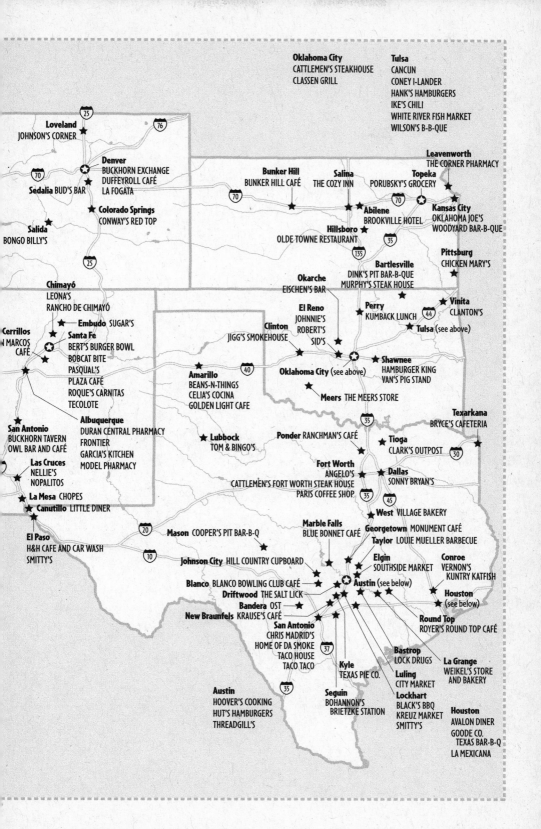

BK Carne Asada & Hot Dogs

5118 S. 12th Ave.   520-295-0105

Tucson, AZ   BLD | $

America's most flamboyant wiener, the Sonoran hot dog, starts as a simple beef frank. It gets wrapped in bacon and grilled alongside other bacon-sheathed hot dogs whose grease drippin's make the process very much like deep-frying. This causes bacon flavor to melt into the dog, leaving the outside patched with streaks of lean that provide marvelous chewy contrast to the frank they embrace. Nestled in a substantial yeasty bun, the frank is topped with tomatoes, pinto beans, onions, mustard, hot green jalapeño sauce, and mayonnaise. Spectacular! On the side comes a roasted guero pepper, which is about the same size, shape, and heat level as a jalapeño, but more yellow than green. At BK, you eat this hot dog at a picnic table on a covered patio and accompany it by cold beer or the refreshing Mexican rice drink known as *horchata*.

While Sonoran hot dogs are the featured attraction here, the other part of the restaurant's name should not be ignored. BK's carne asada is some of the best in Tucson: tender strips of grilled flank steak that are spicy, smoky, and hugely beefy. Order the meat in a taco and it arrives plain in a corn or flour tortilla (your choice), but its flavor is pronounced enough that it flourishes when you dress it to the nines at the copious salsa bar, which includes chunky guacamole as well as salsa verde, chopped tomatoes, pico de gallo, onion, radish, lime, and sliced cucumber.

Cafe Poca Cosa

110 E. Pennington St.   520-622-6400
Tucson, AZ   LD | $$$

There is no printed menu at Cafe Poca Cosa. What's available always changes. Each table is shown a portable blackboard with about a dozen dinners listed on it, virtually all of them in need of explanation. Nothing chef Suzana Davila makes is familiar; certainly there are no tacos, enchiladas, or burritos! Nor are there appetizers and side dishes from which to choose. Each dinner comes complete on a plate with exactly what Suzana believes it should have.

There will be glorious chicken moles, or perhaps the variant of mole known as *pollo en pipian,* for which boneless chicken is cosseted in sauce made from bitter chocolate, crushed red chiles, Spanish peanuts, pumpkin seeds, and cloves. You will always find a tamale pie on the menu as a vegetarian alternative. Even devoted meat-eaters should give it a shot, for this tamale pie is creamy comfort food, tender as a soufflé, always dressed up a little differently, topped, for instance, with a vivid green chile purée or a sweet mango sauce.

There is shredded beef (*deshebrada*) infused with smoky chile flavor; there are seafood dishes and pork, too. Each entree is presented heaped upon a plate along with a bright, fresh salad, so that whatever your main course is, it mixes with the greens and makes a happy mess of things. On the side come small warm corn tortillas; and for dessert, there's Mexican-flavored chocolate mousse (is that cinnamon we taste?) and a sultry square of flan, for which the soft custard is floated on a dish of tremendously sweet burnt-sugar syrup.

The Poca Cosa dining room is a sweeping space with objects of Mexican art on display as if in a museum. "Upscale a little bit, with the times," is how chef Suzana described it after moving here from humbler quarters. It is a good setting for a grand meal, one of the best in the Southwest.

El Bravo

8338 N. 7th St.   602-943-9753
Phoenix, AZ   LD | $$

Chuck Henrickson recommended we visit El Bravo for the "best tamale in Arizona." A worthy suggestion. The chicken and green corn tamales we sampled are earthy, just zesty enough to perk up taste buds, and impossible to stop eating until appetite has become only a dim memory.

Add to that the other AZ-Mex fare on this merry menu and you have a restaurant that is hard to resist. It's not much for looks: decor is piñatas and beer signs. But who needs mood-making ambience when you can choose from among chiles rellenos, enchiladas, burros and burritos, and a fragile-crusted Navajo red beef popover that are all dishes to remember? On the side come super-savory refried beans. We are especially fond of the *machaca*, a.k.a. dried beef, that is available in tacos, burritos, and flautas. For dessert? How about a chocolate chimichanga?

Service is homey, meaning sometimes slow and sometimes brisk. Grandma is friendly, but not cloyingly so.

El Charro

311 N. Court Ave.   520-622-1922
Tucson, AZ   LD | $$

El Charro opened in 1922 and lays claim to many of the dishes that are now taken for granted as classic Mexican-American fare. The tostada grande, first made here by founder Monica Flinn, is a broad cheese crisp known on some local menus as a Mexican pizza. Most people get it with a veneer of creamy melted cheese on top; other options include green chiles, guacamole, air-dried beef, and refried beans. El Charro's round-the-world version is a majestic appetizer, served on a pedestal, garnished with fresh basil leaves.

Carne seca (dried beef) is cured high above the patio in back of the restaurant, where strips of thin-sliced tenderloin hang in an open metal cage. Suspended on ropes and pulleys, the cage sways in the breeze over the heads of customers, wafting a perfume of lemon and garlic marinade into the Arizona air. Sautéed after it is air-dried, *carne seca* is customarily served in concert with sweet onions, hot chiles, and tomatoes, making an explosion of flavor like no other food. El Charro has a full menu of tacos, enchiladas, and chiles rellenos, plus such rarer regional specialties as enchilada Sonorese (a patty of fried cornmeal garnished with chili) and chalupas (small cornmeal canoes filled with chili, meat, or chicken and whole beans). Beyond the indisputable goodness of these meals, the kitchen offers a full repertoire of nutritionally enlightened fare—lo-cal, lo-fat, good for you, and good tasting!

El Charro is noisy and sociable, almost always packed with tourists, Tucsonians, health nuts, and burrito hounds who spoon up fiery salsa picante with corn chips and drink Tecate beer served in the can with a wedge of lime on top. Mariachi music sets the mood as the sturdy wood floors veritably rumble with the crowds and the air fills with the inviting aromas of hot tostadas grandes. Wall decor is a kaleidoscope of vintage south-of-the-border advertisements, straw sombreros and rawhide bullwhips, and years' worth of El Charro calendars, many of which feature melodramatic scenes of Mexican horsemen (known as *charros*), proud steeds, and pretty maidens all making flirty eyes at each other amidst stormy landscapes. The calendars are a house trademark, and a good memento of the high spirits of an El Charro meal.

El Guero Canelo

5201 S. 12th Ave.   520-295-9005

Tucson, AZ   BLD | $

More than any of the hundred places that sell Sonoran hot dogs in and around Tucson, El Guero Canelo deserves the credit for making it popular. Opened in the 1990s, when the *hot-dog estilo Sonora* was strictly a street-cart affair, it is a happy urban picnic more than a restaurant, its totally al fresco dining area shaded by a canopy with nozzles all along the rim that rain down mists of cool water to hydrate the savage desert air. Hot dogs are assembled at a cart adjoining the patio; other Mexican dishes are cooked in a separate kitchen. After you get your meal but before you take a seat, you can gather condiments from the salsa bar to dress your *caramelo,* taco, torta, or quesadilla with salsa verde, chopped tomatoes, pico de gallo, onion, radish, lime, or sliced cucumber.

But you do not dress your Sonoran hot dog. That is done by the hot dog man, and it is almost always done exactly the same way. A beef frank, wrapped in bacon and grilled in a trough, is inserted in a big, soft Mexican bun, then dressed with chopped tomatoes, a scattering of pinto beans, grilled or raw onions, a line of yellow mustard, a green ribbon of hot jalapeño sauce, and an artistic squiggle of mayonnaise. On the side comes a roasted guero pepper, which looks like a pale jalapeño (*guero* = blond) and can be every bit as hot. It would be possible to omit one of the ingredients—onions, beans, or jalapeño sauce, perhaps—but that would be wrong. A Sonoran hot dog with everything is unimpeachable harmony. If you really love the hot-dog-and-bacon duet, El Guero Canelo's cook can make you a Sammy Dog, which is two in one bun, equally well accoutered: a reasonable idea considering the dogs are modest-size and the bun capacious.

El Manantial Tacos Y Hot Dogs

Park Ave. & 36th St.   520-429-4248

South Tucson, AZ   LD | $

We cannot guarantee that El Manantial will be found at Park Avenue and 36th Street in South Tucson. It is a mobile food truck and the location is a vacant lot. If something gets built there or if the proprietors find a better location, the truck may relocate. That's the nature of hundreds of vendors who sell good Mexican food in the Old Pueblo. But El Manantial has been in its current spot for quite a while and it seems extremely popular, so if you are on the hunt for one of the city's best Sonoran hot dogs, it is well worth seeking out.

Like the more permanent places that sell Sonoran hot dogs, El Manantial is two kitchens: one for tacos, burros, *caramelos,* tortas, and quesadillas, the other a small adjoining wagon devoted strictly to hot dogs. The dog is a beauty, completely swaddled in bacon, nestled in a fresh bun, and dressed with the full galaxy of condiments—tomatoes, beans, mustard, mayo, and very hot jalapeño sauce. The roasted guero pepper that accompanies all of Tucson's Sonoran dogs is especially wonderful because it too is wrapped in smoky bacon. As happens on the wiener, the cooking process glues the bacon to the outside of the pepper, creating a lusty laminate of chewy pork and firm-walled vegetable. The bite of the pepper is offset by a droplet of creamy melted cheese stuffed inside the pod.

Dine at picnic tables with a canopy overhead for protection from the desert sun.

El Torero

231 E. 26th St.   520-622-9534

South Tucson, AZ   LD (closed Tues) | $$

South Tucson is surrounded by the City of Tucson but legally and culturally separate. In this part of town, buildings are festooned with brilliant painted tiles, streets hum with low riders cruising in their chopped-roof custom *caruchas,* and at least a dozen different restaurants serve Mexican food that most of us gringos never know.

One of the best is El Torero, a place so inconspicuous that you likely will drive right past it. Once you do walk in, you instantly know you have entered a very inviting region of Mexican-food heaven. The jukebox will likely be belting out party tunes; the bar you walk past to get inside will be occupied by happy people knocking back longneck beers; and at tables in the brightly lit dining room, where the walls are decorated with bullfighter paintings and one large stuffed swordfish, people are plowing into gorgeous plates of expertly prepared true-Mex food.

Start with a wafer-thin tortilla crisp of cheese and green chile strips, presented on a silver pedestal so all at the table can pull away slices. This crisp is among the thinnest and tastiest in a neighborhood full of excellent crisps. The main menu is a broad one, featuring all the familiar tacos, burros, enchiladas, and chimichangas, plus a few items that are truly special. These include off-the-bone turkey topped with a spectacular spicy-rich dark mole sauce or, on occasion, the similar sauce known as *pipian,* which includes pumpkin seeds. Our Tucson friends Ron and Marcia Sparks, who directed us to this out-of-the-way gem, are hooked on the shrimp or flounder Vera Cruz and they also insisted on ordering a *topopo* salad—an amazing site. El Torero's *topopos* are great conical mounds of lettuce and other vegetables packed with your choice of chicken, shrimp, chili, guacamole, or *carne seca,* the sides of the mound columned by logs of hard cheese.

Gus Balon's

6027 E. 22nd St.   520-747-7788
Tucson, AZ   BL | $

Gus Balon's makes great breakfast. The sweet roll is huge, served warm with a big schmear of butter. Seemingly ordinary breakfast sandwiches are elevated to excellence by Gus's homemade bun. Eggs come with American fries freckled with crunchy bits from the griddle. The pancakes, which look commonplace, are light and delicious—far better than you'd ever expect in any typical diner.

Aside from breakfast and inexpensive lunches served in a bare-bones coffee-shop setting (counter and booths), Gus's is known for first-rate pies. It's hard to choose among them (although the freshly made butterscotch is pretty hard to resist) because they all look so good. A few years back, we took inventory of one single day's list: banana, chocolate banana, chocolate peanut butter banana, chocolate peanut butter, chocolate, coconut, lemon, butterscotch, blueberry, peach, raspberry, peanut butter, pineapple, apple, cherry, raspberry, peach, and raisin. Plus crumb-topped apple-cranberry, peach, raspberry, apple, apple-raisin, cherry, and pumpkin!

Waitresses are diner pros who pour coffee and bring food almost faster than you can speak the words to order it, and who refer to newcomers as well as friends as hon, sweetheart, and doll.

Joe & Aggie's Cafe

120 W. Hopi Dr.   866-486-0021
Holbrook, AZ   BL | $

Despite the interstate replacing Route 66, Holbrook remains a town where you can get a real feel for what life was like along western roads in the two-lane days. It still has the famous Sleep in a Wigwam motel; there are some fascinating pawnshops and Native American jewelry emporia; and at Joe & Aggie's—the oldest restaurant in town, since 1946—you can have a real old-fashioned roadside diner meal.

Tables are outfitted with squeeze bottles of honey for squirting onto sopaipillas (puffy triangles of fried bread), and meals begin with a basket of chips and an empty bowl in which you decant some spicy, pepper-flecked hot sauce for dipping. The sign on the front window boasts of "Mexican and American food," but in fact, the menu at Joe & Aggie's is not quite either; it is a blend of Mexican and American that is unique to the Southwest. After the chips and salsa, you move on to such meals as enchiladas made with red or green chili, big stuffed burros, crisp tacos, or chicken-fried steak with potatoes and hot sopaipillas on the side. Roadfood.com user "icrmg" posted a gorgeous photo showing a breakfast of green chili–topped huevos rancheros sided by a cake of hash browns and a side of cheese-dripping refried beans.

La Cabaña

840 N. Grand Ave.   520-287-3249
Nogales, AZ   BLD | $

Our South Arizona friend Margaret Bond took us to La Cabaña when we asked her and her husband, Paul (the estimable boot maker), where to go in Nogales to get a real local meal. Margaret walked into the inviting little cantina with us in tow and she was greeted warmly by the staff, who know her as a regular.

We started with made-to-order guacamole, a bowl of chunky mashed avocado mixed with little bits of cheese and tomato. Margaret advised that we might want to spruce it up with a dab of the hot salsa provided to every table, as well as a spritz of tiny Mexican limes. We also sampled corn tamales, enchiladas, a corn-crusted taco, and a beef burrito filled with meat that was moist and pot-roast tender. Chiles rellenos are packed with deep green-chile flavor, oozing melted cheese, and enrobed in crisp-fried crust. Among the most memorable flavors on the table were the simple flour tortillas, served in a bread basket. They are suitable for mopping one's plate of sauce and refritos, but just by themselves, these are superb tortillas: warm, delicate, with an earthy wheat flavor so rich they taste pre-buttered.

La Cabaña is an inconspicuous little adobe restaurant/bar in a cluster of shops on the main drag. It is outfitted with tables and a couple of comfortable booths. For serious eating, we recommend a booth, where you can lounge like royalty.

Los Jarritos

4832 S. 12th Ave.   520-746-0364
Tucson, AZ   BLD | $

Twelfth Avenue, on the south side of Tucson, bustles with tents and trucks selling corn on the cob by the bushel. One vendor boasts of being "El Rey Del Elote"; another, named "El Frida," has a truck painted with images of corn and chile to advertise "Elote Blanco Mexicano Y Chile Verde." Those last two ingredients—white corn and green chiles—are the makings of green corn tamales, a dish that once was strictly a late-summer treat in the Southwest, made when corn was ripe and chiles were harvested. But now, using corn trucked up from southern Mexico and green chiles roasted and frozen in the fall, many of Tucson's tamale makers make them throughout the year. Only white corn is used to make green corn tamales. They are called green tamales because they traditionally are wrapped in fresh husks with a verdurous appearance unlike the beige dried ones from which ordinary tamales are made.

Los Jarritos, a tiny Twelfth Avenue café, always has green corn tamales on the menu, and they are some of the best anywhere, a swirl of sweet corn and hot pepper flavors steamed to a point of opulent harmony. You must order at least a couple of them to accompany such classic Sonoran meals as carne asada, *nopalitos con chili* (prickly pear cactus with chili colorado), and red or white *menudo,* available in sizes from a pint to a gallon. Most meals are ordered to take out and most tamales are sold by the dozen, but a couple of tables inside and a few on a small patio out front give regulars the opportunity to linger over long breakfasts of huevos rancheros with house-made chorizo and carry on conversations with each other and with strangers.

Mariscos Chihuahua

2902 E. 22nd St.   520-326-1529
Tucson, AZ   LD | $$

Mariscos Chihuahua is a big, bright place with sunlight streaming in picture windows all around, illuminating a tempestuous seascape mural that covers one wall. The staff is friendly, and the tape player belts out Mexican tunes that make every meal feel like a celebration. Seafood stars: oysters raw or cooked, fish grilled or fried, stews and soups. And oh, such shrimp! The menu lists a dozen different styles including cool cocktails and "drowned raw," meaning ceviche-style, i.e., cooked by immersion in a lime marinade.

We stuck to the basics and got an order of cooked shrimp in garlic sauce and an order of shrimp *endiablados,* which means extremely hot. They are presented in a most appetizing way, strewn across a field of crisp French fries on a broad fish-shaped plate that also holds a mound of rice, a green salad, and a warm tortilla wrapped in foil. They are served with the hard tail still on, providing a nice handle for picking them up and nabbing one good mouthful. What's great about the presentation is that whatever the shrimp are sauced with—be it garlic butter, soy sauce, oyster sauce, or that devilish *endiablados*—seeps down and flavors the French fries that are their bedding. That means that as you approach the end of your shrimp, you then get to savor these good, crisp fries infused with whatever flavor it was that gave the shrimp their character.

Beverages include excellent presweetened (and lemon-flavored) iced tea as well as *horchata,* the locally favored sweetened rice milk. A large cooler in the center of the dining area holds bottles and cans of Dos Equis, Tecate, Corona, and Bud and Bud Lite.

There are two other Mariscos Chihuahua in Tucson, located at 1009 N. Grande Ave. and 3901 S. 6th Ave.

Mrs. White's Golden Rule Café

808 E. Jefferson St.	602-262-9256
Phoenix, AZ	L (until 5 P.M.)	$$

Honesty is the policy at Mrs. White's Golden Rule, a cinder-block building where you study the menu written all over the wall (along with celebrity autographs) and order a meal of gravy-smothered pork chops or fried chicken with pork-free-but-nonetheless-luxurious collard greens, sweet stewed tomatoes, and corn bread, followed by hot fruit cobbler, banana pudding, or pineapple cake. No bill is issued. After you've had your fill of homey soul food, step to the cash register and remind Larry White, Mrs. White's son, what you've eaten. He adds it up and you pay what you owe. The price of a meal is between $10 and $15, plus drinks and dessert.

Pico de Gallo

2618 S. 6th Ave.   520-623-8775

South Tucson, AZ   LD | $

This informal, stand-in-line-and-place-your-order café started as a street-corner taco stand and has grown into several small dining rooms. Nothing about the increase in size has impacted its magnificent food. Tacos, constructed in rugged made-here corn tortillas, are among the best anywhere, available with carne asada and *birria* or more exotic ingredients such as tongue, manta ray, and beef cheeks. We love the *coctel de elote* (corn cocktail), which is not quite the beverage its name suggests. It does come in a large Styrofoam cup, the cup filled with an extraordinary stew of warm corn kernels, drifts of soft melted cheese, hot chili, and lime. Spoon it up like soup; it is corn-sweet and lime-zesty. The menu also lists burros, quesadillas, and tamales by the dozen.

Marshaled in a refrigerated case at the counter are red plastic cups filled with the restaurant's namesake, pico de gallo. In this case, the "nip of the rooster" is a bouquet of chunks of watermelon, coconut, pineapple, mango, and even some jicama, all spritzed with lemon and sprinkled with salt and exclamatory chile powder. The red-hot spice elicits the fruit's sweetness and packs its own lip-tingling punch. It is a heady culinary collusion like nothing else we've ever eaten.

Next door to Pico de Gallo is a place that we have a hard time defining because no one there speaks a bit of English, but we highly recommend it for dessert. We believe it is called Paleteria Diana. It is two separate rooms, one of which serves some hot food and big cups of ice topped with sweet-syrup fruits and fillings, the other serving homemade ice cream bars and Mexican ice cream in countless flavors.

Sugar Bowl

4005 N. Scottsdale Rd.   480-946-0051

Scottsdale, AZ   LD | $

A while back, Roadfood.com user Charlene Kingston wrote to tell us, "*The Sugar Bowl* is the name of the ice cream counter that [cartoon character] Dennis the Menace visits, named after this restaurant. Hank Ketcham [Dennis's creator] used to come and visit Bill Keane (creator of *The Family Circus*), who lived in Scottsdale near this famous local landmark, and he used the name in his strip as an inside joke with Keane." So not only is it a good place to eat ice cream; it is a cultural landmark, too!

Few restaurants we know are as pure in spirit and intention as the Sugar Bowl, where everything served is better than it has to be and where the ambience seems like it might not have changed at all since opening day in 1958. With its pink-upholstered booths and counter stools and a swift young staff who look so cheerful carrying raspberry glaciers (Sprite and sherbet), golden nuggets (Sprite, sherbet, and ice cream), and Turkish coffee sodas, it is the quintessential ice cream parlor. In particular, we recommend Camelback sodas, made with either vanilla or coffee ice cream, "extra luscious malts," for which glasses are lined with your choice of marshmallow, hot fudge, or caramel sauce, and a perfect tin roof sundae, made with excellent chocolate syrup (not fudge) and heaped with a bounty of red-skin Spanish peanuts.

There are sandwiches, soups, and salads, too, and those we've tasted are very good; but in truth, when we walk into this happy place, we instantly become too obsessed with ice cream to think much about anything else.

Teresa's Mosaic Café

2455 N. Silverbell Rd.   520-624-4512
Tucson, AZ   BLD | $

Teresa's Mosaic Café bills itself as Oaxacan, and there are some less familiar Mexican dishes on the menu—chiles rellenos stuffed with shredded chicken, marinated pork loin fillets served with squash, and profoundly earthy smoked and pickled pasilla chiles that make a spot-on garnish for anything savory—but much of what's offered is familiar border cuisine (tacos, burros, chimichangas, enchiladas), and Tucson's own personality is reflected in such specialties as *topopo* salad and cheese crisps. Corn and wheat tortillas are made at the back of the dining room and arrive at your table griddle-hot. We love the chunky guacamole and mini chimichanga appetizers; and the green corn tamales, dotted with fresh kernels, are classic Sonoran desert fare.

We found this inconspicuous diner thanks to Roadfood team members and infallible tipsters Chris Ayers and Amy Breisch, who proclaimed Teresa's breakfast worthy of exaltation: "Amy dubbed the huevos rancheros the best ever, while Chris made the same claim for the cheese enchilada." The latter is available as part of a tremendously satisfying combination plate that also includes eggs and a hot tamale. The former, without being outlandish or unique, truly is the model for the way huevos rancheros ought to be: the eggs glistening with butter and perched atop a tortilla that is crisp but also a bit chewy, the salsa hot enough to make you grab for a tortilla from the accompanying basket to tamp your tongue and yet not so hot that the tomato, pepper, egg, wheat, and cheese don't each sing their essential notes loud and clear. There is coffee on the side, but if you've got a thirst to quench, Teresa's makes an intoxicating *horchata*.

Tucson Tamale Company

2545 E. Broadway   520-305-4760
Tucson, AZ   L | $

"The way I see it, the tamale is like a sandwich," says Todd Martin, who started the Tucson Tamale Company in 2008. "You can do anything with it you can imagine." Among his imaginings are vegetarian tamales, vegan tamales, gluten-free tamales, and a thermonuclear Tucson Tamale for which the moist corn masa is supercharged with grilled jalapeños and cheese. We especially love what he has labeled the Arizona tamale—roasted sirloin and smoky chipotle chiles—as well as the Santa Fe tamale, made with pork loin and green chiles. There even is an ode to Tucson's notorious Sonoran hot dog: the dogmale, which is an all-beef hot dog, bacon, beans, and salsa enveloped in corn masa. And in the fall, when corn is ripe and chiles are harvested, traditional green corn tamales are featured for about three weeks.

"Simplify, Sustain and Celebrate" is the motto of Martin's sunny storefront, which vends hundreds of dozens of tamales every week—by mail and take-out for cooking at home, warm for eating on premises at a handful of tables (along with house-made salsas in three heat levels), and at farmers' markets and some dozen grocery stores as far south as Bisbee. Martin is an engaging advocate for the steamed-moist cylinder of cornmeal dough that is most commonly laced with beef and in some places topped with chili. "People think of the tamale as a Mexican thing," he says, "but it goes back to pre-Columbian Mesoamerica, long before the Spanish. So many cultures around the world have their own take on the concept."

Bongo Billy's

300 W. Sackett Ave.   719-539-4261
Salida, CO   BL | $

Thanks to Chuck Henrickson for tipping us off to this cute little sandwich shop in Salida—one of two Bongo Billy's in Colorado. (The other is in Buena Vista.) It bills itself as a café, but it has more of a coffeehouse spirit, with all sorts of whole beans and coffee (and tea) drinks available, as well as an inventory of coffee makers, mugs, and T-shirts. The walls are decorated with a changing display of work by local artists, and bluegrass and folk musicians regularly perform in the evenings. A deck overlooking the Arkansas River provides customers a wonderful opportunity for meditative caffeination.

The menu is a sprightly selection of salads, sandwiches, and such Mexican-accented dishes as a Three Sisters Quesadilla (cheese, corn, beans, squash, and tomatoes) and breakfast burritos. Our pick dish is the Blue Moon Harvest Salad, which is a mesclun mix topped with blue cheese, spicy toasted walnuts, dried cranberries, and sweet peppercorn dressing. On the side comes a length of French baguette.

Beyond coffee, espresso drinks, and tea, drinks include smoothies, Italian sodas, cider, wine, beer on tap, and microbrews by the bottle.

Buckhorn Exchange

1000 Osage St.   303-534-9505
Denver, CO   LD | $$$

Holder of Colorado Liquor License No. 1 (issued in 1893), outfitted with a few museums' worth of antique firearms and furniture, and hung with a menagerie of some five hundred game animal trophies shot by former owner Shorty Zietz, the Buckhorn Exchange is no mere frontier-themed restaurant for tourists. It happens to be a fine place to eat the cuisine of the Rockies.

At lunch, hamburgers, salads, and sandwiches are consumed without ado by a cadre of regular customers inured to the stare of a thousand glass eyes and the creak of wood floors where Buffalo Bill once trod. Tourists like us cannot help but gape and wonder . . . and then tuck into a seriously carnivorous meal. Those who want to eat really wild western fare can start with Rocky Mountain oysters (deep-fried hunks of calf testicle) or rattlesnake marinated in red chile and lime. For the main meat you can choose buffalo tenderloin, elk medallions, Colorado lamb, beefsteaks, or pork ribs. If there's more than a single passionate meat-eater at the table, the dish to have is The Big Steak, a strip steak sized for two to five appetites, cooked to crusty succulence and carved tableside.

Top it all off with a broad slab of hot crumb-topped apple pie and cinnamon rum sauce, and you have eaten a true-West meal.

Bud's Bar

5453 Manhart St.   303-688-9967
Sedalia, CO   LD | $

Bars tend not to be great places to look for excellent food, but if it's a hamburger you seek, they're worth putting on the hit list. For a really excellent bar-burger, we suggest heading south on Highway 85 out of Denver to the town of Sedalia and finding a mid-twentieth-century watering hole named Bud's. Here is served what tipster Mindy Leisure described as "one of the best burgers you will ever eat." It is juicy with a good crust, modest-size, nothing fancy, and no unusual toppings are available. You have a choice of a single or a double with or without cheese. Pickles and onion are the only garnishes available. There's no deep-fryer on premises, so the menu advises patrons, "We don't have no damn fries." Instead, you get a bag of potato chips.

As you might guess by the extremely limited menu—there's nothing to eat other than burgers—Bud's attracts a lot of people for whom the hamburgers are a side dish to the main course, which is beer.

Conway's Red Top

1520 S. Nevada Ave.   719-633-2444
Colorado Springs, CO   LD | $

Conway's hamburgers are genuine whoppers—half a foot across, served on broad-domed buns, accompanied by shoestring French fries and titanic pitchers of soda. Panavision-wide but not gourmet-thick, they are happy lunch-counter patties with enough oily smack to imprint the bun with their savor. They are sold whole or half, topped with cheese (Cheddar, Velveeta, American, mozzarella, or pepper jack), chili, mushrooms, or hickory-flavored barbecue sauce.

One's a meal (that's the house motto), especially if accompanied by good, shrivel-tipped French fries, onion rings, or a combo known as frings. But it would be a shame to visit the Red Top without a taste of the soups and stews that are still made from Grandma Esther's (Phyllis Conway's mom) original recipes. The navy bean soup, for example, is a stout brew with a profound, long-simmered flavor redolent of hickory-smoked ham and spice. With its accompanying sourdough roll, it is hearty enough to be a filling lunch (with a minuscule price tag). Beef stew is another homespun delight—hours in the making, so all the juices of the beef and vegetables have a chance to mellow and blend and soften. It is so thick you only need a fork to eat a bowlful. You can also have a bowl of spicy green chili (made with pork) or a split, grilled hot dog served on a broad burger bun.

Note: There are four other Red Tops in Colorado Springs: at 1228 E. Filmore, 390 Circle Dr., 3589 N. Carefree Circle, and 5865 Palmer Park Blvd. And there is one in Pueblo at 112 W. 2nd.

Duffeyroll Café

1290 South Pearl St.   303-570-2590
Denver, CO   BL | $

Colorado is rich in cinnamon rolls. The most famous is the enormous, plate-size megaroll at the Johnson's Corner truck stop up in Loveland (p. 408). The most elegant is the one at the Duffeyroll Café in Denver. Actually, there are several Duffeyrolls available—crisp-edged swirls of dough drizzled with maple, orange, even Irish cream frosting, but it's our firm belief that such drippy indulgence, while a welcome addition to big, doughy rolls, over-whelms the fragile texture of a plain Duffeyroll. Oh, we do like Pecanilla crunch and the English toffee, which are applied prudently and add a nice extra note. But the regular roll is so perfectly sugary and cinnamony and super-buttery that we cannot bear to adulterate it.

If you do need something denser and more substantial, have a pecan sticky bun, stuck with a thick blanket of nuts. Sandwiches, wraps, soups, and salads are available at lunch.

There is a second location in Denver at 4994 E Hampden Ave.; 303-753-9177.

Durango Diner
957 Main Ave.   970-247-9889
Durango, CO   BLD | $

It was pancakes that made us fall in love with the Durango Diner—plate-wide pancakes, preferably with blueberries, glistening with butter and running rivers of syrup. We branched out to other breakfasts and liked them plenty, especially the "half and half" plate of biscuits with gravy and green chile, and the big warm cinnamon roll. Breakfast is a particularly good meal to eat in this Main Street hash house; you will share it with some locals who claim to have been having coffee an' at these seats since opening day in 1965.

Then we discovered the hamburgers. If you are a connoisseur of hamburger excellence, put Durango on your treasure map, for here they make one really wonderful variation known as the Bonus Cheeseburger Deluxe: one-half pound of meat under a mantle of melted Swiss cheese and a heap of diced green chiles, French fries on the side. We love the Durango Diner's bacon double cheeseburgers almost as much as we love the chiliburgers (available red or green), and although some customers combine all these toppings on one mound of meat, we must confess that bacon and chili together atop a cheeseburger is just too much for our delicate palates.

Johnson's Corner
2842 SE Frontage Rd.   970-667-2069
(Exit 254 off I-25)   Always open | $
Loveland, CO

A favorite truckers' stop along Highway 87 between Denver and Cheyenne since before there was an interstate, Johnson's Corner serves breakfast (and lunch and supper) around the clock and is famous for its colossal cinnamon roll. The roll is fine—probably the most bang for your buck—but when we seek maximum flavor along with maximum calories, we prefer Johnson's chicken-fried steak with eggs, crunchy hash browns, and a biscuit with gravy. The breakfast menu contains all the usual suspects—omelets, pancakes, corned beef hash—as well as buffalo sausage and a breakfast burrito. Non-breakfast highlights include pot roast dinner, hot turkey sandwich, steaks, and pork chops. A full-service soda fountain offers shakes, floats, and malts and one heck of a handsome banana split.

Recently remodeled, the dining area offers hugely spacious booths and counter service. And for truckers and other travelers who want to stay connected, it is a Wi-Fi hot spot.

La Fogata

5670 E. Evans Ave.   303-753-9458
Denver, CO   BLD | $

La Fogata means "the bonfire"; however, the green chile bowl (available with or without pork) served in this bilingual establishment isn't really all that hot. But it is quite delicious: zesty, glowing with sunny chile flavor, and packed with the punch of cumin. If you are looking for excellent Mexican food in Denver, this is the place to be.

Many items on La Fogata's menu are nationally familiar Tex-Mex staples—enchiladas, chiles rellenos, tamales—expertly made and served in abundance; but this is also an opportunity to be adventurous. If you are blasé about beef in your taco, you can order tacos filled with crisp-roasted pork (wonderful!) or with beef tongue (spicy!) or ceviche tostadas; or you can spoon into a bowl of *menudo,* the Mexican tripe-and-hominy stew that is alleged to have magical powers to cure a hangover. To drink, there are imported beers, plenty of tequila cocktails, and the true-Mex nonalcoholic favorite, *horchata,* which is sweet rice milk.

This is a fun place to dine, where the crowd is equal measures of downtown business executives, blue-collar beer drinkers, and foodies who appreciate a taste of high-quality but unpretentious and inexpensive Mexican food.

There are two other locations in Denver: at 8090 East Quincy Ave. and 16600 Washington St.

Brookville Hotel

105 E. Lafayette Ave.   785-263-2244

Abilene, KS   LD | $$

Buffalo Bill slept at the Brookville Hotel in the small town of Brookville, as did untold numbers of cowboys when Kansas was the end of the line for trail drives up from Texas. It was opened in 1870, and it has built a reputation for its bountiful family-style chicken dinners since 1915.

The old Brookville Hotel closed a few years ago and a new version opened in Abilene, right near I-70. It's a modern building with a design that is almost an exact duplicate of the old facility; however, the charms of the old railhead town of Brookville are absent. For travelers who considered a visit to the restaurant part of a genuine visit to old Kansas, the reborn facility will be a disappointment—more like a theme park. Still, the menu remains the same one that made Brookville a destination for generations of hungry Kansans who think nothing of driving two hours each way for Sunday supper. Fried chicken is the main attraction—half a bird, skillet-fried and served with mashed potatoes and chicken gravy, with side dishes of corn, cottage cheese, baking powder biscuits with sweet preserves, sweet slaw, and ice cream for dessert.

Bunker Hill Cafe

6th & Elm Sts.   785-483-6544
Bunker Hill, KS   D Wed-Sat | $$$

Located in a blink-and-you-miss-it crossroads community, the Bunker Hill Cafe is a rugged limestone building that opened as a drugstore, then became a pool hall. Today it is a destination steak house, open for supper only Wednesday through Saturday. It's a small place, no more than a dozen tables, with a menu that includes shrimp, catfish, and chicken, although nearly everybody comes for steak. Filet mignon is available in sizes that range from two to sixteen ounces, sirloin from four to sixteen. There's also bacon-wrapped ground beef and, on occasion, Kansas elk and buffalo. Our sirloins were laden with juice, tender but not at all tenderized, a joy to slowly savor. It was late summer, and on the side came beautiful, full-flavored tomatoes and corn on the cob, as well as the house specialty, honey bread (available for purchase by the loaf).

Decor is Plains rustic: lots of mounted trophies and naturalist pictures on the wall and a couple of wood-burning stoves for warmth in cool weather. As seating is limited, reservations are advised.

Chicken Mary's

1133 E. 600th Ave.   620-231-9510
Pittsburg, KS   D | $$

"It's crazy, isn't it," Chicken Mary's son mused to us one hot summer day many years ago. "What's all this fried chicken doing out here anyway?"

It was a rhetorical question. The man knew perfectly well why the narrow lane off Highway 69 between Frontenac and Pittsburg, Kansas, is known as the Chicken Dinner Road, but he also knew that a couple of strangers highballing up toward Kansas City had to wonder: Why, in the middle of nowhere, are there a handful of flourishing restaurants—Chicken Mary's and Chicken Annie's foremost among them—that specialize in nearly identical dinners of deep-fried chicken?

Mary and Annie have long ago gone to their reward, so Mary's son—no spring chicken himself—explained that in the hard times of the 1930s, his father and Annie's husband both worked in a nearby mine. In 1934, Annie's husband lost a leg in a mine accident. To make ends meet, Annie opened a little restaurant and served her specialty, fried chicken. Only a few years after that, Mary's husband had to quit work, too, because of a bad heart. "There were three of us kids to feed," the old man recalled, "and my mother could see how well Annie was doing selling chicken dinners out here. She took a hint and opened her own place, Chicken Mary's, just down the road."

A tradition was begun. The rivalry has made this unlikely farm road a chicken-lover's mecca for six decades. The meals are ritualized family-style feasts, centered around chicken that arrives glistening with grease. The skin is chewy and luxurious, the meat below moist and tender. You can order whichever parts you want in whatever quantity: dark, white, wings, backs, even livers, gizzards, or hearts. On the side you want German potato salad and/or coleslaw. Poultry-frowners can order chicken-fried steak.

Note: Chicken Annie's is a few hundred yards up the road, at 1143 E. 600th Avenue. We've never eaten at both in the same trip, nor have we done enough research to rate one place above the other.

The Corner Pharmacy

429 Delaware St.   913-682-1602
Leavenworth, KS   BL | $

Located in a well-tended Victorian building that dates back to the beginning of the twentieth century, The Corner Pharmacy is a trip back in time not only for its soda fountain treats and breakfast-served-all-day (to 6 P.M., closing time), but for the low-single-digit prices for meals. A cup of coffee costs less than a dollar, including refills.

Have a seat on a bentwood stool. The countertop is faux marble, but the food is real. Watch the mixologist create a Green River or a phosphate and see milk shakes assembled scoop by squirt, then whirled in the multi-wand mixer and served in their ice-frosted silver canisters. Hamburgers are lunch-counter-thin and just greasy enough to leave a savory imprint on the bun. A plate of biscuits and gravy is one of the best dollars-for-calories deals in the nation.

Beyond the counter is a full-service drugstore, where pharmacist Ron Booth was quoted as saying, "My customers are also my friends and neighbors. They can come in and talk to me about anything."

The Cozy Inn

108 N. 7th St.   785-825-2699
Salina, KS   LD | $

When the McDonald Brothers opened their first hamburger stand in California after World War II, The Cozy Inn had already been around a quarter century. This is one of America's original hamburger stands, and although its management has changed over the years and it was threatened with extinction (but saved by a consortium of local hamburger patriots), it serves burgers that are pretty much the same as they were in 1922.

Here are archetypal sliders. The first great thing to praise about them is their smell. As you approach the compact diner, the scent of grilling onions and beef with a hint of dill pickle tickles your senses like exotic hash-house perfume. Sit at the counter on one of six stools for a ten-minute lunch of maybe a half-dozen little sliders and a bag of potato chips, and that smell will saturate your clothes and stay with you the rest of the day. Freeze a bag of Cozies, then heat them in the microwave oven six months later, and their perfume will billow out when you open the oven door.

The second exceptional thing about them is their taste. These are no Salisbury steaks or quarter-pounders. They are thin-as-a-nickel, one-ounce patties in little buns that somehow form a perfect combination with pickle, mustard, and ketchup. It is a configuration so consecrated that, according to Cozy Inn folklore, some years ago when a Cozy cook tried to put a piece of cheese on his own personal burger, he was fired on the spot.

Oklahoma Joe's

3002 W. 47th Ave.   913-722-3366
Kansas City, KS   LD | $

A gas station, convenience store, and cafeteria-style barbecue restaurant, Oklahoma Joe's offers traditional KC barbecue by the pound and sandwich as well as such specialty sandwiches as the Z-Man, which is brisket and provolone cheese topped with onion rings, and Hog Heaven, which is pulled pork *and* sliced sausage.

Unless you are a purist, you might want to try the fine Smokie Joe, which is a combo sandwich of beef and pork. While the plain pulled pork is great sauceless—sweet, juicy, and radiant with smoke flavor—Joe's peppery, slightly sweet sauce, included in the Smokie Joe, makes the meat duo sing.

Tables are outfitted with paper towels, and myriad banners hung around the interior celebrate the victories of OK Joe's barbecue men in competitions far and wide.

Olde Towne Restaurant

126 N. Main St.   316-947-5446
Hillsboro, KS   BL Tues-Sat, D Fri & Sun, Sunday supper | $$

In a big old limestone building on Main Street in downtown Hillsboro, Olde Towne Restaurant really is Olde! Located in what was built in 1887 as the town's bank (with a vault in the basement), it served for many years as an egg factory where women candled, sorted, and crated eggs. Lower-story decor includes vintage egg crates made of wood as well as antique farm implements and a mural of old Hillsboro showing the great yellow bank building.

Olde Towne is the one nice restaurant in Hillsboro, and so it has a menu with something for everyone, from sandwiches, soups, and hamburgers every day at lunch to an all-you-can-eat Mexican smorgasbord on Friday nights and a Saturday night Low German buffet. Hillsboro is the heart of America's Mennonite community, and many of today's three thousand citizens are descended from Germans who came to the USA (some via Russia). One of those who upholds the culinary heritage is Linden Thiessen, proprietor of Olde Towne and a man who makes a point of serving such melting-pot dishes as *verenika* (cottage cheese dumplings), zwieback bread, beet borscht, and New Year's cookies as well as locally made German whole-hog sausage and slow-smoked beef brisket reminiscent of Texas Hill Country cuisine (where the original settlers brought some of the same likings). Dessert measures up to grandmotherly standards and includes an array of cream pies, bumbleberry pie, hot fruit cobbler, and elegant cream puffs.

Porubsky's Grocery

508 N.E. Sardou Ave.   785-234-5788
Topeka, KS   L Mon–Thurs | $

For over half a century, customers have been coming to the dining room at the side of Porubsky's Grocery store to eat cold-cut sandwiches and chili (the latter during chili season only—October to March). Curiously, no coffee is served for the simple reason that this is an eat-it-and-beat-it type of establishment where few midday customers have long lunch hours to while away sipping coffee. Regulars include a large blue-collar crowd as well as Kansas politicians and other public figures whose autographed pictures, inscribed with praises of the place and the family that has run it since 1950, line the walls.

The sandwiches are well apportioned and low-priced, but it's the extras that make lunch worth a detour off Highway 70. The most famous of the extras are Porubsky's pickles. These big, firm disks, which start as dills but are then infused with horseradish, mustard, and hot peppers, are guaranteed to snap your taste buds to attention. They are a favorite complement, along with crumbled saltine crackers, atop a bowl of Porubsky's chili. Before the hot pickles are applied, the chili is a fine bowl of heartland comfort: ground chuck cooked with a judicious measure of chili powder and other spice, then added to a battered old pot of simmering beans.

Note: In season, chili is served only Monday through Thursday. The Porubsky family likes to keep the store aisles clear on Friday and Saturday for neighborhood residents who still come to shop for their groceries.

Woodyard Bar-B-Que

3001 Merriam Ln.   913-362-8000
Kansas City, KS   LD | $$

The Woodyard is in fact a wood yard selling hickory, cherry, pecan, and applewood logs to pitmasters and backyard barbecuists. It is also a restaurant that serves fine Kansas City barbecue, which you can enjoy at tables inside a country wood-frame house or on a patio built around an open-air smoker. From the smoker emerge splendid baby back ribs sheathed in meat that pulls right off the bone in big, juicy ribbons.

Smoke profoundly infuses the Woodyard's burnt ends (tips, squiggles, shreds, and nuggets of barbecued meat), which are available in a sandwich or on occasion as the topping for multi-bean chili. Burnt ends are powerful stuff. For those less extreme in their barbecue lust, the pulled pork here is nothing short of magnificent, just-right smoky and so full of juice and flavor that sauce is entirely optional. Other items on the menu include hot legs—like wings, but meatier—and a Friday special of pecan-smoked salmon.

Hash House

2605 S. Decatur, Suite 103
Las Vegas, NV

702-873-9479
BL | $

If we were sticklers for our own rules, one of which defines Roadfood as fare of the region where the restaurant is located, the Hash House would not be included in this book. It's in Las Vegas and boasts of serving midwestern food. But because Las Vegas is a city where normal rules of life don't always apply and, more important, because it is a city with a dearth of normal restaurants (what is native Las Vegas cuisine, anyway?), we include it here as a service to hungry travelers in search of something other than an all-you-can-eat buffet or yet another celebrity chef's high-priced eating shrine.

We might never have found it were it not for the intrepid appetites of Roadfood.com's Bruce Bilmes and Sue Boyle, who wrote, "The simple, unflashy home-cooking, served in a simple, unflashy room, plays well in megaflashy Vegas." They noted that it really is a hash house, its breakfast-all-day menu featuring corned beef hash, ham hash, roast beef hash, and chicken hash, as well as Super Hash, which blends them all. A good-size portion, including a couple of side dishes (fried potatoes, grits, fresh fruit, toast) will get you plenty of change from a $10 bill: one of the city's true dining bargains. Bruce and Sue emphasized that just about everything at the hash house is made right there. The hash, of course, which you can have with (or without) peppers, onions, mushrooms, or even eggs scrambled in, but also an amazing array of jellies and jams, including hot habanero, not-quite-as-hot jalapeño, peach, strawberry, and watermelon.

The menu extends far beyond hash. Omelets, pancakes, waffles, eggs Benedict, Alaskan salmon, and perch with eggs for breakfast; soup, salad, sandwiches, fried chicken, and hamburgers for lunch.

Louis' Basque Corner

301 E. 4th St.   775-323-7203
Reno, NV   LD | $$

We ate at Louis' Basque Corner on our first trip across the USA in the early 1970s. At the time, Louis' was only about five years old—Mr. and Mrs. Louis Erreguible, who had only recently come to Reno from southern France, were ebullient hosts in their New World dining room. After supper, we walked out utterly inspired, thinking that *someone* really ought to be writing about marvelous local restaurants in unlikely places across the country. We've been writing about such restaurants ever since, and Louis' Basque Corner continues to serve what Mrs. Erreguible described long ago as "simple food cooked to perfection."

By average-American-meal standards, the food at Louis' is far from simple. What you eat at the long, family-style tables are copious feasts that start with soup, salad, bread, and beans, then move on to a plate of beef tongue, paella, oxtails, lamb stew, or Basque chicken. That's the *first course*! After that comes the serious eating: an entree of sirloin steak, paella, pork loin or pork chops, lamb chops, or a fish of the day.

Louis' is a colorful place with waitresses outfitted in native attire and walls decorated with travel posters of the Pyrenees as well as pottery from Ciboure. Its clientele is a mix of travelers passing through for whom a meal here is a special treat as well as plenty of locals who make Louis' a regular part of their regime.

Martin Hotel

94 W. Railroad St.   775-623-3197
Winnemucca, NV   LD | $$

Bring plenty of appetite if you plan to eat dinner at the Martin Hotel, which has been serving big Basque feeds to locals for well over a century. The copious meals start with soup, salad, herbed carrots, Basque beans, garbanzo beans with sausage, garlic mashed potatoes, and bread, all accompanied by basso profundo burgundy wine. That panoply of food and drink is only a prelude to the main course, which can be steak, lamb shank, pork chops, pork loin, sweetbreads, or salmon, accompanied by excellent French fries cut from local potatoes. There is good bread pudding for dessert, and you must also consider a glass of Picon punch, the bittersweet Basque *digestif*.

The hotel is a humble stucco building that still has hitching posts outside. Dining is at long communal tables that seat up to a dozen people. At lunch, normal-size plates of food are served.

Bert's Burger Bowl

235 N. Guadalupe St.   505-982-0215
Santa Fe, NM   LD | $

Bert's says it invented the green chile cheeseburger, and while we cannot confirm or deny the claim, we can tell you that the one made here is good. Flat patties of beef are sizzled on a grate over charcoal, from which flames lick up and flavor not only the meat, but also the bright orange cheese laid upon it. Dollops of fiery minced green chile are mounded atop the cheese from a bucket near the fire, and unless you say otherwise, your burger will come dressed with mustard, pickle, lettuce, onion, and tomato. Experienced customers, who dine under umbrellas on a sun-drenched patio overlooking Guadalupe Street, gradually peel back the wax paper in which the sandwich is wrapped as they eat, thus avoiding too much spillage.

Other popular burger configurations include BBQ and mayo/relish; and if the normal quarter-pounder seems insufficient, a half-pound hamburger is available. Anyone who eats four half-pound burgers in thirty minutes gets them free. The menu also lists *taco carnitas, flautas de pollo,* chile dogs, and Fritos pie.

Bert's is a quick-order joint, but the food doesn't come right away. You tell them what you want; they take your money and give you a number. Then you hang around listening to hamburgers sizzle. Every one is cooked to order. A sign on the cash register advises: "All our food at Bert's is specially made for you and the approximate wait is twelve minutes once order is placed."

Bobcat Bite

420 Old Las Vegas Hwy.   505-983-5319
Santa Fe, NM   LD | $

While some hash slingers put chiles atop the cheese to make their green chile cheeseburgers, at Bobcat Bite, a comely diner on the outskirts of Santa Fe, the cook secretes a lode of fire-flavored chopped chile underneath the cheese. The creamy cheese melts among the peppers and into the crevices of the crusty ten-ounce burger down below to create a fusion flavor that is pure Land of Enchantment, and perhaps the definitive green chile cheeseburger.

Bobcat Bite is itself an extremely enchanting place, offering lovely rib-eye steaks in addition to the legendary burgers. It is a vintage roadside diner packed with customers through the dinner hour, with a sign-up board outside for those willing to wait. Inside there are about a half-dozen seats at the counter and five or six tables and not much room to move around. Throughout the mealtime, there is a considerable amount of shuffling sideways at the counter seats so parties of two can sit together.

Since it opened in the middle of the last century, Bobcat Bite has maintained a country coziness that makes newcomers and old friends always feel at home. For us, the experience of eating here has a strong nostalgic air, like we've somehow stepped into a shipshape roadside diner in the mid-1950s. In its modest way, it is a beautiful place, with clean varnished wood tables and counter and pictures of bobcats and other wildlife on the walls.

Buckhorn Tavern

68 US Hwy. 380   575-835-4423
San Antonio, NM   LD | $

Expect to wait for a table at the Buckhorn Tavern. Having been in the spotlight of a TV food show and named the seventh-best hamburger in America by *GQ*, the little place has been overrun with pilgrims eager to eat its green chile cheeseburger. Boob-tube and press puffery notwithstanding, it really is a terrific burger. The meat is a wide, rugged patty, about a half-inch thick, cooked medium so it is moist but not dripping juice, redolent of beefy flavor. As for the full-dress Buckhorn Burger, it is a devastating tsunami of beef, melty cheese, hot green chile, lettuce, tomato, and pickle chips on a broad, tender bun. There are more elegant GCCBs in New Mexico—there are some that are beefier or oozier—but this one earns kudos for harmony.

Buckhorn's Fritos pie is a very good one, another example of multiple-ingredient poise. When you order it, you must choose among green chile, red chile, or the combination of both—known as Christmas. Chile cheese fries are a good idea, but the ones we ate were limp and not cooked through. Maybe it was a bad deep-fryer day, or perhaps our extremely early arrival fifteen minutes before opening (to avoid the line) meant the cooking oil wasn't yet hot enough.

Chope's

16165 S. Hwy. 28   505-233-3420
La Mesa, NM   LD | $

There is no better way to taste the long green chiles of New Mexico's Mesilla Valley than as Chope's chiles rellenos. Stuffed with mild cheese, battered, and crisp-fried, the fleshy walls of the pod have a strapping vegetable punch. As for red chiles, their ultimate taste is in the cream-thick, fruit-bright vermillion purée that is scrupulously hand-made in the kitchen every Monday. It is pretty hot, the kind of lip-searing hot that any restaurant outside New Mexico would warn customers about. But in this area, it's normal. The really hot stuff on the table is the green salsa, made entirely from Mesilla Valley jalapeños. Chope's will oblige those who insist on maximum heat by offering special four-alarm chili in a bowl or on enchiladas. The chilecentric menu also includes gorditas, tacos, plates of chili con carne, tamales, and green chile–draped cheeseburgers.

Duran Central Pharmacy

1815 Central Ave. NW   505-247-4141
Albuquerque, NM   BL | $

One of our favorite views in the scenery-rich Southwest is from a stool at the lunch counter in Duran Central Pharmacy. To the right is the kitchen, where you can view one of the staff using a dowel to roll out rounds of dough into broad flour tortillas that are perfect tan circles. Straight ahead is the grill where they are cooked. To see them puff up from the heat and blister golden-brown, then to smell the warm bready aroma fill the air, is to know for certain that good food is on its way.

These superlative tortillas, available plain or glistening with butter, come on the side of most lunches, including the wondrous Thursday-only *carne adovada* (chile-marinated pork). They are used to wrap hamburgers and as the base of quesadillas. We like them best as a dunk for Duran's exemplary red or green chili, which is available either plain (nothing but chiles and spice) or loaded with your choice of ground beef, beans, potatoes, or chicken. The green is hugely flavorful, hot and satisfying with an earthy character; the red is pure essence of plant life, liquefied with a full measure of sunshine.

Duran, by the way, is a full-service pharmacy.

Frontier

2400 Central Ave. SE   505-266-0550
Albuquerque, NM   Open daily, 5 A.M.–1 A.M. | $

The Frontier boasts that it is "home of the latest in broiled food and the Frontier sweet roll." We're not up on broiled food trends and the famous Frontier sweet roll, while awesomely sized, is not on our top ten list. Nevertheless we love this place—not only because it is cheap, informal, and open before dawn, but also because the New Mexican food is first-rate.

At breakfast, for instance, huevos rancheros are available with a choice of four toppings: salsa, green chile stew, red chile, and green chile. The last one is the hottest, with a full-tilt chile punch, giving the plate a roasted, earthy aroma that is insanely appetizing. Cheddar cheese is technically an option, but should not be left out of this big platter that looks like a mess but eats like a dream. On the side comes a puffy, just-cooked flour tortilla (you can watch the man make them behind the counter) that is almost too hot to handle. Orange juice is fresh-squeezed. Quart pitchers of coffee are available for $2—a good deal for the students who come to pore over books early in the morning.

The lunch menu includes such Land of Enchantment specialties as a *carne adovada* burrito, green chile stew, and, naturally, a chile cheeseburger, here dubbed the Fiesta Burger. Homemade lemonade is available to drink.

One thing that makes dining at the Frontier fun is its breakneck pace. Because meals are ordered fast, cooked fast, and served instantaneously, you are guaranteed that things that are supposed to be hot are piping hot; we've gotten hamburgers still sizzling from the grill. Although many students come to linger over coffee and homework, it is possible to be in and out, with a good meal under your belt, in five minutes. The system is serve-yourself. While you wait in line, study the overhead menu and make your decision. When the green light flashes, indicating someone is ready to take your order, step up to the counter and say what you want. Approximately two minutes later, you are carrying your meal to an open table.

Garcia's Kitchen

1113 4th St. NW   505-247-9149

Albuquerque, NM   BLD | $

Garcia's Kitchen has been around since 1975 and there now are seven locations in Albuquerque. All are bright and festive, from Fiestaware dishes to colorful murals on inside and outside walls. The menu is big, including such New Mexico signature dishes as blue corn enchiladas, green chile cheeseburgers, and stuffed sopaipillas. There is Tex-Mex chili con carne and true-Mex *menudo,* as well as a full array of burritos available "chili in," "chili & cheese over," or "smothered."

It is breakfast, served anytime, that we enjoyed. With hungry companions to split dishes (an excellent strategy here), we savored a bowl of *chicharrones,* which are a bacon-lover's fantasy: whole nuggets of crisp-fried pork rind that are about half meat, half fat—unbelievably delicious when eaten still melt-in-the-mouth warm, still irresistible as we devoured the last of them at the end of the meal, our appetites only a memory but taste buds still ravening. It was especially fun to tear off a small piece of sopaipilla, insert a single *chicharrone,* then drizzle on some honey: sweet, wheat, and meat, all in one!

Then there is the glorious *carne adovada*: hunks of pork saturated with sunny chile flavor and bathed in red purée—so much so that the yolks of two sunny-side-up eggs on the plate barely poked up through the chile. On the side came good fried potatoes and lard-rich *refritos.* Huevos rancheros was an equally over-abundant plateful. You get your choice of red or green chili; say "Christmas" and you get both—two soupy brews that magically arrive perfectly separated on the plate, but then swirl together as soon as you attack with a fork. A huge breakfast burrito came similarly dressed, half and half.

Leona's

4 Medina Ln.   505-351-4569

Chimayo, NM   LD (closed Tues & Wed) | $

The village of Chimayo is off a winding road in the foothills of the Sangre de Christos, but it isn't obscure. Generations of weavers have made its cloth a western legend, and its early nineteenth-century *santuario* is a destination for religious pilgrims who believe that dirt from the earthen floor has miraculous healing powers. For four decades, hungry travelers have come to Chimayo to eat Leona's tortillas.

The first time we drove through New Mexico in the mid-1970s, Leona had a roadside stand on Highway 76 where she sold tortillas and chiles.

At harvest time in the fall, you could pull over and get a sandwich of just-roasted chiles wrapped in a fresh tortilla—one of the great roadside snacks of all time. She now makes and sells flavored tortillas (apple cinnamon for breakfast; onion, garlic, piñon, or pesto) and she runs a little, mostly take-out eatery shaded by an ancient catalpa tree just below the *santuario*. Here you can enjoy tamales that radiate corn flavor, red and green chile stew, posole, and the traditional hangover cure of posole and tripe known as *menudo*.

Leona's makes exceptional burritos stuffed with fiery *carne adovada* (chile-marinated pork), rice and beans, or *chicharrones* (rendered pork fat like nuggets of bacon, only piggier). The one that knocks our socks off is the chile relleno burrito. Rellenos, which are cheese-stuffed, breaded-and-fried chiles, are popular throughout New Mexico, but too often the chile and its crust turn to mush. Leona's has crust with crunch; the chile pod it sheaths is al dente and full-flavored, with enough mellow melted cheese inside to balance the heat. Wrap it in one of her tortillas and you have what Leona calls a "hand-held burrito," meaning it's easy to pick up and eat with no utensils. This is a valued quality to pilgrims for whom Leona's sanctuary is a blessed part of the walk through Chimayo.

Model Pharmacy

3636 Monte Vista Blvd. NE   505-255-8686
Albuquerque, NM   L | $

You enter this neighborhood pharmacy past the drug counter, navigate among perfumes, soaps, and sundries, then find the little lunch area: a few tables scattered about and a short marble counter with a Pueblo-Deco knee guard of colorful enamel tiles. If you are like us, your attention will be drawn to the right of the counter, where the cobblers are displayed under a spotlight. Three or four are made every day—geological-looking strata of flaky crust atop syrupy tender hunks of apricot, peach, blackberry, or a mix thereof—and they are available simply warm or warm with a globe of ice cream melting on top.

The soda fountain is impressive: a fully stocked armory of milk shake mixers, syrup dispensers, and soda nozzles, plus a modern espresso machine (so you can get an espresso milk shake—mmm). As for lunchtime entrees, locals love the walnut chicken salad, and some come to eat hamburgers and cold-cut sandwiches; but we'll choose green chile stew every time. It is more a soup, actually, chock-full of carrots, tomatoes, and bits of green chile, with good flavor and alarming heat.

Nellie's

1226 W. Hadley Ave.　　　　575-524-9982
Las Cruces, NM　　　　　　BL | $

Inside this snug, cozy cinder-block and glass-brick restaurant, a sign on the wall clearly declares the kitchen's priorities: "A day without chile is like a day without sunshine." Danny Ray Hernandez, Nellie's son, makes vivid salsas using five to seven different types of chile and specializes in such eye-opening breakfasts as huevos à la Mexicana (scrambled with jalapeños) and eggs with chile and meat. For the latter you can get red or green or a combination of the two (known as Christmas). The red tastes of pure pod; the green is hot enough to require tongue-tamping with the kitchen's pulchritudinous sopaipillas. Mr. Hernandez speculated that dry growing conditions over recent years have produced chiles in which the heat is more concentrated.

Years ago, Nellie's and its offspring, Little Nellie's Chile Factory, served dinner. Today it is strictly a breakfast-and-lunch eatery.

Nopalitos

310 S. Mesquite St.　　　　575-524-0003
Las Cruces, NM　　　　　　LD | $

Las Cruces is in the heart of chile-growing country, and Nopalitos is a family-run restaurant (actually two restaurants; the other is at 2605 Missouri) where you can count on excellent chile-based food. This is not Tex-Mex nor Arizona-Mex nor California-Mex nor Sonoran Mex, but the unique cuisine of New Mexico. That means that nearly every meal poses the question: red or green chile? There is no rule about which is hotter. The day we came to Nopalitos (which means "little cactus"), the waitress assured us that green was the hot stuff, but that red was more delicious. What to do? "Christmas!" she replied, which is the term for a dish topped with both.

We had ours on a stacked enchilada with the works, meaning beans and cheese and a fried egg on top and rice and salad on the side. We also savored excellent chiles rellenos, fried to a fragile crisp and oozing warm cheese.

Before the main course, everybody gets crisp, warm tortilla chips and a set of salsas, red and green. The green is served hot (temperature-wise) but is fairly mild. The red is served cool but is very, very hot. We also ordered what the menu lists as avocado salad but looked and tasted a lot like chunky guacamole.

The broad, airy dining room with its adobe mission-style decor is a pleasant place to relax and enjoy native foods. The staff was kind and helpful, seats were comfortable, and we relished the aroma of other people's chilecentric meals—gorditas, chile con carne, tacos, tamales, rolled as well as stacked enchiladas—wafting past us on their way from the kitchen to tables.

Owl Bar & Cafe

79 Main St.   575-835-9946
San Antonio, NM   BLD | $

"Masterpiece! Masterpiece!" sings the waitress at the Owl Bar as she carries a green chile cheeseburger from the kitchen to the bar at 8:30 A.M. While the menu does have a couple of egg-and-bacon breakfasts as well as a few steaks and sandwiches, the unique New Mexico hamburger is what has put this out-of-the-way watering hole on the good eats map. Since at least the early days of atomic bomb tests at nearby White Sands, when scientists used to come here for an explosive meal, the Owl Bar has built such an exalted reputation that aficionados drive from Texas and Colorado to eat 'em two by two.

Crusty, gnarled patties of beef are covered with chopped green chiles (moderate heat) and the chiles are in turn topped with a slice of cheese that melts into them and the crevices of the hamburger. Customary condiments include raw onion, lettuce, tomato, and pickle chips. It is a glorious package.

Pasqual's

121 Don Gaspar Ave.   505-983-9340
Santa Fe, NM   BLD | $$

Pasqual's looks like a modest corner café, and in some essential way, it is. But the food is too good to be modest and if you eat dinner here, you'll spend as much as in a top-notch steak house. At any mealtime in the crowded, split-level dining room, you are lucky to find a seat at a small table or at the large shared one, where a local or a stranger from just about any part of the world might break bread with you.

At breakfast, we love the pancakes, the blue and yellow cornmeal mush, big sweet rolls, and giant bowls of five-grain cereal with double-thick cinnamon toast on the side, accompanied by immense bowls—not cups—of latte. And for lunch, we can never resist the expertly made soups. Little things mean so much: fresh bread for sandwiches, flavorful roasted chiles on quesadillas; even the coffee is a tasty surprise.

After a few meals at Pasqual's, it is easy to feel affection for its sometimes clamorous ambience; this is a restaurant with character that perfectly complements the good stuff from the kitchen.

Plaza Café

54 Lincoln Ave.   505-982-1664
Santa Fe, NM   BLD | $

Although many of the businesses that now surround Santa Fe's plaza are trendy and high-priced, the Plaza Café, established in 1918, is what it's been all along—a three-meal-a-day town café frequented by locals as well as travelers, who come for dishes that range from American cheeseburgers to Greek souvlaki to New Mexican green chile stew. The sopaipillas that come with the stew are hot from the fry kettle, perhaps the best in town; and please have the quesadilla, a griddled tortilla sandwich filled with soft, shredded pork and little nuggets of caramelized garlic.

Rancho de Chimayo

Santa Fe County Rd. 98   505-351-4444
Chimayo, NM   LD | $$

Built a century ago by the Jaramillo family, whose ancestors arrived in the 1600s, Rancho de Chimayo is a spacious home of wide wood planks and low-beamed ceilings, hammered tin chandeliers, and a capacious fireplace. It became a restaurant in 1965, and since then it has gained fame not only for its charm and ambience, but also for a kitchen that exalts the cuisine of New Mexico.

Native New Mexicans seldom sit down for a "bowl of chili." In fact, chili as a meal isn't listed on the Rancho de Chimayo menu. But there are few dishes this kitchen makes in which the chile pepper doesn't play a vital role, foremost among them *carne adovada,* which is pork marinated in chile purée and sizzled until it glistens red. The marinade turns it tender, and its pepper heat is balanced by a serving of posole (hominy corn)—mild little lumps of tenderness to soothe the tongue. For those who want something a little less inciendiary, Rancho de Chimayo's menu also offers sopaipillas rellenas, in which the triangular fried breads are stuffed with beef, beans, tomatoes, and Spanish rice, and topped with red or green chile sauce. There are flautas, too—rolled corn tortillas filled with chicken or pork and fried crisp, topped with cool sour cream.

For us, it is a special joy to drive to Rancho de Chimayo through the foothills of the Sangre de Christo mountains in the cool of an autumn evening. Chile *ristras* (wreaths) decorate the adobe homes and late-day autumn light makes sagebrush shimmer. Candle-lit tables are arrayed on a stepped patio outdoors, strolling guitarists strum southwestern tunes, and the air smells of sagebrush and native cooking.

Roque's Carnitas

Washington & Palace
Santa Fe, NM   L (closed in winter) | $

Roque's is a jolly little chuckwagon that serves a sandwich made with a sturdy flour tortilla that has been heated on a grate over a charcoal fire. Inside the warm tortilla is succulent beef, and plenty of it—top round thinly sliced and marinated, sizzled on a grate along with onions and chiles, topped with fiery jalapeño salsa. As soon as you peel back the foil and try to gather up the tortilla for eating, chunks of salsa tumble out, meat juice leaks, onions slither, and plump circles of earth-green chile pepper pop free. There are a few yellow plastic stools for seated dining, but the choice location for eating is a bench in the nearby Plaza of the Governors, which is the heart of the old city. Here you can sit and lean far forward as you dine, thus sparing your shirt and lap and providing resident pigeons the carnitas banquet to which they are now accustomed.

Roque, a fifth-generation Santa Fean and a fount of local lore, goes to Mexico each winter, where he runs a pizzeria. To our noses, the smell of his sizzling carnitas on the Santa Fe Plaza is as much a sign of spring as singing robins and blooming lilacs.

San Marcos Café

3877 NM 14   505-471-9298
Cerrillos, NM   BL | $

The San Marcos Café is a popular destination eatery and a convenient stop for folks on their way to Cerrillos or Madrid. If you plan on eating here on a weekend morning, it's best to call ahead and make sure there's room. Breakfast can be a mob scene. We were thrilled with the cinnamon rolls—taller than they are wide, and rather than being dense and doughy like so many others, they are crisp and lightweight, almost croissant-like in character. Other dandy breakfast items are eggs San Marcos, which is a large serving of fluffy scrambled eggs wrapped inside a tortilla and sided by beans, chili, and guacamole under a mantle of melted cheese; biscuits topped with spicy sausage gravy; and *machaca* (beef and eggs with pico de gallo).

A cozy, charming ranch house decorated in country-kitchen style (old enameled stoves, wooden cupboards, knickknacks galore), the café also happens to be a veritable bird jungle. Peacocks and peahens, wild turkeys, and roosters all cavort around the front and back, and while they are not allowed inside the restaurant, there are pictures on the wall of the most famous chicken of them all, a leghorn rooster named Buddy, who served a long tenure as unofficial maitre d'. Dressed in black tie, Buddy cheerfully greeted guests at the door and crowed through the breakfast hour. Years ago, when Buddy passed away, customers mourned. And although a few other roosters have been named to take his place, none has ever had the people skills that Buddy did.

Sugar's

1799 NM 68	505-852-0604
Embudo, NM	LD | $

Fusion cuisine: Texas and New Mexico. The Texas part is brisket: thick flaps of juice-heavy beef so painfully tender that they fall apart when handled, pervaded by sweet smoke and rimmed with an edge that is blackened, crisp, and succulent. The New Mexico contribution is roasted green chiles with sunny flavor and the kick of capsicum. Intertwine these two items with cheese that melts because of the meat's heat and roll them inside a soft, flaky flour tortilla and you have a magically delicious burrito that is a prototypical wrap.

Eat this superb sandwich at a picnic table adjoining the tin-sided trailer that is Sugar's kitchen or ensconced in your vehicle. There are no indoor seats at this remote Land of Enchantment gem. Sugar, by the way, is a muscular bulldog bitch whom you can usually see in the yard to the left of the trailer, where you place your order at a window and then wait while they cook it inside. Her picture also adorns the wall-mounted menu, which is a roadside roster of burgers and green chile cheeseburgers, corn dogs, burritos, and, of course, Fritos pie.

Tecolote

1203 Cerrillos Rd.	505-988-1362
Santa Fe, NM	BL | $$

Tecolote is a great breakfast destination in Santa Fe. Our favorite thing to eat is pancakes made with blue cornmeal and studded with roasted piñon nuts. Pale blue inside with a faintly crusty exterior from the grill, each cake is ethereally fluffy; and gosh, what joy it is to bite into a little lode of those roasty-rich nuts! There are blueberry hotcakes, too, made with a similar from-scratch batter, and plain ones—each available singly, as a short stack (two), or a full stack (three).

Of course there are omelets galore and eggs of every kind, including shirred on a bed of chicken livers; as the crown of corned beef hash; "rancheros" style—fried on a corn tortilla smothered in red or green chile and topped (at your request) with cheese. One nontraditional meal we hold dear at Tecolote is a gallimaufry called Sheepherder's Breakfast—new potatoes boiled with jalapeño peppers and onion, cooked on a grill until crusty brown, then topped with two kinds of chile and melted Cheddar cheese.

Cancun

705 S. Lewis Ave.   918-583-8089

Tulsa, OK   LD (closed Wed) | $$

Cancun is a neighborhood Mexican restaurant where English is a second language. It is a welcoming little place with a handful of tables, those along the front window offering a view of the bumpers of cars in the parking lot. We plowed into a super burrito stuffed with *carnitas* (shredded pork), rice, and beans, smothered with shredded cheese and warm salsa and decorated with dabs of sour cream and guacamole. It's a grand meal, the savory roast pork packing heaps of flavor. On the side you can have *horchata,* the cool, sweet rice beverage that is so refreshing with spicy food, Jarritos-brand mandarin orange soda, or, of course, beer.

The menu is frustratingly tempting for those of us just passing through town with time for a single meal. Beyond the big burrito, choices include tacos filled with a wide range of ingredients from spicy pork to tongue, cheek meat, tripe, fish, chicken, and goat. Other temptations: enchiladas, chili verde and chili Colorado, fajitas, and chimichangas. Seafood specialties include *camarones al Tequila* (shrimp with green salsa and tequila) and *pescado frito* (whole fried fish).

Cattlemen's Steakhouse

1309 S. Agnew Ave. 405-236-0416
Oklahoma City, OK BLD | $$

A sign outside says "Cattlemen's Cafe," and yes, indeed, this is the café to which people who work in and around the Oklahoma City stockyards come for 6 A.M. breakfast as well as for lunch and supper. It is also a top-end steak house, serving some of the best cuts of beef you will find in the West. Top of the line is a big, boneless sirloin that comes from the kitchen alone on a white crockery plate, surrounded only by a puddle of its translucent juices. It is charred on the outside, but not drastically so, and you can see by its glistening, pillowy form—higher in the center than around the rim—that this hefty slab has been seared over a hot flame. Cattlemen's provides each customer a wood-handled knife with a serrated blade. The blade eases through the meat's crust and down into its warm red center—medium-rare, exactly as requested. You don't really need the sharp edge—a butter knife would do the job—but it sure is mouthwatering to feel the keen steel glide through beef that, although tender, has real substance.

Two other specials worth knowing about are steak soup, which is fork-thick, crowded with vegetables and beef, and lamb fries. The latter are testicles that are sliced, breaded, and deep-fried. Gonads are a highly regarded delicacy in much of the West; when young livestock are castrated on the range, it is traditional for cowboys to fry their harvest as a treat at the end of the day. Cattlemen's lamb fries are served as an appetizer: a mound of them on a plate with a bowl of cocktail sauce for dipping and half a lemon to squeeze on top. They are earthy-tasting inside their golden crust, the exquisite organ meat quivery and moist, with nut-sweet savor.

While you can spend $20 to $30 on a steak dinner, lunch can be one-third that price. We like the steak burger in particular. It is juicy and radiant with big beef flavor. While dinner patrons tend to be a dress-up group, the crowd at lunch is an amazing mix of rich ranchers in 100X beaver hats and fancy boots, huge blue-collar guys in overalls, and skinny blue-haired ladies out with their friends.

Clanton's

319 E. Illinois Ave. 918-256-9053
Vinita, OK BLD | $

Clanton's chicken-fried steak starts with what proprietors Melissa and Dennis Patrick call an "extra tenderized" cube steak they get from Tulsa. The beef patty is dipped in a mixture of egg and buttermilk, then dredged once in seasoned flour. "If you double-dip," Patrick says, referring to a common practice of repeating this process a second time, "you will get a steak that looks bigger. But it takes you farther away from the flavor of the beef." The steak is cooked in vegetable oil on a flat griddle until the blood starts rising up through the flour, then flipped and finished. The edge of a fork effortlessly will sever it into a bite-size triangle with beefy, crisp-crusted luxury that is ineffably amplified when it's pushed through mashed potatoes and peppery cream gravy. Whatever else you eat (the roast chicken and dressing is terrific), save room for pie: chocolate cream, coconut cream, or banana cream, all poised atop the most fragile foundation of crust.

Route 66 sightseers who get off the interstate to explore the original roadbed often find their way to Clanton's, which is one of the oldest continuously operating restaurants along the old Mother Road. When Sweet Tater Clanton (Melissa Patrick's granddad) opened for business in 1927, most of the highway was not yet paved, and it said that to attract customers Mr. Clanton used to walk out the front door and bang a pot and pan together when he spied someone about to drive past.

Classen Grill

5124 N. Classen Blvd.   405-842-0428
Oklahoma City, OK   BLD | $

We love to start the day at Classen Grill with a glass of fresh-squeezed orange juice and a plate of *migas,* the Mexican egg scramble that includes strips of tortilla, chunks of tomato, nuggets of sausage, and a mantle of melting shredded cheese. Chinook eggs are salmon patties topped with poached eggs and accompanied by a block of cheese grits. *Taquitas* are tortilla-wrapped packets of eggs, cheese, and vegetables. When we arrive with insatiable appetites, we go for "biscuits debris"—two big ones split open and mounded with gravy chockablock with ham and sausage chunks, cloaked with melted Cheddar cheese.

On the side of breakfast, it is possible to enjoy some serious potatoes—either home fries or the specialty known as Classen potatoes, which are mashed, seasoned with garlic, and rolled into little balls, then deep-fried until brittle gold on the outside. The result is a kind of prairie knish.

The place is an ultra-casual one-room café with paintings of fruit and other gastronomical items hanging on its pink stucco walls. During Sunday breakfast, nearly half the customers sit at tables reading the morning paper while leisurely enjoying their meals.

Coney I-Lander

7462 E. Admiral Pl.   918-836-2336

Tulsa, OK   LD | $

In 1926, Christ Economou came to Tulsa from Texas, where he had run a few hot dog restaurants, and opened the city's first Coney I-Lander. There are now a handful of these cheap chili-dog restaurants in Tulsa and environs, all based on the formula of a small hot dog in a steamed bun topped with mustard, raw onions, and no-bean chili. Shredded cheese is a popular option, and some folks get theirs with a sprinkle of cayenne pepper.

The chili is vivid but not combustible, and it is nothing like the stuff you would spoon up from a bowl as a meal. It is more a beef paste that is both hot (cayenne pepper) and sweet (cinnamon), eminently suited as a dressing for a snappy little weenie or as a topping for a plate of tamales. A Coney I-Lander Coney is a two- or three-bite affair. Three or four is a modest meal in the single-digit price range; it's not uncommon to see a runner from a nearby business walk out with dozens to take back for lunch with colleagues.

Ambience is drive-in, fast-food plain. Service is immediate. The menu is minimal. One dandy alternative to a Coney is the Southwest's beloved hot lunch, a Fritos Pie.

Dink's Pit Bar-B-Que

2929 E. Frank Phillips Blvd.   918-335-0606

Bartlesville, OK   LD | $$

Dink's barbecue selection is broad. Hickory-cooked pig dinners (pork loin), ham, turkey, chicken, sausage, spare ribs, brisket, and back ribs all are available, and while the menu advises that brisket is the specialty, we like the pork better. The brisket can be dry—not a horrible problem, considering that Dink's red-orange sauce beautifully revives it and adds a welcome tangy punch. The spare ribs were so good that we left only bare bones on the plate, and the pig dinner is succulence squared. Each dinner includes a choice of two side dishes from a roster that includes baked beans, pinto beans, green beans, coleslaw, curly-Q fries, baked potato, potato salad, and cottage cheese, plus bread, pickles, green onions, and sauce.

A Bartlesville fixture since 1982, Dink's is a family-friendly, multi-room establishment with buckaroo decor: mounted steer horns, pictures of hunters, cowboys, and Indians, and displays of the "Barbed Wire that Fenced the West."

Eischen's Bar

108 S. 2nd Ave.
Okarche, OK

405-263-9939
LD (closed Sun) | $$

Opened in 1896 and touted as the state's oldest bar, Eischen's is a Wild West destination a half-hour northwest of Oklahoma City. The brick-front bar is patronized by locals at lunch and is almost always crowded with pilgrims at suppertime, especially weekend nights, when it is not uncommon for strangers to share the big tables in the back dining room. Everybody comes for fried chicken of succulent meat and bacon-rich skin that is made to be eaten by hand (plates and silverware are nonexistent). The chicken comes with pickles, onions, and bread as well as fried okra. The beverage of choice is cold beer from the tap. The only other thing on the menu is chili-cheese nachos, another no-utensil food.

Classic road-trip tunes blare from the jukebox and when you wait for a seat, you may be able to avail yourself of one of two available pool tables to pass the time.

Hamburger King

322 E. Main St.
Shawnee, OK

405-878-0488
LD (closed Sun) | $

There used to be a handful of Hamburger Kings in Oklahoma; now there is only one other, in Ada, and it is no longer in the same family as the Shawnee one. We love the look of this vintage lunchroom with its tall ceiling and long rows of tables, each equipped with a direct phone line to the open kitchen. The menu refers to this as the "electronic order system."

The walls are decorated with pictures that show the history of Oklahoma in general and Hamburger King in particular, the showstopper being a blown-up photo of founder George Macsas flanked by King of Western Swing Bob Wills and movie star Jack Hoxie. Wills once wrote a song to celebrate his favorite eatery, its lyrics reading:

When you're feelin' blue, and hungry too
Here's a tip to make you sing.
Pick up your hat, close your flat
Go down to the Hamburger King.

Right up front behind the counter and cash register where the broad, medium-thick burger patties sizzle on the grill, you can watch each one assembled by a cook skillful enough to bun, dress, and garnish one faster than it takes to name its components. The result is a classic lunch-counter hamburger: not too thick, not thin, oily enough to imprint the bun with juice, crusty enough to provide textural contrast to the lettuce, tomato, and pickle on top.

Hank's Hamburgers

8933 East Admiral Pl.   918-832-1509
Tulsa, OK   LD | $

Burger central: have a single, a double, a triple, a Big Okie (four patties), or a Hank's Special, which is a single half-pound patty. Each normal patty is a quarter-pound, and while the avoirdupois of a Hank's Special is awe-inspiring, we prefer the multiple-patty configurations. The interleaved meat and cheese, especially on the one-pound Big Okie, provide a textural adventure that a large single patty cannot. Unless you say otherwise, each hamburger is dressed with mustard, pickle, grilled onion, raw onion, lettuce, and tomatoes.

Hank's is a tiny place with just a few booths around the counter, which is high enough that no seat affords a good view of Mr. Felts, chef and owner, orchestrating events at the griddle. We recommend standing up, or going to the walk-up to-go window at the front, because watching him create his burgers is short-order ballet. As is the custom down in the town of El Reno, onions are pressed hard onto the surface of each patty before it hits the hot surface so that as the burger cooks under a heavy iron, the onions caramelize and virtually become one with the hamburger itself. When the iron is lifted and the burger is flipped, Felts sprinkles on some of his secret seasoning, then cheese. If he is creating a double, triple, or quadruple, he applies the bun top to one patty, uses a spatula to lift it onto another, and so forth until the pile is ready to be placed onto the bottom half of the bun, which has been arrayed with all other condiments.

Everything is cooked to order, and while the half-pound hamburger takes a full fifteen minutes to cook, even the quarter-pounders are not served lightning-quick. "Please allow us a few minutes to prepare your order for you because we don't cook ahead," the menu asks. "Please call early and tell us what time you would like your order. We will try our BEST to have it ready for you right on time and FRESH off the grill." A sign above the counter advises, "We will call your name & bring your food to you as fast as possible . . . Hank's a lot."

Ike's Chili

5941 East Admiral Pl.   918-838-9410
Tulsa, OK   L | $

According to a 1936 article in the *Tulsa Daily World* reprinted on the back of Ike's menu, "When the original Ike Johnson established his first modest little 'parlor' down by the old Frisco depot twenty-five years ago, there was no lowlier food than chili. . . . It was openly sneered at by the Social Register and the hot dog was much higher up on the social scale." To this day, chili maintains a plebeian aura, and there's no better place to savor that aura, and a classic bowl of chili con carne, than Ike's. We thank Tulsan Jim Oakley for tipping us off to this excellent Southwestern chili parlor.

Made from a recipe supposedly secured from a Hispanic Texan employee named Alex Garcia, Ike's chili is a viscous dish of ground beef and a peppery jumble of spice. It comes plain in a bowl, with spaghetti noodles, or three-way, meaning with noodles and beans. Cheese, jalapeño peppers, and onions are extra-cost options, but even a double three-way with everything is scarcely more than $5. Chili is also the star of Ike's Fritos pie and Coney dog. The latter is described on the menu as being built upon a "large Oscar Meyer."

Jigg's Smokehouse

Exit 62 off I-40   580-323-5641
Clinton, OK   L Tues-Sat | $

Jigg's beef jerky is one tough chaw, and that's the way it is supposed to be. Slices of loin as big as a handkerchief are desiccated in a dry mix of brown sugar, garlic, and cayenne pepper, then slow-smoked over coarse-ground hickory sawdust for up to twenty-four hours. The result? Gnarled burnt-sienna-colored patches that pack a resounding harmony of beef, pepper, and smoke. Chew, chew, chew: the waves of flavor are relentless.

Unlike the mighty jerky, Jigg's barbecue is tenderness incarnate, although some of the specialty sandwiches are a real challenge to eat. The Wooly Burger, for example: thirty-one ounces of smoked ham and seven slices of summer sausage plus Cheddar cheese, chowchow relish, mayonnaise, and barbecue sauce. The menu calls it "2 lbs of fun!!!" Jigg's pigsickles, which are slabs of rib meat (no bones) with Cheddar cheese and sauce, come in as doubles and triples. Normal-size sandwiches also are available; sausage and beef brisket are exemplary. No vegetables are available other than beans, potato salad, and potato chips.

Accommodations in the weather-beaten Okie snack shack include a front porch where you can sit in the shade and construction spool tables inside, where the paneled walls feature portraits of meat-eaters' heroes John Wayne, Bob Wills, and Marty Robbins.

Johnnie's

301 S. Rock Island   405-262-4721

El Reno, OK   BLD | $

A sphere of beef is slapped onto a hot griddle. Onto the beef goes a fistful of ultra-thin-sliced yellow onions—about the same cubage as the beef. The grill man uses a spatula to flatten the onions and the meat together, creating a broad circular patty with an uneven edge; he presses down three or four times, slightly changing the angle of attack with each press, and pressing only one-half to two-thirds of the patty each time. The ribbons of onion get mashed deep into the top of the soft raw meat, which assumes a craggy surface because of the uneven, overlapping use of the spatula. Once the underside is cooked, the burger is flipped. The air around the grill clouds with the steam of sizzling onions. After another few minutes, the hamburger is scooped off the grill with all the darkened caramelized onions that have become part of it and is put on a bun, onion side up. Lettuce, tomato, mustard, and pickles are all optional if you like them, but no condiment is necessary to enhance this simple, savory creation.

Beyond its four-star onion-fried burgers, Johnnie's is a good place to eat El Reno's own version of a Coney Island hot dog, topped with meaty chili and a strange, soupy slaw that local epicures hold dear. (Some customers get this slaw on their burger, too.) We also like breakfast at Johnnie's, when the little place is packed with locals eating Arkansas sandwiches (that's a pair of pancakes layered with a pair of eggs) and all-you-can-eat platters of biscuits and gravy. It was at breakfast one day that we decided we had to stick around El Reno for a midmorning pie break, for as we were finishing our coffee, in walked Everett Adams, Johnnie's baker, wedging his way through the thirty-seat restaurant toting a battered tray above his head on which were set the coconut meringue pies and Boston cream pies he had made that morning for the lunch crowd.

Kumback Lunch

625 Delaware St.   580-336-4646

Perry, OK   BLD | $

Kumback Lunch was founded in 1926 in a town created by the 1893 Cherokee Strip land run. So says the very informative menu, which also notes that among the interesting moments in Kumback history is the night in the early 1930s when gangster Pretty Boy Floyd came in brandishing a gun—not to rob the place, but to demand that proprietor Eddie Parker cook him the biggest steak in the house. Mr. Parker is something of a legend in these parts, known for giving free steak dinners to soldiers returning home after World War II as well as to sluggers on the town's semi-pro baseball team every time one hit a home run. Kumback's walls are covered with pictures and memorabilia of "Perry Heroes," including local athletes, several governors of the state, and Oklahoma Highway Patrol officer Charlie Hanger, who captured Oklahoma City bomber Timothy McVeigh and brought him to the county jail in Perry.

Fascinating history and beautiful art deco facade aside, Kumback Lunch is a swell place to eat. And everyone in the town of Perry (and beyond) seems to know that fact, because the place seems always to be crowded with happy eaters and coffee drinkers. For breakfast, we recommend blueberry and pecan pancakes, swirly warm cinnamon rolls, biscuits and gravy, egg-stuffed burritos, and crisp-crusted chicken-fried steak. That steak also makes a fine lunch or supper; or you can choose from among a dozen different hamburgers, barbecued ribs and brisket, and a selection of Mexican meals that includes a baked potato stuffed with seasoned beef, cheese, and salsa.

The Meers Store

26005 OK Hwy. 115   580-429-8051
Meers, OK   BLD | $

Tulsa World magazine once declared the hamburger at The Meers Store the best burger in Oklahoma, which is a bold pronouncement. Border to border, Oklahoma is crazy for all kinds of interesting and unusual burgers, including the unique giants—seven inches across—known as Meersburgers.

A Meersburger is special not only for its size, but also because it is made exclusively from Longhorn cattle that are locally raised. Longhorns are less fatty than the usual beef stock and supposedly have less cholesterol than chicken, and yet the meat has a high-flavored succulence for which no excuses need be made. In addition to Meersburgers, The Meers Store has a menu of steak, chicken-fried steak, prime rib, and barbecue, plus a salad bar; and, being the only place in town, it also serves breakfast: biscuits or pancakes with sausage, cured ham, or thick-sliced smoked bacon.

Meers itself is a sight. In the southwest corner of the state, it is a ghost town that sprung up in the wake of a gold strike in the 1890s, but is now populated by exactly six citizens—the Maranto family, who run The Meers Store. The Store is the only open business, located in what was once a mining-camp emporium. Its walls are blanketed with antiques, memorabilia, pictures of famous and not-so-famous customers, and business cards left behind by happy Meersburger and Meerscheeseburger eaters.

Murphy's Steak House

1625 SW Frank Phillips Blvd.   918-336-4789
Bartlesville, OK   LD | $

Murphy's calls itself a steak house, but to us it looks more like a diner: counter and stools, bare-tabled booths, and a staff of superquick waitresses who git 'er done. The menu does include a bevy of steaks in the double-digit price range—sirloins, filets mignons wrapped with bacon, T-bones and rib eyes— and those that we've seen on other people's plates look good. Nevertheless, it's not for steak that we recommend a visit to this 1940s-era eatery just east of the Osage Indian reservation. It is for a hot hamburger.

If you picture in your head some sort of beef patty in some sort of bun, erase that image and consider this: pieces of toasted white bread spread out on a plate, topped with a large hamburger that has been hacked into pieces, the burger topped with a mountain of French fries, and the French fries topped with a large spill of dark, beefy gravy as rich as Mexican mole. It's a transcendent combination: crisp logs of fried potato softened in places where the gravy blankets them, imbibing a rich beefy savor for which squiggles of onion (an optional component) are an ideal accent. Even folks who come for steak instead of chopped-up hamburger know to order a side dish of fried potatoes with gravy. Variations on the theme include a hot cheeseburger, hot beef, hot steak, and hot ham. Extra gravy is available at 35¢ per bowl.

The front of Murphy's menu is emblazoned with a motto that is one of our favorites: "Gravy Over All." When anyone orders a hot hamburger, the motto becomes a question. The waitress asks, "Gravy over all?" We can't imagine saying no.

Robert's

300 S. Bickford Ave.   405-262-1262
El Reno, OK   BL | $

Robert's is El Reno's oldest hamburger shop, going back to 1926. Starting at six in the morning, its fourteen-stool counter is occupied by regulars who come for coffee and eggs and home fries or—even at dawn—a brace of onion-fried burgers. Proprietor Edward Graham, who started in the business by slicing onions as a kid, slaps a round of beef on the grill and cooks it with a fistful of onions until the onions become glistening, limp squiggles that only partially adhere to the meat and tend to fall from inside the bun as soon as the sandwich leaves its plate. The hamburger, infused with the sweet taste of onions, is juicy and rugged-textured. Some people add bacon and cheese, but we recommend this burger au naturel.

Robert's is a good place to sample El Reno's second passion (after onion-fried burgers), slaw-topped hot dogs, which are known here as Coney Islands. Mr. Graham makes a coarse, pickly slaw that seems to be an ideal complement for the chili sauce that tops the dog.

Sid's

300 S. Choctaw Ave.   405-262-7757
El Reno, OK   LD | $

Sid's is one of El Reno's legendary hamburger restaurants, where onion-fried burgers are cooked so that onions mashed into the patty of meat get charred from their time on the grill, giving the sandwich a sweet and smoky zest. Non-burger-eaters get two or three Coney Islands, which are bright red weenies topped with chili and a superfine slaw with a mustard punch. Milk shakes are thick enough to require a spoon as well as a straw.

Other than the exemplary burger-shop menu, Sid's is noteworthy for its amazing interior decor, which is a virtual museum of El Reno history. Using eleven gallons of clear epoxy to seal some 450 pictures onto the top of the counter and the tops of tables, proprietor Marty Hall has arranged his visual gallery in chronological order starting at the far left of the restaurant. Here are pictures of the Oklahoma land lotteries and cowboys on horseback, as well as nostalgic ephemera from the early days of car culture, when El Reno was a major stop along Route 66. No matter where you sit at Sid's, images of olden days in Oklahoma will surround you.

Van's Pig Stand

717 E. Highland St.   405-273-8704
Shawnee, OK   LD | $$

If you like barbecue, you need to eat at Van's. The rustic, wood-paneled eatery, where tables are outfitted with rolls of paper towels and sheaves of toothpicks and the woodwork is covered with volumes of graffiti, is the oldest barbecue joint in Oklahoma (since 1935) and one of the best anywhere. It offers a large menu of smoked meats, hamburgers, and Sunday chicken dinners, but the essential thing to eat is pork, either as ribs that are crusty with glaze and packed with flavor or in a pig sandwich, which is vividly sauced hacked hunks of pork in a bun with Van's own zesty relish. Superb sides include "Curlie Q fries," which are a variegated tangle of honeytone twigs, and a bacon-flavored, twice-baked potato invented by the current Van's grandma and listed as "Vanized" in the menu.

"The pie lady goofed," said the girl taking our order at Van's counter. "She put coconut meringue on the chocolate pie and regular meringue on the coconut pie." This heinous error—which, in fact, made the chocolate pie extra-good—was the worst thing that happened during an exemplary meal at one of the great barbecue outposts of the Southwest. Opened in 1928 in Wewoka, Van's now has four locations in Oklahoma, including one in Norman, one in Moore, and the one in Shawnee.

White River Fish Market

1708 N. Sheridan Rd.   918-835-1910
Tulsa, OK   LD | $$

Surrounded by light industry and warehouses, the White River Fish Market is not where anyone would expect to eat well. Outside, it looks like a hardware store in a strip mall; inside, there is no printed menu—just a posted list of items on the wall above the counter where customers stand in line to place orders. Meals come at fast-food speed to boomerang-pattern Formica tables, some of which are private, some communal; the brightly lit dining room sounds like a rowdy factory mess hall, occupied by blue collars and Oxford shirts, blacks and whites and Native Americans. For all its indecorous democracy, this unlikely outpost is a seafood-lover's destination.

At the order counter just inside the front door is a long glass case with trays of raw sea scallops from Boston, catfish live-hauled from Arkansas, rainbow trout from Idaho, red snapper, frog legs, colossal shrimp and popcorn shrimp, salmon steaks, tilapia, orange roughy, perch, and whole Gulf Coast flounders. Select the item you want and tell the server your preferred cooking method. If you want it fried, the piece or pieces you have chosen are immediately dipped into salted cracker meal; if it is to be broiled, your selection is put directly onto a broiling tray. The ready-to-cook order is then handed through a large pass-through portal straight to the kitchen. Meanwhile, you pay and find a seat. The servers will make note of where you've gone, and by the time you're comfortable and sipping sweet tea, the meal will be carried from the kitchen trailing wisps of savory smoke.

The dish at the top of our must-eat list is broiled flounder. It is one fish, weighing over a pound and wider than a large dinner plate. Its flesh is scored in a diamond pattern, making the display of several raw ones on ice in the glass case resemble a shimmering ocean jewel box. When broiled, the flesh firms up and contracts so it forms a pattern of bite-size diamonds of meat arrayed neatly atop the skeleton. The tail, hanging over the side of the large oval plate on which it is served, is blackened by flame and provides its own smoked scent; and each juicy nugget you lift—using the gentlest upward pressure of a fork slid underneath—has a delicate ocean sweetness that disallows fancying up.

Wilson's B-B-Que

1522 E. Apache St.
Tulsa, OK

918-836-7020
LD | $

A recording of Chicago blues emanated into the parking lot at Wilson's on East Apache, a Tulsa street that sports a handful of interesting barbecue parlors. Inside the door, the blues were louder, but another rhythm was even more compelling: the whack-thud-whack of a meat cleaver hacking hickory-cooked beef into shreds. "U Need No Teeth to Eat Our Beef" is one of Wilson's several mottoes (others being "U Need A Bib to Eat Our Ribs" and "U Need No Fork to Eat Our Pork"), and sure enough, that hacked-up beef is ridiculously tender. Moist, velvet-soft shreds are interspersed with crusty strips from the outside of the brisket; the flavor is quintessentially beefy, well salted, and fatty. Wilson's sauce is tongue-stimulating hot with vintage savor that reminded us of fine old bourbon.

Hot links are terrific: snapping-taut, dense, and peppery. Another house specialty is a huge smoke-cooked spud that is presented splayed open and lightly seasoned, available "plain" with just butter and sour cream, or stuffed with your choice of brisket, cut-up hot links, or bologna.

J. B. Wilson, who opened the place in 1961, passed away in 2004; but it is now run by Amos Adetula, whom the menu describes as "a good friend to J. B. [carrying on] the same values and traditions." It is now a modern two-room eat-place with wood-paneled walls, table service, and a counter where people come for take-out orders. Decor includes signs that read, "Our cow is dead. We don't need no bull" and "The bank and I have an agreement. They will not sell bar b que and I will not lend money or cash checks." Tulsa law enforcement officials who dine at Wilson's are entitled to a 10 percent discount for their public service.

Angelo's

2533 White Settlement Rd. 817-332-0357
Fort Worth, TX LD | $

"You are in the Land of Brisket," proclaims the counterman when an out-of-towner gets to the head of Angelo's line and innocently asks what type of meat is served on the beef plate. Watching brisket being cut is a joy of standing at the order counter. As the knife severs the dark crust and glides into the meat's tender center, each slice barely stays intact enough to be hoisted onto a Styrofoam plate, where the meat is sided by beans, potato salad, coleslaw, a length of pickle, a thick slice of raw onion, a ramekin of sauce, and two pieces of the freshest, softest white bread in America. Tote your own meal to a table, and if you pay an extra 25¢, you can stop at the bar along the way and fill a small cup with scorching hot peppers.

Sliced brisket stars at Angelo's, but the hickory pit also yields pork ribs with meat that slides easily off the bone, as well as hot link sausages, ham, and salami. In the relatively cooler months of October through March, Angelo's posts a sign below its regular menu advertising chili. Strangely, a simple bowl of red is hard to find in modern Texas. The kind Angelo's serves is an unctuous soup/stew of ground beef and plenty of pepper, here served in a plastic bowl with plastic spoon and little bags of oyster crackers on the side. Most people get an order to accompany a rib or beef plate or a few sandwiches . . . along with a few of Angelo's huge, cold mugs of beer.

Avalon Diner

2417 Westheimer Rd.   713-527-8900
Houston, TX   BLD | $

Although it is in the deluxe neighborhood of River Oaks and extravagantly manicured, big-haired ladies come to lunch here, the Avalon Diner isn't the least bit fussy. Eating here is a happy event—for singles, couples, families, and businessmen who toss their ties over their shoulders to shelter them from burger-juice drippings.

It is a great place to fall in love with Texas drugstore chili or to sample such Dixie delights as smothered pork chops, chicken-fried steak, or a pimiento cheese sandwich. Hamburgers are lunch-counter classics, just thick enough that a hint of pink remains in the center, their crusty outsides glistening with oil from the griddle. The configuration is deluxe, meaning fully dressed with tomato, lettuce, pickle, onion, mustard, and mayonnaise; and the bun has been butter-toasted crisp on the inside but is ineffably soft where you grab it. Burgers are available with American cheese, of course, as well as with Swiss; and their possible companions include French fries, chili fries, chili cheese fries, wet fries (topped with brown or cream gravy), and onion rings.

Avalon is one of our favorite Houston breakfast spots, mostly because it serves elegant, small-tread waffles, all the better to hold countless pools of swirled-together syrup and melted butter. Not-to-be missed beverages include vibrant squeezed-to-order lemonade and milk shakes served in the silver mixing container.

Note: There is a second Avalon Diner in Stafford at 12810 SW Freeway; 281-240-0213.

Beans-N-Things

1700 Amarillo Blvd. E.   806-373-7383
Amarillo, TX   BLD | $

We came across Beans-N-Things a few decades ago when it was run by Wiley Alexander, a Marine whose no-nonsense personality dominated the barbecue parlor. Mr. Alexander is gone, but this Amarillo lunchroom is still a fine stop for plates of hickory-smoked brisket or mesquite-smoked ribs with sides of exemplary beans and coleslaw. Two sauces are available—hot and mild—and beer is the preferred beverage.

It's good barbecue, but a recent visit reminded us that Amarillo is also a significant Fritos pie place. Beans-N-Things' version is a Southwest classic, heaped with cheese that melts into the meat that softens the chips directly underneath.

Beans-N-Things opens at 7 A.M., so if you're blasting along old Route 66 and need a quick breakfast, it's a good place to stop for biscuits and gravy or a triple-meat egg-packed burrito.

Black's Barbecue

215 N. Main St.   512-398-2712
Lockhart, TX   LD | $

Most barbecue restaurants sell little more than meat, bread, and beans, but at Black's, you can stroll through the cafeteria line and choose hard-boiled eggs stuck on toothpicks, little garden salads in bowls, and fruit cobbler for dessert. You can even have the man behind the counter put your meat into a sandwich and your sandwich on a plate—a "deluxe" presentation unheard-of in more traditional barbecues where meat is sold by the pound and accompanied by a stack of white bread or saltine crackers. Furthermore, Black's dining room actually has decor—another smoke-pit oddity—in the form of game trophies and pictures of the high school football team on its knotty pine walls.

All these luxuries, nice though they may be, have no bearing on the superiority of Black's pork ribs, the meat of which pulls from the bone in flavor-dripping strips, sausage rings that burst with flavor, and brisket slices bisected by an ethereal ribbon of translucent fat that leaches succulence into every smoky fiber of the meat. Black's has been one of Lockhart's great smokehouses since 1932, and if you want to know why Texas barbecue inspires rapture, here is a place that will make you understand.

Black's will ship ribs overnight to most places in the United States. Although the cost of sending them is nearly as much as the ribs themselves, this is a good emergency source to know about when the craving for great barbecue strikes.

Blanco Bowling Club Café

310 Fourth St.   830-833-4416
Blanco, TX   BLD | $

The Blanco Bowling Club Café is a real bowling alley where the ninepin league rolls at night. The rest of the day the alleys are curtained off, although customers in the back dining room do enjoy such decor as bowling trophies, racks of balls, and ball bags piled atop league members' lockers. Accommodations are basic: wood-grain Formica tables set with silver wrapped in paper napkins. There is a short counter in the front room with a view of the pass-through to the kitchen and one big table where locals come and go for coffee and cinnamon buns and glazed donuts all morning.

The lunchtime menu includes hamburgers and hot beef sandwiches and an array of tacos, chalupas, and enchiladas, and a recent visit at breakfast time featured huge warm biscuits. But it's pies that are the big allure, some boasting meringue tops that rise three times as high as the filling. And the fillings are delicious. Coconut pie has an indescribably creamy flavor, accented by little bits of toasty coconut scattered across the top of the meringue. Fudge pie is dense, rich, and super-chocolaty. If you are a pie fancier, put this bowling alley on your must-eat list.

Blue Bonnet Cafe

211 Hwy. 281   830-693-2344
Marble Falls, TX   BLD | $

The Blue Bonnet Cafe menu has something for everyone, from salads and sandwiches to big, beautiful hot plates of chicken-fried steak, pot roast, and rib-eye steaks accompanied by a choice of three vegetables from a long and inviting list. Our favorites are fragile-crusted fried okra, pork-rich pinto beans, and butter-sopped leaf spinach. Lunch and supper begin with a basket of excellent rolls, including 4x4-inch yeast rolls with a bakery sweetness that perfumes the whole table as soon as you tear one apart. With the rolls are rugged-textured corn-bread muffins. At breakfast, eggs are accompanied by hash brown potatoes or grits and your choice of thin toast, biscuits, or double-thick Texas toast.

The only problem about eating breakfast at the Blue Bonnet Cafe is that the pies may not be ready to serve until after 11 A.M., and in this place it behooves diners to heed the sign posted on the wall that implores "Try Some Pie." Eight or ten are available each day, plain or à la mode; and while we enjoy the apple pie and pecan pie, the one we'll come back for is peanut butter cream. Smooth and devilishly rich, topped with a thick ribbon of white cream, it is accompanied by a small paper cup full of chocolate sauce to either pour on or use as a dip for each forkful: an inspired condiment!

Bohannon's Brietzke Station

9015 FM 775   830-914-3288
Seguin, TX   BLD | $

A while back Cheryl Speakman wrote to tell us about a place we had to visit on our next trip to Texas. "If you think you have already experienced pie bliss, you haven't yet experienced one of Mutsie's pies," she wrote to us. She said that the next time we visited Texas we had to visit Bohannon's Brietzke Station, where the pies are served, and which she described as "a foodie's dream."

What a great tip! Although the official address of the café is Seguin, in fact it is in New Berlin, a Guadalupe County mini-municipality so small it doesn't have its own zip code. To say Brietzke Station is an inconspicuous eatery hardly does justice to its humble looks. Driving past, you might think it was just a gas station, but a small sign on the wall outside says "Cafe." Opened in 1977 by John and Mutsie Bohannon, it is a treasured town gathering place where citizens come for coffee and homemade biscuits every morning, and for meals of chicken and dumplings, steak and gravy, and fish specials every Wednesday and Friday night. Half the pleasure of eating here is getting to know Big John and Mutsie. Mutsie, who was recognized as New Berlin's Citizen of the Year in 2005, is known to regular patrons as the "town mom."

Her cream pies are modest but masterful. The one that made us swoon was chocolate: not spectacular to look at and not at all sinfully fudgy, but totally satisfying in an old-fashioned milk-chocolate way.

Bryce's Cafeteria

2021 Mall Dr. (Interstate 30, exit 222)   903-792-1611
Texarkana, TX   LD | $

Here is cafeteria heaven, featuring more vegetables than most Yankees see in a year: purple-hulled peas, fried green tomatoes, red beans, turnip greens cooked with chunks of ham, and a full array of potatoes, ultracheesy macaroni casseroles, rice casseroles, buttered cauliflower, sauced broccoli, pickled beets, etc., etc. . . . Main-course highlights include fried chicken that is stupendously crunchy and big slabs of sweet ham sliced to order. There is roast beef and gravy, chicken 'n' dumplings, turkey with all the fixins, fried and broiled fish. Among the multitude of pies, we like Karo-coconut and chess. Excellent alternatives include hot fruit cobbler with a savory crust and traditional banana pudding made with meringue and vanilla wafers.

Bryce's has been a Texarkana landmark since it opened downtown in 1931. Now in modern quarters with easy access from the interstate, it remains a piece of living culinary history. They don't make restaurants like this anymore! Among amenities are a smartly uniformed dining room staff (to carry your tray and remove all the dishes from it when you arrive at your chosen table) and servers who address men as "sir" and ladies as "ma'am." Bryce's also offers drive-through service, which, although convenient for travelers in a hurry, eliminates the joy of browsing along one of the nation's most appetizing cafeteria lines.

Cattlemen's Fort Worth Steak House

2458 N. Main St. 817-624-3945
Fort Worth, TX LD | $$$

Full-body black-and-white portraits of monumental Herefords, Anguses, and Brahmans decorate the walls at Cattlemen's Fort Worth Steak House, located in the historic stockyards district since 1947. At the back of the main dining area, known as the Branding Room, raw steaks are displayed on a bed of ice in front of a charcoal fire where beef sputters on a grate. Before placing a dinner order, many customers stroll back toward the open broiler to admire the specimens on ice and compare and contrast rib eye and T-bone, demure filet mignon and ample porterhouse, K.C. sirloin strip and pound-plus Texas strip.

Texas sirloin is the steak-lover's choice, a bulging block of aged, heavy beef with a charred crust and robust opulence that is a pleasure simply to slice, and sheer ecstasy to savor. And who can resist the warning on the "Heart O' Texas Rib Eye": *Not to be ordered by those who object to heavy marble.* Sweet dinner rolls make a handy utensil for sopping up juices that puddle onto the plate. Start with a plate of lamb fries—nuggets of quivery organ meat sheathed in fragile crust—get the zesty house dressing on your salad, plop a heap of sour cream into your baked potato, and accompany the big feed with frozen margaritas, longneck beers, or even a bottle of Texas's own Llano Escatado cabernet sauvignon. It's one fine cow-town supper.

Celia's Cocina

2917 SW 6th Ave. 806-322-0375
Amarillo, TX LD | $

For a quarter century, Celia Flores ran Los Insurgentes, which had become a necessary stop for excellent Mexican food in Amarillo. In 2007, when sale of the property forced her out, Celia got some help from longtime customers and moved to Sixth Avenue, opening a new cantina with the same great menu. Meals start with baskets of thin, warm tortilla chips (replenished as needed), bowls of hot sauce, and thick, creamy guacamole. The must-eat dishes are Celia's chicken mole and some of the best chiles rellenos in the Southwest, made with firm-fleshed Anaheim peppers. Be sure to have some tamales, laced with succulent shreds of roast pork, and no matter what else you eat, *refritos* (refried beans) must not be missed. They have a luscious avoirdupois that had us scooping the last of them from the plate with tortilla chips.

Chris Madrid's

1900 Blanco Rd.   210-735-3552
San Antonio, TX   LD | $

An efficiency expert might blow a gasket looking at Chris Madrid's, a chaotic multiroom tavern/burger joint where the modus operandi makes no sense but works beautifully. First, squeeze into a line that heads toward the order counter, where you tell the lady what you want and pay for it. You are given a vibrating pager, and while the food is being cooked, it is your job to hunt around for space at a table (outdoors or in). When the pager vibrates, return to the pick-up counter and carry trays full of burgers back to your place.

Madrid's hamburgers are broad and beautiful, not too thick, but juicy enough to ooze the moment finger pressure is applied to the big-domed bun that holds them. A normal quarter-pound version is hearty enough; a macho burger, twice the size, extends far beyond its bun. Several variations are available, including a flaming jalapeño burger, a Porky's Delight layered with bacon, and a super-goopy Cheddar Cheezy; but the house specialty, not to be missed, is a tostada burger. Silky refried beans and massive amounts of Cheddar cheese form a luxurious crown for the big hamburger, which also is layered with a sheaf of tortilla chips that offer earthy corn flavor and intriguing chewy crunch. The great condiment for this one is salsa, to which customers help themselves near the pick-up window. French fries are fresh-cut and delicious. Margaritas, wine, beer, and cocktails are available.

Dining at Chris Madrid's feels like a cross between a frat party and a family reunion. Decor is beer signs and signed T-shirts; when it's really crowded (and it usually is), strangers frequently share tables.

City Market

633 E. Davis St.   830-875-9019
Luling, TX   LD | $

The dining area at the City Market in Luling is cool and comfortable. To fetch the food, however, you must walk into hell. A swinging door leads into a back-room pit, a shadowy, cavelike chamber illuminated by the glow of burning logs in pits on the floor underneath the iron ovens. It is excruciatingly hot; but apparently at ease in their sweltering workplace, pit men assemble meats on pink butcher paper with gracious dispatch. They take your money, then gather the edges of the paper together so it becomes a boatlike container you easily can carry back into the cool, pine-paneled dining room.

The brisket is terrific, as are the pork ribs, but City Market's great dish is a sausage ring. Even when the long communal tables are crowded and a dozen conversations are in full sway all around, you cannot help but hear the crunch and snap as diners' teeth bite into the unbelievably taut casings of a City Market sausage ring. These horseshoe-shaped, string-tied guts are a lean, rugged grind with only the echo of pepper laced through their mineral-rich muscularity.

Uncharacteristically (for Texas), the City Market also makes a significant barbecue sauce—a spice-speckled, dark orange emulsion that is so coveted by customers that signs on the wall above every booth implore "Please Leave Sauce Bottles on Tables."

Clark's Outpost

101 Hwy. 377   940-437-2414
(at Gene Autry Dr.)   LD | $$
Tioga, TX

Clark's Outpost, a good hour north of Dallas, is a Lone Star legend patronized by local horse breeders, city folk hungry for a country meal, flamboyant high rollers who arrive by helicopter in the field across the road, and good-food pilgrims from all over the United States in search of Texas on a plate.

Its fame is built on brisket, slow-cooked for days until it becomes beef and smoke laced together in an exquisite harmony that words cannot convey. Rimmed with a crust of smoky black, each slice is so supple that the gentlest fork pressure separates a mouthful. The warm barbecue sauce, supplied on the side in Grolsch beer bottles, is dark, spicy, and provocatively sweet. Pork ribs are another treasure, rubbed with a seasoning mix and cooked until tender. Rib dinners arrive at the table severed into individual bones, each one lean and smoke-flavored, glistening with its own juice but also begging for some of that good sauce.

Country-style side dishes include crisp-fried okra, jalapeño-spiked black-eyed peas, and French-fried corn on the cob, the last a length of corn, unbattered and unadorned, that has been dipped in hot oil just long enough for the kernels to cook and begin to caramelize. The result is corn that is quite soft with a mere veil of a crust, and is astoundingly sweet. Each piece is served with blacksmith's nails stuck in its ends to serve as holders.

Despite success and renown, Clark's is deliciously rustic. Located in a town that is little more than a farmland crossroads, it is a small agglomeration of joined-together wood buildings surrounded by a gravel parking lot and stacks of wood for the smoker, with the flags of Texas and the United States flying above.

Cooper's Pit Bar-B-Q

US Hwy. 87
Mason, TX

325-347-6897
LD | $$

At the northern edge of the Hill Country in Mason County is a grand barbecue shrine, Cooper's, where the ritual is that you eyeball the meat on its grate, tell the pit man what you want, and he hoists it off. Once it is sliced and priced, you find a seat at one of a handful of tables inside the cinder-block dining room (or at a picnic table outside) and feast. The repertoire of meats is huge, including brisket, all-beef sausage, pork chops, pork tenderloin, and lamb ribs. The brisket is among the best in the state: dripping-moist, radiant with beefy flavor, and so tender that it literally falls to pieces when you lift it toward your mouth. There's a tangy sauce that is delicious, but we recommend a few good samples of this meat without it. Sided by coleslaw and jalapeño-spiked pinto beans, it is the foundation of an only-in-Texas feast.

Although they were originally related and do business pretty much the same way, this Cooper's is now an entirely different operation than the one in Llano. The Llano one tends to be much more mobbed at mealtime, and while some local connoisseurs consider this Mason store to be far superior, we've had great meals at both of them.

Golden Light Cafe

2908 West 6th Ave.
Amarillo, TX

806-374-9237
LD Mon–Sat | $

Opened in 1946 as a hamburger stand, the Golden Light really does glow in the afternoon light along old Route 66. The hamburgers off its vintage griddle are just what you want when you are highballing into the Texas Panhandle: medium-thin patties cooked through but still juicy, at their best when topped with cheese and chile (hot jalapeños or milder greens) and sided by fine, thin-cut French fries. An alternative is to have the burger wrapped in a giant tortilla along with hot sauce and sour cream. We are also big fans of the Fritos pie (here known as "Flagstaff Pie")—a large oval plate of Fritos chips topped with the stout house red chili, cheese, and onions. What's great about Fritos pie is how different every chip is, depending on how close it gets to the chili. Those corn ribbons that are totally smothered turn to soft, salty cornmeal; some remain untouched and crisp; most are half-and-half crisp and tender, or on their way to delicious disintegration.

Next door to the café is the Golden Light Cantina, a live music venue that features Texas Red Dirt band music.

Goode Co. Texas Bar-B-Q

5109 Kirby Dr.	713-522-2530
Houston, TX	LD | $$

Goode Co. isn't exactly an obscure name in the Houston food world. Driving south on Kirby from the city center, you pass Goode Co. Seafood and Good Co. Tacqueria, and there is another branch of Goode Co. Bar-B-Q on Katy Freeway. The place on Kirby is a large eating barn (with a nice covered outdoor patio) surrounded by stacks of wood and the perfume of smoldering mesquite. Inside, there's always a line leading to the cafeteria-style counter. The line moves fast because nearly everyone knows exactly what they want when they come here. Once you've eaten at Goode Co. barbecue, chances are good you will return for more.

Goode Co.'s fame is well deserved, especially for its brisket. This long-smoked meat is velvet-soft and so moist that sauce is superfluous (although Goode Co. does offer fairly spicy red stuff to pour on it if you wish). You can get the beef as part of a platter with superb, slightly sweet baked beans, potato salad, and jambalaya; or you can have it in a sandwich. While blah bread is de rigueur in most great barbecue parlors, Goode Co. offers a fantastic alternative: thick slices of fresh, soft jalapeño corn bread that make a first-rate mitt for the smoky beef.

Other than brisket, the smoke pit menu lists Czech sausage, pork sausage, lean pork ribs, ham, chicken, sweet water duck, spicy pork, turkey breast, and turkey sausage. The pecan pie served for dessert is legendary.

H&H Cafe and Car Wash

701 E. Yandel Dr.	915-533-1144
El Paso, TX	BL | $

If you are hungry and your car is dusty from traveling southwestern roads, the place to go is the H&H Cafe and Car Wash, where table seats in the little joint afford a view of your vehicle being scrubbed and dried. We prefer counter stools with a vista of chiles rellenos getting battered and fried and huevos rancheros being topped with a curious buttery gravy flecked with onions and hot peppers. Artemisa, who has been a waitress here for years, frequently conjures up her own special salsa, which capsicum addicts know to request. "It will hurt you," warns proprietor Kenny Haddad, who offers curious visitors a few spoonfuls in a saucer. It is flecked with seeds and pod membrane (the hottest parts) and glistens seductively. Artemisa, who is normally a stern sort of person, broke into a broad grin when she watched us wipe the last of it up with warm tortillas, then wipe the beads of perspiration from our brows with napkins.

Not everything posted on the H&H wall menu is four-alarm. You can eat ordinary eggs for breakfast or a hamburger for lunch (the café closes at 3 P.M.). Burritos are available seven ways: stuffed with chiles rellenos, egg and chorizo sausage, picadillo, red chile, green chile, carne picada, or beans. Specials include chicken mole, red and green enchiladas, and—always on Saturday—*menudo,* the tripe and hominy stew renowned for its power to cure a hangover.

Hospitality at the well-worn cook shop is enchanting. If you speak Spanish, so much the better: You will understand the nuances of the chatter. But if, like us, you are limited to English, you will still be part of the action. The day we first visited, many years ago, we were wearing ten-gallon hats, so we soon became known to one and all as the cowboys. "*Vaqueros,*" called a waitress as we headed out the door, "*vaya con dios.*" With our car newly cleaned and the radio tuned to the rollicking Mexican polka rhythms of Tejano music, we highballed north along the Rio Grande.

Hill Country Cupboard

101 S. US Hwy. 281	830-868-4625
Johnson City, TX	BLD | $

Chicken-fried steak is bedeviling. There are so many bad ones that one could lose one's faith. But then you come across one such as that served at the Hill Country Cupboard and you are a believer once again. This big barn of a restaurant claims to serve the world's best. Two sizes are available: regular and large, the latter as big as its plate. Neither requires a knife; a fork will crack through a golden brown crust that is rich and well spiced, a perfect complement to the ribbon of tender beef inside. Alongside the slab of crusty protein comes a great glob of skin-on mashed potatoes, and of course, thick white gravy blankets the whole shebang.

Beyond chicken-fried steak, Hill Country Cupboard has a full menu of Southwest eats: barbecued beef, sausage, turkey, and ribs; catfish fillets; grilled chicken with jalapeño cheese sauce. There are even salads, available topped with hunks of chicken-fried steak or chicken-fried chicken!

The Cupboard is where locals eat. Two airy dining rooms are crowned with circulating fans, illumination provided by fluorescent tubes shaded by what appears to be burlap feed-sack material. Service is no-nonsense; checks are put down on the table along with the meal.

Home of Da Smoke

13433 US Hwy. 87 S.   210-649-2498
Adkins, TX   LD | $

Pitmaster Robert Norman does it all: smokes the meat, makes the side dishes, and frequently strolls around the dining room to make sure guests are happy. Even desserts, billed on the menu as "Oice Mae Desserts—Made Fresh Daily," are his, although named for his mother.

There is nothing deluxe about this bunker-like eatery on Highway 87 east of San Antonio. Miscellaneous tables, topped with red-checked oilcloth, are arrayed with rolls of paper towels and jugs of liquid hand sanitizer in lieu of napkins; decor is a multicultural rainbow of pictures and bric-a-brac representing cowboys and Indians, the old West and the new, John Wayne and Bill Pickett (the latter was rodeo's first African American star); prices are solidly in the under $10 range. But unlike the Spartan barbecue parlors farther east, Home of Da Smoke does offer amenities: a printed menu with choices that extend beyond smokehouse meats to include fried chicken and catfish; a plethora of such soulful side dishes as greens, braised cabbage, mac 'n' cheese, and okra; those fine desserts—especially a cherry cobbler luxified with coconut, pineapple, and nuts—and table service by a kindly staff.

Still, it's barbecue that stars. Brisket and sausage are especially good, served with a thin, complementary sauce that has a vinegar tang and a jot of heat. Ribs are almost too tender, if such a thing is possible, the meat sliding off the bone at the slightest provocation. We've yet to try the catfish, but did notice on the way out that Mr. Norman was taking a break from his kitchen duties, sitting at a table and eating a basketful.

Hoover's Cooking

2002 Manor Rd.   512-479-5006
Austin, TX   LD | $$

Chef Hoover Alexander says, "I am an Austin native with deep Central Texas roots that run from Manchaca and Pilot Knob, to little o' Utley, Texas. All of the recipes we use here were inspired by both my mother Dorothy's good cooking and the styles and spices native throughout Texas itself. I grew up on home cooking—nicely seasoned vegetables, smoked foods, pan-fried dishes and spicy foods with a nod toward Tex-Mex and Cajun. I also have never forgotten eating a lot of Mom's fresh baked rolls, corn bread and desserts. . . . After you've had one of our freshly made meals and washed it down with a nice cool beverage, you'll understand why I like to call the restaurant my 'Smoke, Fire, and Ice House!' "

We knew we were in for a bigger-than-life treat as soon as our glass of lemonade arrived. In fact, it arrived not as a glass, but as a pitcher with a straw. We had to ask if a glass would be forthcoming; our waitress told us that the pitcher *is* the glass: a quart of lemonade to be drunk straight from the tankard. And it is good lemonade—sweet, fresh-squeezed, refreshing.

The choice of meals is wide. Hoover's has its own smokehouse, perfuming the parking lot outside, from which come pork ribs, Elgin sausage, highly spiced Jamaican jerk chicken, and lesser-spiced (but nonetheless delicious) barbecue chicken. In addition to smoked fare, the menu lists chicken-fried steak (perhaps the best one anywhere), meat loaf, catfish, and an array of sandwiches that range from a meatless muffuletta (made with a portobello mushroom) to half-pound hamburgers. On the side of any meal, choose from a large selection of vegetables that include chunky mashed potatoes, macaroni and cheese, black-eyed peas, sweet and hammy mustard greens, crisp-fried okra, and jalapeño-accented creamed spinach. The vegetables are so good, and served in such abundance, that Hoover's offers a three- or four-vegetable plate, with no meat at all.

Hut's Hamburgers

807 W. 6th St.   512-472-0693
Austin, TX   LD | $

Hut's is a burger joint with nineteen different varieties of hamburger listed on its menu (not to mention the options of buffalo meat, chicken breast, or veggie burgers), each one topped with a different constellation of condiments that ranges from hickory sauce (delicious!) to cheeses of all kinds to guacamole to chipotle mayonnaise. We are particularly fond of the Buddy Holly Burger with the works, the double-meat Dag Burger, and the Hut's Favorite with bacon, cheese, lettuce, and mayonnaise. The French fries are very good, and the onion rings have a peppery zest that makes them a joy to overeat. Beyond burgers, there are other sandwiches, a different blue-plate special every day (chicken-fried steak, meat loaf, catfish, etc.), and a beverage list that includes cherry Coke, pink lemonade, and a root beer float.

Decorated to the rafters with neon beer signs, team pennants, and clippings celebrating its long-standing fame—since 1939—it is a small place that is always overstuffed with people, with noise, and with a spirit of fun. You will likely wait for a seat in the small vestibule or on the sidewalk outside, but once seated, the food comes fast.

Krause's Café

148 S. Castell Ave. 830-625-7581
New Braunfels, TX BLD | $

Historians have not yet convincingly documented the history of chicken-fried steak, which native Texans consider their fundamental comfort food, but it has long been our contention that this pounded-tender beef cutlet, breaded and fried crisp and served with mashed potatoes under a blanket of cream gravy, most likely traces its heritage back to the many well-trained European cooks who found themselves in Texas but without the fixins for a fine, tender wiener schnitzel. Instead, they took a hunk of cow and beat the chaw out of it, then fried it up like southern-style chicken.

Our genealogical speculation is supported by the fact that the Hill Country, with its preponderance of German great-grandmas, is home of the best chicken-fried steaks anywhere, among them the one served at the venerable Krause's Café. This place has been a New Braunfels town favorite since 1938, and its old/new-world menu lists both wiener schnitzel *and* chicken-fried steak (as well as homemade sausage, old-world potato pancakes, and red-white-and-blue blackened Cajun catfish).

Kreuz Market

619 N. Colorado St. 512-398-2361
Lockhart, TX LD | $$

Kreuz (rhymes with *bites*) started as a downtown meat market over a century ago, and it was one of the places that defined Texas barbecue. A short while back, owing to a complicated family feud, it moved out of town to an immense roadside dining barn with all the charm of an airplane hangar.

But if it lacks the ambience of a good old Texas pit, there is absolutely no denying that its pit-cooked prime rib is among the most carnivorously satisfying foodstuffs on earth. Brisket, sausage, and ribs all are superb. Despite its modern facilities, Kreuz has maintained pit-cook tradition: a limited menu that is meat, bread, and condiments (plus ice cream cones at a separate counter), and tote-your-own service from a ferociously hot pit where meat is sliced to order and sold by the pound.

La Mexicana

1018 Fairview St.   713-521-0963
Houston, TX   BLD | $

Sometimes we feel sorry for our friend Jim Rains. He's got a beautiful wife, a great job, and a bucolic home; but he's a Texan and he lives in Connecticut. Not that there's anything wrong with that, but Jim grew up eating excellent Mexican food whenever he wanted it. And in our neighborhood—and virtually the entire Northeast—it is a rarity. Well, Jim's loss was our gain, at least on a trip we took a while back to Houston, where he highly recommended we stop into a restaurant called La Mexicana. "It's nothing fancy," he warned. "It's plain and it's cheap . . . and it's goo-ood." We had it in our crosshairs as soon as we arrived in the Lone Star State.

It started a quarter-century ago as a corner grocery store and now offers sit-down meals in a festively decorated dining room and bar, as well as take-out meals from a cafeteria line and all sorts of interesting pastries from the in-house bakery. When you sit down for a lunch or dinner, a waiter (outfitted in white shirt and tie) brings a basket of thin, elegant tortilla chips, still warm, along with a mild red sauce and a hotter, lime-tinged green pepper sauce. The chips are large and somewhat fragile; if you eat your way through half the basket so that only smaller, broken half-chips remain, the old basket is whisked away and a new one of full-size, warm chips takes its place.

The menu is huge, including fajitas à la Mexicana, for which the beef is stewed rather than grilled, tacos, flautas, tamales, enchiladas, and chiles rellenos. We began with an order of chile con queso, which comes with a large bowl of jalapeño slices to heat it up, then went on to an all-seafood meal: fish tacos made with succulent strips of grilled (not deep-fried) mahimahi, and shrimp in a chipotle chile sauce. The tacos were light, refreshing, and hot (we asked for them that way), the fish, cabbage, tomato, and cilantro laced with little nuggets of tongue-searing pepper. They were accompanied by Mexican rice and a bowl of creamy-smooth, blue-black *refritos*.

La Mexicana's breakfast starts at 7 A.M. and the choices include all sorts of huevos rancheros, eggs scrambled with chorizo (Mexican sausage), *migas* (a sort of tortilla omelet) and, on Saturday and Sunday only, *menudo,* which is a bowl of stewed honeycomb tripe. *Menudo* has long been considered a sure cure for hangovers.

Little Diner

7209 7th St. 915-877-2176
Canutillo, TX LD | $

Lourdes Pearson's Little Diner, also known as the Canutillo Tortilla Factory, is far off I-10 in an obscure residential neighborhood north of El Paso, but her crisp-skinned gorditas (stuffed cornmeal pockets) are worth getting lost to find. The normal filling is ground meat, but the great one is chili con carne. Tender shreds of beef become an ideal medium for the brilliant red chili that surrounds them with a walloping flavor of concentrated sunshine. You can also get the chili con carne in a bowl—one of the few classic "bowls of red" still to be found in all of Texas. Its flavor is huge, and you wouldn't think of adding beans or rice to this perfect duet. Of course, you do want to tear off pieces from Lourdes's wheaty flour tortillas to mop the last of the red chili from the bottom of the bowl.

We love everything about this friendly diner, where you step up to the counter and place your order before sitting down. The tortilla chips that start each meal have an earthy corn character and are scarcely salty—all the better to taste the essence-of-red-chile salsa served with them. Flautas are crunchy little fried tortilla tubes (like flutes, which is what the name means) packed with moist shreds of chicken or succulent pot roast. The last time we visited, the green chili was even hotter than the red (this varies with the harvest); it adds potatoes and onions to the basic meat-and-chile formula.

The broad Tex-Mex menu includes burritos, enchiladas, tapatias, and tacos. Tamales—red chili pork, green chili cheese, green chili chicken, and green chili chicken with cheese—are generally made once a week, but Lourdes told us that in December, they are a menu item every day.

Lock Drug

1003 Main St. 512-321-2422
Bastrop, TX $

Texas food fans know Route 183 as an essential detour off I-10 between San Antonio and Houston into the town of Lockhart, which is to Lone Star barbecue what Milwaukee is to Dairy State butter burgers: source of the best. Of Lockhart's world-class smoke pits, which include Kreuz Market, Smitty's, and Black's, only Black's offers a meaningful dessert (hot cobbler), so we recommend travelers save their sweet tooth for a half-hour's drive northeast to Bastrop, where you will find Lock Drug.

In this vintage drugstore that still displays its remedies in exquisite carved wood fixtures, the marble counter up front is strictly for soda fountain fare; there are no sandwiches or hot food. The menu warns that "malts and shakes cannot be made with ice cream that has nuts, as it will break our machine"; but that's fine with us, because we're ordering a magnificent black-and-white soda (topped with crunchy fresh chopped peanuts) and an item we've seen nowhere else, a frosted Coke. The latter is built just like a milk shake with an ice cream of your choice (smooth ice cream, please!) and flavored syrup, but it is blended with Coca-Cola instead of milk. The result isn't as thick as a regular shake, but it is rich and effervescent and candyland sweet—essence of soda fountain.

Louie Mueller Barbecue

206 W. 2nd St.   512-352-6206
Taylor, TX   LD | $$

Louie Mueller's, which we have long considered the best of all Texas barbecue parlors, has added a modern dining room that lacks the smoky patina of the original brick-walled restaurant, but no matter where you eat in this august temple of meat, the flavor is historic. Here is a restaurant where beef brisket (as well as sausage, ribs, and mutton) is cooked and served the way Texas pitmasters have been doing it for decades. Step up to the counter that separates dining tables from the smoke pits. Place your order by pound or plate. Carry it yourself to a table.

Louie Mueller's brisket is a thing of beauty. It is sliced relatively thick, salt-and-pepper-crusted, each individual slice halved by the ribbon of fat that runs through a brisket, separating the leaner, denser meat below from the more marbled stuff on top. It is served with a cup of sauce reminiscent of au jus, and there is some hotter sauce set out on the table—but forget sauce, forget inconsequential side dishes. Meat is what you want to eat: brisket, sausage, ribs, and ultra-luxurious pit-cooked steak.

Monument Cafe

500 S. Austin Ave.   512-930-9586
Georgetown, TX   BLD | $$

Three meals a day are served at the Monument Cafe, and we recently enjoyed a swell chicken-fried Kobe steak for a mere $11 and a whole fried catfish ($14); but it is breakfast we like best. The kitchen's *migas* are exemplary: eggs scrambled with cheese, diced tomatoes, and small ribbons of tortilla that variously soften and turn crisp depending on where they are in the pan, giving the dish an earthy corn flavor. On the side comes a nice red salsa to heat it up if desired, along with grits or hash browns and a soft flour tortilla that is good for mopping and pushing food around on the plate. Pancakes and waffles are lovely, as are the big squarish biscuits; the pastry that makes us swoon is sour cream coffee cake, its top blanketed with sugar and frosting, its inside layered with local pecans.

"Our pies, cakes, and cookies are made here fresh every day," the menu notes. "We use only the best ingredients, including real butter, yard eggs, and real whipping cream." Of this boast you will have no doubt if you order a piece of cream pie. Here is some of the best pie in Texas, some of the best *anywhere*! Chocolate pie with a toasted pecan crust is inspired and devilishly chocolaty. Coconut cream pie is equally amazing, but at the opposite end of the pleasure spectrum: angelically light, silky, fresh, and layered on a flaky gold crust.

Oh, one more thing: lemonade, limeade, and orange juice are *fresh*.

OST

305 Main St.
Bandera, TX

830-796-3836
BLD | $$

OST (Old Spanish Trail) has been Bandera's town café since 1921, and its roomy cypress booths and bar stools made of western saddles make it an especially appealing destination for hungry travelers in search of cowboy culture. One whole room is devoted to images of John Wayne; its spur collection includes rowels dating back to frontier days; and the buffet is set out under a downsized covered wagon. The buckaroo trappings make a lot of sense in Bandera, which is surrounded by dude ranches and has proclaimed itself "The Cowboy Capital of the World." The No. 1 cowboy dish in these parts is chicken-fried steak, and OST makes a good one: a tantalizing balance of crunch and tenderness with gravy that is cream-soft but pepper-sharp. Beyond that, menu highlights include such Tex-Mex stalwarts as enchiladas, fajitas, and chilis rellenos.

Paris Coffee Shop

704 W. Magnolia
Fort Worth, TX

817-335-2041
BL | $

The day starts early in cattle country, so it should be no surprise that Fort Worth has always been a good breakfast town. By 7 A.M., the Paris Coffee Shop on the south side is bustling, and some days you will have to wait for a table (seldom for too long, though). A convivial wood-paneled room with a counter, booths, and tables, Paris smells delicious in the morning, its air fragrant with the piggy perfume of sausages, bacon, and pork chops, as well as tangy biscuits smothered with gravy. Beyond biscuits, breadstuffs include soft glazed cinnamon rolls and a choice of eight-grain, sourdough, or sun-dried-tomato toast.

The Paris Coffee Shop is also a legendary lunchroom (since 1926), known for meat loaf, fried chicken, and chicken-fried steak with mashed potatoes and gravy as well as one of the best bowls of chili in the Metroplex. The café's signature dish is an Arkansas Traveler: hot roast beef on corn bread smothered with gravy. Such Lone Star comfort fare is accompanied by your choice from a wide variety of southern-style vegetables such as turnips and/or turnip greens, pole beans, and butter beans. And every meal *must* be followed by a piece of Paris pie. One morning, when we spotted a single piece of custard pie we wanted behind the counter and ordered it for break-fast, the waitress warned, "It's not today's." (Today's pies were still in the oven.) But then she thought a while and agreed with our choice, declaring, "Hey, yesterday's egg custard pie is better than no pie at at all!"

Ranchman's Café (a.k.a Ponder Steakhouse)

110 W. Bailey St.   940-479-2221
Ponder, TX   D (reservations advised) | $$

In a sleepy encampment by the train tracks at the northern fringe of the Dallas/Fort Worth Metroplex, the Ponder Steakhouse (actually named Ranchman's Café) has been a meat-eaters' destination since 1948. Indoor bathrooms were added many years ago, but the steaks are still hand-cut and the ambience is Lone Star to the core.

There's a full menu that ranges from quail quarters and Rocky Moun-tain oyster hors d'oeuvres to fabulous made-from-scratch buttermilk pie, but it is big, butter-glistening steaks that motivate us for the drive. Porterhouse, T-bone, club, rib eye, and sirloin are sizzled on a hot griddle until they de-velop a wickedly tasty crust. Although tender, they are not the silver butter-knife cuts of expense-account dining rooms; they are steaks of substantial density that require a sharp knife and reward a good chew with tides of fla-vor. French fries come on the side, but if you call an hour and a half ahead, they'll put a baked potato in the oven and have it ready when you arrive.

Royers Round Top Café

105 Main St.   979-249-3611
Round Top, TX   LD | $$

Bud Royer has described his menu as "contemporary comfort food," but no single category of cuisine begins to describe his kitchen's boundlessly creative bent. Yes, there are such square-meal classics as filet mignon, rack of lamb, a fourteen-ounce pork chop, and Sunday's garlicky, buttermilk-battered fried chicken, but nearly everything has a Royer twist: grilled pork tenderloin is topped with a peach and pepper glaze, quail comes stuffed with shrimp and wrapped in bacon, and Bud's salad includes both grilled beef and bacon.

If you know Royers Round Top, you know we haven't yet mentioned its flagship dish: pie. Bud (who goes by the moniker Bud the Pieman) offers big country-style classics with ribbons of baked fruit oozing out over the edge of knobby crusts as well as several pies of his own design. We believe the pecan pie, made with giant halves of Texas-grown nuts, is the best anywhere—a perfect balance of toasty nut flavor and syrupy sweetness. And the chocolate chip pie, loaded with pecans and super-chocolaty—really more a huge, thick cookie than a pie—is nothing short of devastating.

Royers is so deeply into pie that the menu threatens to charge customers 50¢ extra if they do not get it à la mode. "It is so wrong to not top your pie with Amy's ice cream!" (Amy's is an Austin brand started in 1984 by Amy Miller, who earned her chops working at the legendary Steve's in Boston.) If you come with a group of people, you can order a pie sampler for dessert: four different kinds à la mode. Those who cannot come to Round Top should know that Royers is set up to mail-order pies anywhere in the United States, and pie devotees can enroll in one of the café's Pie-of-the-Month plans. They range from six pies delivered every other month for a year to Pie-of-the-Month-for-Life!

The Salt Lick

18300 FM 1826   512-858-4959
Driftwood, TX   LD | $$

Our first review of The Salt Lick, in the earliest edition of this book, described a place that began with neither four walls nor a restroom—just a smoke pit and makeshift tables on Thurman and Hisako Roberts's six-hundred-acre ranch. My, how it's grown! Located in the Hill Country west of Austin, it is a lovely theme park of barbecue with seats for 2,000, its limestone buildings surrounded by rough-hewn log fences, the air smelling of slow-smoked meats. Compared to the region's back-of-the-butcher-shop barbecue parlors, it's a fairly civil place with an ambience you might call Rustic Deluxe. There is a printed menu; there is waiter service; and the kitchen's repertoire extends beyond meat to include all sorts of side dishes and desserts.

Meats come pre-sauced, which is good, because Salt Lick sauce is terrific: a tangy-sweet glaze with perhaps a hint of mustard. In fact the sauce is good enough to use as a between-meat dip for the slices of good white bread that come alongside the meal. Sausage is kielbasa-rich, made from equal amounts of pork and beef, more sophisticated than the primal beefy hot links sold in butcher-shop barbecues. The brisket, slow-smoked for sixteen hours, comes from the pit lean and polite, and if it lacks the succulence of fattier meats, Salt Lick sauce snaps it up to speed. Pork ribs drip juice from the tender meat at the bone and deliver a stupendously concentrated smoke-pit flavor in the chewy burnt ends.

Among the worthy side dishes are an intriguing cabbage slaw flecked with sesame seeds and cool German-style potato salad. And of course, pickles and sliced raw onions are available with every meal.

Smitty's

6219 Airport Rd. 915-772-5876
El Paso, TX LD | $

Smitty's is a kick-ass barbecue favored by soldiers stationed at Fort Bliss, and it makes an easy quick-stop for people on their way to or from the El Paso airport. (Take-out orders are a specialty, as is custom barbecue: "You bring it, we'll BBQ it!") The spacious dining room smells of smoke from the pit; decor is a combination of beer signs and Wild West imagery; and the background music is just right for knocking back longnecks and engaging in full-volume palaver with tablemates.

The meat selection is vast: regular beef or lean beef, corned beef or lean corned beef, ham, turkey breast and turkey sausage, chicken, sliced pork and chopped pork, pork chops, pork ribs and beef ribs. Most of these items can be had on a lunch plate or larger dinner plate (with German fried potatoes, slaw, and beans), in a sandwich or stuffed into a burrito, or on the "high protein special" plate which is nothing but meat accompanied by a Styrofoam cup full of Smitty's opaque sweet sauce and a few slices of soft white bread.

Tea (unsweetened) is presented to each table in a large pitcher so you can constantly replenish your glass as you dine.

Smitty's

208 S. Commerce St.
Lockhart, TX

512-398-9344
LD | $$

The atmosphere at Smitty's backroom barbecue is tangible: Eye-stinging clouds of smoke rise from wood fires around the indoor pit where you order meat by the pound. It is cut and assembled and wrapped in butcher paper so you can carry it to a communal table in the dining room. The pork chop is swell, but the Texas beef is definitive: brisket so tender it falls apart when touched and barbecued boneless prime rib (cut extra-thick, please) that has got to be the ultimate in pit-cooked luxury, pink in its center, saturated with juice and giddy with carnivorous energy. The sausage rings are insanely succulent, so loaded that if you plan to snap one in half, you must be sure to push out and away from you, lest its juices splatter your shirt.

Smitty's operates from the oldest barbecue facility in Lockhart, the building in which Charles Kreuz opened his grocery store over a century ago. In 1948 Kreuz sold the business to the Schmidt family, but several years back, a feud split the Schmidts and sent the Kreuz Market out to a big new building (p. 457). Smitty's retains a charismatic historic feel; to walk in off Commerce Street through the age-burnished dining room with its benches along the wall is to see a virtual museum of Texas foodways. The room, now idle, was still in use when we first dined at Smitty's in the 1970s. The long counters were equipped with sharp knives attached by chains long enough for customers to cut their meat but too short for a knife fight.

Sonny Bryan's

2202 Inwood Rd.
Dallas, TX

214-357-7120
LD | $

At Sonny Bryan's in Dallas, the brisket sandwich is simplicity itself: beef in a bun. But oh, what beef! Bathed for hours in a lazy veil of hickory smoke until it verges on disintegration, this is definitive Lone Star barbecue. The slices so drip with flavorful juice that no sauce is required. However, Sonny's sauce is a beautiful thing: opaque red with a tang made to complement the booming protein punch of the brisket. Turkey, ham, pulled pork, pork ribs, and sausage are also on the menu, available in a sandwich or on a plate with a couple of side dishes, and every one is superb. One plate can include three different meats, and you can add cheese to a sandwich. But if you are coming to Sonny Bryan's for the first time, please have brisket—chopped or sliced, it doesn't matter—and you will understand why Texans are passionate about barbecue. Available sides include French fries, onion rings, barbecue-sauced beans, potato salad, black-eyed peas, fried okra, mac 'n' cheese, coleslaw, potato chips by the bag, and in-season corn on the cob.

Dating back to 1910 when Elijah Bryan opened a smoke shack in Oak Cliff, Sonny Bryan's is now a small chain in the Dallas area and a well-known tourist attraction. We most enjoy the oldest of the restaurants (since 1958), on Inwood Road, where dining accommodations include awkward but irresistibly charming school-desk seating. For other locations, see www .sonnybryans.com.

Southside Market

1212 Hwy. 290 E.	512-281-4650
Elgin, TX	LD | $

In the geography of American sausage, no town holds more respect than Elgin (with a hard *g*, as in *gut*), known for hot beef sausages since the Southside Market opened in 1882. About ten years ago, the sawdust-floored house of meats moved from its original location to a huge, spanking clean, barn-size building on the outskirts of town. While the new place lacks the charm of a well-aged and charmingly dilapidated barbecue, it maintains a working butcher shop, and it still smokes sausage and beef brisket the old-fashioned way, in big iron pits over slow-smoldering post oak wood. Order your meat by the pound at the pit and carry it to a table.

The sausage is spectacular—vividly spiced, taut, and moist beyond description. But don't ignore the sliced beef; it too is luscious and flavorful, needing no companion other than a few slices of white bread just to mop its juices.

Taco House

6307 San Pedro Ave.	210-341-3136
San Antonio, TX	BL | $

In some places, breakfast tacos are a novelty. In San Antonio, they are a passion, served in dozens of little eateries all over the city. The best of the taquerias—seemingly most of them—use tortillas that are rolled out and griddle-cooked on the spot, just minutes before construction. Taco House, which has been a destination for decades, offers more than a dozen different kinds, from bacon and egg to *carne guisada* (gravy-sopped beef) and *lengua* (tongue). Fresh, chewy flour tortillas make a big difference, delivering even the most plebeian filling with high honors. But Taco House's plebeian fillings are far from drab. Eggs are buttery; bacon is thick and smoky; nuggets of potato are cooked to a perfect point of inside creaminess and outside crunch.

If you're going to have only one breakfast, consider chorizo and eggs, which, per local custom, is not eggs with a side order of chorizo sausage, but rather eggs scrambled with ground-up sausage to become an entirely new and different food: juicy, spicy, and cream-rich. It's great on a plate with refried beans and potatoes or as the filling of a taco.

Lunch is a full roster of Tex-Mex fare including not just tacos but enchiladas, flautas, and chicken mole. If you order chili, you will be asked whether or not you want beans. Say no and you are presented with an enormous bowl of true chili con carne, a minimalist dish of meat and red chile. Fajitas, like tacos, are available with crisp or puffy tortillas, the latter another San Antonio fave—quickly fried so they blow up like a flat sopaipilla.

Taco Taco

145 E. Hildebrand Ave.   210-822-9533
San Antonio, TX   BL | $

Service is swift at Taco Taco, but if you come at peak hours for breakfast or lunch, you will have to wait for a table. The goodness of its tacos is no secret among San Antonio Tex-Mex aficionados, who have a huge number of excellent taquerias from which to choose. As in all the good places, Taco Taco rolls out its tortillas by hand and griddle-cooks them as breakfast and lunch are served. This means yours will be warm and fresh—delicious to eat with no filling whatsoever.

It is customary for local taquerias to offer *barbacoa* on the weekend, and it's hard to imagine a more delicious version than Taco Taco's. It is the tenderest, most unctuous smoky beef imaginable, slowly roasted and loaded into the taco in heaping shreds that audibly ooze when bitten. No other ingredients are warranted in this taco, as might be right in, say, a chicken taco where a layer of *refritos* and a sprinkle of cheese are a nice complement, or a potato and egg breakfast taco gilded with the kitchen's marvelous salsa. Puffy tacos, a San Antonio passion, also are available—the same ingredients but enveloped in a tortilla that has been fried just enough to swell and soften. And thumbs up to specialty tacos that are made on tortillas that are double-wide: El Norteño contains sizzled chicken (or beef) with beans, slices of avocado, cheese, peppers, and onions. Fiesta is fajita-grilled chicken with chunky pico de gallo.

Meals begin with excellent tortilla chips and that house salsa—utterly impossible to stop eating until all chips are gone or the main course arrives.

Beyond tacos, the menu offers weekend *menudo* and such fine borderland dishes as chicken mole, enchiladas, gorditas, and flautas.

Texas Pie Company

| 202 W. Center St. | 512-268-5885 |
| Kyle, TX | L \| $ |

There is no chance you will miss the Texas Pie Company if you drive through Kyle along West Center Street. Looming over the roof that shades the sidewalk is an immense, colorful sculpture of a slice of cherry pie. Behind that, the house motto is written in bright red letters: "Life Is Short. Eat More Pie!"

This dessert-focused café is especially convenient for travelers just passing through because it makes single-serving mini-pies as well as big ones. Crusts are terrific—not all that pretty, but light and savory. Lemon chess pie radiates dazzling citrus flavor with a buttermilky cushion; coconut is supremely toasty, its fleshy white shreds packing full nutty richness; and the nuts that crowd the top of the pecan pie are rich and sweet and taste fresh enough to have just come out of their shell. We also highly recommend the strawberry cake, which is audibly moist and crowned with a heap of fruit-flavored frosting.

In addition to dessert, the Texas Pie Company sells simple lunches to eat here, including sandwiches and salads, and sells hot meals to take home and eat. Among the latter is that central Texas specialty, King Ranch casserole.

Threadgill's

| 6416 N. Lamar Blvd. | 512-451-5440 |
| Austin, TX | LD \| $ |

In the years we've been eating at Threadgill's, portions have gotten noticeably smaller. Now one full meal is big enough to feed only a couple of people. Still, this boisterous restaurant remains a bonanza for endless appetites, particularly appetites ravening for southern and/or Texas cooking.

Vegetables are vital here, from virtuous (okra with tomatoes) to wicked (garlic cheese grits). Many fans come to Threadgill's to eat *only* vegetables, accompanied by big squares of warm corn bread. If you choose right, a meal of five vegetable selections is, in fact, every bit as satisfying as a few pounds of beef. Among the excellent choices from the regular list are the San Antonio squash casserole, turnip greens, and definitive crisp-fried okra.

As for entrees, we tend to pull out all stops and go for chicken-fried steak or an impossibly rich plate of fried chicken livers with cream gravy.

Those of lighter appetite can choose a very handsome (albeit quite gigantic) Caesar salad piled with grilled chicken, and there are a couple of unfried fish items.

Aside from big, good food, Threadgill's is worth visiting for its history (the Austin music scene started here; Janis Joplin used to be a waitress) and its Texas-to-the-max ambience. Although the original beer joint/gas station that Kenneth Threadgill opened in 1933 burnt down twice and virtually none of it remains, the restaurant today has the feel of an antique: creaky wood floors, wood-slat ceilings, and a devil-may-care floor plan that gives the impression the sprawling space just kept growing through the years. The main decorative motif is beer signs.

Tom & Bingo's

3006 34th St.   806-799-1514
Lubbock, TX   L | $

A wood-slat shack surrounded by a parking lot, Tom & Bingo's serves heaps of tender, moist beef brisket in a bun. That's the menu. Plus chips. And, of course, pickles and onions and relish, if you'd like. The sauce is good, but hardly necessary to enhance the taste of this succulent meat after its long hickory-smoke bath. Seating is spare, along benches that line the walls.

Whole briskets are available if you order them in advance, and Meg Butler, who tipped us off to this place, reported that after she and her husband shared four sandwiches at Tom & Bingo's, they were so enthusiastic that they bought one to carry home. "Security screeners at the airport didn't blink," she said.

Vernon's Kuntry Katfish

5901 W. Davis St.   936-760-3386
Conroe, TX   LD | $

Hugely popular—you will wait for a table any weekday at lunch—Vernon's Kuntry Katfish serves not only Mississippi-raised catfish, but also a passel of country-style vegetables every day. Mustard greens or turnip greens, northern beans, field peas, fried okra, mashed potatoes, and cheese-enriched broccoli are some of the selections; and crunchy, dark-cooked hush puppies, studded with bits of onion and jalapeño pepper, are accompanied by bowls of pickled green tomatoes. If catfish is not your dish, try the chicken-fried steak. It's one to make Texans proud, gilded with pepper gravy and served with biscuits or corn-bread squares on the side.

Dessert is significant: fruit cobbler, banana pudding, or an item known as "good pie," which is a uniquely American pastry edifice of pineapple chunks, bananas, cream cheese, nuts, and chocolate syrup.

Village Bakery

108 E. Oak St.   254-826-5151
West, TX   B | $

The *kolache,* brought to Texas by immigrants from central Europe, has become a morning pastry more popular than donuts in some towns. It is like a fruit-filled Danish, but made with sweeter dough and so delicate that you need to hold it tenderly lest you compress it with brutal thumb and fingers. For some of the best *kolaches,* go to the town of West, Texas, just off I-35, and visit the Village Bakery. "Kolače [Czech spelling] are sold warm from the oven," assures the movable-letter menu above the counter. Apricot, prune, and poppy seed are standard-bearers from the old country. More modern variations are fruitier, filled with apple, strawberry, or blueberry preserves.

While fruit and cheese *kolaches* are traditional, the Village Bakery added a Texas twist to tradition in the early 1950s when baker Wendell Montgomery, worrying that his big loaves of sausage bread weren't selling well, asked his mother-in-law to come up with a snack-size version that included the sausage links that are another passion of Eastern Europeans who settled the heart of Texas. Her creation was a gloss on Czech *klobasnek,* which are customarily made with ground sausage. Purists still refer to them as that or, possibly, as pigs in blankets, reserving the term *kolache* for those filled with fruit, cheese, or poppy seeds. Savory *klobasnikis* have become a staple of *kolache* bakeries throughout the state. The Village Bakery makes regular and hot sausage versions, the latter marked by two slits in the top of the bun, and you'll find bakeries that add cheese and jalapeño peppers and even sauerkraut, too.

More a bakery than a full-service restaurant, this welcoming little shop will sell you a cup of coffee and offers three small dining tables and one circular ten-seat table occupied by gabbing townsfolk most mornings.

Weikel's Store and Bakery

2247 W. State Hwy. 71   979-968-9413
La Grange, TX   BL | $

A Danish-like pastry with Czech lineage, the *kolache* has become a tasty symbol of the Eastern European roots that have helped make this part of Texas such a culinary adventureland. One of the least likely places to find superior *kolaches* is Weikel's Store and Bakery, a convenience store attached to a gas station by the side of the highway. While it might at first look like any other quick-shop highway mart, bakery cases toward the back tell a different story. Here are handsome cakes, rolls, and cookies, plus several varieties of *kolache* from a house repertoire of about a dozen. Prune, cream cheese, apricot, and poppy seed are fluffy-crumbed but substantial, and superior coffee companions.

You know Weikel's is serious about its *kolaches* when you consider the house motto: "We Gottcha Kolache." In addition to its pastry treasures, one other house specialty worth sampling is the house-made pig-in-a-blanket. It is a taut-skinned, rugged-textured kielbasa sausage fully encased in a tube of tender-crumb bread that is finer than any hot dog bun we've ever eaten.

Capitol Reef Inn and Cafe

360 W. Main St.   435-425-3271

Torrey, UT   BLD | $$

At the west end of the town of Torrey in the wilds of south-central Utah, the Capitol Reef Inn and Cafe is an oasis of good food and elevated cultural consciousness. It is not only a restaurant; it is a lovely (and inexpensive) motel with hand-hewn furniture in the rooms; it is a bookstore featuring practical and meditative volumes about the West; and it is a trading post with some intriguing Native American jewelry and rugs.

The restaurant serves three meals a day and appears to be as informal as any western motel dining room, except for the fact that you are likely to hear the gurgle of an espresso machine in the background and Bach played to set the mood. The house motto is "Local, Natural, Healthy"; and while you can have a fine breakfast of bacon and eggs, you can also choose to have those eggs accompanied by smoked local trout, or you can have an omelet made with local cheeses . . . with fresh-squeezed juice to drink.

At lunch and dinner as well as breakfast, the Capitol Reef dining room is a blessing for traveling vegetarians. A few notable meatless menu items include spaghetti with marinara sauce (also available with meat), fettuccine primavera, and plates of steamed, stir-fried, or shishkebobbed vegetables. Beef, chicken, and seafood are always available for vegetable-frowners (that trout, broiled with rosemary, is what we recommend), and desserts include a hot fudge sundae and/or apple pie.

Hires Big H

425 S. 700 E.
Salt Lake City, UT

801-364-4582
LD | $
(two other locations)

Ever since the success of nickel-a-glass root beer at A&W stands during Prohibition, "the temperance beverage" has been an axiomatic drive-in drink. At Hires Big H, with three curb-service outlets in Salt Lake City, it comes in five sizes, from "baby" to "large," and of course there are root beer floats; or you can sip a limeade or a marshmallow-chocolate malt.

The juicy quarter-pound Big H burger is available plain or topped with bacon, ham, pastrami, Roquefort cheese, grilled onions, or a trio of crunchy onion rings, and it is brought to the car in a wax paper bag that makes a handy mitt. The bun is gentle-tempered sourdough with a floury top (as opposed to what the combative menu describes as "some preservative-enhanced, wilted crust studded with obnoxious seeds"), and French fries and onion rings are served with a dipping sauce reminiscent of French dressing. Correspondent Mel Fullmer informed us that the sauce was invented at Utah's Arctic Circle Drive-In in 1948 and is known throughout the region as "Fry Sauce." Utah's fry sauce has become a thing of pride among burger joints as far away as California, Oregon, and Washington.

Idle Isle

24 S. Main
Brigham City, UT

435-723-8003
BLD | $

Ahh, idleberry pie! A sultry, dark extravaganza that resonates with the profound fruitiness of blueberries, blackberries, and boysenberries, all packed into a crust that complements the berries with savory luxury, this pie is so complete that even à la mode seems superfluous. Utah's third-oldest restaurant (since 1921) is the sort of cordial town dining room once found on Main Streets everywhere. In the twenty-first century, its charm is a rarity.

You can have a lovely burger and a malt at the marble and onyx soda fountain; and there is a slightly more boisterous back room with oilcloth-covered tables where regulars congregate at noon; but the choice seats, at least for us travelers, are in polished wood booths up front, each outfitted with a little ramekin of Idle Isle apricot marmalade for spooning onto fleecy rolls. The rolls come alongside dinners that are a roster of blue-plate fundamentals, including divinely tender pot roast with lumpy mashed potatoes shaped like a volcano crater to hold gravy, as well as such daily specials as Wednesday braised beef joints, Friday trout, and Saturday prime rib.

Lamb's Grill Cafe

169 S. Main St.   801-364-7166
Salt Lake City, UT   BLD | $

Utah's oldest restaurant hasn't changed much since we first ate here some three decades ago, at which point it was celebrating sixty years in business. Liquor is more readily available (although you still have to make a special request to see the booze menu), but it remains a house of family-friendly meat-and-potatoes classics, some of which have all but vanished from modern restaurants' repertoires. Poached finnan haddie, anyone? Beef tenderloin à la stroganoff? None of it is self-consciously old-fashioned. These simply are dishes that never have been dropped from a menu that has indeed changed with the times to include the likes of Cajun salad with blackened chicken breast and portobello mushroom ravioli.

Still, it's the old-fashioned dishes we like to see on our plate at this well-aged diner/coffee shop in the heart of Salt Lake City: broiled chicken with lemon caper sauce, triple lamb chops, mountain trout, or chicken-fried steak with garlic-tinged whipped potatoes. Meals come with sesame-seeded Greek bread, which is at once wispy and chewy—great to use for mopping gravy or for eating with or without butter.

If Utah has one distinguishing culinary characteristic (other than scones and fry sauce to accompany French fries), it is a love of sweets. You will appreciate that at Lamb's, in the dark, chocolaty five-layer cake thick with icing, in the homey baked apple, and in the unusually al dente rice pudding heaped with powdered cinnamon.

Maddox Drive-In

1900 S. Hwy. 89   435-723-8545
Brigham City, UT   LD | $

The Maddox Drive-In, attached to the Maddox Steak House, serves lots of hamburgers but specializes in another drive-in delight, the chicken basket: fried chicken and French fries piled into a woven plastic trough. The beverage of choice is known as "fresh lime," which tastes something like lime-aided Sprite with extra sugar. The long, covered tramway where you park at Maddox is festooned with enthusiastic signs apparently meant to stimulate appetites: "We serve only grain-fed beef . . . We invite you to visit our entire operation." What we remember best about this mid-century showpiece is the huge sign high above the restaurant, where futuristic letters boast of MADDOX FINE FOOD.

There used to be a feedlot right in back, allowing customers at the adjoining steak house to look out the window at future steaks on the hoof as they dined. Today the cows are gone, but pound-plus T-bones remain the order of the day, accompanied by a basket of crunchy corn pone and glasses of pure drinking water drawn from Maddox's own well. Beef alternatives include skinless fried chicken, chicken-fried bison, and turkey steak.

Mom's Cafe

10 E. Main St.   435-529-3921
Salina, UT   BLD | $

At the crossroads in the old cowboy town of Salina, Mom's Cafe isn't really all that motherly, and several moms have come and gone, but it's been a worthy Roadfood stop since long before we hit the road many years ago. In fact, this square brick edifice has been a gathering place for travelers and ranchers for more than seventy years now, and it bears the well-weathered look and seeming permanence of the rock mesas that surround the town.

Mom's offers a full menu, including excellent liver and onions at supper, but we like breakfast best, for that is when the scones are fresh and hot. The scone is a Utah specialty, and always on the menu in this true Utah café. It is similar to New Mexican sopaipillas and to the Indian fry breads served at roadside stands throughout the Southwest, but generally big enough and weighty enough to be a nice little meal all by itself. Any time of day, pie is a good choice. It's homemade, and one of the great house specialties is blueberry sour cream.

Navajo Hogan

447 E. 3300 S.   801-466-2860
Salt Lake City, UT   LD | $

Few foods served in modern restaurants actually are native to America; nearly everything we eat is the product of immigrants bringing their recipes (and sometimes their seeds, livestock, and spices) and mixing them with what's available across the fruited plains. Navajo Hogan's tacos are, in fact, exactly the sort of melting-pot, mix-n-match dish that characterizes our nation's cuisine at its most exuberant: Mexican, New Mexican, and Utahan with a measure of fast-food brio.

The Navajo taco, popular throughout the Southwest, is built upon fry bread: excellent stuff here, made using flour and cornmeal that gets slid into a pan of hot oil and fried into a pliable disk ready for anything. Atop the bread goes your choice of ingredients, ranging from what the menu calls "traditional" (beans, beef, lettuce, tomato, shredded cheese, and sour cream) to dessert versions topped with honey butter or cinnamon sugar. You can get green or red chili from New Mexico (the owners' original home), vegetarian toppings, or grilled chicken. That is the extent of the menu, except for Saturday-only mutton stew, a true Navajo dish that goes back at least a millennium.

Roadfood.com tipster Dale Fine, who goes by the screen name wanderingjew, noted that Navajo Hogan is the sort of place "you're likely to pass by without realizing it's there": a windowless cinder-block bunker with fabric signs hung outside. We thank Mr. Fine for discovering it.

Great Plains

Idaho * Montana * Nebraska *

South Dakota * Wyoming

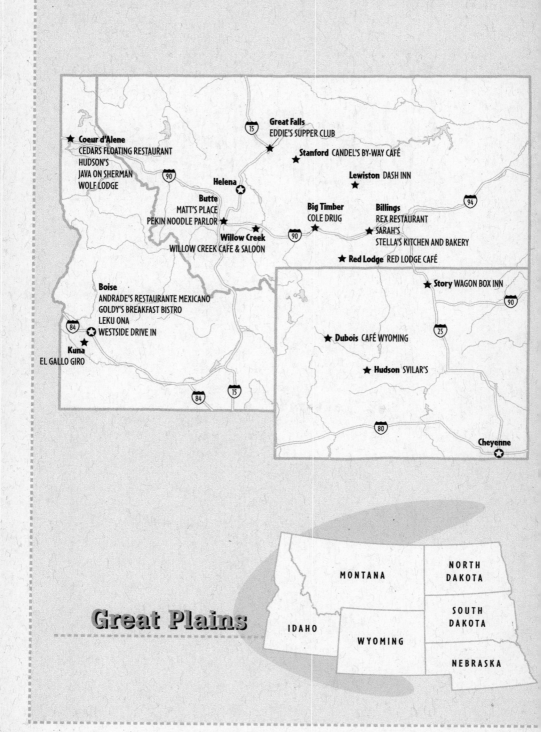

Coeur d'Alene
CEDARS FLOATING RESTAURANT
HUDSON'S
JAVA ON SHERMAN
WOLF LODGE

Great Falls
EDDIE'S SUPPER CLUB

Stanford CANDEL'S BY-WAY CAFÉ

Lewiston DASH INN

Helena

Butte
MATT'S PLACE
PEKIN NOODLE PARLOR

Big Timber
COLE DRUG

Billings
REX RESTAURANT
SARAH'S
STELLA'S KITCHEN AND BAKERY

Willow Creek
WILLOW CREEK CAFE & SALOON

Red Lodge RED LODGE CAFÉ

Story WAGON BOX INN

Boise
ANDRADE'S RESTAURANTE MEXICANO
GOLDY'S BREAKFAST BISTRO
LEKU ONA
WESTSIDE DRIVE IN

Dubois CAFÉ WYOMING

Kuna
EL GALLO GIRO

Hudson SVILAR'S

Cheyenne

Great Plains

MONTANA

NORTH DAKOTA

IDAHO

SOUTH DAKOTA

WYOMING

NEBRASKA

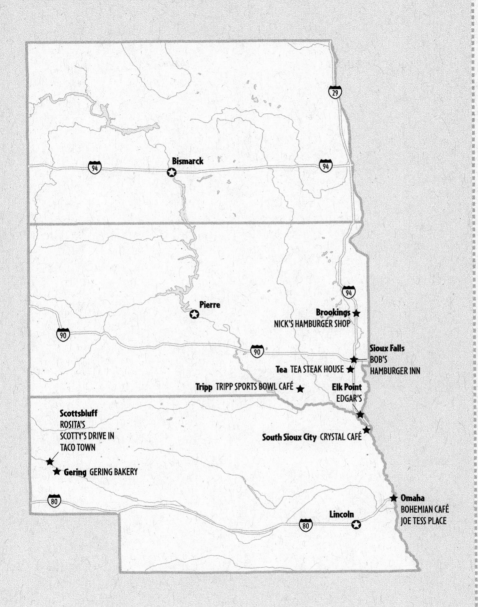

Bismarck

Pierre

Brookings ★
NICK'S HAMBURGER SHOP

Sioux Falls
BOB'S
HAMBURGER INN

Tea TEA STEAK HOUSE ★

Tripp TRIPP SPORTS BOWL CAFÉ ★

Elk Point
EDGAR'S

Scottsbluff
ROSITA'S
SCOTTY'S DRIVE IN
TACO TOWN

South Sioux City CRYSTAL CAFÉ

★ **Gering** GERING BAKERY

Omaha
BOHEMIAN CAFÉ
JOE TESS PLACE

Lincoln

Andrade's Restaurante Mexicano

4903 W. Overland Rd.   208-424-8890
Boise, ID   LD | $$

It used to be that the only good food to eat while traveling through southern Idaho was Basque. But now Mexican food abounds, and one of the best places to enjoy it is Andrade's Restaurante Mexicano in Boise (with a second location in Meridian). Javier Andrade is known for his salsa bar, where diners help themselves to chunky salsa roja, pico de gallo, four-alarm habanero purée, and a large variety of other tongue-tinglers that are just right for dipping tortilla chips. Our one caution is to note that the salsas are not clearly labeled, so it's hit or miss, heat-wise, and in our experience, some of these are hair-raising.

Two great ways to start a meal are fish tacos and *chori queso,* the latter a dense, delicious cheese melted and mixed with chorizo sausage. Favorite dinners include a powerhouse chicken mole, carne asada with grilled onions, and *puerco Michoacan,* which is pork stewed in a tomato sauce with peppers, onions, and sweet corn.

Cedars Floating Restaurant

1514 S. Marina Dr.   208-664-2922
(Blackwell Island)   D | $$$
Coeur d'Alene, ID

Rugged as it is, the landscape of northern Idaho can be irresistibly romantic—especially when appreciated at dinner hour from a table in Cedars Floating Restaurant, which is one of the few eateries that take full advantage of the city's auspicious setting at the north end of Coeur d'Alene Lake. In fact, Cedars is located *in* the lake, moored about a hundred yards out at the head of the Spokane River and reachable by a walk down a long, narrow gangplank from the parking lot. Permanently berthed on three hundred tons of concrete, the dining room does not bob with the waves (as the original structure did in the 1960s!), but the window tables are virtually on the waterline. Our first visit was on a drizzly September evening when the lake was steel gray, reflecting stormy skies and low clouds creeping down over a forested horizon.

A crackling fire and the lively sounds of an open kitchen provide cozy ambience to the spacious circular dining room, where every seat affords a view of waterfowl skimming over waves and the distant rocky shoreline. Cedars specializes in fresh fish from Pacific waters. Salmon, ahi, sea bass, halibut, shark, and mahimahi are some of the frequently available choices; they are cut into thick fillets and charcoal broiled, served with a choice of clear lemon butter caper sauce, tropical fruit salsa, or cucumber dill sauce.

We started our meal with a pound of steamed clams lolling in a garlicky wine broth and accompanied by toasted French bread, and a plate of fresh-seared calamari with garlic aioli and red pepper remoulade. Our fillet of Hawaiian wahoo was a handsome piece of meat, well over an inch thick: firm and sweet-fleshed with a savory crust from the grill. It was accompanied by a baked potato with tawny skin and flavorful insides. "An Idaho potato?" we asked the waitress. Blushing, she confessed the spud was grown in Washington State. On a subsequent visit, we decided to try the beef and were thrilled by a one-pound prime rib, roasted for twelve hours and rubbed with herbs. A marinated "biergarten" filet mignon was deliriously tender . . . if somewhat painfully priced at $39.

The dessert list is short, and it includes huckleberry cheesecake and Cascade Creamery huckleberry ice cream.

El Gallo Giro

482 W. Main St.   208-922-5169
Kuna, ID   LD | $

A cheerful restaurant whose name translates as "the fighting rooster," this Treasure Valley gem southwest of Boise and just a few minutes from I-84 serves superb true-Mex food. Start with hominy-pork soup (posole), *campenchana* (octopus and shrimp in a garlic-lime marinade), or freshly made guacamole accompanied by chips and salsa. Quaff a Mexican beer or creamy-sweet *horchata* (rice milk), then move on to a beautiful plate of chicken mole blanketed with intense chile-chocolate sauce or fish tacos on soft tortillas. We loved our *carne borracha,* which is shredded beef besotted with hot peppers, onions, and tomatoes; served in *molcajetes* (lava rock bowls), it is a dining event. Even the refried beans are extra-good, sprinkled with crumbled cotija cheese.

From what we could see on other people's tables, the more familiar Tex-Mex meals are mighty tempting: enchiladas, chimichangas, fajitas, etc. El Gallo Giro's little tacos, selling for a dollar apiece, are local legend. You can have them filled with steak, pork, goat, cheek, tongue, chicken, or tripe.

One reason people return again and again, other than the food, is the hospitality of Enrique Contreras, who is known for circulating around the dining room throughout mealtime to say hello to old friends and welcome new ones.

Goldy's Breakfast Bistro

108 S. Capitol Blvd.   208-345-4100
Boise, ID   BL | $$

Who couldn't love Goldy's "Create Your Own Breakfast Combo"? Select a main course, which can be eggs, chicken-fried steak, or a salmon fillet, then take your pick from long lists of meats, potatoes, and breads. Among the not-to-be-missed meats are habanero chicken sausage, Basque chorizo, and pork sausage infused with sage. The potato roster includes not only hash browns and sweet potato hash browns but also red flannel hash (spuds, beets, and bacon) and cheese grits. The six available breads include fresh-baked biscuits, sourdough, and cinnamon raisin walnut.

Hollandaise sauce is fantastic: smooth and fluffy with an ethereal lemon perfume. It comes on several variations of eggs Benedict: There's eggs Black-stone (Black Forest ham and tomato); a dilled salmon fillet blanketed with slivers of cucumber and sauce; even a veggie benny, which is sauce over broccoli, asparagus, and tomato. Other choice breakfast items include frittatas, breakfast burritos, cinnamon rolls, and sticky buns; and a full-service espresso bar offers cappuccinos, lattes, and flavor shots from amaretto to passion fruit. Orange juice is freshly squeezed.

A stylish little place with an open kitchen that affords diners a view of breakfasts being cooked and plated, Goldy's can be maddeningly crowded, making meal service less than speedy, and on weekends you will likely wait for a table. But if your goal is having the best breakfast in Boise, this is the place to go.

Hudson's

207 Sherman Ave.   208-664-5444
Coeur d'Alene, ID   L | $

"Pickle and onion?" the counterman will ask when you order a hamburger, a double hamburger, or a double cheeseburger at Hudson's, a counter-only diner that has been a Coeur d'Alene institution since 1907, when Harley Hudson opened a quick-eats lunch tent on the town's main drag.

Your garnish selection is called out to grill man Todd Hudson, Harley's great-grandson, who slices the raw onion to order, using his knife blade to hoist the thin, crisp disk from the cutting board to the bun bottom; then, deft as a Benihana chef, he cuts eight small circles from a pickle and arrays them in two neat rows atop the onion. When not wielding his knife, Todd hand-forms each burger, as it is ordered, from a heap of lean ground beef piled in a gleaming silver pan adjacent to his griddle. All this happens at warp speed as customers enjoy the mesmerizing show from the sixteen seats at Hudson's long counter and from the small standing area at the front of the restaurant where new arrivals await stool vacancies.

Each patty is cooked until it develops a light crust from the griddle but retains a high amount of juiciness inside. One in a bun makes a balanced sandwich. Two verge on overwhelming beefyness. Chef Hudson sprinkles on a dash of salt, and when the hamburger is presented, you have one more choice to make: which condiment? Three squeeze bottles are deployed adjacent to each napkin dispenser along the counter. One is hot mustard, the other is normal ketchup, the third is Hudson's very spicy ketchup, a thin orange potion for which the recipe is a guarded secret. "All I can tell you is that there is no horseradish in it," the counterman reveals to an inquisitive customer.

There are no side dishes at all: no French fries, no chips, no slaw, not a leaf of lettuce in the house. And other than the fact that a glass case holds slices of pie for dessert, there is nothing more to say about Hudson's. In 104 years it has honed a simple perfection.

Java on Sherman

324 Sherman Ave.   208-667-0010
Coeur d'Alene, ID   BL | $

Several years ago during a week in Coeur d'Alene, we started every day at Java on Sherman, and fell in love with it. We sampled breakfast at other cafés and diners around town, but none were as compelling as this stylish storefront coffeehouse (one of a handful of Idaho Javas) where Seattle-level caffeine connoisseurship combines with muffin mastery. All the usual drip-brewed and espresso-based beverages are expertly made, supplemented by house specialties that range from the devastating "Keith Richards," made from four shots of espresso and Mexican chocolate, to the sublime "bowl of soul," which is a balance of coffee and espresso with a tantalizing sprinkle of chocolate and cinnamon served in a big ceramic bowl.

Java offers a repertoire of hot breakfasts, including bulgur wheat with apples and raisins, non-instant oatmeal, and eggs scrambled, then steamed at the nozzle of the espresso machine, but it's the baked goods that have won Idahoans' hearts: handsome scones, sweet breads, and sour-cream muffins, plus a trademarked thing known as a "lumpy muffin"—big chunks of tart apple with walnuts and raisins all suspended in sweet cinnamon cake. Considerably more top than base, this muffin breaks easily into sections that are not quite dunkable (they'd fall apart) but are coffee's consummate companion.

Leku Ona

117 S. 6th St.   208-345-6665
Boise, ID   LD | $$$

Located on what Boisians know as the Basque Block, Leku Ona is both a five-room boutique hotel and an adjoining restaurant celebrating the hearty, high-spiced cuisine of the people of the Pyrenees. Unlike many of the region's Basque restaurants, which serve only groaning-board, family-style meals, this old-world ode offers a regular menu from which each customer is free to choose appetizer (perhaps Urdaiazpikoa, a.k.a Serrano ham), soup (red bean and chorizo, please), and entree, which can range from whole squid cooked in its ink to honeycomb tripe or lamb shank. Prices are high on the Roadfood scale (dinner entrees in the $20+ range), but service is suave and each dish is exemplary.

For those who want the more traditional Basque-hotel experience, Leku Ona does offer family-style feeds of soup, salad, hot bread, and French fries followed by battered codfish and paella and your choice of lamb stew, pork chops, or roast chicken, sirloin steak, pork loin, or meatballs. Drink choices include Pagoa (a Basque beer) in lager, red ale, and stout. There's also a *pinxtos* (a.k.a. tapas) bar featuring small portions of such savories as leek pancakes, beef tongue, and cod croquettes. For dessert, *madari egosiak* is a lurid dish of sweetened pears poached in red wine.

Westside Drive In
1939 W. State St.   208-342-2957
Boise, ID   LD | $

A drive-in owned by "Chef Lou" Aaron, who has a regular cooking segment on Boise television and is creator of a dessert called the Idaho Ice Cream Potato, Westside is a place people come to eat (off their dashboards or on the patio's picnic tables) and to take home such Chef Lou specialties as prime rib, pastas, and salads. The drive-in fare includes crisp-fried shrimp and fish and chips and a roster of extraordinary made-to-order hamburgers that are thick and crusty and juicy inside, nothing like franchised fast-food junkburgers. There are doubles, deluxes, Cajun burgers, guacamole burgers, and Maui burgers. We like a good ol' cheeseburger, preferably with lettuce and tomato. It comes wrapped in wax paper for easy eating.

In honor of his home state, Chef Lou offers "the biggest bakers in the valley," which are one-pound Super Spuds available simply saturated with butter or loaded with chili, cheese, and onions. To drink, there are fine milk shakes, including huckleberry and black raspberry.

Wolf Lodge
12025 E. Frontage Rd.   208-664-6665
(Exit 283B off I-90)   D | $$$
Coeur d'Alene, ID

Here are meat-and-potatoes meals of Homeric scale. A vast red barn-board roadhouse just yards from the highway, this exuberant Wild West domain features oilcloth-clad tables and walls festooned with trophy animal heads, bleached bovine skulls, antique tools, old beer posters, and yellowing newspaper clippings of local-interest stories. It is a sprawling place with miscellaneous booths and dining nooks in several rooms; at the back of the rearmost dining area is a stone barbecue pit where apple wood burns a few feet below the grate. On this grate sizzle slabs of beef ranging from a ten-ounce filet mignon to the Rancher, which is forty-four ounces of porterhouse and sirloin. (Seafood is also available, cooked over the wood.)

Cowboy-cuisine aficionados start supper with a plate of "swinging beef"—sliced and crisp-fried bull testicles, served with cocktail sauce and lemon wedges. We relished a bowl of truly homey vegetable beef soup that was thick as stew with hunks of carrot, potato, beef, green pepper, and onion. Dinners come with saucy "buckaroo" beans, a twist of *krebel* (fried bread), and baked or fried potatoes, the latter excellent steak fries, each of which is one-eighth of a long Idaho baker that has been sliced end-to-end and fried so that it develops a light, crisp skin and creamy insides.

A second Wolf Lodge—Wolf Creek—has opened in Spokane, Washington.

Candel's By-Way Café

487 W. 37 N.   406-566-BYWA

Stanford, MT   BLD | $

We arrived at Candel's By-Way Café mid-morning, just as the pies were coming out of the oven. They are homely pies and each piece fell apart on its way from tin to plate, but the sour cream raisin pie turned out to be one of the best anywhere, with a wicked tangy-sweet character. The crust underneath the warm peach pie is the melt-in-mouth kind, so fine that we found ourselves hunting stray little slivers on emptied plates, gathering them up by pressing down with our forks' tines. "Why are these pies so good?" we called out from our counter seats, quite literally ecstatic from finding them. Sheila Candelaria, who runs the place with her husband, Mike, credited them to her mother, from whom she learned to bake growing up on a ranch seventeen miles south of town. But it turned out that pies aren't the only reason to inscribe this place on the honor roll.

"We cut the steaks, we make our seasoning mixes, even our chicken fingers are from scratch," Sheila told us, singing especially high praises of the chunky, garlic-studded salsa that accompanies the Mexican food Mike makes. At this point, post-pie lunch seemed essential.

Mike's beef-and-bean burrito is smothered with orange-hued chili Colorado that tastes like nothing more than pure peppers and spice. We could hear our chicken-fried steak getting pounded tender through the pass-through window to the kitchen, and rather than coming sheathed in the typi-cal thick batter coat and smothered under gluey gravy, this one has a thin, brittle crust. It sits atop a puddle of refined white gravy with a pepper punch.

Sitting at a table where the view out the front window is the fronts of pickup trucks pulled up in the lot and Highway 87/200 beyond them, a few everyday customers told us just how much they appreciate this place. Everyone in Stanford comes here to eat and to meet and linger over coffee and conversation. As we paid our bill at the cash register, we noticed a book of blank, non-personalized checks from the Basin State Bank: for customers who don't have cash.

Cole Drug

136 McLeod St.   406-932-5316
Big Timber, MT   L | $

Cruising through the lovely little town of Big Timber, we could not resist stopping at the good old lunch counter in Cole Drug Store. The menu remains the same as it was some dozen years ago when we first faced the challenge of a Big Timber sundae (nine scoops of ice cream and all the toppings in the house). This time we ate more modestly and enjoyed a perfectly made black-and-white soda and a huckleberry sundae. Huckleberries are big in the Plains states, and their bright, sweet, fruity flavor makes for an ideal ice cream topping. We were also impressed with the good crunch of the nuts on top.

It was a quiet, soul-satisfying pleasure to sit at the boomerang-pattern Formica counter and chat with the soda-fountain mixologists and a few other customers who walked in for sodas and sundaes. This is a nice place in a nice town in a very nice part of the world.

Dash Inn

207 NE Main St.   406-535-3892
Lewistown, MT   LD | $

One reason we love Roadfood.com so much, other than it being a soapbox from which we can pontificate about our favorite eateries, is that it is a forum where others can pay homage to their favorites, too. We might never have known about the Dash Inn and its fine hamburgers were it not for a review of it posted on the website by Blythe Butler, who described it as a "tried-and-true drive-in: no waitresses, no light-up graphic menu, no affili-ation with a national chain, not even a logo on the napkins; just a square wooden building full of grills, deep fat fryers, and ice cream, next to a row of covered parking spaces offering a view of teenagers cruising the Main Street drag."

The place of honor on the Dash Inn menu belongs to a hamburger known as a Wagon Wheel. That's a modest-size patty sandwiched in two pieces of bread, toasted in a press. Architecturally, it is like a panini, but you won't hear that word used by the disembodied voice with which you speak when you place your order at the beginning of the line. Wagon Wheels (or chicken or ribs) are delivered through your car window in white paper bags, accompanied by memorable beverages. These include rum-flavored Mountain Dew and Cokes doctored up with chocolate or cherry syrup, as well as the spicy Hot-N-Tot, which is Coke kicked up a notch by an infusion of tongue-tingling cinnamon.

Eddie's Supper Club

3725 2nd Ave. N.   406-453-1616
Great Falls, MT   LD | $$

Eddie's is supper-club heaven, loved by generations of Montanans and visitors (it opened in 1944) as a comfortable place to go for cocktails and campfire steaks. There are two halves to it: a coffee shop, which is lighter-feeling, more casual, and with a varied menu that includes sandwiches; and the more serious restaurant, which is atmospheric and has a big-deal menu of beef and seafood.

We like sitting in the supper club if only for its decor: large, handsome pictures of horses, all kinds of them: trotters in action, a bucking horse tossing a cowboy, western horses at work tending cattle. The picture at the back of the room, which has a horse's head in the foreground and a herd of cows in back, is especially beguiling. "We call him Mr. Ed," our waitress said. "His eyes follow you all around the room."

Booths are supremely comfortable, lights are low, and the staff are able pros. Steaks are grand. "Tastes just like that old Marlboro Cowboy cooked it over the campfire," advises the menu. Our waitress told us that the secret of the steaks is not the fire over which they are cooked, but the house's special wine marinade. This seeps into the meat and gives it a special tang, also coating the surface so the exterior of the steak develops a crunchy caramelized crust as it cooks. The T-bone we ate was spectacularly good. And an off-the-menu hamburger, which has the marinade folded into the meat, was wild.

Matt's Place

2339 Placer St.   406-782-8049

Butte, MT   LD | $

A virtual time machine, Matt's Place looks like it might not have changed at all since opening in 1930. The state's oldest drive-in has a short curved counter and a bright red waist-high Coke machine from which you fetch your own bottle from icy waters. Hamburgers sizzle in the back kitchen, milk shake mixers whir, and soda jerks ply the wands of seltzer and syrup dispensers to brew effervescent potions. If you are not in the mood for a pork chop sandwich (Montana's passion) or an ordinary hamburger, Matt's offers a wild array of custom burgers, including one topped with fried eggs and a nutburger spread with mayonnaise and a fistful of chopped peanuts.

Pekin Noodle Parlor

117 S. Main St.   406-782-2217

Butte, MT   D | $

Pekin Noodle Parlor is a relic of Butte's boom days as a mining town, when the small street out back was known as China Alley. An ancient sign on the wall says "Famous Since 1916." Climb a small dark staircase to the second floor and you will be escorted to your own curtained dining cubicle. The setting suggests exotic intrigue, like an old Montana version of *Shanghai Express*. When the food comes from the kitchen, it is announced by the rumble of the waitress's rolling trolley along the wood-plank floor; the curtain whisks aside, and behold! Here is a vista of foreign food the likes of which most devotees of Asian cookery forgot about fifty years ago.

Chop suey and chow mein are mild, thick, and harmless; fried shrimp are girdled by a pad of breading and served on leaves of lettuce with French fried potatoes as a garnish; sweet-and-sour ribs drip pineapple-flavored syrup; and the house specialty—noodles—comes in a shimmering clear broth with chopped scallions on top. Get the noodles plain or accompanied by strips of pork, beef, or chicken served on the side in a little bowl with half a hard-boiled egg.

The after-dinner drink-menu-that-time-forgot includes Separators, Stingers, White Russians, and Pink Squirrels. The thing to drink before a meal is a Ditch—Montanese for whiskey and water.

Red Lodge Café

16 S. Broadway Ave.   406-446-1619
Red Lodge, MT   BLD | $

The Red Lodge Café is eager to please with all modern facilities, yet ingenuous like a mid-twentieth-century tourist stop. For breakfast, you'll want to eat jumbo omelets or blueberry buckwheat pancakes, and to sip coffee long enough to eavesdrop on the conversations of locals and passers-through. The lunch menu features such stalwart items as country-fried steak and potatoes and buffalo burgers, as well as some fine deluxe hamburgers. For dessert, everybody has pie: apple or berry pie or, best of all, banana cream pie, which is so jiggly that it eats better with a spoon than a fork.

The restaurant itself has a western theme, but there is something for everyone from morning to night: keno, weekend karaoke, and the strangest-shaped pool table we've ever seen. Lighting fixtures above the dining room are made of wagon wheels, the ceiling is stamped tin, and the walls are bedecked with painted wooden totem poles and spectacular murals of scenery along the 11,000-foot elevation of the Beartooth Highway that leads from here to Yellowstone. The two-lane highway is closed by snow in the winter, but once it's open, it is a spectacular trip. Charles Kuralt once called it "America's most beautiful road."

Rex Restaurant

2401 Montana Ave.   406-245-7477
Billings, MT   LD | $$

Montana Avenue in Billings has become something of a restaurant row with a handful of trendy places drawing people back downtown for dinner. One of the old reliables in the area is the Rex, a vintage hotel dining room that has been cleaned up but not drastically modernized to be one of the city's most respected upscale eating establishments. Unless you sit on the breezy patio, accommodations are dark and clubby, all varnished wood, brass, raw brick, and cut glass under an old stamped tin ceiling.

Beef is king, and the prime rib we had was one of the best around: thick, juice-laden, and full-flavored. For those not intent on ingesting maximum red-meat protein, the broad menu includes pizzas made to order, sandwiches and big salads, shrimp, crab, and lobster. Lunch can be as inexpensive as an $8.95 burger or $8.50 Caesar salad; beef dinners range to near $30.

We were introduced to the Rex many years ago by a local saddle maker whose doctor had told him he needed to eat less beef, so he ordered cream-sauced pasta, which looked to us like it was richer than a rib-eye steak!

Sarah's

310 N. 29th St.

Billings, MT

406-256-5234

BLD | $

Sarah's is a little hard to figure out, but worth the effort for some of the best Mexican food in the Plains. Here's the way it works. Upon entering, go to the back of the room to an order window. At the right of the window is a large posted menu. Choose your burritos, tacos, or enchiladas and tell the nice lady who steps out of the kitchen what you want. Then go to the cash register and pay for it. Now move over to the condiment bar and help yourself to Styrofoam cups full of hot sauce or mild sauce, onions, or jalapeños to carry to a table, where a basket of chips is set out along with lots of napkins. When you are halfway through the chips, the meal arrives.

We especially love the taquitos, which would be called flautas in much of the Southwest: tightly wrapped, crisp-fried tortilla tubes containing moist shredded beef. They are served with a cup of garlicky guacamole. The red smothered beef burrito is a mighty meal, loaded with big hunks of beef. Our one complaint is that the plastic forks provided are only barely up to severing the tortilla wrap and beef inside.

Stella's Kitchen and Bakery

110 N. 29th St.

Billings, MT

406-248-3060

BL | $

The back of Stella's is a large bakery that supplies breads, cakes, cookies, bagels, and rolls to local restaurants and stores, but if you're in town for breakfast, there's nothing better than eating at the source. The cinnamon rolls are monumental, each one bigger than a softball and enough breakfast for two or more hungry people. The rolls are made fresh each day, but when you order one, it is microwaved so a big glob of butter set atop it is melting when the roll arrives at the table. Heating also tends to give the caramel glaze on top a chewy texture that makes it a fork-and-knife pastry. Even bigger than the cinnamon roll is Stella's giant white caramel roll—fourteen ounces of sweet dough served with a small tub of whipped butter.

Everything is large at Stella's, especially the pancakes, which are known as Monster Cakes. "You've got to see 'em to believe 'em" the menu boasts. Each one is a good twelve inches, edge to edge; and yet they have a nice light texture that makes it easy to eat a couple, or maybe even three. You have your choice of buttermilk or wheat batter; and if you can polish off four of them in a single sitting, you get a free cinnamon roll! We are especially fond of the very small print underneath the pancake listing on the menu: "Diet Smuckers jelly & syrups available upon request." So these would qualify as diet food??

There are normal-size breakfasts at Stella's: omelets, hot cereals (oatmeal, seven-grain, and Stella's homemade grits), and egg sandwiches; and the lunch menu includes such regular-size items as club and sub sandwiches, chili by the bowl, and a French dip as well as hamburgers that range up to the half-pound Ziggyburger, served on an outsized bun to match.

For dessert? Bread pudding made with Stella's homemade breads, please.

Willow Creek Cafe & Saloon

21 Main St.
Willow Creek, MT

406-285-3698
LD (reservations advised) | $$

Reservations advised? In Willow Creek, population 209?

You bet. Here is a way, way out of the way restaurant that attracts customers from Three Forks and Manhattan, even Bozeman, some fifty miles away. They come for pillowy beef steaks and chicken-fried steaks, hamburgers and homemade soups, pies and cakes made that day, even such upscale suppers as pork marsala and saltimbocca. There's always prime rib on weekend nights, but the one never-to-miss meal is barbecued ribs, anointed with a brilliant honey mustard glaze that teases maximum flavor from the pork. A chalkboard lists the day's specials and featured wines, which oenophile friends tell us are a good deal.

The place itself is a hoot: a sunflower-yellow house that started life in 1912 as the Babcock Saloon and has been a pool hall, barber shop, and butcher shop. Dining facilities are small indeed, with room for only a few dozen customers at a time. The old-fashioned print wallpaper and antique wood fixtures make it feel like a trip back in time. If you're heading for Willow Creek, don't worry about finding it. It is the only business in town.

Bohemian Café

1406 S. 13th St.   402-342-9838
Omaha, NE   LD | $$

The Bohemian Café is an immensely cheerful place, a vast, multiroom eating hall decorated with colorful old-country woodwork and pictures of men and women in traditional peasant attire; tables are patrolled by veteran professional waitresses in bright red dirndl skirts. "Vítáme Vás," meaning "We welcome you," is the house motto of this 1924-vintage Omaha landmark. Whether you are an old-timer who came with your parents decades ago or a visiting fireman who wants a fun-time meal with polka music setting the beat in the dining room, you will feel welcome.

The traditional way to begin a meal is with a cup of liver dumpling soup, which is homely and homey; we also love the plain-dumpling, chicken-stock soup that is often available as an alternative. Every meal begins with a basket of chewy sour rye bread. The big menu includes American-style steaks and seafood, a quartet of specials every day, and traditional Czech specialties. Foremost among the kitchen's accomplishments is roast duck—half a bird with crisp skin and flavorful meat that pulls off the bone with ease. We are fond of the sauerbraten, which is a stack of pot-roast-tender hunks of beef that are a joy to pull apart with the tines of a fork. We also like the Czech goulash, a vivid red, smoky pork stew. There is a large choice of side dishes, but the two for which the Bohemian Café is best known are dumplings and kraut. The former is a pair of saucer-size slices of doughy matter covered with whatever gravy your main course demands; the latter is a fetching sweet-and-sour mix, thick as pudding, dotted with caraway seeds. Whatever entree you choose, it will come flanked by dumplings and kraut—an awesome presentation that is a challenge to all but the mightiest appetite.

Paper place mats remind diners that this restaurant is home of the Bohemian Girl Jim Beam commemorative bourbon bottle (there is a huge collection of Jim Beam commemoratives in the entryway); and the mats also list the lyrics to the house song, which has been used in radio advertisements:

> *Dumplings and kraut today*
> *At Bohemian Café*
> *Draft beer that's sparkling, plenty of parking*
> *See you at lunch, Okay?*

Crystal Café

4601 Dakota Ave. 402-494-5471
South Sioux City, NE Always open | $

At 8:30 in the morning at the Crystal Café, men and women who are starting the day (and some finishing a long night) converse about issues that include jackknives, deadheading, log books, and speed traps. They are professional truckers; the Crystal Café is where they come not only to eat, but for fuel and over-the-road supplies. It is an open-all-night truck stop just west of the Missouri River.

Each place is set with a clean overturned coffee cup and a water glass. The waitress flips your cup right-side up and pours coffee and refills throughout breakfast. The cuisine is haute highway: big food, served in abundance. Plate-wide buttermilk pancakes, chicken-fried steak with a patty of oily hash browns, and sausage gravy on big, crumbly biscuits are some of the morning specials. The Texaco Deluxe is an omelet with ham, bacon, or sausage plus cheese, tomato, onions, and green peppers. The morning item we especially like is the caramel sweet roll, which is thick and goopy. At lunch, you can have a breaded pork tenderloin, a bowl of chili, or a ten-ounce king-of-the-road Texaco Burger. Crystal Café's sour cream raisin pie is one of the Midwest's best: dense, creamy, and sweet, crowned with ethereal meringue.

Gering Bakery

1446 10th St.   308-436-5500
Gering, NE   BL | $

A small sign in the window of the Gering Bakery advertises cabbage burgers. Considering that we were in Nebraska, home of the *runza* and the
bierock—bread pockets stuffed with ground beef, cabbage, and spice—the
sign caused us to come to a sudden halt and investigate. *Runzas* and *bierocks*
are nineteenth-century immigrant fare, but in the mid-1950s, the name
Runza was trademarked and is now the lead item at the eponymous restaurant chain. Runza's are okay, but the monotony of the identical restaurants
makes us depressed.

Gering Bakery, on the other hand, is the real deal. Sure enough, the
advertised cabbage burger is a non-corporate *runza,* and a delicious one at
that. Available in bulk to take home or one at a time, and heated up by the
kind lady behind the counter, they are fully enclosed pillows of tender bread
inside of which is a spill of juicy beef and peppery bits of cabbage and onion.
Delicious—real comfort food.

Our hearts won over by the cabbage burger, we had to sample some of
the good-looking sweet pastries on the bakery shelves. We liked the crisp-
edged old-fashioned cake donuts and fell instantly in love with something
called a peanut butter pretzel. That's a twisted piece of pastry dough generously frosted with sweet peanut butter icing.

Most business is take-out, but Gering Bakery offers a few window tables
as well as help-yourself coffee and a cooler full of soda for those who want
to dine here.

Joe Tess Place

5424 S. 24th St.   402-731-7278
Omaha, NE   LD | $

Roadfood warriors Bruce Bilmes and Sue Boyle pointed us to Joe Tess Place,
which bills itself as "Home of the Famous Fish Sandwich." It is a restaurant,
tavern, and fresh seafood market on the south side of Omaha that serves a
fish little known on dining tables outside the region: carp. Like the herring
that swim upriver in North Carolina, carp are fish-flavored fish that get
deep-fried long enough that their fine bones become part of the soft, juicy
flesh underneath the crunchy batter crust. The fried pieces of carp are available on rye in the famous sandwich or doubled up in the double fish sandwich. (The connoisseur's condiment is hot pepper sauce.) Or you can have a
dinner-size portion bedded on rye on a plate with coleslaw and disks of fried

potato, the latter known here as jacket fries. Catfish is another specialty. Like the carp, mudpuppies are trucked in live from Minnesota and you can see them swimming in the tanks of the live fish market. For those with a less adventurous palate, the Joe Tess menu offers chicken (white or dark), grilled salmon, and fried shrimp.

There is a full bar's worth of beverages to drink, plus the western working man's version of a Bloody Mary, known as red beer: beer and tomato juice. Bruce and Sue noted that "any restaurant that serves upside-down cake gets bonus points from us." Besids pineapple upside-down cake larded with pecans, the dessert menu includes a swell cream cheese bundt cake.

Ambience is all-fish, all the time and everywhere. The bar is shaped like a boat and walls are decked with taxidermized fish of every size and shape as well as pictures, posters, and nautical memorabilia celebrating underwater life.

Rosita's

1205 E. Overland Dr.   308-632-2429
Scottsbluff, NE   LD | $

What great corn chips, nearly as three-dimensional as a sopaipilla, fried so they puff up and become airy triangles with fragile skin! An order arrives almost too hot to handle; they come plain or as the foundation for the house specialty called panchos—a circle of them topped with frijoles, melted cheese, guacamole, and jalapeños. Panchos are like nachos, but the chips' refined texture and their perfect poise between breakable and bendable give panchos character far more satisfying than any bar grub.

The same quick-fry technique makes Rosita's taco shells an ideal crispy-chewy wrap for beef or chicken with plenty of garnishes; flat tostadas are made the same way; and even taco salad includes the fine, fluffy chips.

Proprietor Rosemary Florez-Lerma credits her mother-in-law with the recipes that make this friendly Mexican café a standout in an area with an abundance of Mexican restaurants (the legacy of field workers who came to pick beets). The cinnabar-red, garlic-charged salsa that starts every meal and the chunky pico de gallo that dresses up any dish with a stunning spicy punch are especially memorable. We were also quite fond of Rosita's garlicky *menudo,* thick with puffs of posole and strips of tripe, sparkling with fresh-squeezed lemon.

Rosita's has a second location in Scottsbluff at 710 W. 27th St.

Scotty's Drive In

618 E. 27th St.
Scottsbluff, NE

308-635-3314
LD | $

Scotty's menu features a picture of an anthropomorphic serving of French fries talking to an equally humanoid beverage, the scene captioned, "This spud's for you." These are indeed very good potatoes: thin and crisp-edged with earthy flavor. They're an ideal companion for burgers that come in configurations that range from singles to bacon-double-cheese to quarter-pounders and half-pounders and a Bluff Burger, which is three meat patties, cheese, and all appropriate condiments.

The menu lists lots of sandwiches beyond burgers, including fish, chicken, pork, and shrimp. The most interesting alternative is Scotty's Tasty Tavern, a sloppy joe that echoes the passion of neighboring Iowa's Siouxland for ground meat sandwiches. Scotty's Taverns are small (and cheap: 95¢ each); we saw a group of large local boys each ingesting a half-dozen of them along with a family pack of French fries for supper.

Taco Town

1007 W. 27th St.
Scottsbluff, NE

308-635-3776
LD | $

Since the mid twentieth century, Taco Town has been a favorite gathering place for locals, many of whom are descendants of the Mexican families who settled here to work on the vast beet farms surrounding Scottsbluff. While the inside seats are frequently buzzing with table-to-table conversations (a sign outside boasts "We're the Tac-O the Town!"), many customers simply drive through and pick up food at the window just as one would do at any humdrum Taco Bell. But this is hardly junk food! Pork chili, sold by the pint and quart, is a full-flavored homey stew. There are handsome plates of burritos, enchiladas, and flautas; and for $6.75 you can have a combo meal with all of the above plus rice and beans. The taco is a simple delight, its earthy corn shell audibly crisp but pliable enough that it doesn't shatter, loaded with a heap of ground beef filling that is creamy-rich and peppery. Each taco comes wrapped in paper that is twisted tight at both ends to keep it secure until you've found a parking place and are ready to unwrap it and dine off the dashboard.

South Dakota

Bob's

1312 W. 12th St.   605-336-7260
Sioux Falls, SD   BLD | $

Fans of diner food will think they've entered heaven the moment they walk
into this place and sniff bacon sizzling and burgers grilling in the morning.
A tiny diner with a curvy counter and a mere dozen seats, all with a view of
the grill, Bob's specializes in plentiful hash-house breakfasts, burger baskets,
broasted chicken, fried shrimp, and slabs of ribs.

Hamburgers start as a round ball that gets placed on the griddle and is
then flattened with a spatula—but not too hard—to form a thick patty with
a good crust and a load of juice. If you are very hungry, you'll want to know
about the Mega Bob Meal, which is a three-quarter-pound hamburger along
with three-quarters of a pound of French fries, a twenty-ounce soda, and a
couple of cookies. Good as the burgers are, it's chicken that is Bob's main
attraction—pressure-cooked to concentrate the flavor of the meat and create
a sturdy envelope of crust around it. You can buy it by the piece or in a basket with spuds, slaw, and a roll, or as a 250-piece order to feed one hundred.
For dessert, ice cream is noteworthy: made here.

Edgar's

107 E. Main St.

(I-29 Business Loop)

Elk Point, SD

605-356-3336

L | $

Have a seat on one of Edgar's steel-banded counter stools and watch a soda being made. This is no haphazard process. First, syrup and a little ice cream are smooshed together at the bottom of the deep vase-shaped glass to form a kind of sweet-shop roux; next, soda is squirted in and mixed vigorously; penultimately, a globe of ice cream is gingerly floated on top; finally, a crown of whipped cream is applied and, to that, a single cherry. It's a beautiful sight, and while much of the soda will drip and spill down the sides of the glass as soon as it is touched by a spoon, one cannot help but admire the confectionery perfectionism.

The same high standards apply to tulip sundaes, malts and shakes, and a long roster of more elaborate, daring delights that range from the relatively familiar turtle sundae (vanilla ice cream with hot caramel, chocolate syrup, and pecans) to the Rocket, a vertical banana split that the menu promises "will send you for a blast!"

With its pink-and-white tin ceiling, quartet of creaky wood booths, and steel rod chairs for a scattering of tables, Edgar's is an absolutely charming little place inside the Pioneer Drug store on the main street of Elk Point. Its nucleus is a soda fountain that was first installed in Schmiedt Drug in Centerville in 1906. In the 1960s, the old marble fountain was removed and put into storage. It was only recently discovered by Edgar Schmiedt's granddaughter, Barb Wurtz. Barb brought it to Elk Point, where it is once again part of a pharmacy (run by Barb's pharmacist husband, Kevin) and general store.

The back of Edgar's menu is a marvelous page from soda fountain history that features practical how-to articles taken from the 1906 *Standard Manual of Soda and Other Beverages*. Among the suggestions are that a soda fountain attendant "should never display soiled towels or dirty sponges," "should never stand watching the patrons drinking," and "should study each customer's desire and endeavor to remember the particular way in which he likes his drinks mixed and served." The year all this was written, the *Centerville Journal* declared Edgar's soda fountain one of the finest in the state. Over a century later, once again it is.

Hamburger Inn

111½ E. 10th St. 605-332-5412
Sioux Falls, SD L | $

Mel "Nels" Nelson and his wife, Bev, are no longer at the helm of this charming Depression-era twelve-stool diner, and for several weeks early in 2006 it was closed altogether. But hail Jason Bensen and Kelly Torberson, who took over and have promised to keep the Sioux Falls hamburger landmark running for at least a few more decades. They have increased the size of the hand-formed hamburgers from sliderhood to patties of well over a quarter-pound, making the old tradition of getting triples or even quadruple burgers in one bun somewhat ridiculous, although doubles still are available. We prefer a couple of single original cheeseburgers or, better yet, bacon cheeseburgers with a side of onion rings. To drink? A chocolate milk shake made the old-fashioned way and served not too thick. Regulars are loyal to the egg burger, which includes a fried egg on top. Other optional dressings include bacon, onions, cheese, lettuce, tomato, and mayonnaise.

Nick's Hamburger Shop

427 Main Ave. 605-692-4324
Brookings, SD LD | $

Nick's is a Roadfood landmark for the itty-bitty hamburgers it has served since the early days of the slider, in 1929. The price of a Nickburger has gone up from a nickel to $1.48 in the last fourscore years, and the restaurant, officially listed on the National Register of Historic Places, has gotten bigger, but the burgers are still buy-'em-by-the-sack lovelies, hand-formed and cooked on a grill with so much oil that they are virtually deep-fried. Onions are part of the formula, so the burger as well as Nick's itself is perfumed with the sweet smell of onions caramelizing. They're small and wieldy enough that plates are extraneous; Nickburgers are presented on wax paper. We'd say three to five or a couple of doubles makes a nice meal. The ingestion record is thirty-four in a single sitting, set by a student from South Dakota State. Owner Dick Fergen says that anyone who can beat the record will eat for free.

Tea Steak House

215 S. Main St. 605-368-9667
Tea, SD LD | $$

Who can resist a restaurant with the motto "Bring your sugar to Tea"? We love the pound-plus T-bone, a cushiony slab of meat that oozes juice at the first poke of a knife. It's a good thing to order hash brown potatoes on the side to soak up the beef's seepage; crisp and oily, they are great potatoes in their own right (much better than the foil-wrapped baked potato or uninteresting French fries). We also ordered filet mignon, which came splayed open and wrapped in bacon, and it was amazing just how different these two cuts of beef were: each excellent, but while the T-bone had a vivid, almost gamey smack and tight-knit texture that rewarded serious chewing, the filet was cream-gentle in flavor and wanted to melt on the tongue.

The Tea Steak House serves more than steak. You can eat chicken or ham, halibut, perch, lobster tails, or a Saint & Sinner supper of one lobster tail and one small sirloin. Don't ask us how any of that stuff tastes. When we're in Tea, we'll eat beef. And don't ask about dessert, either. This kitchen doesn't bother making any. You need something sweet, you go next door to O'Toole's Bar and have a Grasshopper or a Pink Cadillac.

Tripp Sports Bowl Café

210 S. Main St. 605-935-6281
Tripp, SD L | $

Tripp, South Dakota, population 631, is a small town in big country. A short jog off the highway takes you to Main Street, where the bowling alley and town café are one. We love this place where the locals eat (few travelers pass through Tripp at all) and where decor includes not only the bowling alleys themselves, but also trophies won by the likes of Doug Janssen (a 300 game!) and Dorothy Schnabel (267). The day we came across it, a blackboard in the dining area listed the day's special as creamed chicken on toast, which was delicious—quintessential comfort food—but we were also intrigued by a menu item listed as the Dakota Burger.

The Dakota burger turned out not to be a hamburger at all—not, at least, if you define hamburger as a patty of ground beef—but rather, Tripp's version of that upper Midwest pleasure, hot beef. Junellia Meisenhoelder, chef and proprietor at the Sports Bowl Café, didn't tell us why the sandwich is known as a burger, but there is no point quibbling about labels; it is swell.

Hot beef served with mashed potatoes and gravy is a frequent daily special at the Sports Bowl Café, and the Dakota burger is a somewhat more wieldy variation on the theme: chunks of ultra-tender roast beef, warm enough to melt a slice of bright orange cheese placed atop them, piled into a grill-warmed bun. Simple and excellent!

Café Wyoming

106 E. Ramshorn St.   307-455-3828

Dubois, WY   LD | $$

"Very Wyoming" is how our California tipster described this log cabin adjoining a True Value hardware store parking lot overlooking Horse Creek. The note said that the chef made deluxe dinners every night for which reservations were advised. It sang of homemade soups and salad dressings, and a whole repertoire of house-smoked meats.

While the menu is broad and sophisticated, ribs made the deep impression on us. They are beautiful racks of bones heavy with smoke-infused meat and spiced and sauced with brio. A smoked pork chop was equally delicious, and the steaks that others around us were eating looked great. Sandwiches are served on homemade bread, and there is a BLT and a catfish sandwich in particular that are numbers one and two on our list to eat next time we visit.

Svilar's

173 S. Main St.   307-332-4516

Hudson, WY   D | $$$

Hudson is hours from any interstate on the south edge of the Wind River Reservation, where shaggy horses graze the flatlands by the Little Popo Agie

River and derelict oil works are strewn across the hills. It is nothing but a short strip of bedraggled buildings with businesses that look to be defunct. But in the evenings, Friday and Saturday in particular, the old Main Street comes alive. A sign in one parking lot boasts "Welcome to Hudson: World's Finest Food." An overstatement, perhaps, but High Plains folk who travel the two-lanes through the land of the Arapahoe to dine at Svilar's gladly attest to the fact that the little community is home to the finest beef in the Cowboy State.

Svilar's, a supper club that has been a culinary High Plains magnet since the middle of the last century, serves a full-course dinner that starts with relish tray and salad, then moves on to a hot-appetizer course of ravioli and stuffed cabbage (Serbian-style). Although chicken, shrimp, and lobster tails are available, the only appropriate entree is red meat; steaks range in cuts from wee fillet to multipound rib eye or great mesas of prime rib large enough to overhang a good-size dinner plate. Maybe there's dessert, maybe not. We've never even bothered to inquire, figuring that if we have any appetite for it at the end of the meal, we probably didn't order a large-enough piece of cow.

Wagon Box Inn

108 N. Piney Creek   307-683-2444
Story, WY   D | $$

A rustic inn with cabin accommodations, the Wagon Box also is a restaurant that attracts beef-eaters from miles around. Most of the menu is devoted to big cuts of cow, including filets mignons that come plain or peppered or with mango relish. The handsome XIT Striploin is a boneless sirloin named for the XIT ranch of Texas, which sent its cattle up this way when the West was young. The house specialty is juice-heavy prime rib that delivers maximum beefy savor. It is served with epicurean mashed potatoes (with a few lumps and flecks of skin) and a nice salad garnished with crisp red tortilla strips. Accommodations include a civilized dining room with a big stone fireplace and a cool outdoor patio surrounded by fragrant ponderosa pines.

West Coast

California * Oregon * Washington

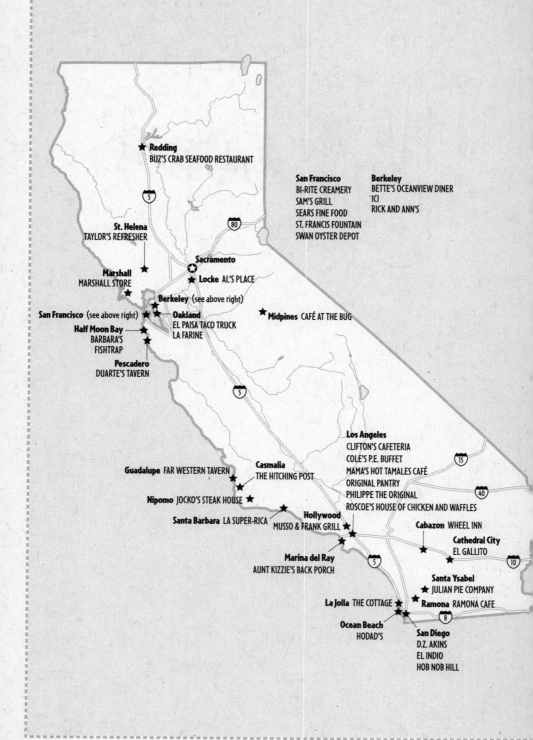

Redding
BUZ'S CRAB SEAFOOD RESTAURANT

San Francisco
BI-RITE CREAMERY
SAM'S GRILL
SEARS FINE FOOD
ST. FRANCIS FOUNTAIN
SWAN OYSTER DEPOT

Berkeley
BETTE'S OCEANVIEW DINER
'ICI
RICK AND ANN'S

St. Helena
TAYLOR'S REFRESHER

Sacramento
Locke AL'S PLACE

Marshall
MARSHALL STORE

Berkeley (see above right)

San Francisco (see above right)
Oakland
EL PAISA TACO TRUCK
LA FARINE

Midpines CAFÉ AT THE BUG

Half Moon Bay
BARBARA'S
FISHTRAP

Pescadero
DUARTE'S TAVERN

Los Angeles
CLIFTON'S CAFETERIA
COLE'S P.E. BUFFET
MAMA'S HOT TAMALES CAFÉ
ORIGINAL PANTRY
PHILIPPE THE ORIGINAL
ROSCOE'S HOUSE OF CHICKEN AND WAFFLES

Guadalupe FAR WESTERN TAVERN

Casmalia
THE HITCHING POST

Nipomo JOCKO'S STEAK HOUSE

Hollywood
MUSSO & FRANK GRILL

Santa Barbara LA SUPER-RICA

Cabazon WHEEL INN

Cathedral City
EL GALLITO

Marina del Ray
AUNT KIZZIE'S BACK PORCH

Santa Ysabel
JULIAN PIE COMPANY

La Jolla THE COTTAGE

Ramona RAMONA CAFE

Ocean Beach
HODAD'S

San Diego
D.Z. AKINS
EL INDIO
HOB NOB HILL

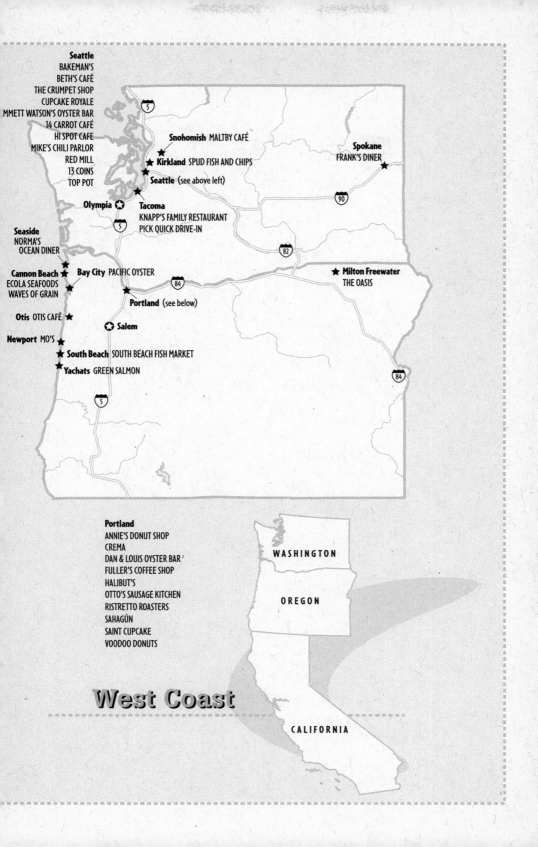

Seattle
BAKEMAN'S
BETH'S CAFÉ
THE CRUMPET SHOP
CUPCAKE ROYALE
MMETT WATSON'S OYSTER BAR
14 CARROT CAFÉ
HI SPOT CAFE
MIKE'S CHILI PARLOR
RED MILL
13 COINS
TOP POT

Snohomish MALTBY CAFÉ

Kirkland SPUD FISH AND CHIPS

Seattle (see above left)

Spokane
FRANK'S DINER

Olympia

Tacoma
KNAPP'S FAMILY RESTAURANT
PICK QUICK DRIVE-IN

Seaside
NORMA'S
OCEAN DINER

Cannon Beach
ECOLA SEAFOODS
WAVES OF GRAIN

Bay City PACIFIC OYSTER

Portland (see below)

Milton Freewater
THE OASIS

Otis OTIS CAFÉ

Salem

Newport MO'S

South Beach SOUTH BEACH FISH MARKET

Yachats GREEN SALMON

Portland
ANNIE'S DONUT SHOP
CREMA
DAN & LOUIS OYSTER BAR
FULLER'S COFFEE SHOP
HALIBUT'S
OTTO'S SAUSAGE KITCHEN
RISTRETTO ROASTERS
SAHAGÚN
SAINT CUPCAKE
VOODOO DONUTS

WASHINGTON

OREGON

West Coast

CALIFORNIA

Al's Place

13936 Main St.   916-776-1800
Locke, CA   LD | $$

If you are traveling the Central Valley in search of tasty meals served with heaps of personality, find Locke, a hidden-away little town in the Sacramento Delta. Originally built by and for Chungshan Chinese, the old levee community was once notorious for its gambling halls, brothels, and last—maybe least—of its pleasures, Cantonese food. Locke's weathered main street of wood-plank sidewalks and shuttered emporia with swayback second-story balconies remains a magical sight. In the middle of it is Al's Place.

The building housed a regular Chinese restaurant from 1915 to 1934, when Al Adami, fresh out of prison as a convicted bootlegger, came up the river and took over. Al had no menu—he asked you how you liked your steak, which was the only thing to eat amidst the slot machines and card tables in the dining room behind the front-room bar. Legend says that at some point in time, a hungry crop duster came in with jars of peanut butter and marmalade and asked Al for some toast to spread them on. Al liked the idea, and started putting peanut butter and marmalade on every table, a tradition that endures.

Al's Place still feels illicit. You enter past the beer and shooter crowd who occupy a dimly lit bar hung with dusty game trophies and memorabilia, into a bright backroom dining area lined with worn laminate tables equipped with shared benches instead of chairs, seating anywhere from two to eight friends or strangers, depending on how crowded Al's is.

The menu remains simple, now including hamburgers, cheeseburgers, steaks, and one amazing steak sandwich. It is amazing because it is only barely a sandwich. In fact, what it is is a sandwich-size steak on a platter accompanied by a second plate of toasted pieces of sturdy Italian bread. Horseradish or a dish of minced garlic is available to spread on the meat. "Most people put the peanut butter or jelly on their toast," proprietor Stephen Gionetti advised us when we asked him what to do with it. "But I've seen some spread peanut butter right across their steaks!"

Aunt Kizzy's Back Porch

523 Washington Blvd.   310-578-1005
Marina del Rey, CA   LD | $$

The back porch is actually just inside the door at this unlikely shopping-center restaurant with a sign outside that boasts of "Down-Home Cooking." Inside, the menu located underneath each glass table-top offers such comfort-food classics as chicken and dumplings, meat loaf, and barbecued ribs served with collards, black-eyed peas, green beans, smothered cabbage, and/or mac 'n' cheese. We are particularly fond of the crisp-fried catfish, sided by a pair of sweet-corn hush puppies. Lemonade is served in mason jars.

Sweet potato pie is not to be missed . . . unless you prefer the inviting frippery of pineapple coconut cake or peach cobbler pie.

Ambience is a curious Los Angeles mix of neighborhood soul and photos of celebrities, especially of the Lakers from when they used to play in Inglewood.

Barbara's Fishtrap

281 Capistrano Rd.   650-728-7049
Half Moon Bay, CA   LD | $$

Fish and chips alert! Barbara's makes it with rock cod, a.k.a. Pacific snapper, which is cut thick enough to remain extremely moist, its natural sweetness underscored by a gold coat with light, oily crunch. You get four large tiles, hot from the fryer, accompanied by a pile of thick fried potatoes. Tartar sauce is fine but unnecessary with fish this flavorful, and ketchup for the fries is irrelevant. (California malt vinegar is supplied for the spuds, too, but why moisten their crisp skin?)

To precede fish and chips, you want a cup or bowl of clam chowder. This is good stuff, its heartiness very much of the northwestern variety, meaning it is creamless but nearly fork-thick, loaded with large pieces of tender clams as well as potatoes and celery: a winning balance of elements.

Barbara's menu is big, including linguine served with your choice of clams, mussels, prawns, or calamari as well as full-bore cioppino with Dungeness crab. There is shrimp and/or crab Louie, and vegetable plates that come steamed, sautéed, or tempura-fried. Meals begin with baskets of fresh, chewy sourdough. At $12.50, fish and chips is the most affordable meal on the menu. Most entrees are in the $20+ range.

Barbara's is casual with a charming nautical dishevelment about the decor, and it is small enough always to seem crowded. It offers a lovely view overlooking the boats in Pillar Point Harbor. But windows remain closed. It became obvious why when, mid-meal, we watched a very large seagull swoop down and perch on a rail just outside. It seemed all too clear that he had come to watch us fork up dinner with his beady, greedy little eyes.

Bette's Oceanview Diner

1807 4th Street   510-644-3230
Berkeley, CA   BL | $

We first found Bette's Oceanview Diner while looking for macaroons at Bette's-To-Go, the bakeshop next door. Aside from the magnificent macaroons and trompe l'oeil chocolate espresso Twinkies, which are, without doubt, the finest snack cake on earth, the bakery shelves' delights include pecan-topped red velvet cake and twin-layer lemon bars (creamy on top, crunchy below).

Anyone with an appetite and a functioning olfactory system would be hard-pressed to visit the bakery without being seduced by aromas from the diner next door: potato pancakes grilling to a crisp, waffles pried fresh from the irons, and eggy oven-baked pancakes.

All these and a full menu of diner classics are dished out in a restaurant that is a savvy gloss on the vintage diner. We usually are skeptical about retro restaurants, diners in particular. Even if their heart is in the right place, all too often the food is not. But a first meal at Bette's disabused us of all prejudice. Here is a modern diner with classic values . . . and really good buttermilk pancakes, usually available in a special flavor each day. For our first visit, around Christmas, the day's pancake (and waffle) was eggnog. Mmm-good. The extra egginess was quite subtle, adding an intangible richness to the cakes, all the better when drowned with the pitcher of real maple syrup provided.

Another compelling breakfast highlight is scrapple, which is some of the best anywhere, including the Delaware Valley. Part of a "Philadelphia breakfast" with poached eggs, it is made from pork butt and hock meat, cornmeal, sage, and plenty of pepper, and sliced thick enough that while the outside gets nice and crisp, the interior virtually melts into nothing but flavor. If you get a fruit salad, fruits are cut and peeled to order.

Bi-Rite Creamery

3692 18th St.   415-626-5600
San Francisco, CA   LD | $

We've never had a banana split we did not like. Even so, we've never had one in the same league as the one made at Bi-Rite Creamery. The vanilla ice cream is a shocking reminder that it is, in fact, chilled cream, suffused with liquor of vanilla beans. The chocolate sauce is cocoa turned to liquid velvet; the bananas are caramelized in amber syrup; the walnuts are toasted crisp; the whipped cream—out of Straus Family Creamery dairy cows that graze on grass above Tomales Bay—is as dense as crème fraîche. Dazzling!

Boasting that it makes "small-batch, artisanal ice creams," Bi-Rite offers such unusual flavors as salted caramel, strawberry balsamic, honey lavender, and chocolate soy, as well as a sundae made with bergamot olive oil (!) and a lemon-gingersnap pumpkin ice cream sandwich. Still, we recommend you start with vanilla ice cream . . . and the best banana split in the universe.

Buz's Crab Seafood Restaurant

2159 East St.   530-243-2120
Redding, CA   LD | $$

Thanks to Roadfooders Karen Meyer and Paul Duggan for clueing us in to Buz's as one of the essential Roadfood experiences of Northern California. They especially recommended cracked Dungeness crab (fresh from November through May), fish and chips, and charbroiled salmon; and they noted that Buz's kitchen is supplied by its own fishing boats out of Eureka on the coast. Calling itself "Redding's own Fisherman's Wharf," Buz's truly is a seafood bonanza, being not only a restaurant but a fish market, a deli, a crab feed caterer, and a mail-order source of cooked crab, smoked salmon, and sourdough bread.

In the restaurant, you'll find something on the menu for every kind of seafood fancier (and even charbroiled chicken and chicken nuggets for fish-phobes), ranging from the copious fisherman's stew known as cioppino to fish tacos and salmon burgers (the latter advertised as low-fat and low-cal). When Dungeness crab is coming in fresh from the cold Pacific, that's all we care to know about, but any other time of year, we will gladly plow into one of Buz's umpteen different kinds of fried seafood basket, featuring prawns, oysters, catfish, and calamari (or all possible combinations thereof). In addition, there are seafood wraps, salads, sandwiches, and burritos, and a long list of fish available charbroiled with barbecue sauce, teriyaki sauce, garlic sauce, or lemon butter.

To accompany meals, Buz's "almost famous" sourdough bread is baked in outdoor ovens throughout the day.

Cafe at the Bug

6979 Hwy. 140   209-966-6666
Midpines, CA   BLD | $

If you are coming to Yosemite to hike, bike, swim, or otherwise savor the wilderness, but want to stay in a room or tent cabin for the evening, you won't do better than the Yosemite Bug Mountain Resort. And if you're looking for a nice place to eat other than around a campfire, the Cafe at the Bug is swell.

It's a three-meal-a-day place with outdoor patios and a glassed-in deck for scenic dining and a menu with choices that range from carnivorous to vegan. You can start the day with a giant buckwheat pancake (available vegan or not), muesli, or eggs or tofu egg substitutes. And while you are having breakfast you can have the kitchen prepare a boxed lunch for the trail. We relished our dinner of stuffed trout with rice and seasonal vegetables and a handsome sirloin steak with potatoes. We were especially fond of the chocolate cake served for dessert; while we cleaned the last of it from our plates, we listened to neighbors rave over their cheesecake.

Service is casual, semi-cafeteria style. Order at the counter and pick your own table. It is customary for customers to bus their own tables at the end of a meal.

Clifton's Cafeteria

648 S. Broadway   213-627-1673
Los Angeles, CA   LD | $

Clifton's Cafeteria is an amazing place to eat. Built to represent the Golden State's redwood forests, its interior decor includes faux granite cliffs and boulders, babbling brooks, walls that resemble tree trunks, and stunning (if faded) murals of forest scenes. Food line choices include fried chicken with buttermilk biscuits, oxtail stew, turkey and dressing, side dishes ranging from whipped or fried potatoes to "cranberry jewel gelatin," and cheerfully corny desserts such as fruit cocktail torte and strawberry pie. For those with fond memories of school lunch, Clifton's also offers grilled cheese sandwiches cooked crisp and pressed flat as a pancake. As of autumn 2010, a new owner has promised to open a lounge and tiki bar upstairs, serve meals 24/7, and restore Clifton's to its full glory.

We like Clifton's plenty, but its surroundings stink. Once you get to Clifton's, though, you cannot help but love Los Angeles all over again, especially when you gaze down at the sidewalk below its marquee. Here, a magnificent tile mosaic shows the many scenic wonders that long ago made this sunny part of the world such an alluring place: the Rose Bowl, the Hollywood Bowl, the oil fields, the deserts, the missions, City Hall, the movie studios, and Catalina Island. To walk across the tiles and enter the redwood forest dining room, then tuck into a meal of meat loaf and mashed potatoes and gravy, with millionaire pie for dessert (mounded with whipped cream, crushed pineapple, and pecans), is to revisit a time when California seemed full of promise.

Cole's P.E. Buffet

118 E. 6th St.   213-622-4090
Los Angeles, CA   LD | $

Cole's P.E. Buffet says it invented the French dip sandwich in 1908, ten years before Philippe's (p. 529). The story here is that a hungry man with sore gums was so impressed by the way Cole's chef, Jack Garlinghouse, carved a roast that he beseeched him to make a sandwich he could chew without pain. The compassionate Mr. Garlinghouse dunked a hard roll in natural gravy to soften it and then filled the roll with tender flaps of beef. The soft and juicy sandwich required little in the way of dental might.

Cole's claim to primacy feels right when you descend a short flight of stairs into the gauzy-aired commissary where wood-paneled walls are imbued with the savory aroma of countless steam-table meals. Decor includes panoramic photos of Miss California contests held long ago in the Santa Monica sun. Tables in some of the cloistered back dining areas are made of oak salvaged from the sides of Pacific Electric Railway Red Cars, source of the "P.E." in Cole's full name: Cole's P.E. Buffet. When it opened, and until the Pacific Electric ended service in 1953, Cole's clientele was mostly commuters traveling what used to be the world's largest interurban rail line.

The French dip is particularly well executed here, where carvers stab slabs of hot brisket from the steam box and hand-slice mounds of thick, juicy pieces, spearing each half of the sliced roll and holding it in a pan of dark gravy long enough to fully flavor the soft part of the chewy bread but leave the crust crisp. The moistened bread melds with the mellow beef it wraps, and the result is a delicious mess. Pork dip might be even better, the meat so tender that it seems to transform from substance into pure flavor. French dip—also available made with turkey, lamb, or pastrami—is the only main course, but there are fork-worthy side dishes, including creamed spinach and garlic fries at dinner and mac 'n' cheese all day.

The Cottage

7702 Fay Ave.   858-454-8409
La Jolla, CA   BL | $$

Here is Southern California at its brightest: fresh and supremely casual and always delicious. Located on a quiet corner in the village of La Jolla, it offers vividly flavored meals in either a sun-drenched dining room or a breezy patio outdoors.

Breakfast is especially wonderful. As you walk in the door, look right. There's the bakery case holding the nut-topped cinnamon rolls, muffins, and buttermilk coffee cake with cinnamon and walnut crumb topping. The pastries are superb . . . but so are the hot meals. In particular, we recommend Cottage Irish oatmeal, served with a full complement of brown sugar, sliced bananas, raisins, milk, and a dish of sensational sticky-crunchy caramelized walnuts. Also grand are meat loaf hash crisped with cottage-fried potatoes and topped with eggs, French toast stuffed with strawberry compote and mascarpone, and "crab Benedict," which is like eggs Benedict but heaped with pure rock crab instead of Canadian bacon. Cottage granola is extra-special—dark and toasty, a delightful chew.

Lunch is an opportunity to taste a high-tone version of San Diego's favorite fast food, the fish taco, here built around grilled mahimahi, dressed with cilantro-avocado sauce, and accompanied by bowls of creamy black beans and chunky papaya relish. The pork and beef chili has a true-Southwest pepper zest, and the hamburger is a SoCal classic, served with an abundance of Cheddar cheese, tomato, lettuce, onion, and mayo. The BLT, augmented with avocado, reigns supreme.

The restaurant is in a bungalow that was built early in the twentieth century and served as a private home in the days when La Jolla was a little-known community of sun-and-surf worshippers. It still exudes the end-of-the-earth charm that makes this seaside community so appealing.

Duarte's Tavern

202 Stage Rd. 650-879-0464

Pescadero, CA BLD | $

We weren't yet driving around looking for Roadfood in 1894 when the Duarte family opened a tavern in Pescadero (nor were there any automobiles to drive around in; it was a stage stop), but we can tell you that the rugged old tavern hasn't changed much at all since we first came across it in the mid-1970s. It is still a place where locals come for coffee in the morning and to eat three square meals a day at mismatched tables and chairs in a knotty pine–paneled dining room or at the short counter opposite the kitchen.

Travelers have come to know it as a place to savor artichokes, which are farmed just south of Pescadero around Castroville, and which grow into gorgeous globes in the Duarte family's abundant garden behind the restaurant. The pick of the backyard crop is available simply steamed—you won't believe how much flesh you can scrape off each petal—and you can have artichokes stuffed with fennel sausage, in breakfast omelets, or as the foundation of blissful cream of artichoke soup.

Most of the menu is down-home dining, California-style: pork chops with homemade applesauce and chunky mashed potatoes; chicken and dumplings; roast turkey with sage dressing. Even the house salad—a perfunctory gesture in so many restaurants—comes topped with beets and tomatoes from the family garden. The kitchen's respect for its provender's seasonal correctness rivals that of any highfalutin bistro in wine country. Ron Duarte, who took over the business in the 1950s from his parents (and whose kids, Kathy and Tim, now run it), cannot hide his happiness as Dungeness crab season starts in November, because that means the restaurant's legendary cioppino will be at its best. "We don't buy frozen or precooked," he says. "We like to get them live."

To conclude any meal at Duarte's, you must have pie. We are gaga over the one made using olallieberries from nearby Watsonville; but they have a short season in early summer, so after that, they are replaced by marionberries from farther north. The last time we visited, Mr. Duarte showed off a big box of just-picked pears and a handsome pie the kitchen staff had made from them.

D.Z. Akins

6930 Alvarado Rd.   619-265-0218
San Diego, CA   BLD | $$

As folks who frequently complain that urban delis aren't what they used to be, we were thrilled several years ago the moment we walked into D.Z. Akins. The air was perfumed with spiced beef and the bakery shelves up front held a spectacular array of ryes, pumpernickels, bagels, hard rolls, and challahs, plus countless macaroons and cookies, all baked right here. The sandwiches we got were fantastic: hot, fat-striated corned beef radiant with flavor, cut thick and piled between two slices of good, old-fashioned deli rye: soft inside with a nice sour smack and a hard savory crust. Full-flavored roast beef was presented in a poppy-seed-spangled hard roll that was also impeccably fresh. At breakfast you can feast on matzoh brei, blintzes, or bagels and lox. Nothing is short of excellent.

The full-service restaurant also features a soda fountain, the menu of which includes sundaes and sodas of all kinds, from a traditional banana split to one called Prenatal Silliness: chocolate ice cream and pickles, with your topping of choice!

El Gallito

68820 Grove St.   760-328-7794
Cathedral City, CA   LD | $

So popular that it is frequently wait-for-a-table crowded, El Gallito has been serving California-style Mexican food in the Coachella Valley since 1978. It has a broad menu of familiar dishes such as tacos, chiles rellenos, enchiladas, and burritos. They're all quite good, in our experience, but we are especially fond of daily specials that include *carnitas* (shredded pork) every Thursday, chicken mole (Friday), and *menudo* (Saturday). The mole is smoky with a pepper zest, cosseting on-the-bone chicken that is ridiculously tender.

We also like El Gallito's bowls of chili. They are not fire-hot, and they are mighty tasty: either chili Colorado, which is bite-size pieces of beef in a peppery red sauce, or chili verde, which is beef cooked with green peppers, onions, and shreds of tomato. The El Gallito Especial is a half-and-half plate of both kinds of chili. It is also worth nothing that breakfast is available, but starting at 10 A.M., when the restaurant opens: huevos rancheros, shredded beef and scrambled eggs, and egg burritos with ricé and beans.

El Gallito is an extraordinarily clean and tidy place, outfitted in classic Mexican-restaurant decor (serapes, sombreros, velvet paintings). It operates according to a lot of rules that are posted throughout the dining room and written in the menu. A sign above the cash register warns, "Cash only." A placard hanging over the dining room notes: "If you have reservations, you are at the wrong place." To discourage unsavory clientele, a sign in the entryway advises: "WE ARE NOT A BAR. Beer/wine is only served to those who dine with us." And on the menu, the management notes that daily specials are in limited supply, so customers who want them should come early; it is further noted that "it is impossible to debone the chicken entirely, so it is possible that you may find a bone in your chicken entree." Finally, be advised that there is a limit of three drinks per customer, and "persons who seem to have been drinking will not be served."

El Indio

3695 India St.   619-299-0333
San Diego, CA   BLD | $

El Indio is a quick-service, cafeteria-style taqueria adjacent to Interstate 5. Meals are served on Styrofoam plates with throwaway utensils. There are a few seats at a counter and some tables to the side of the order line, but many people choose to eat on the sunny, fenced-in patio across the street. Here, one is serenaded by vehicles passing on the raised highway.

The menu is Cal-Mex. An on-premises tortilla press turns out warm wheaty ones for burros and chimichangas; there are freshly fried, hot corn tortillas and deliciously crunchy taquitos; and there are all sorts of combo plates topped with gobs of sour cream. El Indio's fish taco is a hefty meal served in a foil wrapper along with a wedge of lime. When the foil is pulled back, you find a double layer of warm corn tortillas loosely wrapped around a log of crisp-fried cod with a golden crust. The fish is nestled on a bed of ruggedly shredded cabbage, a few tomato shreds, and a faintly peppery pink sauce. Give it a spritz or two from the wedge of lime provided—an ideal complement for the sweet meat of the white fish and its savory crust.

Above the windows where you order your food at El Indio are portraits of fierce Mayan gods, including the god of war, the gods of rain and wind, and the god of Mexican food, who according to this portrait goes by the name of El Indio. We are not up-to-date on our Mayan theology, but there is no doubt in our minds that El Indio is indeed a deity in San Diego's Mexican food scene.

El Paisa Taco Truck

| 2900 International Blvd. | 510-384-5465 |
| Oakland, CA | LD \| $ |

Oakland's International Boulevard is well populated with taco trucks. Tacos El Paisa is the one to know. Proprietor Abel Lopez and his staff offer a wide array of fillings that include chicken, carne asada, beef tongue, head, and brain. There is spicy pork (*al pastor*) and pork *carnitas,* the latter crusty-edged, big-spiced, and juicy nuggets of fried meat. Tacos are built in double-layer corn tortillas and garnished with parsley and pink salsa chopped so fine it looks like caviar. Surrounded by crisp radishes, hot peppers, and slices of tomato, these are some of the most beautiful of all street-served tacos. The good *carnitas* also are available as the stuffing of a quesadilla, which is a super-thin flour-tortilla sandwich containing not only the pork but also melted cheese, bits of onion, and tomato.

This is great food, and at the right price. Tacos are $1.25 each (plus 50¢ if you want sour cream or cheese), and a couple makes a nice lunch. The quesadilla, cut into five good-size triangles, is a very big meal for all of $3.50. A can of soda is 75¢, meaning you will find it hard to spend $5 on a meal. El Paisa has no formal seating, just a few available curbs in the lot where the truck parks.

Far Western Tavern

| 899 Guadalupe St. | 805-343-2211 |
| Guadalupe, CA | LD \| $$ |

The Far Western Tavern is a place to eat barbecue, California cowboy–style. The dining room features a spectacular suite of hairy brown-and-white cowhide curtains, and meals are served on cowboy-fantasy dishware festooned with little images of brands, spurs, and cows' heads. The wall across from the bar is one sweeping painted mural of ranch life; other displays include a portrait of Will Rogers, a poster that shows how to break a wild pony, an autographed 8x10 of Ralph Edwards (from *This is Your Life*) praising the steaks, and a photograph of the all-woman bowling team sponsored by the Tavern along with a display of their trophies.

Specialty of the house is a Bull's-Eye Steak, a boneless rib eye cooked over flaming live-oak wood, served Santa Maria–style, meaning sided by firm pinquito beans, French bread, and salsa. Filets, strips, sirloins, and chopped steaks also are available, as are buttered sweetbreads, pork chops, rack of lamb, and baby back ribs. The Bull's Eye is available for late-morning breakfast and Sunday brunch in a smaller version, served alongside eggs, hash browns, beans, and biscuits.

The Hitching Post

3325 Point Sal Rd.   805-937-6151
Casmalia, CA   D | $$$

Unlike barbecue in the South and Southwest, where meat is cooked for hours in the smolder of hardwood coals, Santa Maria barbecue is always done in the open on a grate over flaming red-oak logs. While much of it is served al fresco from mobile cookeries in local parking lots, the best restaurant source is The Hitching Post, where gorgeous, high-priced T-bones, sirloins, and filets mignons are served as part of a full dinner that starts with a relish tray and shrimp cocktail and includes a green head-lettuce salad, garlic toast, and potatoes, either baked or French fried (the latter are wonderful). The meat glows with the flavor of the fire and with the piquant smack of a wine vinegar and oil marinade that is applied as it cooks. "The trick is in how the steaks are handled," proprietor Bill Ostini explained. "You've got to know how to cook which steak which way—some are made to be cooked rare, some well-done; it depends on the marbling, and how much age they have. It takes two to three years to train a cook to do it the right way."

Ambience in this old, family-run roadhouse evokes a forgotten California, when the Golden State was cattle country and its people were frontier types. Above the bar, a TV is always playing; the mirror is plastered with decals from NASA, *Voyager,* and the Army Corps of Engineers; a bison head on one wall wears a Buffalo Bills cap. In the dining room, which affords a view of the kitchen, there are mounted deer heads and old black-and-white family photos of the proprietors on hunting and fishing trips with their dad when they were young. The hallway that leads to the restrooms is lined with cattle hides.

Hob Nob Hill

2271 First Ave.   619-239-8176
San Diego, CA   BLD | $

The California coffee shop is a unique style of square-meal restaurant, but there aren't a lot of them left. Hob Nob Hill is classic, a three-meal-a-day place where the food is homey, the service fast, and the prices low. At mealtimes, especially breakfast, chances are you will have to wait in line. But the line moves quickly, and once you are seated you are set upon by a team of waitresses who could not move faster if they flew through the aisles—taking orders, filling coffee cups, making sure everyone is happy.

Hob Nob Hill's repertoire is broad, and there isn't a clinker on the menu. There are pecan waffles, pigs in blankets (buttermilk pancakes rolled with ham, sausage, and sour cream), blueberry hotcakes, grilled smoked pork chops, etc.—plus a bakery's worth of coffee cakes, muffins (try carrot), and a not-to-be-missed pecan roll. Even little amenities are special: Syrup is served warm; jelly comes in hollowed-out orange halves; coffee is strong and rich.

At dinner, it's meat-and-potatoes time: leg of lamb with sage dressing and mint jelly, chicken and dumplings, roast tom turkey with giblet gravy, corned beef and cabbage, pot roast and buttered noodles every Sunday. There are turkey croquettes with cranberry sauce, a nursery-nice breast-of-chicken curry, and baked ham with fruit sauce and yams on Thursday. Accompaniments are such comfort-food side dishes as warm applesauce (homemade, of course), marinated bean salad, and puffy yeast rolls.

Hodad's

5010 Newport Ave.   619-224-4623
Ocean Beach, CA   LD | $

Hodad's motto, on a sign above the cash register: "No Shirt, No Shoes, No Problem!"

This ultracasual beachside eatery offers hamburgers in three sizes (mini, single, and double) and as cheeseburgers and bacon cheeseburgers. They come solo or as part of a basket with a pile of French fries, and they are sights to behold. The double, which is two good-size patties, is huge beyond belief, piled inside a broad sesame-seed bun with lettuce, tomato, onion, pickle, mayonnaise, mustard, and ketchup. The menu warns that all burgers come with all condiments "unless you say otherwise"; and frankly, we suggest that unless you are allergic, all the way is the only way to go.

The hamburger is presented partially wrapped in yellow wax paper, which provides a way to hoist it from the table and to keep it relatively together as you try to eat it. The French fries in the basket are thick wedges of potato with pleasantly tough skins and creamy insides. To drink on the side, we recommend a milk shake or malt (vanilla, chocolate, strawberry) served in a glass and silver beaker with a straw and a necessary spoon.

Just getting to Hodad's is a blast. Lined with palm trees and with a gorgeous ocean view, Newport Avenue is a colorful part of the city. It is occupied by surf shops, alternative hair salons, juice bars, and high-proof bars, and this rockin' joint fits right in. Its walls are festooned with vanity license plates from around the nation; surfboards are strung above the dining room. Seating includes hardwood booths and a counter along the wall with stools plus a special booth made from the front end of a VW minibus. Each booth is outfitted with a cardboard container that once held a six-pack of beer bottles. The half-dozen compartments are now used to store sugar and sweeteners for coffee.

Ici

2948 College Ave.   510-665-6054
Berkeley, CA   LD | $

First, a warning: If you want an ice cream cone or cup, you almost surely will wait in line at Ici. The line moves slowly because once a person gets to the head of it, he or she is allowed—even encouraged—to try little spoonfuls of different kinds of ice cream before committing to one. This is a very good thing, because so many of Ici's flavors are ones you likely never have tried, such as mocha salted almond, sesame praline, Santa Rosa plum, or peach habanero sorbet. If that is daunting, we have an insider's tip (straight from niece Nina, who works at Ici): Those with ice cream hunger so great that it precludes waiting can bypass the line and step right up to the counter, where they are free to buy and instantly consume an ice cream sandwich, such as fudge-streaked vanilla ice cream between two devil's food cookies or lemon ice cream sandwiched in tiles of gingerbread.

Still, the weird and original flavors are good enough to wait for. And they demand slow savoring. As much as we like ice cream cones (Ici's are particularly nice: homemade, of course, with a nugget of rich chocolate in the point at the bottom), we suggest getting your chosen flavor in a cup. That allows for very slow licking—an unnatural act that is well worth practicing, for as this ice cream warms, its flavors blossom.

Jocko's Steak House

125 N. Thompson Ave.   805-929-3686
Nipomo, CA   BLD | $$

We found Jocko's many years ago while we were students at Gary Leffew's bull-riding school north of Santa Barbara. (That's another story . . .) When the week of riding rank bulls was over, cowboys who hadn't broken too many bones and had some jingle in their jeans headed for Nipomo to eat beef at Jocko's on Saturday night.

Nipomo isn't much of a town, but cars from afar crowd around Jocko's on weekends, and even if you've made a reservation (highly recommended), you will likely wait for a table. Waiting allows time to belly up to the bar and imbibe a colorful tavern atmosphere of taxidermized animal heads on the wall and the good-time shenanigans of California country folk (a whole 'nother breed from those who live in the big cities). Although the steaks are first-class, the experience of dining at Jocko's is absolutely nothing like a meal in one of the high-priced, dress-up steak house chains. Wear your jeans and boots and Stetson or farm cap and you'll be right at home.

Meat is the only thing to eat. (One Roadfooder wrote to us suggesting that this must be the place where bad vegetarians go when they die, for it truly is a kind of beef-frowners' hell, where smells of roasting meat permeate the air.) Shockingly thick steaks and hefty lamb chops and pork chops are cooked on an open pit over oak wood and served Santa Maria–style, meaning accompanied by tiny pinquito beans and salsa. It's a great, filling meal; and even if you get a relatively modest-size filet mignon, chances are you'll be taking meat home in a doggie bag for lunch the next day.

Julian Pie Company

21976 Hwy. 79
Santa Ysabel, CA

760-765-2400
$

Apple pie is the specialty of the Julian Pie Company, a sweet oasis at the western edge of the desert. Merely walking into the big modern building is an olfactory joy—the air is thick with the aroma of cooked apples, cinnamon, and hot crust. You can watch the pies being made behind the counter; you can buy whole pies to take home; or you can get a single slice and a cup of coffee and find a seat at the counter and indulge.

Varieties of apple pie in the Julian repertoire include Dutch apple with a crumb top, boysenberry apple crumb, natural strawberry apple, and apple rhubarb. Also on the regular menu are peach, peach melba, blackberry, and pecan. Basic apple pie with a pastry top is the classic, and we can't think of a better pie anywhere. Its crust is flaky, and the insides powerfully fruity/sweet. When you choose to dine here, you have the option of getting it à la mode, which is nice . . . but unnecessary.

While not a full-service restaurant by any means, this bakery does have a few other excellent food items worth knowing about. One unusual snack is pie crust—two-bite-size, heart-shaped pieces of crust that are baked in a veil of cinnamon sugar to become irresistibly delicious cookies that fall into flakes as you bite. The other handsome things in the glass display cases are donuts. They are plump cider donuts enrobed in either cinnamon sugar, chocolate, or supersweet (and super-good!) maple frosting.

The other store is at 2225 Main Street in Julian.

La Farine

6323 College Ave.   510-654-0338
Oakland, CA   B | $

A French pastry shop in Roadfood? We debated whether or not to include La Farine, and we are not listing it here for its fruit tarts and frangipanes or brandy cherry truffle tortes . . . although all those things are drop-dead good, as is the flaky morning bun. No, it earns its place in the Roadfood pantheon because it is a super source of the signature bread of San Francisco: sourdough. Available as a baguette, petit pain, or bâtard, with or without Kalamata olives laced into the dough, it is fantastically chewy with a crisp crust. Sour but not overwhelmingly so, this is bread that asks no condiment or complement whatsoever.

Nearly all business is take-out, but there is a large round table inside where customers can sit and nosh on bread and pastries and sip coffee. A great perk of sitting here is that the staff frequently brings out plates of little samples of the bakers' work to try.

La Super-Rica

622 N. Milpas St.   805-963-4940
Santa Barbara, CA   LD | $

La Super-Rica is barely a restaurant. It is a taco stand where service is do-it-yourself and customers are expected to clean their own place when they're finished eating. All plates and utensils are disposable, and seating is at wobbly tables on a semi–al fresco patio. Since Isidoro Gonzalez opened for business in 1980, this extremely modest eatery has built a reputation as a source for some of the very best Mexican food anywhere in the USA.

Using made-here tortillas, tacos can be had with beef, with green chile and cheese, or as a "chorizo especial" of spicy sausage, melted cheese, and tomato. We are especially fond of the taco *adobado* (grilled pork) and the frijol Super-Rica (chorizo and pinto beans with bacon and chile). In addition to tacos, La Super-Rica makes some sensational tamales; and beverages of choice include *horchata* (sweet rice milk), hibiscus, and Mexican beer. Each of the three kinds of salsa is excellent: chunky tomato, spicy red chile, and even spicier green chile.

Expect to wait in line at mealtime. The line is actually a good thing. La Super-Rica has no signs outside, so the crowd of people you see on N. Milpas Street will let you know you have arrived.

Mama's Hot Tamales Café

2122 W. 7th St.   213-487-7474

Los Angeles, CA   L | $

Gracias to Chris Ayers and Amy Breisch, the endlessly adventurous team who sign their Roadfood.com reviews "ayersian," for tipping us off to Mama's Hot Tamales Café in general and Mama's Mexican Mocha in particular. The tamales reflect cuisines of South America and Central America beyond Mexico. Some come wrapped in banana leaves or avocado leaves rather than corn husks; there are sweet ones as well as savories. Altogether, the kitchen's repertoire includes fifty varieties, about a dozen of which are available at any one time.

Any day, you can step back to the coffee bar and order Mexican Mocha, which is latte made from syrupy, licorice-dark espresso and chocolate, infused with steamed milk and shot through with a full measure of cinnamon. There's no better beverage for after a multi-tamale meal, or as a companion to a guava tamal from Colombia or a peach tamal from El Salvador.

Mama's Hot Tamales is more than a restaurant. It is a community center that hosts art shows and adjoins Bohemia Books, where you can buy Latino literature and art. Bohemia's gallery of work by local artists changes every month, and the bookstore hosts an open-mike "Street Dialogue" night once each month.

The Marshall Store

19225 State Route 1   415-663-1339

Marshall, CA   L | $$

The Marshall Store, which gets provender from the Hog Island Oyster Company up the road, brushes just-opened oysters on the half-shell with butter and cooks them on a grate only until they are warm. They are then dabbed with barbecue sauce and served with garlic toast. There are few simple pleasures more so right as this, the experience amplified by the casual magic of the al fresco dining facilities, which are boards set out on wine barrels where the Tomales Bay breeze wafts over your meal.

There is more on The Marshall Store menu, including raw oysters on the half-shell, chowder (dip your own), sandwiches, and salads. It's those barbecued oysters that will keep us coming back.

Musso & Frank Grill

6667 Hollywood Blvd.   323-467-7788

Hollywood, CA   LD | $$

When Musso & Frank opened for business in 1919, Hollywood was young and fresh and Hollywood Boulevard was a magic address. The boulevard went to honky-tonk hell in a handbasket and is now trying to rebirth itself with entertainment complexes and shopping malls competing for attention with cheap souvenirs and hookers' wig shops, but the moment you step inside Hollywood's oldest restaurant, the battle of the lifestyles is left behind.

In fact, now that meat and potatoes have enjoyed a well-deserved renaissance, this vintage eatery almost seems trendy. The menu is printed every day, but Musso's is known for dowdy kinds of meals: thin flannel cakes (for lunch), Welsh rarebit, chicken pot pie on Thursday, classic corned beef and cabbage every Tuesday, lamb shanks, baked ham, chiffonade salads. Please pay special attention to the potatoes. Ten different kinds occupy the menu, from mashed and boiled to lyonnaise and candied sweet. Steaks and chops, cooked on an open broiler where those sitting at the counter can watch, are splendid. From the dessert list, note bread and butter pudding, and its deluxe variant, diplomat pudding—topped with strawberries.

Many adventurous gourmets of our acquaintance do not understand the appeal of Musso & Frank. They compliment its antique Tudor decor and comfortable red leather booths but complain that the food is ordinary. Yes, indeed! It is some of the tastiest ordinary food anywhere.

Original Pantry

877 S. Figueroa St.   213-972-9279

Los Angeles, CA   Always open | $

Not far from the Staples Center, the Original Pantry is a choice stop for fans after Lakers games. Never having closed its doors since opening in 1924, this round-the-clock temple of honest eats is renowned for buckwheat hotcakes and full-bore egg breakfasts accompanied by sourdough toast, thick slabs of bacon, and piles of really excellent hash brown potatoes. OJ is freshsqueezed and the coffee keeps coming. At supper, you can't go wrong with a steak platter or such stalwarts as roast beef or liver 'n' onions; and the favorite dessert is hot apple pie with rum sauce. Sourdough bread and coleslaw are served with every meal.

When the Original Pantry was threatened by developers in 1980, former mayor Richard Riordan bought it, and His Honor's aura helped make it a destination for city politicians, bigwigs, and wannabes, especially at breakfast, when people-watching is a sport. A relatively small place, it is always bustling, and service, by hash-house pros, is nearly instantaneous.

Philippe the Original

1001 N. Alameda St.   213-628-3781
Los Angeles, CA   BLD | $

Genesis, according to Philippe's: One day in 1918 Philippe Mathieu was preparing a beef sandwich at his proletarian eat-place when the roll fell into the gravy. Fetched out with tongs, the drippings-sopped bread looked good enough that an impatient customer said, "I'll take it just like that." And so the French dip sandwich was created.

Philippe's moved to its current location in 1951, but it remains a sawdust-on-the-floor people-watcher's paradise. Place your order with a salesperson at the counter, then carry it to a tall chair at a chest-high communal table where your dining companions will range from racetrack touts and refugees from the nearby courthouse to SoCal creative types desperately seeking a dose of old-fashioned reality.

Dips are made from pork, beef, ham, lamb, or turkey. The beef is soft and tender, the pork even tenderer, and the lamb equally tender but with a tangy flavor twist. The sliced meat of your choice is piled into a fresh roll and sopped with gravy that is radiant with protein. You can get cheese on top, which we consider superfluous; but you must apply some of Philippe's hot mustard, a roaring-hot emulsion that is meat's best friend. Beyond the famous dips, there is a full menu of breakfasts, salads, sandwiches, and two soups each day. The price of coffee remains 9¢ per cup. Decaf is 60¢.

Ramona Cafe

628 Main St.   760-789-8656
Ramona, CA   BLD | $$

Here is a menu that honors potatoes. No mere side dish, Ramona Cafe's glistening chunks of home-fried potato are the underpinnings of whole breakfasts piled into ceramic skillets. Design your own, selecting four toppings from a list that includes ham, bacon, taco meat, chorizo sausage, four kinds of cheese, crushed garlic, and jalapeños. Or choose the Kitchen Sink, which is a panful of hunky home fries loaded with some of everything, including sausage gravy and a couple of eggs, and sided by an immense squared-off biscuit. If you want a meal that is less complicated but nearly as satisfying, consider Ramona Cafe's "blue ribbon" cinnamon roll: a half-pound circle of hot, sweet pastry veined with cinnamon sugar and accompanied by two paper cups of butter.

Other good breakfast options include omelets of all kinds. Of special note is the Gilroy Omelet, named for the California town that has proclaimed itself the garlic capital of the world: ham, bacon, mushrooms, Cheddar, and jack cheese, plus lots and lots of garlic.

While breakfast is the meal by which many travelers know Ramona Cafe, it also happens to be a fine place for a hearty lunch. There are good-size cheeseburgers, hot meat loaf sandwiches, turkey pot pie, and fine fried chicken that is crusted with breading made from the cafe's breakfast biscuits. The list of pies is a long one, including apple and rhubarb and a chocolate peanut butter pie that we once had as dessert for breakfast before a long drive inland, where good eats grow scarce.

Rick & Ann's

2922 Domingo Ave.   510-649-8538
Berkeley, CA   BLD | $$

Rick & Ann's is not Bay-Area hip, so we really like it. Hey, what's not to like about a place that's proud of its fried chicken supper with macaroni and cheese and corn bread?

We are not its only fans. You almost surely will wait for a table in this admirable coffee shop across from the Claremont Hotel, especially on weekends. Breakfast (or brunch) is the beacon meal, featuring gorgeous red flannel hash made with sweet and new potatoes and enough beets to turn it brick red. With eggs and toast, it is part of a breakfast known as The Northeast, but you'd be hard-pressed to find red flannel hash this good in New England. As devoted waffle folks, we heartily endorse the thin, crisp gingerbread-corn waffles (regular buttermilk waffles also are available); and on a return visit, we swooned over the fragile, painfully flavorful lemon ricotta pancakes. For dinner, if fried chicken is not your idea of comfort-food heaven, how about chicken pot pie or meat loaf with mashed potatoes?

Rick & Ann's website (www.rickandanns.com) changes each day to list such specials as shrimp tacos, summer caprese salad with heirloom tomatoes, and springtime crepes with roasted artichokes, fava beans, asparagus, portobello mushrooms, and goat cheese. And let's have a plum strawberry tart for dessert!

Roscoe's House of Chicken and Waffles

5006 W. Pico Blvd.   323-934-4405
Los Angeles, CA   BLD | $

Waffles have nearly vanished from lunch and supper menus, where they used to be a staple at tea rooms, department-store lunch counters, and home-cooking diners. One of the few places that honors them is Roscoe's of Los Angeles. Actually, there are five Roscoe's in Southern California. The one we know and love is on West Pico in Los Angeles—a location movie buffs know from its appearance in *Pulp Fiction*. A soulful eatery that looks a little scary from the outside but takes good care of customers, Roscoe's dishes out thin, crisp, butter-dripping waffles with a bit of cinnamon in the batter as a companion to pieces of crisp-skinned fried chicken. Whatever pieces you like are available: breasts, thighs, legs, wings, livers and giblets, even chicken sausage; and the menu offers all sorts of ready-made combos of chicken parts and side dishes. The latter include "candy yams," red beans, mac 'n' cheese, corn bread, and biscuits. We think collard greens provide ideal soulful harmony to the chicken and waffle combo. Of course, gravy is available, but butter and syrup are the condiments we like at Roscoe's.

Sam's Grill

374 Bush St.   415-421-0594
San Francisco, CA   LD Mon-Fri | $$$

Food trends come and go, and hot restaurants appear and fizzle. Sam's never changes. Tracing its history back to the 1860s, it is at once deluxe and informal, featuring high-priced, top-quality groceries prepared simply. It looks the way you want a great old California restaurant to look: outfitted with yards of thick white linen, brass hooks for coats, and private wooden dining booths for intimate meals.

The printed-daily menu is divided into such enticing categories as "Fish (Wild Only)" and "From the Charcoal Broiler," and the big rounds of sourdough bread brought to the table at the beginning of the meal are among the best anywhere. It's a frustrating place to eat because the menu lists so many things that are intriguing, from the unknown (what is Chicken Elizabeth? what are Prawns Dore?) to such bygone classics as Hangtown fry and mock turtle soup to ultra-exotica (fresh abalone meunière). It is possible to order charcoal-grilled steaks and chops, sweetbreads done three ways, or short ribs of beef with horseradish sauce, or just bacon and eggs, but nearly everybody comes to Sam's for the seafood. Our favorites have all been sole: rex sole fillets glistening with butter (perhaps the tenderest seafood we've ever slid onto the tines of a fork), charcoal-broiled petrale sole, and delicately fried fillets.

Sam's is open only on weekdays, only until nine at night; it caters to a clientele of people who work downtown and come every day for lunch, or for an early dinner before heading home. At noon, it is mobbed with successful-looking types jockeying for a table or crowding three deep against the bar. Once you are seated, it is an immensely comfortable place to eat. The staff of impeccably dressed waiters are consummate professionals, treating out-of-towners in jeans with as much respect as the important guys in business suits.

Sears Fine Food

439 Powell St.   415-986-0700
San Francisco, CA   BLD | $$

It was worrisome late in 2003 when it looked like Sears was about to vanish from the San Francisco landscape. While not the most exciting or innovative restaurant in town, nor an undiscovered gem, this comfortable storefront facing the cable cars on Powell Street has been Old Reliable since it opened in 1938, especially for breakfast. In fact, three meals a day are served and the lunch and dinner menus are extensive; but like most other tourists who find their way here, when we think of Sears we think of little Swedish pancakes served eighteen to a plate, sourdough French toast as tender as custard, non-Belgian waffles (from an old Fannie Farmer cookbook recipe), and thick, crisp bacon or plump sausage links alongside.

Happily, reports of Sears's death were greatly exaggerated; and while new owners took over in 2004, the traditional specialties remain reassuringly unchanged and the vintage dining room decor sets a cozy tone.

St. Francis Fountain

2801 24th St.   415-826-4200
San Francisco, CA   BLD | $

"Where have you been all our lives?" we wondered as we finished off a Forty-Niner at the St. Francis Fountain, a charming little ice cream parlor that opened in 1918, closed in 2002, but then reopened with a fresh coat of paint and a retro-hip attitude, but with the same sweet lunch-counter menu. All of what the St. Francis Fountain serves is familiar and comforting—omelets and egg scrambles for breakfast, bacon Cheddar burgers and legendary homemade soups, swell milk shakes and real egg creams—and, best of all, the Forty-Niner. This is a sandwich that combines two comfort foods in one: the basic BLT and superb egg salad. It is not a dramatically unusual egg salad, but it is just right: the eggs well chopped but not pulverized, delicious mayo (homemade?), and a shot of relish to perk it up. The eggs are what star, which is why the salad is such a good match for a BLT well endowed with bacon.

Seating is at a counter or in wooden booths. Be prepared to wait, especially on weekends.

Swan Oyster Depot

1517 Polk St.   415-673-1101
San Francisco, CA   L | $$

Swan is an urban seafood shack that is a combination oyster bar and storefront market. Seating is limited to a nineteen-seat counter, where your chances of walking in and finding a seat at mealtime are near zero. It is relatively expensive, uncomfortable, and noisy. And yet somehow its inconvenience is part of its charm (as is the ebullience of the Sancimino family, who have run the lunch counter since 1946). For devotees, it is simply the best place in San Francisco to eat fresh seafood. Fans have been crowding in for nearly a century to feast on oysters from the East and West Coasts, whole lobsters, salads of shrimp or crab, and smoked trout or salmon. Also, New England–style chowder. The marble counter is strewn with condiments: Tabasco sauce, lemons, oyster crackers.

Dungeness crab is served in season (generally, mid-November through May), available "cracked," meaning sections of cooked, cooled claw, leg, and body ready to be unloaded of their sweet meat. Crab Louie is a regal dish in which large chunks of sweet meat are cosseted in a condiment compounded from lemony mayonnaise spiked with relish and olive bits, enriched by hard-cooked egg.

Side your meal with sourdough bread and wash it down with Anchor Steam beer.

Taylor's Refresher

933 Main St.   707-963-3486
St. Helena, CA   LD | $$

This picnic-table oasis opened in St. Helena 1949 and has since earned a stellar reputation for one-third-pound, flame-broiled hamburgers (topped with bacon, Cheddar, barbecue sauce, mushrooms, and mayo, please!), chicken tacos, and fish tacos. We like the tuna burger best of all, which is not ground-up tuna but a broad steak minimally seared so the outside becomes a firmed-up envelope for the dense, succulent interior. It is dressed with a scattering of crisp greens known as Asian slaw and woo-hoo spicy ginger-wasabe mayonnaise. The egg bun is toasted warm; and on the side, you absolutely need an order of garlic fries and a milk shake.

Taylor's Refresher has branches in the Oxbow Public Market in Napa and in the San Francisco Ferry Building.

Wheel Inn

50900 Seminole Dr.　　　　　951-849-7012
Cabazon, CA　　　　　　　　Always open | $

The Wheel Inn is the great American truck stop, featuring round-the-clock hours and full-size statues of a *Tyrannosaurus rex* and a brontosaur that you can walk inside. In the mini-mart adjacent to the restaurant, travelers can buy candies, smokes, and sundries; the knotty-pine walls of the café are arrayed with merchandise for sale: fancy cowboy-style belt buckles, novelty clocks, scenic hand-made oil paintings (some on velvet). There is a short counter facing the pie case, and leatherette-upholstered booths are outfitted with Formica tables on which the wood-grain pattern has been worn out in places by decades of heavy plates and diners' elbows.

Pie is the specialty of the house. They are truck-stop pies—not elegant or fancy, but satisfying in a big, extra-sweet sort of way. We like the banana cream filling, the sturdy apple pie, and the fresh strawberry made with firm berries.

Much of the food on the Wheel Inn menu is shockingly real. In a diner where the seasoned highway traveler would expect to find a kitchen using fast-food shortcuts, you find instead Karel Kothera, the chef who bought the Wheel Inn in 1992 and now runs it alongside his wife, Marie, who serves as hostess. The Kotheras are a class act, both in the dining room and in the kitchen, and their efforts transform a basic truck stop into a really fine place to eat. The hot turkey sandwich is a good example. It is made of meat from a roasted bird (not from a "turkey loaf"), and it is accompanied by mashed potatoes actually made from potatoes (not dehydrated potato flakes). French fries to accompany hamburgers or other sandwiches are hot and salty, just oily enough to make perfect culinary sense alongside a half-pound Dino burger (two quarter-pound patties) on a whole-wheat sesame bun with tomato slices, lettuce, pickle, a small cup of Thousand Island dressing, and (optionally) raw or grilled slices of onion.

The preferred beverage for many of the working clientele is coffee, which is served in a bottomless cup; but if you want a true local treat here at the edge of the Coachella Valley, order a date shake. It's a milk shake supercharged with shreds of locally grown dates.

Annie's Donut Shop

3449 NE 72nd Ave.   503-284-2752
Portland, OR   B | $

There's been a donut renaissance in the Pacific Northwest. Seattle and Portland are bonanza cities for sinker-lovers, especially those who like their morning pastry with excellent coffee. For all the new, fashionable, retro, vegan, and Goth donuts available in both cities, we have a soft spot for traditional ones that go great with morning coffee (not latte!). These you will find at their best at Annie's. They are fresh and the variety is tremendous. Old-fashioned cake donuts have the double-circle shape so popular in the Northwest that provides twice the crunchy exterior of a simple round one. Glazed and maple-frosted OFs are especially swell, and although the price is plebeian, the taste and mouthfeel are aristocratic. Cream puffs are light and impeccably fresh-flavored, the only way a cream puff ever should be. The wickedest variety we sampled was a raspberry fritter—unctuous, super-sweet, slightly fruity, and monumentally filling.

Annie's has none of the amenities of upscale coffee and donut shops: no art on the walls, no Wi-Fi, no couches or lounge chairs, and, of course, no barristas. You sit in molded plastic booths that look out on the parking lot and are served by a staff with no attitude other than pride in the donuts they make and sell.

Crema

2728 SE Ankeny St.   503-234-0206

Portland, OR   BL | $

Crema is among the crème de la crème of Portland coffeehouses. It features French press coffee brewed so strong that hot water is made available for those who need to weaken it. The espresso is thick and syrupy, black as licorice; and among the fancy drinks is a dazzler called Spanish latte, which is made with sweetened condensed milk, adding extra body and luxe. Were the espresso not so strong, the supermilk might be overwhelming, but the two extremes form an infinitely satisfying yin-yang morning beverage. As gilding for this lily, the barristas at Crema know how to add the foam on top in lovely leafy patterns, making each drink a potable work of art.

We also like this large, enthusiastically caffeinated coffeehouse for its pastries. Among the wide assortment of sweet ones are Mexican chocolate cupcakes, green tea cheesecake, orange cinnamon buns, cranberry-caramel pecan bundt cake, chocolate bread pudding studded with bananas, and a double-chocolate, powder sugar–dusted Earthquake cookie complete with fault lines. There are all sorts of savory breakfast pastries made with eggs and veggies, our favorite being the ruggedly handsome Cheddar corn biscuit, a squat circle that is all crusty and chewy with baked cheese and dotted with sweet corn kernels.

Dan & Louis Oyster Bar

208 SW Ankeny St.   503-227-5906

Portland, OR   LD | $$

Warm milk, melted butter, and lots of little oysters: This is Dan & Louis's oyster stew, which the menu says was invented by Louis Wachsmuth long ago on a cold winter day. The oysters are Yaquinas from the restaurant's own beds. On the half-shell, they are gentle-tempered and ocean-sweet; in a stew, their oceanic aplomb is pillowy. While it is possible to get the stew with a double dose of oysters, we prefer having a half-dozen or a dozen on the half-shell, then having the stew with its normal number. If we're really hungry, we'll follow that with a plate of pan-fried oysters. Yaquinas fry up beautifully with a toasty golden crust. They are sent to the table with ramekins of tartar sauce and Thousand Island dressing, as well as a pile of lettuce shreds heaped with small shrimp and a length of chewy sourdough bread.

Beyond oysters, Dan & Louis sells Dungeness crab, shrimp Louis, halibut fish and chips, even a hamburger for those who accidentally find themselves in this thoroughly nautical eat-place. Among the non-oyster items, we are fond of the dowdy creamed crab on toast, a dish that one might expect to have been served in a department store lunchroom seventy-five years ago.

The interior of Dan & Louis is mesmerizing, its handsome sailing-ship wood walls bedecked floor to ceiling with an inexhaustible accumulation of nautical memorabilia and historical pictures, notes, and maps that tell of Portland since Louis started serving food here.

Ecola Seafoods

208 N. Spruce St. 503-436-9130
Cannon Beach, OR LD | $$

Cannon Beach is one of the most picturesque places on the Oregon coast, known for the awe-inspiring haystack-shaped rock a couple hundred yards out beyond the shoreline. It is a quiet hamlet and a grand destination for eaters because of Ecola Seafoods (named for nearby Ecola State Park). Ecola is total Roadfood—extremely casual and extremely local, a no-frills seafood market and restaurant where fresh is all. We love simply browsing the cases of Dungeness crab, oysters, scallops, and flatfish that we seldom see back East. And for those who arrive with a good appetite, what fun it is to choose from a broad menu of "fish and chips," the former part of the equation including Willapa Bay oysters, Oregon albacore tuna, razor clams, and troll-caught Chinook salmon. Plus Pacific cod, halibut, jumbo prawns, and ocean scallops. Each is available as a lunch or dinner (bigger portion), and you can get the cod, halibut, salmon, or oysters fried up and put into a toasted, buttered bun with lettuce, tomato, and a couple of lemon wedges.

We feasted on a crab cocktail, which was a sweet pile of cool, pearly meat in a bowl along with zesty red cocktail sauce. And we liked the chowder, too: fine-textured, creamy but not heavy, its ocean savor highlighted by a fine jolt of pepper.

The market's own fishing boats *Legacy* and *Legacy II* bring in wild salmon that can be had in the form of a grilled salmon taco, a salmon burger (a couple of big chunks in a bun) topped with mango salsa, or encased in crusty batter on a fish and chips plate. Smoked Chinook salmon is dense and heavy, falling into moist, bite-size forkfuls as fully satisfying as prime aged beefsteak. If you doubt that this place is serious about its salmon, consider the sign on the wall warning, "Friends don't let friends eat farmed salmon."

For picnickers, sandwiches and whole ready-to-eat dinners are available to go, as are all manner of cook-it-yourself fish.

Fuller's Coffee Shop

136 NW 9th Ave.   503-222-5608
Portland, OR   BL | $

Off the tourist path but loved by locals, Fuller's is the sort of high-quality urban hash house now nearly vanished from most American cities. A man sitting near us at one of the two U-shaped Formica counters mopped the last of some yolk off his plate with a forkful of pancake and declared that he used to eat at Fuller's nearly every day thirty-two years ago, and as far as he could see, nothing's changed but the prices. "This is a diner where they know how to fry bacon!" he declared. Yes, indeed. An order of bacon is four medium-thick ribbons that are crisp but retain enough pliability so they don't break at first bite. And the hash browns are a short-order delight, fried so they are a mix of golden crust and soft, spuddy shreds of buttery potato. The pancakes are good, too; and the cinnamon roll, baked fresh each day, is yeasty and tender.

Our favorite thing at Fuller's is the bread. It's not artisan bread; it's not fancy at all. You get white or whole wheat. These slices are simple and perfect, especially so when toasted and buttered and accompanying a big, well-rounded breakfast. Jelly and marmalade are set out in ramekins along the counter.

Lunch consists of such blue-plate specials as hot beef and gravy (on the good bread) with mashed potatoes and a corned beef sloppy joe. There is always interesting seafood: salmon steaks in season, batter-dipped fish and chips, fresh-fried oysters, and big, slightly scary (but easy to eat) egg-battered fried razor clams with French fries and coleslaw.

Green Salmon

220 Hwy. 101 N.   541-547-3077
Yachats, OR   BL | $

The Green Salmon serves great coffee and espresso, but that's just the beginning. How about a Cafe Oregonian with hazelnut milk, a Cafe Mexico with pepper, brown sugar, and cocoa, or a Kopi Jahe, which is a double-strength brew infused with the sparkle of ginger and sweetness of cane sugar?

Enticing as these coffees are, it's for the food we direct you here, especially if you happen to be passing through in summer berry season. That is when the menu offers an item called triple berry toast: crunch-textured whole wheat spread with creamy Italian mascarpone, topped with freshly picked blueberries, strawberries, and raspberries, each at the peak of their

sunny fruitiness, and finally drizzled with honey and sprinkled with powdered sugar. Breakfast opportunities include a panini-grilled Sicilian egg
sandwich on multigrain bread, granola baked with maple syrup and moistened with steamed milk, and a wide-bodied croissant frosted with a thick
glaze of maple (the Pacific Northwest is crazy for the flavor of maple).

Crowded and sociable, the Green Salmon is more for lingering than a
quickie coffee. Partly, this is because drinks and hot dishes all are made
to order, but also it is because the place is infused with the life-savoring
rhythms of the slow food movement . . . despite all the caffeine consumed
on premises.

Halibut's

2525 NE Alberta St.   503-808-9600
Portland, OR   LD | $$

The best fish and chips in the West? This very well might be the place. When
we walked in, owner Dave Mackay was at the left side of the restaurant
behind the counter where the row of fry kettles are, proclaiming aloud the
beauty of a particular side of salmon. Oh, and it was: vivid pink with dense,
heavy flesh fairly dripping fatty savor. It was from the Copper River, of
course (Alaska's coldest), and while broiling or grilling it would be grand,
this restaurant's deep-fry skills are equally brilliant, encasing the kingly meat
in a thin, fragile crust that is amazingly grease-free and only enhances the essential taste of the fish within. Dave cut the side of fish with aplomb, creating
chunks about 2 x 2 x 4-inches for frying.

All kinds of fish are fried here. Halibut comes as four heavy blocks that
are moist and sweet, big white hunks of their flesh flaking off with pieces of
crust when you hoist them from the basket that also contains crunch-crusted
French fries. (Malt vinegar is supplied for dressing the spuds.) Also of note
on the menu are Dungeness crab cakes, which is a sheaf of four flat ones,
very crabby and nicely spiced with a red-gold crust. The restaurant's subtitle
is "Fish/Chips and Chowder," and the chowder is not to be missed. It is
ridiculously thick with clams and potatoes and a surfeit of rich becon, available plain in a bowl or with Alaskan bay shrimp added.

Halibut's is a casual bar with raucous blues playing on the speakers (or
performed live many nights). There is a happy hour menu and a long list of
such whoop-de-doo cocktails as the Ultimate Margarita, a mai tai, and a
refreshing Lemon Drop, made with fresh-squeezed lemons, Absolut Citron,
Triple Sec, Bacardi Limón, sweet and sour mix, and sugar and served in a
goofy-stemmed martini glass.

Mo's

622 SW Bay Blvd.   541-265-2979
Newport, OR   LD | $$

There are a handful of Mo's along the Oregon coast. The Newport original is surrounded by a dockside sprawl of fish markets, seafood packing companies, and stores that advertise they will smoke any fish, meat, or fowl you bring in. The most famous dish on the menu, and the one you must try, is Mo's chowder—smoky and fork-thick, loaded with pieces of clam and potato. Mo's slumgullion is the chowder enriched with shrimp—a terrific combination, and with a salad and a hunk of bread, a royal supper. Comfort-food aficionados will want to know about scalloped oysters, a lavish baked-together combination of butter, cream, crackers, and oysters. You can also order oysters "barbecued," for which they are sauced, smothered with cheese, and baked. The menu includes a mighty bouillaibasse thick with clams, shrimp, oysters, crab, cod, halibut, and salmon in a light tomato sauce.

Across the street, at Mo's Annex, you get all this hearty fare plus a wonderful view of Yaquina Bay, where customers look out over the water and the commercial fleet berthed at its dock, and watch sport fishermen cleaning their day's catch.

Norma's Ocean Diner

20 N. Columbia St.   503-738-4331
Seaside, OR   LD | $$

Seaside is a semi-honky-tonk town in a divinely beautiful location along Oregon's seashore. You can buy all kinds of T-shirts, fudge, and saltwater taffy; and at Norma's, you can have a real Northwest meal. We knew we were going to like this place the moment we walked in and saw the chalkboard near the pass-through window to the kitchen. It lists which fresh seafoods are available and where they are from: salmon from the Oregon coast, steamer clams and oysters from Willipa Bay, halibut from Alaska, and local petrale sole. Even the featured wine was Oregonian: Duck Pond Merlot.

The waitress congratulated us on our choice of petrale sole mid-April: "Oooo, it's in season right now," she said. And it was wonderful: delicate-flavored, buttery-rich, ocean-sweet. Nor could we resist Dungeness crab, which is available here in all sorts of ways. We chose the "Louis" presentation, which turned out to be about a dozen big, pearly hunks of white meat arrayed atop a pile of lettuce with all the proper garnishes, plus garlic toast made from fresh-baked bread and a ramekin of excellent house-made Thousand Island dressing.

People at a nearby table were all eating fish and chips. The menu lists cod, salmon, halibut, and even albacore available as the fish part of the equation. We asked our dining room neighbors how they liked it. Between bites, they were able to exclaim that this is the best fish and chips they have eaten anywhere, any time.

The Oasis

85698 Hwy. 339	541-938-4776
Milton Freewater, OR	BLD | $$

A short detour off the main road at the Washington state line leads to The Oasis, a sprawling roadhouse that seems to have expanded room by room over the last seven decades. It is ramshackle and rugged, a favorite destination for locals in search of meat and potatoes, live music on the weekends, and Texas hold 'em.

Sirloin steaks come branded with a neat field of crosshatch char marks on their surface. These are cuts of beef with some chaw to them, available in all cuts and sizes, eclipsed in their beefiness only by the kitchen's grandiose prime rib. Many customers who come from afar to dine at The Oasis make a special night of the occasion by treating themselves to the most celebratory of all restaurant meals, surf and turf, which is such a house specialty that an entire section of the menu is devoted to its various permutations. Prime rib or sirloin is available alongside a jumbo Australian lobster tail or with prawns, scallops, or grilled oysters.

Breakfast at The Oasis is a roll-your-sleeves-up kind of meal, served all day with the exception of pancakes and biscuits, which are available only until 11 A.M. The biscuits are extraordinary, a single order consisting of three behemoths and a cascade of thick gravy. This is a meal of caloric content suited to the eater who plans to flex muscles all day.

Otis Cafe

1259 Salmon River Hwy.	541-994-2813
Otis, OR	BLD | $

The Otis is an undersize roadside diner serving oversize meals. Located next to the post office, featuring a picnic-table patio as well as counter and table seats inside, this modest eat-place has received national acclaim for great pies and lumberjack's (or more accurately in this case, fishermen's) breakfasts. Sourdough pancakes have a tang beautifully haloed by lots of melting but-

ter and a spill of syrup. Eggs come with hash browns, the potatoes preferably blanketed with melted cheese, and excellent homemade black molasses
bread or a jumbo cinnamon roll.

Our lunch was a two-fisted BLT made with full-flavored slices of beefsteak tomato plus a bonus layer of cheese, and a goopy cheeseburger on a
hefty bun with Otis's homemade mustard. On the side were dreamy fried red
potatoes. Pies are gorgeous, especially the West Coast rarity, marionberry. A
more intense, supremely aromatic blackberry, the marionberry was made to
be put in a pie. That the crust here is crisp and aristocratic makes it all the
more perfect a dessert.

Otto's Sausage Kitchen

4138 SE Woodstock Blvd.   503-771-6714
Portland, OR   L | $

While it is a full-scale meat market and smokehouse with cold cuts and sausages of all kinds to take home and cook, Otto's is also a fantastic place to
eat lunch—either deli sandwiches (like the great Reuben) or Otto's superior
hot dogs. Whether you choose an ordinary beef-and-pork frankfurter (with
snap to its skin that is far from ordinary) or an extra-large sausage made
from chicken or pork, you might just find yourself amazed, as we do, by just
how much better these fresh, homemade tube steaks taste than factory-made
ones from the supermarket. The progeny of Otto Eichentopf, who opened
this neighborhood meat market in 1927, maintain the highest standards of
old-world sausage making. The beauty of the links they make for lunch is
that you really taste the meat of which they are made. Spices are used to
accent rather than overwhelm the primary ingredient. Served in soft buns
with a choice of onions, kraut, relish, mustard, or ketchup for you to apply
yourself, Otto's sausages can be enjoyed with a beverage chosen from a vast
cooler full of local soft drinks and imported and regional beers.

Otto's appeal has a lot to do with its casual ambience. Dining facilities
are nothing more than a bunch of wooden tables arranged on the sidewalk
outside, as well as a handful of places to sit indoors. It's a neighborhood
picnic every lunch hour.

Pacific Oyster

5150 Oyster Dr.   503-377-2323
Bay City, OR   BLD (closed Sat) | $$

Attached to a very large oyster processing plant on the ocean side of Route 101 is a little bare-table dining area and fish market where you can find a table and feast on Northwest seafood.

All kinds of raw oysters are available: mediums, petites, or the alluring little Kumamotos—freshly opened and served on the half-shell or in shooter glasses for easy gulping. And, of course, there is oyster stew, fried oysters, and even an oyster burger (four fried ones on a bun). Dungeness crab is available in a crab melt made with Oregon's own Tillamook Cheddar cheese. Another treat is a salmon stick, a staff of salty/sweet smoked salmon that is like beef jerky, but easier to chew.

Ristretto Roasters

3520 NE 42nd Ave.   503-284-6767
Portland, OR   BL | $

Ristretto Roasters is a modest establishment, just a small storefront with three counter stools, three tables, a single booth, and a few sidewalk seats. And yet, in a city with more than its fair share of excellent coffee sources, there is a line here all morning long: caffeine-hungry Portlanders waiting for cups of delicious coffee and espresso, the beans for which are roasted in the back room that is visible through a glass window.

The espresso is a perfect balance of caffeinated punch and smooth, chocolaty flavor; the regular coffee has a good kick, too, but is not so strong that a second and third cup don't seem like great ideas. You want to be able to drink a lot of this coffee because Ristretto offers excellent companion pastries, including a creamy and substantial "pound and a half cake" and slices of chocolate espresso bread. The latter is moist, profoundly dark, and an ideal companion for at least two cups of coffee.

Sahagún

10 NW 16th Ave.   503-274-7065
Portland, OR $$

Chocoholics, beware. Come to Sahagún, a low-key, high-quality storefront in Portland, and you easily can overdose. For hot chocolate alone, we'd walk barefoot on broken glass to get here. Made not with syrup or powdered cocoa but with melted chocolate (single origin, of course) and hormone-free half-and-half, it is thick, dense, and supremely satisfying, sweet but not cloying, the paradoxical soothing/exciting essence of pure chocolate.

That's just one item in the dazzling repertoire of chocolatier Elizabeth Montes, who is a woman on a mission. Her goal: to cultivate an appreciation for cacao as something more significant than Easter bunnies and Count Chocula cereal. Some examples are Colombian chocolate–covered cocoa nibs, salted chocolate caramels rolled in Oregon hazelnuts, barks built around local marionberries and sour cherries, bittersweet chocolate-covered Meyer lemon peels, and candy bars from the best chocolate-producing places around the world.

Saint Cupcake

407 NW 17th Ave. 503-473-8760
Portland, OR B | $

What sweet-toothed traveler can ignore a bakery devoted to cupcakes? Yes, here is cupcake heaven. As you walk in toward the counter and cases straight ahead, the kitchen is visible to the right. Customers in line observe batter being mixed and scooped into tins and baked, and chances are that at least one of the types you like to eat still will be warm when you place your order. You'll find chocolate, toasted coconut, and vegan cupcakes, and, best of all, shockingly tinted red velvet cupcakes crowned with a spire of sweet cream cheese frosting. While lots of business is take-out by the dozen, tables for indulging here are available, as is good Stumptown coffee and cold milk by the carton.

Note: There is a second location in Portland at 3300 SE Belmont.

South Beach Fish Market

3640 S. Coast Hwy. 101 541-867-6800
South Beach, OR L | $$

South Beach is an eat-in-the-rough roadside café and seafood store with a vast oceancentric menu of mostly fried fare that ranges from clam strips to halibut and chips. Normally, we wouldn't think of halibut as a fish-and-chip candidate, but these batter-cased hunks of fish retain utmost juiciness, and their subtle sea flavor is enhanced by the surrounding crust. The crab cocktail is swell—a cylinder of shreds and chunks of meat packed into a plastic cup and crowned with a slice of lemon—but we would advise against the salmon burger, which is ground-up fish formed into a patty that gets deep-fried until most of its succulence is gone.

Meals are served in throwaway baskets and eaten at counters equipped with stools. If you've caught a fish that you need smoked, these guys will be happy to do that for $2.50 per pound. The management also sells really good canned tuna—Oregon albacore, packed in its natural juices (nothing added) and cooked in the can. It is dense, rich, and far superior to anything found on supermarket shelves.

Voodoo Donuts

22 SW 3rd Ave.   503-241-4704
Portland, OR   B | $

When Roadfood.com's Mr. Chips wrote to tell us that Voodoo Donuts, a block away from the estimable Dan & Louis Oyster Bar (p. 536), was a "great place to view Portland's strong Goth culture as well as sample tasty donuts," we were intrigued. We generally don't think of Goth culture as a source of good eats, and while we cannot say for sure if the ambience of this brick-walled ex-warehouse indeed is true Goth, we can tell you with certainty that the donuts are swell.

There are beautiful old-fashioned cake donuts with crunchy crust and creamy insides, puffy raised donuts, one glazed behemoth as big as a pizza labeled a Tex-Ass donut (and costing $3.95), and donuts topped with powdered sugar, multicolored jimmies, and all sorts of flavored glazes. The menu lists such mysteries as a No-Name donut, a Dirt donut, a Cock & Balls donut, a Dirty Snowball, and a Diablos Rex. Our favorite item on the menu above the counter was Non Existing Fritter, its cost nil. We suspect that may be Goth humor.

The one pastry we shan't forget is a bacon-maple bar. It is a substantial buttermilk long john frosted with maple glaze and festooned with strips of bacon that somehow, magically, retain a welcome crunch. What a dandy all-in-one breakfast!

Waves of Grain

3116 S. Hemlock St.   503-436-9600
Cannon Beach, OR   BL | $

We don't know too many bakeries where the proprietors' family grows the wheat from which the breads and pastries are made. In fact we know just one: Waves of Grain, in the achingly scenic oceanside community of Cannon Beach. Jason and Hillary Fargo buy their wheat out Pendleton way from Hillary's second cousin, Fritz Hill, who is a fourth-generation farmer.

The Fargos will tell you that it's the wheat, a variety known as dark northern, that gives character to their biscuits, breads, muffins, sticky buns, and cheese sticks. It's also talent and passion, all of which result in the most delicious baked goods north of the San Francisco Bay Area. During a long visit to Cannon Beach, we had breakfast here every morning and managed to nab focaccias and quiches for lunch, followed by dessert of chocolate buttermilk cupcakes and blueberry cream cheese bars.

Of particular note is the big Tillamook cheese biscuit with its crisp edges and creamy inside, the crusty cheese sticks, and the elegant sticky bun (which, if you get here early enough, will still be hot from the oven). Good coffee and espresso drinks are made from organic, fair-trade beans roasted in town by an outfit called the Sleepy Monk.

Bakeman's

122 Cherry St.
Seattle, WA

206-622-3375
L Mon-Fri | $

A working-class cafeteria with a menu that is pretty much limited to soup and sandwiches, Bakeman's is open only for lunch, Monday through Friday. Its claim to fame is the turkey sandwich on white or whole wheat. The bread is homemade, stacked up at one end of the cafeteria line. It is not artisan bread, just good sandwich bread: tender slices that come to life when spread with mayo and/or mustard and/or cranberry and/or shredded lettuce, then heaped with turkey or—almost as wonderful—slabs of meat loaf.

The meat loaf is tightly packed but tender, gently spiced, and with a delicious aroma. As for turkey, get it any way you like because this is superb, *real,* carved-from-the-bird turkey with homey flavor. The dark meat is lush; the white meat is moist and aromatic; either variety has an occasional piece of skin still attached, a nice reminder of just how real it is. The way we like it is, in the words of the countermen who hustle things along at breakneck pace, "white on white; M & M," which means white meat turkey on white bread with mustard and mayonnaise. You can also get it dressed with shredded lettuce and an order of cranberry relish. Turkey sandwiches get no better than this!

Bakeman's offers a couple of good soups each day, such as turkey noodle or beef vegetable, plus a nice chili, or, on one memorable occasion, Chinese eggflower—an egg drop variation. There are Waldorf and potato salads and such, but they aren't all that interesting. But dessert can be wonderful— carrot cake, cookies, or chocolate or lemon poppy-seed cake, sliced like bread.

Beth's Cafe

7311 Aurora Ave. N.   206-782-5588
Seattle, WA   Always open | $

Are you hungry? Really, really hungry? If so, eat at Beth's. Order the twelve-egg omelet. Yes, that's an even dozen, served not on a puny plate but on a pizza pan. If you're only half-hungry, Beth's offers six-egg omelets. Each comes with a heap of hash brown potatoes—all you can eat—and, if desired, bacon strips that have been cooked under a weight so they arrive flat and fragile. Biscuits and gravy is another of Beth's monumental meals, but if you arrive with only a tiny appetite, the menu offers mini breakfasts that are merely a single egg with hash browns and your choice of bacon or sausage.

Lunch isn't so awesomely large, its flagship meal being a half-pound Mondo Burger with cheese, bacon, lettuce, and tomato, fries on the side. There's a great big Reuben sandwich as well as normal-size burgers, BLTs, and French dips.

Beth's is open 'round the clock and is not a place to please a fastidious epicure. It is what some have called an "alternative greasy spoon," attracting wee-hours diners from the fringes of city life. And in Seattle, those fringes are pretty far out!

The Crumpet Shop

1503 1st Ave.   206-682-1598
Seattle, WA   BL | $

Located at the entrance to the Pike Place Market, The Crumpet Shop is a small café that serves crumpets for breakfast, brunch, and lunch. In case you don't know, a crumpet is thick like an English muffin but poured out and cooked on a griddle, coming off chewy and rich-flavored with a craggy-textured surface that begs to be heaped with butter and fruit-clotted marmalade. You can have one simply buttered, or with butter and maple syrup, or with your choice from among nearly two dozen different sorts of sweet and savory toppings, including honey, Nutella, local jams, ham, cheese, and smoked salmon. On the side, have espresso, cappuccino or, better yet, imported tea. If crumpets are not your cup of tea, The Crumpet Shop also bakes terrific loaves of bread, including a rugged groat bread that is an apt foundation for a hefty sandwich.

Cupcake Royale

1101 34th Ave.   206-709-4497

Seattle, WA   BL | $

Whoever invented the cupcake was a genius, providing eaters the opportunity to have a whole cake of their own without feeling like too much of a pig. Seattle's Cupcake Royale makes the situation even better by offering mini cupcakes as well as full-size ones, thus making a snack of two or three cakes a reasonable proposition. On the other hand, the bakery's inventory almost inevitably leads to piggishness on the part of cake-lovers. There are so many good ones that must be tried.

In addition to the regular varieties, which include carrot cake, double chocolates, lavender and lemon drop cakes, and a wicked-good salted caramel-topped one that is especially fudgy, Cupcake Royale offers a cupcake of the month. In January, as an ode to the fried banana and peanut butter sandwich that was a favorite of Elvis Presley (whose birthday is January 8), the spotlighted feature was a banana cupcake with chocolate peanut butter frosting, crowned with a crisp banana chip.

If there is a complaint to be made, it is that the cakes sometimes can be too fresh, so warm and moist that if you are not extremely careful, one bite will detach the top from the stump, or the stump itself can disintegrate between thumb and fingers. Some complaint! The point is that these cupcakes are best eaten at a table or counter rather than from an automobile dashboard.

Note: There currently are four cafés selling Cupcake Royale cupcakes and Vérité coffee. We visited the one in Madrona. Other locations are West Seattle (4556 California Ave. SW), Ballard (2052 NW Market St.), and Capitol Hill (1111 E. Pike St.).

Emmett Watson's Oyster Bar

1916 Pike Pl., Suite 16   206-448-7721

Seattle, WA   LD | $$

A laid-back eatery just across the street from the Pike Place Market in a back-street nook inside the Soames-Dunn Building, Emmett Watson's can be maddening if you are an efficiency nut in a hurry. For leisurely enjoyment of oysters, clams, and mussels, or baskets of fish and chips, or wonderful soups and chowders, this brash little place is a Seattle treasure. There is a sunny, flower-adorned courtyard behind the building for warm-weather dining at rickety little tables, and an indoor area with small booths.

For many regular customers, Emmett Watson's is a place to come for several beers accompanied by oysters on the half-shell, either raw or broiled. We have spent many a happy afternoon at a patio table enjoying a drawn-out "grazing" meal of oysters, then shrimp, then a cup of chowder, and an occasional order of garlic bread. For appetites in search of well-balanced meals, we recommend anything fried (fish, clams, shrimp, oysters) or the steamed mussels or clams in garlic broth. Soups are notable, too, including a spicy shrimp soup Orleans, Puget Sound salmon soup, and a classic cioppino stew of cod, shrimp, clams, and mussels. Meals are accompanied by slices of excellent French bread and butter, and there is good Key lime pie for dessert.

14 Carrot Cafe

2305 Eastlake Ave. E.   206-324-1442
Seattle, WA   BLD | $

Casual and comfortably disheveled, nutritionally enlightened, and perfumed inside and out by coffee, here is an echt Seattle dining experience. Although lunch includes excellent salads and soups as well as vegetarian plates and no-beef hamburgers, most fans of the 14 Carrot Cafe consider it a breakfast place. Omelets are big and beautiful, served with good hash browns and a choice of toast, English muffin, or streusel-topped coffee cake. The coffee cake itself is something to behold: a moist crumble-topped block, served with a sphere of butter as big as a Ping-Pong ball. Other notable bread-stuffs include blueberry muffins and cinnamon rolls. The latter, described as "large and gooey" by our waiter, is a vast doughy spiral with clods of raisins and veins of dark sugar gunk packed into its warm furrows. It, too, comes blobbed with a ball of melting butter.

If eggs aren't your dish, how about hotcakes, sourdough or regular, with sliced bananas, apple slivers, or blueberries, with bacon on the side or cooked into the 'cakes? You can order hot oats with soy milk, dates, and cashews, homemade granola, sourdough French toast, or a grand version of French toast known as Tahitian toast, gilded with a thin layer of sesame butter.

Frank's Diner

1516 W. 2nd Ave.   509-747-8798

Spokane, WA   BLD | $

Anyone who arrives in Spokane with an appetite that demands attention needs to know about the King of the Road omelet at Frank's Diner. This big boy is made from six eggs, ham, Cheddar and Swiss cheese, peppers and onions, and is served with hash brown potatoes and toast.

Not quite that hungry? How about a Joe's Special, named in honor of the "New Joe Special" that is so popular in the San Francisco Bay Area. At Frank's, the Joe's Special is a mere three eggs scrambled with ground beef, spinach, and onion, flavored with Parmesan cheese. There are plenty of normal-size breakfasts, too, from hefty biscuits and gravy to eggs Benedict, and from silver-dollar pancakes to French toast made with cinnamon swirl bread. The breakfast menu boasts that Frank's serves twelve thousand eggs per month.

Our tipster, Charlie, told us that breakfast is the meal to eat at Frank's, but the lunch selection looks pretty inviting, too. It includes, and we quote from the menu, "the best hot turkey sandwich ever," made from turkey roasted in Frank's kitchen, as well as a grilled meat loaf sandwich, chicken pot pie, and a large assortment of one-third-pound Vista Cruiser Burgers made with assorted combinations of cheese, dressings, bacon, and barbecue sauce.

Grand food! But what will strike you even before you eat is the place itself, which is the state of Washington's oldest diner. It really was a railroad diner, Car #1787, built in 1906, and now completely restored in hash-house configuration with a counter that provides a view of the grill. Frank's was located in Seattle from 1931 to 1991, at which point it lost its lease and was moved to Spokane.

Hi Spot Cafe

1410 34th Ave.   206-325-7905

Seattle, WA   BL | $$

The only problem with this very nice, very Seattle breakfast-and-lunch café in the Madrona neighborhood is that too many locals know and like it. Expect to wait for a table, especially if you are coming for weekend brunch. It's located in an old home, so the configuration is curious: a few tables and a long counter on the main floor, then more tables up a flight of stairs (where the kitchen is), and a bathroom with a tub on the floor above that!

Upon entering, glance right. Here you see the pastries, which are a primary Hi Spot attraction: huge flavor-packed scones, huger buttermilk biscuits, and ridiculously big cinnamon rolls that are packed with sugar and slivered nuts. Attractive as the jumbo breadstuffs may be, it's the omelets that won our hearts, especially El Pacifico, which is full of smoked salmon, dill cream, capers, and scallions and topped with more dill cream. The Round-Up is another winner built of chicken sausage, goat cheese, tomatoes, and basil. Both come with home fries and toast. Egg dishes are served until closing at 2:30 P.M. The lunch menu, which becomes available at 11:30 A.M, includes soups and salads and sandwiches on superb Macrina Bakery rolls.

Among the attractive drink options are freshly squeezed limeade, mimosas, and Fonté coffee. Fonté is a local microroaster; the espresso we had was rich, dark, and smooth.

Knapp's Family Restaurant

2707 N. Proctor St.   253-759-9009
Tacoma, WA   BLD | $

All kinds of people give us all kinds of suggestions of places to eat; but when one of the nation's great restaurateurs tells us where to go, we pay special attention. Hap Townes, who for many years ran an estimable cafeteria-style lunchroom in Nashville, Tennessee, tipped us off to Knapp's. "It's your kind of place," Hap said with assurance born of watching us eat many of his fine meals.

The setting of Knapp's in the Proctor District helps create an aura of small-town charm in the midst of big-city life. Walking into the old brick building is like going back half a century. The dining room is patrolled by teams of waitresses who wait tables for a living—pros who refill coffee and replace needed silverware with the grace of a four-star sommelier.

The menu is nostalgic, too. This is a place to have a platter of liver 'n' onions or turkey with sage-flavored dressing and a pile of mashed potatoes with a ladle of gravy on top. Every Tuesday, Knapp's serves corned beef and cabbage; every Wednesday, roast pork loin. Begin your meal with a shrimp cocktail or an iceberg lettuce salad topped with thick dressing, and top it off with homemade peach pie. It is an all-American experience, not necessarily for the fussy epicure, but a treasure for aficionados of square meals.

Maltby Cafe

8809 Maltby Rd. 425-483-3123
Snohomish, WA BL | $

If ever we write a book called *Really Big Food,* the Maltby Cafe will be featured for its breakfast. Its cinnamon roll is less a roll than a loaf—a massive circular coil of sweet pastry scattered with bits of walnut. It is served on a dinner plate, which it fits edge-to-edge, and it is at least a couple of good breakfasts unto itself.

You must get a cinnamon roll at the Maltby Cafe, but there are some other terrific meals, too, and while none is quite so flabbergastingly immense, they are satisfying in the extreme. The Maltby omelet, for example, is another plate-filler, loaded with ham, beef, peppers, and onions. Maltby oatmeal is served with melted butter running all over the top of the bowl; the French toast is double-thick; and, lest we forget, the strawberry jam on every table is homemade and especially delicious when liberally spread on a big, oven-warm biscuit along with—are you ready?—crème fraîche.

After breakfast, there is lunch, which looks good . . . although we must admit that cinnamon rolls and omelets have pretty much put lunch out of the question for us. The menu includes pasta plates, homemade soup, and a piled-high hot Reuben sandwich.

The Maltby Cafe is a most unusual place (a former school cafeteria) in an amazing little town of nostalgic mise-en-scène that includes strategically situated old farm machinery, a few windmills, and an uncounted number of vintage gasoline station signs. Other than the café, the town has a few knick-knack shops and a drive-through espresso stand shaped like a big-gulp cup.

Mike's Chili Parlor

1447 NW Ballard Way 206-782-2808
Seattle, WA LD | $

Outfitted with a billiards table, video games, an ATM station, and pull-tab lotto, decorated with beer signs and festooned with announcements warning that only cash is accepted and touting such specials as a Big Ass Bowl of Chili, Mike's is a personality-plus chili parlor. The chili is a he-man brew of coarse-ground beef with bright Greek seasonings, saturated with enough grease that when it is served by the bowl, your spoon will slide through a glistening layer on top before it hits meat. (Oyster crackers are provided, and they are the connoisseur's way to soak up excess grease.) Beans are optional, as are grated cheese and chopped onions.

You can have this stout stuff in a cup or bowl, as the dressing for burgers, hot dogs, and steak, and in concert with spaghetti noodles. You also can buy it by the gallon (at about $50), but for that, you must bring your own container.

Pick Quick Drive-In

4306 Pacific Hwy. E.   253-922-5599
Tacoma, WA   L (closed in winter) | $

Here's a roadside joint from 1949 that is especially alluring in nice weather when you can sit outside and enjoy a tasty triple cheeseburger, chili fries, and milk shake . . . all of that still in the single-digit price range.

Honestly, the hamburgers wouldn't win first prize in our Best of the Northwest burger awards. They are of modest size and uniform shape, but they have a nice savor from the well-aged grill that imprints itself into the toasted bun. And they come dressed quite royally with mustard, mayonnaise, relish, pickles, onion, lettuce, and tomato. Of course, bacon, cheese, and grilled onions are options. French fries are very good and the milk shakes can be extraordinary as they are made from fresh fruit in season—strawberries, blueberries, blackberries, cherries, raspberries. Any time, you can have fresh banana added to your shake or malt.

Pick Quick is a minuscule establishment that originally served as the canteen for a now-defunct drive-in movie. There is plenty of dining room in the great outdoors with picnic tables of all shapes and sizes.

Red Mill

1613 W. Dravus St.   206-284-6363
Seattle, WA   L | $

There was a diner called the Red Mill in Seattle for thirty years starting in 1937. Twenty-seven years after it closed, a new Red Mill opened in Phinney Ridge, and a hamburger legend was born. No doubt, Seattle is a significant burger city, and many of its connoisseurs believe Red Mill's rate near the top. Flame-broiled to a smoky savor, they come in many configurations from the basic version (lettuce and sauce) to deluxe (lettuce, tomato, pickle, onion, and sauce) and include patties topped with blue cheese or barbecue sauce. You can get a double—that's a half-pound of meat—and you even can get a meatless garden burger. We are fond of the Verde burger, which is topped with roasted green chiles, jack cheese, red onion, lettuce, tomato, and the Red Mill's proprietary sauce. Condiments and dressing are applied in abundance, so while the meat patty itself is good, it's all those extras that put it over the top.

On the side, onion rings are essential. They are big crunchy hoops with ribbons of sweet, caramelized onion inside. And there is a whole menu of milk shakes and malts, plus fresh-squeezed lemonade.

And as if burgers, o-rings, and shakes weren't enough to love this place, we should also add that it has a strict no-cell-phone policy, allowing all of us to dine well and in peace.

Seattle's first Red Mill is in Phinney Ridge at 312 N. 67th St. The phone is 206-783-6362.

Spud Fish and Chips

9702 NE Juanita Dr.   425-823-0607
Kirkland, WA   LD | $

When he found out we were in the Seattle area, Roadfood.com contributor Wanderingjew sent us an urgent note advising we head to Kirkland for fish and chips. We now pass along this advice to anyone eager for cod, halibut, shrimp, scallops, or oysters, hand-breaded and fried in fresh oil until crisp, served alongside first-rate French fries. Spud Fish and Chips, a local destination since 1935, has a limited menu, with salad and chowder just about the only non-fried items; but you can be sure these folks know how to fry. The crust on each piece of fish is thin and crunchy; the cod is cream-moist; the halibut falls into elegant flakes; the shrimp snap. Onion rings also are excellent: individual hoops with severely crunchy exteriors holding ribbons of onion that have caramelized to tender sweetness. You will pay extra for tartar sauce (25¢), but it's worth the splurge; this homemade stuff is studded with al dente bits of pickle. Last but not least, while the iced tea and lemonade are fine, we also recommend the milk shakes, which are too thick for a straw.

Service is do-it-yourself. Place your order at the counter, pay, then wait until the order is put on a tray and ready for you to carry to a booth inside or to the exterior counter and picnic tables. Signs atop each napkin dispenser ask customers to please bus their own tables when they've finished eating.

13 Coins

125 Boren Ave. N.   206-682-2513
Seattle, WA   BLD | $$

At 13 Coins, you can spend $15 for breakfast or $150 for dinner and fine wine, and you can do either 24 hours a day, 7 days a week, 365 days a year. Opened over forty years ago, this favorite haunt of journalists from the nearby *Seattle Times* is not for trend-seekers or effete gourmets. But if you appreciate a square meal composed of quality ingredients cooked to order and served by a staff of pros, there's no finer place north of Hollywood's Musso & Frank.

Decor is a jaw-dropping anomaly of Tudor weight with mid-twentieth-century frivolity. Booths have upholstered backs that soar toward the ceiling; counter seats are not stools but rather huge padded thrones that swivel to make for easy conversation with a neighbor and provide full-access vision of the short-order chefs at work in the vast open kitchen. It is a pleasure to watch the cusiniers shuffle sauté pans on the stove, poach eggs, grill meats, and griddle-cook potatoes.

The menu is gigantic, ranging from a grilled cheese sandwich to surf 'n' turf, including likeable versions of the West Coast specialties Joe's Special (ground sirloin, spinach, and eggs topped with shredded Parmesan cheese) and Hangtown fry (oysters, bacon, and eggs, here cooked frittata-style). The one must-eat dish, whatever else you get, is hash brown potatoes. They are cooked on the griddle with plenty of clarified butter in cakes thick enough for the outside shreds to turn hard and chewy while the inside softens but doesn't become mush. Other allures from the multipage menu include French onion soup, a Joe's Special made with sausage, Dungeness crab Louie, chop-chop salad, and smoked Cheddar and prosciutto macaroni.

Top Pot

2124 5th Ave.
Seattle, WA

206-728-1966
$

If all you know about Top Pot is the leaden sinkers sold at Starbuck's, you might think we are crazy to recommend this place. But at the source, a Top Pot donut is one of the nation's best. First and foremost, there's the crunch of its skin, crisp enough to feel like your teeth are breaking something, after which they slide into the creamy cake interior just below the golden crust. Now, encase the top half with silky dark chocolate, coconut shreds, maple frosting, or a glistening thick sugar glaze and this modest-size circular pastry becomes sheer ecstasy.

There's nothing froufrou or pretentious about these lovelies. They are good ol' cake doughnuts, the kind you want to have with morning coffee, but by any meaningful standard—taste, texture, heft, even good looks—they are world-class, far superior to any of the national chains, as well as to their inferior doppelgangers sold around the country.

New England

Connecticut

Abbott's Lobster in the Rough
  Noank, 5
Big Dipper   Prospect, 6
Blackie's   Cheshire, 6
Carminuccio's   Newtown, 7
Clamp's Hamburger Stand   New
  Milford, 7
Coffee An'   Westport, 8
Colony Grill   Stamford, 8
Doogie's   Newington, 9
Dottie's Diner   Woodbury, 9
Dr. Mike's   Bethel, 10
Harry's Drive-In   Colchester, 10
Kitchen Little   Mystic, 11
Laurel Diner   Southbury, 11
Lenny & Joe's Fish Tale Restaurant
  Madison, 12
Lenny's   Branford, 13
Letizia's   Norwalk, 13
Louis' Lunch   New Haven, 14
Modern Apizza   New Haven, 14

The Olive Market   Georgetown, 15
Pepe's Pizzeria Napoletana   New
  Haven, 16
Pizzeria Lauretano   Bethel, 16
Rawley's Drive-In   Fairfield, 17
Ridgefield Ice Cream Shop
  Ridgefield, 17
Roseland Apizza   Derby, 18
Sally's Apizza   New Haven, 19
Shady Glen   Manchester, 19
Shiek's Sandwich Shop
  Torrington, 20
Super Duper Weenie   Fairfield, 20
Sycamore Drive-In   Bethel, 21
Ted's   Meriden, 21
Zip's Dining Car   Dayville, 22
Zuppardi's Apizza   West Haven, 22

Maine

Beal's Lobster Pier   Southwest
  Harbor, 24
Becky's   Portland, 24
Bet's Famous Fish Fry   Boothbay, 25
Bob's Clam Hut   Kittery, 25

Clam Shack   Kennebunkport, 26
Cole Farms   Gray, 27
Colucci's Hilltop Market
    Portland, 27
Dolly's   Frenchville, 28
Doris's Cafe   Fort Kent Mills, 29
Five Islands Lobster Co.
    Georgetown, 29
Flo's   Cape Neddick, 30
Harmon's Lunch   Falmouth, 31
Harraseeket Lobster   Freeport, 32
Helen's   Machias, 32
Hodgman's Frozen Custard   New
    Gloucester, 33
Lobster Shack   Cape Elizabeth, 33
Long Lake Sporting Club   Sinclair, 34
Maine Diner   Wells, 34
Moody's Diner   Waldoboro, 35
Nunan's Lobster Hut
    Kennebunkport, 36
Rock's Family Diner   Fort Kent, 36
Sea Basket   Wiscasset, 37

Massachusetts

Baxter's Fish & Chips   Hyannis, 38
Christina's Homemade Ice Cream
    Cambridge, 39
Clam Box   Ipswich, 39
Donut Dip   East Longmeadow, 40
Durgin-Park   Boston, 40
Essex Seafood   Essex, 41
Graham's Hot Dogs   Fall River, 41
Hartley's Original Pork Pies   Fall
    River, 42
J.J.'s Coney Island   Fall River, 42
Kelly's Roast Beef   Revere, 43
Marguerite's   Westport, 43
Marty's Donut Land   Ipswich, 44
Nick's   Fall River, 44
Nick's Famous Roast Beef   North
    Beverly, 45
Red Skiff   Rockport, 46
R.F. O'Sullivan & Son   Somerville, 46
Santarpio's   East Boston, 47
Toscanini's   Cambridge, 48

Turtle Alley   Gloucester, 48
The Village Restaurant   Essex, 49
Wenham Tea House   Wenham, 49
The White Hut   West Springfield, 50
Woodman's of Essex   Essex, 50

New Hampshire

Bishop's   Littleton, 52
The Friendly Toast   Portsmouth, 53
Gilley's PM Lunch   Portsmouth, 53
Hart's Turkey Farm   Meredith, 54
L.A. Burdick   Walpole, 54
Polly's Pancake Parlor   Sugar Hill, 55
Sunny Day Diner   Lincoln, 55

Rhode Island

Allie's Donuts   North Kingstown, 57
Bocce Club   Woonsocket, 57
Champlin's Seafood Deck
    Narragansett, 58
Evelyn's Drive-In   Tiverton, 59
Gray's Ice Cream   Tiverton, 59
Haven Brothers   Providence, 60
Mike's Kitchen   Cranston, 60
Olneyville N.Y. System
    Providence, 61
Stanley's Famous Hamburgers
    Providence, 62
Wein-O-Rama   Cranston, 62
Wright's Farm   Harrisville, 63

Vermont

Baba-À-Louis   Chester, 64
Blue Benn Diner   Bennington, 65
Chelsea Royal Diner   West
    Brattleboro, 65
Curtis' BBQ   Putney, 66
Dot's   Wilmington, 66
The Mill at Quechee   Quechee, 67
Mrs. Murphy's Donuts
    Manchester, 68
P&H Truck Stop   Wells River, 68
Putney Diner   Putney, 69

Up For Breakfast   Manchester, 69
Wayside Restaurant   Berlin, 70
White Cottage   Woodstock, 70

Mid-Atlantic

Delaware

Capriotti's   Wilmington, 77
Charcoal Pit   Wilmington, 78
Countrie Eatery   Dover, 78
Hadfield's Seafood   New Castle, 79
Helen's Sausage House   Smyrna, 79
Woodside Farm Creamery
      Hockessin, 80

District of Columbia

Ben's Chili Bowl   Washington, 81
Florida Avenue Grill   Washington, 82

Maryland

Bear Creek Open Pit BBQ
      Callaway, 83
The Breakfast Shoppe   Severna
      Park, 84
Chubby's Southern Style Barbeque
      Emmitsburg, 84
The Cove   Crisfield, 85
Crisfield   Silver Spring, 85
Faidley's   Baltimore, 86
G&M Restaurant & Lounge
      Linthicum Heights, 87
Jerry's Seafood   Lanham, 87
The Narrows   Grasonville, 88
Park-N-Dine   Hancock, 89
Randy's Ribs & Barbecue
      Hughesville, 89
Seaside Restaurant & Crab House
      Glen Burnie, 90
St. Mary's Landing   Charlotte
      Hall, 90
Suicide Bridge Restaurant
      Hurlock, 91

Waterman's Crab House   Rock
      Hall, 91

New Jersey

Charlie's Pool Room   Alpha, 93
Charlies Hot Dogs   Kenilworth, 94
Cliff's Dairy Maid   Ledgewood, 94
De Lorenzo's Tomato Pies
      Trenton, 95
Dickie Dee's   Newark, 95
Harold's New York Deli   Edison, 96
The Hot Grill   Clifton, 97
Jimmy Buff's   West Orange, 97
Libby's Lunch   Paterson, 98
Rutt's Hut   Clifton, 98
White House Sub Shop   Atlantic
      City, 99
White Manna   Hackensack, 100

New York

Aléthea's   Williamsville, 101
Antoinette's   Depew, 102
Barney Greengrass   New York, 102
Burger Joint   New York, 103
Café Edison   New York, 103
Carnegie Deli   New York, 104
Charlie the Butcher's Kitchen
      Buffalo, 105
Clare and Carl's   Plattsburgh, 105
Condrell's   Buffalo, 106
Don's Original   Sea Breeze, 107
Doug's Fish Fry   Cortland, 107
Glenwood Pines   Ithaca, 108
Gus's Restaurant   Plattsburgh, 109
Heid's of Liverpool   Liverpool, 109
Hubba   Port Chester, 110
John's Pizzeria   New York, 110
Katz's   New York, 111
LDR Char Pit   Rochester, 112
Magnolia's   Patterson, 112
Margon   New York, 113
McSweeney's   Plattsburgh, 113
Mike's Candy   Buffalo, 114
New Way Lunch   Glens Falls, 115

Nick Tahou Hots   Rochester, 115
Papaya King   New York, 116
Patsy's   New York, 117
Phil's Chicken House   Endicott, 117
Red Rooster Drive-In   Brewster, 118
Schwabl's   West Seneca, 118
Second Avenue Deli   New York, 119
Sharkey's   Binghamton, 120
Shortstop Deli   Ithaca, 120
Ted's Jumbo Red Hots
    Tonawanda, 121
Texas Chili   Port Chester, 122
Tino's   Bronx, 122
Walter's   Mamaroneck, 123

Pennsylvania

Center City Pretzel Co.
    Philadelphia, 124
Chink's   Philadelphia, 125
DeLuca's   Pittsburgh, 125
Dutch Kitchen   Frackville, 126
Enrico Biscotti   Pittsburgh, 127
The Family Diner   White Haven, 127
Famous 4th Street Deli
    Philadelphia, 128
Geno's   Philadelphia, 128
Glider Diner   Scranton, 129
Jimmy's Hot Dogs   Easton, 129
Jim's Steaks   Philadelphia, 130
Johnny's Hots   Philadelphia, 130
John's Roast Pork   Philadelphia, 131
Jo Jo's   Pittsburgh, 132
Leo's   Folcroft, 132
Longacre's Modern Dairy Bar
    Barto, 133
Lorenzo's Pizza   Philadelphia, 133
Mama's   Bala Cynwyd, 134
Marrone's Cafe   Girardville, 135
Original Hot Dog Shop
    Pittsburgh, 135
Pat's King of Steaks   Philadelphia, 136
People's Restaurant   New
    Holland, 137
Primanti Brothers   Pittsburgh, 137
Robert Wholey & Co.   Pittsburgh, 138

Salerno's Café   Old Forge, 139
Steve's Prince of Steaks
    Philadelphia, 139
Tony Luke's Old Philly Style
    Sandwiches   Philadelphia, 140

Mid-South

Kentucky

Bell's Drug Store   Sebree, 145
Heaton's   Princeton, 146
Homemade Ice Cream and Pie Kitchen
    Louisville, 146
Lynn's Paradise Café   Louisville, 147
Marion Pit   Marion, 147
Mike Linnig's Restaurant
    Louisville, 148
Moonlight Bar-B-Q   Owensboro, 148
Mr. D's   Henderson, 149
Peak Bros.   Waverly, 150
Thomason's Barbecue   Henderson, 150

North Carolina

A&M Grill   Mebane, 152
Allen & Son   Chapel Hill, 153
Bar B Q King   Charlotte, 153
Bill Spoon's Barbecue   Charlotte, 154
Bridges Barbecue Lodge   Shelby, 154
Brownie-Lu   Siler City, 155
Bum's   Ayden, 156
Bunn's Bar-B-Q   Windsor, 156
Chicken Box   Charlotte, 157
Cypress Grill   Jamesville, 157
Dip's Country Kitchen   Chapel
    Hill, 158
Jarrett House   Dillsboro, 159
Jay-Bee's   Statesville, 159
Keaton's   Cleveland, 160
Lexington Barbecue #1
    Lexington, 160
Lupie's   Charlotte, 161
Parker's   Wilson, 161
Penguin Drive-In   Charlotte, 162

Ruby & Ketchy's   Morgantown, 208
Stewart's Original Hot Dogs
    Huntington, 208

Deep South

Alabama

Bob Sykes Bar B-Q   Bessemer, 213
Bogue's   Birmingham, 214
The Brick Pit   Mobile, 214
Dew Drop Inn   Mobile, 215
Isaiah's Restaurant   Montgomery, 215
Jackson's Family Restaurant
    Madison, 216
Martin's   Montgomery, 216
Niki's West   Birmingham, 217
Pete's Famous Hot Dogs
    Birmingham, 218
13th Street Bar-B-Q   Phenix City, 218
The Waysider   Tuscaloosa, 219
Wintzell's Oyster House   Mobile, 219

Arkansas

AQ Chicken House   Springdale, 221
Cotham's Mercantile   Scott, 222
Craig's Bar-B-Que   DeValls Bluff, 222
Doe's Eat Place   Little Rock, 223
Ed & Kay's   Benton, 224
Family Pie Shop   DeValls Bluff, 224
Feltner's Whatta-Burger
    Russellville, 225
The Grapevine Restaurant   Paris, 225
McClard's   Hot Springs, 226
Mickey's BBQ   Hot Springs, 226
Rhoda's Famous Hot Tamales   Lake
    Village, 227
Stubby's Bar-B-Que   Hot Springs, 227
Wagon Wheel   Greenbrier, 228

Florida

Barnacle Bill's   St. Augustine, 229
Blue Heaven   Key West, 230

El Siboney   Key West, 230
Ernie's Bar-b-que & Lounge   Fort
    Lauderdale, 231
Jenkins Quality Barbecue
    Jacksonville, 231
Jerry's Drive-In   Pensacola, 232
La Teresita   Tampa, 232
Louie's Backyard   Key West, 233
Old Spanish Sugar Mill Grill and
    Griddle House   De Leon
    Springs, 233
O'Steen's   St. Augustine, 234
Pepe's Cafe   Key West, 235
Saltwater Cowboys   St. Augustine, 235
T-Ray's Burger Station   Fernandina
    Beach, 236
Vega's Cafe   Orlando, 236
Whitey's Fish Camp   Orange Park, 237

Georgia

Blue Willow Inn   Social Circle, 239
The Crab Shack   Tybee Island, 240
Dillard House   Dillard, 240
Dinglewood Pharmacy   Columbus, 241
Don's Bar-B-Que   Pooler, 241
Edna's   Chatsworth, 242
The GA Pig   Brunswick, 242
Harold's Barbecue   Atlanta, 243
Hot Thomas' Barbeque
    Watkinsville, 243
Mamie's Kitchen   Conyers, 244
Mary Mac's Tea Room   Atlanta, 244
Melear's   Fayetteville, 245
Mrs. Wilkes' Dining Room
    Savannah, 245
Nu-Way Weiners   Macon, 246
Old South Bar-B-Q   Smyrna, 246
Peachtree Cafe   Fort Valley, 247
Sconyers Bar-B-Que   Augusta, 247
Silver Skillet   Atlanta, 248
Skipper's Fish Camp   Darien, 248
Smith House   Dahlonega, 249
Varsity Drive-In   Atlanta, 249

Louisiana

Bon Ton Café New Orleans, 251
Borden's Lafayette, 252
Boudin King Jennings, 252
Bozo's Metairie, 253
Brenda's Diner New Iberia, 253
Café des Amis Breaux Bridge, 254
Café du Monde New Orleans, 255
Casamento's New Orleans, 255
Central Grocery New Orleans, 256
Champagne's Breaux Bridge Bakery
    Breaux Bridge, 256
D.I.'s Basile, 257
Domilise's Po-Boys New Orleans, 258
Don's Specialty Meats Scott, 258
Dupuy's Oyster Shop Abbeville, 259
Dwyer's Café Lafayette, 259
Earl's Lafayette, 260
Galatoire's New Orleans, 260
Jerry Lee's Baton Rouge, 261
Johnson's Boucanière Lafayette, 262
Lasyone's Meat Pie Kitchen
    Natchitoches, 262
Middendorf's Akers, 263
Moody's Minden, 263
Mosca's Avondale, 264
Parkway Bakery & Tavern New
    Orleans, 264
Prejean's Lafayette, 265
Robin's Henderson, 266
Rocky and Carlo's Chalmette, 266
T-Boy's Slaughterhouse Ville
    Platte, 267

Mississippi

Abe's Bar-B-Q Clarksdale, 268
Abe's Grill Corinth, 269
Blue & White Restaurant Tunica, 270
Crystal Grill Greenwood, 270
Dilworth's Tamales Corinth, 271
The Dinner Bell McComb, 272
Doe's Eat Place Greenville, 272
The Elite Jackson, 273
Giardina's Greenwood, 274

Hicks' Clarksdale, 274
Lusco's Greenwood, 275
Phillips Grocery Holly Springs, 276
Ramon's Clarksdale, 276
White Front Cafe Rosedale, 277
White Trolley Cafe Corinth, 277

South Carolina

Beacon Drive-In Spartanburg, 279
Bertha's Kitchen North
    Charleston, 280
Bowens Island Restaurant
    Charleston, 280
Charlie's Steakhouse Greenville, 281
Dave's Carry-Out Charleston, 282
Duke's Orangeburg, 283
82 Queen Charleston, 283
Ernie's Charleston, 284
Fishnet Seafood Johns Island, 285
521 B-B-Q & Grill Indian Land, 285
Hominy Grill Charleston, 286
Hyman's Seafood Charleston, 287
Middleton Place Restaurant
    Charleston, 287
Scott's Barbecue Hemingway, 288
SeeWee Restaurant Awendaw, 289
Sgt. White's Restaurant Beaufort, 290
Shealy's Bar-B-Que Leesville, 290
Summerton Diner Summerton, 291
Sweatman's Holly Hill, 291
The Wreck Mount Pleasant, 292

Midwest

Illinois

Al's #1 Italian Beef Chicago, 299
Ann Sather Chicago, 300
Army & Lou's Chicago, 300
Byron's Dog Haus Chicago, 301
Charlie Parker's Springfield, 302
Cozy Dog Drive In Springfield, 302
D&J Café Springfield, 302
Garrett Popcorn Shop Chicago, 303

Gene & Georgetti Chicago, 304
Gene & Jude's River Grove, 304
Harry Caray's Chicago, 305
Joe Rogers Original Recipe Chili Parlor
    Springfield, 306
Johnnie's Elmwood Park, 306
Lagomarcino's Moline, 307
Leon's Chicago, 307
Manny's Chicago, 308
Mr. Beef Chicago, 309
Paradise Pup Des Plaines, 310
Patty's Diner Skokie, 310
Poochie's Skokie, 310
Stashs Highland Park, 311
Superdawg Chicago, 312
Uncle Johnny's Chicago, 312
Vienna Beef Café Chicago, 313

Indiana

Coney Island Wiener Fort Wayne, 314
Gray Brothers Cafeteria
    Mooresville, 315
Hollyhock Hill Indianapolis, 315
Jamie's Soda Fountain Kokomo, 316
Joe Huber's Starlight, 316
Jonathan Byrd's Cafeteria
    Greenwood, 317
JWI Confectionery Madison, 318
King Ribs Bar-B-Q Indianapolis, 318
Main Cafe New Harmony, 319
Mr. Dave's North Manchester, 319
Mug N' Bun Indianapolis, 320
Nick's Kitchen Huntington, 320
Shapiro's Indianapolis, 321
Teibel's Schererville, 322

Iowa

Archie's Waeside Le Mars, 323
Bob's Drive-Inn Le Mars, 324
Coffee Cup Cafe Sully, 324
Darrell's Place Hamlin, 325
The Farmer's Kitchen Atlantic, 325
Grove Cafe Ames, 326
In't Veld Meat Market Pella, 327

Larsen's Pub Elk Horn, 327
Miles Inn Sioux City, 328
Milwaukee Wiener House Sioux
    City, 328
Off the Hook Des Moines, 329
Smitty's Tenderloin Shop Des
    Moines, 329
St. Olaf Tap St. Olaf, 330
Tastee Inn & Out Sioux City, 330
Wilton Candy Kitchen Wilton, 331

Michigan

Bortell's Fisheries Ludington, 332
The Cherry Hut Beulah, 332
Don's Drive-In Grand Traverse, 333
Gustafson's Brevort, 333
Johnny's Ham King Detroit, 334
Juilleret's Charlevoix, 335
Juilleret's Harbor Springs, 335
Krazy Jim's Blimpy Burger Ann
    Arbor, 336
Lafayette Coney Island Detroit, 337
Northside Grill Ann Arbor, 338
Yesterdog Grand Rapids, 338
Zingerman's Deli Ann Arbor, 339

Minnesota

Al's Breakfast Minneapolis, 340
Betty's Pies Two Harbors, 341
Bloedow Bakery Winona, 341
Cafe Latté St. Paul, 342
Convention Grill Edina, 342
Hell's Kitchen Minneapolis, 343
Lange's Café Pipestone, 344
Maverick's Roseville, 345
Mickey's Dining Car St. Paul, 345
Northern Waters Smokehaus
    Duluth, 346
Tavern on Grand St. Paul, 347
World's Best Donuts Grand
    Marais, 347

Missouri

Amighetti's   St. Louis, 349
Arthur Bryant's   Kansas City, 350
Booches   Columbia, 350
C&K Barbecue   St. Louis, 351
Carl's Drive-In   Brentwood, 351
Crown Candy Kitchen   St. Louis, 352
Goody Goody Diner   St. Louis, 352
Jess & Jim's   Kansas City, 353
LC's Barbeque   Kansas City, 353
Niecie's   Kansas City, 354
Snead's   Belton, 355
Stroud's   Kansas City, 356
Ted Drewes   St. Louis, 356

Ohio

Al's Corner Restaurant   Barberton, 358
Babushka's Kitchen   Northfield Center, 359
Balaton   Cleveland, 359
Balyeat's Coffee Shop   Van Wert, 360
Belgrade Gardens   Barberton, 360
Camp Washington Chili Parlor Cincinnati, 361
Crabill's   Urbana, 362
Flury's Sandwich Shop   Cuyahoga Falls, 362
Freddie's Southern Style Rib House Cleveland, 362
G&R Tavern   Waldo, 363
Hathaway's Coffee Shop Cincinnati, 363
Henry's   West Jefferson, 364
Kennedy's B.B.Q.   Canton, 364
Liberty Gathering Place   West Liberty, 365
Little Polish Diner   Parma, 366
New Era Cafe   Akron, 366
New Sandusky Fish Company Sandusky, 367
The Pine Club   Dayton, 367
Putz's Creamy Whip   Cincinnati, 368
Slyman's Restaurant   Cleveland, 368

Sokolowski's University Inn Cleveland, 369
Swensons   Akron, 370
Taggarts Ice Cream   Canton, 370
White House Chicken   Barberton, 371
White Turkey Drive-In   Conneaut, 372
Young's Jersey Dairy   Yellow Springs, 372

Wisconsin

Anchor Bar   Superior, 374
Beernsten's Candy Store Manitowoc, 375
Bendtsen's Bakery   Racine, 375
Benji's   Shorewood, 376
Chili John's   Green Bay, 376
Jack Pandl's Whitefish Bay Inn Whitefish Bay, 377
Jake's   Milwaukee, 377
Jo's Café   Milwaukee, 378
Klinger's East   Milwaukee, 379
Leon's   Milwaukee, 379
Maggie's   Bayfield, 380
Mazo's   Milwaukee, 381
McBob's   Milwaukee, 381
Mr. Perkins' Family Restaurant Milwaukee, 382
Plaza Tavern   Madison, 383
Real Chili   Milwaukee, 383
Serb Hall   Milwaukee, 384
Sil's Drive-Thru   Milwaukee, 384
Solly's Grille   Milwaukee, 384
Speed Queen   Milwaukee, 385
Three Brothers   Milwaukee, 386
Watts Tea Shop   Milwaukee, 386

Southwest

Arizona

BK Carne Asada & Hot Dogs Tucson, 393
Cafe Poca Cosa   Tucson, 394
El Bravo   Phoenix, 394

El Charro   Tucson, 395
El Guero Canelo   Tucson, 396
El Manantial Tacos Y Hot Dogs   South
   Tucson, 397
El Torero   South Tucson, 397
Gus Balon's   Tucson, 398
Joe & Aggie's Cafe   Holbrook, 399
La Cabaña   Nogales, 399
Los Jarritos   Tucson, 400
Mariscos Chihuahua   Tucson, 400
Mrs. White's Golden Rule Café
   Phoenix, 401
Pico de Gallo   South Tucson, 402
Sugar Bowl   Scottsdale, 402
Teresa's Mosaic Café   Tucson, 403
Tucson Tamale Company   Tucson, 404

Colorado

Bongo Billy's   Salida, 405
Buckhorn Exchange   Denver, 406
Bud's Bar   Sedalia, 406
Conway's Red Top   Colorado
   Springs, 407
Duffeyroll Café   Denver, 407
Durango Diner   Durango, 408
Johnson's Corner   Loveland, 408
La Fogata   Denver, 409

Kansas

Brookville Hotel   Abilene, 410
Bunker Hill Cafe   Bunker Hill, 411
Chicken Mary's   Pittsburg, 411
The Corner Pharmacy
   Leavenworth, 412
The Cozy Inn   Salina, 412
Oklahoma Joe's   Kansas City, 413
Olde Towne Restaurant
   Hillsboro, 413
Porubsky's Grocery   Topeka, 414
Woodyard Bar-B-Que   Kansas
   City, 415

Nevada

Hash House   Las Vegas, 416
Louis' Basque Corner   Reno, 417
Martin Hotel   Winnemucca, 417

New Mexico

Bert's Burger Bowl   Santa Fe, 419
Bobcat Bite   Santa Fe, 420
Buckhorn Tavern   San Antonio, 420
Chopes   La Mesa, 421
Duran Central Pharmacy
   Albuquerque, 421
Frontier   Albuquerque, 422
Garcia's Kitchen   Albuquerque, 423
Leona's   Chimayo, 423
Model Pharmacy   Albuquerque, 424
Nellie's   Las Cruces, 425
Nopalitos   Las Cruces, 425
Owl Bar & Cafe   San Antonio, 426
Pasqual's   Santa Fe, 426
Plaza Café   Santa Fe, 427
Rancho de Chimayo   Chimayo, 427
Roque's Carnitas   Santa Fe, 428
San Marcos Café   Cerrillos, 428
Sugar's   Embudo, 429
Tecolote   Santa Fe, 429

Oklahoma

Cancun   Tulsa, 431
Cattlemen's Steakhouse   Oklahoma
   City, 432
Clanton's   Vinita, 432
Classen Grill   Oklahoma City, 433
Coney I-Lander   Tulsa, 434
Dink's Pit Bar-B-Que   Bartlesville, 434
Eischen's Bar   Okarche, 435
Hamburger King   Shawnee, 435
Hank's Hamburgers   Tulsa, 436
Ike's Chili   Tulsa, 437
Jigg's Smokehouse   Clinton, 437
Johnnie's   El Reno, 438
Kumback Lunch   Perry, 438
The Meers Store   Meers, 439

Murphy's Steak House
   Bartlesville, 440
Robert's   El Reno, 440
Sid's   El Reno, 441
Van's Pig Stand   Shawnee, 441
White River Fish Market   Tulsa, 442
Wilson's B-B-Que   Tulsa, 443

Texas

Angelo's   Fort Worth, 444
Avalon Diner   Houston, 445
Beans-N-Things   Amarillo, 445
Black's Barbecue   Lockhart, 446
Blanco Bowling Club Café
   Blanco, 446
Blue Bonnet Cafe   Marble Falls, 447
Bohannon's Brietzke Station
   Seguin, 447
Bryce's Cafeteria   Texarkana, 448
Cattlemen's Fort Worth Steak House
   Fort Worth, 449
Celia's Cocina   Amarillo, 449
Chris Madrid's   San Antonio, 450
City Market   Luling, 450
Clark's Outpost   Tioga, 451
Cooper's Pit Bar-B-Q   Mason, 452
Golden Light Cafe   Amarillo, 452
Goode Co. Texas Bar-B-Q
   Houston, 453
H&H Cafe and Car Wash   El
   Paso, 453
Hill Country Cupboard   Johnson
   City, 454
Home of Da Smoke   Adkins, 455
Hoover's Cooking   Austin, 455
Hut's Hamburgers   Austin, 456
Krause's Café   New Braunfels, 457
Kreuz Market   Lockhart, 457
La Mexicana   Houston, 458
Little Diner   Canutillo, 459
Lock Drugs   Bastrop, 459
Louie Mueller Barbecue   Taylor, 460
Monument Cafe   Georgetown, 460
OST   Bandera, 461
Paris Coffee Shop   Fort Worth, 461

Ranchman's Café   Ponder, 462
Royers Round Top Café   Round
   Top, 463
The Salt Lick   Driftwood, 463
Smitty's   El Paso, 464
Smitty's   Lockhart, 465
Sonny Bryan's   Dallas, 465
Southside Market   Elgin, 466
Taco House   San Antonio, 466
Taco Taco   San Antonio, 467
Texas Pie Company   Kyle, 468
Threadgill's   Austin, 468
Tom & Bingo's   Lubbock, 469
Vernon's Kuntry Katfish   Conroe, 469
Village Bakery   West, 470
Weikel's Store and Bakery
   La Grange, 470

Utah

Capitol Reef Inn and Cafe   Torrey, 472
Hires Big H   Salt Lake City, 473
Idle Isle   Brigham City, 473
Lamb's Grill Cafe   Salt Lake City, 474
Maddox Drive-In   Brigham City, 474
Mom's Cafe   Salina, 475
Navajo Hogan   Salt Lake City, 475

Great Plains

Idaho

Andrade's Restaurante Mexicano
   Boise, 481
Cedars Floating Restaurant   Coeur
   d'Alene, 482
El Gallo Giro   Kuna, 483
Goldy's Breakfast Bistro   Boise, 483
Hudson's   Coeur d'Alene, 484
Java on Sherman   Coeur d'Alene, 485
Leku Ona   Boise, 485
Westside Drive In   Boise, 486
Wolf Lodge   Coeur d'Alene, 486

Montana

Candel's By-Way Café   Stanford, 488
Cole Drug   Big Timber, 489
Dash Inn   Lewistown, 489
Eddie's Supper Club   Great Falls, 490
Matt's Place   Butte, 491
Pekin Noodle Parlor   Butte, 491
Red Lodge Café   Red Lodge, 492
Rex Restaurant   Billings, 492
Sarah's   Billings, 493
Stella's Kitchen and Bakery
     Billings, 493
Willow Creek Cafe & Saloon   Willow
     Creek, 494

Nebraska

Bohemian Café   Omaha, 495
Crystal Café   South Sioux City, 496
Gering Bakery   Gering, 497
Joe Tess Place   Omaha, 497
Rosita's   Scottsbluff, 498
Scotty's Drive In   Scottsbluff, 499
Taco Town   Scottsbluff, 499

South Dakota

Bob's   Sioux Falls, 500
Edgar's   Elk Point, 501
Hamburger Inn   Sioux Falls, 502
Nick's Hamburger Shop
     Brookings, 502
Tea Steak House   Tea, 503
Tripp Sports Bowl Café   Tripp, 503

Wyoming

Café Wyoming   Dubois, 505
Svilar's   Hudson, 505
Wagon Box Inn   Story, 506

West Coast

California

Al's Place   Locke, 511
Aunt Kizzy's Back Porch   Marina del
     Rey, 512
Barbara's Fishtrap   Half Moon
     Bay, 512
Bette's Oceanview Diner   Berkeley, 513
Bi-Rite Creamery   San Francisco, 514
Buz's Crab Seafood Restaurant
     Redding, 514
Cafe at the Bug   Midpines, 515
Clifton's Cafeteria   Los Angeles, 515
Cole's P.E. Buffet   Los Angeles, 516
The Cottage   La Jolla, 517
Duarte's Tavern   Pescadero, 518
D.Z. Akins   San Diego, 519
El Gallito   Cathedral City, 519
El Indio   San Diego, 520
El Paisa Taco Truck   Oakland, 521
Far Western Tavern   Guadalupe, 521
The Hitching Post   Casmalia, 522
Hob Nob Hill   San Diego, 522
Hodad's   Ocean Beach, 523
Ici   Berkeley, 524
Jocko's Steak House   Nipomo, 524
Julian Pie Company   Santa Ysabel, 525
La Farine   Oakland, 526
La Super-Rica   Santa Barbara, 526
Mama's Hot Tamales Café   Los
     Angeles, 527
The Marshall Store   Marshall, 527
Musso & Frank Grill   Hollywood, 528
Original Pantry   Los Angeles, 528
Philippe the Original   Los Angeles, 529
Ramona Cafe   Ramona, 529
Rick & Ann's   Berkeley, 530
Roscoe's House of Chicken and Waffles
     Los Angeles, 531
Sam's Grill   San Francisco, 531
Sears Fine Food   San Francisco, 532
St. Francis Fountain   San
     Francisco, 532

Swan Oyster Depot   San
    Francisco, 533
Taylor's Refresher   St. Helena, 533
Wheel Inn   Cabazon, 534

Oregon

Annie's Donut Shop   Portland, 535
Crema   Portland, 536
Dan & Louis Oyster Bar
    Portland, 536
Ecola Seafoods   Cannon Beach, 537
Fuller's Coffee Shop   Portland, 538
Green Salmon   Yachats, 538
Halibut's   Portland, 539
Mo's   Newport, 540
Norma's Ocean Diner   Seaside, 540
The Oasis   Milton Freewater, 541
Otis Cafe   Otis, 541
Otto's Sausage Kitchen   Portland, 542
Pacific Oyster   Bay City, 543
Ristretto Roasters   Portland, 543
Sahagún   Portland, 543
Saint Cupcake   Portland, 544
South Beach Fish Market   South
    Beach, 544

Voodoo Donuts   Portland, 545
Waves of Grain   Cannon Beach,
    545

Washington

Bakeman's   Seattle, 547
Beth's Cafe   Seattle, 548
The Crumpet Shop   Seattle, 548
Cupcake Royale   Seattle, 549
Emmett Watson's Oyster Bar
    Seattle, 549
14 Carrot Cafe   Seattle, 550
Frank's Diner   Spokane, 551
Hi Spot Cafe   Seattle, 551
Knapp's Family Restaurant
    Tacoma, 552
Maltby Cafe   Snohomish, 553
Mike's Chili Parlor   Seattle, 553
Pick Quick Drive-In   Tacoma, 554
Red Mill   Seattle, 554
Spud Fish and Chips   Kirkland,
    555
13 Coins   Seattle, 555
Top Pot   Seattle, 556